THE ECONOMY OF
ROMAN PALESTINE

THE ECONOMY OF ROMAN PALESTINE

Ze'ev Safrai

London and New York

First published 1994
by Routledge
11 New Fetter Lane, London EC4P 4EE

Simultaneously published in the USA and Canada
by Routledge
29 West 35th Street, New York, NY 10001

Typeset in Garamond by Florencetype Ltd, Kewstoke, Avon
Printed and bound in Great Britain
by T.J. Press (Padstow) Ltd, Padstow, Cornwall

British Library Cataloguing in Publication Data
A catalogue record for this book is available from the British
Library

Library of Congress Cataloging in Publication Data
Safrai, Ze'ev.
The economy of Roman Palestine/Ze'ev Safrai.
p.   cm.
Includes bibliographical references.
1. Palestine – Economic conditions.   2. Palestine – History
– 70–638.   I. Title.
HC415.25.S25   1994
330.933′ 05 – dc20   93-12941

ISBN 0–415–10243–X

Contents

v

Figures

Acknowledgements

It is with much pleasure that I thank all those who have helped with the publication of this book, and with the research which preceded it. The research and especially the field work were sponsored by the National Academy, The Israel Science Foundation and the A. I. and C. Z. Moskowitz Chair and S. Kroutheimer Foundation, both of the department of "Land of Israel Studies" in Bar Ilan University. I thank them for this assistance, without which it would have been difficult to complete this project.

Many friends came to my assistance, and I can mention only a few of them. My friend Professor Y. Schwartz read the manuscript and made many enlightening suggestions as to style and content. Mrs M. Waldman adapted the figues to the text. I also consulted extensively with Professor S. Dar and A. Kloner, and of course my father and teacher Professor S. Safrai.

Much praise is due to the staff of Routledge, and especially Dr. R. Stoneman, the chief editor, and H. Perkins and S. Bilton who corrected many stylistic errors. And above all I thank my family, my wife Dina and my dear children, Na'ama, Eli, Osnat and Adi, who helped me so much.

Abbreviations

Names of ancient authors or works, unless listed below, are abbreviated according to *Oxford Classical Dictionary* (2nd edn, ed. N. G. L. Hammond and H. H. Scullard; Oxford, 1970).

Details of Rabbinic texts, and explanations of the abbreviations cited, may be found in Appendix II on pp. 463–4.

AAASH	*Acta Archaeologica Academiae Scientiarum Hungaricae*
AASOR	*Annual of the American School of Oriental Research*
AJA	*American Journal of Archaeology*
AJP	*American Journal of Philology*
ANRW	*Aufstieg und Niedergang der römischen Welt* (Berlin, 1970–)
Ant.	Josephus, *Jewish Antiquities*
BAR	British Archaeological Reports (Oxford); 'S' = supplementary (international) series
BASOR	*Bulletin of the American School of Oriental Research*
BJ	Josephus, *Jewish War* (*Bellum Judaicum*)
BSA	*Annual of the British School at Athens*
BZ	*Byzantinische Zeitschrift*
CCSL	*Corpus Christianorum, Series Latina*
CIL	*Corpus inscriptionum Latinarum* (Berlin, 1863–)
CJ	*Classical Journal*
Cod. Just.	*Codex Justinianus*
CP	*Classical Philology*
CSCO	*Corpus Scriptorum Christianorum Orientalium* (Scr. Syr.)
CSEL	*Corpus Scriptorum Ecclesiasticorum Latinorum*
CSHB	*Corpus Scriptorum Historia Byzantinae*
C. Th.	*Codex Theodosianus*
DJD	*see* Benoit *et al.* 1961 (in Bibliography)
EcHr	*Economic Historical Journal*
EI	*Eretza Israel* (in Hebrew and English)
Gr. Schr.	*Griechischen christlichen Schriftsteller*
IEJ	*Israel Exploration Journal*

IGR	*Inscriptiones Graecae ad res Romanas pertinentestes*, i–iii, ed. R. Cagnat *et al.* (Paris, 1906–27)
INJ	*Israel Numismatic Journal*
JEA	*Journal of Egyptian Archaeology*
JJP	*Journal of Juristic Papyrology*
JQR	*Jewish Quarterly Review*
JRS	*Journal of Roman Studies*
LA	*Liber annus* (Studium Biblicum Franciscanum)
MGH	*Monumenta Germaniae Historica*
MGH (AA)	*Monumenta Germanaie Historica Auctores Antiquissimi*
NC	*Numismatic Chronicle*
Or.	Choricius, *Orations*
PBSR	*Papers of the British School at Rome*
PCZ	*Zenon Papyri*, i–iv, ed. C. C. Edgar (Cairo, 1925–31)
PEF	*Palestine Exploration Fund*
PEQ	*Palestine Exploration Quarterly*
PG	*Patrologia, Series Graeca* (ed. Migne)
PL	*Patrologia Cursus, Series Latina* (ed. Migne)
PO	*Patrologia Orientalis*
P. Oxy	*Oxyrhynchus Papyri* (ed. B. P. Grenfell, A. S. Hunt, *et al.*; London, 1898–)
P. Ryland	*Catalogue of Papyri in the John Rylands Library at Manchester* (1911–)
P. Strasb.	*Strasburg Papyri*
PW	G. Wissowa *et al.*, *Paulys Real-Encyclopädie der classischen Altertumswissenschaft* (Stuttgart, 1893–1981)
QDAP	*Quarterly of the Department of Antiquities of Palestine*
RB	*Revue biblique*
REJ	*Revue des études juives*
RIDA	*Revue internationale des droits de l'antiquité*
SEG	*Supplementum epigraphicum Graecum* (Leiden, 1923–)
TAPA	*Transactions of the American Philological Association*
TU	*Texte und Untersuchungen*
WA	*World Archaeology*
ZAW	*Zeitschrift für die alttestamentliche Wissenschaft*
ZDPV	*Zeitschrift des deutschen Palästina-Vereins*
ZPE	*Zeitschrift für Papyrologie und Epigraphik*

Introduction

The Hasmonean kingdom was established in the Land of Israel at the end of the second century BCE and began a series of conquests which changed this small state into one of the most powerful political forces in the ancient Middle East. With the Roman conquest in 63 BCE, the Land of Israel became a vassal state which in the year 6 CE or a little before became Provincia Judaea. In 135 CE, after the Bar-Kochba revolt, the name of the province was changed to Palaestina (Palestine) or Syria-Palaestina. The boundaries of the province changed from time to time and took on a final form really only at the end of the first century CE. The province of Palestine was further divided in the fourth century CE into Palaestina Prima and Palaestina Secunda. In spite of this administrative division, both Palestines continued to be basically one geographic-historical unit (Avi-Yonah 1963).

The Land of Israel is known in the history of mankind as the source, birthplace and original sphere of action of the great monotheistic world religions and as the "Holy Land" of Judaism and Christianity. None of this, however, resulted in political importance during the Roman period. The province of Judaea or Palestine was only about 18,000 sq. km and was a small and economically unimportant province. In spite of all this, the study of the economic history of Judaea during the Roman period is different by its very nature from the study of the same topic in any other province of the Roman Empire. The unique nature of the province was in a number of spheres.

(1) Almost no remains of great wealth have been found in the province of Judaea. The various public buildings which have been discovered were apparently not particularly elegant and their level of preservation is also not very high in comparison with other areas of the Empire (Tsafrir 1985). Thus, a number of farmsteads (or *villae*) have been discovered in the Land of Israel, but none as large or fancy as some of those found in other provinces such as Gaul, Germany or Britain (Chapter 1.V below). Moreover, very few inscriptions have been found in the Land of Israel which add important information to the study of the economic history of that land.

(2) In spite of all this, there has been a good deal of excavation of the rural

1

sphere in the Land of Israel. This attention may be the result of the relatively poor amount of remains found in the city sphere.

(3) Historical-economic research in most provinces of the Roman Empire is based on the study of literary documents, inscriptions and archaeological remains. Talmudic material serves as an outstanding source of information on the Land of Israel. It is impossible to stress enough the importance of this type of literature. The nature and type of information which can be derived from this literature is what makes the study of the Land of Israel different and unique in relation to the study of any other Roman province. Usually, there is a good deal of information on the lifestyle of the rich and upper classes. The life and situation of these upper classes is what is usually reflected in literary and epigraphical source material, and archaeological remains and excavations usually reveal the dwellings of these classes and the public buildings in which they based their power.

Thus, most of the research dealing with the economy of the Roman Empire usually deals with cities (*polis*, pl. *poleis*) and with the upper classes. The Roman "village" or "rural sector" in research usually refers to farmsteads or *villae* of the rich. This is even the case regarding the papyri of Egypt which reflect the realities of the upper classes much more than those of lower classes. Syriac and Egyptian Christian material and particularly the biographies of the Church Fathers do portray local conditions, but most of this type of material is presented from the viewpoint of Christian monastic circles.

Talmudic material, however, basically reflects the realities of the rural sector. This type of literature serves as a tremendous source of information on the everyday life of the village and city in the Land of Israel, on agriculture and the crops cultivated there, and on a whole host of economic and technical problems. The combination of Talmudic sources with archaeological remains and in conjunction with the information known about economic life in general in the Roman Empire, offers a unique chance to add additional data to the socio-economic "mosaic" which makes up the study of everyday life in the Land of Israel. All of this might also add to what is known about economic life in general in the eastern provinces of the Empire.

There are, however, difficult methodological problems with the use of Talmudic material for the study of the matters mentioned above. In this we can add little and our use of Talmudic material *per se* is based on the important studies and methodologies of such scholars as Büchler, Alon, Klein, S. Safrai, Sperber, Feliks, and others. We shall refrain in the course of our present study from dealing with the details pertaining to these methodological issues.

(4) The province of Judaea may have indeed been small, but it did have a rather high population density. Jones (1971, pp. 523–62) lists fifty-one cities in both Palestines of the Byzantine period and this is more than any other eastern province such as Thracia with five, Asia with forty-eight, Lydia with

twenty-eight, Caria with thirty-five and Prima and Secunda Syria with seventeen. The territory of Sicily is one-third greater than that of Palestine, but there are many fewer cities there. The density of population in the Land of Israel is reflected in the great number of villages there and in intensive use of land. This is not to say, though, that Palestine was a rich province, as we have indeed mentioned above.

The Land of Israel is shaped like a rectangle or trapezoid. Its length is approximately 225 km and its width in the south is about 130 km, and between 50–60 km in the north. The country can be divided lengthwise into zones. The westernmost zone is along the coast of the Mediterranean Sea and includes the coastal plain. Eastward is the *shephelah*, the hill or mountain region which is about 30 km wide and the desert which is about 35 kms wide in the south and becomes narrower in the north.

The Jewish settlement, whose literature serves as our main literary source, was the major ethnic and religious population component in the Land of Israel until the Bar-Kochba revolt (132–5 CE). Until this time, pagans were found only in cities. After the Bar-Kochba revolt things began to change. The Jewish population was now centered in the rural sphere of the Galilee. The cities of the Galilee as well as Lod (Diospolis) in Judaea were also basically Jewish. There were also Jewish centers of population in the coastal plain of Judaea and in southern Mt Hebron. The Jewish population began to decline from the mid-fourth century CE and the Jewish sources became silent.

Our present study deals with the Land of Israel during the Roman period, from the destruction of the Second Temple until the mid-fourth century CE. However, we have at times made use of the few available Byzantine sources which contain information on events and life in Palestine during that period (324–637 CE). Naturally, the rural and village sector will occupy most of our attention, and relatively little time will be spent on the urban sector. This does not necessarily reflect economic reality. It does, however, reflect the interest of the Talmudic source material upon which we are almost entirely dependent.

We should really begin our present study with a political and historical survey of the period under discussion. However, there is a good deal of excellent material on these matters (see, for example, Schürer 1973; Avi-Yonah 1963; Z. Baras *et al.* 1982), and we shall therefore begin our work straightaway with economic and social matters.

THE RABBINIC SOURCES

On the question of the reliability of the Talmudic texts as historical sources.

The Talmudic texts are the main basis of our study and the source of information for most of the questions, answers and hypotheses put forward. In terms of the utilization of such sources, we have added nothing new, and we confidently follow a path that has been paved by many students of Jewish history, such as Büchler (1906, 1909), Alon (1957, 1958, 1977, 1980), Epstein (1948) and others. This approach can be summarized as follows.

(a) Every source must be thoroughly checked, examining the original version against manuscripts and quotations of the "Rishonim" (interpreters of the early Middle Ages), as well as additional evidence. After this, parallel sources are used to determine that this is really the original version of the law. Is the text different or distorted? What can be learned from the differences between the sources and from the ensuing questions and investigations?

(b) Almost all Talmudic texts that meet the examination outlined in (a) should be accepted. However, each text should also be examined in the light of related historical sources to establish whether the picture portrayed makes sense according to all other available information.

(c) Naturally, one should suspect texts of exaggeration and excessiveness, and of changes made to correspond with the esthetic and theoretical framework of the story and anachronistic descriptions (mainly of the Biblical period). Such exaggeration is, of course, more common in legends than in *halacha*, and the latter can be expected to be much more accurate. The researcher must identify the historical core in the text; it is this information that can serve as a source of knowledge.

(d) After the authenticity of the source has been established, the researcher must study it and determine its significance and the conclusions that can be drawn. In this context, a number of questions will be asked, and related options will be examined. For example, does the text represent something customary or something exceptional? Is the story an exceptional example that tells us about a general occurrence, or does it refer to an isolated incident or episode? Was the decision of the beit midrash actually carried out? What period does the source represent? What does it incorporate from earlier times and what new elements did the rabbis of the period add? The answers to such questions, in turn, lead to further investigation.

(e) All these tests apply to the Palestinian texts. We treated the Babylonian texts differently, as discussed below.

(f) This method of study based on deduction and analogy serves as an alternative to two other main methods. On the one hand, there is the traditional method, which is based on absolute belief in every source. Accordingly, the research focuses on application of the information. In addition, since all sources are considered indisputable truth, it is necessary to explain the discrepancies between them. These explanations generally ignore the constraints of reason and logic, and require a willingness to reject some other sources such as manuscripts, texts from the Geniza

4

(the Jewish archive found in a synagogue in Cairo dating from the early Middle Ages), some of the midrashim, and the like.

In contrast, another method challenges the belief in the rabbinic literature and its use as a historical source. We discuss this below.

In the context of the present research, it is not necessary to discuss the methodological assumptions presented. After all, this is not the first study of the history of the people of Israel and of Palestine. With all due respect, this is just one of dozens of similar projects, and an extensive discussion of the issue of methodology is beyond our scope.

Nevertheless, this does not excuse us altogether from the need to address the question of method. The main conclusion that arises from this essay is likely (or liable) to seem utopian. The summary seems too neat, and therefore it is not credible. Thus we must defend the way in which we utilized the sources, in general and in principle.

For this purpose, we consider an alternative method of studying ancient sources. Using this method, numerous respected researchers, such as Goodenough (1967), Neusner (1979, 1990), and many others, have presented arguments that question the validity of using rabbinic texts as a source of social history. The major arguments are as follows.

(1) In the Mishnah and Talmud periods, the rabbis headed isolated *batei midrash*. The laws that they developed emerged in these detached, isolated "islands" of study. Thus the rabbis neither understood nor knew the reality of their times; it was not the background to their decisions, their attitudes nor even the legends told in the *batei midrash*. Sometimes this argument is presented in an even more extreme manner. The Talmudic literature is depicted not as a summary of opinions of a group of rabbis, but as personal literary creations. Accordingly, the Mishnah is not a public text, but the work of a single editor or group of editors. Consequently, each book or part of a book has a different social background, which must be discussed separately. Obviously, this type of research does not require the knowledge of all Talmudic texts, and such study becomes simple, one-dimensional and unequivocal.

Applying this theory to our study, the image that emerges of the economy, the community and the settlement would not be true history but "literary history," or "economics of the *beit midrash*."

(2) The public at large did not obey the rabbis. Among the Jews, only a minority followed the rabbis, obeyed their decisions and was influenced by their sermons and moral teachings. It was also this small group that influenced the outlook of the *beit midrash*; its customs and attitudes constitute the social and historical background for the decisions made in the beit midrash. According to this perspective, then, the texts do not provide a true image of the community, but that of a small group, a social stratum whose ties with the wider public were few and

5

problematic. Levine, who takes a compromise stand on this subject, calls Alon's approach "romantic," and sees the stratum of rabbis as an elite who claimed leadership but achieved this only partially (Levine 1985).

These two perspectives are similar, but they are also separated by significant and complex differences.

As noted, although we will not discuss these broad methodological issues, brief discussion of those subjects directly related to our field of research seems warranted. Some of the following comments are restricted to this area and some also have more general theoretical significance. Prior to the discussion, another aspect, more psychological than scientific, should be considered. The Talmudic texts pose an extremely difficult challenge to the scholar. The archaic Hebrew and Aramaic integrated with Hebrew are a primary hardship. Moreover, the texts are written in a sort of inner code, the code of the beit midrash (school). All the interpretive and traditional Mishnaic texts assume that this code is known to the reader, so instead of interpreting it they use it. Thus the first sentence in the Mishnah Brachot 1, 1 would be translated literally as "From when they call: listen!," when it actually means "From when people have to pray the Prayer of Shema [a well-known prayer which every Jew must recite twice a day]." In addition, the corresponding scripture for many of the passages is not clear; sometimes the textual basis for whole chapters is not explicitly mentioned. The material is not organized by subjects and the same issue appears in numerous sources. Conflicts between the sources, errors in a version and later editing of some of the texts all create additional difficulties. Furthermore, until recently there was no lexicon (although now a number of computer programs have been distributed that partially solve this problem), and most of the essays have not yet been published in scientific, or even semi-scientific editions.

It is no wonder, then, that many scholars have erred in their understanding of the texts and made mistakes in using them. Someone who does not know the Talmudic texts intimately will have difficulty making full use of all the rabbinic literature.

Needless to say, in this respect, graduates of the Jewish religious institutions have a distinct advantage. In modern institutions of this type, two to five hours a day are devoted to studying the Talmud. In the more traditional schools, the entire day is devoted to learning the Talmud. On the other hand, students of the latter are exposed to the misleading influence of the traditional method of teaching mentioned earlier.

These "technical" difficulties must not influence our position regarding the reliability of the rabbinic sources. After all, difficulty in reading an inscription does not dissuade researchers, but actually stimulates them to make greater efforts to utilize the hidden information and to determine its implications.

For our purposes, a distinction should be made between three types of conclusions that may arise from the study of rabbinic texts.

(a) Did the rabbis succeed in changing or influencing the social environment through their teachings? For example, did the prohibition against charging interest have an impact on lenders and borrowers? Did the rabbis' utopian position (and their opposition to trade and urban lifestyles) affect the public? Did their moralistic policy and their desire to help the poor and the weak influence the economic structure? We further discuss this group of questions below. These questions actually apply to only a small group of subjects, as the rabbis generally did not try to mold economic life or to pronounce utopian commands; they did not consider it their role to decide what to grow, how to produce, how to sell or to interfere in other purely economic matters.

(b) In the course of their writings, the rabbis refer to a certain religious-social background as though it were real. Thus, for instance, the rabbis assume that the entire public observes Kashrut, keeps the Sabbath and attends synagogue. These assumptions relate to matters that were important to the rabbis. They considered these aspects of life as their realm, and in this respect the distance between themselves, their students and the general public was prominent. After all, the whole community could not be holy. Regarding these matters, the rabbis' writings reflect the customs only of those who were accepted in the stratum of rabbis. Accordingly, one might expect that the background described in the texts applies to the society of the beit midrash (school) alone. This suggestion is also discussed below.

(c) In the course of their discussions, the rabbis relate *by the way* to the situation outside the beit midrash. Thus, for instance, when they discuss the obligation of tithing, they assume that in some places most of the produce is sent to market (M Maasrot 1:5; PT 11, 49c). Perhaps the laws of tithing were theoretical and most of the public paid no attention to them at all, but is there any reason to doubt that there were places where most of the harvest was sent to the market? In this case it might still be argued that the description is theoretical and is presented as a dialectic possibility alone. Even more notable an example is the rabbis' description of the sale of a house, in which they assume that it includes a cooker and stove (M Baba Batra 4:3). We still do not know how common the sale of houses was, but there is no reason to doubt that the cooker and stove were an integral part of a residential dwelling, and it is also clear that they were considered the most characteristic components of such a house.

The decisive majority of subjects with which this work deals belong to the latter type and resemble the last example presented here. A small portion are similar to the previous example of tithing laws. In these cases we must clarify whether the background to the text is realistic, or whether it was presented for the purpose of a theoretical dialectic discussion.

Only very few of the references in this book belong to type (a) or (b) above. In general, the rabbis did not deal with *formation of the economic structure* but with *personal behaviour and lifestyle* within the economic structure of their time. The rabbis were interested in questions of ritual, ceremony, morals and social justice, and economic circumstances only served as a framework, a setting for them. It is actually because the economic, technological and agricultural subjects were not generally the focus of the rabbinic literature that it can be used as a source for the study of the economy.

A reliable historian may draw a wealth of historical information from the satires of Juvenal, or from the stories of Bernard Shaw, despite the clearly fictional nature of these works. Perhaps paradoxically, the less important a subject to the author, the more realistically it is presented as a setting, and the more reliable it is as a source for the researcher of the period.

We now review the arguments on which we base the use of rabbinic literature as a historical source for study of the Roman era.

EVIDENCE FROM EXTERNAL SOURCES

It might be expected that the historical description that emerges from rabbinic literature would be supported, echoed and confirmed by parallel external sources of information, such as Roman and Christian documents, contemporary texts, archeological findings and other sources. Before examining the external sources on this subject, it is important to consider the unique nature of the rabbinic literature as compared to all other historical and archeological sources available for the study of the Roman Empire. The Roman sources reflect the experience of the aristocracy, those people associated with the imperial and urban establishment. All Roman literature was written by members of this stratum, was intended for readers who were also members of this stratum, and was often written directly or indirectly under the patronage of the establishment. The vast majority of epigraphic literature was also written by wealthy people, such as members of the government, the army and the like. Not all the Egyptian papyri represent the leadership; some were produced by merchants or members of the ministries that administered activity throughout the empire. However, they still contain little expression of the simple farmer or the relationships between peasants within their communities.

With the emergence of the literature of the Christian church (particularly that of the East – the Syrian, Armenian and Egyptian church), this situation was slightly altered. The clerical literature also reflects rural life to some extent, but the total knowledge that can be drawn from these sources is not great, as most of the work and writing of the fathers of the church was devoted to church matters. Even the little information that deals with the village and the masses is presented from the religious point of view, and the church perspective is influenced by the principles and views of the Christian religious establishment. The Christian literature reflects the situation from the fourth century on, and so is much later than the Talmudic literature.

The rabbinic literature reflects a completely different social stratum. These texts are the creation of a social group that was completely unknown to the authors of the other sources on the Roman Empire. This is the only literature from that period that represents the native residents, and not the establishment, which was saturated in Greek and Roman culture. The Talmudic literature emerged mostly in the rural community, out of a struggle against the imperial culture, literature and religion. It reflects an entirely different social experience; it deals with different subjects, a different type of people and a different economic, religious and social experience. It is unlikely that any external sources would deal with the rural and Jewish subjects discussed in these texts.

Nevertheless, in the course of this work we do occasionally refer to evidence derived from external sources. In general, the comparisons and parallels with non-Jewish evidence are extremely limited and cast no doubt on our conclusions. Most of the relevant external sources confirm the implications of the rabbinic literature. An example is the reference to life in a private "town" which is interpreted as dealing with a Roman villa. Similarly, the description of a "fair," fits descriptions of the Roman market-day (see also Chapter 3.IV.3 below, describing the "trade," which is identical to the "emporium").

In the present research we gained only little help from non-rabbinic Jewish sources. For the most part, Josephus, Philon, the evangelists in the New Testament, the Qumran texts and external literature deal with the late period of the Second Temple. This period precedes that of our study and that in which the rabbinic literature was produced. Therefore we can not expect much information regarding our subject. Moreover, without entering into a detailed discussion of each of the texts, it can be said that most do not even deal with the social aspects of the rural village. Thus there are very few parallels between these and the rabbinic literature.

THE ARCHEOLOGICAL DATA

The subject of the Palestinian village in the Roman period has recently received increased attention among researchers. Public buildings (synagogues), private buildings, agricultural facilities and a few residential neighborhoods have been excavated. A number of well-preserved settlements have been surveyed, and their buildings measured. Thus we have an additional independent source of information on the rural economy and community life at that time. This evidence has been presented and integrated throughout these pages. In general, the information derived from these remnants corroborates and supports the conclusions drawn from analysis of the texts. In addition, many inscriptions, particularly dedications from synagogues, were discovered; this information is also presented in the discussion. As noted, these findings widely agree with the rabbinic literature. For instance, (1) the inventory of rural roads fits that indicated by the rabbinic literature, revealing a large number of roads and their physical character (Chapter 3.VII.12, below). The large number of roads also testifies to the organizational and communal ability of the villagers, including their ability to expropriate agricultural land, and to prevent damage to roads by farmers whose fields bordered the road (this subject is discussed in Chapter 1.IV.2). (2) Public cisterns were found on roads outside the village, at the "entrances" and in squares within the village. The same is indicated by the rabbinic literature, as we show (Chapter 1, ibid.). The archeological finding proves, then, that the Talmudic literature does reflect the real setting. (3) In most of the rural villages no walls were discovered, and this is also indicated by our sources. On the other hand, security arrangements and installations such as those described by the rabbinic literature were found (Chapter 1.III.2.3). (4) Synagogue inscriptions reveal the custom described in the rabbinic literature of donating money to the city, or of supplying products out of goodwill to the community and the synagogue (Chapter 1.III.2). (5) Weights that were issued by Jewish agronomists (evidently in semi-independent communities) that operated in the *polis* cities were found (Chapter 1.III.3.3). (6) The evidence regarding the village of Kefar Hananiah and the trade in ceramics is clearly proven by the archeometric findings from that region (Adan Bayewitz 1985). (7) The rabbinic texts indicate a rural settlement whose residents traded intensively. This may seem exaggerated and utopian. However, the papyri found in the Judean desert prove that land and agricultural and industrial products were indeed purchased and sold in these small villages in the Jordan Rift (Lewis 1989; Eshel 1992; 1992a). (8) The rabbinic literature contains a great deal of agricultural information, and most of it is realistic, absolutely reasonable and valuable to the study of history (Felix *et al.* 1963). (9) The rabbinic texts describe agricultural installations, such as wine presses and olive presses. The descriptions are sometimes schematic but they are credible. However, they do not express the full technological wealth of the time.

The last points presented deal with the reference in rabbinic texts to the real setting, as an aside (see section (c), p. 7 above). However, points (1) to (5) involve subjects that the rabbis addressed directly and preached about, and they also provide some evidence of the degree of public discipline regarding the instructions of the rabbis.

The general question of comparison between the rabbinic texts and archeological findings is beyond the scope of the present work. This is not a simple issue, and the circumstances are not always consistent. However, with respect to our research, the archeological findings fit well with the information derived from the rabbinic literature. This notwithstanding, it would be a mistake to go too far and accept all rabbinic texts at face value. In our discussion of the roads we showed that the Talmudic source exaggerated a little in the measurements of the width of the roads. The Talmud also refers to four roads that were paved to each estate, and this is also an exaggeration. The Talmud notes ten public installations and services that every town must have (PT Ridushin IV, 66a; BT Sanhedrin 17a, *et al.*). Of these, a synagogue and a bathhouse were found in many places. However, a lavatory has not been found in any of the settlements, although it was also included in the list. It may be, of course, that these lavatories have not yet been excavated, but it is likely that they were actually not so commonplace, or that they were not constructed facilities.

To sum up: in general, the archeological findings confirm and validate the rabbinic texts, and the use of these sources in our work. In the course of the discussion the relevant archeological evidence is of course presented.

INTERNAL EVIDENCE

Its importance notwithstanding, the external evidence by nature encompasses only some of the items presented in our work. The central question is whether the credibility of the rabbinic texts can be corroborated from within the texts themselves. It may seem that a source cannot be used to prove its own credibility, as it is this very evidence that must be corroborated and credited. However, we present a number of points that we believe are significant in this respect. Although they are not sufficient to eliminate any doubt regarding our sources, they do indicate that the rabbinic texts were not detached from the practical world and the real environment.

(1) There is no doubt that the rabbis were familiar with the nature of the country and its inhabitants (Klein 1939). They were familiar with the customs of the general society in Palestine, and they knew the landscape, the flora and the fruits. The discussions of technological agricultural subjects, the design of houses, graves, the wine press and the olive press are, in the majority of cases, completely realistic. Numerous books and essays dealing with this field of research testify to this (see above).

(2) *Did the public listen to the rabbis?* The rabbinic literature indicates that the wide masses in general obeyed the instructions of the rabbis. This situation was not, however, consistent. In the Talmudic literature we find evidence that the majority of the public refused to accept the rabbis' opinion in a number of areas. "Amei Ha-aretz" did not observe the laws of purification, and did not practice tithing, nor did they obey the teachings in some other areas (Oppenheimer 1977). In the Tannaic period, the masses had a particularly negative attitude toward learning the Torah. However, there is no indication that the general public did not observe Kashrut, the Sabbath,

purification of the family ("Nidda"), the laws of festivals and other laws. The archeological findings testify to widespread observance of the Scriptures in several respects (such as the form of the synagogue, the number of ritual baths and more). However, these findings do not refer to the details of the laws, and this subject merits further study (Goodman 1983).

The division between the areas in which the rabbis were obeyed, and those in which compliance was limited to a specific group, is logical in terms of both the law and the society. The rabbinic literature does not present a uniform stereotypical picture. This lends it greater credibility. If this were not the true situation, the rabbis would have presented the entire public as being obedient. The lack of uniformity provides internal proof of the general reliability, although separate examination of each of the subjects of the Mishna is still warranted. Levine and Goodman devote a detailed discussion to this subject, citing many examples of disobedience of the rabbis (Goodman ibid.; Levine 1985). In our opinion, it is the inconsistent picture that is most realistic and is proven, in a general sense, from within.

(3) *The community in the rabbinic literature and in reality*. The description of the community and its customs that arises from the rabbinic literature is also not stereotyped. Our sources include much evidence of difficulties in enforcing procedures. Thus, for instance, the rabbis are asked to ease the sentence of people who have been ordered to destroy their houses. We hear about deviations from planning laws, dumping of garbage in public areas, planting trees too close to a built-up area, building a ledge that protrudes into public property and failure to send a child to school (Chapter 1.III below). There are also cases in which the community as a whole disobeyed the rabbis, as, for instance, when the members of the community dismissed a rabbi who refused to cut out verses in prayer, even though he acted according to the law and was supported by the other rabbis (PT Meg. IV, 75b, BT ibid. 22a), and other similar problems. Again, these are realistic difficulties, and it is hard to understand their inclusion if they did not really exist.

(4) *The status of the rabbis*. The rabbis assumed extensive rights, saw themselves as the leaders of the public and demanded that the masses honor them on the basis of their being scholars. It was typical of them to demand that others stand in the presence of a rabbi, and to expect the daughter of a rabbi to be considered a preferred candidate for marriage, as well as to demand other expressions of preferred status (Levine 1985, pp. 26–32). On the other hand, their actual status in the community was modest and marginal. The rabbis in Palestine did not head the community (in contrast to the demands of the Babylonian rabbis); they did not appoint the community leaders and did not demand control of the leaders' actions. The rabbis did not consider themselves worthy of determining the customs of the state, but believed it their role to formulate and enforce the accepted custom (Elon 1988, I, pp. 740 ff.).

12

A typical example is their status regarding the court. This community matter, which by nature was related to the men of the Scriptures, was left quite open. In our discussion of this subject (Chapter 1.III.2 below), we show that the rabbis found themselves in an uncomfortable position regarding this matter. On the one hand, they supported the community institutions and on the other they assumed the right of judgment. For this reason their stand was not clear-cut.

Once again we reach the same conclusion: the picture portrayed is not stereotypical. In the community in which they were wanted, they and those of their status enjoyed greater influence. Thus, the image of the community in this period is realistic and reflects the status of rabbis, including their limitations.

(5) *The Babylonian community as a test case*. In the following we briefly discuss the reliability of the Babylonian texts, and the nature of the Jewish community in Babylon. In this discussion we show that the community in Babylon had a different character to that in Palestine, and we point out the methodological difficulties in using the Babylonian Talmud as a source.

The Babylonian texts are similar in style and nature to those from Palestine, and accordingly they constitute a sort of test case. The conclusions that arise from the corpus of the Babylonian Talmud are different, and there is a great difference between the use of the Palestinian texts and that of the Babylonian Talmud as a historical source. This distinction reveals the quality of our research tool and criteria, and constitutes a sort of internal evidence of the reliability of the methods that we have applied.

In summary, we see the rabbinic texts as a reliable historical source. In this respect, they are as valuable as the Roman legal texts. The Roman law literature is also not an absolutely reliable historical source; here too, we can assume that not all the laws were observed to the word. Yet no researcher would consider neglecting these texts, even though he or she would try to confirm them in light of other knowledge of daily life of the time. We have adopted the same approach to the rabbinic texts. In general, we accept them as a reliable historical source, with the limitations and reservations already noted.

Different weights should be accorded theoretical law and indications of day-to-day life. A distinction should be made between a source that describes what was probably an unusual incident and one that describes a daily custom. A description in a legend should be treated differently to evidence of actual activity.

Every source requires examination and clarification, but we do not believe that there is any reason to reject the use of a Talmudic saying as a historical source without valid, proven textual, philological, historical or logical objections.

THE BABYLONIAN TALMUD AS A
HISTORICAL SOURCE

To this point we have dealt with texts from Palestine. It seems that the Babylonian texts should be treated differently; their use requires particular caution. In this area we have also followed numerous scholars, and have not sought any methodological innovations. Our position on this subject is summarized by Gafni in his discussion of the Babylonian texts in general, and the Jewish community in Babylon in particular (Gafni 1991, pp. 19–30). The text of the Babylonian Talmud is a conglomeration that seems edited and complete from the outside but which is actually composed of a number of different elements, as follows:

(1) Palestinian texts, as described above.
(2) The Babylonian situation as known by the rabbis of Babylon.
(3) The rabbis' utopia, that is, the reality desired by the residents of the beit midrash (school).
(4) The rabbis' interpretations. The Babylonian rabbis were not always familiar with the situation in Palestine and therefore they interpreted these texts, at times, according to and inspired by the Babylonian situation, and at other times according to their own understanding and rules of interpretation. Needless to say, the result was not always realistic.
(5) The inner dialectic of the Talmud and the objectives regarding the issue at hand, the desire to present the discussion of the law in the form of a dialogue (question and explanation), the aim of harmonization, literary needs and other rules of dialectics of the Babylonian issue.
(6) The literary considerations of the last editor, and the last group of editors (the Savoraim).

Another question is: to what extent were the rabbis of Babylon involved in Jewish life of their time?

Our knowledge about Babylon refers mainly to the life of the Amoraim; we learn about life in the villages only from the Palestinian texts. A typical example is that a book was written about the economy of the Babylonian Amoraim, and this research and others were conducted on the economy in Palestine in general, but not on the economy of the rabbis.

In the course of the present work we refrain from dealing with texts that refer to life in Babylon, or the positions of the Babylonian rabbis, the editors of the Talmud. On the other hand, we do use those texts that seemed to us to fit with the Palestinian material, or quotations from the Palestinian texts that do not seem to have been altered by the editors of the Talmud. Moreover, it can be assumed that the Babylonian discussions of economic sectors that prospered in Babylon were also influenced by the situation in Babylon. Thus we limit our use of the Babylonian material that deals with such industries as flax-growing, fishing and so forth. We also consider the clear Babylonian formulations in those cases in which the Babylonian tradition differs from that in the Palestinian sources. Because of the limitations of the present work, we could not provide a detailed discussion of every case, pointing out the most prominent differences.

THEORY AND REALITY

The evidence that arises from the literary sources is to a great extent theoretical and schematic. As every researcher knows, there is a difference between the society as portrayed in literature and legal texts on the one hand, and the society in reality. In this respect the rabbinic texts do not differ greatly from every other literary stratum of the Roman era. The differences between the reality and the literary works have been dealt with extensively by researchers of the empire (MacMullen 1990, pp. 56–67). There are many examples, such as the difference in the position of women in the economy as portrayed in the Roman literary texts and the epigraphic evidence, the existence of small cities in the western empire, the vague distinction between city and village (Chapter 1.III.4 below), and many other subjects.

Discrepancies of this type also appear to some extent in the Jewish texts. An example is the utopian objection to trade and the preference for self-sufficiency. This utopian view is expressed in the rabbis' teachings, in the works of Roman authors, as well as by the fathers of the Christian church (Chapter 3.XI below). However, in the rabbinic texts we can see that this economic system is purely utopian.

The rabbinic literature is clearly popular literature, and it is possible to determine which sayings are theoretical and which are more realistic. Discrepancies do, however, still exist and they present the challenge that makes historical research interesting and exciting.

The rabbinic literature is literature, but this does not detract from its historical value. A book has recently been written on economics in the Mishna (Neusner 1990) as though the Mishna is an independent creation, detached from reality. It is as if a book was written on the economy according to Cicero, or the economy according only to Lucius Apuleius, or according to the body only of laws of Theodosius. Examinations of this sort are good for what they are (Millar 1981), but those interested in learning about the economics of the period should concentrate on using all the literary and archeological material to construct a full, complete picture, tested according to internal and external evidence and according to the mutual fit between all parts of the picture.

In this work, Chapter 5 provides empirical evidence of the correctness of the method employed, as it presents an overall picture in which most of the building blocks we used are integrated into a single, clear, developed structure. In this chapter the evidence combines to produce a general picture of an open, developing economy, either generating, or resulting from demographic growth.

1

Settlement patterns

I. CLASSIFICATION OF SETTLEMENTS

Classical culture recognized three different levels of settlement: (1) the independent *polis*; (2) the "town" or agricultural village; (3) the "villa" or rural farmstead. Talmudic literature also dealt with the classification of the different types of settlement. The sages often refer to the tripartite distinction between town (*kerakh*), *'yr*, and village (*kfr*) (Krauss 1929, pp. 1–50). The *kerakh* was a large, fortified (walled) settlement, populated by non-Jews. Thus, one who would enter such a settlement was required to recite a special prayer in view of the dangers of a large city. In terms of settlement status, the *kerakh* was similar to the non-Jewish *polis* in Palestine, although the two need not always have been the same.

According to Krauss (ibid.), the *kerakh* was a walled settlement. We shall not, however, deal with this point in detail. In any event, it is clear that one of the major characteristics of this type of settlement was the great number of luxury items available there (see, for example, T Miqva'ot 4:6; T Shabbat 4:3; BT Shabbat 41b; T Eruvin 9:18; PT Eruvin VIII, 25b; T Avodah Zarah 6:6; BT Avodah Zarah 12a; T Bava Metzia 3:20; BT Bava Metzia 52a; T Berachot 7:16; BT Berachot 60a; T Avodah Zarah 1:6; T Kelim Bava Metzia 10:6; T Pesahim 1:13 and parallels; T Nidah 6:9).

The village in this context is a site, a number of buildings or a small settlement without public or communal institutions (see below). The town (*'yr*) includes all of those settlements somewhere in between the "village" and the gentile *polis*. This type of settlement complex was called *'yr* (singular), *'yyrot* (plural) and in Aramaic *krt'* (singular), *kryyt'* (plural). Talmudic traditions also distinguish between a "large *'yr*" and a "small *'yr*." We shall return to deal with this distinction in the course of our discussion.

The Sages did not always adhere strictly to these distinctions in terminology. In addition to the tripartite division discussed above, there was also a dual division: *kerach* and village. The former was a rich and developed settlement while the latter had a much lower standard of living. The women in the *kerach* were more wont to frequent bathhouses. The bakers in the *kerach* baked more and more often than those of the village. There were many other similar distinctions (T Pesahim 1:13 and parallels; T Niddah 6:9 *et al.*). There were also distinctions between the residents of the various types of settlements. The resident of the *'yr* (*krtny* – from *krt'*) is often juxtaposed to the resident of the city. The urban dweller is accustomed to wealth and power associated with the government while the rural *krtny* is naive and ill at ease with life in the big city. The *midrash* describes how a rural bumpkin (*krtny*) came to the city and proceeded to break expensive glassware. The owner, an urban resident, did not ask for payment since the *krtny* had neither any idea of the value of the glass nor the means to pay anyway (Bereshit Rabbah 19:6, p. 175; see also T Kiddushin 2:7; BT Hagigah 13b *et al.*). It should be pointed out, however, that the Rabbinic sources were not always consistent in their use of the terminology and sometimes the village and *'yr* are interchanged.

This lack of consistency on the part of the rabbis, as well as on the part of gentile authors, can lead to a degree of confusion. *'yr* or town may refer a few times to a *polis*, to a farmstead or to a village. *Kryyt'* can refer to a small village or to large villages with thousands of inhabitants. The various phrases and concepts can even be interchanged at times in the same source.

Of course, the modern-day scholar cannot make do with the ancient and occasionally confusing system of antiquity. The ancient system may, however, still serve as the basis for the classification of settlements. This question of definition between town (village) and city will be discussed below in III.4. We should like to propose the following levels of settlement:

(1) *polis* (a) metropolis (capital of a province)
            (b) important cities such as Joppa, Eleutheropolis, Diospolis, Neapolis (second century), Gaza, Ascalon, etc.
            (c) smaller cities such as Jamnia, Azotus, Sebaste (from the second century), Diocletianopolis, Aelia Capitolina (in the Roman period), Nicopolis, and other cities.

This subdivision represents the varying sizes of cities, but not administrative or municipal differences.

(2) town (a) "large town" (local center – capital of an area)
          (b) "medium-size town" – large village or local center
          (c) "small town" – small village town.

This second category is found in the sources themselves. A *baraita* in BT Ta'anit 21a explicitly differentiates between a "large town" and a "small town." Eusebius in his Onomasticon differentiates between a village, large village, and town (*policne*). The Madeba Map (Avi-Yonah 1953) distinguishes between *poleis*, large towns, small towns, villages, and plain rural buildings. Essentially, the classification described here is based on an analysis of the size and transportation networks of the various settlements in the

Galilee and Samaria. The major differences between the settlements are found in the levels of transportation networks pertaining to the individual settlements. The ancient sources also refer to different levels of "cities," such as the capitals of toparchies like Jericho, Gofna, Thamna and Lod (before it became a city), or to settlements which are described as a "town and its satellite (or offshoot) settlements" such as "Sikhnin and its satellite settlements," "Beth Hananiah and its satellite settlements" or "Ginossar and its satellite settlements" (S. and Z. Safrai 1975). It is clear, of course, that in addition to these large settlements there were medium-sized and smaller settlements, and for this reason we have proposed our own system. The differences between the settlements mentioned above (2a–c) are in respect to size and population, but not in essential matters. Therefore, in the course of our discussion we shall be able to refer to the different types of settlements cited in (2) as one basic unit.

(3) village   (a) a village composed of a small number of private houses
               (b) the private " 'yr" or Roman villa, usually a house or a number of houses belonging to a wealthy landowner.

The village is a branch, as it were, of the 'yr. Farmers whose land is far from the mother settlement and who find it difficult to return to their homes every day would build a temporary domicile outside the mother settlement. On the other hand, the rich landowner does not want at all to be connected to the mother city and prefers to maintain his distance.

The term 'yr in Talmudic literature refers at times to the private farmstead of a landowner, while the village (kfr) can refer to (3a–b). We shall discuss this further in the course of the book.

II. THE POLIS

II.1 Introduction

As in the rest of the Roman Empire, the cities in Palestine were also the backbone of the province. Municipal activities, government functions, economic affairs, the cultural and intellectual life of the provinces all revolved around the city. The Roman Empire can be defined as a system in which the cities rule the rural population. In this respect, Provincia Judaea-Palastina was no different from any other province of the Roman Empire. The economic structure of the Palestinian polis can, therefore, be studied within the context of the cities of the Empire.

Many studies have examined the phenomenon of the polis at this time. Some studies deal with the polis in the context of the Roman Empire in general (Jones 1971; Claude 1969) while some deal with local problems of cities in the provinces or with specific provinces (Magie 1950; Wacher 1975). There is, as yet, no complete collection of the material on Palestinian cities and, therefore, there is no purpose in dealing with these cities as a separate unit. In this chapter we shall attempt to point out the general characteristics of the city during the Roman period in Palestine.

II.2 Urbanization

II.2.1 The Hellenistic period (before the Hasmonean revolt)

The Hellenistic period begins, for our purposes, in the middle of the Persian period when the coastal cities mentioned in the description of Pseudo-Scylax first appear. It is clear that there were many changes during the Hellenistic period (lasting about four hundred years), but it is not always possible to determine all the details regarding these urban developments. Even so, it is possible to deal with this period as one unit. The cities which were built during this time can be divided into three basic categories (Avi-Yonah 1963, pp. 17–35; Z. Safrai 1982).

II.2.1.1 Coastal cities

The Greeks established colonies along the coast from Achzib in the north to Raphia in the south. However, the ancients did not really know which were the appropriate spots in which to set up a port or harbor city. They also did not always know where such cities were unnecessary. As a result of this ignorance, many cities were founded in the Hellenistic period, but only few of these cities survived beyond that time. Cities like Achzib, Haifa (or Shiqmona), Crocodilonpolis and Adaroth disappeared after this time. The coastal cities during this period were generally established at distances of 8–16 kilometers from one another. The smallest distance is between Crocodilonpolis (at the mouth of Nahal Taninim) and Straton's Tower (later Caesarea), a mere 5 kilometers, and the 2–3 kilometers between Anthedon and Maiumas Gaza. The greatest distance between coastal cities is the 25 kilometers between Straton's Tower and Apollonia. Not all the cities were built at the same time during the Hellenistic period, nor were they all similar in size. It is clear that Straton's Tower and Apollonia were built later on. Apollonia, Shiqmona, Crocodilonpolis and Bucolonpolis were, it appears, very small (Avi-Yonah 1963, pp. 25 ff.).

Paradoxically, Beth She'an should also be added to the list of coastal cities. All the coastal cities were located on important highways and enjoyed excellent agricultural conditions. Beth She'an, throughout all the periods under discussion here, fulfilled both of these conditions and, therefore, for the purpose of our discussion, should be added to the list of coastal cities. Its commercial importance was the result of the fact that it was located at an important commercial intersection leading to the cities of the Transjordan.

II.2.1.2 Cities of the mountainous regions

At this time there were four administrative units: Galilee, Samaria, Judaea and Idumaea. The "city" need not always have been the capital of the district, or region. It is doubtful whether Beth Yerah belonged to the Galilee from an administrative point of view, but it is clear that economically speaking, it should be considered part of that district. Among the cities of the mountainous regions, only Samaria (the future Sebaste) was a large and strong *polis* and this was the case only because the government established a Macedonian colony there. Beth Yerah and Adora did not survive beyond the Hellenistic period. Jerusalem did survive, and more or less functioned as an urban center, but the Greek community there did not develop.

II.2.1.3 Cities of the inner plain

Pegai, Maresha and Geba belong to this category. All of these cities were founded after the Greek conquest of Palestine and are not listed in Pseudo-Scylax. Many of these cities tried to secure control over the mountainous regions, in spite of the difficulties (economic and political) in building cities in this area.

II.2.2 The Hasmonean kingdom

The Hasmoneans conquered most of the coastal cities. These cities also suffered damage as a result of this conquest. The status of these cities during the Hasmonean period is not clear, but it is certain that they all suffered difficulties during this time and it was as if urban development came to a standstill in spite of the economic growth of that period. Only Joppa continued to function as a harbor city at that time (Applebaum 1980).

Pompey and Gabinius

Pompey (63 BC) restored many Greek cities. However, it seems that he did not found or build new cities. Rather, he restored some of the Greek cities from the pre-Hasmonean days. Pompey's decision regarding individual cities can be seen as a process of selection whereby it was decided which cities were viable and could survive, and which small artificial cities could not. Another process of selection was undertaken by Gabinius a few years later. Thus a drop in the number of cities in Palestine does not indicate a drop in the level of urbanization or a halt to urban development. On the contrary, the criteria for the establishment of cities became much higher. Small cities like Pegai, Crocodilonpolis and others were not restored and continued to function only as villages. It should be pointed out that Joppa did not become a *polis*, but remained in Jewish hands and continued to function as a Jewish port (Avi-Yonah 1963, p. 49).

Herod

Herod built three entirely new cities: Caesarea (Straton's Tower), Sebaste (Samaria) and Geba (as well as Antipatris which, however, did not become a *polis*). All three were actually ancient cities which Herod restored and built almost completely anew in elaborate and ornate form. Herod, in spite of all his building activities, never really built a completely new city. He did, however, spend a good deal of money on the construction of Sebaste and Caesarea and built an extensive harbor for that last city, providing it with an important economic base.

II.2.3 The sons of Herod (4 BCE–4 CE)

The sons of Herod ruled over Galilee and the Golan which had been considered marginal until this time in terms of geo-political interests. Thus no cities were built there up to this time (except for Beth Yerah or Philoteria during the Hellenistic period, which did not survive beyond that time for lack of the appropriate basis for urban survival). The attention that these regions now received resulted in the construction of a number of new cities, some of which existed almost down to modern times. The building of Julias was an absolute failure. Herod Antipas apparently thought that the city could survive in a fertile agricultural region even if it was not built near major roads. Julias is near a number of secondary routes, but it seems this was not enough.

Livias, built in the Transjordan, also did not survive too long. The two cities that were built in the Galilee, however, Sepphoris and Tiberias, soon became the major settlements of their regions and continued as such till the beginning of the twentieth century. Tiberias is still the central city of the eastern Galilee. It is possible that a *polis* was established in Joppa at that time (Applebaum, unpublished), but that matter still requires further study.

II.2.4 Vespasian and Hadrian (70–135 CE)

The most far-reaching change was the destruction of Jerusalem, which had been the metropolis as well as the most important urban center of the mountainous region, in the year 70 CE during the Great Rebellion. It was rebuilt as a smaller city in about 130 CE. During this period new cities were founded. This was not the actual construction of new cities, but rather the granting of the rights and status of *polis* to already existing ones (Joppa, Schechem (Neapolis) and possibly also Antipatris). This period marked the further development of the cities of Palestine and in particular the cities of the hill or mountain region. Thus Neapolis was founded as a small city, but quickly began to grow. Sepphoris received a gentile name and the gentile aspects of the city were further stressed. At the same time, however, a number of cities declined in their fortunes or were destroyed. Such cities, for example, were Dor, Geba, Apollonia, and Sebaste, which did not lose their status of *polis*, but became much smaller. Julias and Livias ceased to exist as cities and survived only as villages.

It is possible, though, to find an explanation for this phenomenon. Dor and Apollonia declined on account of the success and growth of nearby Caesarea. The same is true regarding the decline of Sebastea and the growth of Neapolis, only nine kilometers away (Z. Safrai 1986b). Perhaps the decline of Geba is associated with the success of Legio which until now had simply been the base of a Roman legion (the Sixth), but became the city Maximianopolis by the end of the third century CE. There may be individual reasons for the decline of individual cities, but the phenomenon was general and a general reason should be found. There are two possibilities. Either there was an economic decline at this time which resulted in the decline of the small cities, or the process of selection continued, favoring and strengthening stronger cities at the expense of the weaker ones. It would seem likely that the second possibility is correct. The general economic advancements and developments there could not have taken place within the context of an urban recession. Moreover, as we shall see below, urbanization is connected to the strengthening of the non-Jewish population of Palestine and, in fact, derives its momentum from that population, which increased in strength and power at the end of the first century CE and at the beginning of the second century CE. It is thus unlikely that exactly then there was a decline in urbanization.

The Bar-Kochba revolt (132–5) also played a role in the events we have described. There is no reason to claim or assume that these cities were destroyed during that revolt. However, the difficult economic situation in the wake of the revolt may have contributed to their decline. The strong cities quickly recuperated, while the weak ones disappeared.

II.2.5 The third century

Cities built at this time in the plain include Beth Gubrin (Eleutheropolis), Emmaus (Nicopolis), Lod (Diospolis), and Legio (Maximianoupolis, built at the end of the third century). It is likely that Antipatris was also built at this time, although there is no definite proof. The common denominator of all these cities is that they serve to connect the mountain region cities (built, for the most part, earlier) and the coastal cities. We shall discuss this point further below. Some cities which had begun to decline in the second century now lost the official status of *polis* and became villages (Geba, Dor, Apollonia). This represents the end of the period of their decline which had started over a century before.

II.2.6 The Byzantine period

This period saw the rise of a great number of small cities which lacked the natural urban qualifications to survive. Diocletian was the emperor who began this urban building in Palestine. At the beginning of his reign, Maximianoupolis was built in the Jezreel Valley. This city did, apparently, have the proper natural qualifications. Next, Diocletianopolis was built, 2–3 kilometers from Ascalon. It is obvious that two cities cannot function within such a small area. Some of the cities which were built now were cities which had ceased to function or had disappeared during the second or third centuries (Dor, Apollonia and Geba). Some were the result of a bifurcation of existing cities (Azotus Paralius, Maiumas Gaza, etc.). This perhaps might explain the relationship between Ascalon, a port city, and Diocletianopolis, the corresponding inland city. Some of the cities were actually built anew (Bethulia, Helenoupolis and a number of cities whose location is unknown). All of this is the result of the hyper-urbanization which took place in the Byzantine period. Palaestina Prima became one of the most urbanized provinces in the Byzantine empire, second to Pamphilia (Koder 1986). Palaestina Secunda was a little less urbanized. Characteristic of this process is the construction of artificial cities which had no chance of survival. The new cities were, to be sure, built in economically developed regions, but they were also built in areas already dense with urban construction. It is not surprising that they ceased to exist a short time after they had been built.

Many of these new cities were built in the Gaza Strip. This phenomenon requires some explanation. Moreover, throughout the entire period, Anthedon, only 2–3 kilometers from Gaza, continued to function. The city also had a small harbor which naturally would have served to compete with the harbor of Gaza. At first glance it would seem that Anthedon should be defined as an artificial city which should not have been rebuilt during the time of Gabinius, or which should have ceased to exist in the second century. The city, however, did survive. It is true that we lack information regarding the area in the second or third centuries, and perhaps the city did suffer some type of decline. It appears, however, in all the lists of cities from the Second Temple period onwards and is certainly functioning as a city from the time of the Council of Ephesos (431) and afterwards.

This would seem to prove that the Gaza region was quite conducive to urban development. The following factors may explain this phenomenon. (1) The region contained important intersections of the routes leading from spice and gem centers (Arabia); (2) The major route from Egypt to Syria passed through this area. Needless to say, this route also had a positive effect on more northern regions; (3) This is the only region in which the shore is suitable for the construction of harbors, and the area is also quite fertile. The ground water in the Gaza region is at a particularly high level, but there is little flooding. It would seem certain that the ancients knew how to utilize this water-supply.

All of this, however, only partly explains the great degree of urbanization in that region, and actually only explains why the emperors felt (incorrectly) that this was the best region in which to build additional cities. Our discussion above perhaps partly solves the problem of Anthedon, but it is hard to believe that even in that case this is sufficient. The solution may be found in the political sphere. Maiumas was founded in order to protect the Christian inhabitants there from pressures exerted by pagan Gaza (Avi-Yonah 1963, p. 117). Based on this assumption, we can perhaps offer an additional suggestion. Gaza was certainly a non-Jewish center. Perhaps Anthedon was more of a Jewish center. Anthedon was built by Herod, perhaps to compete with non-Jewish Gaza. Gaza, it should be remembered, was connected both politically and economically to the Nabatean kingdom. Herod did not enjoy very cordial relations with the Nabateans. It is not inconceivable, then, that Herod constructed an artificial city in order to weaken Gaza. There are a number of indications that this may be so, but it cannot be proven. We have no clear-cut reason, in any event, for the continued existence and success of Anthedon during this period, and the matter warrants further study.

II.2.7 The early Arab period

We shall not really deal with this period. However, it should be pointed out that it was a period of decline and destruction in terms of the settlement history of Palestine. Most of the cities in Palestine were destroyed. Only the largest and most established continued to function. During such difficult times only those cities with natural characteristics tended to survive. Thus, the following cities were destroyed: Geba, Dor, Apollonia, Javneh-Yam, Anthedon, Antipatris, Sebaste, and others. The coastal cities suffered in particular, on account of the economic recession there due to the collapse of international sea trade. This phenomenon, however, requires separate study.

II.2.8 Summary of the geo-historical process

Urban development in Palestine was the result of two processes: economic development and internal migration (which could change or affect the balance of power in internal power struggles). Most of the cities were, in one way or another, non-Jewish (except for Jerusalem up until 70 CE and Joppa from 141 BCE–70 CE). It can be stated with a fair degree of certainty that the economic process was the most important factor in regard to urbanization, while political problems tended to hinder the natural outcome of this economic process.

The process of urbanization was almost continuous. It ceased only during the Hasmonean period. The fact that there was an urban crisis, even though there was economic development at the same time, resulted in a greater tendency towards the process of selection whereby the weaker cities were not restored. As we have seen above, crisis conditions speed up the process of urban selection and highlight the differences between cities which have the natural characteristics to survive and artificial cities.

If it were not for Pompey and Gabinius, the process of urban restoration would probably have been much slower. Political considerations of the Hasmoneans hurt the cities. Roman political considerations, however, resulted in precisely the opposite and brought about widespread restoration of the cities. Thus, except for the Hasmonean period, the process of urbanization was continuous. This was the case in spite of the occasional rebellions and difficult security conditions in Palestine. These difficult conditions may have slowed up the process, but did not entirely stop it. Thus, for instance, the period of the anarchy (230–80 CE) did not mark the construction of any new cities. The dying out of cities then must be explained in a different manner.

From a geographic point of view, there are three general characteristics of urbanization: (1) the founding of new cities; (2) the development and growth of existing cities; (3) selection. Selection is an integral part of urban development, even if it results in fewer cities. This selection is a necessary weeding-out process. Perhaps in controlled city-planning mistakes could have been avoided and artificial cities would not have been built. When the building of cities is spontaneous, however, and cities are constructed without always paying heed to geographic considerations, mistakes are inevitable. Hindsight can determine these urban mistakes, but infallibility cannot be demanded of the ancients. Moreover, it is likely that the construction of artificial cities is a necessary stage in rapid urbanization. The very existence of small urban centers is, most likely, necessary for the development of the larger urban settlements. It is difficult to know the exact situation in a city caught up in this process of selection. Did the population and level of services decrease, or did the city simply maintain its status quo while other cities grew and developed? In any event, the decision to transform a city into a *polis* is not based solely on settlement or geographic considerations. It is clear that political considerations were also important and the emperor, relying on the advice of his advisers or the requests of his friends, would decide whether to transform a city into a *polis*. This administrative decision was at times based on whim. Even so, there are a number of geographical stages evident in this stage of urbanization:

(1)   The establishment of small cities on the coast (many of which were artificial cities and many of which had been established as early as the Persian period).

(1a)   The establishment of additional coastal cities and the strengthening of existing cities having the qualifications of survival and growth.

(2)   The process of selection among the coastal cities and the establishment of the first mountain region cities (from the Hellenistic period until the Hasmonean revolt).

(2a)   The continuation of the process of selection among the coastal and hill cities, including the strengthening of central urban sites (from Pompey to Herod).

(2b)   The completion of selection among the coastal cities and the re-establishment of urban hill country centers (from the end of the Herodian period to the reign of Hadrian).

(3)   The construction of cities in the transition or intermediary area (from the second to third centuries), and the further development of the hill or mountain region cities.

(4–4a) Over-urbanization in the plain and the establishment of new cities, including many that failed in stages 2a–2b. Some cities that failed in stage 2, such as Tabor, were also restored. In this case, though, there were reasons particular to that site, apparently connected with its sanctity.

These stages are similar to the stages of urbanization as determined by scholars such as Taaffe (Taaffe and Gauthier 1973). For the sake of comparison, we shall illustrate the situation in Palestine graphically on the basis of Taaffe's model. However, in this representation, there is no relevance assigned to the individual locations of the cities or to the distances between them. This fact requires further study (Figure 1).

Taaffe's model is based on the development of the road network in relation to urban development. It is difficult to examine this model in Palestine for the following reasons. (1) It is very difficult to know exactly when each road was constructed. At best we can sometimes determine the possible time when construction began, but the road could have existed previously in some other form. (2) It is impossible to determine the individual major arteries, or to determine if there were changes in the levels of their function or technological innovations which affected their function. (3) The road network was constructed for the most part by the authorities or by the army. Usually, economic considerations dictated the necessity for construction, but sometimes there were also defense and administrative considerations. The connection, therefore, between the road network and the urban situation is not always clear. For example, Legio took on major importance in the road network already in the second century because it served as the base for the Sixth Roman Legion. The Roman army constructed roads from its base at Legio to the cities of the Galilee. Legio, however, became a city only 150 years later. Lod also occupied a central and important position in the road network by the beginning of the second century. The Via Maris, as well as a number of roads from the base

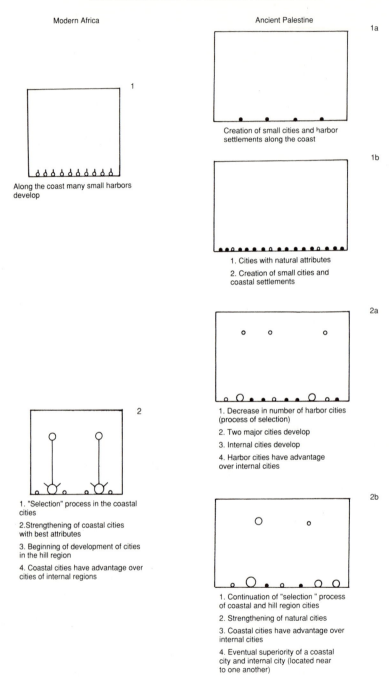

Figure 1 Geographic model of urban development in the Land of Israel during the Hellenistic, Roman and Byzantine periods.

2c

1. Continuation of selection process in coastal cities and strengthening of coastal cities

2. Renewed building of hill cities

3. Increasing power of coastal cities

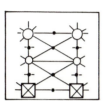

3

1. Coastal cities grow. Selection process ceases

2. Internal cities grow

3. Creation of intermediate cities

4. Roads to intermediate cities and connection to a number of coastal cities. Roads to internal cities and connection to one coastal city

5. Small settlements established at intersections

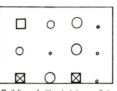

3

1. Building of cities in intermediate zone. These cities usually become powerful quite quickly

2. Further development of coastal and hill cities

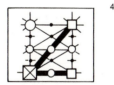

4

1. One coastal city achieves priority

2. One hill city achieves priority

3. High-grade roads between various urban centers

4. Superiority of coastal cities

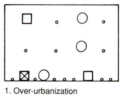

4

1. Over-urbanization

2. Further strengthening of hill cities and cities of intermediate zone

•	Settlement
○	Small city
◯	Medium city
▢	Large city
⊠	Very large city
—	Road
▬	Main road

•	Small settlement
∘	Very small city
○	Small city
◯	Medium-sized city
▢	Large city
⊠	Very large city

Figure 1 cont.

of the hill country, also passed by that site. Lod, however, became a *polis* only much later. It is also clear that in some cases there is a direct connection between the construction of a road and the development of a nearby city, although it is not always easy to distinguish this phenomenon. Therefore, we cannot utilize the road network of Palestine to analyze or improve the model (Figure 2).

II.3 The nature of a Roman *polis*

It is very easy to define a city in the Roman period. An official city is one which received the status of *polis*, and this status was given by the emperor. This administrative definition is most precise, but it does not define the nature of a city sufficiently. The settlements which received this status were generally located near major intersections and became large and important settlements even while they were still villages (A. H. M. Jones 1971, pp. 261–94). The emperor's considerations are beyond the scope of our study. However, it is still necessary to determine the nature of the city after it had been established.

As is well known, the phrase "city" has no exact definition. Scholars have enumerated a number of urban "characteristics," and only those settlements having a great many of those were generally considered, in a geographic sense at least, to be cities. Different periods had different quantitative requirements regarding these characteristics. Thus, for example, a large population is generally considered one of the characteristics of a city. In the Biblical period, however, a large population for a settlement could be several hundred. In classical antiquity, the necessary number may be a few thousand, while in modern times a large population might number several hundred thousand, or even millions.

We shall enumerate below the characteristics of the Palestinian "polis" (apart from the Negev) during the period under discussion. The list is based on the various discussions concerning the modern city, taking into consideration those elements particular to the ancient world (Mumford 1966; Finley 1973, pp. 123–7):

(1) Large population. It is impossible to determine exact numbers, although a small city probably had anywhere from 8,000–20,000 residents. This number is based on the estimated size of cities (see Figure 3).

(2) Institutional structure. The city would have high-functioning and independent administrative bodies as well as a town council (*boule*). This is the major characteristic of a *polis*. Essentially, a *polis* can be defined as a self-ruled settlement possessing the necessary institutions required of the *polis*.

(3) Control over the neighboring region. During the Roman period the

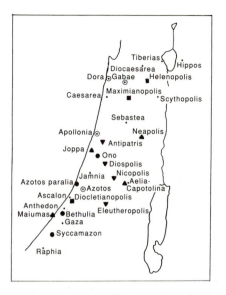

- City founded before the destruction of the Second Temple

▲ City founded between 70–160 CE

▼ City founded between 160–284 CE

■ City founded between 284–350 CE

● City founded in Byzantine period

⊙ City founded during the Second Temple period, destroyed and rebuilt during the Byzantine period

Figure 2 Map of cities in the Land of Israel.

Figure 3 The size of cities in the Land of Israel.

31

polis ruled over the adjacent rural territory. Before that time there was a different municipal system. In that previous system, every district (*toparchy* or *nome*) had a local capital, but that capital as well as its municipal institutions did not control the entire region (Schalit 1969, pp. 100–20).

(4) Architecture. The city had its own unique architectural nature. It had, for instance, many public or community buildings (theatre, stadium, gymnasium, etc.). It usually provided a central supply of water, bath-houses, sewage system, walls and other services. It often had rather crowded residential quarters (see no. 5) and multi-storied buildings (Tsafrir 1984, pp. 59–128).

(5) Social stratification. The city had both rich and poor, nobility and commoners. During the classical period, especially prominent were the rich landowners, their tenants and slaves.

(6) The city was larger than the rural settlement (in accordance with nos. 1 and 4). A middle-sized city was somewhere between 200–300 dunams. The large rural settlements were between 100–120 dunams (see below).

(7) Sources of employment. In the classical city, as well as in the village, the economic system was based on agriculture (see Chapter 4). The city differed in that it was more industrialized, relatively speaking, than the village.

(8) Local mercantile and economic center.

(9) The level of services was relatively high (in accordance with nos. 1, 2, 4 and 5).

(10) Hellenistic population, whether in terms of the origins of the inhabitants or in terms of outlook or culture. This factor is listed last because it is not one of the general characteristics of a city and is particular to antiquity. It is, however, of paramount importance in the case of the cities of Palestine. Actually, a city never existed unless it had a non-Jewish element which eventually, at least, became dominant. The gentile element, however, did not have to be a majority. Thus, for example, cities such as Sepphoris, Tiberias, Lod (Lydda), Schechem and others were established with a majority Jewish or Samaritan autochthonous population. This majority was generally hostile to the gentile (or Samaritan) minority, and opposed the establishment of Hellenistic institutions or Hellenistic practices. It was this Hellenistic population, however, which determined the nature of the city and the establishment of institutions there. Thus, for example, the coins of Sepphoris and Tiberias have imperial and pagan motifs which certainly would not have been acceptable to the Jewish population.

The cities in Palestine were built for the gentile and hellenized population. When the city was established, a gentile population was often brought in, even if it was not indigenous to the region. When he restored the cities in

Palestine, Pompey particularly chose the Hellenistic cities which had been destroyed by the Hasmoneans. This was also the policy of Herod who developed Geba and Sebaste as gentile urban centers. This was not stated specifically regarding Caesarea, and later on the Jews of the city would actually claim that the city was theirs since, as they would state, the founder of the city (Herod) was theoretically Jewish (Josephus, *Antiquities* 20. 173, Levine 1975). In spite of this and in spite of the large Jewish population, the city was essentially non-Jewish. The growth of the foreign community constituted another factor in the openness of the *polis* (city) to the influence of the Hellenistic culture. There were many natives in the *polis*, but it was a Hellenistic settlement, like Roman cities throughout the empire. Thus the *polis* served as a channel for the penetration and dissemination of Hellenism throughout Palestine. A similar process took place, of course, throughout the empire, but in Palestine this cultural-political process also had an ethno-national aspect. It seems that this latter aspect is crucial to understanding the history of the province. In the kingdom of Herod, which was for the most part Jewish and, in fact, in all of Palestine until the Bar-Kochba revolt, the gentile population was found essentially in the cities. In the Second Temple period, however, there were a number of Jewish cities. Jerusalem until 70 CE was Jewish, although it is not clear whether it had the administrative status of a *polis*.

Centers of autochthonous population (Jews, Samaritans and perhaps Edomites) retarded the growth and development of cities and this is one of the reasons why it took so long to establish them in the hill or mountain regions, where the Jewish and Samaritan populations were very strong. This is an example of local political interests affecting the geographic process we described above.

As stated previously, the city controlled the adjacent territory from an administrative as well as from an economic standpoint. This control, however, was not just geographic in nature. There were also social and ethnic implications to the control of the city, since the Hellenistic city, by controlling the countryside, also had control over the Jewish population. Thus, the classic conflict between city and country also took on a social and ethnic guise. This last element, however, requires separate study.

The major source of material for the study of the economy of Palestine is the corpus of Talmudic literature. This material indicates that Jewish settlements were for the most part rural. However, there were Jewish communities in the cities and Talmudic literature occasionally gives a glimpse into the life and customs of the *polis*. The majority of the material, however, deals with the rural and village economy and therefore the bulk of our discussion regarding the economy of Palestine will deal with this sector. We shall deal with the urban economy in Chapter 4(VI).

As mentioned above, the city controlled the adjacent territory. The suburbs of the city may be divided into a number of different types.

(1) Villas belonging to the wealthy (V.5). (2) What may be described as service suburbs, as, for example, the harbors near the coastal cities (Maiumas Gaza, Javneh-Yam, Azotus Paralius, etc.). Hamath Tiberias and Hamath Gader were of a similar nature. These sites had well-known *thermae*. (3) In the rural sector of the city there were villages, both large and small. Thus, for example, within the agricultural periphery of Neapolis were 5 major settlements and 15 satellite villages (Z. Safrai 1986, p. 106, Figure 4). This phenomenon was also especially prominent in the Jerusalem area. Hundreds of graves have been found in the area around Jerusalem. According to Jewish law, these tombs had to be outside the actual settled area. The walls of the city include within them an area of about one square kilometer. To the north and west of the city within an area of 3–4 kilometers very few graves have been found (Kloner 1980, pp. 268–96). These northern and western regions were probably the suburbs of Jerusalem and densely constructed, although not as densely as the city itself. As just stated, the necropolis of the city extended a distance of 3–4 kilometers. According to Kloner, this was the agricultural hinterland of the city. Beyond this were a large number of towns and villages. There were also additional sites within the agricultural region. Kloner (1980, pp. 320–1) counted some 16 sites, some towns and some farms or satellite settlements. In addition, reference should be made to Bethphage (Beth Pagi) which was a suburb, or possibly a neighborhood of the city (S. Safrai 1965, pp. 153–5), even if it was located some 500 meters from the city walls and a deep and steep valley separated it geographically from Jerusalem (Figure 5).

II.4 Economic services provided in the *polis*

The *polis* enjoyed, for the most part, autonomy. Even if the Roman authorities attempted in some ways to limit this privilege, the city still retained a highly developed mechanism for independent self-rule. The local administrative system was also highly efficient and encompassed many aspects of life. The involvement of the city in the economic sphere, the topic of our study, was quite pronounced and even if there are only a few clear-cut specific indications of this regarding the cities of Palestine, there is no reason to assume that the situation there was different from that in the rest of the Empire. Thus the material regarding the Empire in general, pertaining to this point, can also be used for Palestine (A. H. M. Jones 1966, pp. 211–19, 250, 259–69; 1974, pp. 35–61; Magie 1950).

II.4.1

The *polis* owned lands, in the agricultural hinterland as well as in the city. Residences or stores were often built on the municipal lands. The rents for these plots were an important source of income for the city. There are two

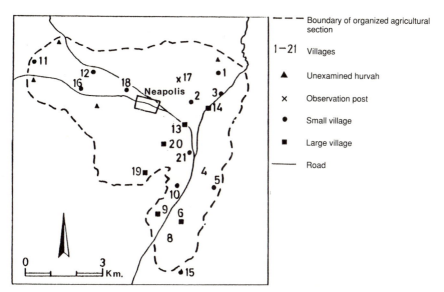

Figure 4 Neapolis: city, suburbs and satellite settlements. After Z. Safrai 1986b, Figure 5.

Figure 5 Necropoleis (ancient cemeteries) in the Jerusalem area at the end of the Second Temple period. After Kloner 1980, Figure 3.8.

35

testimonies to this practice from the Byzantine period regarding the cities of Palestine. In Ascalon, for instance, there was a law that three-quarters of the property of a landowner who was not survived by a male would be forfeited to the city (Procopius, *Anecdota* 29. 17; A. H. M. Jones 1966, p. 200). Choricius seems also to refer to municipal land in Caesarea (*Or.* 2. 19). There is no clear indication that the Jewish town owned land, although one source does mention that a store belonged to an *'yr* (T Avodah Zarah 6(7):1). On the one hand, it is possible that the *'yr* refers to a *polis*, while on the other hand it is also possible that the reference is to a Jewish town having a highly developed and independent level of self-government (pp. 46–61 below). Talmudic traditions also possibly relate an instance of the confiscation of a house for a *polis* (T Avodah Zarah 6:2).

The city, too, had a monopoly on a number of elements associated with business and trade. The selling or renting out of these monopolies was also an important source of income for the city.

II.4.2

The *polis* could also levy duties or taxes on internal trade in the city, and especially on items imported into the city. There is no clear-cut source pertaining to this practice as regards the cities of Palestine, but neither is there reason to think that this province was different from any other province in the Empire. Midrash Psalms 118:18 (p. 243) describes a merchant who had already paid the levies to the customs agents along the road. When he reached the city (lit. *medinah*, meaning *polis*), he had to pay the *eparchos* (prefect) at the gate of the city. The source is not clear as to whether the levies were municipal or imperial, but the distinction between those who collected the levies on the road (*haragim* and *haramim*) and "*eparchos*" in the city (*medinah*) possibly indicates that it was a city tax. Another *midrash* mentions the "*fensor*" or the *defensor* who stood at the entrance to the city (Tanhuma Deuteronomy, Shoftim; PT Shabbat VI, 8d). This would also seem to be dealing with a municipal customs agent (Dan 1984, pp. 103–6; Lieberman 1963, pp. 114–15; Rees 1952; Abbot and Johnson 1922, p. 93). A *defensor* of the *demos* is mentioned in reference to Gaza (Marcus Diaconus, *Vita Porphyrii* 25 (fifth century)). Jewish sources also mention the *ekdikos* – perhaps the Greek equivalent of the *defensor* – Bereshit Rabbah 12, p. 108). Procopius of Gaza sent a letter to his brother with a recommendation regarding the *ekdikos*, although it is not clear from the context where this official was (*Letters of Aeneas* 43, 44 (fifth to sixth centuries)). This reference does indicate that the official seemed to function specifically in the judicial sphere (cf. *C. Th.* 1. 29. 3 – Rees 1952, pp. 44–90). An inscription from Gerassa in the Transjordan mentions a *scholasticus* (lawyer) who was also an *ekdikos* and responsible for the construction of the stoa in the city (Welles 1938, no. 275).

II.4.3

The *polis* also supplied the economic infrastructure of the city. It constructed city streets and roads, provided water, built a market (*agora*) and other business installations. The stores in the city were usually found along the main streets, and some were also concentrated in the market (*agora*) area. In Palestine, stores have been found in Herodian Jerusalem along the main street of the city (as yet unpublished in scholarly literature). Such stores are also depicted in the Byzantine representation of Jerusalem in the Madeba Map (Avi-Yonah 1953, p. 147) and have also been found in Sebaste as well as in Antipatris (Kochavi 1989, 2111; see also Hirschfeld 1987, p. 50). A building from an *agora* was excavated in Mampsis (Negev 1988, pp. 163–7) in Palaestina Tertia, and an *agora* is mentioned in relation to Gaza (fifth century – Choricius 1. 17–18; Caesarea, ibid. 3. 39–41) and it is likely that such buildings were also constructed in other cities. The city had mercantile quarters devoted to a single trade or industry. In Jerusalem at the end of the Second Temple period, for instance, there was a quarter in which all the textile stores were centered (wool and clothing), and another with the shops of the smithies (Josephus, *BJ* 5. 331). Tiberias had a tailors' market (PT Erubin V, 22d) and Beth She'an had a district where wheat was sold (*SEG* VIII. 43).

Such districts were also found in the suburb or harbor cities such as Javneh-Yam (Mahoza D'Javneh), the harbor of Ascalon, Azotus Paralius and Maiumas Gaza. Some of these suburbs eventually achieved independent municipal status even though, for all intents and purposes, they remained suburbs. Some of the cities of Palestine had *stationes municipiorum*, business offices, in some of the other major urban centers of the Empire (see Chapter 3.VI). Therefore it is likely that cities from other provinces, or other cities of Palestine had such *stationes municipiorum*. There are also what seem to be a number of references to such business offices of local villages in the local urban center (Chapter 3.III below).

The most important official in the economic sphere was the *agoranomos*, also referred to as the *logistes*. The Talmudic literature of Palestine mentions the *agoranomos* quite often (Sperber 1977), and it would seem that the Jewish town also had such an official. It is therefore not always easy to distinguish whether the sources are referring to this official in a *polis* or in a Jewish settlement. The large number of traditions concerning this official, however, indicate the importance of the function. The *agoranomos* was generally elected by the inhabitants of the city. The sons of Herod, however, were usually involved in this official's appointment. Thus, for instance, Herod Antipas appointed Agrippa to the position in Tiberias (*Ant.* 18. 149) and II Maccabees 3:4 relates a dispute between the *prostates* (administrator) of the Temple and the High Priest regarding control of the market in Jerusalem; this would seem to indicate a relationship between this economic function and the Temple authorities.

However, in most cities this was a municipal appointment. The duties of the *agoranomos* were as follows.

(1) The supplying of goods to the city. This was particularly important regarding those cities which were not located in agricultural districts. In Palestine, this duty was of less importance and there are no clear-cut traditions referring to it. Other officials mentioned in a similar capacity were the *astinomos* and the *sitonoi*. The *sitonoi* were responsible for supplying the city with flour (Chapter 2.I.2 below). In the course of our discussion in another chapter, when we discuss whether there are any indications that wheat was given out gratis or at a subsidized price, we shall see that there are no traditions relating to this aspect of the *sitonoi*'s job. The phrase, though, was well known to the rabbis, and it eventually came to mean simply large-scale merchants in the Palestinian traditions.

The *astinomos* was also apparently connected to some aspect of food supply. Originally this function related to building bridges and supplying water. In smaller cities, however, the *astinomos* also fulfilled this additional function (A.H.M. Jones 1966, pp. 214–15). In Gaza, for instance, there was an *astinomos* who was responsible for a water installation (Choricius 34. 1). PT Ma'aser Sheni V, 56b mentions three *astonansin* (= *astinomoi*) in Lod and they were considered, in the framework of their function, as experts regarding the price of fruit. Thus, it would seem likely that they dealt with some aspect of food supply or the setting of prices (see below).

(2) Setting prices. In the *halachah* as related in the Palestinian traditions, the *agoranomos* was not in charge of setting prices (Chapter 1.III below). This, however, would seem to apply only to the Jewish town where the *agoranomos* was bound by *halachah*, and would not, most likely, be the case in the *polis*. This situation is reflected in the law that states that a large merchant (*tgr*) can sell fruits even if tithes had not been set aside from them, since "the *agoranomos* was a non-Jew and he forced him to sell at a cheap price" (PT Demai II, 22c). The fact that the non-Jew is mentioned shows that this practice goes against the usually accepted law. It also indicates that the tradition refers to a *polis*, in which case the *agoranomos* would certainly be non-Jewish.

(3) Certifying weights and measures, as well as providing them. There is not much literary evidence, but the numerous weights which have been discovered and which had the seal of the *agoranomos* on them is ample proof of this function. The weights of Palestine have not yet been fully catalogued and studied and there is, to date, no single comprehensive work on the matter. A number of studies, however, have dealt with some collections of weights (Lifschitz 1976; S. Qedar 1978, 1981, 1983; Manns 1984, *et al.*). Other weights have been published and studied in the various reports on excavations. Most of the weights were produced by the *agoranomos*, although a few seem to have come from other officials, such as the functionary in charge of fairs (Qedar 1978, p. 56), the proconsul himself (Qedar

1981, p. 45; 1983, p. 57), the XV Roman Legion (Qedar 1981, p. 45), the *eparchos* (Qedar 1981, p. 57), the *episcopus* (of a farm or a church) (Qedar 1978, p. 65), and other officials (Qedar 1979, p. 36, etc.). The setting of standards for weights was of great importance on account of the many types of metals in circulation. It does, however, require separate study.

(4) Checking the quality of produce and supervising the activities of the market-place. This was probably the most important, as well as the most commonplace, activity of the *agoranomos*. Thus, for example, R. Meir establishes that a sponge made from rubber is to be considered an implement because the *agoranomos* uses such a sponge to taste wine and determine its quality (T Bava Kama 6:9). Another story relates that a *logistes* was angry with the bakers who baked their loaves from low-quality wheat (Sperber 1970; Lieberman 1944–5; T Avodah Zarah 7:6, concerning the non-Jewish *agoranomos* who tasted wine, and other examples in Sperber 1977).

The Palestinian Talmudic traditions do not provide much information regarding economic life, trade and services in the city. It is clear that the cities of Palestine had vibrant economies, but much of the details can be learned only through comparison with the other provinces of the Roman Empire.

III. THE TOWN

As we stated above, this type of settlement is the *'yr* (pl. *'yyrot*) in Hebrew, while in Aramaic it is called the *krt'* (pl. *kryyt'*). Most of the towns in Palestine in the Roman period were not established at that time, but rather were the continuation of the Israelite or Hellenistic period settlements. New settlements were often located on the remains of an older site from the Israelite period. The continuity of settlement can be established through the study of archeological remains as well as from the fact that the ancient name was often preserved in one form or another.

III.1 Description of the town

III.1.1

The usual location for such a settlement was at the top of a mountain or at the edges of a slope. The residents of the ancient settlement usually sought out the most fortified point in the area. During the Roman period the settlements began to abandon the fortified peaks, preferring the more level area below. This process, which began in the Roman period, continued with greater intensity in the Byzantine period. New settlements were no longer built in the fortified area, while the established sites began to expand towards more level ground. Thus pottery sherds from an ancient settlement are often found in the high fortified area, while Byzantine sherds are to a great extent found below this original settlement.

Until the Roman period, each individual settlement was responsible for its own defense. The small town was supposed to be capable of defending itself as well as of serving as a base for the defense of the area and the country at large. The situation changed after the Second Temple period. Military defense became the responsibility of the state, and the Roman army was now responsible for dealing with the threat of invasion. Moreover, the inhabitants of the local settlements generally had no interest in defending the state against invasion and would usually support the invader and not the Roman army. Individual settlements did have to defend themselves against bandits, but this was not particularly difficult as gangs of marauders were generally not large and did not have much fire power. Thus, in terms of settlements, the defense factor became somewhat secondary and continued to be of influence only in a more "historic" sense: the inhabitants simply preferred to make use of existing buildings, often in the old fortified area, and not to rebuild the settlement.

In spite of abandoning the fortified peaks in the Roman period, the new settlements were not built on the most level land of the plain below. This was usually the fertile farm land, and there was no reason to lose it to urban construction. If there was a well in the village, the houses were usually built above the line of the well so that they would be near it, but would not lose the use of arable land which could be irrigated. Interesting examples of this type of construction are villages like Chorazin in the Lower Galilee, Habalta in Benjamin, and Fukhin and Bethther in the Judaean Mountains (Figure 6).

Until the Bar-Kochba revolt, all towns were Jewish. There were no mixed or non-Jewish towns. Mixed settlements were either in the periphery or in those regions that were not completely part of Palestine. As is well known, the Jewish population suffered reversals in the wake of the Bar-Kochba revolt. Many towns were now settled by non-Jews, and Talmudic literature began to describe the new reality of mixed settlements even though most of the information in Talmudic literature regarding non-Jews pertains to the *polis*. In any event, in the Galilee the Jews remained the major component of the population until the end of the Talmudic period, and the towns in this area also remained almost completely Jewish. Therefore, most of our discussion will center around the "Jewish town," since this was the reality with which most of Talmudic literature was acquainted. For the most part, the data regarding the Jewish town is the same as that of the mixed town. If this is not so, we shall comment on that particular point.

III.1.2

The population and size of the Jewish town was not fixed. Josephus relates that every village in the Galilee had at least 15,000 inhabitants (*BJ* 3. 43). This figure is of no value and is certainly exaggerated, as are most of the other population figures in Josephus. Population figures, however, are found in

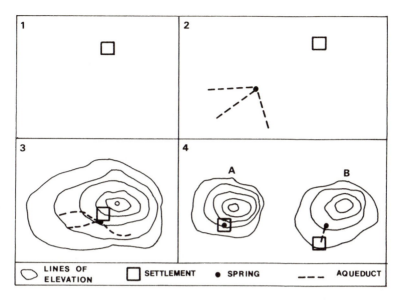

1. Settlement without a spring

2. Settlement and spring in agricultural area – normal situation

3. Settlement above a spring. Spring waters mostly agricultural terrain

4. Settlement around a spring. The spring provides water for the settlement – most unusual

Figure 6 The village settlement: the location of fountains.

Talmudic literature. BT Ta'anit 21a (according to readings in the manuscripts) states that a large city has the capacity to send forth 1,500 men of military age, while a small town can send forth 500. The language of the Talmud literally refers to those who could serve in the infantry. It is difficult to know what percentage of the population was included in this phrase. It would seem likely, though, that all males from the ages of 16–18 until about 55–60 should be included. If so, a large town would have about 1,000 families, while a small one would have about 350. All of these figures are, of course, estimates. Seder Eliyahu Rabbah (ch. 9, p. 48) mentions a "little town" with 60 houses, but it is difficult to estimate how many inhabitants lived in such "houses." Although it is difficult to date this tradition, it would seem that this work reflects the period of the Roman anarchy and represents a depressed situation.

A survey undertaken in the Golan and Galilee has established three levels of settlements which could be included within our definition of a town

(Yeirin 1971). The largest settlements were about 90–100 dunams and had about 1,000 rooms (used as residences). There were, of course, families which used more than one room, and a number of domiciles were undoubtedly more than one storey high. Thus, we can estimate that the large town had about 1,000 small families.

The second settlement level was about 30–45 dunams and had approximately 300 rooms. This is more or less the equivalent of 350 families and is also in keeping with the number cited in the Talmud for a "small town." This is, too, the "medium-sized town" that we mentioned at the beginning of our study. Studies and surveys have shown, however, that the settlements in the Galilee were about 25 per cent larger than the settlements in the rest of the country. Thus, for instance, Um Rihan in Samaria was 40 dunams (Dar *et al.* 1986). The small towns, according to the classification suggested above, would be represented in the Galilee by such settlements as Hirbet Shema' (10 dunams), in the Carmel by a site such as Hirbet Ali a-Din, and in the hills of Lod by such settlements as Hirbet Najar, Hirbet Hamam and Hirbet Yeqavim, and many other small settlements which were 5–8 dunams in size and had 100–250 families, according to the number of rooms there. Later on we shall prove that 100–120 males was the minimum number of men in a settlement in order for it to have been considered a town. Any settlement with less than that number of males was considered a village (Z. Safrai 1983b, pp. 173–5).

The external form of the town

A complete settlement has yet to be excavated. A number of groups of buildings have been excavated in Capernaum (Corbo 1975, Figure 7). At Meiron a small quarter was excavated (Meyers *et al.* 1981), and in Chorazin a number of buildings were excavated together with the synagogue which, all told, give the impression of a limited quarter (Yeivin 1971, Figure 8). Most recently, Negev and Yeivin have undertaken extensive archeological excavations in Hirbet Susyah, in the southern region of Mt Hebron (Negev 1985). A number of settlements, though, have been surveyed. One of the most extensive surveys was that of Um Rihan in the northern region of Samaria (Dar *et al.* 1986, Figure 9), and the authors of that survey also included a discussion of the pertinent Talmudic references. A number of smaller settlements were surveyed and measured by Dar (Dar 1986, Figure 10), and Frankel measured a settlement in the north-western Galilee (Frankel 1987, 1992, I, Figure 11).

The basic building unit is the "courtyard" (the term "courtyard" includes a number of rooms serving as residences, a number of other rooms serving some non-residential purposes, and an open courtyard). The impression from Talmudic literature is that in the average courtyard there were more than 10 residential rooms. This is undoubtedly an exaggeration. There were

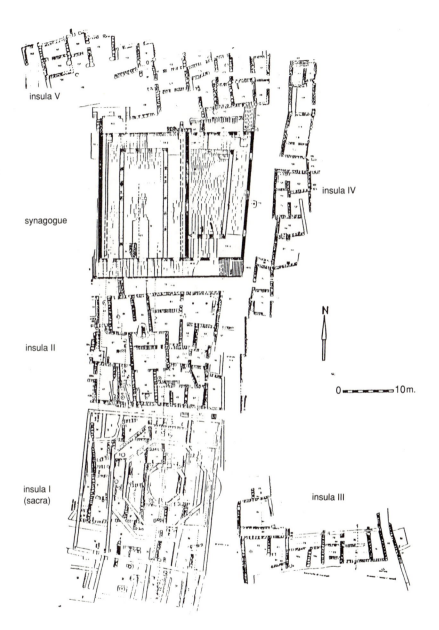

insula V

insula IV

synagogue

N

insula II

0 ▬▬▬▬▬10m.

insula I
(sacra)

insula III

Figure 7 Residential quarter of Capernaum. After Corbo 1975, Tavola 1.

43

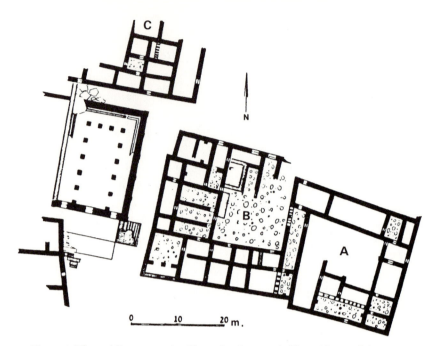

Figure 8 The public quarter in Chorazin, Lower Galilee. After Yeivin 1973, Figure 11.

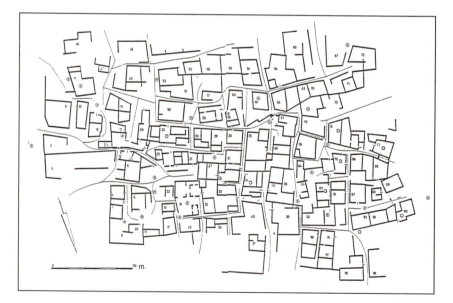

Figure 9 The settlement at Um-Rihan, northern Samaria. After Dar *et al.* 1986, Figure 2.

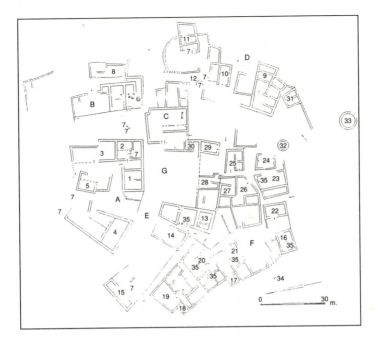

Figure 10 The settlement at H. Najar, Samaria. After Dar *et al*. 1986, Figure 3.5.

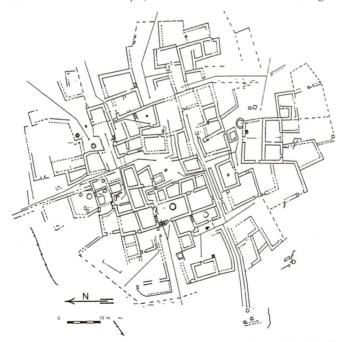

Figure 11 The settlement at H. Dan'ila, western Upper Galilee. After Frankel 1987.

45

usually no more than 3–6 rooms (as was the case, for example, in Meiron, Hirbet Najar, Hirbet Yeqavim, Yattir, Hirbet Susyah, Hirbet Ali a-Din and other such settlements). On the other hand, rather large courtyards have occasionally been found and, indeed, entire settlements based upon these large courtyards (Hirschfeld 1987; Z. Safrai (unpublished survey)).

A single family generally lived in every courtyard. In addition to the room serving as a residence, the family domicile usually included an auxiliary or service room (kitchen or storeroom). The courtyard was considered the shared property of the family. At times an entire *hamulah* lived in the courtyard, which was then considered as regular common property. Occasionally a rich family would live in a number of rooms, but this was not very common.

Between the courtyards were empty passages and lanes. The width of a lane usually ran from 2–4 meters. Some alleys, however, were narrow and measured no more than half a meter in width. In the larger cities it was possible to distinguish neighborhoods and districts (*suqim*). These terms have not been adequately defined, and it would seem that they were, in some form or another, groups of courtyards that faced or belonged to the same lane or passageway.

The courtyards belonging to the same lane were constructed quite close to one another in such a mannner that they could be closed off and defended. The more external courtyards were also built close together in such a manner that they seemed to form a wall. Such a town is referred to in Talmudic literature as "a town whose roofs are its wall."

The Jewish city or town was not planned. Therefore its streets and thoroughfares often meandered with no clear purposes. Jewish laws regarding planning only dealt with extreme ecological disturbances or threats such as the removal of trees, furnaces, and tanneries. There were also certain rules regarding the building of a synagogue. Occasionally, though, it is possible to see evidence of planning in a Jewish settlement (as, for example, a main thoroughfare), and some settlements even sought to imitate the basic Hellenistic town plan known as the Hippodamic plan. This was the case, for instance, in Hirbet Shema' in the Galilee. Outside the town were country houses belonging to farmers, both rich and poor, who to all intents and purposes lived in the city but chose to build their houses closer to their fields. Of course they utilized the network of social and economic services of the mother city.

III.2 Community activities in the town

III.2.1

The Romans granted the Jewish town a tremendous degree of autonomy. This autonomy was based on the one hand upon the inability of the Romans to supervise every aspect of day-to-day life, and on the other hand on the Roman recognition of Judaism as a legitimate religion. Apart from unusual cases or occasional periods of political or religious oppression, the Romans never got involved in the everyday affairs of the Jewish town, although at times, in a limited manner, they may have supported the communal institutions in a dispute with an individual.

The representative body of the local Jewish community was the institution of the "seven town elders" (literally "virtuous men," in Hebrew *tuvey h'yr*). This council controlled the financial aspects of the town and made most of the necessary municipal decisions. Either alongside the council or as an integral part of it, there was a smaller group of three "archons" led by a mayor (*rosh ha-'yr*). These institutions derived their mandate from the local town assembly which served as the legal organ of the "men of the town" (*anshei ha-'yr*) (S. Safrai 1976a). The town assembly was an active participant in municipal affairs and voted not only on matters of great importance, but occasionally on more mundane affairs. Thus, for example, the seven town elders or the three archons can sell municipal property, but the sanctity may be taken away from a synagogue only after the vote of the entire town assembly (PT Megillah III, 74a; BT Megillah 26a–b). The division of authority in all this is not terribly clear. From the source cited above, it would appear that the town assembly could intervene in the actual management of the town. It apparently had some kind of veto power over the decisions of the town leaders, and they also apparently had to ratify these decisions (T Sanhedrin 2:13).

It is not clear how the members of the various town institutions were chosen. The national Jewish leadership had, it seems, some kind of control over local Jewish affairs. Thus, for example, the Patriarch, in this case Rabban Gamaliel of Javneh, deposed Shazfar, the mayor of Gezer, and a number of sources attest to rabbis appointing *parnasim* or *archons* (PT Rosh Ha-Shanah I, 57b; cf. BT Rosh Ha-Shanah 22a; PT Peah VIII, 21a; PT Sheqalim V, 48d; V, 49a *et al.*). It is, however, difficult to know whether these were official actions with official authority, or whether these actions represent individual cases and succeeded only because of the personal, and not the official, prestige of the rabbi or patriarch. It is likely that the appointment of the *parnasim* mentioned above was made simply to instigate the local community to undertake their charitable and social obligations. Since the town assembly had so much power, it would seem likely that many of the town officials were elected by that body.

The residents of the Jewish town could vote or be elected regardless of social or economic position. This was certainly not the case in the non-Jewish *polis*. Realistically, however, most of the town offices were held by the more well-to-do, since only they had the free time to engage in municipal affairs. This, though, was not a formal restriction.

In addition to the elected officials, there were other town functionaries such as, for example, "dispensers of charity" (*parnase zedakah*), the "head (*rosh*) of the synagogue," who occasionally also served as mayor, "*hazzanim*," "*haver 'yr*," whose function is not clear, and other functionaries whose jobs will be discussed below. There were also no restrictions regarding appointment to these positions. These appointments appear to have been made by the national leadership in conjunction with the local assembly. This is the intent of the *midrash* that "*parnasim* (functionaries) should not be appointed for the community unless the community is consulted first" (BT Berachot 55a; BT Shabbat 104a; T Ta'anit 1:7).

III.2.2 *The legal status of the town leadership*

The town leadership was not considered an independent legal body, but rather a partner of every citizen of the town. This partnership provided everyone with an equal share of the common town property, even if that property could not always be defined. On the other hand, the national Jewish leadership was considered an independent legal entity whose members represented the community *in toto*. Every partnership, though, has its limitations. Thus the city, or all the partners, could not force an individual, or one of the partners, to do something that was beyond the specific requirements of this municipal partnership at its outset. The town, therefore, was prevented from taking certain actions *vis-à-vis* its inhabitants. The town's right to force its residents to undertake actions was based on two principles (M Bava Bathra 1:5; T Bava Mezia 11:23–6: (1) State custom, whereby the town could force its residents to do those things which were within the commonly accepted sphere of municipal action; (2) *Halachah*, as determined by the rabbis. Needless to say, the first principle was also determined by *halachah*.

These two principles might seem to be somewhat contradictory. Medieval scholars spent much effort on trying to work out this contradiction and set up a complex legal system in which state custom became dependent on the approval of the sages. The matter was much simpler in the Mishnah and Talmud period. "State custom" was the determining factor and it would seem likely that only on very rare occasions was this not accepted. The opinion of the sages in such matters usually only reflects the reality with which they were familiar, and at most they attempted to change a particular custom. A clear-cut *halachah* was usually established only in those instances in which no custom had taken root.

Thus, for instance, Talmudic literature records a dispute as to whether every city or town could construct its own wall (M Bava Bathra 1:5). The Mishnah really reflects a transition period between the time when settlements put up walls and when they decided that they were superfluous. The dispute should not be seen as a binding legal decision, but rather as a reflection of the times with an occasional educational or informational message added.

III.2.3 Communal services

The network of communal services in the Jewish town was quite developed and extended to most aspects of life in the large towns and villages. We shall discuss below the major services offered by the town (M. Weinberg 1897; S. Safrai 1974a; Z. Safrai (in press)).

III.2.3.1 Education

The Jewish town mandated a degree of obligatory education. In the period after the Destruction of the Temple this mandatory education was expressed in three spheres (S. Safrai 1983, pp. 171–90). (1) Parents (or more particularly fathers) were required to send their male children to school. There is no evidence of sanctions against those who did not do this, and it would appear that it was just a religious obligation. The Palestinian Talmud is even specific in stating that this requirement should not be forced upon parents. Rather, they should be peacefully convinced to fulfill the obligation (PT Kiddushin I, 61a). (2) The town provided the opportunity for study, providing, for instance, teachers, the *sofer* who taught Torah on a more elementary level, and the *meshaneh/mashneh* who taught *mishnah* on a more advanced level. Anything on a more advanced level was voluntary. The town also provided a place of study. Generally the children studied in the synagogue, although in larger settlements there were *bate midrash* (houses of study) or even separate school buildings. (3) The town supported this entire infrastructure, unlike the Jewish communities in Babylonia (Z. Safrai 1987, p. 78).

There were laws in the Jewish town regarding the times of study, vacations, duration of studies and the manner of instruction. The local leadership, as well as the rabbis, set great store by formal and regular instruction, and there are many Talmudic traditions praising the *sofer* and the *mashneh* (Mekhilta D'Rabbi Ishmael, Pis'ha, Bo 18, and see also PT Hagigah I, 76c and parallels. For study in the synagogue see, for example, PT Megillah III, 72a).

The teacher taught Torah every day, except for the Sabbath and festivals, from the first hour of the day until the sixth hour. Only during the summer (from the seventeenth day of Tammuz until the ninth of Av) did school finish any earlier. The teacher received a salary, although not very much, since it was clear that his teaching duties did not leave him time to engage in outside work. From a technically halachic point of view, there are problems in taking a salary for the teaching of Torah. The reality of the situation, however, required that the teachers be paid and legal solutions, somewhat far-fetched, were found.

Because of this system of education, almost every male Jew was able to read the Torah (but not to write, since writing was not stressed in the school), pray, understand the *derashah* and observe the commandments. It was the educational system which expressed the unique nature of the Jewish people and which also guaranteed that this unique nature would be maintained by creating an educated and enlightened workforce. Needless to say, in this sphere the Jews were unique in the classical world.

III.2.3.2 Charity (*zedakah*) or the social welfare system

Welfare was a rather difficult problem, because of the vast degree of poverty, often the result of the utter dependence of the farmer on the vagaries of nature. Therefore, the town set up a rather developed system of charity institutions. One such institution (*kupah*) gave weekly financial support, while another (*tamhui*) provided daily food portions. Those in need were also provided with a place to sleep (T Pe'ah 4:8 and parallels). These were the regular day-to-day activities of the charity institutions. There were also special services such as burial, providing for a bride and the redemption of prisoners (PT Brachot III, 6a; Moed Qatan I, 80a; M Ketubot 6:5; T Pe'ah 4:9; PT Pe'ah IV, 21a *et al.*). An interesting papyrus discovered in Egypt tells of a member of the town council (*boule*) of Ono who went to Egypt to redeem a woman who had been captured and enslaved. It is likely that the woman came from Ono and the local community was willing to spend the time and effort needed to redeem her, even if it involved going to Egypt.

The *gabbaim* (sing. *gabbai*) were in charge of the charity institutions. According to the *halachah*, charity was collected by two *gabbaim* and dispensed by three, just like any other court-sponsored activity.

Poor widows and orphans were given special consideration. They were exempted from many of the municipal taxes and were given special legal protection. The court also required that a guardian (*epitropos*) be appointed for them until they could take care of their own affairs (Gulak 1922, IV, p. 43).

The great number of traditions regarding all of these charitable activities, whether regular or extraordinary, would seem to indicate that this was one of the main spheres of activity in the town. In addition to charitable activities organized by the town, many private individuals were active in charitable affairs, as were some non-municipal institutions. One of the semi-formal institutions that did much in this area was the *haver 'yr* which we mentioned above.

The Jewish community had a great degree of social awareness and responsibility, and the sages further encouraged this. It is no coincidence that the two general terms of *zedakah* and *mizvah* (lit. commandment) came to be technical phrases for the giving of monies, usually for social welfare purposes, and this certainly indicates the importance of this activity.

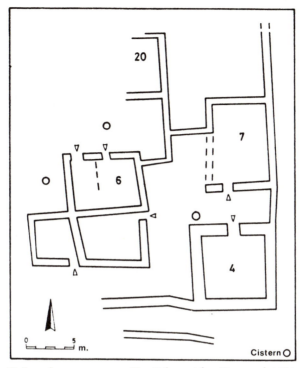

Figure 12 Security structures at Um-Rihan. After Dar *et al*. 1986, p. 28.

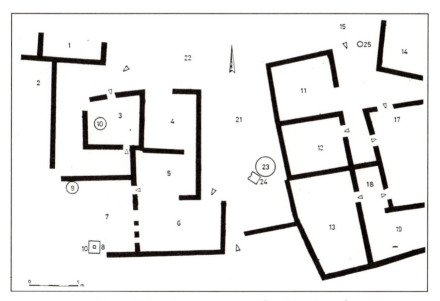

Figure 13 Security structures at Ali-a-Din, Carmel.

III.2.3.3 Defense

Generally, the defense of the province was the obligation of the Roman army, and it was successful in keeping out foreign invaders. However, its success in dealing with brigandry was much more limited. These brigands (Hebrew: *gaysot*, lit. columns of forces) were a constant danger to both property and life (generally through kidnapping for ransom). Thus, constant guard was necessary (Isaac 1984). During normal times the large settlements did not fear direct attack. The smaller towns and villages, however, fortified their settlements in order to be able to withstand attack by the brigands. The defense of their settlements consisted of a number of actions (Z. Safrai 1982). (1) Guard units were established. There were guards during the day and during the night, as well as special guard forces placed at various posts in the fields. These constituted a local militia, more or less. There was also a local police force ("the guards of property" – T Sukkah 2:3; PT Sukkah II, 53a; PT Hagigah I, 76c and parallels. See also Figures 12 and 13). (2) During periods of tension or disturbance, the town levied special duties for the building of *pasei ha-'yr*. The sages had a number of different explanations for this term. One explanation was the digging of trenches for defense. Another was the sealing of all spaces in the outermost courtyards, thus creating something similar to a wall (T Pe'ah 4:9; PT Bava Bathra IX, 12d; Pe'ah 8:21; T Sotah 7:23; Z. Safrai 1982). (3) A wall was built. During the Hellenistic and early Roman periods there were many settlements with walls. After the Destruction of the Temple most settlements were built without walls, and according to certain rabbis the town could not force its inhabitants to build or contribute towards the building of a wall (see above). In any event, when a wall was built during periods of disturbance, the wall was considered a service within the financial sphere, and not in the realm of defense. Thus the residents had to contribute towards the building of a wall based on their projected profit from it (BT Bava Bathra 7b; see Figure 14).

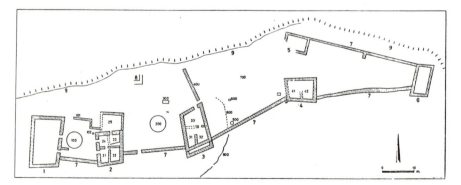

Figure 14 H. Tefen, western Upper Galilee. After Z. Safrai 1985, p. 218.

III.2.3.4 Planning, building and infrastructure

As stated above, the Jewish town was generally not planned. However, a number of basic ecological requirements were observed. Moreover, in those settlements which were especially organized, there was supervision regarding building standards, and a house in danger of collapse was destroyed (T Bava Mezia 11:7; PT Bava Mezia X, 12c; BT Bava Mezia 118a). The town provided basic services such as bathhouses and lavatories. The town also dealt with transportation, and constructed roads within the settlements as well as in the agricultural fields. These roads were built on a fairly high level and much effort was expended on their construction. They were 2–4 meters wide, wide enough for beasts of burden to pass through (see, for example, M Bava Kama 6:4; BT Bava Kama 80b; Bava Bathra 100a; PT Bava Bathra V, 15a; below, Chapter 3.VII.1). The roads between the various settlements were the responsibility of the regional or national leadership (see below). In addition to building the road, the town also provided or built those necessary elements to service the road or those who used it. Thus, cisterns were dug, inns were built both in the town and outside it, and fruit trees were even planted alongside (T Bava Mezia 11:28–32).

The city was also responsible for the hospitality of the visitor, either in the inn or through private hospitality. The synagogue often served as a place of lodging for the guest, and the city often provided food both for the guest and for his beast.

An interesting service provided by the city was the provision of lighting for public buildings or for dark streets. This service was hardly ever provided even in the largest *poleis* of the Roman Empire (A. H. M. Jones 1966, p. 214). It is, of course, unlikely that every Jewish town provided this service, but the larger settlements certainly did, for at least some of the streets (M Terumot 11:9; M Pesahim 4:4; T Pesahim 2:17; PT Pesahim IV, 31a; Leviticus Rabbah 9:2, pp. 175–6).

Hygiene As stated above, the town maintained bathhouses and lavatories. The city also supported private bathhouses. The town also provided the services of a doctor and a bloodletter (*uman* – the ancients set much store by this procedure). These professionals need not have worked only for the municipality, but the town provided their services when necessary (T Bava Mezia 27 *et al.*).

III.2.3.5 Law

There were two parallel legal systems. One was the municipal court system and it is likely that the seven elders served as judges. Additional courts, composed of the notables of the settlement, also existed and operated in this sphere. The other system operated within the sphere of the rabbis of the town, and especially the "elders" (members of the Sanhedrin). This judiciary system derived its authority from the Sanhedrin as a religious institution whose decisions were binding. Therefore the rabbis, as against the other residents of the town, were not interested in the further development of the municipal court system. On the other hand, there were not sufficient sages to set up their courts in every settlement (Alon 1980, pp. 217 ff.).

The two parallel systems and the strengthening of the one or the other caused a degree of confusion and, undoubtedly, tension between the sages and the municipal leadership. Characteristic of this situation is the somewhat unclear status of the judges of the second tier court system. The auxiliary services provided to these judges, however, are mentioned in a number of sources, and this seems to be much clearer. Thus the judges in a Jewish settlement enjoyed the aid of a police force and scribes of the court. The *hazan* of the synagogue also gave assistance. In large settlements there were also professional witnesses (Naveh 1978b), who functioned as types of notary.

III.2.3.6 Religion

Every one of the topics discussed above was part of the greater sphere of religious life, at least as far as the ancients were concerned.

In the Jewish town there was no official appointed for the specific purpose of dealing with religious affairs. The concept of "town rabbi" is medieval in origin. It is clear, however, that if a prominent rabbi lived in the city or in the general area, he undoubtedly influenced life there and enjoyed at least a degree of moral authority. Religious services such as the provision of the *eruv* and supervision regarding the observance of the various religious precepts were the responsibility of the municipal court, or, in other words, of the municipal leadership. The problems of the Sabbatical year were especially dealt with within this system. During this year, a special system of supervision and regulation was developed in which the produce was marketed together and distributed to the poor. It is possible, however, that this was simply an extension of regular economic activity, although there are no clear-cut indications of this in the sources (T Shevi'it 8:1 and parallels).

Contrary to the *polis*, the Jewish settlement did not engage much in the construction of elaborate buildings. The only building which could really be included in such a category is the synagogue. The major function of the synagogue was not prayer; indeed, this was only one of its many functions. The phrase "synagogue of *Bet Kenesset*" literally means "House of the Community." Many of the municipal institutions and the functionaries attached to them operated from the synagogue. The *sofer* or elementary school teacher taught his pupils here. The court mentioned above met here and guests and laborers visiting the city often slept in the synagogue.

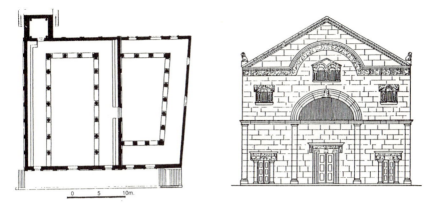

Figure 15 Synagogues in the Land of Israel. After Mazar 1970, p. 277.

Non-official community activities such as festive meals or public eulogies also took place in the synagogue (S. Safrai 1976c, pp. 904–44).

One of the major components of the synagogue was the central hall. This hall served for communal assemblies, whether for prayer, or for a *derashah*, or for any other purpose. At these times official municipal matters were discussed, and communal appeals also took place.

The varied functions of the synagogue dictated its architectural forms. At the center of the synagogue was the central hall, which we have just described, which served for assemblies (and for prayer). Rooms were built next to the hall which served the various municipal functionaries. We shall not, however, delve too much into the architectural details of the synagogue which, after all, is beyond the scope of this study (Figure 15).

The synagogue was built in an elaborate manner and towered above the houses of the settlement. Theoretically, it was supposed to have been constructed at the highest point of the town, but this was not always the case.

The synagogue represents the joint activities of the *kehila* functioning as a unified community, and serves as a monument to a wonderful achievement in the face of difficult economic and political conditions. All this was possible, however, only in the framework of the community organization which we have described, and as part of the religious beliefs of the residents of the town.

III.3 Community activities associated with economics and trade

Up till now we have discussed the activities and policies of the rabbis in light of a general survey of Jewish communal organization in the Jewish city. Now we shall see how the town leadership operated in the economic sphere.

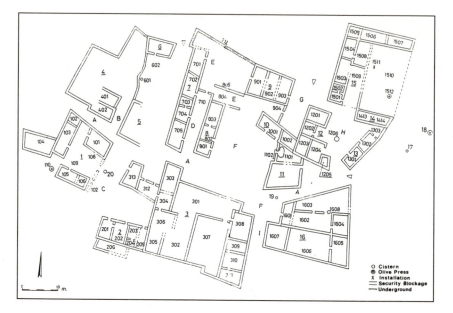

Figure 16 Plan of settlement at H. Ta'mur, Samaria.
Note: Building D may be an *agora*.

III.3.1 The building and maintenance of markets

As we shall see in Chapter 3.IV.2, there were regional Jewish markets even before the Bar-Kochba revolt. These markets were basically the equivalent of Jewish fairs. The *midrash* refers to this type of fair: "He said to him [God to Esau] – you will have fairs and he [Jacob] will have fairs" (Bereshit Rabba 67:7, p. 762). This type of market did not usually require special buildings or organization, unless it offered rebates of customs tax or benefits. In such a case some degree of political lobbying would also have been necessary to acquire these benefits, in addition to the administrative organization necessary to maintain the tax reductions.

Buildings associated with the market-place have almost never been discovered in rural settlements, with the possible exception of Um Rihan in Samaria, where remains of a rural market may have been uncovered (Dar *et al.* 1986, pp. 37–8). An *agora* is also mentioned in Jewish En-Gedi (Lewis 1989). Another market may also have been uncovered in Hirbet Ta'mur, a small satellite village in Samaria (Dar and Safrai, in press). The building found there has two rows of stores, similar in structure to the *agora* of Mampsis (Negev 1988, fig 8; Negev gives no explanation of this building).

56

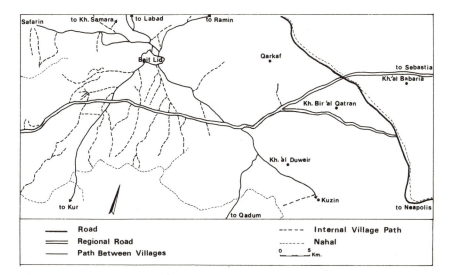

Figure 17 Road networks in the Beth Lid area, Samaria. After Z. Safrai 1986, p. 44.

III.3.2 *Construction of road networks*

Throughout Palestine, and especially in the mountainous areas, there was an extensively developed network of rural roads. This network has hundreds of roads. Every village was connected to its immediate neighbors a distance of 3–4 kilometers away, and the road network to more central settlements extended even further. We shall discuss this topic further in Chapter 3.VII.1. The Rabbis dealt with the various laws governing the expropriation of lands for the construction of roads and their maintenance. It is clear that such projects could be undertaken only by autonomous governing authorities. In Jewish areas, this was the responsibility of either the local or national Jewish leadership (Chapter 3.VII. 3). In this case, we have clear-cut testimony to the attempt of Jewish authorities to facilitate inter-regional trade and to aid in the incorporation of Jewish rural settlements within the economic framework of the Empire. Talmudic sources indicate that the sages encouraged the building of roads, recognizing their social and economic importance and considering the construction of roads as part of "the settlement of Eretz-Israel" (Figure 17).

III.3.3 *The supervision of business morality and ethics*

The Jewish community regulated business morality and ethics, particularly regarding weights, measures and coins. This was always a serious problem since each district usually had its own system. Supervision, then, would have been of the utmost importance. The official in charge of the supervision of this sphere on the part of the community was the *agoranomos* (Sperber 1977). He was aided by a number of other officials such as the *resh kuri* (lit. head of the heap or measure) and possibly also the "measurers" (*kayalin*) (T Bava Mezia 9:14; PT Bava Mezia IX, 12a and VIII, 11a). A number of studies have dealt with this official, so we shall not discuss all the details here. Suffice it for the moment to state that originally, of course, this function pertained to the *polis*. Later on, the Jews incorporated it into their communal and economic organization. The large number of sources and laws regarding his functions and the duty of the court to appoint him (PT Bava Bathra V, 15a; BT Bava Bathra 90a; Sifre Deuteronomy 294, 14, p. 313; Sifra Kedoshim 8:8) would seem to indicate that the *agoranomos* was appointed by autonomous Jewish institutions. However, it is not always easy to differentiate in the Talmudic sources between the *agoranomos* in the Jewish settlement and the *agoranomos* in the *polis*. We shall discuss this problem further in the course of our discussion. It is clear, though, that as far as the sages were concerned, the appointment of the *agoranomos* was a religious obligation and he functioned within the realm of religious law. It would also appear likely that *agoranomoi* were appointed in villages. Although there are no clear-cut sources attesting to this assumption, the great number of traditions stressing the requirement to appoint this official would indicate that this was so. There is therefore no reason to assume that the *agoranomoi* functioned within the framework of the Jewish community only in the *poleis*. It is not exactly clear how an autonomous Jewish community functioned in a *polis*, but the assumption that the *agoranomos* sources relate to a Jewish official operating in a parallel capacity to the *agoranomos* in the *polis* is unfounded and does not relate to the matter we are studying.

III.3.4 Supervision of prices

There is a dispute in the various traditions whether the *agoranomos* is responsible only for the standards of weights and measures, or also for the levels of prices. All of the Palestinian sources, though, would seem to indicate that he was not responsible for prices. This function was within his responsibility only in Babylonia (PT Bava Bathra V, 15a–b and parallels). In any case, even if this was not the function of the *agoranomos*, there was a certain degree of price control in the town; the town at least had the right to supervise the level of prices as well as salary levels of the workers. Thus, for instance, it is stated: "The residents of a town are allowed to make conditions regarding prices and measures and the salary of laborers and they are allowed to enforce their decisions against those who deviate" (T Bava Mezia 11:23; Bereshit Rabbah 98(99), p. 1255). It is also possible that this function was fulfilled by the *astinomos*, whose role we shall discuss below. Relevant here is an interesting law of Arcadius from 396 CE which grants the Jews economic autonomy and states: "One who does not belong to the religion of the Jews shall not establish prices for the Jews when merchandise shall be offered for sale" (C. Th. 16. 8. 10). This would seem to be a ratification of an accepted and ancient law, since it is difficult to assume that the Jews would first receive this privilege in the fourth century when their situation worsened. The law does not state to which Jewish community in particular it refers, but it seems likely that it relates primarily to Palestine and especially to the rural or village sector there. Such a law would be in contradiction to the official function of the *agoranomos* in the *polis*, and it is difficult to imagine that the emperor would authorize two contradictory sets of rules regarding prices in the same settlement. It is more likely that the prices for the Jews referred to in the law of Arcadius were established by some sort of regional or national authority.

III.3.5 Common marketing of produce

The town sometimes arranged the marketing of agricultural produce. In fact, during the Sabbatical year this became accepted practice. All agricultural produce was handed over either to the town or regional leadership (T Shevi'it 8:1), and they organized and controlled the distribution of the produce and the sale of the surplus. The town also posted watchmen in the fields during this year. It is related regarding R. Tarfon that he refused to accept this framework and once attempted to pick fruit from his own field during the Sabbatical year, and was beaten by the watchman who did not recognize him (S. Safrai 1966–7). Thus it seems clear that the town posted regular guards over the produce and also had the power to enforce its regulation (as well as that of the sages) even against such an important sage as R. Tarfon. The town organ that was apparently responsible for this was the municipal court and the *hever ha-'yr*. Regarding the fruits of the Sabbatical year, it is stated that "They give them to the *hever ha-'yr be-tovah*" (T. Shevi'it 7:9) (*be-tovah* is the phrase referring to the framework described above).

The framework described above derived from the particular problems of the Sabbatical year. It is difficult to assume, though, that such a complex framework of guarding, harvesting and marketing would be set up only for the purpose of one year. Therefore, it is likely that this framework, at least in some partial form, also existed during the other years of the Sabbatical cycle. We know, for instance, of joint marketing in Gush Halav during the War of the Destruction. Johanan, the leader of the town, brought all the agricultural produce of the site to a place where the demand for it was great (*Vita* 13). This, however, took place during unusual times and may not have been common practice. It might, however, indicate that such a practice was possible; it was certainly profitable.

If the town did organize the marketing of produce, then it is possible that the "measurers" mentioned above were the officials who were responsible for measuring the quantities of the produce and perhaps also the quality of the goods sent by individual farmers. Olive presses, mills and similar installations seem, though, to have been private, and there is no indication that the town dealt with these matters.

III.3.6 Trade rights

In Babylonia the community appears to have given out trade rights or monopolies to favored individuals (sages), but there is no indication in the sources that such a situation existed in Palestine.

III.3.7 Supply of merchandise

The *polis* took care of the supply of staples and sometimes even distributed them gratis or at a subsidized rate. The functionary responsible for this was either the *agoranomos* or the *'istinomos*. This function may be mentioned once in Talmudic literature. PT relates that R. Hoshaiah used to redeem the second tithe based on the evaluation of three *'istonansin* (= *'astomoi*?). If our interpretation is correct, these officials evaluated the worth of the fruit so the sage could then redeem it. It is logical that someone redeeming this tithe would make use of such officials (PT Ma'aser Sheni V, 56b). This tradition, of course, can hardly be considered clear-cut proof that such an institution existed in the Jewish community. R. Hoshaiah lived in Lod which was a *polis*, and afterwards in another *polis* – Caesarea. Since most of the inhabitants of this *polis*, however, were Jewish, it would not be too hard to find Jewish *'istinomoi*. The situation in Lod is also not necessarily analogous to the reality of the average Jewish village.

Another name for the *agoranomos* was *logist* (Sperber 1970; Lieberman 1944–5). The *midrash* has detailed descriptions of how this official supplied bread for the market and also supervised aspects relating to its quality (Yalkut Deuteronomy 808). However, it would seem that the story relates to a Roman *polis*, since the official threatens to inflict corporal punishment or the death penalty, and such behavior would be highly out of place in a Jewish town.

Thus it would appear that there are no references in our sources to the Jewish municipality dealing with the supplying of commodities. It should be remembered, though, that the autonomous Jewish town was a rural settlement and belonged to the territory of a *polis*. The supplying of commodities or merchandise for market would therefore be the responsibility of the *agoranomos* or the *logistes* in the city. It would also be difficult for a village to bear the burden of such an undertaking. The position of an autonomous Jewish community in a *polis* is less clear. In the economic sphere, at least, there had to be some kind of understanding regarding the roles of the various economic institutions of both the *polis* and the Jewish community. This would certainly also be the case even in those instances in which the Jewish community had recognized autonomy. Therefore, lack of information regarding the supplying of merchandise by the Jewish community would seem to indicate that in this sphere the community was dependent on the *polis*.

III.4 Definition of the *polis*

The *polis* (city) and the townlet as depicted in the sources and particularly in Jewish sources, and as presented in this work, form two distinct and separate types of settlements. They differ from one another in size, in economic level and in architecture, in their ethno-demographic stratification and, particularly, in the degree of Hellenization, or the degree of openness to the Greco-Roman culture and integration in the life of the Hellenized elite in the eastern empire. The description suggested is to some extent schematic and theoretical. In reality, the situation was more varied, and the distinction between types of settlements was at times complex and unclear. Our brief discussion of this question should begin with the days of the Second Temple.

III.4.1

In the days of the Second Temple, the term "polis" was somewhat arbitrary. It seems that in the region under discussion, a "polis" could be defined as a settlement whose residents defined it as a "polis" or that authors and writers of the time defined as such (Corbier 1991). For instance, we find mention of "cities" such as Bukolonpolis and Sikymonpolis on the coast of Palestine. The ruins in this area reveal a small settlement, and its Hellenistic character is somewhat doubtful (Avi-Yonah 1963 p. 24; Strabo 16. 2. 27, Pliny *HN* 14. 75). These cities are mentioned as early as the later Persian era and until the end of the days of the Second Temple. Similarly, the excavations of Shiqmona clearly show that there was a fairly prosperous settlement at this location throughout most eras, but it was not a "polis" according to the above description (see the *Encyclopedia of Archeological Excavations*, under Shiqmona). Herod and his sons also built cities: Caesarea, Geva, Sebastea, Sepphoris and Tiberias were evidently *poleis* (cities) in every sense. This is not true of Antipatris, which was also built by Herod as a *polis* (*Ant.* 16. 142; *BJ* 1. 417). Excavation of the city reveals a residential quarter, a commercial street and an odeon (Kochavi 1989, pp. 97–108), but this settlement did not even enjoy the status of the capital of Toparchia until the year 70 (Z. Safrai 1980, p. 81), and it is clear that it is not possible to speak of a "polis" without territory. In Josephus, the term "polis" is not precise; he uses it interchangeably with the terms "city" and "village," without distinction. Antipatris was, then, a rural settlement built by the king which had an urban quality, including some penetration of Hellenism, but it was not a "polis" in the full administrative sense of the word.

Similarly we are familiar with Migdal (Tarichea), near the Sea of Galilee. In this settlement there were, among other things, a hippodrome (*Vita* 27; *BJ* 2. 549) and a wall. The settlement also had a Greek name, the translation of the Hebrew-Aramaic name (the Aramaic name was Migdal Nunia – the Tower of Fish). However, it is doubtful whether Migdal was the capital of Toparchia, and it was certainly not a "polis." Its population made its living by fishing and textile production, and the town numbered about 200 to 300 households, approximately 1,000 men (Z. Safrai, 1985, pp. 86–8).

Like Migdal, Gabara was also located in the Lower Galilee. It was the most important rural settlement in that region. Josephus called Shimon, the leader of the town, "proton-polis," the head of the city (*Vita* 124) and his home, situated at the top of the hill on which the settlement lay, is described as a "baris," that is, something between a wealthy home and a fortress. According to Josephus, there were four cities and two hundred townlets in the entire Galilee. The "cities" were Sepphoris and Tiberias, which were *poleis* and Tarichea and Gabara, two townlets that adopted some of the features of a *polis* (Z. Safrai 1985, p. 59).

In addition to Gabara in Lower Galilee, Josephus mentions Yafa, which he describes as the largest townlet in the Galilee (*Vita* 230), and we also know of Yodaphata in this area, which was supposed to be less important geographically. Excavations of this settlement began in 1992 and the findings have not yet been published (Adan-Bayewitz *et al.*, in preparation). The area of Yodaphata was about 100 dunam and it was surrounded by a wall and impressive fortifications. If a settlement like Yodaphata was this strong, we can assume that Yafa and Gabara were even larger and more developed.

Gamla in the Golan Heights (Gutman 1981) and Bethther (Ussishkin 1992) were townlets of similar dimensions. Bethther was also surrounded by a wall and in part by a ditch; in Gamla streets were found but the wall was evidently built or only fortified before the revolt. No signs of Hellenization were found in these last three towns, but the excavation of Bethther has not yet been completed.

All these large settlements, then, had an urban quality, but they did not enjoy the formal status of "polis," did not mint coins and, evidently, their Hellenization was slower. It seems, then, that in reality the distinction between a small *polis* and a large townlet was somewhat unclear. Thus it seems that the learned discussion of Tcherikower (1951) on the question of whether Jerusalem was a *polis* is somewhat insignificant. Functionally, Jerusalem was a *polis* in every sense, but it is very likely that formally it was not defined as such. Its residents did not classify themselves according to the division of townlets and *polis* cities and Jerusalem had no formal territory, and no assembly of elected officials.

After the fall of the Second Temple we also find settlements that are difficult to define in terms of status. Rihll and Wilson use the extent of traffic to a settlement as the indicator of its status in the hierarchy; in their opinion a settlement that served as a central crossroads is considered a *polis* (Rihll and Wilson 1985). According to this criterion, Lod of the second century was the primary crossroads (Roll 1976), but became a *polis* (Diospolis) only in the early third century.

An extremely interesting townlet is H' Samara. This settlement was included in the British survey (Conder *et al.* 1883, II, pp. 182–3). As early as this, a series of elegant buildings and public buildings were found. In later excavations, Y. Magen found a large public building, perhaps a pagan temple, from the first or second century (for Magen's first report, see Magen 1992). The settlement gives the impression of a village or townlet that was greatly Hellenized, expressed in the construction of massive secular and religious public buildings (Magen 1992).

In the Byzantine period we know of Prophirion, known sometimes as Prophirionpolis (Honigmann 1939–45). This large townlet, situated on Mt Carmel, was a private village (see Chapter 4.I.6 below), but it had a council, and a bishop (*episkopos*) led the Christian community there. The name of the town and its status in the church administration testify to a settlement that was more respected than a regular townlet.

On the other side of the settlement hierarchy, we know of Byzantine cities where settlement was very sparse, which evidently had only a shell of an urban settlement. Antipatris is included in the administrative lists of Hierocles Synekdemus and Georgius Cyprius, and it sent a bishop (*episkopos*) to the Christian synods (Z. Safrai 1980, p. 92), but the excavations of the settlement reveal no evidence of a significant settlement in the Byzantine period (Kochavi 1989, p. 121). Perhaps the city moved to a nearby site, but it is difficult to imagine that an entire city could have disappeared, leaving no trace.

The situation regarding Dora is similar. This city declined in the third century (E. Stern 1992). Evidently the Byzantine settlement grew beyond the ancient tel; a church was found at the foot of the tel. Here too, however, it is doubtful that the Byzantine settlement that was renovated in the sixth century succeeded in becoming a true city. Nevertheless, Dora is mentioned as a *"polis"* in the secular and Christian administrative lists of the sixth century (Z. Safrai 1980, p. 154). Thus it seems plausible that this too was a rural townlet with an urban administrative "shell."

Thus, despite the clear formal distinctions between *polis* and townlet, in practice the differences were less clear and less absolute, and types of settlements with intermediate status also emerged. As shown below, there were only minor differences between cities and large townlets in terms of types of industry (Chapter 4.VI.2), and this also blurred the distinction between them. The above notwithstanding, according to the available information, the number of such settlements of the "middle" status was very small. In general most of the cities were *"poleis"* in every sense and most of the townlets did not include the architectural and social elements that were typical of the *polis*. Thus, for instance, the signs of Romanization, such as ornate construction, planning, and public buildings such as a theatre or hippodrome were constructed, and orderly *agora* were typical only of cities (it will be recalled that at Ein Gedi there was also an *agora* (Lewis 1989, nos. 11, 16), but it seems that this term is borrowed and does not refer to a Roman-style *agora*).

This blurring and the difficulty of defining the *polis* are not restricted to the province of Judea, but are widespread throughout the empire (see, for instance, Rodwell and Rowley 1975). In fact, it seems that in Palestine it was less common than in other provinces, as the process of Romanization in the rural sector in Palestine was relatively limited and slow. Thus the distinction between the Roman *polis* and the culturally autochthonic rural settlement was relatively clear-cut. Perhaps the good condition of the evidence also contributes to clearer distinctions between the *polis* and the large townlet. However, as noted, these distinctions were not valid in every case, for all settlements, and throughout the period.

IV. THE VILLAGE

IV.1 Definition of the village

There were a number of halachic distinctions between the village and the town or Jewish city. The *halacha* defines a village as a small settlement which did not have "ten *batlanim*" (M Megillah 1:3). Scholars have argued as to the meaning of the term. The most likely definition is that of S. Safrai (1976a), based on the medieval *Halachot Gedolot*, that the ten *batlanim* (lit. inactive, in modern usage more in the sense of lazy) were the municipal institutions of the Jewish town. Thus, the "village" is a settlement without local municipal institutions. This definition becomes clearer in light of the situation in the Jewish town which we have already discussed. As we have seen, the Jewish town had municipal institutions and provided a great number of services within the framework of an autonomous community organization. The village had none of this, or at least not the minimal level that existed in the Jewish town. A number of other explanations have been given for the phrase in the Mishnah, but we shall not discuss them at present.

The definition of a village as a settlement without a framework of community services is found a great number of times in Talmudic tradition. As we have already seen, the *halachah* required that every Jewish town have a municipal court which served to some extent in a leadership capacity (Alon 1980, I, pp. 217–25; 1984, II, pp. 15–57). The sages of the Usha period expressed a number of opinions as to the minimum number of residents required in order to set up a *Sanhedrin*, which in this case was the local court. The figures cited were anywhere from 100–230 residents (M Sanhedrin 1:6; T Sanhedrin 3:9; BT Sanhedrin 17b–18a). Some of the numbers are certainly schematic and some are a combination of a schematic and Biblical motif with the reality of the times. Thus, for example, 120 residents is based on the assumption of 12 officers of 10. Twelve, of course, was a number that often figured in town councils, while officers of 10 was based on Biblical precedent. It is interesting to note that Christian communities chose leaders when the number of believers in the community reached 120 (Acts 1:15).

In actuality, the dispute centers around the demographic criterion for defining a Jewish "city." The sages refer only to males, or in other words, 100 men represent 80–100 nuclear families. This would imply a settlement of 8–10 dunam (according to a figure of 10 families to a dunam). The sages give various reasons for the figures they cite, but it is clear that this or that Biblical verse is not the dominant factor in their computations, but rather the reality of their own days. A similar figure appears in relationship to the 'yr nidahat or the city which was to be destroyed because its inhabitants had adopted idolatry. A settlement could not become an 'yr nidahat unless it fulfilled the halachic definition of an 'yr or Jewish town. A kerach or a "village" could not become an 'yr nidahat. Therefore, Midrash on Deuteronomy 13:14 states: "until the majority shall be ensnared to idolatry. And those ensnared are from 10 to 100, according to R. Josaiah. R. Jonathan says, from 100 to the majority of a tribe, as it is written: 'the inhabitants of that town,' not a small village and not a large kerach" (Midrash Tannaim on Deuteronomy 13:14, p. 66). R. Josaiah's comments are not really relevant for our purposes. According to R. Jonathan, the population of a village was less than 100 males.

The smallest settlement having a synagogue, at least that with which we are familiar, is Hirbet Shema'. Yeivin (1971, pp. 39–44) estimated that the settlement was 10 dunams. Yeivin's figure was somewhat schematic and in actuality the site is only 7 dunams. The synagogue is a good indicator for establishing whether a site is a village or a town since, as we have seen, the village is defined as lacking the community institutions and officials who fulfilled their functions in the synagogue. Personal observation at a great number of sites has convinced us that community building and structures were quite rare in a site smaller than 7 dunams, although the village did provide some services as we shall see. In any event, a synagogue has yet to be discovered in a smaller site. The situation is different in Christian communities, where churches are found in settlements smaller than 7 dunams. The explanation for this phenomenon would seem to be that the synagogue was a community institution and structure which was essentially related to community services, while the church was a basically religious structure.

There is, then, a relationship between the size of a settlement and its communal organization. That is not to say, however, that the relationship always functions on a consistent basis. If the definition of the village was

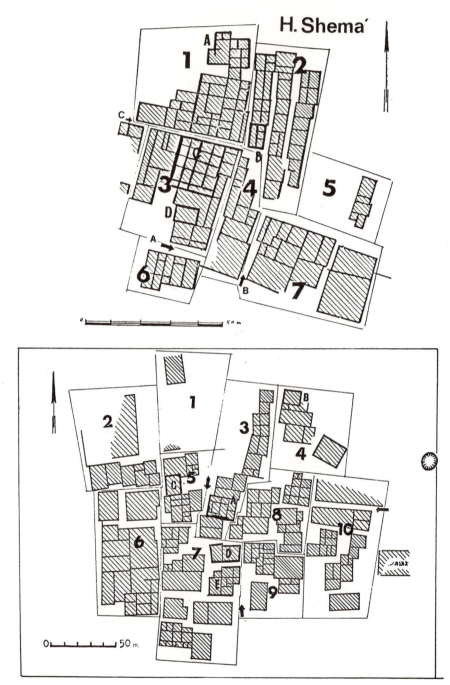

Figure 18 H. Shema' and Kh. Usha, Upper Galilee. After Yeirin 1991, Figure 12.17.

based simply on the size of the settlement and not on the existence or lack of communal organization, the sages would not have made the definition of the town dependent on such. Therefore it is quite possible that there actually were villages with a certain degree of communal services, and perhaps even a synagogue.

IV.2 Village communal organization

In the course of examining the remains of ancient villages, we have been able to determine that there were certain communal services in the village, and the residents apparently had a degree of community consciousness (Z. Safrai, unpublished survey). Thus, for example, there was a *miqveh* or ritual bath in Hirbet Tuqim. Pools and public water cisterns were found in many such similar settlements. In Hirbet Levad (Figure 19) streets, public water-cisterns and a watch-tower were found. There are also other apparent remains of some sort of defense system. Signs of a degree of planning were found in Hirbet Ta'mur (Figure 16), and some sort of fortifications were found in Hirbet Tefen (Figure 14). This is the case also in other similar settlements.

An interesting phenomenon has been found in the *shephelah* of Samaria. Near satellite villages larger settlements were found which were apparently small independent towns (7–12 dunams). The satellite villages, however, were in no way connected with these settlements, but rather with the large villages which served as their mother settlement. Thus, for example, Hirbet Levad was apparently not connected to nearby Hirbet Anusha, but to the mother settlement of Luban. Hirbet Tuqim was similarly not connected to Hirbet Ta'mur or to Hirbet Yeqavim nearby, but to Dir Balut. This is clearly indicated by the network of village roads which connect the satellite settlement with the large mother settlement, but not with those other settlements nearby (Z. Safrai, unpublished survey).

Some of those village roads were built by the residents of the respective towns in order to get to their fields. Some, however, were built in order to reach the satellite village. Such is the case, for instance, at Hirbet Shem Tov, Hirbet Muntar and Hirbet Tefen. A specific road to reach Hirbet al-Harev was built in the territory of Kefar Thulth, the mother settlement. The road did not reach other satellite settlements, however, such as Hariqat Abu-Far, Hirbet el-Qulub and Hirbet Biyad (Grossman and Safrai 1980, Figure 20). This would seem to indicate that this particular road was not built for the benefit of the village, but rather by the town residents for their own particular purposes, and the inhabitants of Hirbet el-Harev were lucky enough to be able to enjoy use of it. There are numerous similar instances of such a phenomenon. It should also be clear that the building of a road is a good indication of the existence of community organization, while the lack of such construction would also indicate the absence of organization. Thus, at Hirbet Shem Tov (Kloner and Tepper 1987, pp. 226–7), which was a

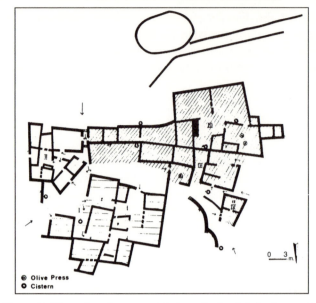

Figure 19 Plan of settlement at H. Levad, *shephelah* of Samaria.

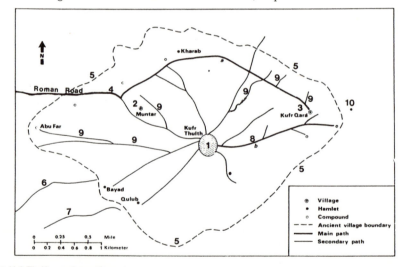

1. Kufr-Thulth – mother settlement

2. H. Muntar – a large satellite settlement (5 dunam)

3. H. Kafr Kera – a large satellite settlement (5 dunam)

4. Roman road from Schechem to coastal plain

5. Boundary of settlement according to roadways and topographical conditions

6–7. Paths from neighboring settlements. They do not reach Kufr Thulth

8. Roads from Thulth to neighboring settlements

9. Agricultural paths within territory of Kufr Thulth

10. Iyyun Kafr Kera – site outside the boundaries of Kufr Thulth

Figure 20 Road network in the vicinity of the village of Thulth, Samaria.

medium-sized village, there was a road that led to a nearby spring, proof of a fairly high level of local community development.

It is most likely that the village did not have a school. Thus, for example, the children in the settlements near Caesarea studied in the city (PT Ta'anit IV, 68d). Granted that this source might refer to those villages close to that *polis*, it would still seem to serve as proof that the village itself did not have schools.

IV.3 The satellite village

IV.3.1

The *halacha* cited above, which discussed the definition of a village, referred to the reading of the *megillah* on *Purim*. The assumption is that a prayer quorum (*minyan*) could not be assembled in such a settlement and in any case there was nobody there capable of reading the *megillah*. The *megillah*, therefore, was read in the town on the day before *Purim*. Market-days were Monday and Thursday, and it was on one of these days that the *megillah* could be read for the villagers. In any case, all of this shows that the village was also economically dependent on the town (Z. Safrai 1983b).

The satellite or offshoot settlement has of late been much discussed in scholarly research. This settlement is a sort of branch of the mother (and founding) settlement. The residents of the village continue to be dependent on the mother settlement in terms of community, public organization and economics, and perhaps even legally. In those societies which are based on extended families (*hamulah*), the residents of the offshoot settlement usually belong to a branch of one of the extended families (*hamulot*) in the mother settlement. During the course of time the offshoot village is likely to grow and develop, and may even become an independent village (Boserup 1965, pp. 68–75; Birch 1967; Siddle 1970; Hudson 1969).

In order to examine the ancient village in the light of modern scholarship, it is first necessary to determine whether these villages are satellite or offshoot villages in the modern sense of the word. It is of course impossible to examine each and every village. Many of them, however, were, in our opinion at least, satellite settlements. This can be determined in those few sites in which it is possible to ascertain the extent of the farm area of the village. The only real data at our disposal is the network of village roads.

Such networks of roads leading from the mother settlement (the *'yr*) to farm areas have been preserved in a number of villages. These roads reach the end of the agricultural region of the settlement as seen in Figures 20–22. These roads served to connect the mother settlement, its fields and the offshoot settlement. They are similar to the roads between the various settlements themselves (Chapter 3.VII below). A late Byzantine law provides literary proof of the fact that the satellite settlements were within the

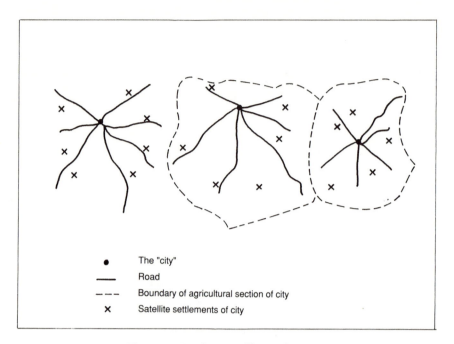

Figure 21 Roads to satellite settlements.

territory of the mother village and belonged to it at least concerning the payment of taxes (C. M. Brand 1969, p. 49).

Thus, small villages located within the farm territory of a settlement were, mostly likely, offshoot settlements. Good examples of this phenomenon are found in the region of Kefar Thulth in western Samaria (Grossman and Safrai 1980), Bet Lid near Schechem (Figure 17), Kefar Aziz in the Hebron Mountains and Hirbet Tefen (Figure 14) in the western Upper Galilee. The *shephelah* of Samaria has been examined by Safrai and Grossman (not yet published), and the boundaries of many villages were determined. Within their territories were a number of smaller villages which are certainly satellite or offshoot villages. In addition, somewhat larger villages (7–10 dunams) were found in the region between the various mother settlements.

It is also likely that there were small villages which sprang up without any connection to a mother settlement. These villages are generally located in the area between the various mother villages and therefore are outside their territories. Such a village would be the small site, not much larger than a single building, near Mitzpe Tura'an (unpublished). This site is located in the intermediate territory between the boundaries of ancient Tura'an and 'Uzeir.

The road network reflects the transportation needs of local inhabitants. The roads to which we referred above might indicate that the small village had economic ties, and perhaps social ties, only with the mother village. If ties with other settlements existed, it is probable that roads would have been built leading to them. This would indicate that the villages which we have discussed were normal satellite or offshoot settlements. It is impossible to know whether the residents of these small villages had family connections, whether in terms of the nuclear or extended family, with the residents of the mother settlement. The limits of the extended family at that time are not clear, and in any event the lack of sources does not enable us to reach conclusions regarding such ties between any of the different levels of settlements (Rubin 1972; Z. Safrai 1983a).

IV.3.2 The factors leading to the establishment of offshoot settlements

We have examined the development of satellite settlements in relation to the mother settlement and as a phenomenon within the territory of that mother settlement. It is not necessary to determine the reason for the establishment of the individual satellite settlement in the ancient world. Scholarly research dealing with the phenomenon in the modern world has cited the following factors:

(1) Economic pressure which results in a shortage of land. Some of the residents of the mother settlement move to the fringes of the territory of the mother village in order to use the lands there. Very often these lands are either deserted or cultivated only in a marginal manner. The residents of the about-to-be-formed offshoot settlement wish to cultivate these lands in a more intensive manner and move to that area in order to be closer to their lands.

(2) Internal social strife in the mother village forces some residents to leave. These found an offshoot settlement.

(3) Lack of land for construction. As the population grows, a shortage of land ensues. The majority of residents are also not willing to allow construction on arable farm land. As a result, the price of all land rises. New residents prefer to move to a new site in which they can build their homes on cheaper non-arable land.

In addition to the above, the following factors have an effect on the rate of the establishment of satellite settlements:

(1) Difficult defense conditions. The satellite settlement, having a small population, faces greater dangers. In extremely difficult defense situations, no satellite settlements will be established because of the inherent danger. During less pressing, but still precarious situations, the process may be slower, but usually the economic pressure prevails.

(2) Low level of community services. Those used to a very high level of community and public services do not usually establish offshoot settlements. Such services, if they even exist, are always on a low level in the

satellite settlement. Residents used to such services will not often establish an offshoot settlement.

(3) Alternative solutions. If the residents of the mother settlement can find alternative solutions to the problems mentioned above, they will not establish offshoot settlements. Such a solution might be the development of some branch of local industry or migration to a city or any other acceptable solution.

The main question, of course, is the particular reason for the establishment of such villages in the Mishnah and Talmud period. Thus, the above factors must be examined in light of their applicability to that period.

The security situation in Palestine at that time was generally quite good. The Roman army for the most part was responsible for matters of defense. The Jewish inhabitants of Palestine may not have liked the Roman army very much, but they could not deny that it brought a *"Pax Romana"* to Palestine and that there was no danger of external invasion. Even so, brigandry was quite common (Herr 1961; B. Isaac 1984). Marauding robbers could undoubtedly attack small villages, but they most likely would have refrained from attacking larger settlements. A reference to this situation is found in the *midrash* which describes the residents of "small villages" (*kufrny' dkyky'*) not leaving their homes after dark (PT Berachot I, 2a).

The defense system in the Jewish town has been discussed in scholarly literature (Z. Safrai 1982) and it was shown that the residents of smaller settlements were much more sensitive to defense matters than those of the larger settlements. Those sensitive to such matters would especially evince their concerns through choice of location (at the top of a hill or some other spot offering a view of the area, etc.). It is impossible, though, to state that small villages were built as fortresses. In fact, they were usually unwalled. More often the settlement was built in a crowded and close manner intended to provide some feeling of security. An example of this would be the manner of building at Hirbet Levad (Figure 19). An example of an offshoot settlement with a radical awareness or sensitivity to defense matters was Hirbet Tefen in the western Upper Galilee (Figure 14). This small village is located on a steep peak on the edge of an abyss. After its initial construction, a massive fence was later built which protected some of the buildings of the settlement by blocking the passageways between the buildings. Apparent attention to choice of location with a view toward defense needs was found in a great number of settlements examined for the purpose of this study. On the other hand, Hirbet Tuqi, for instance, was neither enclosed nor fortified.

An important factor in determining the location of the settlement was its proximity to farm lands. The settlement was very often established as near as possible to good farm land, taking defense considerations into account, of course. Both these factors were important in the location of a settlement, and usually some operative compromise was reached. An awareness of defense and security needs did exist, but, as we have seen, it did not always prevent the establishment of offshoot settlements. The residents were sometimes willing to take risks in security matters, and organized themselves accordingly.

As mentioned above, the greatest danger was not from foreign invaders but rather from brigands. These brigands were more of a danger to property than to life and limb; thus the economic factors affecting the establishment of offshoot settlements often prevailed.

The system of community services in the Mishnah and Talmud periods was, as we have seen, quite developed. The residents of satellite villages had to give up this comfort. As we have stated, this was also likely to slow down the process of establishing satellite settlements. Those same economic factors discussed above often prevailed over the comforts of community services. A possible solution was for the villagers to make use of the social, religious and communal services of the mother settlement. We shall discuss traditions pertaining to this below.

The Mishnah and Talmud period, therefore, did not lend itself particularly to the establishment of satellite settlements. However, the great number of satellite settlements in ancient Palestine would seem to indicate intense economic pressure, which only the establishment of such settlements could relieve.

IV.3.3

We do not have literary sources describing the actual process of the establishment of offshoot settlements at this time or indicating the particular reason for the establishment of these settlements. It would seem, though, that the economic reason was the major force behind the establishment of this type of settlement. One of the most important developments at this time was the marked increase in population. Scholarly research has basically been devoted to the political situation, and did not deal very much with this aspect of history. Today it is clear that peak settlement population was reached in the Roman–Byzantine period. The various surveys undertaken in the last few years have shown this to be an uncontestable fact (Chapter 6 and Figures 102–3). It is likely that this development resulted in the quest for new lands, as well as in intensified cultivation of existing lands. As we have seen above, this is one of the main reasons for the establishment of offshoot settlements.

We also discussed above two additional factors regarding this process. There is no proof, however, that they played a role in the early period under discussion. We have no sources of any kind indicating that there was internal strife within the mother settlement which resulted in the establishment of an offshoot settlement. Moreover, the extended family structure (hamulah) was not, after all, that strong, and it is therefore difficult to imagine a situation in which this aspect would be instrumental in resulting in the splitting up of the village.

There would also hardly be a shortage of land for building in the hill or mountain regions of Palestine. Most of the settlements border on good arable land, either on land that could not be cultivated or at the fringes of a valley. Inspection of numerous sites has rarely indicated a lack of available building land. Satellite settlements which are established because of a lack of land for building are usually built very close to the mother settlement. The offshoot settlements which we examined were usually located at the periphery of the territory of the mother settlement and in relation to the best arable land in that territory (Grossman and Safrai 1980). Thus, for example, the offshoot settlements of Kefar Thulth in the *shephelah* of western Samaria were built in the best farmland area and at the fringes of the territory of the mother settlement.

It is possible that in a few cases there were instances of a shortage of land for building. Proof of this phenomenon would be the construction of settlements 200–400 meters from the mother settlement, as is the case regarding a number of settlements in Palestine (Kefar Aziz, Amudim, Hirbet Hamam *et al.*) (unpublished). It is difficult to assume, though, that this was the major reason for the establishment of satellite settlements in Palestine.

Needless to say, neither all the mother settlements nor all the offshoot settlements have been examined. The above-mentioned studies, though, indicate that the mother settlement still had a reserve of building land left. Offshoot settlements were also found to be built on land of similar quality to the land of the mother settlement. In almost every settlement examined, there was land available for building quite close to the mother settlement. The sources, moreover, do not indicate any shortage of land for building. There are traditions which relate *halachot* forbidding the turning of building land into farm land (M Arachin 9:8; T Arachin 5:18; Sifre Behar 4 (end)), but these laws were designed to encourage the "settlement of the Land of Israel" and do not indicate any shortage of land for construction.

A Byzantine law, albeit somewhat later than the period under discussion, gives an interesting insight into this phenomenon (C. M. Brand 1969, p. 49). According to the author of the law, satellite settlements were established because residents of the mother settlement wanted to live near their far-away fields. Thus, after the death of the father of the family, the son who received the fields furthest away went to live near them (reason 1). Another instance cited is a person becoming rich, acquiring many sheep and slaves and finally, when he considered his house in the village to be too small, went and built himself a new house outside the village (reason 2). The third instance is judicial in nature. Land that was abandoned within the territory of a village was, after thirty years, transferred to the government which then sold the land. The buyer, being an outsider, built his house near the land.

IV.4 The ties between the village and the town ('yr)

IV.4.1

As we have stated, the satellite village is connected to the founding mother settlement or the 'yr of the rabbis. The town provided the services which the village residents needed which they could not receive in the village. We shall attempt to understand the nature of this relationship. The farmer in the ancient world did not usually market fresh produce, but rather preserved or processed produce. Grapes were marketed as wine or as raisins, olives as olive oil, figs and dates were dried and sold in various forms and wheat was sold in seed form (Chapter 2). The residents of the village undertook these processes themselves. The wine press in the Mishnah and Talmud period was privately owned, either by the owner of the vineyard or by a number of partners. The wine press was generally located in the agricultural area and not in the settlement itself. There is no reason to assume that villagers did not have their own wine presses. Wine presses have even been found near small villages. An interesting phenomenon was discovered in Hirbet Muntar, an offshoot settlement of Kefar Aziz in the Hebron Mountains. A large number of wine presses were found at the fringes of the offshoot settlement. Most of these were of the simple or basic type, and it is clear that they were used by the residents of the small village and possibly even by farmers living in the town who preferred to have a wine press next to the offshoot settlement. A similar situation was found at Kasr Farjas in the Judaean *shephelah* (Kloner and Tepper, 1987, pp. 202–3).

Most satellite settlements which we examined had at least one olive press and often many more. Thus, for example, Hirbet Muntar and Hirbet Levad each had two olive presses. The olives were processed into oil in the villages themselves. Threshing-floors were also found in the farm regions and it is therefore likely that there were threshing-floors near the villages. It is difficult, however, to find clear-cut remains of a threshing-floor since there was no actual construction. In any case, though, a threshing-floor was found about 10 meters from Hirbet Levad which apparently served the residents of that village (Figure 19).

The first steps in the processing of agricultural produce were undertaken, therefore, in the village which was not dependent on the mother settlement in this matter. It is hard to know whether this was the case regarding fish. The matter has not yet been studied, but it would appear that all the small harbors on the shores of the Sea of Galilee (*Kinneret*) belonged to the large towns. The matter, though, still requires much more study.

The village was most likely dependent on the town in terms of trade and commerce. No stores have been found in any of the villages which were examined, even in those which have survived almost completely. It is, of course, quite difficult to identify a store without actually excavating. In any

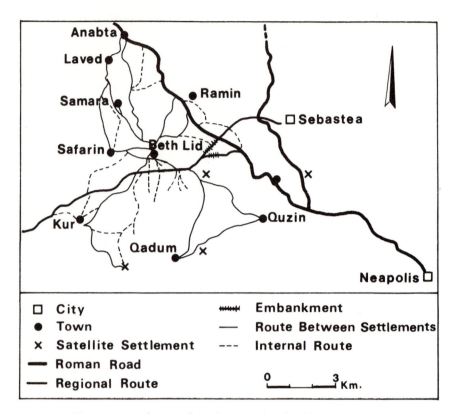

Figure 22 Road network in the area of Beth Lid, near Samaria.

case, it is hard to imagine that 20–40 families could support the existence of a store, or for that matter actually needed one.

The commercial ties between the village and the mother settlement were based on the market-days taking place in the central towns. We shall discuss the issue of market-days further on in our study (Chapter 3.IV). The source material indicates that in addition to the established market in the *polis*, there were seasonal markets in the large rural towns.

During the Second Temple period, and until the first century CE, there were two established market-days – Monday and Thursday. The markets were set up in major towns and villagers used to gather there on those days. These gatherings served as excellent opportunites to make use of the local court system which met on market-days, and to read the Torah. Public functions such as fasts and the reading of the *megillah* on *Purim* were also instituted on these days. This twice-weekly gathering seemed, however, to die out, at least in some regions of the country. The communal aspects of these gatherings apparently ceased to function even earlier. Market-days began to occur when traveling caravans reached the settlement and, in any case, stores in the larger settlements began to function on a regular basis.

Roman administrative policy, and especially Byzantine administrative policy, recognized the town as a tax unit. The offshoot settlement was included within this unit (C. M. Brand 1969, p. 49). Thus the villagers paid their taxes through the town, and their tax assessment was also determined by the town.

IV.4.2 *The traveling salesman* (rochel)

The traveling salesman (*rochel*) represented the most important commercial link between the town and the village. The very institution of the traveling merchant was supposedly one of the *takkanot* of Ezra (BT Bava Kama 82a; PT Megillah IV, 75a). It is clear, though, that the institution at this early time, if it really existed, represented a rather undeveloped trade network. As we shall see, though, the institution continued to exist, although in a different form, in the late Roman period.

The *rochel* is mentioned in a great number of traditions. He is described as traveling from one settlement to another. Thus it is stated in M Ma'asrot 2:3: "The *rochlim* [sing. *rochel*] who travel throughout the towns, eat until they come to a place to sleep. R. Judah says – the first house [which he reaches] is his house." PT Ma'asrot II, 49b on this Mishnah adds: "What is a place to sleep? His own house. R. Simeon b. Lakish stated in the name of R. Hoshaiah – like those [*rochlim*] of Kefar Hananiah who go out and sell in four or five villages and come and sleep in their [own] houses." The matter discussed here relates to the eating of fruit before tithes had been set aside. Tithes had to be removed from the fruit only after it had been brought from the fields to the house. The *rochel* received or bought fruit out in the fields. He is not considered to be an actual fruit merchant, though, since such a merchant does not have to set aside tithes until he reaches his final destination (M Ma'asrot 2:1–3). The sages discuss the status of the *rochel*, and more particularly what is considered to be the permanent residence of this merchant.

The description above, as we saw, refers to the village of Kefar Hananiah in the Galilee. It also fits other settlements quite well, such as Kefar Thulth in Samaria (Grossman and Safrai 1980, Figure 20). The traveling merchant leaves his house in the morning and makes his rounds among the various offshoot settlements, returning home in the evening. The distance from this village to the main offshoot settlements (types 1 and 2) and back is about twelve kilometers. If the merchant spent about an hour and a half in the major offshoot settlements (type 1) and about an hour in the others, he would have to put in a rather long day from early morning to evening. Thus, the merchant may consider whether to sleep over in one of the settlements, and this is the question discussed above. The matter of identifying the offshoot settlements of Kefar Hananiah is not, however, within the scope of our present study (Z. Safrai 1985, pp. 63–6).

Examining the sources dealing with this merchant does much to explain both his various functions as well as the nature of the offshoot settlement. The *rochel* is described as transporting his merchandise in a *kuppah* (box) which had a vast assortment of merchandise. The *kuppah* is cited in legal sources as an example of an object which contains many different "kinds." Thus, for example, "He who takes out [from one domain to another] a *kuppat rochlim* [on the Sabbath], even though it has many kinds [of merchandise], only transgresses on one account" (M Shabbat 9:7).

The *rochel* dealt especially with expensive merchandise which could be easily transported. Spices and perfumes were considered to be common wares of the *rochel*:

> He used to call R. Eleazar b. Azariah a *kuppah* of *rochlim*. And to what was R. Eleazar similar? To a *rochel* who took his box and entered a city. The residents of the city came to him and said: Do you have good oil? Do you have ointment? Do you have balsam? And they take everything out with him.
>
> (Avot D'Rabbi Nathan A 18, p. 34)

The nature of his merchandise brought the *rochel* into contact with women, and his was considered a profession that specialized in the needs of women. Thus, "Ezra established for Israel that the *rochlim* should travel about the towns on account of the honor of the daughters of Israel" (PT Megilla IV, 75a and parallels; T Kiddushin 5:14). The tradition refers to the selling of perfumes and cosmetics and the like. These items would have been unavailable to the women of the towns were it not for this "institution."

The tools of the *rochel* were the funnel and the hook. The first implement served to pour the oils of cosmetics as well as to measure the quantity poured (M Kelim 2:4 and parallels). The *rochel* also allowed the potential customer to smell the perfume.

R. Judah b. Bethyra and R. Akiva dispute as to the reason for allowing the customer this privilege. This, however, would indicate that the *halachah* on this matter reflects the early Javneh period, or perhaps even the Second Temple period. The hook was for the transport of the *kuppah*. The *kuppah* was carried on a long pole with hooks at both ends. According to R. Judah, the one in front was within the halachic definition of an implement or tool and was, therefore, susceptible to ritual uncleanliness. The second one, though, served only "as a guard like a metal roof" (T Kelim 2:4). All this would indicate that the *rochel* would travel with a small box which could be carried on his shoulder without having to be transported on a donkey.

The Jew who searched for the Messiah who was born, according to tradition, on the day of the Destruction of the Temple, is described in terms similar to the description of a *rochel* (PT Berachot II, 5a). He wishes to seek the Messiah in the various settlements and therefore becomes a seller of children's clothes, wanders from settlement to settlement plying his wares, especially among women.

The geographic principle behind this type of trade is that at every station along his way there was no economic justification for the establishment of a permanent store. The traveling merchant then can ply his wares in these settlements. In our opinion, this trade model was the norm mainly in small villages or in satellite settlements. Many of the technical terms regarding the types of settlements frequented by the *rochel* would seem to bear out our assumption. However, as we have already mentioned on a number of occasions, Talmudic literature is not always consistent in its use of such technical terms. Thus, for example, in the tradition cited above regarding the clothes merchant, BT Berachot refers to the settlements as towns (*kryyh* or *krt'*) while the parallel tradition in Lamentations Rabbah (1.16, p. 89) calls them villages. This lack of consistency in the use of settlement terminology makes it difficult for us to claim that the term "villages" of Lamentations Rabbah is conclusive.

The very nature of the type of trade and merchandise of the *rochel* would seem to prove our point that this merchant frequented the satellite settlements. It is hard to imagine that there was a need for this type of merchant in larger settlements with a population of 1,500–3,000. The *rochel* sets out, for instance, from Kefar Hananiah or from Thulth, visits five settlements and returns home. If the *rochel* also visited larger settlements, he would not have been able to finish so quickly. The average distance between settlements in the Galilee is 3–5 kilometers. Thus, the merchant would have to travel at least 25 kilometers, assuming he was walking in a straight line. Winding roads characteristic of the Galilee, however, would probably lengthen the distance to 30 kilometers. When, then, would he have time to sell his wares? If he visited a large settlement, he would certainly need a number of hours in order to sell his merchandise. This, however, is not in keeping with the sources described above. Thus, it would seem that our original assumption, that the *rochel* frequented, for the most part, the small offshoot settlements, is correct. BT Avodah Zarah 61a explicitly mentions the *rochel* in connection with a farmstead, or an *'yr* which had a gate and a bolt, in which it was not customary to find strangers. This is also the impression from the parallel source in PT Avodah Zarah IV, 44b. This type of trade is also mentioned regarding Birat Malcha (also known as Birat Arava) of Beit Lehem (Bethlehem). Since Beit Lehem could be described as a normal type of settlement, perhaps Birat Malcha was an offshoot settlement. The *rochel*, according to Talmudic sources, was also found in the towns near Sepphoris. A *rochel* met the sage R. Jannai there (Leviticus Rabbah 16:2, pp. 349–50 and parallels). Some versions of this tradition state that the meeting took place at Achbara near Safed, which was a fairly large settlement. It would seem, though, that the correct version is "the towns near Sepphoris," and Achbara was mentioned in other versions only because R. Jannai was often associated with that site and the scribe was confused by this (Oppenheimer 1978). An additional *rochel* was apparently a resident of Caesarea and referred to himself in a Greek term which would basically mean *rochel*. It is not clear from the inscription which mentions him, however, where he plied his wares (Lifshitz 1961, p. 120).

According to the decree of Ezra mentioned above, it would appear that women would not have had an opportunity to buy cosmetics and jewelry were it not for the *rochel*. Since there were stores in the larger settlements, the decree would be meaningless if the *rochel* frequented these types of places. Thus, in summary, it would seem to be correct that the *rochel* served as the middleman between the mother settlement and the offshoot settlements.

The phenomenon of the merchant who travels between small villages is known from many other parts of the world and has been studied to some extent, such as in the study of Skinner on China (Skinner 1964). The extent of these merchants' spheres of operation is similar to the extent of the trade networks between the various settlements. The difference is that the villagers do not come to the market in the central urban center. The market, as it were, comes to them. The small trade potential in the village regions hardly made it worthwhile to set up a permanent market.

The *rochel*, as we mentioned, supplied mainly luxury items. The residents of the satellite settlements probably came to the mother settlement for necessary services unavailable in the village and to buy necessary staples. Those satellite settlements located on or near inter-urban routes were also likely to enjoy visits of larger caravans going from city to city (see Chapter 3).

An interesting tradition attests to the dependence of the villagers on the stores and markets of the town during the Roman period. M Bava Mezia 4:6 states: "Until when is it permitted to return [money which turned out to be counterfeit]? In large cities [*kerakhim*] – the time it would have taken to show it to a money-changer. And in villages – until the eve of the Sabbath." The assumption is that there is no money-changer in the villages and therefore the villagers have until the eve of Shabbat. T Bava Mezia 3:20 explains this *halachah* in the following manner: "In the villages until the eve of Sabbath – since the market usually stays in the towns from the eve of the Sabbath to the eve of the Sabbath." The market thus functions until the Sabbath and it is assumed that the villager will get to the market at least once before the Sabbath. The extension given to the villager proves that he does not live near the market. Otherwise there would be no distinction in the time allowed to return the coins. The villager was in no position to simply run back to the market to the money-changer (and it would also appear that there was no money-changer in the towns). It should also be mentioned that in this case the tradition would appear to be quite exact in the use of settlement terminology.

We have no further traditions regarding the dependence of the village on the town. However, the level of dependence, and also of mutual ties, would seem to be very great. This is based both on the geographic logic of the matter and on an analysis of the road network and the literary traditions which we have cited. It would appear that the Aramaic *targumim* provide additional confirmation of this assumption. The Biblical phrase of a city and "its daughters" is translated in the Aramaic as "its villages," reflecting the Targum's understanding of the relationship between town and city. The phrase "mother town" ('*yr 'm*) even appears once in a literary tradition: "R. Samuel b. Nahmani came up from Babylonia to ask three things. He found Jonathan Ish Ha-Birah and said to him: What is the meaning of the verse 'The rulers ceased in Israel, they ceased'? Jonathan said to him: The small towns which were destroyed by Sisera, but which when Deborah arose became mother towns in Israel.' " (The Midrash on Psalms 3, 3). The process hinted at in the *midrash* is quite well known. During periods of tension in defense and security matters, small villages are abandoned. When the emergency is over, however, and during periods of peace, they become stronger and might even become "mother towns." The term "mothers" (or mother towns) corresponds to the Biblical terminology of "daughters," translated as villages, and reflects the ties between the various levels of settlement.

IV.5 Life in the village

If the social fabric of family life in Palestine was based on the extended family, then it is likely that the extended family was also the family unit in the village. The laws relating to the reading of the *Megillah* might reflect this situation. Thus the distinction between the various levels of settlement and on which day they should read the *Megillah* is based on the following verse: "Every family, every province, every city" (Esther 9:28). PT Megillah I, 70b understands the verse in the following manner: family is the villages, the provinces are the towns and the cities are the cities (*kerakh*). The "family" then is the unit identified with the "villages" who read the *Megillah* on Monday or Thursday. All this would seem to imply that the social unit living in the village was the (extended) family. On the other hand, it might be that the connection between "family" and "villages" may simply be coincidence and dependent upon the *derashah*, without reflecting reality.

Talmudic literature usually portrays villagers as poor and as leading rather miserable lives (Derech Eretz Zuta, ch. 10). This is understandable in light of the low level of communal services available in the village, as well as the dangers in terms of security. The archaeological remains in the villages, though, would seem to be less conclusive. Sometimes the villages really do appear to have been poor, with shoddy construction, and life there must have been conducted without community services and organization. On the other hand, in some villages a large, fortified and centrally located building was discovered, apparently the dwelling of a rich family. The residence is usually at the center of the village at the top of a hill. It would seem likely that this family was the founding family of the village and thus managed to secure the best site in the village. The standard of living in the village was lower than that in the town, but not always markedly so.

Krauss, in his attempt to describe the villages of Palestine, made use of those sources mentioning villages as opposed to the *kerakh*. This decision, though, causes many methodological problems. As we have already stated, such sources, citing a "village" in opposition to the *kerakh* (or *polis*), might include within the "village" all levels of settlement between *polis* and village. Thus, for example, one source mentions the bakers in the *kerakh* as opposed to those in the village (T Pesahim 1:13 and parallels). It is hard to imagine, though, that villages had bakers. Moreover, the *halacha* should have also mentioned the baker in a town. Thus, the village in this case is all-inclusive. Such sources, then, must be used with care.

In any event, it is clear that village life was far simpler and poorer than life in the *polis* or in the town. We shall not expand on this point at the moment (Büchler 1900; S. Safrai 1983b, pp. 193–6). In addition to these types of villages and townships there was another form of private village and even private township (discussed below at IV.1.6.4).

V. THE VILLA

V.1 Definition

The farmstead or *villa* was the backbone of the settlement system in the western Empire. In various parts of Italy, Gaul, Germany and other provinces one could travel from *villa* to *villa* and reach a *polis* only after many hours of walking (Percival 1981). White's book on Roman agriculture deals almost entirely with this type of settlement (White 1970). This is, indeed, the impression that one would get reading the works of Varro, Cato and Columella on Roman agriculture. The farmstead was a much rarer phenomenon in Palestine. Even so, both literary sources and archeological remains teach us that it did exist in Palestine. The farmstead, however, is occasionally referred to as 'yr in Talmudic traditions, resulting in some confusion (Gulak 1929, p. 26; Applebaum 1973). Much has been written about the agricultural, architectural and settlement aspects of the *villa* in the Roman Empire. We shall try to summarize this material and point out pertinent material relating to Palestine and Judaea.

The owner of the farmstead was usually rich and lived for the most part in the *polis*. He usually owned much land and maybe even a number of farmsteads. In the center of the farmstead was the *oikos* or the farmhouse, where the workers or slaves lived under the supervision of the *epitropos* or foreman who was in charge of day-to-day affairs. The classic farmstead was essentially autarkic. Many different crops were cultivated in order to reach self-sufficiency, as well as to provide a handsome profit for the owner. The profits, of course, were sent to the city and the owner, and served as his economic support as well as his base for social, political and economic activity. Many farmsteads specialized in one particular crop or sphere such as grapes, olives, pigeons, cattle, etc. However, such a farmstead was also supposed to be self-sufficient, at least according to the various sources dealing with the matter.

The farmstead did not maintain an active series of ties or connections with other settlements in the area. As stated above, it was basically self-sufficient and marketed its surplus in the *polis*. The owner, when in the farmstead, would usually maintain some type of relationship with his neighboring gentleman farmers. This had social value and thus may have contributed to the value of the farm. The real economic effect of such social relationships, though, was hard to determine.

V.2 *Oikos*

The farmhouse fulfilled three basic purposes: (1) it was the residence of the laborers or slaves; (2) it served as the central storage area for implements necessary for farm work or for processing the crops (olive presses, wine presses, clay furnaces, etc.); (3) it was the permanent residence of the *epitropos*, who might have been either freedman or slave (and was very often a freedman). The owner would also stay here if he came to visit the farmstead.

All of this required an elaborate building with all the necessary comforts: a wide courtyard, comfortable or even elegant rooms used as residences, colored mosaic floors and a bathhouse. Some large and elaborate farmsteads found in various parts of the Roman empire had pools, a theater, hippodrome and other types of buildings associated with a luxurious lifestyle.

The functions described above would require a building containing three wings. An elaborate wing would be constructed for the use of the owner, a simple one as a residence for the workers, and the third section would serve for the equipment and farm installations kept there. The location of the *oikos* was chosen to facilitate all of the above-described functions. It was thus built at a central location of the farmstead, usually at an intersection of internal lanes and roads within the farm. The choice also took into consideration the external roads leading from the farmstead, as well as the esthetics of the location.

V.3 The farmstead as an economic unit

The farmstead was of great importance *vis-à-vis* the economic situation of the region. The agricultural system of the farmstead allowed for the cultivation of vast expanses of land, planning agricultural strategy, as well as a chance to use the latest innovations in technology. Thus many of the farmsteads had aqueducts, efficient drainage, constructed bridges and roads, and made use of other installations which increased the agricultural potential of the farm. An example in Palestine would be the royal estates or farmsteads in Jericho or in En Gedi (Porat 1986; Netzer 1984; 1989). A rather impressive series of aqueducts and dams was built in these estates in order to secure water from long distances away and to use it in the excellent farm lands of the valley (Porat 1986). Central planning usually produced better use of the farm land of the estate and thus increased yields and profits. The farmstead enjoyed a strong economic foundation. The owner, usually rich, had at his disposal the necessary funds to meet the expenses of long-term development. This long-term development, of course, allowed for greater exploitation of the farm potential. The small farmer, however, usually had to deal with short-term problems in order to survive and had little money available for long-term development or planning. He thus enjoyed none of the fruits of such long-term development.

The rich landowner also served a political purpose. For example, he usually protected those small farmers in his employ or connected to his estate from instances of local oppression. The political and legal protection offered by the owner of the estate or farmstead made the phenomenon very popular in the late Roman period (see Chapter 4.I.3).

The estate also served a social purpose as the bridge between the high standard of living in the *polis* and the rural sector. The average dweller of the rural sphere would come in contact with some of the niceties of life at that time only in the estate. There he would see fancy pottery and beautiful glassware, and would come into contact with the buildings and the lifestyle of the Hellenistic and Roman world.

The estate or the farmstead system contained a great deal of social inequality, since the laborers usually lived in difficult conditions, with the majority of the profits going to the owner in the city. From an economic point of view, though, this system further strengthened the rich who, of course, were the backbone and foundation of the Greek and Roman cities and, for all intents and purposes, of the entire empire. This system was dependent upon a decent transportation network and a decent level of local trade. The system also provided for and supported unproductive elements of society such as the estate owner, his house slaves living with him in the *polis*, and, in fact, all those providing services in the *polis* who were supported indirectly, at least, by the farm sector.

V.4 *Proasteion*

A different type of estate was the *proasteion*, known basically from the late Roman period (*Cod. Just.* nov. 159, etc.). This was the permanent residence of a rich city dweller who preferred to leave the city and live in the more pleasant surroundings of a countryside suburb. If the rich owner of such a house also possessed lands near the city, then there would also be farm installations near his country residence. Such types of estates without agricultural installations have been found at Beth Gubrin (Vincent 1922), and Beth Shean (Zori 1963, p. 139). A number of such buildings with impressive agricultural installations and dating from the fifth to sixth centuries CE have been found in Geva Hippeum (Z. Safrai and Linn 1988).

V.5 Estates in Palestine

V.5.1

As stated above, the estate was a typical type of settlement in the Hellenistic–Roman world. There were a number of estates or farmsteads in Palestine pre-dating the Hellenistic period. The farmstead in Tirat Yehudah, for instance, was built in the Persian period (Yeivin and Edelstein 1970). A number of farmsteads at Um Rihan in northern Samaria date to the Persian period, or even earlier, and many of them continued to function in the Hellenistic and Roman periods (Dar *et al.* 1986, p. 113). Likewise, dozens of farmsteads which have been surveyed in the Plain (Shephelah) of Lod apparently existed by the Persian period and continued to exist until the Hellenistic–Roman period (Finkelstein 1981; Dar 1986, pp. 2–7).

V.5.2

The estate in the Roman world usually belonged to the rich. In Judaea, or Palestine, the owner of such an estate was usually a rich non-Jew, associated or identified with Hellenistic culture and naturally identified with the interests of the government. Those identified with the government or close to those in power might get large tracts of land in order to build an estate or set up a farmstead. Such people would by their very nature be non-Jews. Often the grant would be for services rendered to the emperor, not a very Jewish avocation. Many of the Talmudic traditions mentioning this type of settlement, therefore, also mention the "king." The "king" need not actually refer to the emperor, but rather to a local official (Ziegler 1903 collected most *midrashim* of this type). There were, however, Jewish estate owners such as Rabbi Judah the Prince who received estates from the emperor (PT Sheviit VI, 36d). It is also clear that other lands owned by this Jewish leader had been given either to him or to his forefathers by the Roman emperor.

Halachic traditions mention one who has either bought or sold an *'yr* and it is clear from the context that an estate is intended (M Bava Bathra 4:7; Gulak 1929, pp. 26–7). It is also taken for granted in these *halachot* that both buyer and seller are Jewish, otherwise there would be no purpose in discussing the matter. A non-Jew would hardly undertake such transactions based on Rabbinic strictures. Another tradition relates the story of a Jew who bought an estate together with non-Jewish slaves (PT Yebamot VIII, 8d). Other laws deal with the roads to an estate that the local Jewish community leaders must build (PT Bava Bathra V, 15a and, somewhat differently, in BT Bava Kama 80b). According to the discussion in PT Bava Bathra, the roads must be built as part of the requirement to "settle the Land of Israel." This obligation was in keeping with the Rabbinic view regarding fostering further development of the Land of Israel and providing adequate services for its inhabitants. The estate owner in these cases is also very likely to be Jewish. It is doubtful that the rabbis would have demanded the comfort and convenience of a non-Jewish and usually hostile landowner.

V.5.3

Very few estates in Palestine have been excavated. The literary traditions, however, provide much more information. The lack of archaeological material probably reflects the low awareness on the part of scholars of this settlement phenomenon. Thus, for example, the early Roman farmstead at Hurvat Murak was called a palace (Damati 1982). It is thus likely that surveys and even excavations have uncovered additional estates and farmsteads that have gone unnoticed by scholars. On the other hand, scholars have also been too free in calling simple buildings constructed in a field either estates or farmsteads (see V.2 above).

V.6 Settlement patterns of estates in Palestine

V.6.1

Most of the estates of Palestine were in the plains in the best agricultural lands. The rich non-Jews who owned most of the estates in Palestine would certainly have preferred such a location, whether in terms of the land or the proximity to the *poleis*. However, most of the known examples of this phenomenon are in the hill or mountain regions. The remains in this region have also survived to a much greater extent than in other regions. A number of such estates were discovered in the emergency survey of 1968 (Kochavi 1972 – such as Hirbet Um Dimnah in the southern Judaean Mountains, no. 244, pp. 80–1; Dir Qal'a', no. 308, p. 233; Hirbet e-Diurah, no. 211, p. 233; Deir Sama'n, no. 203, p. 231, and detailed discussion in Dar 1986, pp. 26–30; Tepper 1986b; Hirbet Al-Mutinah, no. 187, pp. 228–9. Hirbet Al-Habas, no. 199, p. 231 is, however, not an estate, but a small village). The *Survey of Western Palestine* (Conder 1882) lists additional estates such as Deir Arav and Deir Diklah in Samaria (II, pp. 311–13). The *Survey of Western Palestine* also mentions a number of estates which were later surveyed in the emergency survey of 1968 (Deir Sama'an, pp. 319–20; Dir Qal'a', pp. 315–19). Additional estates were found in el-Bastin in Nahal Kanah (Dar 1986, pp. 25–6).

Literary sources mention estates belonging to Rabbi Eliezer bar Harsom in Har Ha-Melekh (northern Mount Judaea, Lamentations Rabbah 2:2). This sage lived during the Javneh period. An early estate from the first and second centuries CE was also found in Hirbet Murak (Damati 1982, Figure 23). Not far from there, at Hirbet el-Hama'm on the border between the hill region and the *shephelah* of Judaea, an additional estate was found (Figure 24, not yet published). Estates have been found and studied in the region of Um Rihan in northern Samaria (Dar *et al.* 1986, pp. 109–13, Figure 25). An estate was discovered in Kalandia in the Judaean Mountains (Magen 1984, Figure 26). A *villa* which later became an estate was excavated at el-Maqarqash in the Beth Gubrin area (Vincent 1922). A number of buildings connected to an estate were found by Finklestein near Schechem in his survey of Mt Ephraim (Finklestein, 1988–9). Procopius (*Anecdota* 11. 29) mentions a large number of Christian estates in Samaria. Novella 144 of Justinian regarding lands of Samaria also seems to refer to the large number of estates in that region. A few centuries before, Ptolemaeus, Herod's commander, had an estate in the village of Haris in Samaria (*Ant.* 17. 289; *BJ* 2. 69). Prophyrion in the Carmel range was a private estate that later became the property of the emperor (Procopius, *Anecdota* 30. 18–19). The village of Tafsha, north of Jerusalem but unidentified, was owned by a rich landowner (Petrus the Iberian, p. 98). In the village of Tekoa was *'a ktêma*, a phrase associated with property belonging to a rich owner and organized in some distinct manner (*Life of Chariton*, in Cyrillus of Scythopolis). Mosaic floors of villas have been found in Hirbet 'aliyah (Judaean Mountains) (Avi-Yonah 1981, no. 388) and Hirbet Mashrav in the Judaean Mountains (ibid., no. 402). An impressive farmstead from the second and third centuries CE has been excavated near Jerusalem at Ein Yael (Ein Yalu) (*Hadashot Archiologiot*, 92, 1988, pp. 37–9).

In the upper Carmel, two possible remains of villas have been found at an unnamed site and at Tel el-Batah (Ronen and Olami 1978, no. 31, p. 14; no. 62, pp. 28–9). A farmstead was excavated at the base of the Carmel Range near Ramat Ha-Nadiv (H. Uqub el-Mansur) (Hirschfeld and Birger 1988). In the Golan, however, which was surveyed in a fairly exhaustive manner (Kochavi 1972), only two farmsteads have been found (nos. 57, 174).

Needless to say, it is not always easy to distinguish between estates and plain rural buildings or small villages. Moreover, a farmstead or estate building is often interpreted as a church or a monastery. Such, for instance,

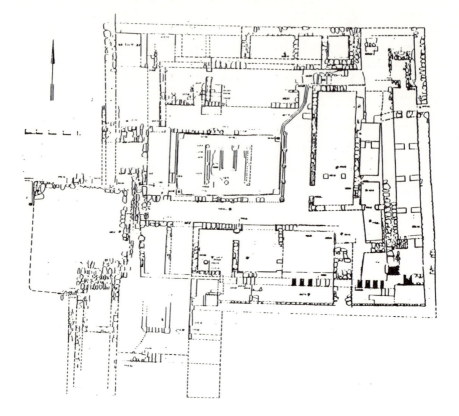

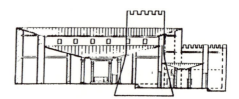

Figure 23 Villa at H. Murak. After Damati 1982, p. 118.

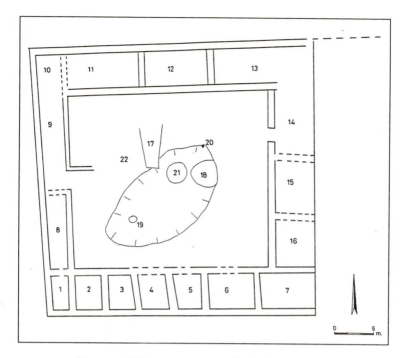

Figure 24 Villa at H. Hamam, *shephelah* of Judaea.

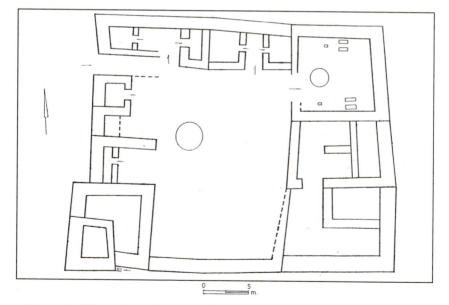

Figure 25 Villa at Qsar a-Lejah, northern Samaria. After Dar *et al.* 1986, p. 111.

012345   10m.

Figure 26 Villa at Kalandia, Judaean mountains. After Magen 1984, p. 62.

is the case regarding Dir Qal'a'. Apart from this site, we have cited examples whose nature is more or less certain.

In spite of all the problems, it is possible to conclude that the estate or farmstead was a common and recognized phenomenon in the hill or mountain regions. An especially large number of estates were found on the slopes of the mountains of Samaria in the transitional region between the mountains and the *shephelah* of Lod (Bastin, Qal'a', Diqlah, Duirah, Arav and additional sites).

In any case, most of the estates were in the plain. This can be determined based both on historical information as well as on the geographic logic discussed above. Estates have been excavated near Caesarea (Levine and Netzer 1986, pp. 149 ff.); and Hofit (*Hadashot Archiologiot* 74–5 (1981), p. 56). Zori excavated a farmstead near Beth Shean (1962, p. 51) and another farmstead was also excavated in this region (*Hadashot Archiologiot* 50 (1974), p. 7). It is possible that the "house of Leontus" was initially also an estate or *proasteion* (Zori 1973). Some estates were discovered in the survey of Emeq Hefer in the Sharon (Porat *et al.* 1986). One dated from the Persian period, another from the Hellenistic period, seven from the Roman period and ten from the Byzantine period. Likewise a large farmstead (approximately 3,000 sq. m) was discovered near Hadera (*Hadashot Archiologiot* 92 (1988), pp. 26–8). A large number of estates were also found in Emeq Jezreel and its environs. There are even scholars who suggested that the entire valley was a royal estate already in the Canaanite period and maintained this status of a royal estate continuously until the end of the Byzantine period (Chapter 4.I below). Herod gave his veterans land in this area at Geva (*Ant.* 15. 294 and parallels; Schalit 1969, pp. 257–62, 365). Bernice also owned lands in this region. The center of that estate was at Beth Shearim (*Vita* 24). Rabbi Judah the Prince also owned a plantation in this region with an estate at Mahalal near Beth Shearim (PT Halah IV, 60a). Two Byzantine farmsteads (*proasteion*) were excavated at Tel Abu Shoshah or Geva Hippeum, the first by R. Giveon (unpublished, see Z. Safrai and Linn 1988), and the second by Safrai and Linn (1988). Raban also examined many buildings of farmsteads in this area (1982, no. 21, p. 16; no. 32, p. 26, etc.). A large number of installations belonging to an estate, apparently that of Rabbi Judah the Prince, were found about two kilometers (north) of present-day Nahalal (no. 82, pp. 68–9, Figure 27; Chapter 4.I.6). Other possible farmsteads were surveyed by Raban in the vicinity of Mishmar Ha-Emeq (unpublished). Farmsteads were excavated in Yoqneam Illit (*Hadashot Archiologiot* 10 (1964)). To these can be added the farmsteads owned by the rich man who met R. Eleazar b. Zadok (BT Sukkah 44b). The tradition does not explicitly state where these estates were, but the sage was a resident of Tivon on the fringes of Emeq Yizrael.

Christian sources dealing with the Ascalon–Gaza coastal plain supply much information about estates in that area. The *Vita* of Petrus the Iberian mentions a large estate at Migdal Tutha (p. 100). Jerome tells of an estate in the vicinity of Gaza (*Vita Hilarionis* 25). The orator Choricius tells of a rich man named Somos who lived in the Gaza region and had lands there. The impression of the literary sources that there were a great many estates is borne out by archeological remains. Thus, a farmstead near Ascalon was examined (*Hadashot Archiologiot* 16 (1966), p. 18) and some others have been mentioned in *Hadashot Archiologiot* 7 (1963), p. 23; near the Erez roadblock, 34–5 (1970), p. 26; near Tel Rukish, 48–9 (1974), pp. 7–8. An extremely large farmstead, located to the east of Ascalon, has recently been excavated (unpublished). The excavators discovered residential quarters,

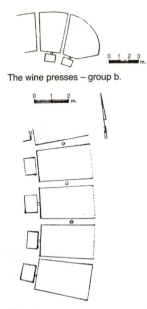

The wine presses – group b.

The wine presses – group a.

Figure 27 Network of wine presses in the Jezreel Valley (apparently estate of Rabbi Judah the Prince, near Nahalal). After Raban 1982, p. 69.

including basilical halls. They also found wine and olive presses, a bathhouse and even lavatories (*latrina*).

V.6.2

The situation is different in the Lod region. In this case it is possible to discern a large number of estates and a great many rich landowners from a relatively early period.

Dozens of farmsteads were found in the hills of Lod dating to the Persian period. They continued to function until the Hellenistic period when many were destroyed, apparently during the Hasmonean revolt (Finkelstein 1981; Dar 1986, pp. 2–7). The estate at Tirat Yehudah, excavated by Yeivin and Edelstein, would appear to belong to this group of estates. This latter estate was very large. The others were quite small and probably belonged to some local rich person.

Talmudic traditions from the Tanaitic period, and particularly from the end of the Second Temple and Javneh period, describe many rich landowners. R. Eliezer b. Hyrcanus was a resident of this city. His family owned many lands as is clear from the Talmudic tradition describing his early years (Genesis Rabbah 41(42):1, pp. 397–8 and parallels). His father, at the end of the Second Temple period, had rather extensive holdings. R. Eliezer himself had a field at Kefar Tov, a site as yet unidentified. A rich landowner living in the city and owning lands in the hinterland was a common phenomenon in the Roman world.

Another rich sage descending from an important family and living in Lod was R. Eleazar b. Azariah. R. Eleazar is basically associated with the Javneh period and, apparently, also with Lod. Talmudic traditions do not mention his lands, but he must have had such possessions, since that is what would have made him and his family wealthy. He did have flocks of sheep, however (BT Shabbat 54b; PT Shabbat V, 7c and parallels). Another rich sage of the Javneh period in Lod was R. Tarfon. R. Tarfon is described as a landowner (see, for example, PT Sheviit IV, 35b; BT Nedarim 62a *et al.*). One tradition relates that R. Tarfon gave R. Akiva money in order to buy an estate ('*usiyah*) for the two of them (Leviticus Rabbah 34:16, p. 812 and parallels). These three sages were priests and came from important families. None of this is coincidence, but this is not the correct forum in which to discuss the matter.

A lesser-known sage called Beytos b. Zonin was also active in this region during the Javneh period. Unlike the other three sages mentioned above, Beytos was not one of the great rabbis of that time. He was, however, a functionary at the court of the Patriarch, having administrative responsibilities there (T Pesahim 3(2):11). Beytos is described as often loaning out large sums of money (M Bava Mezia 5:3 and parallels). He imported dried figs by ship (M Avodah Zarah 5:2 and parallels) and was also apparently a textile manufacturer (T Pesahim 1(2):31). This sage is worthy of a further study. In any case it is clear that he was a rich resident of the Lod-Javneh region.

Literary sources mention another rich person living in the Lod region at the end of the Second Temple period. Joseph of Arimathea or Ramathaim, today's Beth Rimah in the hills of Lod, redeemed the body of Jesus (Mark 15:43 and parallels). There is no specific reference to his lands, but it is hard to imagine that one could have been a wealthy resident of a village and not own lands. It is possible also that Kalba Savua, R. Akiva's employer before he began his scholarly career, lived in this area, although there are no references to this.

During the Javneh period there was a courtyard or structure in Lod called Beth Aris. Klein suggested that this structure referred to or indicated the existence of large tracts of land in the Lod region leased out to tenant farmers (Klein 1939, pp. 69–79). Klein brought two more purported proofs to the existence of this phenomenon in the Lod region. One tradition refers to the "towns" that assembled in Lod for a funeral eulogy. Another tradition mentions the twenty-four *krywt* of Rabbi Judah the Prince that were damaged at Lod. All of his proofs are problematical, even though they would seem to support our general conclusions about land ownership. The "towns" do not necessarily refer to farmsteads or estates, as we have already mentioned above (p. 19). The twenty-four *krywt* do not refer to estates either, although this might be the common meaning of the term. Rather the word should be interpreted as carriages or wagons and part of the large retinue of the patriarch, as Alon has shown (1977, II, p. 98). Beth Aris might indeed be interpreted as Klein suggested (*aris* = tenant farmer), in spite of Epstein's serious objections (1930). However, there is certainly no proof for this manner of interpretation.

There are other traditions referring to rich landowners in the *darom* (lit. south, but often refers to Lod). Thus, for example, there is the laborer from the Galilee who hired himself out to a rich man in the *darom*. According to the version of this tradition in the Babylonian Talmud, this rich man was the grandfather of R. Eliezer b. Hyrcanus (BT Shabbat 127b). This latter aspect is of course legend, but all the traditions indicate that there was a rich landowner in the *darom* (Seder Eli. 16; Derech Eretz Zuta I).

Later on during the Amoraic period, there are traditions which relate that R. Simeon b. Pazi had lands in Har Ha-Melekh, the mountainous region of northern Judaea (PT Demai VI, 25a; PT Avodah Zarah I, 40b). R. Joshua b. Levi, the prominent sage of Lod, deals with the halachic problems of people who obviously do not live in Har Ha-Melekh, but own lands there, particularly olive groves (PT Shabbat I, 3d; PT Avodah Zarah II, 41d). True, the tradition does not relate exactly where these Jews live, but the fact that it is R. Joshua b. Levi of Lod who deals with this matter, as with the previous *halachah* which we cited, would seem to hint at a possibility that they did live in Lod, although it is necessary to remember that this famous sage answered questions from other and more distant regions. Thus once again we have an example of rich landowners living in the city and owning distant agricultural lands. We have also already mentioned the lands of R. Eleazar b. Harzom in Har Ha-Melekh during the Javneh period.

There is not much specific information regarding Lod. The material that there is, however, clearly indicates a large number of rich landowners in the city and its environs. As we mentioned above, a large number of estates were found in this area in the Byzantine period, particularly on the border between Samaria and the hills of Lod. There is possibly a connection between these two phenomena; the region, therefore, was generally associated with estates.

V.6.3

Other estates have been found in the *shephelah* of Judaea. An interesting estate was discovered at Hirbet el-Bas near Moshav Amaziah (Kloner and Tepper 1987, pp. 83–96). This structure – and another one in this region in H. Hazan (ibid., pp. 115–27) – dates to the first and second centuries CE. Hirbet el-Hamam and Hirbet el-Murak (Figures 23–4) which we mentioned above are actually located at the periphery of the hills of the *shephelah* and not really in the mountain region. There was an estate at Kefar Zechariah, north of Beth Gubrin and dating to the fifth century (Sozom. *Hist. Eccl.* 10. 11. 1) in Rasm Dahana in the same region (Kloner and Tepper 1987, pp. 209–16). A rich resident of Beth Gubrin had lands in Beth Zedek to the north of that city (*Vita Epiphanii* 2. 1). At the very beginning of Moslem rule, there was an estate to the west of Beth Gubrin at 'Ajlan. There were *Ktêma* in Socho and Emmaus (Moschus 1938, *Leimanarion*, 80, 181, 165). A *villa* which later was turned into a church was excavated at Emmaus. A number of reports on the excavations of villas in the *shephelah* have been published in *Hadashot Archiologiot*: near Nahalat Yehudah (4, 1963, p. 15); near Nahshonim (5, 1963, p. 22); in Kefar Roth (74–5, 1981, p. 9); Tel Jarmuth (77, 1982, p. 56); Aderet (78–9, 1981, pp. 81–2).

This is, of course, not a complete list, nor was it the intention to provide such a list. Our purpose was to point out the regions in which this phenomenon is especially prominent and at the same time to show that this was a common mode of settlement. Careful attention, though, must be paid to dating. It is clear that information from the Javneh period need not be relevant to the Byzantine period, for instance. It is interesting to note that there is specific information regarding estates that later turned into towns, villas that became churches, and private estates that became crown estates. Talmudic literature also refers to this phenomenon, but we shall not discuss it at present.

In the light of the information which we have presented, it would seem likely that the Lod region could serve as an example of common settlement patterns in the plains and in the *shephelah*. The large number of traditions on this region would seem to be coincidence and would simply seem to reflect the large number of Talmudic traditions relating to this city and its environs. There is also a good level of preservation of the remains found on the hills of Lod.

As we mentioned above, there seem to be fewer instances of estates in the mountain region. This, however, may not actually be the case since the state of preservation of remains there is much less good and scholars have not always paid attention to related structures. Many structures belonging to estates were not properly identified. A good example would be Hirbet Murak which was identified as a "palace." In the Golan, which was surveyed in a rather thorough manner, only two estates were found, one unnamed (Kochavi 1972, no. 57, p. 265), and Rujm Zaki (no. 174, p. 286).

V.6.4

No farmsteads have been found yet in the Galilee. Literary traditions do seem to refer to some farmsteads in the Galilee (Gulak 1929, pp. 26–8). Many Talmudic traditions refer to rich landowners in that region, and this would also seem to indicate that there were farmsteads in that area (see, for example, Büchler 1909, Chapter 3; id. 1912, Chapter 2; Sperber 1978, pp. 19–135). Not all of these references, however, can be proven to refer explicitly to the Galilee and certainly they do not all refer to Sepphoris as Büchler claimed. The fact, though, that such rich landowners are frequently mentioned in literature edited in the Galilee would seem at least to prove that authors were familiar with the phenomenon. Needless to say, not every rich or powerful person mentioned in these traditions owned an estate. However, land was the prime source of wealth and thus we might cautiously conclude that a reference to this type of person was conceivably referring to an owner of an estate.

The parables of Jesus, which reflect to a great extent life in the Galilee, also refer to a rich man owning many farmsteads (Luke 19:12–27, but cf. Matt. 25:14–31). The specific information regarding estates in the Galilee is rather limited. If Krauss is correct in interpreting the phrase "they went out to the *kryyt'* " as referring to visiting farmsteads (Krauss 1924, I, 1, pp. 44–5), then a number of traditions could be interpreted as referring to the farmsteads of such sages as R. Levi b. Sisi, R. Johanan Hakukaah (from Hukuk north of Tiberias) and R. Hiyya who lived in Tiberias. True, not every *kryyt'* can be interpreted in terms of an estate (see I), but the specific term cited above would seem to refer to estates. During the Ptolemaic period there was an estate at Beth Anath (Klein 1930, pp. 127–8, 133–4). There was also a village in the Galilee called Beth Aris or Garis, and Klein, as we have already seen, interpreted such names in terms of tenancy or share-cropping (1930). The site itself is rather small, located on the periphery of the Netufah Valley, and could conceivably be an estate. The "King" (Agrippa II) had an estate in Sihin (T Shabbat 13(14):9; PT Shabbat XVI, 15d; BT Shabbat 121a).

V.6.5

As we have already stated, there are not enough examples of excavated estates, and the information available extends over a great period of time. It is, therefore, difficult to discuss "types" of estates in Judaea. In terms of some general characteristics and on a preliminary basis, it is possible to state that the estate was usually constructed to relatively high standards and columns, capitals and colored mosaic floors in a rural district and in buildings of a non-religious nature could be found only in such a type of building. However, buildings constructed according to the high standards prevalent in other parts of the Empire have not been found. The average estate was 1–2 dunams and none has as yet been discovered which had theaters or similar leisure-time buildings. The palaces of Herod in Jericho are an exception to the rule in terms of their elegance, but these were not really estates in the sense used here, or in the sense that we have discussed. Hirbet Murak (Figure 23, Damati 1982) is also an exception to the rule. The excavations uncovered an elaborate building including a central courtyard and a series of rooms around it. In the west was the residential section, with small rooms for the workers or slaves. These rooms open one into another and each does not have free passage to the courtyard. In front of this row of small rooms were more expansive ones, the residence of the owner and his family. The southern section of the estate was for the bathhouse and storerooms. It is not clear what the northern and eastern sections were used for, but it would appear that they were utilized for storage. At the center of the room was the place where the owner sat. It had a raised platform and was surrounded by water-channels. Agricultural installations were not found in this estate. Likewise, the farmstead located to the east of Ascalon is on an imperial level.

Based on the few existing examples, it is possible to conclude cautiously that in Palestine there were many estates in which the agricultural installations were not in the central building of the estate proper, but in some other additional structure or courtyard appended to it. This is the case, for instance, at Der Sama'an (Figure 28, Tepper 1986b), in the farmsteads near Geva (Z. Safrai and Linn 1988), at the two farmsteads near Anab a-Kabir (Figure 29, Z. Safrai 1986b nos. 10, 18, Figure 9) as well as at the farmstead excavated by Hirschfeld at Hirbet Mansur el Ukuv in the Carmel (Hirschfeld and Birger 1988). If this assumption is correct, it would explain why agricultural installations were not found at Murak and at other sites. However, it is also clear that in many cases the agricultural installations were in the structure itself, such as in the case of Tirat Yehudah, Qsar a-Lejah near Um Rihan where an olive press was found in the building of the estate itself (Figure 25), at Hirbet al-Bas where two olive presses were found in the main structure (Kloner and Tepper 1987, pp. 83–96; H. Hazan, ibid., pp. 115–27), in Gan Hefer in Emeq Hefer where a wine press was found in its main building (Porat *et al.* 1985, pp. 226–8, Figure 30) – this is so far the only instance in which a wine press has been found in this situation in Palestine – and at Hirbet Asilah near Anab a-Kabir, where an olive press was found in the main structure and outside a sheep pen (Figure 29, Z. Safrai 1986, no. 10).

Many of the farmsteads which have been excavated and published are quite early, from the early Roman period or even from the Hellenistic period. This, however, is misleading, at least in our view, since the majority of the farmsteads which have been surveyed, as well as those which have been excavated but not published – and indeed the relevant literary sources – indicate that it was in the Byzantine period that the number of farmsteads began to increase dramatically. It was really only at this time that this particular form of settlement became widespread and accepted in the Land of Israel. All this took place in conjunction with the phenomenon of the increase in tenant farming in the agrarian sphere (see Chapter 4.I.4) on one hand, and urbanization on the other (see II.2 above).

It can be determined from a number of farmsteads that were excavated

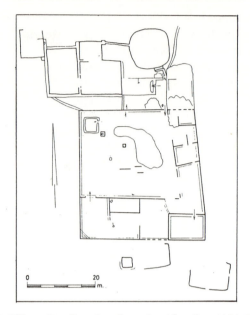

Figure 28 Villa at Der Sama'an, Samaria. After Dar 1986, Figure 28.

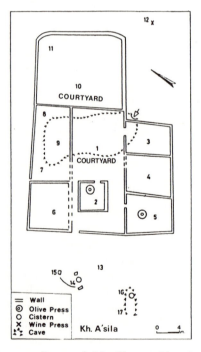

Figure 29 Manor house or house of rich village resident in Anab al-Kabir in the southern Mt Hebron region. After Z. Safrai 1986, p. 121.

98

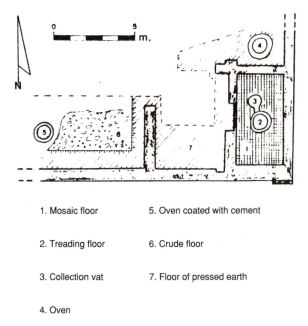

1. Mosaic floor
5. Oven coated with cement

2. Treading floor
6. Crude floor

3. Collection vat
7. Floor of pressed earth

4. Oven

Figure 30 Manor house at Gan Hefer. After Porath *et al.* 1985, p. 226.

that some of them were apparently destroyed during the War of Destruction (66–70 CE). This was the case apparently at Tirat Yehudah, Kalandia, H. Murak and at H. Uqub el-Mansur (near Ramat Ha-Nadiv). However, destruction at this time has not been proven at enough sites to justify considering this to have been a general phenomenon. It is well known that the rich and especially well-to-do priests suffered during this war. They were the target of violence on the part of radical groups such as the Zealots, and it is likely that their holdings also suffered as a result of the war in general. It is not too far-fetched, therefore, to connect the destruction of these farmsteads to the property damages suffered by the upper classes during the War of Destruction, even if it cannot really be proven.

Management and work on the estates had a unique nature. We shall deal with these phenomena in our discussion of agrarian developments in Palestine (Chapter 4.I).

VI. SPATIAL STRUCTURE

Provincia Judaea possessed a wide variation of geographical regions as well as, in the period under discussion, a varied ethnic make-up. Pagan, Samaritan, Jewish and mixed settlements were often located adjacent to one another. There were regions in which the settlement patterns were particularly influenced by nearby Hellenistic elements (such as the coastal plain which had, relatively speaking, more *poleis* and estates). There were other regions such as the Galilee and Golan where these types of settlement were uncommon, and where, in any case, their spatial structure was different.

The number of cities in Palestine differed from region to region as well as during different time periods. During the height of urbanization in the third century CE, there were 15 cities in the coastal plain, 3 in the central mountains (Judaea and Samaria), 3 in the Galilee, 1 in the Golan, 3 in the Jezreel Valley and altogether 22 cities (although there might be a few more, since there is some discussion as to the urban nature of a number of settlements). The model of this spatial structure can be seen in the sketch in Figure 31. The *polis* was at the center of the territory. Around the *polis* were the suburbs of villas (*proasteion*) in which some of the rich citizens of the city lived; and the farm region which included, at times, both large and small towns. The territory was divided into village units, each with a mother settlement and a number of satellite or offshoot settlements. Scattered throughout the entire region were a number of estates, generally related in some manner to the major roads in the region.

VI.1

This structure is modular and the sum total of geographic, historical and ethnic factors of every region determined the particular structure of that region. In the coastal plain there were a great number of cities. Their territories, consequently, were smaller. Therefore the number of towns in the region of a *polis* in the plain was also limited. Thus the territory of Dor which was particularly small, probably no more than 60 square kilometers, had no more than 10 towns (based on the as yet unpublished survey of Olami). The regions of Apollonia, Lod and Joppa have been at least partially surveyed, but the state of preservation of remains does not enable us to determine the exact number of towns in these regions. In any case, it would seem likely that in a territory which extended 100–200 kilometers, there would be no more than 10–20 mother settlements. The excellent agricultural nature of these plains allowed for the development and survival of more agricultural towns than regions which were ecologically poorer.

In spite of all this, in the hill region the territory was very large and the number of towns and villages was great. The territory of Neapolis extended some 540 kilometers. The agricultural region included some 35 square kilometers and had 5 mother settlements and 15 offshoot settlements (Z. Safrai 1986b, p. 106, Figure 4). The exact number of villages in the entire territory is not clear, but it would seem to have included about 60 mother settlements. In the territory of Susita (Hippos) there was only 1 *polis*, but there were apparently more than 60 mother towns (Urman 1985). Maoz claims that there were only 30 such settlements in that territory (Maoz 1986,

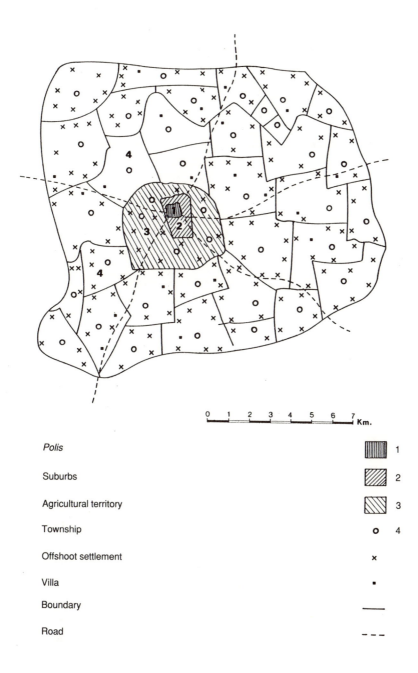

	0	1	2	3	4	5	6	7
Km.

Polis	▦	1
Suburbs	▨	2
Agricultural territory	▧	3
Township	o	4
Offshoot settlement	×	
Villa	▪	
Boundary	———	
Road	– – –	

Figure 31 Regional structure in the village sphere: descriptive model.

101

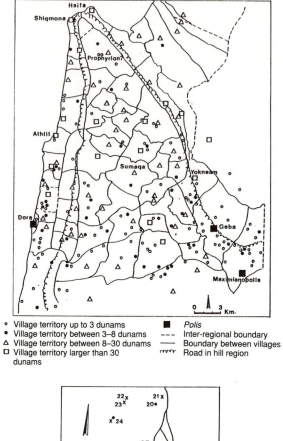

° Village territory up to 3 dunams   ■   *Polis*
• Village territory between 3–8 dunams   – – – Inter-regional boundary
△ Village territory between 8–30 dunams   ⸻ Boundary between villages
□ Village territory larger than 30   ⟿ Road in hill region
     dunams

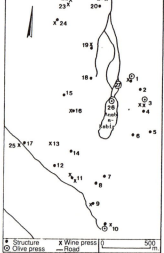

• Structure   ✕ Wine press
⊙ Olive press   — Road

Figure 32 Settlement areas in the Mishnah and Talmud periods. After Z. Safrai 1986, p. 180.

p. 85). Together they were about 50 times larger than the city. There were also a number of regions in the Golan without any urban settlements. In the Jezreel Valley the situation was different. During the height of urbanization there were two cities in the region – Geba and Maximinopolis – which functioned basically as mother towns. There was only one other town in the entire region (Yoqneam-Qamon).

The number of offshoot settlements was also different from region to region. Such settlements have hardly been surveyed in the Golan (Urman 1985). This is also the case in the Upper Carmel region (based on the surveys of Ronen and Olami 1978; Olami 1981; Ronen 1983; and an unpublished survey of Olami). On the other hand, 10–14 satellite settlements per city have been found in the Jezreel Valley (Figure 32, Z. Safrai and Linn 1988).

It is difficult to determine the numerical relationship between the city and village residents. Avi-Yonah, with no basis whatsoever, claimed that the urban sector represented one-quarter of the population of Palestine (Avi-Yonah 1964, p. 121). This estimate reflects the intuition of this great scholar, but it is still only intuition. The data which we have discussed are based on more detailed information, which is, however, at best only partial, since many regions have not been completely surveyed. We can make a somewhat rough estimate and suggest that in the coastal region the ratio was somewhere in the region of between 2:5 to 1:3. In the Dor region which was thoroughly surveyed, the ratio was between 1:5 to 1:7 in favor of the rural district. In the hill regions the ratio was at least between 1:8 to 1:10. In general, it is likely that the urban population of Palestine was less than twenty per cent of the population of the country. We should add that the data are based on the average area settled in a village.

It is, however, difficult to arrive at an estimate of the entire population of Palestine. Broshi has devoted a number of studies to this topic (Broshi 1979). He claims that there were no more than a million people in Palestine even at the highest population levels of the Roman period. Broshi's estimates are based on two factors: (1) those sections of the city containing residences and a density coefficient of thirty people per dunam. Broshi also assumes, without proof, that urban dwellers represented one-third of the population of Palestine; (2) the estimation of average grain production, based on the figures of grain production in Palestine in 1942.

The matter requires further study. In any case, we shall prove in the further course of our study that during tremendous periods of population growth an open farm system was utilized in Palestine and large amounts of wheat were imported into Palestine. In any case, Roman period agriculture in Palestine was more developed than the Arab farm system of the 1940s. It is likely that the population was much higher than the figures suggested by Broshi. At this point we do not have exact information regarding the population of Provincia Judaea during the Roman period.

2

Modes of production

I. AGRICULTURE

I.1 Introduction

I.1.1

Agriculture was the main sphere of production in the ancient world in general as well as in the Roman Empire. Most ancient manpower worked in the various aspects of this field and most of the ancient gross national product was derived from agriculture in one form or another. We shall discuss below the relationship of agriculture in Judaea to the economy in general. In this chapter we shall discuss the various spheres of agriculture. We shall not delve into technical farming matters, but rather concentrate on the economic structure of agriculture in ancient Judaea.

Talmudic literature mentions over 500 types of produce. Of these, about 150 types of cultivated crops, 8 types of grain, 20 types of legumes, 24 types of vegetables, 30 types of fruit and about 20 types of spice plants have been identified. Numerous non-fruit-bearing trees have also been identified (Feliks 1982, pp. 424–7). The three major crops – wheat, olives and grapes – are mentioned in all types of Talmudic literature far more than any other. R. Johanan (third century CE) explains the verse "Blessed are you in the field" in the following manner: "That your possessions should be divided into three parts – one-third in grain, one-third in olives and one-third in grapes" (BT Bava Mezia 107a). When Talmudic literature wishes to describe difficult times, it states: "The world was injured – one-third in olives, one-third in wheat and one-third in barley" (BT Bava Mezia 59b). In this case, barley is mentioned as the third most important crop. Another tradition cites the story of a rich man who wishes to flaunt his wealth and does this by stating that he has estates where olives and many vineyards grow (BT Sukkah 44b).

We have many ancient sources as to the agriculture in Roman Palestine, no less than in Roman Italy (Frayn 1979; Flach 1990) or classical Greece

(Isager and Skydsgaard 1992; Saller 1991; Wells 1992 *et al.*). The Arabs' traditional farming supports us with a lot of additional information. However, this information needs caution (see, for example, Halstead 1987; H. Forbes 1992).

I.1.2

The importance of these crops is further shown by examining the information regarding the various foods eaten at that time, as well as the dining customs of that period. The ancients ate two daily meals during the week and three on the Sabbath. Breakfast, eaten in the third or fourth hour of the day, consisted of bread dipped in olive oil or bread with some type of vegetable. The poor made do with bread and garlic while the wretchedly poverty-stricken ate "dry bread" which they dipped in salt. Supper, eaten during the twilight, was the main meal of the day. This evening meal included bread and some cooked food such as an egg, or some type of cooked legume flour or paste. The Sabbath meal, according to Jewish law, had to be festive. The rabbis, therefore, required that it include two cooked foods. This may have included eggs, fish, legume flour or paste, vegetables, and on rare occasions meat. The rich, of course, enjoyed such festive meals more frequently, and their diet was much more varied (S. Safrai 1983, pp. 91–6; M Peah 8:5–7; M Kelim 17:11; BT Shabbat 117b, 118a; BT Pesahim 12b *et al.*). There were those, however, who ate only one meal a day (BT Sukkah 7b. For a meal of bread and legumes see, for example, M Baba Mezia 7:1).

Talmudic tradition has recorded the basic ancient diet. This diet is mentioned in a number of traditions, proving its wide usage and acceptance. According to the rules governing this diet, food was to be provided to the needy. The rules of the diet also stated the exact and established quantities of food that a husband had to provide his wife if he deserted her. These quantities served as the basis for many other laws and for the establishment of a norm regarding the daily amount of food sufficient for the set "two meals," as this is called in the *halachah*. The wide acceptance of this diet in numerous cases of law would seem to indicate that this was also the norm of the vast majority of people at that time.

Because of the importance of these traditions for understanding the economy of Palestine, especially as it pertained to the rural sector and the common people in general, we shall cite these traditions in their entirety. M Peah 8:7 states: "A poor man who is journeying from place to place should be given not less than one loaf worth a *pondion* (from wheat costing) one *sela* for four *seahs*." The price for a *seah* of wheat is one-quarter of a *sela* = *dinar*. The *pondion* is one-twelfth of a *seah*. Thus, a loaf is one-twelfth of a *seah* or one-half of a *kab*. A *seah* of wheat, therefore, is 6.3 kilograms. Thus, the Mishnah is describing a loaf that weighed 0.525 kilograms.

M Peah 8:5 states:

> They may not give to the poor from the threshing floor (as poorman's
> tithe) less than one-half a *kab* of wheat or a half *kab* of barley. R. Meir
> says: A half *kab* of barley or a *kab* and a half of spelt or a *kab* of dried
> figs or a *mina* of fig cake. R. Akiva says: half a *mina*, a half *log* of wine.
> R. Akiva says: a quarter. Or a quarter *log* of oil. R. Akiva says an
> eighth. Of any other produce, Abba Shaul says: They should be given
> so much that, if they sell it, they can buy with it food for two meals.

The Mishnah lists staples that in each case are equal to two meals, or as a
baraita in PT Peah VIII, 20d states: " 'And they shall eat at your gates and
be satisfied' – give to him in order that he be satisfied." Thus, the nutritive
value of wheat is equal to its cost. This would also seem to prove the
importance of grains in the daily diet as well as in the economy in general.

This list is cited in a number of traditions (T Peah 4:2, 5; PT Peah III, 20c;
M Eruvin 8:2; BT Eruvin 29a). M Ketubot 5:8–9 is especially important for
our discussion:

> If a husband maintained his wife at the hands of a third person he may
> not grant her less than two *kabs* of wheat or four *kabs* of barley [every
> week]. . . . He must also give her a *kab* of pulses and half a *log* of oil
> and a *kab* of dried fruits or a *mina* of fig cake; and if he has none of
> these he must provide her with other produce in their stead. . . . He
> must also give her a cap for her head and a girdle for her loins and
> shoes at each of the three feasts and clothing to the value of 50 *zuz* each
> year. He must give her a silver *maah* for her needs, and she should eat
> with him on the night of every Sabbath.

The Mishnah discusses a person providing for his wife. The money for this
purpose is deposited with another person who transfers it to his wife. The
list of staples applies to the entire week. It may be broken down into the
following components:

(1) two *kabs* of wheat – enough for eight meals;
(2) a *kab* of dried figs or a *mina* of fig cake – enough for two meals
    (according to R. Akiva, as mentioned above);
(3) a half-*log* of oil – enough for two meals;
(4) a half-*kab* of legumes – food for two meals.

True, the Mishnah in Peah does mention a *kab* and a half of spelt, but
examining the two versions in Peah and Eruvin, it would seem that the
legumes are in place of the spelt. The difference between the two *mishnayot*
would seem to relate to the different geographical districts described by the
different *mishnayot* (below we shall see that this Mishnah was edited in the
Galilee). The sum total of the food and meals mentioned in the Mishnah is
fourteen meals, encompassing the entire week including the meal on the eve

of the Sabbath. The phrase "and she should eat with him on the night of every Sabbath" apparently relates to sexual relations, as was understood by the Talmudic discussions on the matter. The Mishnah simply refrains from describing the matter in explicit language. The phrase does not refer, though, to dining habits (PT Ketubot V, 30b). All of the sources cited above, except Mishnah Ketubot, deal with the monetary value of the food sufficient for two meals or, in other words, the cost of a day's fare. M Ketubot discusses the weekly diet and mentions a number of kinds of food. This weekly food schedule includes two *kabs* of wheat. Thus grain constitutes four-sevenths of the weekly diet, as in the whole Roman Mediterranean (compare Foxhall and Forbes 1982). The figure of half a *kab* a day is cited in all the sources dealing with the matter as an accepted figure. M Eruvin 8:2 cites it as the opinion of R. Johanan b. Beroka, but even the different figure cited by R. Simeon is close to the half-*kab*. Actually, it is not really clear whether R. Simeon cites a higher figure (two-thirds of a *kab* or 900 grams a day) or a lower figure (two-ninths of a *kab* or 233 grams a day). The PT and BT have detailed discussions on the matter (BT Eruvin 82b, 83a; BT Ketubot 64b; PT Eruvin VIII, 25a). It would appear that Z. Safrai (1985, pp. 115–16) was right in claiming that the Babylonian Talmud did not really understand the reality of the Palestinian diet at the time and therefore offered explanations for the figures which greatly decreased the daily intake. The discussions in BT on this matter should be seen more in the light of theoretical and dialectical discussions and not as reflecting the actual dietary habits of Palestinian Jewry.

The daily fare as established by the Palestinian sources is sufficient for basic needs and can therefore be seen as the norm, at least for the vast majority of common people. The rich consumed more, but the addition would mostly likely not have been in terms of grain, but rather additional fruits, wine, meat and other luxury items. Thus the sources provide two schedules of diet: one which deals with the monetary value of various staples, and the other which describes the nature of the popular diet.

The standard diet, as we have seen, includes three basic components: bread, usually from wheat but occasionally from barley, olive oil and figs. Wine is mentioned only in a few sources. We shall discuss the implications of this below.

I.1.3

Many sources mention the olive and the grape as the two major orchard or grove crops of that time. Thus, for example, the sages did not allow the branches of the olive tree or grapevine to be used as heating material in the Temple "for the sake of the settlement of Eretz-Israel" (Mishnah Tamid 2:3; BT 29b). On the other hand, the branches of other types of trees could be used for that purpose. The branches of the fig tree or nut trees were frequently used as a source of fire on the Temple altar. These other trees were obviously less important, agriculturally speaking.

The villages in Samaria were surveyed by S. Dar. Dar found that in Kefar Buraq, grains constitute 26.4 per cent of cultivated crops, grapes 20.2 per cent, and olives 12.9 per cent. 5 per cent of the area was for crops needing irrigation, probably vegetables, at least in our view. In Karawat Bani Hasan 52 per cent of the cultivated area was for grain, 22.2 per cent for grapes and 24.8 per cent for olives (Dar 1986, pp. 245 ff.; Dar *et al.* 1986, pp. 57–83). It should be stated, though, that it is not always that easy to determine the exact area in which olives were grown during ancient periods, and the same is true regarding the exact nature of the areas supposedly cultivated with grain. Much of the agricultural determination is based on the nature of the terrain, as well as on the assumption that these were the three major crops. Thus, even if we accept these evaluations of ancient agriculture from the two villages in Samaria, they should not be seen as proof of the actual farm structure, but certainly as an indication of the importance of these crops. More details on the components of the rural farm will be discussed below in Chapter 4.

I.2 Grains

I.2.1

Eight types of grain are mentioned in Talmudic traditions. Five are described as the "five major kinds of grain." Wheat, however, was by far the most important grain in Palestine. Proof of this is the far greater number of times that wheat is mentioned in Talmudic traditions as against barley. The Mishnah, for instance, mentions wheat 88 times, while barley is mentioned only 47 times. It should be stated, however, that the value of this statistical information is somewhat limited by the fact that the traditions which we have in our corpus of Talmudic literature is at best only a fragment of the ancient information, and occasionally mentions wheat or barley in relation to matters not connected to agriculture. The Mishnah in Ketubot 5:8 which discusses the dietary schedule, as we saw above, does mention barley along with wheat, but regarding the barley it adds: "R. Jose [140–80 CE] said: It was R. Ishmael (100–32 CE) who granted her barley [and] who lived near Edom." Thus, only R. Ishmael added barley to the staples. This sage lived in Kefar Aziz in the southern Hebron mountains (M Kilayim 6:4 and parallels; Schwartz 1986, p. 39). This is a rather dry area with inconsistent amounts of annual rainfall. Barley is a major crop of this region even today because the conditions are not conducive for the cultivation of wheat. Only a sage living in such a region would include barley in the list of staples, at least in the view of R. Jose.

The Mishna also states that if someone pledges to do a certain act "before the harvest," he must fulfill his vow "until that time when the people begin to harvest the wheat, but not the harvest of barley – everything in accordance with the place" (M Nedarim 8:4). PT Nedarim VIII, 41a states specifically that the reference to barley ("in accordance with the place") relates specifically to the *Darom*. *Darom* is basically synonymous to Edom or Judah (Klein 1939, pp. 249–54; Schwartz 1986, pp. 35–81). Thus, this mishnah also associates barley just with the southern regions of Israel. Another important testimony on this matter is found in the discussion in PT Orlah II, 62a regarding certain laws relating to the heave-offering (*terumah*): "And it was taught thus that all heave-offerings which the priests are not particular about, such as carobs and barley in Edom." Thus, even in Edom, where barley was widely cultivated, it was not considered important and the priests were willing to forgo their due. T Bezah 1:23 and parallels relate an additional proof regarding the low status of barley: "R. Simeon says – wheat may be sent because it is eaten *asisiot*, *ful* because it is a Lyddan dish, and barley because it is appropriate for animals." The Law cited above is that food may not be sent on a festival from one place to another unless it can be eaten immediately with no additional preparation needed. Wheat fits into this category because it can be eaten *asisiot*, either soaked in water or in a city by that name. *Ful* is eaten raw in Lydda or Lod. Barley, however, was given to the animals uncooked. The Tosefta does not state that barley was only eaten by animals, but it is clear that this indicates its status *vis-à-vis* other grains. This same sentiment is stated in Midrash Samuel 20 that a field of lentils is more important than a field of barley since "lentils are a food for humans while barley is fit for animals."

Barley was also considered to be a food fit for prison inmates, another indication of its limited status in the normal family diet (M Sanhedrin 9:5). Thus, the average person was more accustomed to food from wheat. Wheat is also cited very often in Rabbinic literature as an example of unspecified food or fruit, another indication of its importance (M Demai 3:4; M Ma'asrot 4:5; M Bava Mezia 5:1, 5:8, *et al.*). Most of Palestinian Talmudic literature derives from the Galilee and therefore wheat is cited as the major crop. It is likely that if we had other ancient traditions from Judaea and the *Darom* the descriptions might have been somewhat different. The value of barley was about half of that of wheat (Sperber 1977, pp. 112–13). Its nutritive value was also less than that of wheat (M Ketubot 5:8). It was, however, considered to deplete the soil less than the cultivation of wheat (M Bava Mezia 9:8). It is clear, though, that barley's economic importance was far below that of wheat.

I.2.2

According to the dietary schedules cited above, the daily sustenance of wheat was an amount equal to half a *kab* or 0.525 kilograms or the monetary equivalent. The average yield of a field cultivated with wheat during good years is between 180–360 kilograms or between 90–180 in less bountiful years (Feliks 1963, pp. 160–9). Needless to say, these numbers are no more than estimates, but in any case, they would seem to be fairly accurate. For the sake of convenience we shall use the figure of 150 kilograms per dunam as an average crop yield. This figure may seem to be somewhat high, but reflects the high level of agriculture in Palestine at this time. Crop yields from other provinces in the Empire are not specific enough since they are based on untrustworthy literary references on one hand, or on later sources on the other (Spurr 1986, pp. 28–88; Evans 1981; Garnsey 1992). The yield cited above is sufficient for the sustenance of a person for 300 days. Thus, about 1.28 dunams is necessary to sustain the average person. Because of the system of crop rotation at that time, the land was cultivated only every other year. Thus, in reality, 2.5 dunams was needed to sustain the average person and about 10 dunams for the average family of four. This figure pertains only to basic sustenance. In order to make a living as well as to be able to pay the various taxes, additional sources of income were needed. There was, however, some kind of income from those areas which also lay fallow. All of the above is in accordance with the opinion of R. Johanan b. Beroka. According to R. Simeon, whom we also mentioned above, the average person would need 1.7 dunams and the family 13–14 dunams.

According to the weekly diet schedule cited above, the average person needed 2 *kab* of wheat per week or 2.1 kilograms. The family would consume yearly 438 kilograms of wheat. In order to produce this amount, a little less than 6 dunams had to be cultivated. If it were possible to state that every family grew its own wheat, then it would also be possible to compute the population limits of each region in Palestine.

I.2.3 The importing of wheat to Palestine

I.2.3.1

As stated above, wheat was widely cultivated in Palestine, and was perhaps the most commonly cultivated crop in the period under discussion. The important book of Y. Feliks (1963) discusses the many traditions pertaining to the cultivation of grain in general, and to the cultivation of wheat in particular. However, there still exists a question as to whether Palestine was able to supply its grain needs, or whether it was necessary to resort to imports. There are no significant testimonies regarding the importing of wheat to Palestine during the Second Temple period, or during the first and second centuries CE (Tannaitic period). The various references to the importing of wheat refer to particular difficult instances such as during a drought, or the contributions of Queen Helene of Adiabene or the importing of grain by Herod. These, however, were the exception to the rule (*Ant.*

15. 299–316, 20. 102). There also seem to have been some isolated instances of importing wheat from Egypt (T Machshirin 3:4). It is possible that the attempt of the sages to render as ritually unclean the wheat imported from Egypt reflects their desire to limit the importing of wheat, as does a similar case regarding the ritual purity of imported glassware (T Kelim, Bava Bathra 7:7; PT Shabbat I, 3c; BT Shabbat 14b). However, droughts and famines are not so unusual in Palestine, and it would seem assistance would have to be rendered on a more frequent level. Good examples of this phenomenon in modern Israel are the severe droughts of 1984 and 1985. Much wheat had to be imported and it would seem quite likely that this was also the situation in the ancient world. It is also likely that it would be necessary to import wheat during the Sabbatical Year (T Sheviit 4:16 and parallels). All of this, though, would have a cumulative effect on the economy. Droughts could conceivably have occurred every 2–4 years and the Sabbatical Year, of course, occurred every seven years.

We have a number of traditions from the Amoraic period (or Byzantine period) pertaining to the massive importing of wheat. The *derashah* of R. Hanin, for instance, is repeated a number of times: " 'And thy life shall hang in doubt before thee' (Deut. 28:66) – that is one who buys wheat for the entire year. 'And thou shall fear night and day' – that is one who [buys wheat] from the wholesaler [*sydky*]. 'And shalt have no assurance of thy life' – that is one who buys from the seller of bread [*palter*], and I depend on those who sell bread." (PT Sheqalim III, 47c; VIII, 51a; PT Shabbat VIII, 11a; Esther Rabbah Petihta 1; BT Menahot 103b; Midrash Ha-Gadol on Deut. 28:66, p. 629).

The tradition refers to the "retribution" if the Children of Israel do not observe the Law. Three punishments are cited. In the worst instance it would be necessary to buy wheat from the seller of bread or *palter*. A less serious situation would be the need to buy the wheat from the wholesaler. Finally the lightest punishment of all would be buying a year's supply of grain. This may seem to be a rather light punishment, but it still is considered, after all, to be a punishment. There are two clear-cut conclusions from this *derashah*. (1) As far as the author of this teaching is concerned, the ideal situation would be that everyone should cultivate the amount of grain needed for personal consumption. We shall see below that this utopian ideal was very popular in ancient Palestine, although there were other opinions on the matter. (See Chapter 3.XI.2) (2) The buying of wheat was common and accepted. R. Hanin himself relates that he bought wheat from a *palter*. The sages interpreted the chapter of retribution in Deut. 28 as referring to their own times. Thus, the reality of being dependent on the selling or commerce in wheat was also a common phenomenon, even if it was considered as a punishment.

I.2.3.2

Often the *sydky*, the wholesaler cited above, or to be more exact the "grain market" (where such a wholesaler would ply his wares) is brought as an example regarding the buying of fruits in the market (PT Nedarim XI, 42c). We hear in particular of the grain market of Sepphoris which operated during the entire year (PT Bava Mezia V, 10c). This would seem to imply that in Sepphoris the farmers did not grow grain, but rather bought it in the market. Another tradition relating that the price of wheat in Sepphoris was 25 per cent higher than the price in Tiberias also indicates that wheat was sold in the market of Sepphoris (PT Bava Kama IX, 6d). Thus, it appears that wheat was grown in the Hauran or in the Golan, brought to Tiberias, and from there to Sepphoris. Sepphoris is located near the Beth Netufah Valley and the Tura'an Valley. If a city like Sepphoris could not supply its own grain needs, this was certainly the case regarding other settlements in the Galilee. Thus, at least part of the grain needs of the Galilee came from outside that region.

I.2.3.3

A number of other sources describe the importing of wheat. Thus, for example, late Palestinian halachic traditions mention Edomite wheat brought to Palestine in boats, and wheat brought to Palestine via the desert (Margoliot 1974, p. 41). Byzantine sources also describe the importing of wheat to Palestine on a regular basis and particularly during periods of drought (*Vita Georgii Chozebitae* 25, Cyrillus of Scythopolis, ed. Schwartz, p. 186; ibid., p. 136 *et al.*). One of the orations of Choricius (3:54) states that the governor once imported wheat to Palestine, but since this instance related to a period of drought, it might be argued that this could not serve as proof that the importing of grain was a common occurrence or that this was the accepted role of the governor.

There is also much information regarding the supplying of wheat to specific regions of Palestine. We have already mentioned Tiberias in the second and third centuries. As we stated above, wheat from the Hauran was brought to Tiberias (via Susita). We also mentioned the large wheat market in Sepphoris and that the source of its wheat supply was probably Tiberias. We shall cite a few additional examples.

Beth Shean. The Palestinian Talmud and the Rehov inscription (Y. Sussman 1973–4, pp. 109–14) relate that tithes had to be offered on agricultural produce from the Beth Shean region. Some of the produce was grown in the vicinity of Beth Shean, or in the region which was exempted from the obligations of tithes and the Sabbatical Year. Other produce was imported from the halachic Land of Israel, areas that were not included in the exemption from tithes and the Sabbatical year. This *halachah* gives us the opportunity to examine, indirectly at least, the sources of grain supply for Beth Shean. According to the specific *halachah* in the Palestinian Talmud and the Rehov inscription, wheat was supplied to the city from the area that was exempted from tithes, or the vicinity of Beth Shean. The exemption of Beth Shean from tithes and the observance of the Sabbatical year was established during the time of R. Judah the Prince (third century CE) and the exact geographic boundaries of the area included in the exemption were also, most likely, established at that time. The city of Beth Shean itself had a quarter that was called the Wheat Quarter (*SEG* VIII, Lifshitz 1977, p. 43, 271). It is likely that the wheat merchants of the city were found in this part of town. Thus wheat was supplied to the city from its immediate environs and from that area included in the exemption.

Caesarea. According to the sources cited above, wheat was brought to that city from areas outside the region surrounding Caesarea which was also exempt from tithes and the Sabbatical Year (Y. Sussmann 1974, p. 131). The exemption regarding the Caesarea region underwent a number of stages. The initial exemption apparently dates to the beginning of the Amoraic period when only the coastal plain nearby ("from everywhere where one sees the sea"), or to be exact, until the beginning of the hills some 4–6 kilometers to the east of the coast was exempted. At this time only the fields of the residents of the city, most of whom were non-Jewish, were included in the exemption. Wheat was imported to the city from the eastern and central Sharon, outside the limited region of Caesarea's lands. The Sharon was especially suitable for the cultivation of wheat and, in fact, during the Phoenician period the Joppa-Dor region was referred to as "lands munificent in grain" (Avi-Yonah 1966, p.38). In any case, it would seem that in the third century CE the residents of Caesarea had to supplement their local wheat supply from other areas inside the halachic agricultural boundaries of Israel.

Paneas. According to the Palestinian Talmud and the Rehov inscription, wheat was brought to Paneas from outside the halachic boundaries of Palestine, but not from the Hulah Valley, even if this region, which is near Paneas, was suitable for the cultivation of grain (Y. Sussmann 1973–4, pp. 129–31). It is not clear, however, from when exactly the pertinent section of PT and the Rehov inscription date.

Ascalon. R. Pinehas b. Jair (early third century) relates that on the eve of Passover, the Jewish residents of the city used to sell grain in the *basilicae* of Ascalon, ritually immerse themselves and eat the Passover meal in a state of ritual purity (T Ahilot 18:18 and parallels). From the context of the tradition it is clear that the Jews did not remain in Ascalon itself to eat the Passover, otherwise they would have remained impure on account of "the dwellings of non-Jews." Thus, it would appear that these Jews did not live in the city itself, but rather in the villages or in the surrounding suburbs. The parallel version in PT (PT Sheviit VI, 36c) specifically related that these Jews returned to their own towns and clearly did not live in Ascalon.

The Lod region. As is known, there were three important markets in the northern Judaean mountains, southern Samaria and the region of Lod: Yaashuv (Yassuf), Paetros (Budros) and Antipatris. Fruits were brought to these markets from Har Ha-Melekh (the northern Judaean mountains) and grain and legumes were brought from the plain region or the Lod area (T Demai 1:11 and see also Chapter 3.IV.2). This situation pertained to the period before the Bar-Kochba revolt and the Usha period. It would seem then that by this time the hill and mountain region could not supply its own grain need. Below in Chapter 4.V.3 we shall see that Judaea was considered the grain region *par excellence*, while the Galilee specialized in the cultivation of olives. This testimony also strengthens our point above regarding the difficulties of supplying grain to the Galilee. We shall expand on this point below.

Geba Hippeum. A possible indication of the areas in which grain was cultivated and what happened to them was revealed through the discovery of installations for the processing of flax found near Tel Abu-Shoshah and dating from the Roman and Byzantine periods (Z. Safrai and Linn 1988). Based on the sources which describe the ancient cycle of grain cultivation and the particular use of these installations, it is possible to determine not only the extent of flax cultivation, but also the extent of this cultivation in relation to all grain cultivation in this region. From the various computations it would appear that the local farmers grew enough grain for local consumption, but there was not enough surplus for sale. The Jezreel Valley was a natural grain supplier in ancient times and an explicit reference to this characteristic exists in reference to the Second Temple period. Josephus tells of the gathering of grain from the villages belonging to Berenice in the Beth Shearim region and its transfer to the Galilee (*Vita* 24). It would seem then that grain was widely cultivated in this region during the Second Temple period, but later on the wheat fields were turned into orchards or cultivated with flax which was far more profitable. The installations in Geba reflect the situation in the late Roman and Byzantine periods (from the third century on).

In addition to the material cited above, there are a number of additional testimonies to the growing of wheat or to buying it in a number of regions of Palestine. In order to further expand our discussion, we shall cite these testimonies below.

I.2.3.4

Talmudic literature relates that R. Judah the Prince and R. Jose b. Judah, Galilean sages from the beginning of the third century CE, once went to buy wheat in Javneh (Genesis Rabbah 76:8, p. 906). Other merchants, probably from the Galilee, went to buy wheat in Himonaya in the Javneel Valley (Shir Hshirim Raba 5:13). R. Hiyya of Sepphoris went to buy wheat in a place called Sura or Surta (unidentified – perhaps Sura in Babylonia?) (Pesikata D'Rav Kahana, Va-Yehi Beshalah 18, p. 194; Klein 1966, p. 45; Z. Safrai 1985, p. 118). A fourth-century CE Roman work called *Totius Orbis Descriptio* (c. 31) describes Neapolis, Caesarea and Lod as cities abundant in grain. Ephraim (Taiybeh in Ramat Issachar) was a center of grain cultivation (Genesis Rabbah 86:4, p. 1058; Exodus Rabbah 9:6; Tanhuma Buber on Exodus Vaerah 12). These sources all relate to the Amoraic period (and cf. M Menahot 8:1 and parallels; T Menahot 9:2 – this tradition reflects the end of the Second Temple period and the first century CE). Judaea in general excelled as a wheat growing region. In southern Judaea, however, the cultivation of barley was more prevalent. We shall discuss this matter further in Chapter 4 V.3.

There are more references regarding the growing of wheat in specific sites in Palestine. The coincidental manner in which this agricultural fact is usually mentioned makes these references, however, limited in their importance for our discussion. Thus, a source citing the growth of wheat at a particular place need not indicate that wheat was not grown in other sites not mentioned in the sources. As we remember, wheat was grown in all regions of Palestine. The problem at hand, however, is whether it was necessary to import wheat. Moreover, almost every source on this matter is problematical. Thus, for instance, the wheat bought at Javneh, mentioned above, was purchased at a storehouse (*"otzar"*), which was an official government storehouse used to store taxes paid in kind (T Demai 1:13). This grain served to supply regular rations to soldiers serving in the area (*annona* or *arnona* in Talmudic literature). The surplus, though, was probably diverted to the local markets and sold there.

Thus, it is possible that the buying of wheat by these rabbis from the Galilee in Javneh does not represent regular trade or commerce between the Galilee and the Judaean plain. It may even have been a one-time affair, and thus the event would be devoid of any basic economic importance. The sources cited in previous sections, however, generally represent market conditions in Palestine or in specific regions there. Thus, those sources cited in the previous section are of greater importance for our discussion.

What was the actual extent of the importing of wheat to Palestine? It is difficult to give a clear-cut absolute answer. It would appear that there were regions which were self-sufficient in grain. Other regions in Palestine did have to import grain, either from other areas of Palestine, or from abroad. However, it is important to state that most of the grain consumed in Palestine was, apparently, grown there. The laws of heave-offerings (*terumot*), tithes and the Sabbatical Year would seem to prove this point. The vast majority of the sources on these laws indicate that grain, without specific reference to where it was grown, was included within the complex of the commandments dependent upon the land. The commandments dependent upon the land refer, of course, only to produce grown in the Land of Israel. There are many discussions in the sources regarding the setting aside of tithes by bakers, wholesalers or any kind of bread merchants. All of this would indicate that their wheat was cultivated in Palestine. Even so, care must be taken not to over-generalize from these types of sources, or to see them as reflecting the ancient periods in general. Most of these traditions are Tannaitic (first and second centuries) or Amoraic (up to the third century CE). Some of the Amoraic sources are also influenced by the earlier Tannaitic material, even if their literary formulation is later (see, for example, M Demai 1:1; PT Demai I, 21b; T Bava Mezia 2:3). The traditions relate a reality in which most of the cultivation was by Jews. This might have been the situation in the Tannaitic period, but not in the third century, at least in our view. In any case, however, the fact that these traditions do state that unspecified grain falls within the realm of the commandments dependent upon the land would seem to at least indicate that most of the grain was grown in Palestine. The importing of grain, then, should be considered as supplementary to local cultivation and the rate of importing differed from region to region. Most of these traditions were studied by Sperber (Sperber 1974, pp. 31 ff.). According to Sperber, the importing of grain was a direct result of a decline in agriculture during the period of the anarchy (235–84).

His basic claim regarding the decline in agriculture during this time is beyond the scope of our discussion. In our view, there were no radical changes in the natural conditions of Palestine at that time and the traditions dealing with the importing of grain do not all date to the period of the anarchy. Moreover, during that same time there apparently was a large degree of agricultural export (Chapter 4.VI). It would appear that the importing of grain was not the result of an agricultural decline, but rather related to changes in the mode of land use.

I.2.4 The treatment of wheat

After harvesting the wheat, the farmer would bring it to the threshing-floor (*goren*). There he would smooth out the heap of wheat, thresh it, scatter it to complete the separation of chaff from seeds, and sift it. The final result of all this was a pile of seeds. The farmer did not grind these himself, but sold them in this form or stored them. This is clear from the fact that this pile of seeds is referred to in Talmudic literature as "the finished product." This stage of production is the halachic state whereby the grain can acquire ritual uncleanness if defiled, and is the point from which the obligation of tithing begins (Feliks 1963, pp. 187–289).

The final stage is the *merihah* or smoothing out of the pile of seeds. This was necessary in order to measure the seeds. In those places where the pile of seeds was not smoothed out (*merihah*), the halachic status mentioned above began "when the *alah* was removed" (T Terumot 3:11 and parallels). The *alah* was the utensil used in the final stages of scattering the chaff from the seeds. The wheat was stored as seeds and not as flour. This is clear from the discussion in PT Sheviit V, 36a which assumes that one buys seeds from the wholesaler. The seeds were obviously not bought for planting since they were old. Rather, it is taken for granted that even the wholesaler sells unground wheat. As is known, the volume of flour is 75 per cent of the volume of the seeds. It would, therefore, make more sense to market flour and not the seeds. However, it would have been much more difficult to store flour, and therefore it was preferable not to grind the seeds.

Customers would bring the wheat seeds to be ground. There are many sources describing this. In any event, it is clear that traditions relating to the grinding of wheat are not necessary proof that the grain was cultivated nearby.

I.2.5 Other grains

A number of other grains are mentioned in Talmudic sources. These grains, such as oats, spelt and rye were of limited importance and there are not many traditions which discuss them.

I.2.5.1 Rice

Rice was a rather new crop in the Palestinian agricultural scene. Talmudic literature mentions it for the first time in traditions from the Javneh period (90–132 CE). The sages were not sure whether rice should really be considered a grain, and were of various opinions as to the proper blessing to be recited when eating it. They were also unclear about the status of rice on a number of other issues (Feliks 1963a). Rice was widely grown, and in some instances provided a substitute for regular bread. Rice bread is mentioned a number of times in Talmudic traditions (PT Hallah I, 57a; III, 59a; T Nedarim 4:3 *et al.*). Rice also appears as a supplement to the dietary schedule which appears in PT Peah VIII, 20d (I.I). According to this source, a quarter of a *kab* of rice cost the same as half a *kab* of wheat. Thus, rice cost twice as much as wheat.

Palestine was self-sufficient in rice since it is listed among the produce that require one who buys them to offer heave-offerings and tithes. This would prove that they were cultivated in Palestine (M Demai 2:1 and parallels). The list, though, included produce about which there was some doubt regarding where it was cultivated, and thus it is possible that very small amounts of rice were imported. The discussion of the Palestinian Talmud on this Mishnah does mention imported rice coming from Hulta or Heilat Antioch (T Demai 2:1; PT Demai II, 22b), but this was a different variety. It would appear, then, that plain rice mentioned in the sources was rice cultivated in Palestine.

The reference cited above to rice from Hulta has misled a number of scholars. Avi-Yonah, for instance, indentified Hulta with the Hulah Valley and concluded that all rice mentioned in the sources was grown in Palestine (Avi-Yonah 1963, p. 152). This valley, which is inundated with water, is suitable for the cultivation of rice. However, Heilat Antioch is clearly regarded as being outside the boundaries of the Land of Israel, while the Hulah Valley was considered part of Israel. The rice from this region (perhaps the vicinity of Antioch, the capital of Syria) was considered in the *halachah* to be "permitted," that is, one did not have to set aside tithes from it, and it was therefore grown outside the Land of Israel. There must have been some degree of import from this region, otherwise the source would not have mentioned it.

In Caesarea on the coast the rice was considered to be "forbidden," that is, it came from a region considered halachically to be part of the Land of Israel (PT Demai II, 22d; Y. Sussman 1973–4, p. 130). Caesarea Philippi is located near the Hulah Valley. This is further proof that Heilat Antioch is not to be identified with the Hulah Valley.

We do not have figures regarding the level of consumption or of purchases of rice at markets. It was apparently a profitable crop and as we have stated, Palestine was mostly self-sufficient in its rice needs. There might even have been a degree of export abroad (PT Demai II, 22d).

I.2.5.2 *Ful*

Another important crop mentioned in the sources often together with lentils is *ful* (T Okazin 1:5; T Machshirin 3:6; M Kelim 15:5; T Menachot 10:24; PT Nedarim VI, 40a; T Baba Mezia 3:9). This pulse as well as the lentil served as the basic ingredient for the cereal eaten by the common people for their evening meal (see I.5 below) (M Machshirin 5:9; Tanchuma Acharei I; M Maasrot 5:8).

I.3 Groves

I.3.1 Olives

I.3.1.1

The Middle East is the birthplace of the olive and many wild varieties are found in Palestine. Generally, olives do not flourish in regions having very cold winters or very hot and dry summers, or, as Josephus stated: "Olives thrive on a temperate climate" (*BJ* 30. 517). In spite of this, the olive had adapted to diverse regions of Palestine. The sources indicate a number of regions which had very heavy olive cultivation. Olive presses, however, are found in almost every region of Palestine having undergone even a superficial survey. Thus, it would seem that olives were an important crop in almost every region of Palestine, except in those areas with extreme climates. As we stated above (I.1), the olive numbered among the three most important crops in Palestine and it was of great economic importance.

I.3.1.2 The olive and its oil

The olive was cultivated primarily for the production of oil. Many sources and *halachot* reflect this fact. Thus, for example, "From what point is one required to set aside heave-offerings [*terumah*] on olives? From when they are loaded up? R. Simeon says: From when they are ground" (T Terumot 3:13). The sages argue as to the final stages of work associated with the olives which then make it necessary to offer heave-offerings and tithes. In any case, from the tradition above it is clear that the olives were meant to be used for the production of oil and the sages would probably not have conceived of any other use for them. Another *halachah* regarding tithes and the like gives the same impression. Most fruits become subject to tithes after the harvested fruit have been piled up. Thus, for instance, we find in M Maasrot 1:7 oil, when it has dripped down into the trough (or oil pit), but even though it has already dripped down one may take from the press basket or from between the press stones (*memel*) or from between the press boards. . . ." The oil has already begun to drip into the trough or pit. The oil which has not begun to drip there is not subject to tithes. This is the oil which is between the press boards (the pieces of wood or stone which support the pile of press baskets from the side. The *memel* which is mentioned in this context cannot be the crushing wheel on top of the *yam*, since in the context of the Mishnah it is connected to the pressing and not the crushing procedure.

Another expression of this concept is found in T Terumot 3:15 (and M Terumot 1:4); "One who is setting aside heave-offering [*terumah*] from oil-producing olives for olives to be eaten, sets aside the heave-offering based on the amount of oil that these olives to be eaten would produce." The *terumah* even for table olives is computed based on the amount of oil that they would have produced. It is also clear from the context of the Mishnah that these table olives were of a different variety than the regular oil-producing olives. Hundreds of other traditions associate olives with olive oil. Thus, for example, T Maasrot 3:13 states: "A Levite who had tenant farmers raising olives, sets aside a tenth based on the amount of oil the olives would produce." Once again, it is clear that plain olives are used for oil. The sages also discuss whether a person may sell his olives to one who is not accustomed to offer up tithes. According to Bet Hillel this is permitted. The PT on this Mishnah explains that "the reason of Bet Hillel is that most people eat olives still in their skins only if they have a particular reason for doing so" (M Demai 6:4; PT Demai VI, 25c). Thus, according to Bet Hillel it is possible that someone might eat olives before the oil-producing process, but only under special circumstances. Once again then, it is clear that under normal circumstances olives were meant for oil and were not to be eaten in any other form.

The major use of the oil was for the dipping of bread. Small amounts were used for cooking. Not much of it was used for lighting either, since most people went to sleep rather early. There was light in the house in the evening only on the Sabbath eve for the festive Sabbath meal.

The olive was, of course, of great importance in the normal diet of the time. Olive oil was the major source of necessary fats, since animal fat was hard to preserve in the warm climate of Palestine. It is doubtful, however, that the ancients had a sophisticated knowledge of the major nutritive families. As far as they were concerned, olive oil was the most important dip in their diet.

I.3.1.3 Table olives

In spite of everything mentioned above about the nutritive and economic value of olive oil, there were some instances in which the olives were not processed for oil. Thus, the sources occasionally relate instances of olives that were eaten pickled, boiled, rolled and salted. M Terumot 2:I teaches; "One may set aside for heave-offering (terumah) from olives used for oil for olives to be pickled, but not from olives to be pickled for olives used for oil. . . . This is the rule. . . . One may set aside (for terumah) from the better quality for the poorer quality, but not from the poorer quality for the better quality." Thus, there is a special variety of olives for pickling, but these are considered to be of inferior quality to those olives processed for oil. The Tosefta adds, however, one exception to the rule: "One may set aside kelofsin olives for olives used for oil, but not olives used for oil for kelofsin olives" (T Terumot 4:3). Thus there is a type of olive even more expensive than the oil-producing olive. Other sources mention pickled olives as "olives pickled in their skins" (M Uktzin 2:1; BT Berachot 20a) or "non-sanctified olives which were pickled with olives of terumah" (M Terumot 10:7).

Another type of olive mentioned in Rabbinic sources is the rolled olive or the "geluska." The halacha did not permit one to eat foods pickled or cooked by non-Jews. On the other hand it was permitted to eat "pickled foods in which it is not common to add wine or vinegar." As an example of this type of food the Mishnah cites "olives – geluskaot [MSS. versions keluskaot] which are rolled." The Tosefta adds: "Sheluhin olives which are sold at the entrances to bathhouses are forbidden to eat, but it is permitted to enjoy benefit from them." R. Jose also does not allow one to enjoy benefit from them because they pour on them vinegar in order that they may take out their pits. This halachah is also cited in PT: "These are keluska olives – these are rolled olives and sheluhin olives are forbidden. R. Hiyya (said) in the name of R Johanan – it is a type of olive and they put vinegar on it in order to take out its pit" (M Avodah Zarah 2:7; T Avodah Zarah 4(5):8; PT Avodah Zarah II, 42a. See also M Eduyot 4:6; T Eduyot 2:2; BT Yebamot 15b). Thus, rolled olives are permitted. (This phrase recalls the rolled egg – an egg rolled in ashes or along the sides of the oven.) The rolled olives, as we remember, were also called *keluska* olives. These would appear to be olives pickled in salt, as opposed to those pickled in vinegar mentioned above (Krauss 1929, II, 1, pp. 274–5; Aruch Completum, II, 1955, p. 285).

Another type of olive mentioned above is the *sheluhin* or *shelahin* olive. These olives were soaked in vinegar in order to remove their pits and then sold as a sort of "snack" at the entrances to the bathhouses. It is possible that these were a different species of olive than the others mentioned so far, as can really be understood from the discussion in the PT above. It is also possible that these were regular olives soaked in water (*shalhin* literally means an area that is irrigated). As is well known, olive groves which are irrigated produce less oil in their olives and are considered of lower quality than other types. According to the *halachah*, *bikkurim* or first fruits could not be brought from the fruits of Sepphoris or from those of Beth Shean, even though these were considered to be especially fertile regions. It is likely that these were regions in which irrigated crops predominated and for that reason the fruits were disqualified from being brought as *bikkurim* (PT Bikkurim I, 63.4).

Another type of table olive was the sliced olive, or sliced and salted olive (T Taharot 10:11; BT Shabbat 145a). A different source, though, refers to this type of olive as a raw olive dipped in salt (M Taharot 9:5; T Tahorot 10:10; BT Baba Mezia 89b). We do not really have any information on the boiled olive (*shelukim*). The sources do state: "The added clay rim at the top of a cauldron belonging to olive-seethers (*swlky*)" (M Kelim 5:5; 8:8; M Eduyot 7:8; T Eduyot 3:1; T Kelim Bava Kama 4:5; T Parah 12:10). However, it is possible that this cauldron was used to heat up the squeezed olives in order to produce a little more oil. The following reference is somewhat clearer: "pits of olives and pits of dates which have been boiled" (T Uktzin 2:10). In this case, an attempt is made to get out the last drops of oil from the pits.

Table olives are mentioned a number of times in Rabbinic sources. *Halachot* describe one who was eating an olive and radish, or olive and onion, and it is clear that the person was eating an olive itself, not the oil (BT Berachot 41a; T Hagigah 3:12; BT Erubin 29a). There were also those who ate raw olives, not processed in any manner (see above and see M Maasrot 3:3; PT Maasrot I, 49b). This for the most part represents the traditions mentioning the eating of olives either pickled or in some other form, excluding oil. As we have stated, though, the predominant form in which the olive was used or eaten was as oil.

The Galilee was the major olive-producing region in Palestine. The olives of the Decapolis (in Transjordan) were also of high quality and food olives from that region, as well as from Beth Shean, were exported to Rome (Pliny, *HN*. 15.4, 15).

I.3.1.4

The average yield of an olive grove is mentioned in only one tradition. M Peah 7:2 states that an olive yield of two *seahs* exempts one from the obligation of the forgotten sheaf or fruit which was left for the poor. However, important amounts of crops forgotten in the fields did not have to be left for the poor. There were a number of opinions as to the meaning of the Mishnah regarding olives. According to the Tosefta (Peah 3:9), if the owner had begun to harvest his tree and forgot to complete the job on that particular tree, the remainder had to be left for the poor. However, if a large quantity of fruit remained on the tree (two *seahs*), it need not be left for the poor since the owner of course knew that he had to return and finish the picking of the olives. The PT gives a somewhat different explanation (PT Peah VII, 20a). According to the discussion there, a tree that produces two *seahs* exempts the owner from leaving the fruit for the poor, since any tree that produces a large yield, 1.5 or a little less than the yield of the average tree, exempts the owner. According to the first explanation, a normal tree yields more than two *seahs* (17.08 kilograms) or at least 20 kilograms per tree. According to the second explanation, a normal tree yields 1.4 *seahs* or about 12 kilograms (or a little more).

Cato (*De Re Rustica* 10) states that for 240 *iugera* of olives (= 600 dunams) it is necessary to have receptacles able to hold 4,750 liters (five olive presses, each holding 950 liters). As is well known, the olive tree yields fruit only every other year. Thus, the yield in a good year is 9,500 liters or 15.83 liters per dunam. For the purposes of our discussion we shall use the figure of 16 liters per dunam. The amount of oil in the Italian olive is a little less than 20 per cent of the olive. Thus, according to Cato, every dunam would yield about 80 kilograms of olives. In Palestine, 11–12 trees were planted in each dunam (10 trees in "Bet Seah" 784 m^2, M Sheviit 1:6 and parallels). Thus each dunam had a yield of 132–220 kilograms. Studies of olive yields in primitive Arab farms during the 1950s showed that their trees had yields of 10–30 kilograms per tree (or 100–300 kilograms per dunam). This would also yield 20–60 liters per dunam (Boneh 1953, p. 10; Gur *et al.* 1960). Comparing these figures with those from Italy and others from Palestine leads to the conclusion that the second explanation regarding the Mishnah cited above, with lower estimations of crop yields, should be preferred. Therefore it is possible to estimate the yearly yield as being 132 kilograms of olives or 26.4 liters of oil per dunam. Because a crop is produced only every other year, that would therefore result in a final figure of 13.2 liters of oil per dunam.

The monetary value of this is enough to provide meals for 148 days

$(13.2 \div 0.089 = 148)$. As we remember, the amounts cited by R. Akiva are smaller, and according to his computations there would be enough for 296 days (M Peah 8:5). It is impossible to know which of these computations is correct and in any event it would probably be dependent on conditions in different regions of Palestine. In any case, from the above figures it is possible to state that a single person would need to cultivate 1.23–2.46 dunams of olives to produce a crop to make enough to provide his food needs. A family would need about 4.9–9.8 dunams of olives.

I.3.1.5 The economic importance of the cultivation of olives

It is well known that in the ancient world, the cultivation of the olive was widespread and of great economic importance. We have already mentioned that it was one of the three most important crops in Palestine. We shall now try and construct a model which will enable us to quantify the yield of this crop during the Mishnah and Talmud periods. In order to arrive at this evaluation it is necessary to have three figures on either the local or regional level (depending on the particular case): (1) regional or village olive yield; (2) oil consumption in average village (= family consumption × number of families); (3) value of the oil (yield × price). If we are able to determine these three facts, it is possible to ascertain whether a village was self-sufficient in oil, needed to import oil, or possibly was able to export. We can also determine the monetary value of this economic sphere *vis-à-vis* the village. It should be remembered, though, that the numbers which we shall use are at best estimates. Even though we do not have detailed statistics, the estimates can still do much to help our understanding of the matter.

Olive Yield   The olive yield can be estimated by determining the general extent of the olive groves and the average yield in such instances. Statistics on both of these elements are problematical, as mentioned above. On the other hand, the yield can also be estimated by determining the capacity of the olive presses found in the region. At many sites in Palestine, including well-preserved ones, many olive presses have survived. The survival of such presses can theoretically, therefore, aid in ascertaining the yield in a particular village. Unfortunately, there is no clear-cut indication in literary sources as to the capacity of the ancient press, and the modern calculations on this matter are widely divergent. S. Dar (1986, pp. 182 ff.) has suggested that the olive presses were used about ten weeks a year. 10 per cent of the press time, though, was undoubtedly lost due to mechanical failure. Thus, the capacity of a press during the olive season would have been about 3,600 liters.

Urman (1985, p. 161), using the same time factor, estimated that the capacity of a press was 500–600 kilograms of olives a day, or 30 tons of olives during the season. Both of these estimates are based to some extent on the supposed capacity of the olive press in the traditional Arab village, and not on exact figures pertaining to the ancient world. It would also seem to be difficult, methodologically speaking, to determine ancient capacities based on the traditional Arab olive press. We therefore suggest a different manner of arriving at a reliable figure.

The storage pits in the ancient olive press are somewhat diverse in dimensions, but based on the examination of dozens of these pits it is possible to state with some certainty that they could hold from 40–50 liters. These pits held the distilled water and oil (about 25 per cent). This figure is also in keeping with the height of the olive bales, which can also occasionally be measured.

Every complete turning of the press produced, therefore, 10–12.5 liters of oil. The Arab press had a somewhat more sophisticated pressing device and the complete rotation was finished in about an hour. For the sake of caution we shall assume that in an ancient press with a complex beam-pressing device the rotation took from an hour to two hours. It is also unlikely that the presses were worked during the nights. Thus, on Sunday through Thursday they were worked for about 14 hours per day, while on Friday, because of the approaching Sabbath, they were in use for only 10 hours. Thus the average press was in operation for about 80 hours per week ($5 \times 14 + 10 = 80$) out of a possible 136 hours. During this time there would have been 40–80 complete rotations of the press (see also C. Ben David 1989, pp. 12, 88–100, and compare H. Forbes 1992, pp. 89 ff.). According to these figures, the press produced 400–1,000 liters per week and 4,000–10,000 liters during the ten-week season. These figures represent a minimal capacity which is far lower than the other numbers cited in modern scholarship. It is still not known, however, whether all the presses in a particular village were operated simultaneously. It would appear, though, even if there is no clear-cut evidence, that this was not the case. The capacity was also determined by the nature of the actual pressing device. The screw press was faster than the beam press operated by weights. However, since most of the sites have not yet been fully excavated, there are undoubtedly presses which have not yet been discovered and this would raise the theoretical capacity of oil production in a given village. All of these doubts, though, would seem to cancel each other.

The olive press was a community installation and was meant to serve all of the local growers. It is also likely that the presses were built with a potential capacity to process the local olive crop in a good year.

The minimum amount of oil that a husband had to supply to his wife was half a *log* (M Ketubbot 5:8. See also Z. Safrai 1985, pp. 113–16 and Sperber 1974, p. 112). Parallel traditions record even smaller amounts. Similar amounts are recorded regarding the amount to be provided to the poor, and thus the Mishnah seems to record the minimum required amount. During the year, therefore, an individual needs at least 26 *logs* of oil and a family of four would need 104 logs (4.3 *seahs* = 37 liter). An extended family with 7 members would need 182 *logs* of oil (7.6 *seahs* = 64.8 liters based on 1 *seah* = 24 *logs* = 8.54 liters).

S. Dar (1986, pp. 184–90) has produced a different set of figures. The Mishnah permits one to sell five jugs of oil during the Sabbatical Year on the assumption that this is equal to the yearly supply of oil (M Sheviit 5:7; PT Sheviit V, 36a). The standard Palestinian jugs would contain about 20–25 liters of oil. It is impossible, though, to know the size of the family supposedly referred to in the Mishnah. Based on the first figure cited, though, this would have to be a large family. In any case, the figure cited by Dar would be higher than the one suggested by us. However, M Ketubbot cited above refers, as we remember, to minimum amounts for the lower classes. M Sheviit would seem to refer to the absolute maximum needs of a family (see p. 129).

Price of Oil Scholarly literature on the economy of the Roman Empire contains estimates of prices in dinars based on the price edict of Diocletian (see, for example, Duncan-Jones 1982). In our opinion it is more fruitful to compare prices in relation to the price of wheat or the price of daily sustenance. There are data on these two matters in Palestinian Rabbinic literature. The sources portray a rather constant economic situation not dependent to any great extent on market fluctuations. The reliability of these data has been shown by Sperber (Sperber 1974, pp. 112–27).

According to M Peah 8:5, a fourth or an eighth of oil was equivalent to the monetary value of two meals (or a day's sustenance). As we have stated above, this Mishnah has many parallels and is often cited in post-Mishnaic traditions, indicating that the figures there were the norm during the second and third centuries CE (Z. Safrai 1985, pp. 112–16). Thus, a family of four would need the monetary equivalent of 7.6–15.2 *seahs* of oil or 130 liters of oil per year. The monetary equivalent of that amount of oil refers, of course, only to the cost of food. Actual expenses including clothing and living expenses would be higher. Taxes would also have to be included in necessary living expenses. It is difficult to evaluate this final factor. Hopkins estimates taxes to account for 10 per cent of the gross national income of the Roman Empire (Hopkins 1980). The farmer would probably have to pay up to about 30 per cent of his income toward various taxes. Thus food expenses would amount to about 40–50 per cent of total expenses. Although it is difficult to know the population of the ancient village, it is possible to measure its size. We estimate that the average density was between 30–40 people per dunam. We shall not, however, discuss this last point in detail at this stage of our discussion. In any case, our estimate is rather high. Other estimates in scholarly literature are somewhat lower. According to these, the final conclusions would be far more radical than those suggested here. (The archeological material pertinent to the discussion is presented in Chart 2 (Figure 33).)

It is possible that some of our computations are mistaken. However, we have always tried to use the minimum figures and not the maximum. If, for instance, we should claim that the capacity of the olive presses was greater, or that the population density was lower, then the final figures would indicate a higher rate of production. On the other hand, the assumption that oil consumption was higher than the level we have suggested is not borne out by the sources which have been discussed. Even if we accept the computations suggested by Dar (100–125 liters of oil per family per year), the final figures would still indicate a much higher rate of production than was necessary in terms of consumption. It should be remembered that the presses were built with the maximum yields of bumper crops in mind. The fluctuations in yield as a result of the occasional drought, however, were not great. As we have stated above, the olive trees produced only every other year. However, it can also be assumed that not every tree produced fruit in the same particular year. Thus the yield levels would basically be constant.

Conclusions (1) Most of the oil produced was intended for sale or for export outside the particular town where it was produced and, most likely, outside the local region and the province. This would seem to prove the basic contention that the farmstead at that time was based on open economy. This concept, however, will require further discussion (Chapter 5 below).

(2) The conclusions above pertain to most regions of Palestine. The situation may have been somewhat different in Judaea.

(3) The oil production industry provided, at times, twice the financial remuneration needed to subsist. It would appear, therefore, that the general standard of living was high. Basic expenses (food, taxes, clothing and the like) were only part of the family's general cost of living. As is well known, the higher the standard of living, the lower the percentage of expenses for staples in the family budget. It is possible that it was the landowner and not the individual farmer who enjoyed this higher standard of living. On a national level, though, the standard of living was undoubtedly much higher than has been generally assumed.

(4) This assumption, as well as conclusions based on it, should still be considered tentative since not enough sites have been completely excavated. Hopefully further excavation will shed more light on the matter.

I.3.2.1 Cultivation of grapes

As we have stated above, the most widely grown and important crops in Palestine were wheat, olives and grapes.

The grape was the most profitable crop of these three. In the Syrian-Roman code tax rates on land are recorded: "During the time of Diocletian lands were measured. Five jugers which are 10 *plethra* [12.5 dunams] of vineyards shall be considered one *jugon* [tax unit]. Twenty jugers [fifty

Source	Site	Area (dunams)	Population (rooms counted)	Presses	Minimum production (liters)	Production rate % from estimated consumption	% from complete costs and necessities of settlement	Region
1.a	H. Khurkush	14	600	3	12,000	1. 175	80	Western Samaria
2.b	H. Horah	5		5	20,000	2. 875	400	Shephelah of Judaea
3.a	H. Boraq	25–30	1,000–1,500	5	20,000	3. 116–175		Western Samaria
4.c	Um-Rihan	40		10	40,000	4. 219	100	Northern Samaria
5.b	H. Khaspash	10	320	4	16,000	5. 437.5	153	Shephelah of Lydda
6.b	H. Hamam	5–6		4	16,000	6. 583–700	266–320	Shephelah of Lydda
7.b	H. Levad	3.2	112–120	2	8,000	7. 583–625	205–220	Shephelah of Lydda
8.d	Anab a-Kabir	30		4–5	16,000–20,000	8. 116–146	52–66	Southern Hebron Mtns
9.b	H. Kerach	20		5	20,000	9. 219	100	Carmel
10.g	H. Shev Tov	2–3	50–60	2	8,000	10. 1168–1400	410–492	Shephelah of Judaea
11.e	H. Jerba	25		5	20,000	11. 175	80	Golan
12.e	Zamimra	30		5	40,000	12. 116	66	Golan
13.e	Chalba	10		7	28,000	13. 612.5	280	Golan
14.f	Karkara	18		7	28,000	14. 340	155	Upper Galilee
15.f	H. Mu'ar	3		4	16,000	15. 1166	533	Upper Galilee
16.f	Dan'ila	30		5	20,000	16. 875–1094		Upper Galilee
17.f	Ramah	5		2	8,000	17. 350	160	Upper Galilee

Basic Data:
Consumption of 11.4 liters per person per year;
Olive press capacity of 4000–10,000 liters per year;
Thus, the press provides for 350–877 persons.
The press, therefore, provides for a population living on a built site of 8.75–29.2 dunams.
A family needs 130 liters of oil for subsistence;

Thus, a press would support 30.8 families (123 persons) living on approximately 4 dunams.

Sources
(1)Dar 1986. (2) Z. Safrai survey (unpublished). (3) Z. Safrai 1986. (4) Ben David survey (Ben David 1989). (5) Dar et al. 1986. (6) Frankel 1992, and pers. comm. (7) Z. Safrai (unpublished).

Figure 33 Production and consumption of oil in the Land of Israel.

dunams] of a field [cultivated with wheat] which are forty *plethra* shall be considered one *jugon*. Two hundred and twenty-five choice olive trees shall be considered one jugon." (Sachau no. 151). That number of trees was planted in 18–20 dunams, as we saw above (I.3.1.4). Thus, a vineyard of 12.5 dunams was equal to an olive grove of 18–20 dunams and the cultivation of grapes was about 1.5 times more profitable than the cultivation of olives. Both grapes and olives were more profitable than wheat (this calculation will be discussed in Chapter 4). The *midrash* states a similar sentiment: "The grape vine – one branch goes forth from it and rules over all the trees" (Leviticus Rabbah 36:2, p. 838). Roman farmers reached the same conclusion and stated that the grapevine is the queen of agriculture and the grape grower cannot but profit from his crop. Figures on yields and prices in the ancient sources and especially in the edict of Diocletian mentioned above prove the benefit in cultivating the vine over the cultivation of wheat or olives. "The price of wine was high and a half-*log* of wine (0.18 of a liter) or a quarter-*log* was equal to the price of half a *kab* of wheat" (0.525 kilograms – see I.1 above).

Generally, it was worthwhile for every farmer to cultivate the vine. Two factors, however, limited the cultivation of this fruit in Palestine. (1) The grapevine is rather sensitive and can be cultivated only in particular types of soil. It is also influenced by changes in the weather. (2) The grape was only of secondary dietary importance. Widespread cultivation would imply extensive marketing of the crop and would therefore be subject to the vagaries of the market (similar to modern agriculture but certainly not to the same extent). This last fact requires further discussion.

I.3.2.2 The role of wine in the ancient diet

The dependence upon grain was a reality in the ancient world. Bread was the basic food staple in the entire Roman Empire. The basic minimum need of this food is more or less constant and the possible maximum consumption is also limited. The minimum which can be established both in terms of the caloric requirements of the body and certain requirements of *halachah* was about half a kilogram per day. The maximum consumption was between 1–2 kilograms per day (I.1 above). The basic need for and consumption of olive oil was also fairly constant. This was not the case, however, regarding wine. Modern-day statistics record enormous variations in wine consumption among various peoples and cultures. However, it is possible to estimate the basic wine consumption in the ancient Jewish town and village.

We have already discussed the dietary schedule recorded in M Ketubbot 5:8. We have also seen that this tradition which theoretically pertains to the minimum support granted to a wife by her husband also reflects the common fare of the lower classes. This Mishnah, however, does not even mention wine! T Ketubbot 5:8, elaborating on this point, states: "She does not receive wine because the wives of the poor do not drink wine." PT Ketubbot V, 30b expands further on this point: "She does not receive wine because the wives of the poor do not drink wine. The rich women do [drink wine]." The continuation of the discussion in PT Ketubbot records the famous case of Marta b. Beytus, one of the richest women of Second Temple-period Jerusalem, who was granted by the sages a portion of two *seahs* of wine every day (17 liters). Needless to say, this quantity, sufficient not only for her but also for her servants, is somewhat exaggerated. The sages, further on in the discussion, expressed disapproval regarding the giving of wine to rich women, but this would seem to be more a reflection on their views regarding the propriety of feminine behavior than a true mirror of reality. By the time this matter was discussed in BT Ketubbot 65a, only the rabbinic disapproval of women drinking wine was stated and no differentiation was made between rich and poor women.

A certain amount of information regarding daily consumption of wine can be culled from the laws pertaining to the Sabbatical Year when the fields were not cultivated. According to the *Mishnah*, a potter could sell five jugs of oil and fifteen jugs of wine because this was considered a legitimate amount stored for the needs of the year. Any quantity beyond this exceeded the needs of that particular year and would have been considered hoarding for the period after the Sabbatical Year and was forbidden (M Sheviit 5:7). The ancient jug usually held from 20–25 liters and thus the yearly consumption of wine would have been from 300–375 liters. This figure, of course, can pertain to a nuclear family of about four members, meaning that the consumption per capita would have been 75–94 liters, or to an extended family of about eight which would lower the per capita consumption to 38–47 liters per person. But we know that, through its internal logic, the *halachah* of the Sabbatical Year requires the maximum consumption, thus these figures represent that maximum consumption.

It is also likely that the consumption of wine in the Sabbatical Year was higher during that year than in other years. As we shall see in the course of our discussion, much of the grape crop was intended for sale or for export and not for personal use. Agricultural trade was greatly limited during the Sabbatical Year and thus much of the grape crop during that year undoubtedly went toward personal use, either to use up the existing supply or to compensate for the lack of other crops (particularly grains), since the fields were not cultivated. Thus, wine consumption in other years was in all likelihood much lower.

The laws of the Sabbatical Year provide another important indication of the level of wine consumption. According to the Mishnah discussed above, the consumption of wine was three times that of oil. True, the PT (ibid.) states that the Mishnah refers to different vessels which can easily be distinguished one from another. It would appear that the Talmud had in mind different forms, but not different sized vessels. The daily consumption of oil was set by the Mishnah based on half a *log* per week (M Ketubbot 5:8). If the consumption of wine was three times that of oil, this would have been 1.5 *logs* per week.

True, lower-class women did not receive wine, nor did they drink it at all. The *halachah* states that women should be made happy on Passover: "How should they (= men) be made happy? With wine. . . . R. Judah says women should be made happy with what is appropriate for them . . . such as nibblings and doves, and the children with that which is appropriate for them such as nuts and hazel nuts" (PT Pesahim X, 37b). Thus, men can drink and enjoy wine; women and children make do with other luxury items. Even the very drinking of wine on Passover by women is a matter of dispute among the sages (cf. BT Pesahim 109a). The sages dispute as to whether a woman is actually required to drink the four prescribed cups of wine on Passover. These disputes would certainly indicate that lower-class women did not drink wine at all.

Wine was either drunk neat (the pure grape potion) or diluted with water. Various amounts of water were used to dilute the raw wine, but very often the ration of water to wine was 2:1 (M Niddah 2:7; BT Shabbat 77a; BT Erubin 29b; cf. II Maccabees 15:39), or two cups of water to one cup of wine. Thus, this amount of 1.5 *log* of wine per week was enough to make 1.5 liters per week or less than a cup per day per person. Women, those who imbibed, drank less.

Wine consumption, then, appeared to be rather minimal, at least according to these sources. It would seem, though, that these sources reflect the situation in the Galilee where the vine was cultivated to a much lesser extent than in Judaea. Thus, M Ketubbot 5:8, which has served as the basis for our discussion, is the *Mishnah* of R. Akiva as the *Mishnah* explicitly states: "R. Jose said – it was R. Ishmael who granted her barley because he (lived) near to Edom." R. Ishmael lived and was quite active in the southern Mt Hebron region, residing in Kefar Aziz. This region is often called Edom in rabbinic literature (M Kilayim 6:4; Schwartz 1986, pp. 33–42). Grapes were extensively cultivated in this area (I.3.2.4 below). It is likely, although there are no clear-cut sources on the matter, that wine consumption was higher in Judaea in general and in the Mt Hebron region in particular, where grapes were extensively cultivated.

Rabbinic traditions, which reflect for the most part the reality of the Galilee, associate wine with important and extended banquets. The well-to-do were accustomed to eat their evening meal with much pomp and company. The meal, which began in the ninth hour of the day, continued for many hours and included a wide variety of courses. The Passover meal (*seder*) was modeled on this type of meal. At festive meals and religious banquets wine was a major component of the meal. However, it played a very minor role in the daily fare of the common people.

The laws pertaining to the recalcitrant son (*sorrer u-moreh*) provide an additional indication regarding the small quantities of wine that were consumed. The law states that the recalcitrant son who was liable to be put to death was one who drank large amounts in a coarse manner (*be-gasut*) and against the wishes of his parents. Drinking large amounts "*be-gasut*" is explained in M Sanhedrin 8:2: "When is he liable? When he eats a *tartimar* of meat and drinks a half-*log* of Italian wine. R. Jose says – A *maneh* of meat and a *log* of wine." The measurement of wine according to the Mishnah is equal to 0.18 of a liter of wine at a meal. According to R. Jose he had to drink 0.36 of a liter at a meal. The amount of meat that is mentioned in the *Mishnah* is also somewhat minimal – from 150–300 grams at a meal (PT Sanhedrin VIII, 26a and BT Sanhedrin 70a). This "gluttonous" meal indicates the fairly low level of meat and wine consumption in the period under discussion. Wine, thus, was considered a festive beverage, but not normal fare. This is what made it so prominent in both Jewish and non-Jewish religious ceremonies, in the ancient world (Tabory 1977, pp. 31–6).

I.3.2.3

In order to express our conclusions in numerical form, we shall construct a basic model of wine consumption in terms of grape vineyards, bearing in mind the minimal amount of ancient statistics.

The estimated data is the following: a dunam of grapevines produces 360 liters of wine per year (based on agricultural statistics of Palestine in the 1920s). There were approximately 2.1 million residents in Palestine (the male population can be roughly estimated at 600,000). According to the basic figures regarding the consumption of wine (1.5 *logs* per week or 28 *logs* per year per male), 168 million liters of wine were consumed per year. This amount could be produced from less than 50 square kilometers of vineyards. As stated above, these figures represent wine consumption of the lower classes. In order to reflect the higher rate of consumption of the rich and the upper classes, the figures will be multiplied by a factor of 4. Even so, the entire amount of wine consumed by all the residents of Palestine could be produced from an area containing 200 square kilometers or less than 2 per cent of the potential arable land of Palestine!

According to the maximum figures regarding consumption cited above, the nuclear family would consume 300–375 liters per year and 187.5 liters would be consumed throughout the entire country. All of this could be produced from 520 square kilometers and even if we should double this, and this is undoubtedly a needless exaggeration, only 1,000 square kilometers would be needed, or less than 10 per cent of potential available land. If the Mishnah deals with an extended family, then only half this amount would be needed.

Clearly then, a large amount of wine was not imbibed by the ancients in the Galilee. The importance of a food, though, is not just in terms of caloric content, but also in terms of taste and variety. Wine gave meals that "extra something" both regarding sugar content and a little variety to the otherwise common fare. The phrase "There is no joy except with wine" (see above and (BT Pesachim 109a) sums up this sentiment. At this time there were very few beverages known to Palestinian Jews apart from water and wine (which was diluted with water). Wine was imbibed almost like a soft drink in today's modern culture. In spite of all this, its modest place on the Palestinian table seems strange in light of the numerous rabbinic sources which would seem to indicate that it was cultivated on a much wider basis.

All of the data discussed above lead to the conclusion that much of the wine produced in Palestine was intended for export. The sources also indicate a large degree of wine export to other countries, particularly to Egypt. Most of the sources dealing with the exporting of wine are non-Jewish. We shall discuss this matter further (Chapter 4.VII.3). We do not have reliable information regarding the amount of wine that was exported. However, the role of grape cultivation as an important part of the ancient Palestinian economy can be understood only if the export of wine was undertaken on a large scale.

I.3.2.4 The extent of grape cultivation

As stated above, rabbinic sources deal very often with issues associated with grape growing. Moreover, since the grape is a very sensitive crop and influenced to a great extent by local conditions, many different varieties developed. These are also mentioned in the ancient sources and enable us also to determine the extent to which this crop was cultivated. The sources generally describe the Galilee as the olive-producing region and Judaea as the grape-producing region (Chapter 4.VI.3). It is important to stress, though, that this does not mean that grapes were not cultivated in the Galilee or that wine was not produced there. We hear of a type of wine produced in Sepphoris and Tiberias (PT Megillah I, 72d) and of Galileans harvesting their grapes later than usual, after Sukkot (PT Gittin III, 45b; BT Bava Bathra VI, 15c). Antoninus of Piacenza (sixth century) also relates that grapes were grown in the Galilee (Wilkinson 1977, p. 81). During the course of surveys and field-trips many grape presses were found in the Galilee, and this would seem to indicate that the cultivation of grapes was important there, but not as important as the cultivation of olives.

Hardly any grape presses were discovered in the Upper Golan (Urman 1985, p. 162). It is possible that some wine was produced in wood or clay wine presses which are mentioned in some sources, but it is unlikely that these fragile presses were used much and the absence of presses in the Upper Golan would seemingly indicate that grape cultivation there was limited.

The cultivation of grapes was widespread in Judaea in general and in the Lod region in particular. There are, however, some areas of Judaea in which wine presses have not been found, such as the *shephelah* of Beth Gubrin. It would be extremely worthwhile to produce a catalogue of all those places in which grapes were grown, but this is beyond the scope of the present work.

In Samaria, the grape as well as the olive was cultivated. This situation has been excellently documented by S. Dar (1986, pp. 147–90). In his opinion, 20.2 per cent of the farmland at Hirbet Burak was cultivated with vineyards. An average 25-dunam farmstead usually put aside 5.1 dunams for grapes (Dar 1986, pp. 87 ff.). At Karawat Bani Hasan, another village examined by Dar, a farm with 39–45 dunams devoted 22 per cent of this land to the cultivation of grapes or on the average 9–10 dunams per person (Dar 1986, pp. 245 ff.). Both of these villages serve as excellent examples for the situation in Samaria.

Another proof of the extent of grape cultivation in the region is the great number of towers in the hill region. These towers were related to the wine-producing process and serve as an excellent indication of the widespread growing of this crop in the Hellenistic period, the period in which these towers were built (Dar 1986, pp. 88–125). Similar towers are found on the southern slopes of the upper Carmel range, indicating that wine was also produced in this region (Olami 1981, nos. 38, 39 etc.). "Carmeli" wine is mentioned in rabbinic sources and this probably refers to the Carmel range and not to Carmel in Judaea, which is located near the desert and which was hardly a very suitable region for the cultivation of grapes (BT Niddah 21a). Assaph, the Jewish physician from the beginning of the Middle Ages, also writes about the special wines from Carmel (Muntner 1957, p. 161). In any case, it is clear that Judaea was a major center of grape cultivation, and in particular such sites as Ein Gedi (Shir Ha-Shirim Zuta 14), Beth Rimmah and Beth Laban in northern Judaea (M Menahot 8:6). A number of other settlements in this general region were also known for their grapes.

The vineyard was cultivated rather intensively. The vines were planted much closer to each other than was customary in groves with other fruit trees. The distance between the vines was only 4–8 cubits, and not 16 as was the case regarding trees in other types of groves (M Kilayim 4:2, 8, 9; BT Bava Bathra 82b). A vineyard in which only ten trees were left in a *beth seah* was considered a "poor vineyard" (M Kilayim 5:1). In contrast to the traditional Arab farmstead, the grape vines were planted according to an ordered system (M Kilayim 5:1; 4:5 *et al.*). The amount of land which constituted a vineyard was rather small – 3 *kabs* or 392 square meters. Thus BT states: "I shall sell you a portion in my vineyard, Sumchus said he may not sell less than three *kabs*. R. Jose said: these are words of prophecy [= stated without any particular reason]. And in Babylonia how much [must he sell]? Rava bar Kisna said: three rows containing twelve vinetrees each" (BT Bava Bathra 12a). M Kilayim 4:5–6 implies that five vinetrees were considered a vineyard. It is clear that the cultivation of the vine was quite intensive.

The crop was first of all intended for production of wine. Therefore, the actual production of the wine is considered the completion of the stages of work associated with grapes regarding the requirement of setting aside tithes and the like (M Maasrot 1:7; T Terumot 3:13). Grapes, similar to olives, are not "crops of the threshing-floor" (BT Bava Mezia 88b), that is, the grape in itself is not considered an independent type of fruit, but rather deemed a stage in another process. There was not much of a demand for fresh grapes, and the small demand there was pertained only to the period immediately after the harvest, since the grapes began to rot rather quickly. Thus, after the harvest a person would take his grapes at once to market and if he couldn't sell them he brought them to the press (T Maasrot 2:4 *et al.*). Another option, albeit less profitable, was to dry out the grapes to make raisins (BT Shabbat 45a; BT Bezah 26b *et al.*). Raisins are mentioned quite frequently in Talmudic literature, but it would seem that in spite of this they were not very common. Thus, when an entire "load" of raisins was brought to Tiberias, it was decided that the raisins came from outside the boundaries of the Land of Israel since even though raisins could be found in Palestine, it was not likely that a whole load came from there and, therefore, the raisins had to have been imported (PT Demai II, 22d; PT Nedarim VIII, 41a). The raisins could also be soaked in wine to produce an inferior type of wine. Wine which spoiled could be used for vinegar. We shall not discuss other types of wine mentioned in the sources.

There were some changes in various aspects of the cultivation of grapes or the production of wine during the course of the ancient periods. The towers in Samaria which we mentioned above (Dar 1986, pp. 88 ff.) are from the Hellenistic period. They were hardly used, however, in the Roman period. This may reflect changes in the make-up of the settlement or the transferring of production to the towers. However, it could just as easily reflect changes in land utilization or the demand for wine. The towers in the Carmel range, though, date from the Roman–Byzantine period (Olami 1981).

Rabbinic traditions also refer to a number of changes in cultivation and production: "At first vinegar in Judaea was exempt [from tithe] because it was assumed that it was made from *tamad* [= husks and stalks of pressed grapes] and, therefore, *tamad* is exempted from tithes. Now it is assumed that it is made from wine" (T Demai 1:2; PT Demai I, 21d; PT Pesahim III, 29d; BT Pesahim 42b). R. Judah explains this matter further in PT Demai I, 21d:

> At first vinegar in Judaea was exempt from tithes because they used to make their wine in a state of ritual purity and it would not spoil [and consequently they would not make vinegar from wine]. They used to make it from *tamad*. Now that wine does spoil [and vinegar is made from wine], they must set aside tithes from it.

Thus, before the days of R. Judah (135–80), most likely during the Second Temple period when wine was sent to the Temple and prepared with great care and under much scrutiny, wine did not normally spoil and turn to vinegar. *Tamad* is exempt from tithes since it is only a secondary product of the grape. After the destruction of the Temple, the wine was produced under less stringent conditions and at times turned sour. The difference was not so much in the matter of ritual purity as in the price that superior wine fetched in Second Temple times and the price that was received after the destruction. It should be pointed out, however, that *tamad* in itself did have some importance and a jug with a seal attesting to the fact that it contained *tamad* has even been discovered (Sukenik 1942). R. Judah lived in quite difficult times, a period in which the olive industry had been devastated and great care lavished on those trees which remained, according to his contemporary, R. Jose (PT Peah VII, 20a). Even so, wine at that time was apparently so plentiful and cheap that it was produced under less than stringent conditions, leading occasionally to its turning sour and into vinegar.

M Pesahim 3:1 states that preservatives were added to vinegar made in Edom (southern Judaea) and, therefore, it was forbidden on Passover. PT Pesahim II, 29d connects this Mishnah with the tradition discussed above regarding wine. During the Second Temple period, barley was not added to wine in order that the wine remain pure and be acceptable for libations in the Temple. This pure wine did not turn sour (cf. also BT Pesahim 42b). When the Temple was destroyed, however, the residents of southern Judaea began to mix barley into the wine and it also began to turn sour occasionally. This seems to be the meaning of the Talmudic texts, but there are some problems with this explanation. It is not clear, for instance, why adding barley to the wine should render it potentially unacceptable for Temple use. R. Solomon of Troyes (Rashi) in his commentary states that the barley itself does not render the wine unfit. Rather, during the Second Temple period the Temple, as it were, miraculously prevented wine brought there from turning sour. It is possible then that there is no intrinsic connection between the discussion in Tractate Demai which dealt with tithes and the discussion in Tractate Pesahim which deals with the laws of vinegar. The two matters may have been connected solely because the Temple was discussed in both instances. In any case, it is clear that there were certain changes in the manner of wine production and there was less stringency among the Jews regarding the religious aspects of this preparation.

A development of the Javneh generation was the prevalence of grafting. During the Second Temple period, a vineyard with grafted vinetrees was considered inferior and wine made from such grapes could not be used for the Temple (T Menahot 9:10). During the Javneh generation the sages discussed halachic problems relating to the grafting of vine trees (M Kilayim 6:3). This system, thus, apparently became widespread only at that time. We hear of two "grafters" who lived at this time in the mountain region south of Jerusalem (DJD II, no. 29, p. 142). This development may also be the result of the fact that wine was no longer prepared for the Temple, although it is difficult to prove this point.

The Temple was one of the major consumers of wine grown in Judaea. The destruction of the Temple, however, did not destroy the wine industry in Judaea (as was also the case regarding the dove industry). Rather, new markets were found for Judaean wine. The new developments in wine production which we have discussed may reflect this new situation.

I.3.3 Figs

Figs were not among the three most important foods in Palestine, but they are mentioned in the diet schedules discussed above (I.1). Pressed figs and dried figs are mentioned in many halachic discussions. The fig was apparently an important component of the diet at that time. Figs served as an important source of sugar (in addition to the sugars in grain), and were the most popular fruit eaten on a regular basis. They were eaten in two common forms: dried or pressed. This allowed for preserving the quality of the fruit as well as for a period of storage. The weight relationship between these two forms can be seen in the diet schedules discussed above. The wife received a *kab* of dried figs (2.1 liters) or a *manah* of pressed figs (about 600 grams). The relationship, thus, was about 1:3.5.

The fig was a very profitable fruit. The Mishnah (Sheviit 1:2) describes a field with three trees to a *beth seah* (784 square meters). A "grove" such as this would yield a loaf of about sixty *maneh* or a large full-grown tree would yield twenty *maneh*. A regular sized tree planted in a standard grove (11–12 trees per dunam or as the Mishnah states: "a grove of ten trees to a *beth seah*" – 784–900 square meters, M. Sheviit 1:4,6) would yield about 15 *maneh* (9 kilograms) of fig cake which is equal to 31.5 liters of dried figs. According to these calculations, a dunam of figs would yield about 165 *maneh*. We saw above in our discussion of diet that a *maneh* of fig cakes was the monetary equivalent of two meals. According to R. Akiva, as we also saw above, only half a *maneh* was necessary. Thus, a dunam of figs could support a person for approximately 165 days. A family of four could be supported by cultivating 8.8 dunams of figs (365 ÷ [165 ÷ 4]). In the diet discussed above (Chapter 2.I.1; M Ketubbot 5:8), a *maneh* of fig cake was the amount set for a week and, therefore, 1.2 dunams of figs were required to supply the average family's needs in terms of figs.

As we have just stated, figs were considered to be a rather profitable crop. However, much effort had to be invested in their cultivation. The fruits on the fig trees do not all become ripe at the same time. The ripening process takes about two months. Thus, the fig trees must be checked every day during this period in order to complete the harvest. Such a procedure would require a great deal of manpower. Talmudic literature was aware of this phenomenon. Thus T Peah 1:7 lists the fig among those crops "which are not collected at one time." PT Berachot II, 5c relates the story of a rabbi who sat under a fig tree to teach his students. Every day the owner of the tree would come to harvest his figs. Lest the owner suspect the rabbi of stealing, the sage decided to sit under a different tree. The owner of the tree explained to the rabbi that he did not come to the tree every day because he suspected the rabbi, but rather, that this was the manner in which the fig tree was harvested.

Under the circumstances described above, it is not surprising that in the ancient Jewish farmstead as well as in the traditional Arab farm, the cultivation of figs was not of primary importance. The average farmer usually had a few fig trees but not a grove. M Sheviit mentions different uses of land since there are halachic implications as to whether land is used for the cultivation of grains (a "white field") or for fruit-bearing trees (M Sheviit 1:2–3). The tractate also deals with areas cultivated with a number of crops or with fruit trees scattered among fields generally used for grains. The status of these trees is usually determined by the size of the tree and the amount of fruit that it produces. These laws are applicable to all kinds of fruit trees, but the specific tree cited as an example is the fig tree, illustrating the sporadic nature of the cultivation of the tree. PT Sheviit asks why fig trees were chosen to serve as the example of this law. A number of answers are suggested. One possibility is that the yield of the fig tree is more or less constant, unlike for instance the bi-annual yield of the olive tree (PT Sheviit I, 33b; Feliks 1980, pp. 44–8). It would seem, though, that the real reason is the one which we have suggested above, that this is the most common type of tree which is not cultivated in groves, but rather sporadically.

Palestine was usually self-sufficient in figs. Figs, together with other fruits, are among those fruits found in markets from which tithes must always be set aside ("and these are the products which must be tithed as *demai* everywhere," M Demai 2:1). The list in that Mishnah includes pressed figs, dates, carobs, rice and cumin. The halachic assumption is that all of these products found in Palestinian markets were grown within the halachic boundaries of the Land of Israel.

PT Demai II, 22b does mention pressed figs which came from Bostra in the Transjordan, but these pressed figs were of a different type. Talmudic tradition also attests to at least one case of the importing of dried figs during the Javneh period (90–120 CE). Thus, M Avodah Zarah 5:2 relates that when Beytos b. Zonin, one of the rich residents of Lod at that time, brought dried figs by ship to Palestine, non-Jewish wine was poured on them. The wine would seem to prove that the figs were brought from a non-Jewish region. Since at this time agriculture in Palestine was under Jewish control, the figs had to have been brought from some area outside Palestine (Syria?). It should be remembered, though, that the Mishnah in Demai cited above would seem to indicate that Palestine was self-sufficient in figs and the importing of this product would only be of secondary importance. Figs, however, were exported. The extent of this export cannot be determined. It is known, though, that they were exported to Rome (Pliny, *HN* 13. 51; see also Chapter 4.VII.3).

I.3.4 Dates

I.3.4.1 The cultivation of dates

The cultivation of dates was of great importance in the desert regions as well as in the Jordan Valley (Löw 1924 II, pp. 302–62; Feliks 1968, pp. 40–7). The major areas of cultivation were, therefore, the Jericho region (and Jericho is referred to in the Bible as the "city of dates" (Deut. 34:3 and parallels), Ein Gedi, the Beth Shean Valley and to some extent the Tiberias region. The date requires a great deal of heat and water and, therefore, can be cultivated only in tropical climates. The date is not mentioned in the diet schedules we have studied above, since these mention crops found in all of Palestine, while the date is a regional one. It is likely that the date was an important component of the diet in those regions in which it was cultivated. The monks of the Judaean Desert even used it instead of bread. Palladius, for instance, relates that a certain Cosmus used to give the monks dates because they did not eat bread (ch. 52). The eating of dates alone, and not bread, was considered a mark of monastic privation, and apparently was not a common substitute for bread in those regions in which dates were grown.

The date groves of Palestine had an excellent reputation and foreign visitors were often impressed by them and especially by the groves of Jericho (Löw 1924; see discussion below for a number of these sources). However, the importance of these sources should not be exaggerated. Dates made an impression on these travellers not only because of their economic value, but on account of their attractive and somewhat exotic nature. They were also not very common in the Roman Empire. Most of the date-growing centers were outside the Roman Empire (the Arabian Desert and Parthian Babylonia). Only in Egypt (and to some extent in Palestine) could the Romans see this impressive tree.

The palm or date tree is mentioned quite often in Talmudic literature and like the olive, the dried date serves as a unit of size. We do not know, however, the exact extent to which dates were sent from those regions in which they were cultivated to the markets in Palestine.

I.3.4.2 The selling of dates

Dates are mentioned in M Demai 2:1 as one of the crops which are usually not imported to Palestine. PT Demai II, 22b does mention a type of date imported from Alexandria, but these were apparently of a type not grown in Palestine. (Apicius 7. 11. 2 states that the dates of Alexandria ripened in a rather unique manner. See also Strabo 16. 1. 51.) An interesting Talmudic tradition, though, does relate an instance of importing dates to Tiberias. Thus R. Zeira, a sage of the fourth century CE, sent the following question to R. Alexandri of Zedoka (Beth Zedek): "The local [lit. "of here"] Nicolaus dates, how do you reckon them – the majority as coming from non-Jews, or as from Jews?" (PT Demai II, 22c; Sperber 1978, p. 179). In this particular case it is clear that these Nicolaean dates were grown within the halachic boundaries of the Land of Israel and the only question is whether they were cultivated by Jews or non-Jews.

In order to fully understand this tradition, though, it is necessary to discuss some of the geographic background of the tradition. R. Zeira lived in Tiberias. This particular type of date was usually grown in the Jericho region: *Nicolaum itaque palmulam in Palestinae regione loco, qui sic vocatur Iericho* [Therefore they grow the Nicolaean palm in the land of Palestine, in a place called Jericho] (*Totius Orbis Descriptio*, c. 31, Löw 1923–34, II, pp. 322–4). The location of R. Alexandri's home is less certain. Alon interpreted Zedoka as Beth Zedek near Beth Gubrin (Alon 1984, p. 250). If this is the case, though, it is difficult to understand why this unknown sage from the Beth Gubrin region should be consulted as a specialist on dates from the Tiberias region. It is also clear that R. Alexandri did not live in Tiberias, since it was necessary for R. Zeira of Tiberias to send the query to him, apparently some distance from that city. It is likely that R. Alexandri lived in the region in which these dates were grown, possibly in the Jericho area, and was consulted as a local expert on this particular type of date which was marketed in Tiberias. If this interpretation is correct, the Talmudic tradition would seem to reflect wide-scale importing of dates to Tiberias.

Dates sold in the Caesarea region were also brought from Jewish areas in Judaea and, therefore, these dates were governed by the laws of the commandments dependent upon the land. This was the case even regarding dates in Caesarea itself which was exempted from these precepts (PT Demai II, 22c. This is also mentioned in the Rehob inscription – Y. Sussman 1973–4, p. 131). A similar list of fruits is also mentioned regarding Beth Shean. Most of the dates marketed in this city, located in a date-growing region, came from the date palms in the immediate vicinity of Beth Shean which was included within the region exempted from the commandments dependent upon the land. "*Aphsiyot* Dates," however, were brought from a more distant region which was considered part of the halachic Land of Israel, and therefore were governed by the commandments upon the land (PT Demai II, 22c; Y. Sussmann 1973–4, p. 113; Z. Safrai 1984, pp. 1100–08; Feliks 1986, pp. 456–97, as against Stern 1980, I, pp. 496–9). The *aphsiyot* dates are apparently identical to the *passitacium* also mentioned in *Totius Orbis Descriptio* (c. 31) as growing in the Jericho region (*et alteram palmulam minorem at pasittacium*). This type of date, therefore, was brought to Beth Shean from the Jericho region.

Dates in Palestine were not cheap. Palestinian sages who arrived in Babylonia were often amazed by the plethora of dates as well as by their cheap price at the market (BT Taanit 9b). A Talmudic tradition shows that Palestinian dates were more expensive than figs. The tradition deals with the case of one who has sinned and eaten from *terumah* (heave-offering) which can only be eaten by a priest. The person who has sinned must return the exact amount of fruit eaten by mistake and then the *halacha* adds: "R. Eliezer says, they may repay with one sort for another sort, provided that the repayment is from a superior sort for an inferior sort. How so? If he ate barley, he repays wheat. [If he ate] dried figs he repays dates and he shall receive a blessing. R. Akiva says, they may not repay except from one kind for the same kind." (The rule quoted above is already found in M Terumot 6:6. The example cited above is from T Terumot 7:9; Sifra Emor 6:6; PT Terumot VI, 44b). The plain meaning of the tradition seems to be that R. Eliezer had in mind the repayment of the same amount of fruit, but with a more expensive kind of fruit. BT Eruvin 29a (and BT Pesahim 32a) seems to imply that the amount of dates repaid was equal to the cost of the figs that were eaten. The intrinsic value of the dates, however, was higher since they were more easily sold in the market. It is difficult to know, however, whether this conclusion is based simply on the dialectics of the argument or on actual economic reality. It is also difficult to know whether this was the economic reality in Babylonia or in Palestine. The price of dates in the Edict of Diocletian is almost six times greater than the price of figs, proving once again the more expensive nature of dates.

Palm trees in modern-day Israel yield 90–120 kilograms per dunam (*Encyclopaedia of Agriculture*, III, pp. 211–17). The yield in the ancient world was obviously lower, but certainly higher than the yield of figs. Since the price of dates was also higher than that of figs, it was a far more profitable crop.

The palm tree itself was considered to be of economic value, and therefore it was forbidden to sell superior quality palm trees to non-Jews, just as it was forbidden to sell them land (M Avoda Zarah 1:5; Sperber 1978, pp. 160–76). It is important to remember, though, that a good deal of the lands in the Jericho region were part of royal estates, and thus a good deal of the profits from the date trade went to the Roman *fiscus* (see below 4.I.2). The local residents did not profit from this industry, nor did it have much effect on the local economy. As we have mentioned above, most of the dates in the various Palestinian markets were grown locally. There was, though, some degree of export. A halachic question addressed to R. Helbo bar Keruya (PT Maaser Sheni IV, 54d) mentions the export of dates to Rome. R. Helbo apparently came from Coreae in the Jordan Valley (S. Safrai 1968, p. 110) and therefore it is clear why a question dealing with dates should have been addressed to this local sage. Roman sources also mention the exporting of Palestinian dates to Rome and Italy. Virgil, for instance, mentions the palms of Idumaea (*Georgics* 3. 12). The superior reputation of the dates of Phoenicia in general and the dates of Idumaea in particular proves that these dates reached the markets of the west and were considered to be of high quality (Silius Italicus, *Punica* 3. 6000; Avi-Yonah 1958, p. 323). In the Edict of Diocletian (III.42) mention is made of the honey from Phoenicia. Since dates are not grown in Phoenicia, it would seem that the references to Phoenician dates actually refer to those grown in Palestine and Syria. It is possible, however, that the edict refers to a different type of bee honey than those previously mentioned in the edict. Pliny also mentions wine that was made from these dates (Pliny, *HN* 3. 26. 44; see also Chapter 4.VII.3).

I.3.4.3 Supplementary products

The main product of the palm was, of course, the date which was intended to be eaten either raw or pressed. Talmudic sources also mention date honey (M Terumot 11:2–3 *et al.*). Straw baskets (PT Shabbat II, 5a) and mats were also produced from palms (Midrash Thehilim 92:11 pp. 409–10). A special palm which served for the production of such baskets was the *passitacium* which we discussed above (Avi-Yonah 1958, p. 253; PT Shabbat VII, 11b *et al.*; Avi-Yonah 1964, p. 125; Sozom. *Hist. Eccl.* 8. 13 (*PG* 94:465).

I.3.5 Additional fruits

I.3.5.1

In addition to the three fruits discussed above, Talmudic tradition lists over twenty other different kinds of fruit grown on trees. The diet schedules discussed earlier (Chapter 2.I.1) do not mention these types of fruit. However, a *baraita* in the Palestian Talmud (PT Peah VIII, 20d) adds a number of types of fruit which were considered the equivalent of two meals: "a measure of vegetables, three *kabs* of carobs . . . ten nuts, five peaches, two pomegranates and one *ethrog.*" Being mentioned in the source does indicate some degree of importance, but their overall worth was apparently not very great.

I.3.5.2 The carob

The most common fruit in the list cited above was the carob. We have no information regarding carob groves or plantations, so it would seem that they were grown on trees scattered throughout various types of fields. The carob, quite cheap in relation to the fig (three *kabs* of carobs were the equivalent of a *kab* of dried figs), was essentially the food of the poor. In some circles the eating of carobs was considered an act of asceticism, and ascetics and wretchedly poor such as Hanina b. Dosa and R. Simeon b. Yohai ate, according to some traditions, only carobs. Certain types of carobs such as those from Shiqmona (a coastal town south of Haifa) and Calamon and Gedru in the Acco valley were exempt from the requirements of tithes since they were not even considered food (Sifra Behukotai 12:9; PT Maasrot I, 48c and parallels). Carobs were also considered fit animal fodder (M Shabbat 24:2; M Maasrot 3:4 and parallels). They are also included among the types of produce from which the priests were willing to forgo their tithes "and they are not particular about it" (PT Bikkurim III, 65c; PT Orlah II, 61d–62a). Carobs are also listed among the oaths which are easy to fulfill in the sense that someone who vows not to eat carobs will have little difficulty in fulfilling his vow (PT Ketubbot VII, 31c; PT Kiddushin II, 62c).

In spite of all this, the carob tree was considered to be a fruit tree. Carob trees were planted (and even the carobs mentioned above which were exempt from tithes were not exempt from the requirements of *orlah*, which meant that their fruit could not be eaten for the first three years, since, as the Talmud explains it, the trees were planted by those expressly wishing to plant them (PT Orlah I, 61a). The fruit of the carob tree was considered like any other fruit and was gathered and collected (M Maasrot 1:6 *et al.*). The fruit of the carob was stored on roofs like other fruits (M Maasrot 3:4). The Mishnah, however, states that "carobs which were not yet gathered to the top of the roof and which can be taken down and given to an animal are exempt" (from tithes – M Maasrot 3:4). The exemption was granted because the carobs had not yet been brought to storage on the roof. Once they had been brought there, tithes had to be set aside. Various traditions mention that carobs were also preserved and some were pickled in wine (M Sheviit 7:7). As we have already mentioned above, it was forbidden to use wood from fruit trees as fuel for the sacrificial altar. The Mishnah mentioned only the trunks of the grapevine and olive tree. The Tosefta added additional types of wood such as that of the carob tree (T Menahot 9:14). This does not indicate, however, that the carob was an important fruit since the sycamore is also listed and this tree, of course, did not bear fruit at all.

During the Sabbatical Year when there was a shortage of fruit as well as during years of sparse crops, the carob also served for human consumption. The *halachah* states that during periods of drought or famine it was forbidden to hoard fruit and specifically mentions that "during a famine one should not store even a *kab* of carobs because it brings a curse upon the prices" (T Avodah Zarah 4(5):1; BT Bava Bathra 90b). The use of the word "even" shows that carobs, for all intents and purposes, were considered fit for human consumption only during famines. During the Sabbatical year the carob was even sold by weight to needy people (PT Bezah III, 62a). The fourth century CE sage R. Abahu, who lived in Caesarea, tells of the Hellenistic population there who mockingly used to wish one another "that they not need carobs like the Jews do" (Lamentations Rabbah, Petihtah 17). This was part of a series of anti-Jewish statements characteristic of the residents of Caesarea which were recorded by R. Abahu. The statements for the most part reflected the poverty of the Jews. Eating the fruit of the carob tree was indicative of this poverty. In a similar vein, the third-century CE sage R. Aha somewhat cynically states: "If Israel needs to eat the carob, they shall repent" (Leviticus Rabbah 35:6, p. 824; 13:4, p. 281 and a similar statement in Pesikta d'Rab Kahana 14:3, p. 241). There is nothing like poverty, represented by the carob, to bring about repentance.

In short, then, the carob, as we remember, was listed in the dietary schedule which appears in the *baraita* in the Palestinian Talmud and thus apparently was consumed basically by the poor. It was eaten on a widespread basis only during the Sabbatical Year or during periods of famine.

I.3.5.3

M. Bava Bathra 4:8 differentiates between a grafted carob tree which is considered to be a fruit tree and one which was not grafted and which was not classified as a fruit-bearing tree. The Mishnah is apparently referring to a male tree which grew from a carob seed and which did not always produce fruit until fertilized with a female shoot. This source also proves that the carob was of some degree of secondary importance, at least, and it would appear that its quality was of a higher level than that of the Palestinian carob today. In that sense it would be similar to the carobs grown at present in Greece and Cyprus for export. A carob tree in Cyprus yields today no less than 30 kilograms. The optimum weight of the carob is 0.2 kilogram. According to the Palestinian Talmud (PT Peah VIII, 20d and see I.1 above), three *kabs* were the equivalent of the price of two meals. Thus a carob tree yielding thirty kilograms could support a family for 8.8 days. In order to support itself a family needed forty-one trees growing in an area of 4 dunams. Because of bi-annual yields, twice the amount of trees was necessary (8 dunams). It is clear that the cultivation of this fruit was not much less profitable than the cultivation of olives, grapes or figs which were also grown in groves.

Palestine was generally self-sufficient in carob. Talmudic tradition does, however, mention the importing of carobs. These carobs were apparently somewhat unusual in form (M Demai 2:1; PT Demai II, 22b).

I.3.5.4 Other types of fruit

Ancient tradition also mentions pears, apples, peaches, *ethrogs*, nuts and other types of fruit. It is clear, though, that their economic importance was rather limited. Pears, apples, peaches and nuts require a relatively cold climate, and thus decent yields could be produced only at the high elevations of the Judaean mountains, the Upper Galilee and the Golan. *Ethrogim* grew for the most part along the coast. Caesarea was a natural center for the cultivation of the *ethrog* (Levine 1975, pp. 51–2). These fruits were for the most part, therefore, local crops and their economic importance was probably limited to those regions. Pomegranates grew throughout Palestine and were used basically for the preparation of pomegranate wine. The paucity of reference to them in the ancient sources would seem to indicate their limited economic value.

I.4 Vegetables and the squash family

More than twenty-four types of vegetables are listed in Talmudic tradition. However, most of the vegetables eaten today were not known to the ancients (or did not yet exist). Thus, tomatoes, cucumbers and peppers were unknown to them. Likewise, only the bulbous type of potato, which was of the sweet variety, is mentioned in ancient tradition (Feliks 1982). Most vegetables played only a minor role in the regular diet. In spite of this, vegetables were a regular feature on the table. As we have already seen (I.1.1 above), vegetables were regularly eaten in the morning and evening meals. The Tannaitic appendage to the dietary schedule which we have cited a number of times and which is found in PT Peah states that the price of a "pound of vegetables" [300–360 grams] was the monetary equivalent of the value of two meals (PT Peah VIII, 20d; see above I.3.4). The mentioning of vegetables in this list proves that they were widely consumed. However, the citing of the word "vegetables" ("yrk") without further clarification as to type or quality would seem to indicate that they were not as commonly sold as was the case regarding othe products in this list. PT Kiddushin IV, 66d even states that it is forbidden to live in a settlement in which there are no vegetable gardens.

Vegetables are described in the sources as not regularly being placed in storage and as having a rather short shelf life. Thus, T Peah 1:7 states: "Vegetables – even though they are harvested at one time, one does not bring them in to preserve." Talmudic tradition, therefore, recounts often how they were quickly sold at market, since they could not be stored for a long period of time. Only onions and garlic could be placed in storage for extended periods.

Vegetables had to be irrigated, or were dependent on at least some type of supplementary irrigation, unlike the other crops discussed above which were not dependent on irrigation (see Chapter 4.V below). Vegetables were cultivated, therefore, in a "garden" (ginah), the term commonly associated with an area intensively cultivated and irrigated (Feliks 1963, pp. 311–23). The necessity to irrigate limited the extent of the areas cultivated for vegetable crops, since there was not always a great deal of water available. In many areas of Palestine, the supply of water was dependent solely on rainfall, and therefore vegetables were irrigated by water drawn from cisterns. Lack of sophistication in this process made the work rather tedious and reduced the economic value of such crops.

Vegetables were generally grown for private use or for local markets. There are exceptions such as the type of sweet potato mentioned above, which was grown in northern Judaea in Har Ha-Melekh and marketed in Caesarea (PT Demai II, 22c; Rehov inscription – Y. Sussmann 1974, p. 132). Vegetables were also imported from long distances to the market in Beth Shean (PT Demai II, 22c; Y. Sussmann 1974, p. 112; Lieberman 1976). The Ascalon onion was also sent to distant markets and apparently even abroad (Strabo 16. 229).

I.5 Legumes

Legumes were a regular component of the Palestinian diet. Legume porridge was regularly prepared and the rich were wont to eat vegetables either as an appetizer or for dessert. We do not have much information regarding the cultivation of legumes and it would appear that they were not cultivated on great tracts of land. PT Peah VII 20b relates a story of a man who planted "a *seah* of beans and reaped three-hundred *seah*." The tradition is, of course, aggadic and it is difficult to reach any type of clear-cut conclusion based on it. Talmudic tradition mentions over twenty types of legumes. The most important types of legumes were lentils, green beans, *ful* – and especially Egyptian *ful*, clover, alfalfa and vetch which were used as fodder (M Terumot 9:3; T Terumot 8:3). These types of legumes, therefore, could not become defiled or defile with the impurity of food (a type of defilement which pertains only to food consumed by humans). The discussion as to whether they defile or not (T Uktzin 3:13–14) reflects their customary status as fodder, but the need to actually bring the matter up would prove that during droughts or other such times they were also eaten by humans and, therefore, their status was unclear.

A law pertaining to land tenancy provides some interesting information regarding legumes. In T Bava Mezia (9:32) it is stated:

> One who receives a field from his friend – a place in which they are accustomed to give *ful* in place of barley (as rent) – he gives *ful* in place of barley. [A place in which they are accustomed to give] twice as much barley as wheat, they may give twice as much [barley] in place of the wheat or anything else which can be kept in fiscal storage – "*otzar*," usually the Roman tax storage. R. Judah said – lentils and leeks are like wheat.

The tenant was at times allowed to substitute one type of grain for another. In this case, twice as much barley could be paid for an amount of wheat, since the barley was worth half the value of the wheat (I.2 above). *Ful* could be exchanged for barley since their price was the same. Wheat could also be replaced with lentils or leeks. According to R. Judah, these two types of legumes were also accepted as substitutes for tax payments at Roman storage depots, since they were equivalent to wheat.

Lentils were common fare of the lower classes. They were eaten by the rich only on rare occasions (BT Ketubbot 67b). In the diet schedule (I.1 above), legumes occupy a rather prominent position. A half a *kab* of legumes, which is equal to 0.71 liters, appears in the weekly fare (M Ketubbot 5:8). 140 liters would be needed to support a family for a year. M Peah 8:5 states that a *kab* and a half of spelt is equivalent to the food of two meals and that they are three times cheaper than wheat. All this would seem to show how widespread was their use as food. It is impossible to determine the extent of legume yields and thus it is also impossible to estimate their overall economic importance in the Palestinian economy.

Even though there is no proof of this practice, it appears that legumes were planted in grain fields in the period between the planting of the yearly crops of wheat. This is indeed possible in terms of crop rotation and was common practice in Roman agriculture (Spurr 1986, pp. 89 ff.).

I.6 Herbs, spices, medicinal plants and perfumes

I.6.1 Spices

More than 15 types of spices are mentioned in Talmudic literature. The most prominent ones are mustard, coriander, cumin, the fruit of the caper bush, and most important – pepper. The spice was rather expensive. In the addendum to the dietary schedule in PT Peah, "spices" are included as one of the food components. It is stated there that a *"kulah"* of spices is equivalent to the value of two meals (or the necessary support for a day – see I.1 above). The exact weight of the measurement listed is unknown, but it is probably somewhere between 50–100 grams. This then shows how expensive these spices were. We have no information regarding the extent to which these spices were cultivated. It is clear, though, that they were supplementary crops.

The case of pepper was unusual. Pepper, for all intents and purposes, is a tropical plant and it was somewhat difficult to accommodate it to the conditions of Palestine (Löw 1924, III, pp. 49–64). The rabbis were rather proud of the fact that pepper was grown in Palestine, but being aware of the difficulties in cultivating it, stated that this was one of the successes of Solomon and apparently one needed his wisdom to cultivate the spice: "I [= Solomon] planted every type of fruit tree – even the pepper" (Ecclesiastes Rabbah 2:7). Likewise R. Joshua b. Hannaniah, when expounding the virtues of the Land of Israel, mentions that the Biblical verse states that it is "a land . . . nothing will be missing from it," and mentions "peppers from Natzhanah" (location unknown) or from "Askar" (Sychar near Neapolis – Ecclesiastes Rabbah 2:11; Midrash Ha-Gadol on Deuteronomy 8:9 p. 179).

This aggadic tradition connects the pepper to a sage from the second century and in fact it is mentioned in the course of a dialogue which supposedly took place with the emperor Hadrian. The sources, however, in which it appears are all Amoraic and it would appear, therefore, that it refers to the third to fourth centuries and not the second century. The cultivation of pepper was not very important and it was undoubtedly grown only on a local basis. Those who did grow it, however, probably enjoyed rather high prices.

Ancient sources mention a number of other spices, but they were of secondary importance. Mention should be made of the caper bush discussed by Pliny (*HN* 12. 109) and of cumin.

I.6.2 Perfume plants

I.6.2.1

Among the perfume plants were a number of perfumes which made Palestine famous in the entire Roman Empire. The most famous of these were balsam and myrrh. Many Greek authors cite these plants and especially the balsam. Balsam was of great importance in the Roman Empire. It was imported from Arabia. Its great value and the very long distances over which it was necessary to bring it made it quite expensive in the markets of the Roman Empire. The only area within the Empire in which balsam and myrrh were cultivated was the Jordan Valley in Palestine, and this, of course, made the groves there quite valuable.

Both balsam and myrrh are tropical plants which require a great deal of heat. The Jordan Valley in general and the area in the vicinity of the Dead Sea in particular had the appropriate climate for both of these plants. Modern-day attempts to cultivate this balsam under laboratory conditions by Y. Feliks were not successful (unpublished), although some trial attempts at growing myrrh in the Ein Gedi region did succeed. Apparently, the desert climate and perhaps the low altitude (some 300 meters below sea level) were conducive to its growth.

To some extent, balsam became the representative crop of Palestine. Many authors mention it together with the date, which may have been cultivated to a greater extent but was less profitable. Aristotle (fourth century BCE) mentions the Dead Sea without further elaboration (*Meteorologica* 2). Theophrastus (end of the third century BCE) also mentions the Dead Sea, as well as dates of the area and the Jericho Valley. In spite of his great interest in the flora of the region, however, he does not mention balsam (*Historia Plantarum* 2. 16. 5). Another reference in the same work, however, does mention two balsam groves, one about 4 *plethra* (6 dunams) and the other one somewhat smaller. This is the earliest reference to the balsam groves. It is difficult to expect any earlier reference, since there was only limited interest in Palestine on the part of early writers. In any case, Theophrastus

Galen (end of the second century CE) mentions the balsam region a number of times on account of the medicinal importance of this plant, which it seems was of great interest to this physician (*De Simplicium Medicamentorum Temperamentis*; *De Antidotis* 9. 3. 8; *De Alimentorum Facultatibus* 1. 2. 12). Galen also states that Ein Gedi was the site of the best balsam in Judaea (*De Antidotis* 1. 4). His description seems to indicate that the balsam groves in that region were quite extensive and produced a high-quality product. His comment would also seem to indicate that balsam was cultivated in other regions of Judaea.

Josephus also mentions the balsam groves of the Jericho region a number of times in the course of various discussions on Jericho (*Ant.* 8. 174; *BJ* 1. 138–9; *Ant.* 4. 54). He also mentions the balsam of the Ein Gedi region (*Ant.* 9. 7). Josephus relates that Antony gave the Jericho region to Cleopatra, and Herod had to rent it back from her at a great sum (*Ant.* 15. 96; *BJ* I:361–2). These areas were returned to him by Augustus only in 30 BCE (*Ant.* 15. 296–8; *BJ* I:403).

Other sources mention balsam as a medicinal plant but do not add any new information (*Mulomedicina Chironis* 193, 796). Other authors who visited or described the Dead Sea and its asphalt do not mention balsam in that region. We shall return to discuss the implications of this fact (Paus. 5. 7. 4; Alexander of Aphrodisias, *Commentaria in Graeca* I (1900), III, 2, 163; Aristotelian *Problemata* 3. 49; Olympiodorus, *Commentaria in Aristotelem Graeca* (1900), vol. 13, 2, p. 163). Eusebius (fourth century CE) mentions the balsam in Zoar (§ 193) south of the Dead Sea and in Ein Gedi (§ 428), but not in Jericho.

Talmudic traditions add only a small amount of new material. BT Berachot 43a mentions the balsam of the emperor (Caesar) and the balsam of the House of Rabbi Judah the Prince. The tradition would seem to indicate that balsam of a lower quality was grown in other regions in Palestine. Part of the balsam obviously still belonged to the Roman *fiscus* ("the balsam of the Caesar"), but other balsam groves were apparently privately owned by Rabbi Judah the Prince (third century). The Bible relates that Nebuchadnezzar, who conquered Jerusalem in the sixth century BCE, left "vinedressers and husbandmen" (II Kings 25:12) in Israel. Rav Joseph (third century) teaches and explains: "vinedressers – these are the collectors of balsam from Ein Gedi and until Ramtha" (BT Shabbat 26a). It is clear that Rav Joseph is not describing the reality of the sixth century BCE, about which the rabbis had no extra-Biblical sources, but rather the situation during his time. The source indicates that the balsam was publicly owned and was concentrated in Beth Ramtha, a town opposite Jericho in the Transjordan and in Ein Gedi, as we have mentioned above.

A synagogue inscription from Ein Gedi provides important information regarding balsam in the Ein Gedi region during the sixth century CE. The pertinent section of the inscription reads: "He who steals the *zvwtyh* from

149

his fellow, he who reveals the secret of the town to the non-Jews – He whose eyes look upon the whole world, He will turn His face upon that man and upon his seed and uproot him from under the heavens. And all the people will answer *amen amen selah*" (Naveh 1978, p. 107). There have been many attempts to explain this curse. It would seem that the explanation of Feliks (1981) is correct and that *zvwtyh* refers to palm fibers which were used as a sponge to collect the balsam. Because of the high value of the balsam, stealing palm fibers would be a heinous crime indeed. The secret of the town refers to some secret and apparently local means of production, unknown to competitors.

There have been many archeological excavations in the Jericho area. Installations for the production of balsam have been found in only one such excavation at Ein Boqeq (Gichon and Fisher, as yet unpublished in scientific literature). Other excavations centering around the palaces or around farm-steads in the region shed much light on the agricultural history of the area and are also important to some extent regarding the cultivation of balsam (Porat 1986) (Figure 34).

I.6.2.2

According to the information cited above, the first information regarding the cultivation of balsam in the region dates to before the time in which the area was conquered by the Greeks, and by the time that Alexander arrived on the scene, at least part of the area was being cultivated. Archeological excavations have shown that the region underwent market development during the Hasmonean period and that this development reached its zenith during the days of Herod (Netzer 1984; 1985, pp. 54–61). All of the springs in the region or in the hills nearby were channeled into aqueducts to the agricultural region. The cultivated area was spread out over 15 square kilometers. This is in keeping with the literary traditions examined above. The measurements cited by Theophrastus and Pliny regarding the balsam groves indicate that large tracts of land were cultivated with this crop in the Roman period. The measurements regarding the entire agricultural region of this area cited by Strabo (a length of approximately 20 kilometers) and Josephus (approximately 52 square kilometers) would appear to be exagger-ated (see Figure 35).

Theophrastus and Pliny discuss two balsam groves which apparently took up only a small part of the region or 20 *iugera* (50 dunams). Solinus' comments regarding 200 *iugera* is no more than a literary embellishment. Archeological excavations would seem to indicate a decline in the agricul-ural region after the War of Destruction. We shall return to discuss this matter later on. Suffice it for the moment to say that it is difficult to assume that there would be much of an increase in the extent of the agricultural region after the time of Pliny. In any case, the balsam groves were only a

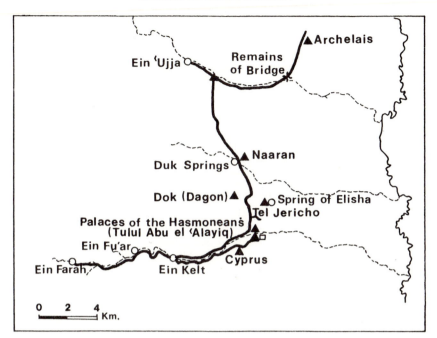

Figure 34 The water systems at Jericho. After Porat 1986, p. 129.

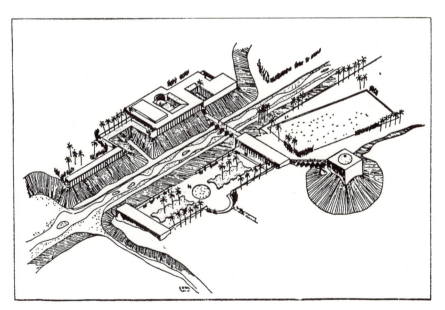

Figure 35 Herod's palace at Jericho.

151

small part of the area cultivated with different types of crops. Thus, for example, we have also seen that dates were grown extensively in this region.

The information regarding the balsam groves until the year 70 CE is quite explicit. This is not so regarding what happened after that time. Pliny tells us that the Zealots attempted to burn the balsam groves so that they not fall into the hands of the Romans. They were, however, unsuccessful and the groves were not damaged.

Pliny also tells of 800,000 sesterces exacted from the region five years after the conquest of Judaea. This would indicate that Pliny refers to 75 CE at the very latest (the War of Destruction ending in 70 CE) or perhaps even 73 CE, five years after the conquest of Jericho in 68 CE. The excavations in the palaces of Herod and the aqueducts indicate that they were destroyed at the end of the first century CE. The destruction of these buildings does not necessarily indicate that the agriculture of the region was also devastated. There is a vast difference, as we shall see, between structures which housed the rich or public buildings and agricultural terrain. However, as we stated, the aqueducts were also damaged at that time, and without a supply of water it is clear that the agriculture of the region could not survive.

The literary traditions regarding balsam in the Jericho region after the first century CE is even more limited. Galen mentions only the Ein Gedi region. Rabbinic sources, as we have also seen, mention Ramtha and Ein Gedi, but not Jericho. Even stranger is the fact that some traditions mention Jericho and the Dead Sea region with no reference to balsam whatsoever. *Totius Orbis Descriptio* (c. 31), for instance, mentions favorably the dates of Jericho and the agricultural produce of Palestine in general, but does not mention balsam.

All this would seem to indicate that the balsam groves in Jericho were destroyed or that their extent was greatly limited. They apparently did suffer some damage, but were not entirely abandoned. Agriculture, it appears, was limited to the area of springs such as Jericho itself and Naaran.

It is difficult to know what caused this decline. Porat claims that it was the result of the War of Destruction (Porat 1986, pp. 132–3). However, as we have seen, the balsam groves were still profitable a number of years after this time. It would seem then that it is necessary to suggest a later date for the decline. R. Judah b. Ilai mentions the orchards (*pardes*) of Jericho as examples of expensive types of land (T Arachin 2:8 – Theophrastus also used the term "orchards" to describe the balsam groves). The specific matter described by R. Judah refers to the Temple. The example itself, though, reflects the situation in his time. This would appear to show that these groves were destroyed only after his time or perhaps somewhat before. R. Judah lived after the Bar-Kochba revolt. The most logical assumption would be, then, that the balsam groves were destroyed during that revolt (132–5 CE).

It is also possible that the agricultural decline was not the result of some military event, but rather of a long period of neglect. The sophisticated water system in the area was very expensive and the Romans, perhaps, were not willing to invest in maintaining it. When the aqueducts were damaged in the First Revolt, the Romans did not bother repairing them. This explanation is, however, not sufficient. All of Palestine had undergone agricultural and economic development. It is hard to understand why the Romans would have given up particularly on this region and on what had been an important source of income. In 106 CE Trajan incorporated the areas under Nabatean control into the Roman Empire. With this act the Romans effectively cornered the spice and perfume trade and it became a Roman monopoly. This may have caused a drop in the price of perfume and made the Jericho produce unprofitable since, after all, it was now competing with the Roman perfumes of Arabia. This hypothesis though is also somewhat problematical, since there was always a great demand for perfumes and we have no sources attesting to the fact that the supply was greater than the demand.

There is no evidence of an agricultural decline in the Ein Gedi region. As we stated above, the literary traditions also attest to continued agricultural development in the region in general and to the continued existence of the balsam groves (Galen, the Ein Gedi Synagogue Inscription; BT Shabbat 26a). The archeological excavations also attest to a continued strong settlement presence there (Mazar 1966, *et al.*). The entire cultivated area in the Ein Gedi region has been estimated to have been no more than 650 dunams (Porat 1986, pp. 133–6). It is possible that the small balsam grove mentioned by Theophrastus, Strabo, Pliny and Solinus was in this region. This area was of great local economic importance, but its impact on national economy was, apparently, limited.

The major economic question is whether the entire Jericho region was state owned or not. If the area belonged to the *fiscus*, then its impact on the economy of Palestine was rather limited since all profits reverted to the Empire. If, however, some of this area was privately owned, then some of the profits were channeled into the national economy.

As far as the matter of balsam is concerned, a number of the traditions examined above would seem to indicate that this was part of the *fiscus*, especially Pliny and BT Shabbat 26a. BT Berachot 43a mentions the balsam of the Caesar and that of the House of Rabbi. This would seem to show that at least part of the balsam, that of R. Judah the Prince, was privately owned. The Ein Gedi inscription regarding the fibers serving as a sponge to absorb the balsam would seem to indicate that the balsam was cultivated by private growers ("He who steals the *zywtyh* of his fellow," etc.). These growers were either totally independent or were tenants who, to all intents and purposes, were independent and their subjugation was reflected in the rent they had to pay the landowner. We shall discuss this matter further later on in our study (Chapter 4.I.2).

Scholarly literature has long accepted the view that the entire Jericho region was state-owned. There is no doubt that there were state-owned estates in the region, but in our opinion, at least, there is not enough evidence to prove that the entire region was state-owned. There is evidence regarding some state-owned estates in the area as early as the Persian period. Proof of this is found in the jars stamped with the inscription "Yehud" or "Pehah" which, according to most scholars, refers to state-owned land during the Persian period (Sukenik 1942; Welten 1969; Lapp 1960; Rainey 1965, 1982). Such stamped jars dating from the Persian period and perhaps even the early Hellenistic period have been found in both the Jericho and the Ein Gedi regions.

The granting of the area to Cleopatra by Marc Antony does not prove that the area was state-owned, since in this instance Cleopatra does not function as a private person but represents the state. This is also the case regarding Herod who had to lease the lands back from Cleopatra. Upon the death of Herod, Phasaelis was bequeathed to his sister Salome (*Ant.* 17. 321; *BJ* 2. 98). It would appear that this is proof that the village belonged to Herod, and thus he was able to bequeath it to his sister. She bequeathed this village as well as neighboring Archelaïs to Livia (*Ant.* 18. 31; *BJ* 2. 161. There is some problem regarding the status of Archelaïs which in *Ant.* 18. 31 is regarded as part of Salome's territory, while in *Ant.* 17. 341 it is a village which is founded by Herod's son Archelaus. This question is beyond the scope of our discussion).

Archeologists have excavated an elaborate tomb belonging to the "family of Goliath" in the area of Jericho. One of those buried in that tomb was referred to as "a freedman of Agrippina." It is likely that this freedman was a foreman or supervisor at one of the estates in the region and most likely one that belonged to Agrippina (Hachlili and Killebrew 1981). This shows that there were estates in the region, but it was only in the Byzantine period that the entire area became a *regio* (Avi-Yonah 1963, p. 119), an administrative term pertaining specifically to area which had taken on the official status of a crown estate. This definition of a *regio* is possible, but not necessarily the only one. We also hear of farm areas that may have belonged to the Temple in Jerusalem (M Pesahim 4:8; T Pesahim 2(3):19). The rest of the *halachot* in this source regarding the men of Jericho seem to describe independent landowners making independent decisions regarding their land or crops. Thus, these farmers appeared to have owned their land, or at the very least were tenant farmers still capable of making independent decisions similar to those in Ein Gedi.

Ein Gedi is also referred to before the Bar-Kochba War as being a village of the emperor. In fact, it is described in such a manner in one of the Bar-Kochba letters (Lewis 1989, p. 42, etc.). However, these same letters also mention independent landowners, buying and selling land, and Babta, a resident of the area, appears to have been a rich and independent woman (Polotsky 1967; Lewis 1989). There was even an *agora* in Ein Gedi as well as a fortress (Lewis 1989, pp. 42, 85, etc.). The lands of Ein Gedi, therefore, were not entirely state-owned. We have no information regarding the status of Zoar before the Byzantine period. It appears that during the Byzantine period it was a royal estate. This status is dependent on the interpretation of a Greek phrase and we shall discuss the matter further on in our study (Chapter 4.I).

Thus, the balsam which was cultivated in this region was grown for the most part on royal estates. Some of the land, however, was privately owned, channeling profits from this valuable commodity into the various markets of Palestine. The royal estates were worked by tenants who had to hand over part of the crop or profits to their masters, but remained with enough to contribute to the economy of Palestine. This is the same regarding dates. The other crops in this area were destined for local markets (Porat 1986).

I.7 Industrial crops

I.7.1 Flax

I.7.1.1 The cultivation of flax in Palestine

Flax was one of the important raw materials for clothing in the Roman Empire (Wild 1980). Flax or *kytn'* in Aramaic is mentioned quite often in the literature of the Mishnah and Talmud period (Hirschberg 1924). The sources describing the economy of Palestine in the Second Temple period, however, do not mention it at all and it would appear that it was not of much importance at that time. Archeological excavations, though, have yielded cloth from flax from as early as the Neolithic period. Such cloth has also been found in the caves of the Judaean desert from the second century CE (Yadin 1971). Early literary sources mention cloth woven from strings of flax (Felix 1968, pp. 279–84). Herodotus also describes flaxen armor as characteristic of the armor of the crews of those ships which the "Phoenicians together with the Syrians of Palestine" supplied to the armies of Artaxerxes (481–479 BCE – Herodotus. 7. 89). However, it is not described in any of these sources as an important cash crop. Josephus, in describing the economy of Palestine (*BJ* 3. 3) mentions various aspects of the agriculture of Palestine, but not the cultivation of flax.

Sources from the second century CE, however, describe flax quite often both in terms of its agricultural importance as well as its industrial significance. It is also described as one of the main export crops of Palestine. Clement of Alexandria (*Paedagogus*. 2. 20), when accusing the women of Egypt of extravagance, claims that they wear flaxen garments from the land of the Hebrews. Pausanias (5. 5. 2) also implies that the flax of Palestine was of rather high quality. Thus, when describing the flax of Greece, he compares it to that of Palestine. The fourth-century CE *Totius Orbis Descriptio* (c. 31) mentions a number of cities in Palestine which exported textiles. The price edict of Diocletian (ch. 26) describes the flax of Scythopolis as the most expensive in all the world. Other laws from the fourth century CE mention the factories in which this cloth was woven and it would appear that it was of great economic importance (*C. Th.* 10. 20. 8; Genesis Rabbah 19:1, p. 170; 20:12, p. 196; PT Ketubbot VII, 31c and parallels; PT Avodah Zarah I, 39c). Many Talmudic traditions describe the cultivation of flax. Flax is considered something likely to be found among Galilean women: "One does not take from shepherds wool, milk or kids . . . but they may be taken from women . . . and utensils of flax in the Galilee" (M Bava Kama 10:9). Also, one of the obligations of a woman to her husband is to weave him clothing from wool (M Ketubbot 5:5). R. Judah (135–80) adds: "One does not force her to weave from flax because it makes the mouth smell foul and stiffens the lips" (T Ketubbot 5:4; PT Ketubbot V, 30a; BT Ketubbot V, 61b). Thus, the weaving of clothes from flax really should have been included among the duties of a wife, but because of the damage that would ensue it was removed from the list of obligations. There are many other such references to flax in Talmudic literature, proving its importance both in agriculture as well as in industry.

I.7.1.2 The history of the cultivation of flax in Palestine

Flax is mentioned in literary traditions as becoming an important crop beginning from the end of the Javneh period and especially after the Bar-Kochba War. By the time Pausanias visited Palestine (175 CE), the flax of Palestine had acquired an Empire-wide reputation. Clement of Alexandria, whom we mentioned above regarding the flaxen clothing worn by the women of Egypt, lived between 150–216 CE. The flax installations found near Tel Shosh, or Gaba Hippeum, date from the beginning of the third century (Z. Safrai and Linn 1988) (Figure 36). Many other traditions also indicate that flax became a prominent crop only after the Bar-Kochba War (135 CE). Before this time, it was cultivated on a rather limited basis. Thus, it would appear that the extensive cultivation of flax began at the beginning of the second century CE, or to be even more exact, at the beginning of the second quarter of the second century CE (Z. Safrai 1985, pp. 148–52).

I.7.1.3 The extent of flax cultivation

As we saw above, flax is cited as a characteristic crop of the Galilee, while wool is more characteristic of Judaea. A number of settlements are mentioned as centers of cultivation or production. The most famous of such sites is Scythopolis. Arbel is also mentioned as a site of production of rough flaxen cloth (Genesis Rabbah 19:1, p. 170 and parallels).

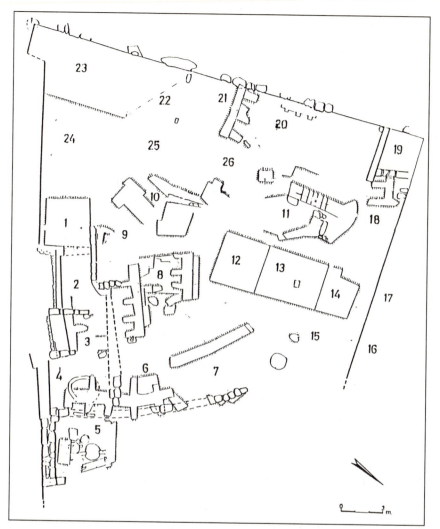

Figure 36 Installations for the preparation of flax at Gaba Hippeum. After
Z. Safrai and Linn 1988, p. 178

Another center for the production of flax was Tiberias and the Kinneret
basin. Thus, an Amora states: Bar Hedaya said – "I saw myself how the Sea
of Tiberias was encircled with washbasins of flaxen clothes on the intermediate days of the festival [*hol hamoed*]" (BT Moed Qatan 18b). Tiberias also
had a guild of weavers (Schwabe 1967, p. 181), and since we have just seen
that there was much flax in the area, it would seem that the guild was of flax
weavers. During the seventh century we hear of a flax merchant from
Schechem who used to sell flax in Tiberias. (Brock 1973, pp. 314–15).

R. Hiyya, a resident of Tiberias, was an important producer of linen (PT Bava Mezia V, 10c *et al.*).

Many installations for the soaking of flax have been found in Mishmar Ha-Emeq (Z. Safrai and Linn 1988). In this area, on the fringes of the Jezreel Valley, dozens of such installations have been found, the earliest of which date to the Talmudic period (third–fourth centuries CE). Most of the installations, however, date to a later period (fifth–sixth centuries). At least some of these installations were abandoned in the sixth century and olive presses (this is the case in two clusters of installations) or parts of a farmstead (the case in another cluster of installations) replaced them. Thus, it would seem that the cultivation of flax was reduced at this time while that of olives was increased. Perhaps the cultivation of flax ceased completely during this period. The entire area of the installations was abandoned in the seventh century with the Muslim conquest of Palestine, but may have been abandoned as early as 614 CE with the Persian conquest. We do not have information yet regarding the switch from flax to olives at that time.

As mentioned above, the literary traditions attest to flax being a characteristic crop of the Galilee. Therefore, it would seem likely that the majority of traditions in Talmudic literature pertaining to the cultivation or production of flax reflect the situation in the Galilee, and that the majority of traditions regarding textiles in the Galilee deal with linen and not wool. Since most of the Palestinian Talmudic literature was written, edited or formulated one way or another in the Galilee, it would seem likely that most of the material in general dealing with the textile industry found in Talmudic literature pertains, therefore, to flax grown in the Galilee.

I.7.1.4 The role of flax in the national economy

Flax is considered to be a crop which depletes the soil and was planted, therefore, only once every four or six years (T Bava Mezia 9:31 and parallels). Thus, after every year of cultivation, the farmer waited another 3–5 years before cultivating flax in the same field again. During those other years, the farmer grew grains and especially wheat in the field used previously for flax (M Bava Mezia 9:9; T Bava Mezia 9:32; PT Bava Mezia IX, 12a). The wheat and other grains were, of course, cultivated within the common cycle of letting the field remain fallow every other year.

Flax, therefore, was likely to be cultivated on a quarter or a sixth of the fields available for the cultivation of grains. Even while growing the maximum amount of flax, it was possible to grow wheat in the other years, in accordance with the cycle of leaving the field fallow every other year, on a quarter or half of all available area. Since, as we shall shortly see, flax was much more profitable than wheat, it would seem likely that the farmer would attempt to grow the maximum amount of flax within the potential of

Planting cycles – including flax

Year	Cultivation of flax	
	Every 4 years	Every 6 years
1	Flax	Flax
2	Fallow	Fallow
3	Wheat	Wheat
4	Fallow	Fallow
5	Flax	Wheat
6	Fallow	Fallow
7	Wheat	Flax
8	Fallow	Fallow
9	Flax	Wheat
10	Fallow	Fallow
11	Wheat	Wheat
12	Fallow	Fallow

Figure 37 Possibilities for planting cycles including the cultivation of flax.

his farm and, therefore, on the average devote a sixth or a quarter of his fields to the cultivation of flax.

Flax was more profitable than any other grain. According to the Edict of Diocletian, the price of a *modius* of wheat was 100 dinars. The *modius* was 8.54 pounds or 6.4 kilograms (according to the calculation that 1 pound = 0.75 kilogram of wheat). If the average yield per dunam of wheat fields was 100–150 kilograms (Chapter 2.I.2), there was a profit of 1562.5–2343.7 dinars. Remembering that wheat was cultivated only every other year, this profit was also cyclical. Figuring out the profit from a flax field is somewhat more difficult. There are no traditions available regarding average yield. The only statistics which may be of help are those regarding flax yields in the 1950s from the State of Israel. These yields were achieved without the aid of supplementary irrigation and before the implementation of methods based on modern research to increase yields. It would seem, therefore, that these statistics might represent the yields of the ancient world (Arnon 1963, II, pp. 591–7; Marany 1955). A dunam of flax yields approximately 500 kilograms. This includes about 50 kilograms of fibers and 20 kilograms of tow (Arnon 1963). According to Hirschberg (1924, p. 60), of the 50 kilograms of fibers, 55 per cent are good strings or even first-class, 24 per cent are second-class and 20 per cent are third-class. The Edict of Diocletian also gives prices for three types of flax fibers.

Calculating the profit is based on the following factors: the profit per *modius* is based on the prices in the Edict of Diocletian (26. 1–12). The edict also gives prices for fibers of a lower standard. We did not take into account the price of straw as well as the costs of labor and production.

Thus, according to the Edict of Diocletian, the profit per dunam of flax is

	Yield per kilo	Average yield (liters)	Price pound fibers	Profit fibers	Price pound cloth	Profit from cloth
Class A	27.5	76.39	24	1833.4	1200	91668
Class B	12	33.3	20	666	960	31968
Class C	10	27.0	16	432	840	22680
Tow	20	55.5	?	?	?	?
Total			2931.4	146316		

Figure 38 Profit from the cultivation and production of flax.

2931.4 dinars. This is 1.2–1.8 times the profit on a dunam of wheat. This is also not taking into account the price of the tow, which is unknown. Once the flax has been turned into the rope, the profit skyrockets to 62.4–93.6 times the profit on a wheat field. This calculation is, of course, not complete since the price of seeds and straw must also be taken into account for wheat. However, there is also the profit of the tow as well as the oil produced from the surplus of flax seeds. All of this makes the cultivation of wheat far less profitable than the cultivation of flax. The only consideration against the cultivation of flax may have been the high labor and production costs compared to those of wheat. This is the result of the spinning and weaving necessary in the production of flax. This, as we remember, also resulted in the vast difference between the price of the fiber and that of the rope. This price gap was approximately 824–1176 dinars per pound, or about 4800 per cent–5050 per cent.

Even so, the difference in price between the fiber and the woven product was not just the result of the price of labor. The edict also established price levels for the labor of wool and flax weavers. A weaver of wool received 15–40 dinars for a pound of wool, while a weaver of flax received 20–40 dinars per day. The weaving, of course, was only part of the necessary stages of production. Additional days of labor or payment were necessary for other stages of production such as dyeing or ironing. Even if we do not possess complete information regarding the cost of all of these additional labors, it is clear that they cannot account for the vast difference in price between the fiber and the woven product. It would seem that in the final result, this was caused by the desire on the part of the grower to receive a rather high rate of profit, whether he participated in all stages of growing and production, or whether hired workers undertook these tasks.

It was also possible to achieve a high rate of profit from the seeds of flax. Half of these seeds were usually not used for cultivation in following years. Rather, oil was produced from them to serve as a base for dyes, for medicines or even for consumption. The great advantage in the cultivation of flax was that the profit was the farmer's alone. One of the great problems for the farmer of the ancient world was how to utilize those periods in which agricultural chores or tasks were not being undertaken. The rate of production of the farmer was determined by the necessities of agriculture during peak seasons. However, conditions in Palestine were such that there are many months in which there was little agricultural work, and the farmer in vain sought some profitable extra activity. The peak period in the production of flax fitted in nicely in the calendar of the farmer *vis-à-vis* the cultivation of grains, olives and grapes. Flax provided many jobs whether in the production of ropes or the weaving of the flax into cloth and even in the sewing of garments. The cultivation of flax then could offer the farmers additional sources of activity and profit during the dead months of the winter. As we saw above, the most profitable stage pertaining to the production of flax was in the weaving of fabric from the fibers. This work took place, most likely, during those winter months when there was not much else to do (Chapter 4, Figure 81). Thus, the cultivation of flax became one of the major industries in the economy of Palestine, as well as one of its major exports and in particular a source of livelihood during those months when not much else was available. Some of the profits from this industry were absorbed by the government, either in the form of taxes or through government-owned weaving factories. Even so, most of the profit did reach the farmer and his neighbors who participated in the various stages of production and thus greatly enriched the agriculture of Palestine.

I.7.2 Industrial plants

I.7.2.1 Silk

The different types of silk are mentioned quite often in Talmudic literature, but usually as an imported product (Hirschberg 1924, pp. 46–55). Many of the names of the individual types of silk are from the Greek. A name like "*Hindoin*" reflects a product originally from India and the name "*Metaxsa*", which refers to plain silk, is Aramaic. There is no doubt that Palestine took part in the international silk trade (Johns 1960; Chapter 3.VI.3). However, very little silk was actually produced in that province and most of the traditions dealing with silk pertain to import. Thus, for example, BT Bava Bathra 143a tells of a person who sent silk to his family from abroad or in particular from countries along the Mediterranean basin. When the sages ponder the meaning of the word "*kalach*," which is a type of silk, or when they are interested in particulars regarding a certain type of silk, they usually turn to sailors (PT Kilayim IX 32a; BT Shabbat 20b). In that same discussion in PT Kilayim, *kalach* is called "cissaros [*agbyn*] of Caesarea," implying that it was brought to Palestine via that major port-city. Indicative of that city in Palestine regarding silk is the complaint of the sage pertaining to the Roman tax authorities that one is hardly able to provide the members of his household with simple woollen garments while the Romans demand silken ones in payment for taxes (Avot D'Rabbi Nathan, version A, chapter 20, p. 71). The demand that provincials pay taxes with products not produced by themselves, but which had to be purchased (usually from official store-houses) is mentioned in Roman literature as one of the worst forms of oppression (Tac., *Hist.*, *Agr.* 15. 19).

It would appear that a small amount of silk was also produced in Palestine. The sages were proud of the fact that almost every conceivable type of crop was cultivated in Palestine. The *midrash* states the following:

> Hadrian, may his bones rot, asked R. Joshua b. Hananiah the follow-ing question – The Torah states that the Land of Israel is a "land wherein thou shalt eat bread without scarceness" [and continues to state that "thou shalt not lack anything in it"]. You [R. Joshua] shall bring me three things that I ask of you. And he said: What are they? He replied: Pepper, pheasant and silk. He brought him pepper from Natzhanah [var. lec. Askara = Schechem], pheasant from Sidon, and some say from Achbara [in the Galilee], and silk from Giscala.
>
> (Kohelet Rabba 2:11; Midrash Ha-Gadol on Deuteronomy 8:9 p. 123)

Thus, the *midrash* describes this silk as being locally produced and secured from Giscala in the Upper Galilee.

During the Middle Ages the Upper Galilee did become a center for the production of silk. In order to facilitate this, many strawberry bushes were planted since this served as food for the silk worms. An aggadic tradition relates that R. Isaac Ibn Daud of Spain (eleventh century) was a descendant of one of those exiled by Titus to Jerusalem and sent to a proconsul at Merida in order to establish the silk industry in Spain (Sefer Ha-Kabbala, ed. G. Cohen 1967, p. 79). This tradition, however, is quite late and apparently reflects the reality of the Middle Ages, but not that of the ancient world. In any case, silk was mostly imported to Palestine and only rarely cultivated there.

I.7.2.2 Hemp and cotton

Hemp is also described as a product imported to Palestine via the various ports of the coastal cities (PT Kilayim IX, 32d; Hirschberg 1924, pp. 95–9). There are, therefore, no traditions regarding cultivation or production of hemp.

Cotton is mentioned a number of times in rabbinic sources (Hirschberg 1924, pp. 92–5). Judging by the minimal amount of references, it would appear that it was not widely cultivated and was of minimal importance. In spite of this, the view that cotton was not cultivated in the Land of Israel is not correct, since in the Mishnah cotton is referred to as "cotton wool" (see, for example, M Kilayim 7:2) (Hebrew: *tsemer gefen* and not *cutnah*).

Moreover, cotton fibers have also been discovered in the Land of Israel, but these were undoubtedly very expensive (Sheffer 1987). In the sixth century it is described as an important crop in the Jericho region (Gregory of Tours, *PL* 71: 721).

I.8 Fishing and grazing

I.8.1 Fishing

Fish were of great importance in the diet of ancient Palestine. Fish may not have been included in the diet schedule discussed above, but it was considered a regular part of the Sabbath meal (Krauss 1929, II, pp. 216–23; Nun 1964, pp. 138–44), and in general an important food. There are no statistics regarding fish consumption at that time, but it certainly was consumed in great amounts. The fish were caught both in the Mediterranean Sea and in the Sea of Galilee. Fishermen along the Mediterranean coast set out either from the large port-cities or from the smaller coastal villages. Ptolemais (Acco) is described as an important fishing center (BT Moed Qatan 13b; Genesis Rabbah 5:10, p. 38; 13:16, p. 125, Exodus Rabbah 9:6, A Shinan ed. p. 211; PT Pesahim IV, 30d *et al.*). There are, of course, numerous traditions regarding fishermen in other cities. Most of the residents of the coastal cities were non–Jews and this would ultimately mean that most of the fishermen in Palestine at that time were non-Jews. However, ancient Palestine was not self–sufficient in its fish needs and many traditions attest to the importing of fish. In fact there are even traditions which describe fish markets of various types of fish in which all the merchandise was imported (see Chapter 4.VI.2).

Fish were sold after being preserved in a briny type of fish sauce. During this process their appearance was changed and it became impossible to identify the species of the fish. Since there are various halachic restrictions regarding the eating of fish and not all types were permitted, fish whose appearance had been altered, such as brine of hashed tarith, could not be bought from non-Jews (M Avodah Zarah 2:6 and parallels).

Most of the needs in terms of fish of the Jewish population were supplied by the fishermen of the Sea of Galilee and particularly those from Tiberias. This area was primarily Jewish. The fishermen of the Sea of Galilee are mentioned in the New Testament as well as in rabbinic traditions, and it is therefore clear that fishing was quite important in the basin of the Sea of Galilee. The boatmen of Tiberias had established work practices (PT Pesahim IV, 30d), and during the War of the Destruction they formed the majority of one of the parties in Tiberias (Josephus, *Vita*, 9. 12). It is impossible to quantify the economic implications of the fish industry in this area, but if the Jewish fishermen did supply most of the Jewish population with their needs in terms of fish, then it is likely that many people were engaged in this activity. Josephus relates important information about Tarichea, a settlement in this region. According to what he relates, Josephus commandeered 230 boats belonging to the extended families of the settlement and placed four boatmen in each one. He then attacked Tiberias with this force (*Vita* 32. 163). These numbers appear to be more or less realistic and do not seem to be as exaggerated as other figures in Josephus. According to these figures, almost every extended family (7–8 persons or 4 males) possessed a fishing boat. This would indicate that almost the entire workforce of the settlement engaged in fishing.

There was great density of settlement along the western bank of the Sea of Galilee. Thus, for example, we find the settlements of Beth Yerah, Hamath (a semi-independent suburb of Tiberias), Tiberias, Magdala, Ginossar and Kefar Nahum. There is a rather limited amount of available land and therefore it would appear that the development of the region could only be the result of the successful fishing industry there. The great number of harbors found along the banks of the Sea of Galilee would seem to prove this point (Nun 1977, pp. 77–92).

There is only a limited amount of material on the fishing industry in Palestine during the Biblical period and it seems that this industry came into its own only in the Second Temple period (Nun 1964, pp. 53–79). The development of the fishing industry is by its nature dependent upon the development of trade and transportation networks. Without such networks it would be impossible to market the fish over long distances. We shall discuss the development of trade in more detail in Chapter 3.

The ancient sources relate that fish were grown in special pools called *bybryn* and *pskyn*. The sources also describe the fish being fed in these pools. One such pool was even excavated in a villa near Caesarea (Levine and Netzer 1986, pp. 151 ff.). A number of others have also been found on the coast near this city (Flinder 1985, *et al.*) (Figure 39). Fishponds are mentioned in a number of *halachot* such as the following: "One may not catch fish from a fishpond on a festival nor give them food, but one may catch venison or game from animal enclosures and one may put food before them. Rabban Simeon b. Gamaliel says: not all enclosures (*bybryn*) are alike. This is the general rule: whenever chasing is still necessary it is forbidden but where chasing is not still necessary it is permitted" (M Bezah 3:1; PT Shabbat XIII, 14a; PT Bezah III, 61d and parallels). The only labors that one may perform on a festival are those which are for the explicit purpose of the festival and only if they do not require preparation. If the preparation can be considered an independent task, the labor itself (as well as the preparation) is forbidden. One may not catch fish from a fishpond on a festival since this is considered to be real labor, which is apparently not the case regarding animal and bird enclosures. Fishponds are mentioned a number of other times (as, for example, in PT Sanhedrin X, 29c). Tacitus also mentions fishponds in Jerusalem at the end of the Second Temple period (*Hist.* 5. 12).

This is probably something of an exaggeration since the supplying of water to Jerusalem was always quite difficult.

The fishpond was more often associated with a *villa* and a high standard of living than with a rural agricultural farmstead. Rabbinic literature mentions the fishpond as a common part of the villa in a number of cases (T Bava Bathra 3:5; PT Bava Bathra, IV 14c). Fishponds were found near a villa in Nabi Yamin and maybe near Kfar Saba (Roll Ayalon 1989, pp. 161, 214). The *midrash* also relates that King Solomon, extravagantly wealthy according to the *aggadah*, built a fishpond (*piskinus – piscina*) (Kohelet Rabbah 2:8). This might also explain the fishponds of Jerusalem in Tacitus. Tacitus probably was told by Roman tourists or travelers of the wealth of Jerusalem and Tacitus naturally turned this into a city with fishponds, a sure sign of wealth (Stern 1980, p. 267). Thus the raising of fish in fishponds never really became economically important. It was, rather, a sign of wealth and a high standard of living.

I.8.2 Grazing

I.8.2.1 The structure of grazing activity

Ancient sources describe three types of sheep grazing: (1) sheep which graze in the desert throughout the entire year; (2) sheep which are grazed in the desert or near the desert during the summer (from Passover until the rainy season begins. During the winter the sheep are returned to the settlement); (3) sheep which are grazed near the settlement itself (M Bezah 5:7; T Bezah 4:11; PT Bezah 63b; BT Bezah 40a and parallels).

These three types represent three different agricultural and economic types of grazing. The first type, in which the sheep are grazed all year long in the desert, typifies nomadic society which also lives for the most part in the desert. This type of grazing was especially prominent in the Judaean Desert, in the Negev and in the region of the Limes which is beyond the scope of our study. The second type is typical of a mixed farmstead in which both agriculture and grazing are of great importance. The seasonal migration of sheep transhumance requires a particular type of settlement network such as is extensively found in Italy, for instance (Frayn 1984), and in a number of other provinces such as North Africa and Greece (Isager and Skydsgaard 1992, pp. 99–101; Whittaker 1988; Hodkinson 1988) for example. In Palestine, such sheep herder settlements have been found in Anab a-Kabir. Around the settlement were sheep-pens usually composed of a room used as a residence and courtyards for the sheep (Z. Safrai 1986; see above, Figure 29, and see Figure 40). These sheep-pens are similar to those found in England or in North Africa (Huntingford 1934). The third type of grazing is typical of a situation in which the grazing of sheep plays only a small or auxiliary role in the economy of the settlement. The land in the vicinity of

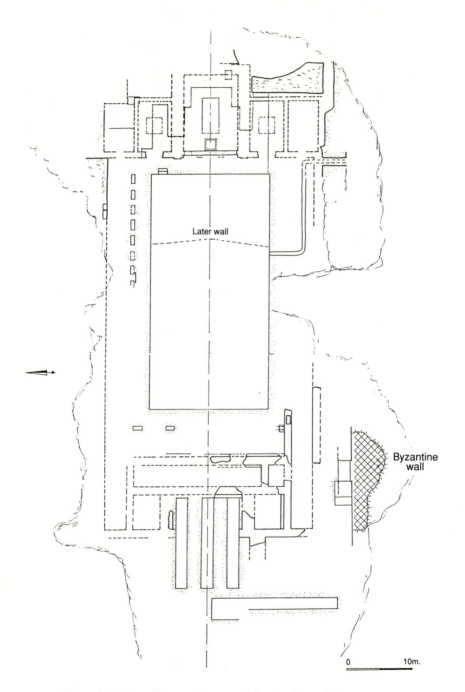

Figure 39 Fishponds near Caesarea. After Levine and Netzer 1986, p. 151.

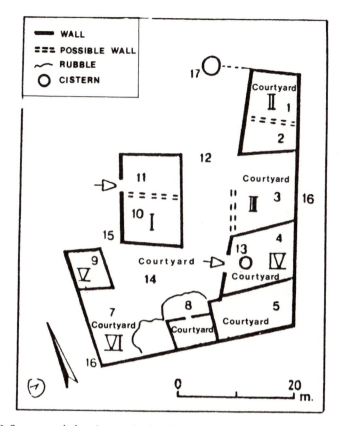

Figure 40 Structures belonging to shepherds at Anab a-Kabir, southern Mt Hebron region. After Z. Safrai 1986, p.120.

the settlement usually did not allow for much grazing since it was necessary for intensive agricultural use.

The picture one gets from the ancient sources is that the average farmer may have had one or two sheep serving only minor economic functions. Not every farmer grazed his sheep. Rather, it was customary for a number of farmers to hand over their sheep to a professional shepherd. The *halachah* at times gives expression to the reality of a professional shepherd grazing flocks which do not belong to him. Thus, for instance, it is stated: "One does not buy wool or milk or kids from a shepherd or wood and fruit from one who guards fruit" (M Bava Kama 10:9 and parallels). The Mishnah indicated that the average shepherd is not usually the owner of the sheep, but considered only their guardian or similar to one who guards fruit. There are dozens of examples in Talmudic literature pertaining to this status of the shepherd (M Bezah 5:3; PT Bezah V, 63b; BT Bezah 37b; BT Avodah Zarah 22b; M

Bava Kama 6:2 *et al.*). On the other hand, there are also sources attesting to the fact that there were farmers who had a great number of sheep and who grazed them themselves. An interesting phrase reflecting this reality is found in a number of *halachot* describing someone who "pens his sheep in his field" (M Sheviit 3:4). This law pertains to the Sabbatical Year when it is forbidden to fertilize fields. It is permitted, however, to "pen" or place sheep in a field in order that they might naturally fertilize it while they stay there. The sheep-pen in such a case would, of course, be a temporary one. The reality described in the *halachah*, however, is that of a farmer in a mixed farmstead who also owns sheep.

The difference between these two types of grazing reflects geographic differences. Most of the grazing in Palestine was centralized in Judaea, while in the Galilee grazing was only of minor importance. The sources character-ize the Galilee as the region of flax production while Judaea is characterized as the region of wool production (see I.7.1 above). This geographic and economic distinction can be proven in another manner. In the 1950s a survey was undertaken to determine the extent of natural pasture land as well as its potential. According to those involved, the Lower Galilee was capable of grazing 4,400 cattle or 24,000 sheep (Seligman *et al.* 1959). In order to compute grazing potential of sheep, it is necessary to take into account 10 rams and 22 lambs for every 100 sheep (see Genesis Rabbah 76:7, p. 905). According to these figures it would be possible for the Lower Galilee to graze only about 19,000 sheep. The real figure was probably lower since some of the areas which could have been used for grazing according to the survey were probably used instead for intensive cultivation. On the other hand, it is possible that the animals of the ancient world were somewhat less developed and therefore required less food. Even so, it is also possible that if these fields were cultivated, it would be possible to find alternate food supply sources for the sheep such as stubble in wheat fields or wild grass in groves or orchards.

In spite of the problems regarding the survey, it is possible to use the data from that study for our purposes, since the various problems seem to cancel each other out. It is likely that the average farmer had at least a cow or ox for agricultural purposes and perhaps even a donkey. We do not know what the population of ancient Galilee was. There were certainly, however, tens of thousands of families that resided there. This would leave only a small amount of sheep-grazing area since the majority of land was cultivated in a rather intensive manner and the household animals also needed some grazing land. Sheep grazing was probably of much greater importance in the Upper Galilee and in Judaea because of the nature of the terrain there.

The *halachah* forbade the raising of sheep (*behemah dakah*) in the Land of Israel (Alon 1980, I, pp. 277–85; Gulak 1941). This *halachah*, dating from the beginning of the second century CE, would seem to be more character-istic of the Galilee. Thus, it is explicitly stated that it is permissible to raise sheep in the deserts of Judaea and in neglected areas on the periphery of settled regions and wells as in "woodland" and "deserts" (T Bava Kama 8:10; Alon, ibid.).

A number of other sources tell of the great number of sheep in Judaea. Thus, for example, the Tosefta states regarding the Temple that "calves were brought from the Sharon and sheep from the desert" (T Menahot 9:13). BT Menahot 87a (= BT Sotah 34b) explains that the "calves came from the Sharon and the sheep from Hebron" and adds that Absalom, the son of David, had gone to Hebron in order to bring sheep from there. A *midrash* on the blessing of Jacob to Judah states in a similar vein that "all the valleys will turn white from the fields of wheat and the flocks of sheep" (Bereshit Rabbati 49:12 and parallels). All this would seem to prove that the raising of sheep in the Hebron mountains was quite prevalent.

Thus, it appears that sheep grazing was rather limited in the Galilee and a rather widespread phenomenon in Judaea. Sheep grazing in this area served as the basis for the extensive industry of woven goods in Judaea (see II.2 below). The "hired" shepherd is characteristic of an economy in which grazing is only of minor importance compared to agriculture and this seems to be the situation in the Galilee. The traditions regarding "mixed" farmsteads (wheat and sheep) probably reflect the conditions of Judaea. The hired shepherd handed over his sheep to their owners in the evening who milked them or cut their wool when the appropriate time came. The structures in Anab a-Kabir and in other nearby regions (Z. Safrai 1986) served as dwellings together with sheep-pens. This would indicate that the householder was also the owner of the sheep which were kept in the pens. This situation would most likely prevail in areas bordering on the desert.

I.8.2.2 The economic implications of grazing

The consumption of meat both in the agricultural sphere as well as among the population at large was rather limited. According to the laws applicable to the "rebellious son," if a child consumed a *tartimar* of meat (150–180 grams) or a *manah* (500–600 grams) against the wishes of his parents, he could be considered "gluttonous" and "rebellious" and put to death (M Sanhedrin 8:2; PT Sanhedrin VIII, 26a and parallels). The Tosefta (T Peah 4:10) tells of a member of a rich family who received extraordinary treatment and "they used to bring up to a certain old man a pound (300–360 grams) of meat in Sepphoris every day." The story is told of an unusual occurrence concerning a poor man who managed to achieve the standard of living of the rich, and the measures are exaggerated on purpose. In Babylonia the story was somewhat misunderstood since meat was always plentiful there and the thrust of the story was changed (BT Ketubbot 67b). In Palestine, meat was usually eaten only on festivals or on special occasions (M Hullin 5(3–4) and parallels). Only the rich could eat meat on a more frequent basis. Jerome relates a fourth-century edict of the emperor Valens forbidding the eating of calves, since they were apparently being eaten out of existence (Hieronymus, *Adversus Iovinianum* 2. 7; Opelt 1971).

Thus, the sheep which were not grazed were probably not used for meat. Of those which were eaten, they were most likely the young lambs (up to the age of about three months). Lambs, however, were also necessary to replenish the flock or replace old sheep. The majority of the sheep were cultivated for wool and milk. It should be remembered that in the ancient world it was possible to raise lambs only by forgoing the milk of the mother which was necessary to nourish the young lamb. If the farmer intended to milk the mother then he had to forgo the continued development of the lamb. The farmer, however, could not have both mother's milk and also raise the lamb to adulthood. Ancient traditions indicate that sheep were for the most part identified with wool, while goats were associated with milk. Thus, for instance, it is stated: "Goats are evaluated in accordance with the fact that they are milked while ewes are evaluated in accordance with the fact that they are shorn" (T Bava Mezia 5:4). Another tradition states: "One who goes to milk his goats and to shear his sheep" (BT Bava Mezia 74a) or "a goat for its milk and a ewe for its fleece" (BT Shabbat 19b *et al.*; BT Ketubot 79b). The Mishnah (M Hullin 11:1 and parallels) explicitly states that the laws pertaining to the first fleece apply only to ewes and not to one who cuts off the fleece of his goat. Regarding the laws of mixed kinds (*kilayim*), PT Kilayim IX, 31d states that "wool is only the wool of rams," meaning essentially that wool came from sheep. Since the first wool shorn from the fleece was considered holy and had to be set aside, wool of a species which was exempt from such a requirement, such as that of a goat, would be rather unimportant. Thus, the grazing industry served as the source of the small amount of meat that was eaten, of milk and its products, and especially of wool.

The ancients attempted to estimate the amount of wool that could be produced by a sheep. Only those sheep which could produce this amount were included within the obligation to set aside a small amount from the first fleece for the priest. The Mishnah states: "R. Dosa b. Harkinas [80–110] says, five sheep which produce each a fleece the weight of a *maneh* and a half are subject to the Law of the First of the Fleece. . . . And how much should one give him [= priest]? The weight of 5 *selas* in Judah, which is equal to 10 *selas* in Galilee, of bleached wool, but not dirty wool, sufficient to make a small garment" (M Hullin 11:2). The weight of a *maneh* and a half cited above is how the Babylonian Talmud understood the Hebrew phrase *maneh*, *maneh ve-peras* written in the Mishnah (BT Hullin 137b). BT also understood the *maneh* to be 40 *selas* or all-told the amount would be 60 *selas*. T Hullin 10:4 understood the phrase in the Mishnah to be two and a half *manehs* or all-told 75 *selas* (based on a *maneh* of 30 *selas*) and on the average of 15 *selas* to a sheep. As can be seen, it is somewhat difficult to determine the weight of the *sela*. The *sela* was the equivalent of a *sheqel* and the *sheqel* of the Bible was 14 grams (Meshorer 1967, pp. 154 ff.). However, the ancient traditions mention lighter *sheqels*. Thus, the average sheep could produce yearly 180–210 grams of wool or 12–15 *selas* (which is quite poor in comparison even with modern minimal standards). The amount of wool mentioned in the Tosefta would be enough for three garments for small children, since M Hullin 11:2 states that 5 *selas* was enough for one small garment (this measurement is also cited as the amount that a woman had to weave according to the Mishnah – M Ketubbot 5:9). It is likely that the garment of an adult weighed three times the amount that a child's garment did. Within four years, therefore, it would be possible to produce the amount of wool necessary to clothe the entire family. However, since most people wore several layers of clothes, it would have taken somewhat longer to produce the wool.

These estimated figures would explain the shortage of garments in Palestine. The sources describing this reality, however, seem to reflect the reality of the Galilee. As we have seen, there were many more sheep in Judaea, and thus there was also a greater supply of woollen garments. The Judaean wool was not only for local consumption, but also served as the raw material of the textile industry producing for export. We shall discuss this point as well as the textile industry in Judaea further on in our study. We shall also examine the possibility that flax served as a substitute for wool later on. In any case, there was not too much profit to be made from sheep grazing. True, R. Johanan did say that anyone wishing to become rich should raise sheep (BT Hullin 84a–b), but this was possible only if large tracts of land were available.

In areas bordering on the desert (such as in the southern Mt Hebron region) or in the Judaean desert itself, there was not too much else that could be done with the land. In settled areas with agricultural potential, however, grazing was a very poor substitute for any other agricultural endeavor. This can be easily shown by examining the prices in the Edict of Diocletian. The minimum amount of wool that can be produced per sheep per year is 200 grams. Modern sheep farmers have managed to raise the figure to a kilogram of wool per year. For the ancient world, therefore, we shall use the estimate of 600 grams of wool per sheep per year (2 pounds). The best price available for wool according to the Edict of Diocletian (paragraph 25) was 175 dinars per pound or 350 per year and this, it should be remembered, was the maximum price. For this price, according to the same price list, one could buy 3.5 modia of wheat (33 kilograms). This is the yield of a quarter-dunam sown with wheat seed. Even taking into account that a wheat field was cultivated only every two years, the figures above would seem to indicate that the profit from one sheep was equal to that of half a dunam of wheat.

The matter, however, was not that simple. A single sheep needed grazing land of 4–5 dunams of untilled land (Seligman *et al.* 1959) and, therefore, the cultivation of wheat would be 8–10 times more profitable than the raising of sheep. The conclusions are somewhat tentative since local farm conditions as well as the profit from the meat must be taken into account. There are, though, additional factors to be computed into the profit from a wheat field such as that from straw, etc. In any case, it is clear that it was far more profitable to cultivate wheat than to graze sheep.

I.8.3 Pigs

In most countries, the pig was considered an integral part of the farm livestock. This was not the case in Palestine in general and in Jewish Palestine in particular. The ordinance against eating the flesh of pigs was considered to be very important by the Jews and was considered also to be one of the distinguishing characteristics of the Jew in the ancient world. Many non-Jewish writers were familiar with this prohibition. Macrobius (*Saturnalia* 2. 41), for example, cites in the name of Augustus that *"melius est Herodis porcum esse quam filium"* (it is better to be Herod's pig [at court] than to be his son). His sons were often put to death. A pig apparently had a better chance to live to old age, not being eaten. Apion, Plutarch and others also testify to the fact that the Jews did not have too much to do with pigs (Josephus, *Contra Apionem* 2. 37; Plutarch, *Quaestiones Convivales* 4. 5. 2). Porphyrius states that there were no pigs to be found in Judaea and Phoenicia (*De Abstinentia* 1. 14 – third century). Later on he does seem to qualify this statement by saying that Jews do not eat pigs (2. 61), but in any case, the gist of the first statement seems to be that pigs were not too prevalent in Palestine.

The Torah specifically forbade only the eating of pigs. It was the rabbis who forbade also the raising of this animal: "In no place are pigs to be raised" (M Bava Kama 7:7). BT explains this aversion to the pig in light of an *aggadah* referring theoretically to the period of the Hasmonean civil war (BT Bava Kama 82b; BT Sota 41b; BT Menahot 64b). In any case the sages were apparently quite familiar with this animal and knew a great many details regarding its form and character (Feliks 1972, I, p. 52). Pigs were occasionally raised by non-Jews and it seems that even some Jewish farmers raised them. Jesus, for instance, met up with a flock of pigs in the eastern bank area of the Sea of Galilee (Matt. 8:28–34 and parallels). This region, which belonged to the territory of Hippos, had a mixed population and therefore it is not too surprising that pigs were raised there.

The Mishnah in Tractate Uktzin 3:3 states as a matter of fact that the carcass of a pig as well as that of a camel, hare and rabbit could be sold to a non-Jew any place in which there were non-Jews. Since the law is dealing with Jews, this would seem to indicate that pigs, after all, were raised by Jews. The Palestinian Talmud deals with damages caused by pigs (T Bava Kama 1:8; PT Bava Kama I, 2a; BT Bava Kama 17b; 19b). A Talmudic tradition even mentions the law regarding the placing of food before a pig (BT Shabbat 155b – it is not clear whether this *sugya* is Palestinian or Babylonian). To all intents and purposes, though, the pig was probably not a common sight on a Jewish farmstead and probably was found more often on non-Jewish farms (PT Avodah Zarah III, 42a; BT Avodah Zarah 39b). Thus, for example, PT Terumot VIII, 46b–c mentions a non-Jewish swineherd in Tiberias who later on became prominent. Three strata of population have been uncovered in Tel Hefer in the Sharon. In the earliest (up to the year 500), many bones were discovered, but none that could be identified with those of swine. In the later strata, pig bones were found in addition to those of other animals. The excavator of the site sees the change in animal bones as representing a change in population from Jews or Samaritans to pagans or Christians (Porath *et al.* 1985, p. 169).

It is likely that the raising of pigs was of great economic importance in the non-Jewish communities of Palestine, but it is difficult to prove this assumption since there is only a minimal amount of material available on these communities.

I.9 Supplementary farmstead endeavors

I.9.1 Animals

The smooth running of a farmstead required animals for plowing and transport. A cow and an ox or a pair of oxen could fulfill the purpose of plowing fields (Feliks 1963, pp. 51–5). Not every farmer owned animals for this purpose, and therefore rabbinic literature records many instances of borrowing or renting animals in order to plow a field (M Bava Mezia 6:4; *et al.*). The donkey was used as a beast of transport, usually for short distances such as between fields and the residence of a farmer, but sometimes to transport over longer distances such as to the nearest city or market. Horses, mules and similar animals were found on a much less frequent basis and only for transport. They served no purpose whatsoever in the Jewish farmstead (Krauss 1924, I, 2, pp. 170–8).

Fodder was generally provided for farm animals and in this context many sources mention grass, leaves and especially legumes, vetch, clover and alfalfa. These were apparently grown in wheat fields during those years in which wheat was not cultivated in them. It is also clear that animals grazed in the fields particularly during the winter when wild grass began to flourish. Animals were also allowed to eat leaves and thin branches of fruit trees after the fruit had been picked.

I.9.2 Doves

I.9.2.1 Columbaria installations

Only a few ancient Jewish sources mention the raising of doves. In order to understand this economic endeavor it is necessary to study the installations referred to in scholarly literature as "columbaria." The columbaria were usually hewn out of the sides of caves in the form of triangular *cochim* or niches (measuring 20 cm in length, 20 cm in height and 15–20 cm in depth) or at times square ones (about 20 × 20 × 20 cm, see Figure 41).

The workmanship of the niches is usually of a high level and quite precise. They are mostly arranged in long lines along the wall of the cave and often contain shelves and troughs. Most of the columbaria caves are located in the *shephelah* of Judaea and only a very few are located in other regions of Palestine (Tepper 1986). Most date to the Hellenistic period and only a very few were used after that (Kloner and Hess 1985; Oren 1968; Siegelman 1970; Yadin 1966, pp. 138–9). Many of the columbaria installations were abandoned, some on quite short notice and even in the middle of their preparation. During a later stage (Roman?) some of these installations were part of olive press installations or quarries.

Scholarship has provided two explanations for the columbaria installations. The first associates them with burial installations of some form or another, while the second explains them in terms of the raising of doves, the manner in which we have explained them up till now. The phrase "columbaria caves" is of course a modern one and reflects the latter explanation. A detailed archeological analysis of these installations is outside the purview of our study. It is necessary, however, to deal somewhat with this matter since unless it can be shown that these installations are connected to the raising of doves or pigeons, it will be impossible to use them in reconstructing the ancient dove-raising industry and it is unlikely that we shall be able to fully understand this industry and its economic implications for the rest of the Palestinian economy.

The basic factor leading scholars to identify these structures with burial installations is the fact that they resemble burial caves of the common people in Italy in such places as Rome and Ostia. The major difference, however, is that in the *shephelah* the niches do not contain a depression in which to place the bottle with the ashes of the deceased. Moreover, the level of building in the Judaean niches is much higher than that in Italy and many more niches are included in the Judaean installations. The possibility that these niches are burial installations has resulted in a number of difficulties. (1) Cremation is forbidden according to Jewish law. There was of course a prominent Idumean settlement in the *shephelah* of Judaea and the destruction of that settlement with the Hasmonean conquest in 125 BCE would explain perhaps the abandonment of these installations. However, the Idumean settlement is

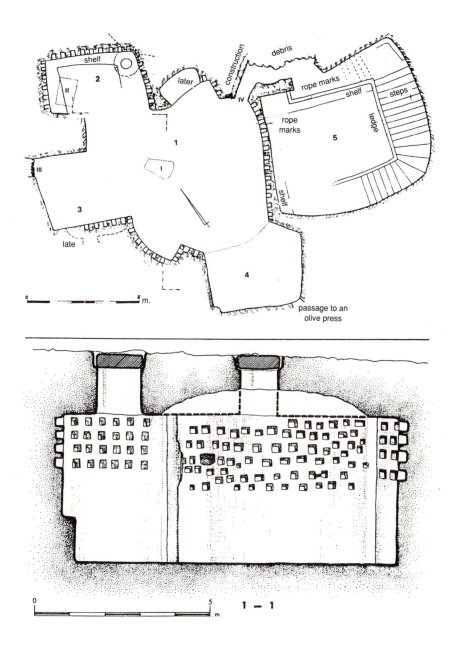

Figure 41 Columbaria at Maresha, *shephelah* of Judaea. After Kloner and Tepper 1987, p. 123.

not exactly contiguous with the area in which the columbaria were found and this certainly does not explain the small concentration of these installations in the coastal region (Seligmann 1970). (2) The number of installations found is very large. According to Tepper, there were in Judaea about 500 such installations containing about 160,000 niches, and it is likely that not all of these installations have been discovered. Around the small settlement of Hellenistic Marisa, for instance, which was only about 120 dunams, some 65 installations have been uncovered containing more than 10,000 niches. Sometimes 10–12 installations have been discovered in rather small villages. It is difficult to assume that such settlements needed so many burial caves. Since the installations are also found in so many settlements, it is also impossible to claim that they are regional burial sites.

A number of scholars such as Oren, Kloner and Tepper claim that these niches were used for the raising of doves and especially those referred to as *hardasiyot*. The information available on these doves can be summarized as follows. (1) The doves or pigeons were considered domestic. They were fed in a regular and orderly manner and many sources relate that they were available for immediate use (M Hullin 12:1; M Shabbat 24:3 *et al.*). (2) The cote of these doves was known to be rather well made and built in the form of long lines. Talmudic tradition tells a number of tales in relation to this particular type of dovecote (BT Hullin 139b). (3) It would appear that by the middle of the third century CE at the latest, these doves were no longer raised in Palestine. Various *Tannaim* dispute as to the exact name of these doves (BT Hullin 139b; Oren cited above; Epstein 1948, pp. 27–9). Rav Kahana, a Babylonian *Amora* who was in Palestine for a time, is able to explain the nature of these birds. All this would indicate, though, that they were not raised at that time (BT Hullin 139b). This seems to fit the information that we have regarding the columbaria installations and particularly the fact that they were not in use during the Roman period.

Most of the dovecotes mentioned in Talmudic literature are not those found in the columbaria caves but rather were built and some, at least, were found in courtyards of residences and discussed in Talmudic literature regarding the laws of partnership in courtyards (M Bava Bathra 2:5 and parallels; M Shabbat 24:3). Some were undoubtedly found in a second storey or attic such as was the case in Egypt (*P.Oxy.* 1207). These doves are referred to in Talmudic literature as "doves of the second storey" (*'aliyah*) (see our discussion below). However, there are also references in Talmudic literature to dovecotes hewn in caves (T Meilah 1:24) and one source says that the regular form of a dovecote (BT Sukkah 7b) was circular, which is in keeping with one of the less common forms, at least, of the columbaria installation.

Yadin discussed an attempt or "experiment" in which he sought to determine if the doves could be raised in the columbaria niches (Yadin 1966, pp. 138–9). However, Yadin's efforts could hardly be described as a scientific experiment. Tepper, however, found columbaria-like installations in modern-day Iran and in Karanis (Roman Egypt – Field 1950). Similar installations have also been found in Cappadocia in Turkey, and in France. The local inhabitants explain that these were used for the raising of doves, but this is only hearsay. Such installations built above ground have also been found in the Cyclades of Greece (Goulandris 1979; Baud 1959). The inclusion of troughs, shelves and cisterns in these installations would also seem to indicate that they were for the purpose of raising doves. Thus it would seem likely to assume that these columbaria were for the purpose of raising doves.

I.9.2.2 Doves and the economics of the farmstead

There are no sources attesting to the raising of doves for profit during the Biblical period. As we have already seen, though, during the Hellenistic period and the early Roman period, the raising of doves was rather widespread in the *shephelah* of Judaea. According to the *midrash*, a pair of doves living in a niche could give birth to a pair of doves a month (Shir Ha-Shirim Rabbah 1:63 and parallels). Needless to say, this number is an exaggeration. Modern-day scholarship would indicate that the dove can produce offspring four times a year. Therefore, in spite of the apparent exaggeration of the *midrash*, there seems to have been a rather high level of cultivation of doves (see below). According to rabbinic sources, the first pair of offspring were not taken out of the nest, but replaced the parents as they aged and lost their fertility (M Bava Bathra 5:3 and BT Bava Bathra 80a). If we assume that during the course of a year there were 5–6 sets of offspring and that the first set remained in the nest, then the dovecotes in the *shephelah* of Judaea produced 800,000 doves during the year and about 120 tons of dove meat (at approximately 150 grams per dove). Additional profit accrued from the accumulated dung of the doves used as fertilizer which was, of course, extremely important for the farmer.

As we have seen, only a minimal amount of meat was consumed, whether beef or dove meat. This would make the above figures somewhat suspect. Oren (1968) has collected a great number of sources regarding the cultic use of doves (cf. Pollard 1977, pp. 89–91). The only expression of the cultic use of doves for the Jews, however, was the Temple in Jerusalem. Tens of thousands of pilgrims used to come up to the Temple in Jerusalem and were required to offer up a number of sacrifices, whether on a festival or on a weekday. Pairs of doves or pigeons were commonly offered up for sacrifice by the common people who could not always afford more expensive animals such as sheep (Lev. 1:14). The regular sacrifice of doves consisted of a pair of young female birds (M Hullin 1:5; T Hullin 1:15; BT Hullin 22a–b). This system of bringing up very young doves to the Temple, and thereby removing them at quite an early age from the nest of their mother, explains the rather high rate of producing offspring mentioned in the sources. In any case, if our assumption that the majority of doves were for sacrificial use in the Temple is correct, the rapid decline of this economic sphere after the year 70 CE or so would be quite understandable.

During the Javneh period (80 CE–132 CE), the attitude of the sources seems to change. A number of *halachot* limit the area in which doves may be raised or the area in which dovecotes may be constructed (M Bava Bathra 5:2). These sources seem to fear the ecological dangers inherent in the raising of doves. The attitude toward the raising of doves reflected these ecological fears and not only the fact that after 70 CE the market for doves had become much more limited. The feeding and raising of doves exacted a rather high economic price. The dove requires a daily fare equal to about 10 per cent of its weight. Only about half of the dove can be consumed. Thus, to produce a gram of meat requires an investment of twelve times that amount (the assumption also being that a dove is slaughtered at about the age of one month and that it is also necessary to feed its parents, all-told about sixty days of food for every dove. These assumptions, of course, represent only estimates and not exact calculations).

The vast majority of the food given to the doves was grown and produced particularly for them (35 per cent–50 per cent of their food consisted of wheat or legume seeds). Part of the food they consumed came from left-over items from the farm or consisted of food that the doves found themselves such as insects. Much of this, such as insects, served no other purpose and would not have been used by the farmer. The seeds, though, probably would have been put to some use. Thus it would seem that the farmer had to grow or produce about half of the food consumed by the dove. The entire dove population would require, therefore, about 1440 tons of food (120 × 12 = 1440). To produce this amount of grain would require about 10 square kilometers (according to the figures cited in I.2 above). In a settlement such as Hirbet Shem Tov, for instance, 2,000–3,000 niches for the raising of doves were discovered. To feed them would require 18 tons of grain growing in an area of 120 dunams or 12 per cent of the entire agricultural region of the settlement. All this would produce 1.5 tons of meat. It is also necessary to take into account the ecological damage caused by the birds by eating seeds etc. Only a unique economic factor such as the Temple could justify such a high investment.

As long as agriculture in Palestine was not too intensive, it was possible to feed the doves and for that matter the populations of most settlements with what was produced in the various large tracts of land without investing additional manpower. As the population increased, however, and as agriculture became more intensive, this method of feeding the doves became economically unfeasible. The same would appear to be true regarding the grazing of sheep and this would explain the traditions from the Javneh period which forbade grazing near settlements.

After the destruction of the Temple, the raising of doves did not cease completely, but had only minor importance in the economic life of the average farmstead. Some of these doves or pigeons were not even domesticated and were raised in second storeys or in nests found by chance. These are the doves who nest in undergrowth (*tfahin*) or those of the *'aliyah* mentioned in a number of sources (T Hullin 10:13; T Shabbat 18:4; BT Bezah 24a *et al.*). The constructed dovecotes were often found in a courtyard with access to them via a ladder (M Bava Bathra 5:2; M Bezah 1:3 *et al.*). These, however, were not fed in a special manner, or special food was not produced for them, and what they consumed was taken from available matter in the fields (BT Shabbat 155b). At the most, the farmers refrained from uprooting wild grass "since they are preserved for doves" (PT Kilayim I, 26d). Even so, the feeding of regular pigeons was incumbent upon man, and it was forbidden to feed them on the Sabbath (M Shabbat 24:3; M Hullin 12:1).

Thus the dove-raising industry was of importance in the *shephelah* of Judaea, at least, from the third century BCE until the first century BCE. The industry declined with the destruction of the Temple, or perhaps even before, and from that time afterwards it returned to its natural place as a supplementary sphere of economic activity in the average farmstead.

I.9.3 Fowl

I.9.3.1 Description

During the Biblical period fowl and poultry were not raised domestically. The first information we have regarding this endeavor is from rabbinic literature dating from the end of the first century CE (T Bava Kama 8:10). The chicken was the most important of the domestic fowl ("the choice among fowl – the chicken" – BT Bava Mezia 86b). In our discussion above regarding doves we discussed a number of sources (I.9.2.1) in which it is also stated that fowl were considered appropriate food normally found at the farmer's home ("at one's disposal"): "Which are they that are not at one's disposal? Such as geese and fowl that made their nests in the open field. But if they made their nests within a house, or in the case of *hardasioth* doves" (M Hullin 12:1). Doves were fed by the farmer and therefore they could also be fed by him on the Sabbath since "their food is your responsibility." M Shabbat 24:3 adds: "And fowls may be made to take up food. Water may be poured into bran, but we may not mix it [into a mass]. And water may not be placed for bees or for doves in a dove cote, but it may be placed before geese, fowl and *hardasioth* doves." A number of sources describe the feeding of fowl such as those laws which relate that they were fed vetch (M Terumot 11:9; M Pesahim 2:1; 2:7; BT Menahot 24a *et al.*). Much of the food for fowl, however, was acquired by the fowl themselves in the course of their wanderings around the various courtyards of the settlement or through the settlement itself. Many laws discuss the damage caused by these fowl in the course of their perambulations through the settlement (M Bava Kama 2:1; M Taharot 3:8; BT Yoma 75b *et al.*).

I.9.3.2 The chicken coop

Chickens were generally found in the courtyard in the "chicken house" or in the "chicken coop" (*lul*). Some of these were rather well built (BT Pesahim 8:1; PT Yoma I, 38c; Bava Bathra III, 13a). The chicken coop was also found in a shared courtyard. R. Jannai (third century) explicitly states that "even the chicken house has four cubits" (BT Bava Bathra 13a). This would imply that the owner of the chicken coop had equal rights in the courtyard four cubits large (2–2.4 sq. m). M Nedarim 5:1 relates that neighbors in a joint courtyard who vow not to enjoy any benefit from one another may not use the courtyard "and both of them cannot put a millstone or oven there, nor can they raise chickens there." This law indicates that under normal circumstances, the chicken coop was to be found in the courtyard, at least at the end of the second century CE, the date of this *halachah* (T Nedarim 2:9).

In the third century, neighbors in a common courtyard who vowed not to derive any benefit from one another began, in the words of R. Eleazar, "to permit such benefit (regarding the raising of) chickens (in the courtyard), in spite of the fact, as R. Jose stated, that this was against the Mishnah (PT Bava Bathra III, 13a–b). In any case, all this would seem to show that it was quite common to raise chickens in the courtyard and problems arose only in those cases such as we saw above. As we have just seen, though, in the third century even the problems of neighbors, vows and courtyards did not apply to chicken coops, perhaps because of the great many chicken coops and the importance of raising chickens, although it is just as possible that R. Eleazar is really expressing a more stringent view to the effect that even under normal circumstances all neighbors must agree before it is permitted to raise chickens in a common courtyard.

Additional sources relate that both chickens and the chicken coop were found in the courtyard (PT Bava Bathra III, 13a–b). This would also seem to be implied in the many *halachot* allowing the chickens to be fed on the Sabbath and the chicken coop to be opened. If chickens or the chicken coop were outside the courtyard it would have been forbidden to carry the food there on the Sabbath (BT Shabbat 122b *et al.*). Raising chickens inside the residence itself was somewhat problematical and usually seen as a sign of poverty (Pirke Rabbenu Ha-Kadosh 3; T Bava Mezia 8:30). There were instances, though, in which the chickens were actually inside the house (PT Bava Bathra III, 14a; PT Eruvin VIII, 25a).

I.9.3.3 Raising chickens in the farmstead

The fact that the chicken coop was usually in the courtyard proves that the raising of chickens was only a supplementary activity in the average farmstead. Even so, it was also a rather important activity. Krauss devoted much energy to studying the various ways of cooking and baking with eggs as recorded in the ancient traditions, and came to the conclusion that the egg must have been rather important in the ancient diet (Krauss 1929, II, 2, pp. 271–6). Hens apparently provided a high yield of eggs. A tradition in PT Bava Mezia V, 10b recounts a case in which two partners divide the profits of their partnership based upon a previous evaluation of profits. The evaluation is based upon an estimation of profit of ten eggs per hen per partner a month, or in other words, the average hen laid 20 eggs per month or 240 per year. This is a high yield, proof of the care and energy which went into this endeavor. This also proves that the major function of the hen was to lay eggs which were collected before they were allowed to hatch.

As we have just seen, the consumption of eggs was very high. If we assume a rate of consumption of about half an egg per day per person, this would require the average village family to own 3–4 chickens (taking into consideration, in addition, the time necessary for eggs to hatch in order to occasionally replenish the group of hens).

The raising of chickens, therefore, was important and had a great influence on diet, even if this endeavor was somewhat auxiliary to the others of the average farmstead.

I.9.4 Other Fowl

I.9.4.1

In addition to chickens and doves, the sources also mention quail, geese, peacocks and pheasants. If we judge by the number of times that the birds are mentioned in Talmudic literature, by no means of course a foolproof method of evaluation, it would seem that the pheasant was somewhat rare, although not that unusual, while geese, ducks, quail and peacocks were rare indeed. The peacock, of course, was considered not only to be food, but also an ornament or decoration. A late *midrash* states:

> A parable is told of a king who told his friend: 'I greatly desire to see a peacock on my table.' The friend went at once and brought the peacock and put it on the table. He then ran to bring the knife to slaughter it. The king screamed and said to him: 'What are you doing? Did I tell you to do thus? Did I tell you that I wish to see a slaughtered peacock on my table? (Rather I said that I wished to see one standing.)

Since you brought the knife, here is a pheasant before you. Slaughter it in place of the peacock'.

(Aggadat Bereshit 31)

The story reflects the dining habits of the upper classes in Palestine and their relation to the two birds. The pheasant was considered excellent fare. The peacock was for something else. The story would of course also imply that both birds were raised in Palestine.

I.9.4.2 Pheasant

As we have just seen, the pheasant was considered somewhat rare, but extremely tasty. R. Joshua b. Hananiah was rather proud of the fact that the pheasant was also raised in Palestine. According to this rabbi, these birds were raised in Saidan or in Akbara (Kohelet Rabbah 2:11; Midrash Ha-Gadol on Deuteronomy 8:9. See above I.7.2.1). Saidan is to be identified with Julias, located to the northeast of the Sea of Galilee in the Betihah Valley which is partly flooded. There is no indication that pheasants were raised there domestically, rather they appear to have flourished there of their own accord. This highly commended food (BT Kiddushin 31a) was apparently hunted and trapped in this swampy region (Felix 1980).

I.9.5 Honey

I.9.5.1 Types of honey

One of the major sources of the necessary sugars required by ancient man was honey. Honey was acquired from both plant and animal. Honey from the plant variety could be produced from dates, grapes, figs or carobs. Honey is mentioned in the Bible as one of the fruits or crops which were the glory of the Land of Israel: "a land of wheat and barley, and vine and fig trees and pomegranates; a land of olive trees and honey" (Deut. 8:8 and parallels; Ex. 3:8). The reference here would appear to be to date honey, since it is unlikely that the Bible mentions carob honey, a rather unimportant fruit as we have seen above (I.3). In the Mishnah and Talmud period, though, date honey was rather rare. M Nedarim 6:9, for instance, relates that one who vows not to eat honey does not refer to date honey. Although it was theoretically possible to make honey from figs and grapes, these, as we have seen (I.3 above) were probably too important as cash crops to "waste" on the production of honey. Thus, in the final analysis, most of the fruit honey probably derived from carobs, which in itself was not a very important fruit (I.3). There were, however, limited amounts of the other types of fruit honey.

I.9.5.2 The honey of bees

An important source of sugar and the sweetening of food was the honey of bees. We know very little about the production of honey in the Roman Empire. There are a few references to it in the Roman agricultural writers (Charles 1942; Fraser 1931) and a small amount of archeological remains (Mellor 1929; Crane 1983; Graham 1975, 1978; J. E. Jones *et al.* 1973). There is also a minimal amount of information on this subject regarding the production of honey particularly in Palestine, but what information there is serves to supplement what we know about the Roman Empire in general (Krauss 1909a; Bodenheimer 1956, II, pp. 317–20; Z. Safrai 1988). The honey of bees was not domestically produced during the Biblical period, but was the product of nature (I Samuel 14:26–30). This appears to be the case in the Hellenistic period as well. The functionaries of Zenon who visited Palestine in the second century BCE imported honey for their use from Syria (*PCZ* 59007). The Zenon Papyri, in fact, mention honey quite often, but not any produced in Palestine. Rather, it was imported from Syria or from Attica (*PCZ* 59680; 69012; 59014; 59426; 59311, etc.). Josephus, however, is apparently familiar with bee honey produced in Palestine, and relates that the date honey of Jericho is just as good as regular bee honey (*BJ* IV:468–9). It is only in the Javneh period, though, that we explicitly hear of the production of honey in the Land of Israel.

The bees resided in a hive. The hive, in the form of an elongated chest or extended cylinder, was usually placed with the entrance facing up. The hive was occasionally cemented to the ground. Other times it was placed on two stakes and sometimes just placed directly on the ground. One tradition describes supports for the hive in which the underneath of the supports was in the form of a cone. The hive was made from all kinds of material: straw or coarse cement referred to as *halma* (Safrai 1988b; T Bava Kama Kelim 6:3; M Oholot 9:1–14, 15; T Kelim Bava Mezia 1:4) or reeds only (M Oholot 15:1; BT Shabat 8:1).

The hive was placed in a field or in the wall of a house, or on the roof. These hives were permanent ones (M Bava Mezia 2:9 and parallels, and the sources cited above). The sources also mention mobile hives, moved perhaps in accordance with the weather or the seasons of the year (BT Shabbat 8a; M Sheviit 10:7; M Uktzin 3:10; T Uktzin 3:15; M Bava Bathra 2:10 *et al.*). The hives in the Roman Empire were generally fixed or permanent ones. In Egypt, however, the hives may have been mobile (*P.Strasb.* 59467), and those found in Greece could also be moved from place to place (Graham 1975). The hives did not require too much attention. The ancients did treat the hive during the periods when new swarms were being formed and protected it against the vagaries of nature and weather (M Bava Bathra 5:3 and BT Bava Bathra 80a).

A number of sources describe the removing of the honey from the hive.

The first stage in this process was to smoke the hive with the help of a *madaf* (a pipe made of skins). The second step was to remove the honeycombs themselves. Two combs were left in the hive in order to provide nourishment for the bees. Unlike the information given in the ancient Roman sources, Talmudic literature does not state how many times a year the honeycombs were removed or when this was done. It would appear from these sources, at least, that the beekeeper would remove the honey whenever he wanted to do this. There were, according to Talmudic literature, two stages in the production of the honey once the combs had been removed: heating (*hirhur*) and cutting (*risuk*). In the first stage, the honeycomb was heated by fire or pierced and the first honey was removed. Afterwards the honeycombs were cut, pressed and the honey was strained (M Bava Bathra 5:3; T Bava Bathra 4:7; BT Bava Bathra 80a; BT Shabbat 43a; BT Bezah 36a; M Kelim 16:7a; M Uktzin 3:11; M Shabbat 22:1; BT Shabbat 145b *et al.*).

Beekeeping was not a major pastime in the ancient Jewish farmstead and belonged rather to the auxiliary or supplementary fields of endeavor there. Some of the honey was apparently marketed. The beekeeper sold prepared honey, honeycombs or even complete hives (M Bava Bathra 5:3; T Bava Bathra 4:7).

The hive, as we stated above, was placed in the wall of the house or on the roof. Such locations are characteristic of the auxiliary spheres of the farmstead. Talmudic tradition mentions only once a rich merchant of honey (PT Peah VII, 20b). This was the situation in the Roman Empire in general. Varro (*Rust.* 3. 16) does mention farmsteads which specialize in honey (see also *P.Oxy.* 85; Johnson and West 1949, pp. 212–21), but in general this would seem to apply to tenants who had a number of hives. The intent seems to be also to the auxiliary or supplementary spheres of agriculture. There is even an inscription which states that the tenant could only maintain five such hives (*CIL* VIII. 25902).

Honey fetched a rather high price (M Bava Kama 10:4; T Bava Kama 10:25–6; Edict of Diocletian 3. 10–11). The honey trade, therefore, was of great economic importance. However, in spite of the fact that there is no clear data regarding the extent of production and trade, honey production was limited compared to the major agricultural pursuits we have described above.

I.10 Quarries

I.10.1

Palestine has very few quarries. During the Biblical period and other early periods there were apparently iron and copper quarries in the Galilee, the coastal plain and in the Jordan Valley. By the Hellenistic period, however, these quarries were no longer operational. There were important copper quarries in Punon in the Negev, but this is outside the area under consideration in our study (Löw 1969).

I.10.2 Salt

An extremely important mineral was salt. Salt was not only a spice, but also a necessary component of one's diet. Modern man receives part of his salt intake through the consumption of meat. The ancients, as we saw, ate meat rather infrequently and therefore it was necessary to find different methods to supply their need for this mineral. The minimum salt requirement per person per day was three grams. If there were approximately two million inhabitants in Palestine, two thousand tons of salt would be required for dietary needs. Additional amounts would be required for the drying of meat as well as for the curing of fish and the processing of olives (Löw 1969, pp. 137–70; Brisay and Evans 1975; Bloch 1976).

The Tosefta mentions two main sources of salt:

> Salt – this is the salt of Sodom, as it is written: 'neither shalt thou suffer the salt of the covenant of thy God to be lacking' – bring salt which is not 'lacking.' And what is this? This is the salt of Sodom. And how do we know that if he did not find the salt of Sodom that he should bring *Istarqanit* (Ostarkine) salt? Thus it is written (Lev. 2:13): 'Salt . . . salt' to include this salt
>
> (T Menahot 9:15 and parallels)

The source deals with the supplying of salt to the Temple, but would seem to be relevant to the use of salt in everyday life. As can be seen, the tradition mentions two sources of salt: *Istarqanit* comes from Sabkhat el Bardawil in the northern coast of Sinai and belonged to Egypt at that time (Dar 1980, pp. 232–5). Sodom, of course, is the famous site near the Dead Sea. The reason cited for the preference of the salt of Sodom is somewhat midrashic, namely that it "is not lacking" or does not cease. The salt from Sabkhat el Bardawil is collected from drained pools. After the pool has been drained and the salt collected, it must be filled again in order to renew the supply of salt. This might give the impression that this salt is lacking or ceases. The salt from the Sodom region is mined from salt mountains which would, of course, give the impression that they never cease. Salt could also be collected in the Sodom region from pools, but this apparently was not too common. Preference for mining salt from the mountains can be seen in the writings of Galen, who in his description of the Dead Sea mentions the salt of Sodom which is mined in the mountains there, and then comments upon the medicinal properties of this salt (*De Simplicium Medicamentorum Temperamentis*, 4. 20, 58–75). The salt from the Sodom region contains many sulphurous elements. The ancients were not fully aware of the health hazards of these sulphites. They did, however, find that this salt burned one's eyes and, therefore, decreed the washing of hands (especially the fingertips at the conclusion of the meal (BT Eruvin 17b; BT Hullin 105b). This *halachah* would also seem to indicate that the Sodom salt was the regular table and cooking salt of Palestine during the Roman period. Since, however, the matter of burning the eyes is found only in the Babylonian Talmud and is a much later explanation to an earlier law, it is doubtful whether this matter of burning eyes is applicable to Roman Palestine.

Another source of salt was the salt pools along the coast. The ancient sources relate that such pools existed along the coast of Caesarea and Dor. PT Demai II, 22c mentions a site called Migdal Malha (= salt) along this coast. Channels and installations have been discovered along the coast north of Dor. These are simple installations composed of a channel and a pool or at the very most two small channels whose volume was no more than three cubic feet (Ronen Olami 1978, no. 100, etc.; Raban 1987). The pottery remains at these sites indicate, however, that they were in use only in the Byzantine period. An important site with such installations was Beth el Meleh (Ronen Olami 1978, no. 99). A large group of installations which served perhaps for the production of salt was found near Dor (Olami, survey unpublished). As we stated above, though, these installations were apparently used only in the Byzantine period. Having examined the site, we come to the conclusion that they were rather small and at most could produce no more than ten tons a year, less than one per cent of the annual consumption in Palestine.

Salt was expensive. Transporting it, as well as trading in it, was often a source for exaggerated profits. Dar is of the opinion that the settlements along the coast of northern Sinai were meant to protect and aid the caravans transporting the salt from Ostarkine (Dar 1980, p. 236). Bloch has suggested that the border settlements generally identified with the network of settlements of the *limes* were in actuality supposed to protect the salt caravans (Bloch 1971). It is difficult, however, to accept Bloch's view, particularly in the light of the great amount of information regarding the role of these sites in protecting the southern border of settled Palestine from nomads and barbarians. The protection of salt caravans may have been a secondary function of the *limes*. In any case, the transport of 1,000 tons of salt required the use of 5,000 donkeys (or 13 a day and 100 a week), and such a vast endeavor would undoubtedly require a large degree of security.

As is well known, the production of salt and the trade in it was a Roman monopoly (Rostovtzeff 1957, p. 341, and pp. 688–9). It is difficult to know, though, whether this was the case in all provinces of the Roman Empire. It is also difficult to know the extent of this monopoly. Did it include only the production level or perhaps also wholesale trade and transport? There is hardly any material whatsoever available on this matter regarding Palestine, and the existence of a special salt tax in the Hellenistic period is of no relevance at all regarding the problem at hand. Peter the Iberian (p. 119) tells of a fifth-century CE Aaron of Acco who was in charge of Malhata (from *melah* = salt), but it is hard to know exactly what he did. The *Midrash* tells of a caravan bringing salt to a *polis*, and it is clear from the tradition that the reference is to independent merchants (Midrash on Psalms, 12:8 pp. 104–5). The Palestinian Talmud knows of a sage by the name of R. Abdimi Malha who was a salt merchant in Caesarea in the third century CE (PT Bava Mezia IV, 9d). From the context of the source it is clear that Abdimi was a private merchant, but it is impossible to determine the level of his trading, whether he was an important wholesaler or a minor merchant.

In summary, there is no proof that salt was exported from Palestine during the Roman period and it would even seem that some of the required amount of salt was imported to this province from Ostracine. It is impossible to determine the extent or the level of importance of the salt trade in Palestine, but it is clear that it was important. It is also impossible to determine how much of the profits went to the Roman authorities and how much went to local merchants or traders.

I.10.3 Asphalt

Greek and Roman sources mention quite often the asphalt and bitumen of the Dead Sea. These served as necessary ingredients of the embalming process, and were also of importance in the preparation of medicines. Asphalt from the Dead Sea is mentioned as early as the first half of the third century BCE by Hieronymus of Cardia (*Historia Diadochorum* 33). The Dead Sea area was considered a rather exotic and attractive area due to its geographic uniqueness on one hand (its salty and heavy waters) and the important agriculture in its adjacent regions (balsam and dates – I.3; I.6 above) on the other. The references to asphalt should be understood in this context. We will list some of these references now in chronological order: Xenophilus, *Historiarum Mirabilium Collectio* 151; Diodorus 19. 98–9; Vitruvius 8. 3, 8; Scribonius Largus, *Compositiones* 209; Dioscorides, *Materia Medica* 1. 3. 1; Pliny, *HN* 5. 72; 5. 2 65; 28. 80; 30. 5 178; Tac. *Hist.* 5. 5. 1; Galen, *De Symptomatum Causis* 3. 7 (a detailed description of the Dead Sea). Galen mentions the Dead Sea and salt in this description, but does not mention asphalt. Asphalt or bitumen are mentioned in a number of other works of Galen (*De Simplicium Medicamentorum Temperamentis ac Facultatibus* 9. 2. 10; *De Antidotis* 1. 2; 1. 12). There are also a number of other authors like Solinus who mention the Dead Sea and its asphalt, and so on, but these authors are usually dependent on earlier authors such as Pliny and there is really no reason to mention all of them. This list cited above is rather impressive. It should be remembered, though, that most of those mentioning the Dead Sea and its asphalt date to before the first century. Those authors after that time who describe or mention the Dead Sea usually do not mention anything about asphalt or bitumen there. It would seem estimated that the areas he described could produce about 14 pitchers worth of balsam (12 pitchers from the larger area and 2 from the smaller one). Each pitcher contains about three pints, or altogether the area would yield about 42 pints. The price of this was twice the price of an equivalent amount of silver (see *Historia Plantarum* 4. 4. 14 and 9. 1. 6).

Diodorus also described the area and states that balsam grew in a particular valley and that it was very profitable (2. 48. 9; 19. 98). Strabo mentions Jericho for the first time regarding the cultivation of balsam and states that the irrigated area of Jericho was only 100 *stadia* (about 20 kilometers). Pompeius Trogus (*Historiae Philippicae* 36. 31) states that the area cultivated was 200 *iugera*. This, however, was the size of a standard cultivated region which was then divided into centuria, and therefore the number is somewhat suspect.

The most detailed description of the area is found in Pliny. Pliny (*HN* 12. 111–24) states that already by the time of Alexander the Great, balsam was cultivated in the area. The large grove yielded 6 *congii* while the small one yielded 2 (*HN* 12. 117). These comments would seem to be simply an elaboration upon Theophrastus cited above. Pliny also mentions two groves, the larger one being 20 *iugera* (50 dunam) and the other one somewhat smaller (*HN* 12. 111), which were the property of the emperor and were part of the Roman *fiscus*. The value of the balsam was twice that of silver and it would appear that this statement was also taken from Theophrastus. Pliny estimates that the balsam groves brought the royal treasury about 800,000 sesterces in five years. He also describes the development of the region as a result of the balsam groves and in spite of Jewish attempts to damage them during the War of the Destruction. Josephus also describes a raid of the Zealots on the balsam-growing region of Ein Gedi (*BJ* 4. 403).

Other contemporary authors mention the balsam groves in the Jericho region (Tac. *Hist*. 5. 6; *BJ* 4. 469). Josephus relates that the area cultivated was 100–120 *stadia* (13–14 kilometers or about 52 square kilometers).

After the first century CE there is less information regarding the balsam groves and many of those who do mention them are dependent on the earlier references and do not reflect contemporary reality. Thus, for example, Solinus (third century CE) devotes a detailed description to the Jericho Valley in the course of his discussion of Judaea (*Collectanea Rerum Memorabilium* 34–5). This description, however, is essentially dependent on Pliny. Solinus states that the cultivated area was about 20 *iugera*. This would seem to be taken from Pliny. He adds that after the War of Destruction the cultivated area was expanded (35, 5). Pliny, however, does not really say this. He seems to imply that the cultivated area was just 20 *iugera* and that this reflected the situation in his time. However, from Pliny's enthusiastic description it is possible to conclude that the cultivated area may have been somewhat greater. In any case, the comments of Solinus are based upon Pliny and should not be seen as an independent tradition.

likely, therefore, that by that time the asphalt supply had been depleted and was taken out from the Dead Sea only on rare occasions. Proof of this is the fact that Galen is familiar with the bitumen of Judaea, but only for medicinal purposes and not that specifically of the Dead Sea. Likewise, Jewish sources do not mention asphalt and it would appear that its importance began to decline in the first century (about the same time that there was a decline in the economic importance of balsam. See I.6 above).

II. CRAFTS AND INDUSTRY

There were many types of labor and crafts in village and *polis*. To discuss them requires first of all that the various types of labor be distinguished. This is more in the nature of economic distinctions than in terms of technology. The various categories of labor are (1) farm produce labors – preserving the crop, transforming it into liquid (oil, wine, etc.) or pressing (dried dates and figs); (2) labors associated with export industries; (3) local industry; (4) labors which consist of providing services (we shall discuss these in our study of the service system later on).

II.1 Farm produce labors

As we have already seen, the processing of agricultural produce served three purposes:

(1) Investing labor in order to raise prices. This was usually the result of the difficulty in realizing profits based on agriculture alone (too many workers and a limited amount of land);
(2) Preserving the crop in order to market it at distant sites as well as maintaining the quality of the crop for greater periods;
(3) Decreasing the volume of the crop (oil, for instance, is 25–29 per cent of the volume of a similar amount of olives. Wine takes up 60 per cent of the amount of grapes from which it is produced). This also makes it easier to transport and to market the produce.

Talmudic literature and archeological remains have shown that there are basically three types of installations: (a) the wine press – usually found in fields (Figures 42–3); (b) the olive press – usually found in an agricultural center or city (Figures 44–5); (c) the mill for grinding flour. The last belongs to the second type of labor and we shall discuss it further on in our study.

In actuality, there were also other types of installations such as one for the preparation of fig honey or for carob and date honey. The purpose of such an installation would be to grind and press the fruit. There were also installations for the processing of flax (I.7 above and Figure 36), for the pressing of figs and for the drying of dates (T Terumot 31:6). Particular installations were necessary to beat wool, and there were even installations

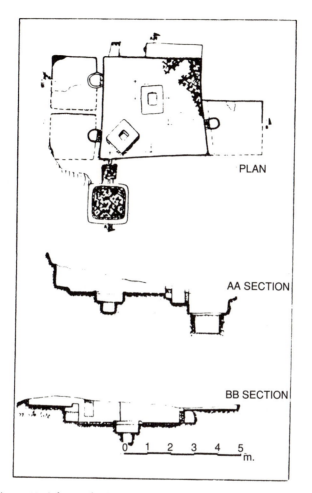

PLAN

AA SECTION

BB SECTION

0 1 2 3 4 5
          m.

Figure 42 Advanced wine press. After Hirschfeld 1981, p. 386.

for the preparation of pomegranate wine. At first, the individual seeds would
be separated from the fruit, and then ground in such a manner as not to
crush the seed, which would have given the drink a rather bitter taste.

In addition to references to such installations in the sources, it is possible
to find remains of such unusual types of installations. They are, however,
much less common than the three most important agricultural installations
discussed above – the wine press, olive press and mill. Needless to say, the
number of installations usually reflects agricultural reality.

From the sources discussed above it would seem clear that grapes and
olives were transformed into wine and oil respectively in the local settlements or offshoot settlements (see I.3 above). There is no reference to an

189

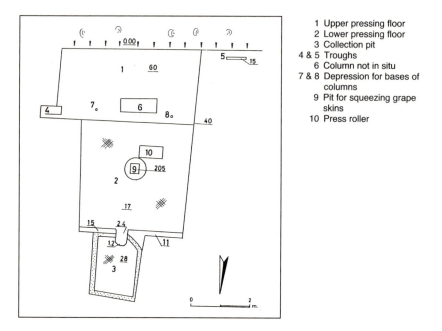

1 Upper pressing floor
2 Lower pressing floor
3 Collection pit
4 & 5 Troughs
6 Column not in situ
7 & 8 Depression for bases of
    columns
9 Pit for squeezing grape
    skins
10 Press roller

Figure 43 Advanced wine press. After Z. Safrai and Linn 1988, p. 183.

unfinished product being sent to a regional center and there undergoing the final stages of wine or oil production. Even spices or perfumes grown in the Jericho and Ein Gedi regions underwent all necessary production stages locally (see I.6 above). In spite of the fact that the procedure was undoubtedly quite complicated, all sources state that the inhabitants of these regions sold balsam and not some sort of raw material. Proof of this general principle is also found in the textile industry. Local farmers did not market raw wool or flax but sought to market a product at the most completed stage possible (see above I.7).

II.2 Industry

There were a number of industries in Palestine which were of importance on a national level: textiles, glass, pottery and perhaps the paper industry. Although the textile and glass industries were meant to supply some local needs, the majority of production was intended for export. Pottery was usually intended for regional markets. There is only a little material available on the paper industry, and therefore it is impossible to determine exactly to which markets the paper was sent.

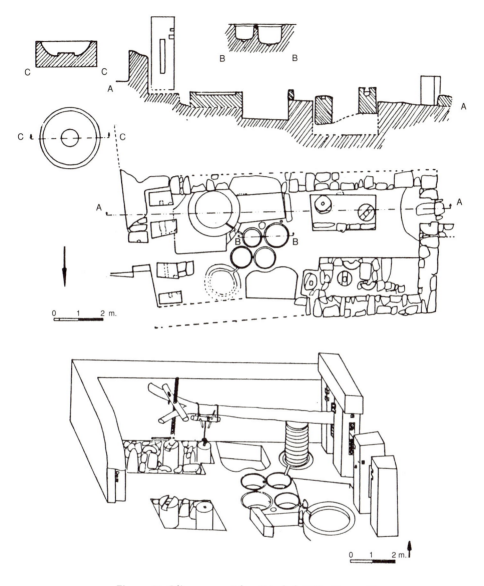

Figure 44 Olive press. After Frankel 1992, Figure 10.

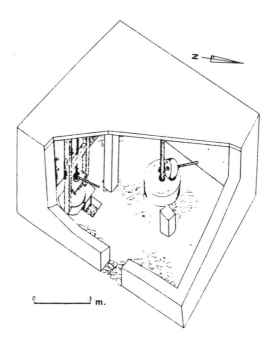

Figure 45 Olive press. After Yeivin 1966, Figure 9.

II.2.1 Textiles

II.2.1.1

The most important industry in Palestine was the textile industry. The basic raw materials were flax in the Galilee (I.7 above) and wool in Judaea (I.8). Secondary raw materials were purple dyes, the dye of the *hilazon* shell and plant dyes (I.7). The textile industry also made use of cotton, cotton wool, silk, etc. (I.7).

Many traditions attest to the importance of this industry. We have already discussed some of them above in our discussion of the flax industry (I.7). From these traditions it is clear that Palestine was considered a first-rate producer and exporter of textiles. Purple-dyed garments and flaxen garments were especially famous. The tremendous number of Talmudic traditions mentioning the weaving, dyeing, washing and sewing of garments as well as garments and textiles in general, would also seem to prove the importance of this industry. These Talmudic traditions were collected by Hirschberg (1924), and are discussed by a number of other scholars (Heichelheim 1938, pp. 189–98; Alon 1980, pp. 108 ff.; Avi-Yonah 1958). We shall not discuss the technical details regarding the production of textiles. There is, though, much information in Talmudic literature regarding such matters. Wild (1980) has pointed out, for instance, that there is very little information available on the production of linen during the Roman period. Hirschberg, however, has shown that Talmudic literature has much to say on this matter (Hirschberg 1924, pp. 68 ff.). The flax fibers had to undergo a great many treatments before the final product could be produced. There was, for instance, controlled soaking in water, removal from the water and the squeezing of the fibers. They were then dried, both in the sun and in an oven, beaten, and the dross was pulled away. At the end of all this there was a pile of clean soft fibers which could then be woven into thread.

There were fewer stages in the treatment of wool. The wool was cut from the animal, washed and spun into fibers. This was also the case with cotton and silk threads. The weaving process was for the most part identical for the fibers mentioned above, barring minor differences resulting from the quality of individual yarns. The following stages were also pretty much identical. This would also seem to be the case regarding the organization of labor and the economic structure of the various branches of the textiles mentioned above. The treatment of fibers in Palestine was essentially the same as that in other provinces, taking into account, of course, various minor differences. At the end of the Byzantine period, however, we hear of a special kind of loom in Palestine (*PG* 128:278).

II.2.1.2

As we saw above (I.7), most of the profit associated with the flax industry went to the person producing thread or fabric from the fibers. This was basically the same in the wool industry. The price of wool was rather low. The most expensive wool mentioned in the Edict of Diocletian (ch. XXV) came from Tarantum and cost 175 dinars for a pound. Wool from other places was cheaper. Weavers also received rather low wages (30–40 dinars a day, ch. XXI in the Edict). The prices of garments, however, were very high (ch. XIX). A soldier's coat, for instance, could cost as much as 4,000 dinars. It thus made a lot of sense for the farmer to undertake as many of the stages of production as possible in order to receive the maximum profit. This also provided the farmer with something to occupy his time during the winter months when there was not much actual farm work to do (see also Chapter 4, Figure 81).

There was additional profit to be made in the sewing of the garment, but this was usually undertaken by a professional tailor. Those stages of production associated with the fiber did not require too high a degree of professional expertise. The average farmer, therefore, could be expected to undertake those stages of production associated with the fiber, at least up to the weaving of the fabric.

The sources state that it is permitted to buy both woollen and linen products from a woman – the assumption being that her husband allows her to sell a small amount of flax (M Bava Kama 10:9). The woman, therefore, brought the flax up to the level of "product" (*kelim*) and was not selling the raw agricultural material. *Kelim* in the Mishnah usually refer to garments or to fabric. The Mishnah cited above, therefore, might indicate that the woman who sold the flax was able to undertake all stages of production necessary to produce fabric or a garment itself. However, M Ketubbot 5:8, which discusses the obligations of a woman to her husband, records the exact number of woollen threads that the woman must weave, and this would seem to indicate that she was able to undertake those stages of production up to the preparation of threads, but no further.

Talmudic literature contains additional material on farmers who grew flax as well as participated in at least some stages of production. PT Megillah IV, 74d relates an *aggadah* in which R. Hiyya is depicted as a farmer who grows flax and turns it into a net which he requires. Talmudic tradition also mentions that a tenant farmer who cultivates flax must treat it "until he has made it into *krzym*" (T Bava Mezia 9:19). It is possible that this refers to the preparation of the stalks (see Lieberman 1988, p. 114). It would seem that it was common practice for the farmer to undertake those stages of production necessary at least to produce thread.

These stages of production were usually the responsibility of the woman. Although R. Judah states that a woman should not be forced to work on flax "since it makes the mouth stink and disfigures the lips" (T Ketubbot 5:4 and parallels), it is implied from the manner in which the *halachah* is stated that the woman was accustomed to undertake this labor which, in any case, had odious side-effects only until the weaving of the thread. The combers, tailors and washers were considered to be professions which "Dealt with women" (T Kiddushin 5:14 and parallels). Talmudic literature also relates an instance in which a young girl went to take flax from the flax or linen worker (PT Yebamot XIII, 13c). Another tradition states that the Prophet Elijah told R. Jose how important are the women who received flax from their husbands and were able to make it into a worthy garment (BT Yebamot 63a).

Hirschberg (1924), however, claimed that the treatment of flax was man's labor. Hirschberg cites as proof the fact that in dozens of instances in which various labors associated with the treatment of flax are mentioned in Talmudic literature, the masculine form is used. This, though, is of no consequence, since the masculine form is very often used irrespective of the gender of the person involved. There were, of course, men who did undertake some of the labors associated with the treatment of flax, but the role of women in this sphere was apparently quite great. Weaving, for instance, was regarded particularly as woman's work or as the tradition states: "the wisdom of a woman is only in her spindle" (PT Sotah III, 19a; BT Yoma 66b).

As we have just stated, weaving was considered to be woman's work, and therefore when the rabbis wish occasionally to describe various positions of the female's body, they might do so in terms of positions of the body during weaving (M Negaim 2:4). A woman who works outside the house is referred to as "weaving in the market," once again demonstrating the female proclivity for this avocation (M Ketubbot 7:6, 9:4 *et al.*; Leviticus Rabbah 17:1, p. 371). The involvement of women in the treatment of flax also proves that these labors were undertaken for the most part in the local household, since women were not wont to seek employment too often outside the house.

II.2.1.3

Talmudic literature mentions many professions associated with the processing of flax such as combers, washers and tailors. The people associated with these labors are usually described as hired workers. Thus, for example, the Mishnah states that "sherds which are taken out by the washer belong to him, but those which the carder removes belong to the proprietor. The washer may remove the three threads at the edge and they will belong to him, but all over and above that will belong to the proprietor. . . . If a tailor left a thread sufficient to sew with, or a patch of the width of three fingers by three fingers, it will belong to the proprietor" (M Bava Kama 10:10; T Bava Kama 11:11–14 which also adds a weaver and a dyer).

In all the examples cited above, the laborers are described as hired workers and the raw material belongs to someone else. We mentioned above the tradition which relates the case of the "young girl who went to take flax from the flax worker," implying that the flax belonged to the girl (or most likely to her husband) and the flax worker had it temporarily in order to undertake some necessary labor.

The *Mishnayot* in Bava Mezia, chapters 6–7 mention laws which deal with artisans and laborers. Textile workers are often cited in the *Mishnayot* (or parallels) as examples of hired workers such as "one who hires . . . workers to take out flax from the soaking pool" (M Bava Mezia 6:1), or a hired worker who received yarn "to weave an outer garment (*talit*) for two *selas*" (T Bava Mezia 7:1 and parallels). A dyer receiving a garment to color is the most often cited example of an artisan receiving something and harming it (M Bava Kama 9:4 and many other traditions). A number of laws in the Tosefta cite the weaver and the sewer as examples of hired labor. Thus, for example, it is stated that "a weaver who left a candle at the side of a garment and it burned must pay for it because he receives payment." The garment clearly belongs to someone else and the worker only has temporary possession. Other laws, for instance, illustrating this point state: "He told him – I told you to prepare a shirt, and he answers that you told me a *talit*" or "I told you I would pay a *sela* and he said that you said two, as long as the garment is in the possession of the artisan, the owner must bring proof of his contention . . . after its time, the weaver swears and he takes it" (T Bava Mezia 7:15–17).

In all the cases cited above, the artisan receives raw material from the proprietor and returns to him an improved product. Another case mentioned in the Palestinian Talmud deals with "the garments of a priest which were being woven together with the garments of an Israelite." The Talmud then goes on to state that the weaver is permitted to use "burnt oil" which is oil that had been set aside as a heave-offering to a priest and had become defiled. Normally only a priest, his partners or those who work for him may make use of this oil. The fact that the weaver is allowed to use the oil proves that he is considered as a hired worker of the priest in preparing his garments as well as of the others whose clothes he makes (T Terumot 10:9 and parallels). This would also seem to be the impression received from many other *halachot* (M Sheviit 7:3 and parallels; M Kilayim 9:10 *et al.*).

The term *kwvs* which we have translated above as washer really included two different tasks: the artisan who washed garments (as we have translated), who certainly was a hired laborer, and an artisan who bleached wool, usually by soaking it in various cleaning and bleaching chemicals and is also called *kwvs* in Talmudic sources (Hirschberg 1924, pp. 106 ff.). The word *kwvs* appears many times in Talmudic literature. Sometimes it refers to the washer while at other times to the bleacher such as in the combination "combers, *kwvsym* and tailors." Both types of *kwvsym* were considered hired laborers.

The Jewish economy was based for the most part on independent labor (see below, Chapter 4.V.2). The use of so much hired labor in the textile industry was certainly an exception to the rule. As we stated above, most of the profits in the textile industry went to those who turned the fibers into fabric. It was, therefore, in the interest of the farmer to continue to process the flax for as long as possible to maximize his profits. However, the great amount of work in the Jewish farmstead as well as the tensions associated with it and the expertise required for some of the tasks associated with the processing of the flax forced the farmer to depend on hired labor.

II.2.1.4

As we saw above, some of those who worked with flax worked at home, such as the flax worker who was working on the flax of the young girl mentioned before (PT Yebamot XIII, 13c), and the worker who wove garments for the priest (see p. 196 above). Sometimes, however, the artisan worked at the house of the proprietor and was paid by the hour or in accordance with the number of pieces produced: "If he said to him – I told you to make a shirt and he [the artisan] replied – you said to make an outer garment [*talit*], if he [the artisan] was at the house of the proprietor . . . and if at the house of the artisan" (PT Yebamot cited above and III, 13a; Bt Bava Mezia 29b *et al.*).

Textile workers did not have much status according to the traditions in Talmudic literature, and their occupations were considered to be base and unimportant: "There is no meaner occupation than that of the weaver [*gardi*]." Only the most depressed types would work as hired labor for a minimal salary in a field in which there was so much profit to be made.

II.2.1.5

In addition to the system described above there are also references to "guilds" of textile workers and textile factories. The institution of the guild was especially important in the Middle Ages, but its origins are in the Byzantine period and are found in a number of provinces of the Empire. Such guilds or groups of workers in various fields are mentioned in Talmudic literature, but as yet there has been no real serious study on the matter. Egyptian papyri mention professional guilds quite often and especially those associated with the textile industry or weavers' industry and headed by an official called the *instonarchos*. It would seem that there were two types of textile guilds in Egypt (Ninnen 1987), one being essentially cooperative. Work in such a guild was undertaken in common. The head of the guild assigned the various tasks to the members and took care to pay the necessary taxes. The other type of textile guild in Egypt was of a less binding nature, and its major purpose seems to have been for the joint payment of taxes. The guild was considered as the taxable unit, and therefore the tax burden was not on the individual workers. All of the tasks associated with the production of the textile were done on an independent basis by the individual members. The source materials from Egypt and Asia deal for the most part with weavers' guilds and do not refer to flax workers. It is also difficult to know if the weavers' guild also included those who produced the thread from raw materials and the nature of the relationship between the various members of the guilds and those cultivating the flax (Wipszycka 1965). There is, however, one reference to a guild supplying merchandise to a weaving factory, and in this case it would seem that the guild engaged in weaving and in, perhaps, the first labors associated with the production of flax or even in a number of agricultural tasks (Wild 1979; *C. Th* 11. 1. 2).

Talmudic sources refer to a guild of linen weavers in Sepphoris (BT Avodah Zarah 17b) and inscriptions mentioning guilds of weavers have been found in Tiberias (Schwabe 1967, p. 181).

There are explicit references to linen weavers in Beth Shean or Scythopolis. A law in the Theodosian Code dating to 374 CE mandates a severe punishment to one who hides or smuggles flax workers. The section of the law which deals with matters concerning us mentions the weavers of the city who are called *linyfos publico*. The beginning of the law deals with *linteones* of other weaving factories without stating where they were located (Dan 1984, p. 197). The law then clearly differentiates between the *linteones* or hired workers in imperial factories and the public weavers in Beth Shean, a different class of weaver according to this law. These workers were required to pay tax or produce a specific number of finished products. Therefore, it would appear that the law makes reference to a professional guild which is required to pay taxes. The status, though, of individual members in this guild does not seem to be clear. Cyrillus of Scythopolis mentions weavers in Beth Shean who were apparently independent and who used to weave curtains voluntarily (*Vita Sabae*, p. 80). These women, it would appear, did not belong to a cooperative guild.

Inscriptions from Gerasa also mention guilds of weavers (Welles 1938, nos. 79–81, 190–2). It is likely that there were such guilds in other cities. There were synagogues of "Tarsians" in a number of cities such as Hamath Tiberias (PT Shekalim II, 47a), Lod (Leviticus Rabbah 35:12, p. 831 and perhaps BT Nazir 52a, but in the parallel in T Ahilot 4:2 the word "Tarsians" is missing) and Jerusalem. It is, of course, possible that the word "Tarsians" refers to immigrants from Tarsus. It is hard to imagine, though, that there were so many immigrants from this city and that they were organized to such an extent. It would seem therefore that "Tarsians" refers to guilds of textile workers.

Talmudic traditions also seem to refer to a guild of flax workers (*kytn'y*). Thus it is stated in PT Peah I 16a: "The guild of flax workers had a meeting and there was one in this guild called Bar Hovetz who did not attend. They said – what are we eating today? One person said "cheese" (*hyzyn*). He said – let Bar Hovetz come." The flax guild workers, according to this tradition, met with a representative of the government. The reason for the non-participation of Bar Hovetz is not mentioned in the tradition, but it is clear that his fellows were upset by his non-appearance at the meeting. It seemed to them that he was trying to avoid payments due from the guild to the government. The members of the guild, though, could not just come out and tell the government representative that Bar Hovetz was absent. The reference to the food, though, was a means of calling attention to his absence. The tradition ends with R. Johanan stating: "This is hidden slander."

As we stated above, in the organized guilds the tax burden was on the guild and not on individual members. The guild, though, could decide how the tax burden should be split up. Since the guild had autonomy in these matters, the representative of the government really had no say in the matter, nor indeed did it concern him, whether Bar Hovetz was present at the meeting or not, and R. Johanan would have seen nothing wrong in forcing him to pay. The government representative must have been present on the matter of an unusual and extraordinary tax which apparently was levied on an individual basis. In spite of the fact that the tradition relates an unusual individual tax, it also shows that the guild was a recognized sector and that there was a degree of unity in its ranks.

A greater degree of professional unity is seen in the following source:

"The wool workers and dyers are allowed to say that every transaction that is in the city (within their own fields), we shall all be partners in it" (T Bava Mezia 11:24). Thus, the wool workers and dyers seemed to exercise some degree of control over raw materials that arrived at a particular settlement. The production in this case seems to have been private, but the workers apparently distributed production quotas and dealt with the various taxes in a united manner.

Another interesting case which is mentioned three times in the Palestinian Talmud deals with groups of weavers who asked R. Ammi, a resident of Tiberias, whether they were permitted to engage in business with non-Jews on the festival days of these non-Jews. R. Ammi forbade them to do so, citing the teaching of R. Hiyya b. Abba: "The festival day of non-Jews is forbidden [for purposes of business]" (PT Avodah Zarah I, 39c and parallels). It is not known which festival this was. It appears, though, that a number of Jewish workers residing in a mixed city wished to profit from selling merchandise associated with or necessary for the non-Jewish festival. The source does not say that these workers were organized in a guild and it does not say in which city they lived, although it is not inconceivable that they formed a weavers' guild of either Tiberias or Beth Shean. According to the excavators of Gaba Hippeum, the installations discovered there belonged to guilds of flax workers (Z. Safrai and Linn 1988, and Figure 36). The installations are divided into units, and there is a clear association between the various installations within the individual units. This association is expressed by the use of a common source of water (a large cistern) and by the fact that excess water is drained off to other installations through a series of channels and ramps from one installation to another. The association between the various installations is most prominent in areas 1, 3 and 4. A large installation for the beating of the flax was discovered in area 3 as well as installations for the combing and subsequent stages of production.

According to our understanding of these remains, the flax was soaked in these areas and the guilds continued to undertake all other labors there, at least through the stages of producing threads. The weights from the spindles and looms found in this area and in other excavations there would seem to indicate that the flax was treated in this region to produce thread and fabric. There is no proof, however, that these later stages were also undertaken by the guilds.

II.2.1.6

The guilds in Beth Shean were called, as we have seen, *linteones* or *linyfus publico*. These workers, according to the Edict of Diocletian, produced completed garments since the edict gives prices only for clothing and not for fibers. Talmudic tradition mentions the sale of thread quite often. Thus, for example, R. Zera sent R. Bibi to buy a small spool of thread at the fair in

Beth Shean (PT Avodah Zarah I, 39c). Likewise, the Amora of "R. Isaac bar Tavlai found a wound spool of thread" and the Amora of R. Johanan found a similar one (PT Bava Mezia II 8b). The decisions regarding the finding of these objects is based on the assumption that the spools contain no distinguishing marks. It is clear, therefore, that these cases refer to thread, since if fabric had been found, there is no question that there would have been distinguishing marks and that it would have had to have been returned to the original owner. The legal decision allowing the finder of such spools of thread to keep them is based not only on the assumption just made, but also on the view of R. Simeon b. Eleazar who stated that: " *'anforia'* vessels need not be announced" (M Bava Mezia 2:1). The Babylonian Talmud had some difficulty in explaining the term *anforia* and eventually understood it to mean new utensils. The word, however, is probably just a jumbled form of "*emporia*," or a large market. The term was quite common in the eastern provinces and was even known to the rabbis (see Chapter 3.IV below). This would seem to imply that the spool of thread was also the type of ware commonly found in such a large market and, therefore, the property of the finder, if lost.

A number of other phrases associated with thread are mentioned in Talmudic literature. Thus, for instance, the rabbis mention a bobbin (for either woof or warp) or *kybwra'* or *sysyn* in Aramaic (Hirschberg 1924, p. 127). There was even a standard weight for such bobbins: "R. Eliezer says, its measure is with warp-clews from four for a *mana* which is forty for a *sela*" (T Kelim Bava Mezia 6:6). In other words, the bobbin of the warp weighed 10 *selas*, while that of the woof weighed twice as much or 20 *selas*. There seems to be a distinct connection between this law and the obligation of the woman to prepare for her husband 5 *selas* of thread in Judaea and 10 in the Galilee (M Ketubbot 5:9). It would seem, therefore, quite clear that the women were required to undertake those stages of production, at least up to the production of thread. The last two sources cited deal with wool. The obligation of the woman to weave pertained only to wool and the source regarding the weight of the warp was stated by R. Eliezer b. Hyrcanus, one of the sages of Lod during the Javneh period. As we mentioned above, Lod was a wool center at this time and in any case, the Javneh period sources deal to a much greater extent with wool than with flax.

II.2.1.7

It would seem, then, that the proofs stated above show that during the Mishnah and Talmud periods there were two major forms of organization in the textile industry in general and in the flax industry in particular. (1) The farmer, either by himself or with hired workers, undertook those stages of labor up to the production of cloth or a garment. The farmer was usually aided by his wife. Often even many of the early stages of production were undertaken within the framework of the flax workers guild. (2) The farmer undertook only those stages of labor up to the production of thread. The thread was bought either by individuals or by guilds or even by government factories and only then was turned into cloth and garments.

Both of these systems were operative at the same time and neither excludes the other. Most of the sources, though, seem to indicate that the first system was more widespread as well as more profitable. It is not impossible, though, that the government encouraged and even forced the implementation of the second system as part of an effort towards super-vision and centralization of agriculture and attendant industries. This would not have been inconsistent with Byzantine imperial policy. Needless to say, this last suggestion is merely a hypothesis and is based on general proofs and information pertaining to the Empire. This hypothesis, however, might be important in explaining the vast difference between the price of thread and the price of cloth in the Edict of Diocletian.

In any case, all of this indicates that most stages of linen production were undertaken by the farmer himself, or at least within the village or rural sphere. Clear proof of this is a *halachah* stated by R. Hoshaiah which is based on the assumption that there were settlements in the *Darom* in which all the men worked in the dyeing industry on a regular basis, and therefore their fingers were always stained (Tanhuma Naso 8).

As opposed to this, almost all the sources dealing with weavers' guilds pertain to the large cities of Palestine such as Tiberias, Sepphoris, Lod, Gerassa, Gaba, Scythopolis and Jerusalem. There are few traditions which do not seem to pertain to any place in particular (such as, for instance, T Bava Mezia 11:24), but this does not change the fact that the weavers' guilds were an urban phenomenon. It is not impossible that just as was the case in Carthage (*C.Th.* 11. 1. 2), the rural growers sent the product to the city after undertaking the first few stages of production. In any case, though, trade and export were undertaken through the cities. Proof of this would seem to be found in Chapter 29 of *Expositio Totius Mundi* which mentions only cities as textile centers.

Despite the fact that Palestine was considered an important textile center, and perhaps the most famous one in the ancient world, there was a chronic shortage in Palestine of garments in general and of linen ones in particular, and such linen garments were quite rare and certainly very expensive. Thus, for example, they are mentioned in BT Pesahim 109a as something that would bring much joy to women at festival times. Since the price for these garments was so high, it made much more sense for the small farmer not to use the garment himself, but rather to sell it. Another possibility is that most of these labors were undertaken as *liturgiae* (a form of imposed labor) and that in the final result, most of the profit reached either the rich or the government. The shortage of clothing would seem also to indicate that most of the workers involved in this trade were either hired workers or tenant farmers. This, though, would seem to contradict our contention that most land in Palestine in the second through fourth centuries was in the private hands of independent or small farmers. This matter will have to be studied further.

II.2.2 Glass

II.2.2.1

Palestine contains one of the most important quarries of sand for the production of glass. This type of sand is found even today in the Acco Valley and the ancient sources mention the mouth of the Belus River or the modern-day N. Naaman in particular.

Strabo already mentions the glass-sand in the Acco Valley (16. 25) and Josephus also describes the region (*BJ* 2. 189–91). Tacitus repeats more or less the same description (*Hist.* 5. 7. 2) and Stephanus of Byzantium does the same in his entry under Acco. The rabbis also describe the Acco Valley as a source of this type of sand. According to the sages this area belonged to the tribe of Zevulun. The Book of Deuteronomy describes his portion as: "The hidden treasures of the sand" (33:19). On this the rabbis stated: "Sand – that is glass." In the continuation of the tradition Zevulun complains: "O Lord of the universe . . . to my brethren you gave fields and vineyards, but to me you gave sand. The Lord said to him – in the end they shall have need of you for the glass-producing sand" (Sifre Deuteronomy 354:19, pp. 416–17 and parallels). We cite the tradition here according to the version in Yalkut Shimoni. Other versions read: "And to me you gave the *hilazon*." It is true that the *hilazon* was found in the territory of Zevulun (along the coast in the vicinity of Haifa), but Zevulun's complaint would not be understandable if this is the correct version, since the *hilazon* was a source of great wealth. The version we cited is much more logical since the sand is, after all, not fertile.

Strabo relates that the sand was taken from the Acco area and served as the raw material for the production of glass in Sidon, a city famous for its glass industry (16. 25–6). Tacitus, however, already stresses the connection of this region to Judaea when he states: *et Belus amnis Iudaico mari inlabitur* (The River Belus also empties into the Jewish Sea). The *midrash* also stresses the connection between Jewish Galilee and the sands of the territory of Zevulun. Although the Acco Valley theoretically belonged to Phoenicia, its population was Jewish and it would appear that much of the raw material from the coast was sent inland to Palestine to supply the glass industry there. From an archeological point of view, it is quite clear that the glass from the northern regions of Palestine is identical in style to that of southern Phoenicia (Barag 1970).

II.2.2.2

Many sources mention the glassmakers, their utensils and the types of vessels produced. Most of these traditions can be found in Brand (1978). Furnaces have been excavated in Beth Shearim (fifth century CE and afterwards), Sebastia, Kefar Yasif in the Acco Valley, Apollonia, Gerasa (Barag 1970, II, pp. 1–5), Jalama (second to fourth centuries CE (Weinberg 1988)) and in Mishmar Ha-Emeq (Z. Safrai and Linn 1988). Moreover, unpublished surveys mention dozens of settlements in the Galilee and in the Carmel, in which glass fragments were found which seem to point to the existence of furnaces. (Much of this unpublished material was discovered during the course of surveys undertaken by the author of the study. However, the conclusions must remain tentative until excavations or more detailed surveys are carried out.)

Most of the traditions do not state whether the glass utensils were for local use or for export. However, since glass utensils were very expensive and since there are so many traditions, it would seem likely that at least some of the glass was meant for export.

During the Second Temple period, glass utensils were still imported to some degree to Palestine. Jose b. Joezer of Seredah and his colleague Jose b. Johanan of Jerusalem (mid-second century BCE) decreed, therefore, that these imported glass utensils were defiled with the impurity of nations (b. Shab. 14.2). This, of course, more or less made it impossible to use these vessels. Not everyone was particular regarding the details of the laws of ritual purity, but many people were – particularly the upper classes, leaders and priests. It was also forbidden to use a defiled vessel in the Temple. The decree of the two sages mentioned above is usually explained in terms of the desire to protect local production by limiting imports. If this is the case, it is possible to ascribe the beginnings of the local glass industry to the time of this decree. The furnaces which have been discovered, though, date to later times. It is also important to point out that the economic implications of this decree are not as far-reaching or stringent as one might think, as we shall see in the course of our discussion regarding the impurity of pottery (II.2.3.3 below).

The glass vessels discovered in archeological excavations in Palestine date from the first century CE onwards, and from this time on and throughout the Byzantine period the glass industry flourished in Palestine. According to Barag, the very technique of glass-blowing was developed in Palestine or in southern Phoenicia and it was from here that techniques and styles were exported to the rest of the world (Barag 1970, pp. 273–7).

II.2.2.3

The sand was collected at the quarries and Josephus (cited above) relates how boats would come to the mouth of a river and there take on a load of this sand. The sand had to be purified in fire. It is not known exactly how this procedure took place. Strabo states that this procedure did not take place near the quarry, but does not add additional information. The burning of the sand produced a chunk of raw glass referred to in many sources as the *"bulos"* (Y. Brand 1978, pp. 156–9). The *bulos* was sold by weight to the glassmakers (M Kelim 29:6). It is not necessary for the purposes of our study to delve into the actual production of the glass. Such chunks of glass have been found at Beth Shearim, Tiberias and Appolonia (Y. Brand 1978, p. 159).

II.2.2.4

There is no information regarding the organization of glassworkers into guilds or similar groups apart from a single source referring to Biri (Baram? – PT Avodah Zarah II, 40c). It is possible that the source makes reference to an extended family of glassmakers. It is likely, though, that glassworkers were organized into some kind of guild since this industry requires a good deal of cooperation. Operating the furnace, for instance, requires the preparation of the raw material as well as of some type of fuel and a small furnace was more expensive to operate than a large one. A private individual or producer could not even fully exploit the potential of the furnace. There is little we can add, though, apart from these theoretical considerations.

II.2.2.5

Archeological excavations have uncovered many imported vessels. It is not known, however, whether these vessels were imported for the express purpose of importing glass, or whether they were simply used for storing something else imported to Palestine. However, some of these glass utensils were undoubtedly imported for themselves, particularly the very small ones which could not really store much. Such small vessels were also indicative of the common trade in small artifacts. Talmudic tradition makes reference to glass vessels from Sidon, an important glass-producing center near Palestine (T Kelim Bava Kama 3:11; Y. Brand 1943, p. 507). It is clear, therefore, that the imported vessels also included high quality expensive wares. On the other hand, there was also a great degree of export from Palestine and southern Phoenicia, and the vessels produced there often served as a source of inspiration for glassworkers in many countries (Barag 1970, pp. 230–77). We shall examine this phenomenon below (Chapter 4.VII).

II.2.3 Pottery

II.2.3.1

Clay pottery was basically an everyday utensil since most kitchen and work utensils were of this type. Pottery is also quite breakable and cannot be repaired. Thus any implement which was slightly damaged was usually discarded or, at the very most, use was made of its fragments. It was also quite difficult to clean clay pottery utensils properly. Thus, such utensils that were for storage or for cooking one particular item or food could not usually be used to store something else, especially liquids. The shape of the clay implements also made cleaning difficult. From a halachic standpoint, a clay pottery implement which had become defiled could not be purified, and there was no recourse but to break it. All of the above explains the high turnover in terms of the usage of these implements.

Pottery was cheap, since the raw materials necessary to produce them were readily found in nature (earth, water and fuel). The labor necessary to produce them was also cheap. This also explains why pottery which broke quite often could be replaced rather easily. In any case, the pottery industry was extremely important even if the pottery was intended for local usage.

The trade in pottery was by its nature regional. On the one hand, the kiln was capable of producing a great quantity of implements, while on the other hand the bulky nature of the utensils, as well as the fact that they were cheap, made it impractical to transport them over extremely long distances. Thus trade in these implements was usually limited to the local region.

II.2.3.2

There is a great deal of information on pottery in Palestinian Talmudic tradition. This literature mentions over 120 different types of pottery (Y. Brand 1953) and there are also references in Talmudic literature to potters, other workers associated with the preparation of clay utensils, kilns and other aspects of this trade – further proof of the importance of the pottery industry. There has not been sufficient research in this field. It is true that Brand studied most of the Talmudic terms associated with the pottery industry, but he made scant use of archeological material. There has been much work done on the technical aspects of pottery analysis, but little attention has ever been paid to its economic implications. Our discussion of the matter, therefore, does not really do justice to this important field, which awaits further detailed study. For the moment, the issue has been studied by Adan-Bayewitz (1985).

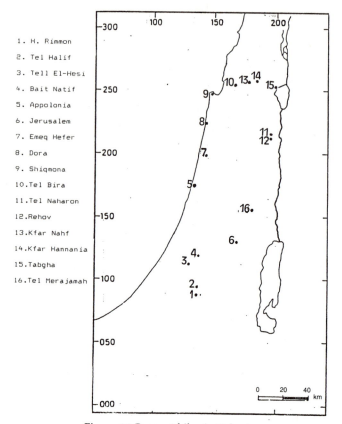

Figure 46 Potters' kilns in Palestine.

II.2.3.3

There is no way to determine the extent of pottery production in Palestine since there is insufficient numerical data regarding such factors as, for instance, the firing of the pottery, production costs, market prices and the rate of production.

Palestine was essentially self-sufficient in its basic pottery. This was not so, however, regarding special utensils. Excavations in both ancient cities and villages have uncovered large amounts of imported pottery from Asia, North Africa and even western Europe. It is true that some items were imported not for themselves, but rather for what they contained (such as wine or wheat – see below). Some bottles, plates, dishes and other implements, however, were imported primarily as pottery. Although, as we just stated, a great deal of imported pottery has been found at archeological excavations, there is not enough data to enable us to gain a full understanding of the matter. From an economic standpoint, the major question is not whether imported wares were discovered in one excavation or another, but the numerical relationship between these wares and local ones, or the relationship between these wares and imported vessels from other sites or different periods. Although this data can be collected, no one has yet made the effort to do so. Moreover, it is often difficult to differentiate between imported wares and local limitations.

The first attempt to answer some of these questions, at least partially, is that of Gunneweg et al. (1983). Gunneweg and his colleagues examined both the eastern (ETS) and western (WTS) terra sigillata pottery found in Palestine, especially that dating to the period before 70 CE. Their study indicated that there was a tremendous amount of pottery imported to the east from the middle of the second century BCE onward (the time of the Hasmonean revolt in Palestine). The pottery was discovered throughout the east, including Palestine. Most of the Palestinian sites, however, were not within Judaea. Most of the ETS reached Palestine from Cyprus and Syria and the WTS also came from the east, mostly from western Asia and a small amount from Italy. All of the Palestinian sites in which it was discovered were either non-Jewish or connected with the government in one form or another, such as Acco, Caesarea, Azotus, or the Nabatean city of Avdat, Samaria. Some of the sites were connected directly with the government such as the winter palaces in Jericho (p. 84), Masada or Jerusalem. Much of this type of pottery has also been found in Tal Anafa, which also had quite a clear Phoenician political orientation. This kind of pottery has also been discovered in Shivta and Nessana which are not real urban settlements, but they are also Nabatean and beyond the scope of our discussion. It is also important to remember that Gunneweg's important work cited above deals with the Second Temple period, which is really before the period under discussion in our work. Recently, imported pottery wares have been discovered in a number of excavations and surveys in the rural sphere, but it is still necessary to wait for the publication of the relevant ceramic material.

There is an additional reason why the economic implications of the importing of this type of pottery are not clear. Negev, who excavated the pottery factory in the Nabatean settlement of Avdat, claims that the pottery produced there was ESA (eastern sigillata A), which previously had been considered a type of pottery that was imported (Negev 1974, p. 24, pp. 34–5; id. 1986). According to Negev, only the raw material was imported to Palestine. The actual production of the utensils, in Negev's view, was a local matter. If this was the case, these "imported" vessels had to be relatively cheap.

Ceramic pottery remains of the late Roman and Byzantine empires in general have been partially examined by Hayes (1972; 1980). His conclusions are obviously based on utensils discovered up to the publication of his books. There have been many excavations in Palestine since the publication of his works, many of them as yet unpublished. Hayes, of course, had no access to any of these remains, and it would appear that he was not familiar at all with the material published in Hebrew, although only a small amount of the research is on pottery. Hayes's conclusions, therefore, should be considered only tentative.

According to Hayes, between 70–250 CE there were more or less no imported ceramic wares in Palestine. From the mid-third century CE, though, there was an influx of such wares from both east and west. As stated above, it is possible that his conclusions are not completely accurate. Elgavish, for instance, claimed to have discovered in Shiqmona imported ASA wares from as early as the second century CE (Elgavish 1977, pp. 9–11), although the majority of the imported pottery dates from the third century. Shiqmona was a small harbor town of regional importance. The discovery of imported ceramic wares here need not be indicative of the situation in the villages in the hills or mountains. Imported wares were also discovered in Caesarea from the second century CE (Levine and Netzer 1986, pp. 161 ff.). Even so, it is understandable that the remains are of great importance since there are so few excavations with remains that can be dated without question to the period of 70–250 CE. It is possible that the paucity of remains reflects difficult economic times. It is also possible, though, that the matter is only a coincidence, and it certainly requires further study.

As stated above, from the middle of the third century CE there was an influx of imported ceramic wares to Palestine, and they have been discovered not only in urban settlements, but in such rural settlements as Capernaum (Loffreda 1970, 1974), Meiron (Meyers et al. 1981, pp. 123–46), Nazareth (Bagatti 1969) and many others. In H. Sumaqa in the Carmel Range, approximately 80 per cent of the pottery discovered so far (third through fifth centuries) is imported (Dar, pers. comm.).

Usually there is no numerical data available regarding the scope of the importing of pottery. This unfortunately prevents us from analyzing the ceramic wares in terms of the amount imported, the direction of the trade and other relevant economic matters commonly discussed in scientific literature (as for example in Morel 1983; Peacock 1977; Garlan 1983, Tchernia 1983; Middleton 1983; and see Chapter 4.VI.2 below).

Importing and long-distance trading in beautiful or special ceramic wares was a common phenomenon in the ancient world, even in the periods which predate those studied in the present work. Imported wares reached Palestine from as early as Biblical times and even before. Even if the trade in this merchandise was rather limited in those times, it appeared to be acceptable for the rich to import or buy such wares. This is also the case regarding the Persian period. According to Stern (1973, pp. 138–44), local wares were for the most part for the use of lower economic or social strata, while those interested in showing off fancier wares imported them from Mesopotamia, Asia Minor or Greece.

All this, therefore, leads us to suggest a degree of caution in attempting to evaluate the importance of the trade in pottery as reflecting economic development of the Empire. Even in basically closed economic systems there was a degree of imported pottery, as we mentioned above. Even so, it appears that imported fancy ceramic wares became more and more commonplace during the course of the Roman and Byzantine periods, not only in the houses of the rich, but to some extent such wares could also be found on the table of the more common strata of society in both city and village.

According to Jewish law, imported pottery is ritually impure. Therefore, that segment of the population which observed the laws of ritual purity could not use this type of pottery. This segment of the population, though, was a minority (although we do not really know its size) and by the fourth century, this *halachah* was apparently not observed. However, the effect of this *halachah* on the importing of pottery vessels might prove to be interesting, and in fact we can hypothesize (but unfortunately not prove) that the small amount of imported pottery, at least until the beginning of the third century, was the result of this *halachah* and the laws of ritual purity in general.

II.2.3.4

Kilns for the production of pottery have been discovered at a number of sites in Palestine such as Beth Shearim and Apollonia (Barag 1970), Nahaf (Vitto 1980, 1986) and Kefar Hananiah (pp. 210–11 below). Literary sources also mention kilns at a number of urban sites and especially at rural ones such as Kefar Hananiah (T Bava Mezia 6:3 and parallels). A kiln in Kefar Hananiah was recently excavated by D. Adan Bayewitz (1987). Talmudic tradition also mentions one in Asochis (T Bava Mezia 6:3 and parallels; Z. Safrai 1985, pp. 44–8), Beth Ramtha (Midrash Tehilim 3:3) and in Sogane (M Kelim 5:4; T Kelim Bava Kama 4:4). Baramki (1936) discovered one at Beth Natif. There were also special ceramic wares named after the site at which they were produced such as the thin delicate "cups of Tiberias" (BT Niddah 21a; Y. Brand 1953, p. 212), the large "Bethlehem jars" and the medium-sized "Lyddan jars" (M Kelim 2:2 and parallels; Y. Brand 1953, p. 146, Figure 46).

It is possible to determine something of the economic organization of this sphere from the archeological and archeometric studies of the pottery of Kefar Hananiah (Adan-Bayewitz 1985) and the archeological analysis of the lamps of Beth Natif (Baramki 1936; V. Sussman 1969, p. 71; V. Sussman 1978). Both of these settlements produced specific types of pottery. In Kefar Hananiah, for instance, it was stew-pots and cooking pots, while in Beth Natif it was lamps. The wares were also sold within a particular area in relation to where they were produced. The Kefar Hananiah wares were sold, for instance, within 20 kilometers or so of that settlement. The Kefar Hananiah wares seemed to have enjoyed an unofficial monopoly within this territory and no other pottery of the type produced in that village has been discovered there. Fewer Kefar Hananiah wares are found in villages outside this radius. It would seem that there were similar arrangements regarding the other pottery workshops and the lamps of Beth Natif, although its sphere of influence has yet to be determined. The "Bethlehem jars" of the Talmud mentioned above would seem to indicate that Bethlehem was a regional center for the production of a particular type of jar. It is possible that other types of jars or utensils were also produced at this site, but they may not have been of much importance. In Kefar Hananiah and at Beth Natif, it would appear that only specific implements were produced. It is possible that the "Samaritan lamps" found throughout Samaria and neighboring regions reflect a similar phenomenon. In this case the lamps would not necessarily reflect ethnicity, but rather regional production in a large workshop in Samaria.

All of this would seem to indicate that in every region there were a number of workshops which specialized in various types of implements. This supposition allows us to reconstruct a system of trade regions. Such a region, for instance, existed in the Golan (Adan-Bayewitz 1985, pp. 198–216. For a similar system in other parts of the Empire, see Harris 1980).

II.2.3.5

An analysis of the laws pertaining to Kefar Hananiah and Asochis might elucidate another aspect pertaining to the pottery trade. The *halachah* forbids setting a final price regarding future merchandise, that is, payment at present for merchandise not yet existing or available. There was a fear that such transactions were simply a way of disguising the taking of interest on loans, which of course was forbidden. However, the *Tosefta* continues and states:

> One does not set a price on the raw unformed clay of the potter until he should make the implement. R. Jose said – when does this law apply? Only regarding the potters who make vessels with white earth. Those, however, who use black earth, such as [the potters of] Kefar Hananiah and its environs and Asochis and its environs can establish a final price because even though one might not have [a chunk of raw clay], his fellow [will have one]
>
> (T Bava Mezia 6:3)

Thus one can set a price on an implement to be fashioned from the unformed clay from either Kefar Hananiah or Asochis because there is never a danger that the potter will not have the clay to produce the utensil. Even if he should temporarily lack it, there are so many potters in these areas that it is always possible to acquire some for the immediate purpose at hand.

The tradition cited above shows that in these settlements there were a large number of potters and that they also maintained friendly relations among one another. It is also important to point out that Kefar Hananiah and Asochis were not isolated settlements producing pottery, but each was the center of a regional network of pottery-producing settlements ("and its environs"). It is interesting to note that a pottery-producing workshop was also discovered at Nehaf near Kefar Hananiah, but this workshop dates to the Byzantine period when the pottery center at Kefar Hananiah no longer existed.

We shall further discuss the matter of the extent of the pottery production industry when we re-examine the question of importing pottery to Palestine (Chapter 4.VI below).

II.2.4 The metal industry

Many traditions mention a metal industry, essentially for local and regional use. Thus, ancient sources mention smithies, smelters, silversmiths, gold-smiths and even forgers of weapons for both local use and for the Roman army (Cassius Dio 69. 12). This industry has not yet been examined in detail (Alon 1980, I, pp. 171–2) and in any case was not very widespread.

II.2.5 The papyrus industry

Another industry mentioned in the ancient sources is the paper or papyrus industry. This industry could, of course, only exist in those areas in which there was a supply of raw material which, in the case of papyrus, meant the Jordan River area or the region of the Sea of Galilee. This industry was studied years ago by S. Klein (1937). A settlement in the Plains of Jericho was called "Papyrion," which would seem to imply that papyrus was prepared there. The *midrash* states that the tribe of Naftali used "to twist the work of paper" (Genesis Rabbah 94:8, p. 1180) and a number of traditions mention that jugs were covered with paper as a matter of course. We have no idea, however, as to the extent of this industry or its economic importance. The traditions mentioned in the literature would seem to indicate that this industry was only of local importance.

II.2.6 Other economic spheres

II.2.6.1

There were other products, usually only of local importance, in addition to those mentioned above. Thus, for example, mats produced in Usha and in Tiberias were renowned in Palestine (or at least in the Galilee – PT Sukkah I, 52c; BT Sukkah 20a–b). It is likely that this is also the case regarding similar utensils such as straw ones made also with date fibers (I.3 above). Along similar lines, dozens of unique installations have been found throughout

Sumaqa (similar types of installations have been found at additional sites in the Carmel – Dar, pers. comm.). Dyes were possibly produced in these installations. Even though we cannot be completely sure as to what was produced, it was apparently of local unique economic importance and the product was known throughout the region. There were other unlikely products in the various regions of Palestine about which we know nothing.

II.2.6.2

The quarrying or stone industry serves as a good example of an industry of secondary importance which later became quite important. The quarrying of stone can be defined as a service industry of the type which we shall discuss below (III). However, in the area of Dor and the Carmel coast (the territory of Dor) this became an extremely important economic endeavor. Due to the survey of Olami (unpublished), it is possible to determine the settlement map of this region to a quite exact level. The quarries were surveyed by my student B. Steinberg for the purposes of the present research. The summary of the data and findings are presented in Figure 47. Some of the settlements in the region existed only in the Roman–Byzantine period, which was the period which represented the pinnacle of settlement of the area. It would seem, therefore, that most of the quarries date to this time. Another manner of dating the quarries pertains to the Roman–Byzantine tombs discovered in many of them. These Roman–Byzantine burial caves are usually located at the bottom of the pit, proving beyond a doubt that the quarrying of the pit itself somewhat predates the burial caves.

Basic assumptions   A half-day's work is needed in order to quarry stone measuring 30 × 20 × 40 cm. Eleven days are needed for a cubic meter of stone. This would also include the time necessary to transport it to the nearest coast.

During the course of a year it is possible for an individual to quarry 30 cubic meters (based on an assumption of 330 days of work).

The quarries were used for a period of 700 years (100 BCE–600 CE). Therefore, a hypothetical worker engaged in this occupation during the course of all these years could remove 21,000 cubic meters of stone.

Summary   The types of labor and industry discussed in the pages above were found both in the urban and rural spheres. The major force in these endeavors was the small producer who operated within an extended family framework or within that of a guild or group of producers. We can conclude that at least 10–20 percent of the entire population of the region (Dor) worked in the quarries.

The textile and glass industries were of major economic importance, since they were export oriented. The pottery industry, as we saw, was more for local use. We also saw a number of other local or regional industries and it is

	Site	Volume per 1,000 cubic meters
1.	Dor	7,000
2.	Tel Abdon (1)	
3.	Drachmon	2,000
4.	Hadarim	29,400
5.	Entire region (2)	38,400
6.	Territory of Dor (3)	38,400
7.	Athlit and Kartah	2,012
8.	Migdal Malha	30
9.	Tel south of Tel Naami	675
10.	Zerufah	3,717
11.	Carmel coast from 1–8	42,792
12.	Carmel coast, including those bordering on hill region	42,792

	Size of settlement (dunams)	Size including satellites
1.	50	55
2.	10	31
3.	10	21
4.	15	22
5.	85	128
6.	361	447
7.	100	102
8.	100	108
9.	18	21
10.	20	36
11.	123	185
12.	399	504

	Number of families (10 per dunam)	Number of those quarrying	% of those quarrying of male population
1.	1,550	333	60
2.	310	95	
3.	210	1,400	45
4.	220	1,400	636!
5.	1,280	1,828	143!
6.	4,470	1,828	41
7.	1,020	96	96
8.	1,080	2	0.2
9.	210	32	15
10.	360	177	49
11.	1,850	2,038	10
12.	5,040	2,038	40

Notes

1 The quarries within the territory of the village are included within the Territory of Dor.

2 Includes the four sites mentioned above and satellite settlements. Dor may have been larger.

3 Includes those hill settlements within the possible administrative territory of Dor. Other villages are too far away and it is difficult to assume that their residents came to work every day at the quarries.

Conclusion: Quarrying was a very important factor in the Carmel plain. In some villages (nos 4, 5) the local population was inadequate and consequently workers from nearby villages were brought in.

Figure 47 Quarries located on the Carmel coast.

more than likely that there were others not mentioned in the sources, and therefore not included in our survey.

III. SERVICES

III.1 Labor-related services

The Jewish town was essentially self-sufficient regarding the provision of various services for its residents. An individual might avail himself of services available in the city or *polis*. The Jewish town, though, clearly provided an established and organized network of services since it was inconceivable that every resident would provide for himself all that was necessary.

Thus, for example, R. Joshua made needles in Pekiin, a site certainly not much more than a small village (PT Berachot IV, 7d and BT Berachot 28a (in BT he made charcoal)). Joseph the father of Jesus was a carpenter in late Second Temple-period Nazareth. In Beth Shearim, which was a large settlement but not a *polis*, there was a large public market with an official announcer (Schwabe 1954a). R. Jonathan b. Harsha who was either a wood or metalworker lived in Ginnosar (T Kelim Bava Bathra 5:6; PT Maasrot 1, 48d *et al.*). Biri (Biriah or Baram) had a family or guild of glaziers and a family or guild of carpenters (PT Avodah Zarah II, 40c). Gobta, within the territory of Ariah (near Tiberias) had a jug maker (Sifre Numbers 131; PT Sanhedrin X, 28d). There were leather workers in Beth Zaida (M Ketubbot 7:10 – although this source could possibly be referring to Sidon). When R. Hanina b. Dosa was in a stone quarry, porters came by to aid him (Kohelet Rabbah 1:1). Throughout Samaria and Judaea there are thousands of quarries and limepits, proof of the many people involved in the stone industry and in providing stones both for local usage and for cities. A document from the Judaean desert mentions two "grafters," those involved in the grafting of grape arbors (DJD II, no. 29) and there are references in the sources to similar types of occupations and services.

Talmudic sources mention many different occupations such as leather worker, plasterer, quarry worker, shoemaker, blacksmith, perfumer, builder, ditch-digger, carpenter, etc. Although it might be possible to claim that these occupations were found only in the large cities, the general tenor of the sources would seem to indicate that this is not so. It is inconceivable that the dozens of Talmudic references pertaining to these occupations refer only to Tiberias and Sepphoris. Thus it is likely that some of them, at least, refer to Jewish towns. The laws pertaining, for example, to the removal of leather-making installations or lime kilns from a settlement do not differentiate between various types of settlements and therefore would also refer to the town (M Bava Bathra 2:9; T Bava Bathra 1:10 *et al.*). Another law states that it is forbidden to sell a white sandal on a festival, since such a shoe is not yet ready for wear and would require a shoemaker to make the final preparations (M Bezah 1:10; T Bezah 1:23; BT Bezah 15a). In any case this would indicate that shoemakers were quite common in a Jewish town. There are no traditions regarding going to these types of artisans in a big city (*polis*), although there are sources pertaining to artisans who travelled from settlement to settlement (Chapter 3.III.3).

Clearly, then, the Jewish town had many types of artisans. The farmer therefore did not have to undertake all labors by himself, but was able to avail himself of a support system of services in the town. It is clear, though, that in the economic sphere the city strove for self sufficiency, and that goods produced there were also marketed there in an organized manner based upon a set and established place of market (see below Chapter 3.III.3).

III. 2 Regular services

The service network in the city was quite remarkable. However, it is important to remember that the difference between the *polis* and the Jewish town became quite pronounced regarding luxury items or services. A good example of this, for instance, is the bathhouse. There is no doubt that every established Jewish settlement had a public bathhouse and this was indeed one of the requirements of an *'yr* (town), which required a degree of communal organization (BT Sanhedrin 17b; PT Kiddushin IV, 66d; Tanna Deve Eliyahu Zuta (Derech Eretz) 1). Bathhouses have been found in such rural settlements as Beth Yerah, H. Hamam, Ramah in the Galilee, etc. Literary sources also mention a bathhouse in Bene Berak and in other settlements. It is clear, though, that there was a difference between the number and type of bathhouses in the *polis* or large city and the town (T Nedarim 2:7; BT Shabbat 40a *et al.*). The sources state, for instance, that the women of the city washed in the bathhouse more than those of the town (BT Shabbat 40a; BT Niddah 48b). Thus there certainly were bathhouses in the Jewish town, but not to the extent that they were found in the *polis* or large city. The bathhouses were sometimes privately owned and sometimes the property of the community (PT Sheviit VIII, 38b; M Nedarim 4:4 and parallels).

Another service in which there is a marked difference between city and town pertains to the baker. Thus, for instance, it is taught: "When is the leavened bread of non-Jews permissible after Passover? That of householders is permitted after three weeks of baking. That of bakers – in the "village" (*kfr*) after three days, while in the *polis* after the baking of three oven-loads" (T Pesahim 1(2):13; PT Orlah II, 62b). In this source, as in the other ones cited above, there are two types of settlements which are mentioned: the *polis* (*kerakh*) and *kfr*. Although *kfr* usually is translated as village, in this case it means any type of settlement that is not a *polis*. There were both bathhouses and bakers in these types of settlements.

From the continuation of the tradition in the Tosefta it is clear that a baker in general would bake in his stove only once a day, while the baker in a *polis* would bake at least three times a day and perhaps even more. It is of course possible that the rural baker would occasionally bake bread more than once a day. It is possible that there was even a guild of bakers, although it is not clear whether the sources allude to such a guild in all types of settlements or only in the *polis* (T Bava Mezia 11:25). There were also other services in the *polis* associated with luxury items which were not found at all in any other kind of settlement.

Most of the traditions pertaining to the service network do not specifically refer to the town, although as we mentioned above in our discussion of labor-related services, this would seem to be the case. It is difficult to imagine that the traditions refer only to the *polis*. Thus, for example, we shall see below that there were stores in the cities which also served as restaurants. It would seem logical, therefore, that this was also the case regarding the town, even if it was not all that common.

We shall discuss below some of the traditions relating to small settlements. We shall not mention those services which belong to the town or are operated by municipal institutions such as the provision of water through aqueducts, education or charity. In the list of services which a Jewish town must provide (see Chapter 1.III.2 above) we find the bathhouse, public lavatory, doctor, bloodletter, scribe and slaughterer. Tanna Deve Eliyahu adds: "chest of spices." This addition is difficult to comprehend, since it is unlikely that spices were provided free to the residents of the town. In our view this version is a mistake based on the "chest of charity" or the "chest of the food plate" which are mentioned before.

Some of the providers of these services are mentioned in other traditions. An interesting *halachah* is mentioned in T Bava Mezia 11:27:

> Whoever was a public bathhouse worker, or a barber for the general public, or a baker for the public, and there were no other such workers there except for him; if the time of festivals arrived and he wished to go home, he can be prevented from doing so until he should find a replacement.

The tradition relates to a small settlement with only one such worker in these endeavors, whose own home was in a neighboring village. He cannot leave the settlement where he is employed until he arranges for a replacement. A similar law mentions four instances in which "the slaughterer is forced to slaughter even against his will" (M Hulin 1:4 *et al.*). The slaughterer is employed in a small settlement in which there are not many other slaughterers. Although the slaughterer is privately employed, there are times when the town imposes by-laws or restrictions regarding his services.

The slaughterer also served as butcher and sold meat, and it seems that occasionally his premises also served as a meat restaurant. Thus, for example,

the sources mention the stove of the cook (M Kelim 6:2) and his preservatives (M Pesahim 3:1). A source also mentions the burning of a dish of a
cook (T Bava Kama 10:9). Another tradition relates that the slaughterers of
Jerusalem used to bake and cook an entire meal (T Berachot 4:8).
Unfortunately there is no proof that the slaughterers in small settlements
also functioned in the additional capacities mentioned above. The slaughterers in large settlements certainly worked more frequently than those in
smaller ones. Thus, for example, it is stated that: "an expert slaughterer who
has ruined the meat is liable, even if he is an expert like the slaughterers of
Sepphoris" (BT Bava Kama 99b – From the continuation of the discussion
there it seems that the slaughterer came from Maon, a small village near
Tiberias). In the final result, it seems that the discussion pertains to a regular
slaughterer from a small settlement who was not particularly expert. It is
also possible to learn that the slaughterers of Sepphoris were considered to
be quite expert, most likely because of their constant experience, as opposed
to those slaughterers who worked in smaller settlements and did not work
too often. In the instance cited above, the slaughterer received an animal to
slaughter and cook, at least as the matter was understood by the *Amora*
Samuel, and managed to render it unfit or as stated: "One who gives an
animal to a slaughterer and he renders it unfit." Thus it seems that the
slaughterer did not only butcher the animal, but also seemed to have cooked
it. A parallel tradition also mentions one who brings flour to a baker in order
that he bake the dough (we have discussed similar matters above). The
bringing of grain to the baker seems to have been a matter of course and is
mentioned in many traditions, such as the one pertaining to the house of
Rabban Gamaliel in Javneh (Song of Songs Rabbah 5:13). It is clear, though,
that occasionally the baker provided his own grain. Both systems seem to
have operated simultaneously.

The sources also mention a poultry merchant who sold slaughtered birds
and poultry. It is not known, however, whether this type of merchant was
found outside the *polis* (T Bezah 3:6; BT Hulin 95a *et al.*).

Additional professions are mentioned in the sources, but there is no proof
that these professions were found in small settlements. Thus, for instance,
the sources mention tailors (M Shabbat 1:3; Mechilta Mishpatim 1; BT Bava
Bathra 21b; BT Shabbat 11b; BT Bava Kama 119b; T Kelim Bava Mezia 2:2;
T Pesahim 3:18; BT Pesahim 55b *et al.*) and perfumers (T Berachot 6:8; BT
Berachot 53a *et al.*). There are also traditions pertaining to "fullers." The
fuller usually was responsible for the cleaning of the cloth and dyeing it at
the end of the other procedures. It is clear that the fuller in this instance was
part of the textile industry. We should point out that we have translated the
Hebrew *kwvs* as fuller. Occasionally the word also pertains to one who
washes garments as, for instance, in the tradition that states: "If one saw his
talit at the *kwvs* [to be translated here as washerman]" (T Bava Bathra 2:6;
BT Bava Bathra 45b; T Shabbat 1:22; BT Shabbat 19a; T Moed Katan 1:2;

T Maaser Sheni 5:13 *et al.*). The large number of sources pertaining to the tailor and the *kwvs* together would seem to indicate that these were, after all, popular professions in the Jewish town. On the other hand, it is clear that most people laundered their own garments and may have even also sewn them (T Pesahim 3:18; BT Pesahim 55b). It is, therefore, possible in summation to see that there was quite a variety of labor services available in the town.

There was also an established court in the Jewish town. Auxiliary judicial services were also provided. We have already mentioned the scribe who prepared documents. There were also professional witnesses in the town. These witnesses apparently functioned in the sense of modern-day notaries, authorizing various documents. This professional is referred to by the Aramaic *shdh* and is found in a synagogue inscription at Susiya and in an inscription from H. Jalama in the Jezreel Valley (Naveh 1978 p. 118–19. According to Naveh, the term *mnhmh* which also appears in a Susiya inscription also refers to this profession). Naveh's assumption might help explain a difficult mishnah (M Sanhedrin 3:1–2), but this is not the place to discuss this matter.

The Jewish city was essentially agricultural and therefore there were many agricultural services.

(1) It was possible to hire laborers in the town. There are many dozens of traditions relating to the existence of seasonal laborers and this matter should be studied separately (Chapter 4.V.2 below).

(2) In the town it was also possible to find workers for hire possessing expertise in particular agricultural tasks. Thus, for example, one of the documents discovered in the Judaean Desert mentions "grafters" or those who specialized in the grafting of grape arbors (DJD II, no. 29). A *baraita* in BT Moed Katan 11b mentions artisans or laborers who are allowed to work even during their period of mourning because there is no one else to fulfill their tasks. Thus, for example, it was permissible for the worker who turned over the olives or for the one who sealed casks or soaked flax to work then. A number of other professions are also mentioned, such as: "those who chisel stones, bind grape arbors, pierce the *higin* (a type of tree or shrub) or pull out weeds" (T Bava Kama 11:18). It is possible, though, that these are not real professions, but are mentioned only on account of the specific halachic problems involved with them.

(3) Another task was that of the guardian of fruits. This, however, does not seem to have been a profession, but rather made use of occasional labor (T Sukkah 2; 3; PT Sukkah II, 53a; BT Sukkah 26a *et al.*).

(4) Providing pasturage was also an important service. Cattle and sheep could be entrusted to the professional shepherd, or in other words there were professional shepherds for hire in the town (I.8 above).

It seems, therefore, that in terms of the service network available in the Jewish town, there was a great degree of self-sufficiency, and in this instance, at least, the town did not maintain ties with a neighboring *polis*. As we have seen, the town maintained quite a widespread and organized service network. Some of these services, though, need not have always been provided on a professional basis and individuals may have taken care of their needs in these spheres by themselves. Thus, one usually laundered one's garments and occasionally even sewed them without the aid of a professional tailor (T Pesahim 3:18; BT Pesahim 55b; M Moed Qatan 1:8, etc.). A person might also occasionally plaster his own roof (M Moed Katan 1:10 and parallels), bake his own bread and even sell it in the market (T Pesahim 3:18), make his own pottery (M Kelim 12:12, 6 *et al.*) or undertake similar types of activities for which there were professional services (M Eduyot 3:9; M Kelim 12:6).

It is also clear that the *polis* offered more services than the town. Thus the portrait painter mentioned in one source was undoubtedly found in the *polis* and would not be found in a town.

In spite of all this, the extent of the services offered in the rural towns was quite amazing, especially in view of the rather modest standard of living at the time. This phenomenon will be examined later (Chapter 5).

APPENDIX:

Grain consumption in the Jewish farmstead system
(see also Chapter 2.I.1)

The starting point for the discussion in the Babylonian Talmud (BT Eruvin 82b) is M Eruvin 8:2. This Mishnah establishes the amount of food on the Sabbath pertaining to the laws of *Eruv*. R. Johanan b. Beroka set the quantity at the regularly accepted measurement of "a loaf costing a *pondion* when four *seahs* are worth a *sela*." According to R. Simeon the measurement was: "two-thirds of a loaf [three of which make a] or [from a] *kab*." A *baraita* quoted in BT Eruvin states that their views are almost identical. R. Simeon's view there is explained as being two-thirds of a loaf, which is a third of a *kab*, or in other words two-ninths of a *kab* or 233 grams. This is quite clearly much less than the half *kab* which R. Johanan requires. The Talmud explains that R. Johanan refers to the amount of flour before expenses and that a third to a half should be deducted for the baker's expenses. Thus, a person really ate a quarter (262.5 grams) to a third (350 grams), and this measurement is close to the one cited by R. Simeon (233 grams).

BT Ketubbot 64b reached a similar conclusion through a different series of questions. The Talmud there understands M Ketubbot 5:8 – "If one supported his wife through a third person, etc." as pertaining to the amount of every kind of food which would be sufficient in itself for the week. In other words, 4 *kabs* are enough for 14 meals or 7 days. The quantity mentioned by R. Johanan is enough for 8 meals while that mentioned by R. Simeon is enough for 18. Thus, it would seem that M Ketubbot 5:8 is in accordance with the view of R. Johanan and goes to great lengths to try and show that the measurement cited by R. Johanan would be enough for 14 meals, or for 12 meals (excluding the Sabbath) or for 16 meals (based on the assumption that it was required to eat four meals on the Sabbath. Needless to say, all of these intellectual acrobatics are hardly satisfying.

The approach of the Babylonian Talmud on this matter is highly unlikely for a number of reasons. As we have already seen, the Mishnah in Ketubbot should be explained in a different manner. All of the foods together mentioned in the Mishnah are enough for exactly one week. Therefore it is incorrect to claim that the woman would be supported only from wheat. Thus the very idea that the quantity of wheat mentioned takes into account payment to the baker is unnecessary.

Moreover, it is difficult to imagine that a pauper who also has to beg would pay part of the grain to a baker. On the contrary: he would make an effort to bake the bread himself in order to save money (or grain). The baker basically invests a great number of man-hours in his labor (grinding, building the oven, finding combustible material, etc.). The poor person usually has a good deal of time on his hands, but lacks capital. Undoubtedly he would prefer to bake himself and save the money. Also, the cost of baking was apparently not as high as the cost of the flour, which was 50 per cent of the price of the loaf of bread and rather steep. Moreover, a quarter of a *kab* or two-ninths of one are not enough to support a person. A hundred grams of wheat have 38 calories, while a normal person needs a minimum of 1,200 a day in order to supply his minimal energy needs. Thus, 233 grams were not sufficient for nutritive requirements.

In our opinion, R. Johanan b. Beroka establishes that a poor person needs half a *kab* of wheat per day or 525 grams (198 kilograms per year) to survive. In our opinion, R. Simeon's view in the Mishnah should be explained as follows: "two-thirds of a loaf, three of which make a *kab*," means two loaves of a third of a *kab*, or two-thirds of a *kab* which is 700 grams of wheat per day. This adds up to 255.5 kilograms of wheat per year and this is the meaning of the *baraita*, which states that the views of R. Johanan and R. Simeon are almost identical, since R. Johanan required a similar amount (525 grams of wheat per day).

At this point it is imperative to examine the discussion of PT Eruvin VIII, 25a on this matter:

And it was taught so – their views are almost identical. Come and see: One makes a loaf the equivalent of twelve eggs [= half a *kab*] and the other makes a loaf of eight eggs [one-third of a *kab*]. Shall we say that this is so. Rav Huna said – figure out the difference [between the greater and smaller sum] as a third for expenses.

The discussion in PT should not be explained in a manner similar to that in BT. PT establishes two principles. (1) There are differences regarding the standard size of a loaf (half a *kab* or a third of a *kab*). R. Johanan requires that the poor man receive a loaf of a half a *kab*, while R. Simeon is of the opinion that he should receive two loaves, each a third of a *kab*. (2) The difference between the views of the particular sages is dependent upon whether the value of the loaf should be taken into consideration (wheat + expenses) or only the quantity of wheat. The different views, though, do not extend to the question of the various standard sizes of the loaves. The difference between the two sizes may be one-third, but it makes no sense to explain this away simply as expenses. Moreover, differences of opinion between the sages as understood by PT are not identical with the manner in which the matter is explained in BT. The difference between the views there, in the manner in which we have explained it, is not one-third but between one-half to two-thirds of a *kab*, since half a *kab* plus one-third of half a *kab* are two-thirds of a *kab*. According to this explanation, the "third" mentioned does not represent a third of total expenses, but the addition of one-third of a loaf (one-third of a half *kab*) to the expenses of the cooking. (For a somewhat different view see Sperber 1974, pp. 112–15.)

3

Trade in the Land of Israel in the Roman period

This chapter will basically deal with the trade system in the Land of Israel in the Mishnah and Talmud period within the economic framework of that time. The Land of Israel was, of course, at this time a Roman province, and therefore the matter at hand must be studied in reference to the economic position both of the Land of Israel and of the Roman Empire.

I. TRADE IN THE LAND OF ISRAEL DURING THE SECOND TEMPLE PERIOD

I.1 The self-sufficient economic system

During the Second Temple period the national Jewish economy was almost entirely self-sufficient within itself and there was very little exporting or importing. Josephus, when explaining the reason that there was no information regarding the Jews, says:

> Well, ours is not a maritime country, neither commerce nor the intercourse which it promotes with the outside world has any attraction for us . . . there was clearly nothing in ancient times to bring us into contact with the Greeks, as the Egyptians were brought by their exports and imports and the inhabitants of the sea-board of Phoenicia by their mercenary devotion to trade and commerce.
>
> (*Contra Apionem* 1. 12. 60–1)

There are, however, a few sources which do indicate that there might have been a limited amount of importing. Thus, T Makhshirin 3:4 mentions some importing of wheat, and the decree of the rabbis that imported pottery and glass was ritually impure would also seem to indicate that these goods were imported to Palestine. It would also indicate that the rabbis opposed this and tried to curtail it (T Kelim Bava Bathra 7:7; PT Shabbat I, 3d; BT Shabbat 14b).

The Hefzibah inscription from the Hellenistic period shows that there was a degree of trade between the various villages of the region and there might have been some export (Landau 1966; Fischer 1979). It is also likely that the Jericho region was a sort of trade enclave, since balsam and dates from this area were sold outside the region and at the same time it is clear that the residents of the Jericho area were not self-sufficient in other respects.

However, all of this was not of much importance when viewing the general economic picture. Thus, for example, the Romans levied on Hyrcanus a yearly land tax and harbor tax for Joppa to the amount of 20,665 *modia* (*Ant.* 14. 206) or approximately 135.5 tons of wheat. Joppa was the major Jewish port and a tax of 135.5 tons of wheat was ridiculously low, proving that there was only a minimal amount of export from the city. Josephus states that it was the Phoenician coastal cities that were the major trade centers. They participated in the international trade of the Mediterranean region and also apparently served as the major ports for the limited import and export needs of the Land of Israel. During the Hasmonean reign these cities were captured. They may not have been entirely abandoned, but their status certainly suffered, as did their economic position. Only Joppa continued to function as a small harbor city and Ascalon also remained independent. When Palestine was conquered by the Romans, the Phoenician coastal cities flourished once again and regained their stature as economic centers (Applebaum 1980; Sperber 1976, pp. 117–19).

Needless to say, during difficult periods of drought or famine it was necessary to import food, as was the case during the time of Herod (*Ant.* 14. 299–316) and of Queen Helena (*Ant.* 20. 102). However, trade at this time was generally a phenomenon of the coastal cities as is clearly seen from the Testament of Job 11:3.

I.2 The period of Herod

During the Second Temple period and particularly during the time of Herod, there developed local centers of consumption. An important center of consumption at this time was Jerusalem at the end of the Second Temple period. This center developed from the needs of those residents who did not engage in agriculture as well as from the needs of the Temple and pilgrims (M Hagigah 3:3–4; T Hagigah 3:30–4). Thus, the doves that were raised in the *shephelah* of Judaea were sent to the Temple (see Chapter 2.I.9 above). All in all, though, trade in Palestine at this time was still on a rather small scale (Broshi 1985).

During the period after the destruction of the Temple, during the time of the *Tannaim* and *Amoraim*, the situation changed and there are many traditions attesting to increasing trade and mercantile activities. The place of trade within the general economic picture will be discussed later on (IV and V below). We shall also attempt to analyze the structure of trade.

II. LOCAL TRADE IN THE RURAL SETTLEMENT

II.1 The farmer as merchant

Part of the produce grown by the farmer was for personal use. The surplus was marketed. Sometimes the bulk of the produce was for personal consumption, while at other times the majority of the produce was intended for market. Both possibilities are mentioned in the sources. The most common occurrence was what is related in the following sources: "What are the circumstances? It refers to one who brings his produce to the market. However, if one brings it to his residence" (M Maasrot 1:5). PT, on a different matter, states: "the Mishnah deals with a place in which most people bring the produce in to their houses. However, in a place in which people bring it to the market" (PT Maasrot II, 49c). Many *halachot* also relate cases of bringing fruit to market (T Terumot 3:16; T Sheviit 5:10; T Makhshirin 3:8; M Demai 5:7; PT Demai V, 24d *et al.*). Other sources also mention the bringing to market of quasi-agricultural products such as wool or milk (M Bava Kama 10:9 *et al.*).

Some of the instances related in the sources, such as the one just cited above, deal with farmers who bring produce to market and stand there themselves and sell it to customers. Thus, for example, the Mishnah relates cases in which the farmer himself sells his produce to the residents of a settlement (M Maasrot 2:1). The Mishnah also relates an instance of a person who bought from a householder and went back again and bought from him (M Demai 5:7). This Mishnah deals with a householder who sells the vegetables which he raises in the private garden next to his house. The householder becomes a merchant, as it were. The farmer could also sell his produce to the small merchant or to the *tagar* (pp. 228–9 below).

II.2 The store

Every town had at least one store and usually many, and these are considered common and recognized institutions of town life. The store usually sold foodstuffs and often doubled as a restaurant.

The store is a permanent structure operated throughout the entire year by the merchant or his representatives. The store was often found in the town and is mentioned in many sources. It was even possible to rent or to hire out stores (M Bava Mezia 8:6). The resident of the town or settlement could usually buy most everyday necessities in the store. The store is usually mentioned regarding the sale of food or foodstuffs such as vegetables, eggs, fruits (usually special or exotic types), etc. The store, however, was not just the site of transactions, but also served as a workplace and at times even as a restaurant: "A storekeeper who was cooking vegetables from the Sabbatical

Year" (T Sheviit 6:22 and also T Kelim Bava Mezia 2:10). Processed foods were also prepared in the store (T Bava Mezia 11:30).

Moreover, a place of work, such as a bakery (lit. store of bakers), in which the final product may ultimately have been sold, was also called a store (T Yadayim 2:16). This is also the case regarding a store of dyers (and bakers – M Bava Bathra 2:3; M Bava Mezia 8:6; T Bava Mezia 8:27), a store of perfume (T Berachot 6:12) and the store of a carpenter and smithy (T Bava Kama 6:26).

An interesting *halachah* is found in M Bava Bathra 2:3:

> If one desires to establish a shop within a courtyard, another may protest against him and say to him – I am unable to sleep on account of the noise of those coming in and because of the noise of those going out. But one who makes utensils in his house and goes forth and sells them in the market – none may protest against him and say to him – I cannot sleep on account of the noise of the hammer or because of the noise of the handmill or children.

Thus the store or shop is synonymous with the workshop. The Mishnah deals with a smithy, a baker (a miller) and a barber-shop. One can complain about the comings and goings of customers, but not about the noise associated with the work itself. The reason that the Mishnah legislates here against commerce while not taking action against the noise associated with the labor is not that it considers the commerce to be inferior, but rather that the customers enter the courtyard, which is the common property of all residents of the courtyard, and the other residents have veto power over its use. This *halachah* is also quite effective in illustrating the difference between the regular or permanent store and the stall at a market mentioned above.

The shop was not usually in the courtyard. Rather it quite often faced the public domain or pathway. In fact, the store or shop is the most frequently cited structure when rabbinic material wishes to describe a building that directly faces the public domain (T Eruvin 10:1; 11:11; T Bava Kama 6:28; T Bava Bathra 1:4; T Moed Qatan 2:13; T Shabbat 1:1; T Tohorot 7:1; M Bava Kama 6:6; M Maasrot 2:2 *et al.*). The shop did not usually double as a residence and its function was basically limited to its professional use (T Ahilot 18:11). Based on all the above, it has been possible to identify a number of structures in the rural sphere as shops or stores (Hirschfeld 1987, pp. 49–51, Figure 48; Dar *et al.* 1986, pp. 34–8, Figure 49).

The shopkeeper was the most prominent personality in the town regarding all matters pertaining to fluid capital, and he appears in the sources in terms of the town hierarchy somewhere between the householder and the moneychanger:

> If one deposited money with a moneychanger and it was tied up, the latter may not make use of it . . . if the money were loose, the

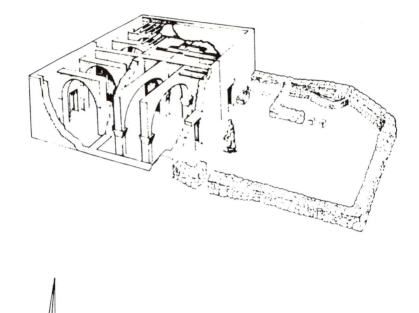

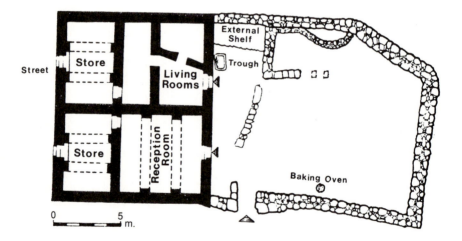

Figure 48 Store at H. Susiya, southern Mt Hebron region.
After Hirschfeld 1987, p. 18.

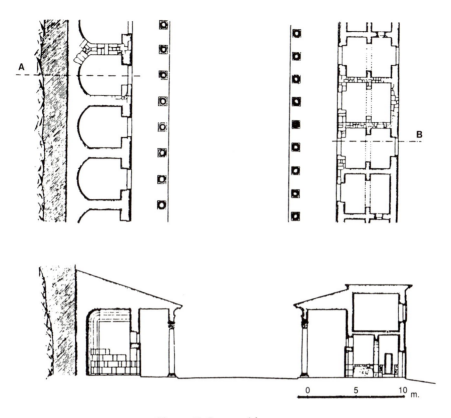

Figure 49 Street with stores.

moneychanger may make use of it . . . if it were left with a private householder, whether tied up or loose, the latter may not use it . . . A shopkeeper is accounted like a private person: this is the view of R. Meir; but R. Judah says, A shopkeeper is to be considered like a moneychanger.

(M Bava Mezia 3:11; M Meilah 6:5; T Meilah 2:11)

The merchant or shopkeeper also serves as the replacement for the moneychanger in a small town (which may not have a moneychanger of its own). Thus, for example, the sources cite the shopkeeper together with the moneychanger as one who would have cash in his store (M Bava Mezia 2:4). They also are cited together in a tradition describing the case in which a customer disputes whether he has already paid for his merchandise or not (M Sheviit 8:5; PT Shevuot VII, 38a). The sources describe both the money-changer and the shopkeeper as likely to grant credit to customers (M Bava Mezia 9:12; T Bava Mezia 10:5; Sifra Kedoshim 2:11). The shopkeeper would at times provide the merchandise before payment by the customer

227

(M Shevuot 7:1 and parallels; M Sheviit 10:1; M Bezah 3:8; Sifre Deuteronomy 276, p. 294; Sifre Deuteronomy 112, p. 173; M Avot 3:16), and at times the customer would also pay in advance (M Eduyot 1:10; M Maaser Sheni 2:9), but this was cited in the sources only as a way of avoiding a particular halachic problem. Moreover, when the Mishnah wishes to cite an example of the cessation of work in a town on account of a fast, the example brought is that: "the shops are closed" (M Taanit 1:6 *et al.*).

All of the sources cited above would seem to indicate that the shop and shopkeeper were far more prevalent in the town than other forms of labor, in spite of the many sources also pertaining to these forms of labor (Chapter 2.II.3 above). The other types of laborers would also most likely receive their salary or payment in cash, but such payment is mentioned only regarding the shopkeeper. It is also likely that most towns had many shops or stores and it was unusual for a town to have only one shop (M Nedarim 11:2; Sifre Numbers 155, p. 206). This also made the shop a rather prevalent institution. Another reason why the shop became the "representative" form of labor or services will be proven below (p. 353). Suffice it for the moment to state that the other forms of labor were usually undertaken by those who primarily worked in agriculture. These other labors were tangential to agriculture and undertaken only in their spare time. This was not the case regarding the shopkeeper (Chapter 4.IV below).

II.3 The *tagar*

The *tagar* was a large-scale merchant. The sources, for instance, occasionally describe him as a regular merchant selling produce such as a melon together with its leaves. (They were necessary either for esthetic purposes or to help preserve the fruit) (M Uktzin 2:1). Other sources, however, describe him as a much more high-powered merchant: "The *tagar* may buy grain from five granaries and put it into one storeroom" (M Bava Mezia 4:11–12), while the regular merchant was not allowed to do so; such a merchant would combine merchandise in order to cheat, while the *tagar* would not do so, being accustomed to work with large quantities. The *tagar* was also mentioned in the sources as being an expert on monetary matters (M Bava Mezia 4, 4), albeit not overly trustworthy in this sphere. It would seem that the *tagar* was not a resident of the rural town, but rather came there in order to buy farm produce directly from the farmer (M Bava Bathra 6:6). The doubts pertaining to the honesty of the *tagar* might indicate that many of them were non-Jewish. This, however, is not explicitly indicated in any of the sources and perhaps the negative traditions simply reflect the tension between the rural towns and the rich merchants of the large cities. The *tagar* is also mentioned in one source in reference to the fair (T Avodah Zarah 1:9 and IV.3 below). It is likely that the *tagar* is identical with the *pragmateutes*, who participates in a more regional level of commerce, and whom we shall discuss below.

II.3.1 The wheat trade

Highly developed stores and shops are mentioned in relation to commerce in grains. There are traditions pertaining to the buying of seeds not only from a shop but also from the bread baker (lit. *nahtom*), the large-scale baker (lit. *palter*) and from the wholesaler (lit. *siton* or *sidki*) (PT Sheqalim III, 47c and parallels; M Demmai 5:6 and parallels; PT Bava Mezia V, 10c *et al.*).

II.4 The marketing of products of labor and services

II.4.1

Until now we have discussed the marketing of agricultural produce. The marketing of products relating to services and labor were apparently organized in a somewhat different manner. Many traditions describe the artisan as marketing his own products.

Thus, there are many sources which relate that the potter brought his jugs and pots to the market and sold them there. When rabbinic literature wishes to bring as an illustration a man going from place to place with large quantities of pottery or glassware, it mentions the potter and the glazier: "two potters who were walking alone" (and broke each other's pottery – M Bava Kama 3:4), or: "A potter who put down his pottery" (M Taharot 7:1 and parallels; Ohalot 16:2; BT Ketubbot 24b). Similarly we find: "A potter who was selling his wares and entered the region from Modiin and inwards" (M Hagigah 3:5). This potter was making his way from the coastal plain to the Jerusalem region. Another source states that a dish found in the public domain is considered to be the property of a potter (M Bava Kama 5:2). It would seem, then, that the potter brought his merchandise to market and sold it there to a shopkeeper or merchant, making an attempt to keep handling commissions down to a minimum. A number of sources also indicate that the wife of a farmer who raised sheep or who cultivated flax, would sell clothes woven from either wool or linen (M Bava Kama 10:9; T Bava Kama 11:9; BT Bava Kama 119a *et al.*).

There were, however, linen or flax workers who apparently did sell the product that they themselves produced directly to customers (PT Yebamot XIII, 13c). A rabbinic tradition mentions also a wool producer who came directly to Jerusalem after the destruction of that city in order to sell his merchandise (Lamentations Rabbah 2:15 and parallels). There were, of course, merchants who came to the city and who had no part regarding the production of the merchandise. Even important manufacturers such as those in Kefar Hananiah and Asochis mentioned above (Chapter 2.II.2), who produced their own pottery on a regional level, apparently sold their wares themselves, and there are *halachot* which deal with the buying of such utensils (T Bava Mezia 6:3 and parallels).

II.4.2

Most of the services were provided in the rural town. There were shop-keepers, artisans, potters, glaziers, goldsmiths, merchants, donkey-drivers, porters, carpenters and other types of laborers in the average town (Chapter 2.II above). There were, however, certain occupations which could not provide for a decent living in a small town. The solution in such a case was for the worker to travel from center to center plying his wares or his trade, thus also saving travel expenses for the potential customer. There are only a few references to this situation in Talmudic literature. Thus, for instance, an *aggadah* relates that Joshua advised the spies to disguise themselves as carpenters, since it was assumed that carpenters traveled from one site to another and this would not arouse suspicion. According to R. Nehemiah, the spies disguised themselves as potters, thus indicating that pottery may have been provided by itinerant potters and not necessarily purchased in the central market (Numbers Rabbah 16:1). This is the manner in which the phrase "an artisan who came to the town" should be understood (Midrash Shir Ha-Shirim, ed. Greenhut 1:1; Ruth Rabbah 2:1).

A similar phenomenon exists today in Judaea and Samaria, particularly in iron goods and a similar situation also seems to exist in China (Skinner 1964). Here there is no single center, but a network of regional fairs and itinerant artisans.

Workshops are also referred to by specific names such as stores or smithies, dyers or workshops (see pp. 224–8 above). An interesting case in M Bava Bathra mentioned above describes a workshop (a smithy or a mill) within a residential courtyard. According to the law as stated in the Mishnah, the residents of the courtyard cannot close down the workshop, but they can prevent customers from entering the court and they can force the owners of the workshop to sell their wares in the market. Thus, within the realm of local trade, the sources mention only primary merchants of ancient industrial goods and not secondary ones.

II.5 Forms of trade

The farmer and the artisan attempted to sell a finished product such as bound vegetables (M Makhshirin 2:10; T Makhshirin 3:8), or olive oil (instead of olives), wine (and not grapes), pressed figs (and not fresh ones) and linen yarns or cloth (and not flax) (M Bava Kama 10:9 and parallels and see Chapter 2.I.2 above). There are, however, cases mentioned in the ancient literature in which someone did bring olives or grapes to market and upon failure to find customers, returned home to complete the processing of the crops. The olives were pressed and became oil, and the grapes were turned into wine (T Maasrot 2:4). This would indicate that there were those who sold fresh produce and the buyer intended to complete any additional processing. Thus, we read in the sources of fresh olives, grapes and flax fibers being sent to a nearby region for continued processing (T Sheviit 4:19). These instances, however, are exceptions to the rule and for the most part the farmer undertook all stages of production in order to save on the costs of transport as well as to increase profits.

It was also possible to sell agricultural produce to a merchant before it was harvested and while it was still in the fields: "If one possesses a garden behind his fellow's garden . . . and he may not bring merchants into it (M Bava Bathra 6:6 *et al.*). Or another source which states: "one says to his fellow – here are two hundred *zuz* based on what your fields will produce (T Bava Mezia 6:7). The sources also mention the selling of wool even before the fleece is shorn from the sheep (M Bava Mezia 5:6). In spite of all this, however, this was not the usual form of commerce and most products were sold at least after a final stage of processing.

II.6 The village market

Villages did not usually have a permanently constructed marketplace with regular stores or stalls as was accepted practice in the Hellenistic–Roman *polis*. In spite of this, an "agora" is mentioned in a source pertaining to Ein Gedi (Lewis 1989, nos. 11, 19, 20) and it would seem that there was some type of permanent market structure in Um Rihan in northern Samaria (Dar *et al.* 1986 and above Figure 9, structure 16). As we have already seen above, the village did have an *agoranomos* who was in charge of the market and local rules of commerce.

The small satellite settlements did not have stores, and the tasks and functions of trade and commerce were for the most part fulfilled by the traveling pedlar (pp. 77–81 above). The pedlar took with him such wares as needles and the like, cosmetics and other such products popular among women, and went from small settlement to small settlement plying his wares, returning home to his house only in the evening. When it was necessary for the residents of these settlements to make a more serious purchase, they would travel to the mother settlement.

The sources record many cases of transactions, both buying and selling, of animals, land, slaves and agricultural produce. Usually the transaction was direct with no intermediary between seller and buyer. It is possible to conclude that most transactions in the village sphere were between local householders, and supplementary to their regular occupations or pastimes. Very few people, such as shopkeepers or pedlars, engaged in commerce or trade as a regular occupation. It is likely that even these professionals engaged in some manner of agriculture, although this is, of course, impossible to prove. We shall return to this matter later on.

III. REGIONAL COMMERCE

Village settlements were not self-sufficient. They needed a trade network in order to market their surplus and buy necessary goods or commodities.

III.1 Trade models

Theoretically, there are two possible models pertaining to the provision of services in a specific region (Bunge 1962).

(1) *The Spider Model.* In this model, a central city is located at the center of a particular region and all the other settlements market their goods there as well as receive goods and services. The road network in such a system will resemble a spider's web, with the major city at the center. In very large regions not all the settlements are directly connected with the major urban center. Rather, there exists a settlement hierarchy with the small villages connected to a major village. A number of such villages are connected to a town and a number of such towns would be connected to a regional urban center, etc. (see Figure 50).

(2) *The Net Model.* In this system, all settlements are connected and there is no clear or central center (Figure 50). It is clear beyond doubt that both systems are theoretical, and it is impossible to find one region or another in which one of these theoretical systems was completely operational. Every road network has elements of both systems. The matter essentially boils down to the level of influence of the local centers at different levels of the hierarchy and the level of trade between the various settlements. Later, we shall try to determine how such spatial approaches functioned in Jewish regions in the Mishnah and Talmud periods.

One of the ways to determine the nature of the systems mentioned above is to study the local road network. We shall deal with this matter later in great detail, analyzing a certain regional model. For the moment, however, we can already state that every settlement maintained close ties with its neighbors, within a radius of 3–4 km in Samaria or 3–5 km in the Galilee. There were undoubtedly central settlements, a matter we shall also discuss in detail later, but it would appear that the essential economic network was based on the net system described above. Every settlement had a path connecting it to its neighbors, undoubtedly reflecting economic ties.

Not all the Roman roads of Eretz-Israel are known (VII.1 below, Figure 56). Even so, and based upon what is known, a glance at the map of Roman roads clearly shows that the net system was predominant in all of Palestine. Every city was connected to neighboring cities, and it is hard to discern a central city or a city which was located at the center of the road network. Every city traded, therefore, with its surrounding region. Proof of this is the fact that a city could at times be connected to a far-off city without being connected to closer cities serving as intermediaries. We shall offer examples

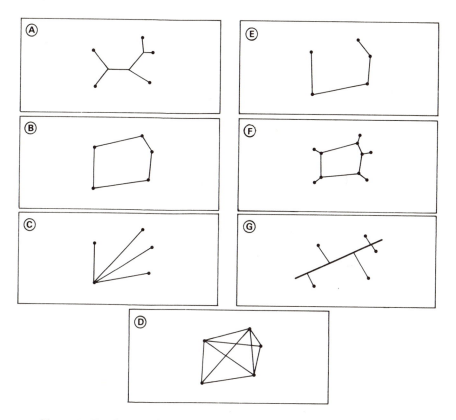

Figure 50 Road network: descriptive model. After Z. Safrai 1983, p. 278.

of the phenomenon below. (1) Jerusalem was connected directly to Lod by a direct road (via Kefar Roth) in spite of the fact that there was a route (or even roads) via the city of Emmaus. (2) Eleutheropolis was connected to Azotus and Ascalon via separate roads even though it was possible to travel to Ascalon via Azotus; the difference in terms of distance between both of these possibilities was quite small. (3) Scythopolis was connected to Caesarea and Ptolemais (Acco) without passing by the road which went through Maximianopolis (Legio); in this case, only a few hundred meters were saved. All of these roads were constructed by the Roman government. Some of them may have originally been constructed as a response to defense needs and considerations, but usually once the situation became calm they fulfilled clear-cut economic functions. This usually also required the construction of new roads while the old ones were cared for with much concern.

III.2 The donkey and camel caravans of trade

The major means of inter-village or inter-regional trade was the donkey or camel caravan (Hebrew: *hmrt* and *gmlt*).

A number of traditions provide information on this system:

> Donkey drivers that came into a town – one said mine is new [= new agricultural produce] and my companion's is old [= last year's produce], mine is not completely tithed, but my companion's is completely tithed, they are not to be believed. R. Judah says, they are to be trusted.
>
> (M Bemmai 4:7)

These donkey-drivers provided agricultural produce (wine). They were not local since otherwise it would be possible to determine whether they were *haverim* or *amei ha'aretz* (in other words could be trusted regarding the produce), as is clear from the preceding mishnah. The sages were in disagreement as to the nature and reliability of the ties between these drivers, and thus whether they could be trusted. It is clear, however, that they were recognized in the source as an established group. The preceding mishnah dealt with similar issues regarding plain individuals who came into a town and concluded that they were trustworthy, once again proving that these donkey-drivers were a set and organized group. PT on this matter (IV, 24b) states that R. Judah was of the opinion that they could be trusted "on account of the survival of the residents of the town" who were forced to buy from these donkey-drivers, implying also that there were no others from whom the people could buy. The sages, who did not trust the donkey-drivers, were of the opinion that "they could receive sustenance from another town," or in other words, that it was possible to go and buy the same produce or wares in a neighboring settlement.

Similarly one finds a tradition that states: "If the donkey-drivers were looking for wine or oil (to buy), one should not tell them go to this or that person when they never sold wine or oil" (T Bava Mezia 3:25; BT Bava Mezia 58b). This source also implies that these donkey-drivers were not local, but went from one place to another buying produce and bringing it somewhere else to sell it. Thus we find in the following tradition:

> R. Hama b. Hanina said – in the case of a settlement which used to receive its provisions from caravans of donkey drivers . . . the drivers who came on the sixth day used to ask those who came on the fifth [what deals could be made there], those who came on the fifth day asked those who had come on the fourth, those who came on the fourth asked those who had come on the third, those who came on the third asked those who had come on the second, those who came on the second asked those who had come on the first, and those who

234

came on the first, whom did they ask? Did they not ask the residents of the town?

(Genesis Rabbah 8:2, p. 57).

The source describes caravan drivers who served as the major providers of commodities and supplies for a settlement.

The caravans stay in the village for a day or so and new caravans come every day. None of the donkey-drivers would appear to be local to the settlement or even to the region. Thus, they do not know what the residents buy and sell. None of the caravans stay in the settlement over the Sabbath since all of the drivers return home by this day. There are other sources which further elaborate on this matter. Thus, for instance, it is stated: "Conjugal rights mentioned in the Torah [that a husband is legally required to join with his wife] – men of leisure, every day; workmen, twice a week; donkey drivers, once a week; camel drivers, once every thirty days; sailors, once every three months. This is the view of R. Eliezer" (M Ketubbot 5:6). Another view found regarding donkey-drivers is that they must engage in marital relations once every two weeks (T Ketubbot 5:6).

There have been many attempts to explain this mishnah. Maimonides, for instance, explains the mishnah almost in terms of modern-day sexual studies saying that the mishnah attempts to measure the sexual potency of those engaged in the occupations listed above. It is difficult, however, to accept his conclusions and it is doubtful whether they reflect reality in any form or fashion. Rather, it is more likely that the mishnah is describing the mobility factor of these professions. Workmen usually labor in the general vicinity of their homes and can return at least twice a week. The donkey-driver travels throughout the entire week going from settlement to settlement (in the view of R. Eliezer mentioned above). The camel driver who engages in international trade returns home only once a month, while the sailor who sails off to the west (to Rome) completes his journey only after six months when he returns home (as can be learned also from many other sources). Thus, the donkey-driver leaves home on Sunday, spends the week buying and selling agricultural produce and returns home for the Sabbath.

Another source along a similar vein states: "And the donkey drivers used to go up from Arab to Sepphoris and they said – R. Hanina b. Dosa has already started the Sabbath in the city" (PT Berachot IV, 7c). This source does not describe a one-time occurrence, but rather a regular phenomenon. The donkey-drivers, it seems, came from Sepphoris, the central city of the central Galilee, and they used to return home for the Sabbath. The distance between Arab and Sepphoris is about 13 km, and taking into consideration the nature of the terrain, the ass could make the trip in 3.5 hours. It is likely that the drivers went directly home on their return journey and in this final stage no longer engaged in business. Otherwise, the source would seem to indicate that R. Hanina began the Sabbath on Friday afternoon.

As mentioned above, the donkey-drivers wandered from settlement to settlement throughout the entire week and returned home for the Sabbath. The source above deals with the final stage of the week. Later, we shall discuss this tradition in greater detail as well as expand upon the role of Araba in the economic network of the Galilee. Needless to say, there were cases in which the donkey-drivers spent a good deal of time in a particular settlement. Thus, for example, the traditions pertaining to the city which has been beguiled and accepted idolatry mention a donkey-driver who spent a month in a settlement, but this would seem to be the exception to the rule. Halachically speaking, these donkey-drivers were not considered residents of the settlement in which they were working at the moment, since it was felt that they spent too short a time there (M Sanhedrin 10:7; T Sanhedrin 14:2; BT Sanhedrin 112a; BT Bava Bathra 8a and additional parallels).

T Demai 1:10 states:

> One who buys from a donkey caravan in Tyre and from stored produce in Sidon is exempt (from tithes). From stored produce in Tyre and from a donkey caravan in Sidon one is required (to set aside tithes).
> . . . R. Judah says – a donkey caravan which goes down to Achzib – tithes must be set aside, since the produce is said to have come from the Galilee. The sages say – it is to be considered exempt, until it is determined from where the produce came.

We shall not delve into all the details pertaining to this very difficult law. Suffice it for the moment to say that the donkey caravans brought produce from the Galilee via Achzib to the coastal cities of Tyre and Sidon. We saw above that there was a view that the donkey-drivers returned home only once every two weeks and it is possible that the law referred to drivers who worked in such a caravan, which probably left from a central point (Sepphoris?), travelled during the week acquiring produce, and reached its designated market (Tyre) by the Sabbath. During the following week it would buy produce in this area, which it would sell as it worked its way home (to Sepphoris?).

The role of the donkey caravan in the economic framework of the period explains many *halachot* which testify to the donkey-drivers being bound together into professional guilds, as it were, offering insurance, aid and cooperation to its members. In the Jewish town and in the *polis* there were other such guilds. The majority of the guild traditions, however, relate to the donkey-drivers. Thus, for instance, another *halachah* describes a system of mutual insurance to provide an ass for a driver in the event that his dies (T Bava Mezia 11:25; BT Bava Kama 116b). Another law relates that it is forbidden for other drivers to pass a slow donkey in a caravan (T Bava Kama 2:10). A different tradition tells of a guild of donkey-drivers which bought merchandise together (salt) (Midrash Psalms 12). This guild apparently had a leader, although it is impossible to determine what his status or responsibilities were.

From all the sources cited above, it would seem that the donkey caravan was the central component in the economic systems described above. By wandering from settlement to settlement, the donkey caravan served as the primary conduit of merchandise, whether agricultural produce or of a non-agricultural nature. It is important to remember, however, that the central settlement as well as the central markets still played an important role in the economic system.

III.3 Direct commerce between village and *polis*

There are not many traditions which specifically mention the direct marketing of agricultural goods from the village region in the city or the direct marketing of city goods in the village. This is not to say, however, that the phenomenon did not exist; in fact, it was probably quite prevalent. Fruits grown within a radius of one day's travel from Jerusalem were marketed in that city (M Maaser Sheni 5:2 – the tradition may relate to Maaser Sheni (the second tithe), produce to be brought to Jerusalem and eaten there, but it is clear that it reflects economic reality in general).

Josephus informs us that the commander of the Gischala region took care to organize centralized marketing of the local produce (Vita 13). Gischala was the capital of a toparchy and thus it would seem that during a state of emergency, the produce of the entire toparchy was brought to the capital settlement and sold there together. An additional expression of the relationship between the city or central settlement and the surrounding region is found in the words of R. Johanan in PT Bava Mezia V, 10c: "all the towns nearby to Tiberias – when the price is set in Tiberias they set their own price [= based on the price in Tiberias]." In other words, the price of merchandise was set in the central settlement and, in any case, most of the economic activity took place there. The *midrash* describes the economic activity of Joseph in Egypt in a similar manner. According to the *midrash*, Joseph collected the produce of the entire region in a central city. The *midrash* cites Tiberias and Sepphoris as examples of such central cities (Genesis Rabbah 90:5, p. 1105).

A more explicit example of this economic practice relates to Ascalon. R. Pinhas b. Yair (beginning of the third century CE) tells of the villagers living in the Ascalon region who used to come to the market in the *polis* during the day and towards evening return to their villages (T Ahilot 18:18 and parallels). Some villages may have maintained courtyards or houses in the larger cities which served as economic or business stations, as, for example, may have been the case regarding the courtyard of Beth Galodah in Lod (T Eruvin 9(6):2), which perhaps belonged to the village of Galodah (DJD II, no. 115) and is identified with Jalud near Akrabim. There was the courtyard of Beth Gadiya in Jericho, which perhaps belonged to the residents of Ein Gedi (T Sotah 13:3; PT Sotah IX, 24b; BT Sotah 48b; BT Yoma 9b; BT Sanhedrin 11a. The name appears in parallels and manuscripts in such other forms as Guriya and Geriya in addition to the other form cited above). It is also possible that the courtyard of Beth Aris in Lod belonged to the village of Aris or Haris in Samaria (Abel 1927). It is also likely that the courtyard of Beth Ya'zek in Jerusalem belonged to the residents of Azeka in the Shephela (M Rosh Ha-Shanah 2:5).

The Sanhedrin also met a number of times in such courtyards. They did not meet in these courtyards because they had to convene in secret as suggested by Klein (1939, p. 161), but rather because these courtyards were semi-public and often empty, which, therefore, allowed for accommodation for visiting sages when not being used by the village owners. Unfortunately, however, there is no real proof that this was the nature of these courtyards.

There are many additional traditions regarding agricultural produce brought to such coastal cities as Tyre, Acco, Caesarea and others, but the high percentage of non-Jews in these cities, and consequently the different economic situation there, makes it difficult to use these sources in relation to the other cities in the Land of Israel (see discussion in Chapter 4.VI below).

Talmudic traditions mention the markets of Tiberias and Sepphoris quite often. Non-agricultural products were the basic products sold in these markets. The sources mention such specific markets as a cosmetics market, a market for animal skins, for wool and for fowl and even a wheat market. Most of the agricultural produce, though, was probably marketed and distributed through the services of the donkey caravans in accordance with the net model discussed above (III.1). Other items produced by the various forms of labor required a central market in order to be sold, and that was basically the role of the market in the central settlement. We have already discussed artisans who travelled from settlement to settlement. We shall return to deal with these matters later on in our discussion of the Roman road network, and we shall show that our conclusions above are correct.

III.4 Trade and commerce in the *polis*

Every *polis* had some sort of constructed market-place (*agora*). This market was usually rather large with a courtyard and space for permanent stores and stalls (Chapter 1.II.4 above). The city also had *basilicae* which served as trade or commercial centers (Krauss 1910–12, II, pp. 365–6; Tsafrir 1985, pp. 89–92).

There were other stores in the city, whether individual or in clusters, in addition to those in the *agora*. Such a group or cluster of stores is referred to in Talmudic literature as a "*shuq*" (Hebrew: lit. market). A large city usually had a number of these specialized markets for individual products such as a fish market, or fowl or wool markets. The "*shuq*" of Talmudic literature is the equivalent of the *"emporion"* (emporium) of non-Jewish sources of the Empire and Syria (A. H. M. Jones, 1964, pp. 855–8, 864–72). Talmudic sources also refer to *"emporim,"* or large-scale merchants, and the vessels or implements which were sold in the marketplace are described as *"anporia"* – vessels or literally "merchants" vessels, implying that they were "mass produced" and as such had no unique or distinguishing marks which could be found, for instance, on the vessels of a small workshop or factory (M Bava Mezia 2:1; T Bava Mezia 2:1). BT Bava Mezia 23b explains *"anporia"* as meaning "new vessels," but this is a rather liberal interpretation. See also Midrash Psalms 118, p. 486, ed. Buber. Cf. also Krauss 1910, II, p. 686, n. 301).

Another term in Talmudic literature for a large market was the *"durmos,"* such as the one in Tiberias (BT Bava Mezia 72b; A. H. M. Jones, 1964, p. 284).

The economic activity of the *polis* was organized and supervised by the *agoranomos*. The hundreds of weights found throughout Palestine with the seal of this official serve as proof of economic activity, as we have already seen above (Chapter 2.III.4).

IV. REGIONAL MARKETS AND FAIRS

IV.1 The market on Mondays and Thursdays

IV.1.1

Some Talmudic traditions mention a regional market which operated on Mondays and Thursdays. These traditions are found within the following contexts.

(1) Courts used to convene in the various towns on Mondays and Thursdays (M Ketubbot 1:1; BT Bava Kama 82a; T Taanit 2:4). This practice was ascribed to Ezra. Needless to say, this is hardly historical fact, but it does indicate that the practice was quite ancient. The traditions do not explicitly state why the courts met on these days, but it would seem that the days were chosen because many people assembled in towns on those days to go to market.

(2) A virgin was wed on Wednesday (M Ketubbot 1:1). The mishnah states that this day was chosen in order to allow the husband to be able to complain the next day in court if he found that his wife was not a virgin. The Tosefta and Talmuds bring additional reasons for the choice of this day, but it would seem that the matter was basically rooted in popular custom of unknown origins. In any case, it provides additional proof for the meeting of the court on Thursdays.

(3) Talmudic tradition states that Ezra decreed that the Torah was to be read on Mondays and Thursdays (M Megillah 3:6; 4:1; T Megillah 4(3):10;

PT Megillah IV, 75a; Tractate Soferim 10:1; BT Bava Kama 82a *et al.*). To be more explicit, it is the Babylonian Talmud which ascribes the decree to Ezra. However, in the continuation of the discussion there and in the Mekhilta, the decree is ascribed to "Prophets and Elders" (Mekhilta Va-Yisa 1, p. 154). The parallel in Mekhilta of R. Simeon b. Yohai (on Exodus 15:22, p. 103) ascribes it only to the "Prophets". In any case, all of this would indicate that the custom to read the Torah on these days was quite ancient (on the unique nature of these days see also M Taanit 4:3 and parallels). The Talmuds explain that these days were chosen in order that three days should not pass without the reading of the Torah. It is possible to discern, though, that this custom was also connected to public gatherings. A veiled reference to this is the explanation that ten verses should be read "in reference to the ten *batlanim.*" The *batlanim* were "men of leisure" in the sense that they served as municipal functionaries. In any case, the tradition connects between the reading of the Torah and municipal institutions (BT Megillah 21b).

(4) The residents of villages celebrated the festival of Purim on the nearest Monday or Thursday to the fourteenth of Adar. The explanation given for this custom is that there was nobody in these villages who could read the megillah scroll for the community and perhaps they did not even have a "community" at all. Monday and Thursday were chosen because they they were the "days of assembly" (M Megillah 1:1). The Talmuds add another reason stating that these days were chosen because the residents of the agricultural villages come to the towns in order to supply the markets with fresh produce (PT Megillah I, 70b; BT Megillah 4b).

(5) From all of the above it would seem clear that Mondays and Thursdays were market and "assembly" days.

(6) Mondays and Thursdays were also the days on which public fast days were to be declared if there was a need to do so (M Taanit 2:9 and parallels). The sources state a number of reasons for this custom. The major reason, though, would seem to be the public gatherings which took place in any case on these days. The assembly and public prayer which took place in the "town courtyard" were the basic elements of such public fasts.

The tradition above regarding Purim connects the market-days with the rural sector or with villages (Chapter 1.IV above). The law pertains to the residents of the villages and not to the townspeople. As far as this law is concerned, a "village" is a settlement which does not provide community services (the ten *batlanim* mentioned above) and this is clearly one of the characteristics of the village.

IV.1.2

The descriptions of the market-days above reflect a rather undeveloped commercial and judicial framework and certainly are not in keeping with other information regarding the level of the economy and management in

Jewish settlements in the Mishnah and Talmud periods. Clearly, there was not a market in every small town or settlement, since the assembled population there would not justify such an economic outlay. It is also fairly clear that the market on Mondays and Thursdays was not intended for the residents of the town itself, since they could buy what they needed on any other day of the week.

In the Mishnah period (at least after the destruction of the Temple and apparently already at the end of the Second Temple period) every town had established stores, was visited by caravans and set up at least a small market on the days that these caravans came. The courts probably also met every day of the week, as we shall shortly see, which would not be in keeping with the traditions pertaining to Monday and Thursday as market-days and as days on which the courts convened. During the course of the Mishnah and Talmud periods later on there were "market-days," but these generally related to regional fairs in which there was rather large-scale trade and commerce. These fairs also benefited from the support and aid of the government (see below IV.3) and in any case, they had nothing to do with the market-days mentioned in the traditions above.

It would seem, therefore, that the market-day traditions above refer to a rather early period (Hellenistic) before the success and development of the economy during the Roman period. As we saw above, all of the *halachot* in these traditions are rather ancient and this, of course, is in keeping with our claim. Moreover, there are Talmudic traditions attesting to the fact that already by the Javneh period the market-days of Monday and Thursday had lost much of their importance. Talmudic tradition also relates a clear objection to the Monday–Thursday rule regarding the reading of the megillah for villagers, based, as we remember, on the ancient market-days. Thus, it is stated: "R. Judah said – When [do we follow the rule that the megillah is read for villagers on the Monday or Thursday nearest Purim]? In a place where they assemble on Mondays and Thursdays. Since they already assemble there, they should assemble only at the correct time" (T Megillah 1:3). R. Judah then seems to refer to areas in which the market-days did not take place only on Mondays or Thursdays, but rather that the villagers came to town more frequently, indicating a greater frequency of market-days. If such is the case, the megillah should be read at the correct time, the 14th of Adar and not the Monday or Thursday before.

There were also problems later on regarding the custom of wedding a virgin on Wednesday. T Ketubbot 1:1 relates that: "from the danger and afterwards they used [to wed virgins] on Tuesday and the sages did not object. If, however, he wished to wed her on Monday, they did not allow it." The original custom was apparently changed during the period of the Hadrianic persecutions, but interestingly enough, once the danger passed, they did not revert to the original custom. The change during the persecution probably came about as a result of the desire to minimize the fanfare attendant upon the wedding ceremony, and thus it was rescheduled to a day before the villagers began assembling in the town. After the persecutions had subsided, though, the original custom was not reinstituted.

PT Ketubbot I, 24d qualifies this *halachah* "according to the view of R. Eliezer (quoted in the Mishnah and who had explained the law in relation to the days on which the court convened) – in those places in which the court meets every day, she may be married on every day of the week." Thus, the Talmud describes the possibility of the courts actually convening on a daily basis. In PT this possibilty is theoretical; BT relates the matter to actual practice:

> Rav Samuel bar Isaac said – this was the case [regarding the wedding days of a virgin]: only from the period of the decree of Ezra when courts met on a regular basis only on Mondays and Thursdays. Before the time of Ezra's decree when the established courts used to convene every day, the woman could be married on every day of the week.
>
> (BT Ketubbot 3a)

In any case, the connection between the day on which the virgin could be wed and the days on which the court convened was questioned in Talmudic tradition and eventually the connection was abandoned. The Talmud then had to seek the basis of the law in various legendary traditions, some of which were cited not as additional explanations for the law in the Mishnah, but in place of the attempt to connect the practice to the meeting of the court (PT Ketubbot I, 24c; BT Ketubbot 3a).

According to what we have seen so far, it is possible at this stage to summarize and state that during early periods there were many regions in which the settlement pattern was based on small satellite villages around a central regional settlement. Under these conditions, the market-day, in addition to its prime economic purpose, served as a day of communal and municipal assembly.

During the Roman period, with the further development of settlement, a new economic system was instituted and developed. As the settlements expanded, the municipal and economic institutions also grew. This made the old market-days obsolete, and in many places they were completely abandoned (see below). In spite of this, the *halachot* attendant upon this obsolete reality continued in many instances to exist, perhaps explaining the need in Talmudic literature to find new or additional reasons for their observance. The sages may have realized that the initial reasons for the existence of these laws no longer applied, but in spite of this they did not change the law, even if they stated that this was possible because conditions had changed. According to our understanding of the situation, there were two parallel developments or processes. One was in the realm of economy and communal services and organization, the other was related to the development of *halachah.* Both of these processes, however, are well known in scholarly literature.

Thus, the market-days of Talmudic literature do not reflect the relationship between town and village during the Roman period, the period which concerns us in our study, in spite of the fact that the village remained dependent on town or city throughout the entire period. Villagers, for instance, continued to remain dependent on the town for the reading of the *megillah*, although the reading for these villagers did not now have to take place on the old market-days of Monday or Thursday.

IV.2 Regional markets

T Demai 1:11 lists three markets: "the 'dome' (Hebrew: *kupat-kipat*) of Yeshuv and the 'dome' of Antipatris and the market of Patros." According to the Tosefta, fruits sold at these markets came from Har Ha-Melekh (from northern Judaea) and wheat and legumes came from Judaea. The markets mentioned in this Tosefta were, therefore, large regional ones and apparently located near or on important local roads. From the continuation of the *halachah* it becomes clear that these markets no longer functioned after the Javneh period since R. Judah states – "and 'now' the sages said all the towns of the Cuthim along the road." R. Judah (and 'now') refers to the Usha period (138–80), thus the beginning of the *halachah* refers to the Javneh period (70–132). Since the markets were apparently destroyed, the continuation of the Tosefta no longer refers to them, but rather to the villages "along the road." These three markets were located in the rural sphere and, in fact, it is important to point out that fairs were often located in rural districts (as was the case, for instance, regarding Woodeaton in England, located in an open rural district or *Beth Ilannim* (= Terebinth) (see below IV.3).

There were large commercial centers in other sites such as in Javneh or in Regev, mentioned in T Demai 1:13–14, but these were permanent markets and not seasonal fairs.

IV.3 Fairs

IV.3.1 Major characteristics of the fairs in the Land of Israel

IV.3.1.1

The Roman fair was referred to as *"paneguris"* in Greek, occasionally as an *"agora"* and sometimes in the Latin form of *"nundinae"* or the more neutral *"mercatus"*. In Talmudic literature the forms *"atlis"* (*'tlys*), *"atliz"* (*'tlyz*) and *"yerid"* are found. The *"atlis"* was apparently a local form of a Greek term, meaning exempt (from customs excises), and as we shall see later on, such exemptions were an important component of the fair (Lieberman 1959).

The form *"atlis"* is rather rare in Greek literature, but was apparently more common in the East. *"Yerid"* is simply a translation of the Greek word meaning to go down, which is also the meaning of the root *yrd* in Hebrew. This word is likewise rather rare in Greek regarding the phenomenon we are discussing. *Paneguris* and *nundinae* do not appear in Talmudic literature. Thus, one of the Talmudic terms is simply a transcription of a rare Greek phrase, while the other Talmudic one is a translation of another rare Greek term. The common and accepted Greek or Latin words were apparently not too frequently used in Palestine (Z. Safrai 1984b).

The fair in Palestine had a number of common characteristics. (1) The fair was "seasonal" in that it took place either only once a year or a limited number of times. (2) The merchants at the fair received a tax and customs exemption from the emperor. The rate of the exemption is not known, but it certainly was of great economic importance. (3) There was large-scale trade, including rather expensive items. (4) The fair had religious overtones; it was dedicated to a god and during the course of the fair there were various religious rites and ceremonies. (5) The fair also served as a forum for social gatherings as well as for amusement (including the sexual variety) and leisure. (6) The fair could take place either in a *polis* or nearby one, or in the rural sector. (7) Only the emperor could grant permission to establish a fair, and this permission was of great importance. Sometimes the emperor was personally involved in the establishment of a fair and, through legislation, provided for the supply of goods to it.

It is now necessary to examine Palestinian Talmudic literature regarding fairs in light of the factors mentioned above, in order to determine the role of the Jews in this branch of economic activity. It is also important to point out that Talmudic literature may add significant data to the information about fairs at this time in general. Due to various problems related to the presentation of this material, we shall diverge somewhat from the order of characteristics cited above.

IV.3.1.2.1 The first two characteristics we shall discuss are the religious nature of the fair and the tax reductions or exemptions.

Talmudic literature sees the fair as a market dedicated to some form of idolatry, and most Talmudic references deal with this aspect of the fair. Thus, for example, M Avodah Zarah 1:1–2 deals with the prohibition against engaging in commerce with non-Jews on their festival days. In spite of the fact that at first glance the prohibitions seem quite severe, the festivals on which commerce was forbidden seem to be only those connected with the cult of the emperor. The Mishnah mentions three festivals in particular, and perhaps a number of private festivals should be added to the list.

M Avodah Zarah 1:4 states the following rules:

(1) "If there be idolatry in a town, it is permitted [to have business dealings

with the idolaters] outside the town. If there was idolatry outside the town, it is permitted [to have business dealings with idolaters] inside the town."

(2) "Is it permitted to go there? When the road leads only to that place it is forbidden, but if one can go on it to some other place, it is allowed."

3. "If a town has idolatry and some shops in it are decorated and others are not – and there was such a case in Beth Shean – the sages said: Those that are adorned are prohibited and those that are not are permitted".

Although the Mishnah does not explicitly state that these laws pertain to a fair, this seems quite clearly to be the case based on the parallels as well as on the logic of the matter. We shall cite a number of reasons for this conclusion. (1) The Mishnah could not possibly intend to prohibit business in every city or town which had a pagan temple ("If there be idolatry in a town"). The preceding *mishnayot* discuss the prohibition against engaging in business with pagans on their festivals and the details of these *mishnayot* are different from those discussed in the present Mishnah. Therefore, it would seem that M Avodah Zarah 1:4 is not discussing festival days. (2) The parallel to the Mishnah in T Avodah Zarah 1:5–6 adds a number of pertinent details. Thus, in relation to no. 2 of the Mishnah cited above, the Tosefta explicitly states that it relates to a "fair in that city." No.1 of the Mishnah is also described in the Tosefta within the framework of "a fair in that city" (and at this point the Tosefta adds no. 3 of the Mishnah). The Tosefta, in any case, understood the entire Mishnah as referring to a fair. (3) Resh Lakish explains no. 1 of the Mishnah in PT Avodah Zarah I, 39c as referring to a fair ("it was taught relating to a fair"). (4) In BT Avodah Zarah 11b Resh Lakish mentions the "*atliz*" of Gaza as an example for rule 1 of the *mishnah*. All of this would seem to prove that M Avodah Zarah 1:4 deals with a fair.

PT Avodah Zarah I, 39c explains the reason for the prohibition: "Inside [the town] it is forbidden [to engage in business with them] because he enjoys customs benefits. Outside [the town] it is permitted because he does not enjoy customs benefits." Thus, the reason for the prohibition seems to be that tax or customs benefits were offered at the fair in honor of a pagan divinity. Since it was forbidden for a Jew to derive benefit from idolatry, he could not derive benefit, in this case, from the fair. BT Avodah Zarah 12a provides other explanations, but it would seem that BT was not aware of the reality of the situation.

Since the fairs in the Empire were indeed dedicated to pagan divinities, it would seem that the explanation in PT fits in quite nicely with the general information regarding fairs. The claim that the tax or customs benefits were dedicated to a pagan god is repeated a number of times in Talmudic literature. Thus, for example, the fair of Tyre was prohibited because it was dedicated to the "Gad [= fortune, Tyche] of Heraclius, Diocletian's partner in rule" (PT Avodah Zarah I, 39d), and the prohibition was explained as relating to the fact that "one benefited on account of idolatry." The fair in Acco was referred to in Talmudic literature as *Ntbr'a* or *Ntbh'a*, apparently derived from the Aramaic *mdbh'a* meaning altar, which undoubtedly testifies to the cultic nature of the fair (BT Avodah Zarah 11b).

A clear combination of the economic element of the fair together with the cultic (including a temple) is found at the fair of Beth Ilanim or Botnah (and we shall discuss this matter in detail later on). R. Nathan, one of the sages of the Usha period (*c.* 135–80 CE) relates an interesting custom pertaining to the cult at these fairs (and in fact hinted at in M Avodah Zarah 1:4 discussed above):

> R. Nathan says – the day on which the pagans set aside the customs excise. They announce and say – everyone who takes a crown (wreath) and puts it on his head and on the head of his donkey in honor of the divinity – the customs excise will be set aside. And if not, the customs excise will not be set aside. How should a Jew at such a fair act? If he places a crown on his head, he derives benefit [from idolatry]! If he does not [he pays the excise] and causes benefit.
>
> (BT Avodah Zarah 13a)

On account of this dilemma the rabbis declared that it was forbidden to derive benefit at all from a fair and the merchandise purchased there had to be destroyed.

The law stated above by R. Nathan regarding crowns is quite interesting. An active participant of the cult, who expresses his participation by placing the crown on his head, is exempt from tax. Everyone else was required to pay it. Part of these taxes were apparently diverted to the particular cult in question and this is probably the meaning of the phrase "if he does not and causes benefit." Similar laws existed at the beginning of the Middle Ages in Europe when the profits from a fair were given to a particular monastery or church. In the Roman world, however, such practice was not accepted. In spite of the fact that R. Nathan came to Palestine from Babylonia, it is hard to imagine that the law related above in his name reflects Babylonian practice, since as we shall see below, the Babylonian sages were not familiar with the reality of the Roman fair. It would appear that R. Nathan was describing a custom prevalent in the Roman East which, for some reason, did not receive sufficient or clear expression in the epigraphic or literary sources of the Empire.

As we saw above, the fair presented a number of halachic difficulties and the rabbis, as was their custom, analyzed the particulars of a number of pertinent cases. The rabbis, in the course of their deliberations, provide a goodly amount of material on fairs that were quite unique. Thus, for example, T Avodah Zarah 1:7 states: "A fair given by the kingdom and one given by the city [= *polis*] and one given by prominent citizens of the city are permitted. Only a fair of idolatry is forbidden." The Tosefta mentions here four types of fairs. The last one on the list was the common fair mentioned above. The other three types are not mentioned in other Talmudic sources. As we stated above, a fair could be established only by the emperor. The Tosefta, on the other hand, mentions fairs established by the *polis* or by prominent citizens there. The differentiation between the cultic fair and the fair set up by the government or emperor as found in Tosefta is also unknown in other sources. A fair established by a municipal senate in Africa apparently did exist (Johnson *et al.* 1961, p. 207). The first three types of fairs mentioned in the Tosefta were apparently not dedicated to any divinity or cult, and this is the reason why they were permitted, even if there may have been some cultic trappings during the course of the economic gatherings. Perhaps also these first fairs offered no tax benefits and for this reason were permitted. It is interesting to note that the rabbis had some doubts regarding the fair at Tyre, whether it was dedicated to a divinity or simply in honor of the emperor Heraclius; or in other words, the rabbis debated whether this fair was one "given by the government" and thus permitted (PT Avodah Zarah I, 39d).

There is no reason to reject the historicity of the tradition in the Tosefta. On the other hand, it is likely that the differentiation mentioned there was not common in Palestine or the surrounding areas. Both PT and BT had difficulty in harmonizing the various *baraitot* which permitted one to go to fairs with the vast majority of halachic tradition which forbade it. Never was it suggested, however, to solve this problem based on the criteria set up by the Tosefta discussed above. It is likely, therefore, that non-cultic fairs were quite rare or perhaps existed only very early.

IV.3.1.2.2 The "*atliz*" As we saw above, the fair was usually associated with paganism, and therefore it was forbidden to derive benefit from it. No traditions, however, forbid one to frequent the "*atliz*." Thus, for example, R. Akiva met Rabban Gamaliel and R. Joshua at the *atliz* of Emmaus. It is inconceivable that three of the greatest sages of this period knowingly transgressed the law. Halachic tradition stated that animals intended for sacrifice, for instance, which had become unfit could be sold at the *atliz* (M Bechorot 5:1 and parallels). M Arachin 6:5 mentions the opportunity of selling a cow at an *atliz* and that "if one kept a cow till the *atliz* took place, its value goes up." Similar cases and instances of transactions in the *atliz* are mentioned in numerous other Talmudic traditions (Midrash Psalms 86:2, p. 373; Pesikta D'Rav Kahana 'Aser Te'aser 7, p. 168).

In view of all this, it would seem that the *atliz* had no connection to any pagan cult. Perhaps the *atliz* should be identified with the fairs "set up by the city (*polis*) and by prominent residents of the city" mentioned above, although it is impossible to prove this (Safrai 1984b, p. 145). The sources do not specifically mention the tax exemption at the *atliz*, but it is certain that it existed since, after all, the word derives from the Greek phrase meaning tax exemption. The full or partial tax exemption explains the somewhat difficult source that the *atliz* offered the opportunity to sell goods at an expensive price (see above and see also the contribution of the discussion below), even though at such popular fairs goods were usually sold at lower prices. The source apparently reflects the fact that the merchant made a rather good profit because of this tax exemption, in spite of the fact that he sold at a low price.

IV.3.1.3 Seasonal activity

Roman fairs, as we remember, were seasonal and those fairs mentioned in Talmudic literature were also seasonal. This is clear, for example, from Mishnah Avodah Zarah 1:3–4 discussed above and T Avodah Zarah 1:9 mentions, for instance, those "merchants (Hebrew: *tgryn* – see above on the *tagar* [*tgr*] who arrived early for the time of the fair and those who arrived late – it is permitted [to do business with them]. It is only forbidden [to do business] during the time of the fair itself." Thus, it is possible that the *atliz* was also seasonal, although there are no clear-cut references to this fact.

IV.3.1.4 Large-scale commerce and expensive items

The fair appears in the sources as a place where one can find or sell such expensive goods or commodities as houses, fields, vineyards, slaves, hand-maidens and pepper, which was rather expensive. The sources also mention the sale of clothing, utensils, metal implements and fruits as well as shoes, "*keluskin*" (*klwskyn*), an expensive type of cake or roll, and regular bread (T Avodah Zarah 1:8; 3(4):1; PT Avodah Zarah I, 39c–d; BT Avodah Zarah 13b; Genesis Rabbah 47:10 (p. 476–7)). As we saw above, the *atliz* is mentioned specifically regarding the sale of animals and clothing.

Many sources mention caravans with large-scale and important merchants (*pragmatotes*) traveling through the Empire and going from fair to fair. It was the merchants in these caravans who brought the exotic and expensive gifts to the fairs. An inscription has even been found in Italy with a map indicating a thirty-day itinerary of such a caravan (see Figure 52), based on the premise that the fair took place one day a month. The map is also quite schematic, based on a comparison of it with the map of Italy (Snyder 1936).

Talmudic sources relate information regarding such mercantile caravans in Palestine. Thus, for instance, we saw the source above (T Avodah Zarah 1:9; BT Avodah Zarah 13a) regarding large-scale merchants (Hebrew: *tgryn*) who came early, or late, for a fair. The *tgr* appears in Talmudic literature as an important merchant operating on a rather large scale, and it is likely that he should be identified with the *pragmatotes* of the non-Jewish sources (II.3 above).

It should be pointed out, though, that not every *tgr* mentioned in

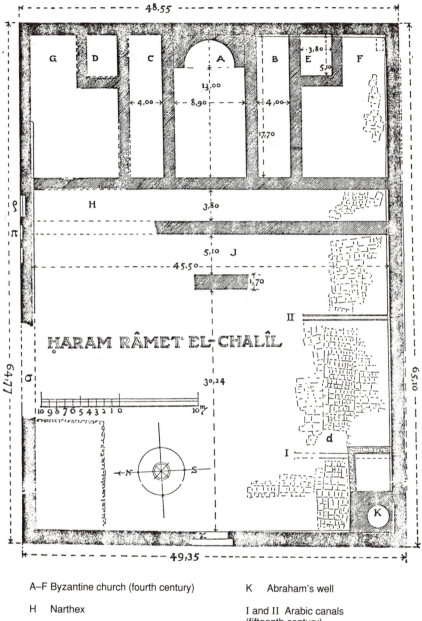

A–F Byzantine church (fourth century)

H   Narthex

J   Abraham's altar

K   Abraham's well

I and II Arabic canals
(fifteenth century)

Figure 51 The fair at Botnah. Plan of *Haram Ramet el Khalil* after the excavations. After Mader 1957, Plate 37.

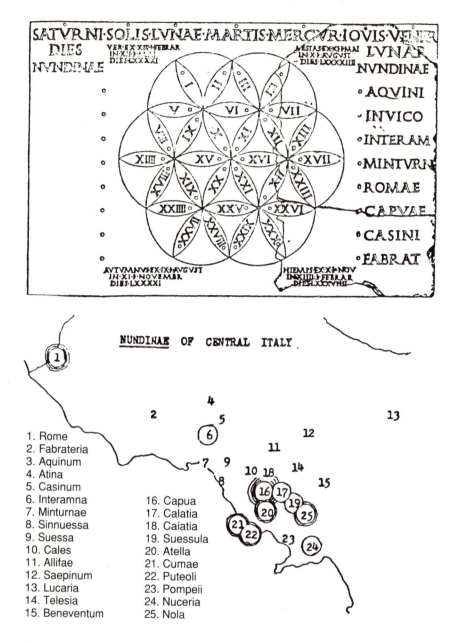

Places circled once (twice, etc.) occur
twice (thrice, etc) on the *nundinae* lists

Figure 52 Fairs in central Italy. After MacMullen 1970, p. 340.

250

Talmudic literature was connected with fairs, and there were undoubtedly some who operated on a regular basis in the various *poleis*. The majority, however, were apparently connected to fairs, traveling from one to another, and thus much of the information regarding this group found in Talmudic literature can add to our store of knowledge concerning fairs in general.

IV.3.1.5 Forum for social gatherings and amusement

In addition to its economic and religious functions, the fair also served as an amusement center of sorts. Thus, for example, Sozomenos states that prostitution was not prevalent at the fair at Beth Ilanim (*Hist. Eccl.* 2. 4), implying that at other fairs this was not the case. Talmudic literature was also aware of this aspect of the fair, mentioning, for instance, bear-baiting in the market-place as well as acts of "heroism" and other such attractions there (Genesis Rabbah 86:4 (p. 1056); 87:3 (p. 1063); Choricius, *Or.* 13. 2. 1). In spite of the fact that in the last sources cited, the market and not the fair was mentioned, it hardly seems likely that this was the reality of the common market-place.

Everyday life in the market-place is described rather nicely in the *midrashim* which describe the sin of Israel at Baal Peor in terms of their own contemporary reality:

> The Amonites and Moabites went and built small stalls from Beth Ha-Jesimoth all the way unto the Mount of Snow and put there women selling all kinds of sweets. And Israel used to come to eat and drink there. At that time one Israelite would enter the market and seek to buy something from an old woman and she would sell it to him at its real value. And a young girl would call him and say – come inside and buy it at a lower price . . . and he would enter her stall and the pitcher was full of wine.
>
> (Sifre Numbers 131, p. 170–1 and parallels)

The presence of small stalls, prostitutes plying their wares, the selling of wine and foods was characteristic of the large market or fair but certainly not of the common or regular market.

Talmudic literature also provides references to promiscuity in the *atliz*: ". . . 'and Casluhim (Gen. 10:14)' – they used to set up *'utlisin* [= a plural form of *atliz*] and they would steal each others' wives" (Genesis Rabbah 37:5 (p. 348)). In spite of the fact that the source refers explicitly to adultery and not prostitution, and in spite of the fact that it is not possible to prove from this source that this was the situation in every type of fair, it would seem quite likely that there was a degree of sexual promiscuity at every type of mass gathering which would, of course, include the fair. Such was apparently also the case regarding the inn.

An interesting combination of a fair with elements of amusement and leisure was found at Hamat Gader. This suburb with its hot baths was an important and well-known bathing center in the East and during the bathing season, which was quite short, there was also a fair at Hamat Gader (Epiphanius, *Panarion* 80. 7). It is difficult to determine whether this combination was planned or coincidental. In any case, Epiphanius, who provides the information on the matter, states that the fair took place every year because of the great number of people coming to bathe in the hot springs.

IV.3.2 *The location of the fair*

Talmudic traditions take it for granted that the fair was located in a *polis* or at least in a town ('*yr*) (T Avodah Zarah 1:5–6 and parallels). This would seem to indicate that fairs were located in some sort of settlement or another. We shall return to deal with this matter when we discuss the fairs in Eretz Israel. However, there were also fairs outside the city or settlement (such as Gaza – see above).

The Mishnah and Tosefta also inform us of an otherwise unknown fact, that the exemption from taxes was not applied to every store in the town. Those stores which benefited from the exemption were decorated with garlands (M Avodah Zarah 1:4), thus indicating that the stores participating in the fair were not concentrated in one section of the city, but rather were spread out throughout the entire settlement. The Tosefta refers to these as "mixed stores" (T Avodah Zarah 1:6) within the context of the *halachah* cited above in the name of R. Nathan (BT Avodah Zarah 13a) that those participating in the fair would place crowns or garlands on their heads as well as on those of their animals. All this indicates that participation in a fair was a special privilege enjoyed only by some of the merchants in the town. It is understandable that there is not much epigraphic information on this aspect of the fair, and therefore the Talmudic evidence on the matter should be accepted.

IV.3.3 *Participation of Jews in fairs*

As we have seen above, according to the *halachah*, not only is it forbidden for a Jew to go to a fair, but it is also forbidden to even appear to be going to one: "If a fair is in that city [= *polis*] – one does not go there or even to the towns nearby, since he would in such a case appear to be going to the fair. This is the opinion of R. Meir. The sages say that the prohibition applies only to that city" (T Avodah Zarah 1:5).

A similar view is expressed in the Mishnah (Avodah Zarah 1:4): "It is permitted to go thither? When the road leads only to that place it is prohibited, but if one can go thereon to some other place, it is allowed." BT Avodah Zarah 12a brings a *baraita* showing that the sages and R. Meir also disagreed regarding this matter. The Mishnah is in accordance with the teaching of the sages. R. Meir (c. 138–80 CE) was more stringent in his view. Thus it would seem quite clear that it was forbidden for a Jew to participate in a fair. This, however, was not always the case. There are traditions which relate that in spite of the many *halachot* on the matter, Jews did frequent fairs. Thus, for example, it was necessary for Tosefta Avodah Zarah 3(4):19 to state that if someone went to a fair and bought or sold an object, the object was to be destroyed and no benefit could be derived from the money. The way the *halachah* is phrased is clear proof that Jews did frequent fairs.

Other traditions, particularly from the Amoraic period (third to fourth centuries CE) seem to indicate that the prohibition began to be considered outdated and eventually was ignored (on the stages of this development see Safrai 1984b, pp. 147–51). Not only did the people at large begin to participate in these fairs, but even the sages of those times, who did not apparently object to this participation, frequented them themselves.

The fair at Botnah (Beth Ilanim) near Hebron offers a marked and clear-cut example of this development. Various Amoraim cite this fair as the most pagan one in Palestine. Thus, for example, R. Johanan said: "The sages forbade only a fair like that at Botnah. And thus it was taught – There are three fairs: The fair at Gaza, the fair at Acco and the fair at Botnah. And the most famous one (also in terms of its pagan nature) was the one at Botnah." Thus, it would appear that R. Johanan forbade only those fairs which were especially pagan such as the one at Botnah (PT Avodah Zarah I, 39d). Sozomenos (*Hist. Eccl.* 2. 4), however, tells us that during the time of Constantine (mid-fourth century CE) there was at the site a large fair and, as it happened, an inter-denominational festival, frequented by Jews, pagans and Christians. There is no reason to reject this testimony, and it thus seems clear that despite all the prohibitions, large numbers of Jews frequented this fair, which as we just saw, was considered to be the most pagan of them all. Later on, Sozomenos relates that the emperor forbade non-Christians to participate in the festival and also abolished the pagan and Jewish cult there.

The emperor's edict seems to have been effective and Jews apparently ceased to frequent the site, since Jerome relates that the Jews hated this fair in particular (Hieron., Commentary in Jeremiah XXXI,15).

As stated above, the sources clearly indicate that the prohibitions against frequenting these fairs were gradually abolished. The prohibition was quite clear during Tannaitic times. By the second generation of Palestinian Amoraim, there were a number of partial exemptions to this rule and by the days of R. Abahu (end of the third century), the prohibition extended only to special cases. The exemptions to the prohibition undoubtedly reflected the growing economic importance of these fairs on the Palestinian scene. The fair at Botnah, which had been explicitly prohibited in the third century, was in the final analysis permitted, although the particular halachic formulation of this innovation has not survived. However, it should be pointed out that there is also the possibility that the sages really never permitted the fair and the Jews frequented it anyway. We have seen more than once in the sources we have studied that there was at times a gap between the teaching of the sages and the socio-economic reality of the times.

IV.3.4 The fairs in the Land of Israel (Figure 53)

The Fair at Botnah (Beth Ilanim). The fair at Botnah was "the most famous" of them all, both in terms of its pagan nature and in terms of the amount of information available about it. Many ancient traditions pertaining to the fair have survived and it has also been studied and excavated (Bacher 1909; Krauss 1909; Mader 1957–8, II; Figure 51). The site has also been excavated quite recently by Y. Magen (1991). The fair at Botnah is the best example there is of Roman fairs throughout the Empire. In view of the great amount of scholarly material on the site we shall make do with a brief presentation of the relevant data.

The fair at Botnah is referred to in Greek as a *paneguris* and in Latin as *mercatus*. In Hebrew it is called a *yerid* (fair) or *shuq* (market). The use of the word in Greek clearly shows that the fair at Botnah belonged to the "*paneguris*" type of Roman fair discussed above and that the Hebrew *shuq* may also refer to a fair.

The holy place at Botnah was located at an intersection which without a doubt was the transport and communications center of the southern Judaean mountains. During the Second Temple period the site was called Beth Ilanim and Herod built an impressive enclosure there, and this is only one of the proofs of its important cultic function at that time. The enclosure measured 3,200 square meters and was surrounded by a massive wall. Mader's excavations have shown that the Herodian construction was destroyed during the War of the Destruction. Hadrian rebuilt it and founded a fair there. The Church Fathers tell of the great number of Jews sold there as slaves after the Bar-Kochba War for a rather cheap price.

As we saw above, the fair at Botnah is referred to in Talmudic literature as the most pagan of all the fairs in Eretz-Israel. One of the *midrashim* brings the fair of Botnah as an example of a site in which there was large-scale trade, even more than in Caesarea, the capital of the province (Sifre Deuteronomy 306 (pp. 338–9) and parallels). We shall see later on that the *midrash* is accurate in its description.

Sozomenos (*Hist. Eccl.* 2. 4), as we saw above, states that until the time of Constantine, an important combined fair and inter-denominational festival took place at the site with the participation of Jews, pagans and Christians. The emperor was angered by this situation and forbade all cults there apart from Christianity. This put an end to the inter-denominational nature of the festival and the fair became Christian. Constantine renovated the enclosure and in the east built a large church which took up about one-third of the

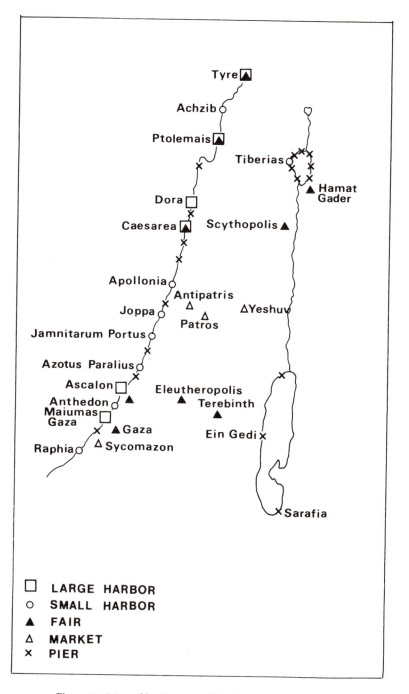

Figure 53 Map of harbors and fairs in the Land of Israel.

entire enclosure. In the southwest section of the enclosure was a sacred well and the ancient terebinth. Along the walls there were apparently stores, and the center of the enclosure was the open courtyard which actually was the courtyard of the church. Two of these stores have been preserved. One measured 16 × 11 meters while the other measured 9 × 10 meters, apart from the section in front of the church where it had a length of 16 meters. There was room, therefore, for another three stores in the enclosure itself. Most of the commerce probably took place in stalls in the open area outside the immediate enclosure. Sozomenos tells us that the fair took place in an agricultural area and those who came there set up tents, in spite of the fact that there apparently was a settled village right nearby.

The coins discovered at the site indicate that merchants came from Syria, Asia Minor, Egypt, Greece and Italy and even from as far away as Spain and Gaul to participate in this fair. All together, approximately 1,287 coins predating the Muslim period have been discovered at the site and 1,275 of them date to the Roman–Byzantine period. Of these coins, 201 come from cities, the majority from provinces outside Palestine and only a few from the cities of Judaea. International trade (= transit) in general and especially that with the eastern part of the Empire played an important role in the commerce there. Among fourh-century coins discovered, comparatively many were struck in distant mints. However, several questions remain to be answered before it is possible to use this information. Comparison of these findings with the fair at Woodeaton in England is quite interesting. The remains there show that there was very little external trade and that the majority of the commerce there was internal, with only a small amount directed to Gaul (Milne 1931).

The large number of coins found at Botnah give a good indication of the extent to which the fair was frequented. Thus, for instance, the many coins from the Constantinian age show that the fair was of great importance at this time. The reference in Jerome, cited above, that during his time there was a famous fair there which the Jews detested, would seem to be proof of this fact. The numismatic remains indicate that the apex of economic activity at the fair was during the first half of the fourth century.

Based on these same remains it would seem that the fair began to decline around the year 400 CE. This decline apparently reflects the general economic decline in Byzantine Palestine at this time. There are no Byzantine coins there after the time of Justinian. The small number of Arab coins discovered indicates that Botnah continued to serve as a cultic site during the seventh and eighth centuries and even later on in the Middle Ages. Contemporary pilgrims, though, refer to it only as a cultic site and not as a fair.

Gaza. According to the Chronicon Paschale (224), the fair in Gaza was established by Hadrian and those Jewish slaves which he could not sell at Botnah were sold here: "And even today that fair is called the 'Hadrianon'."

We have already discussed a number of additional references to this fair. During the Byzantine period, the famous Maiumas festival took place here (Choricius 13. 2. 1).

Hamat Gader. We have already discussed the reference to this fair in Epiphanius above.

Ascalon. One of the permanent pagan cultic sites was Sarafia in Ascalon. The Talmudic reference to the site would seem to indicate that it was rather important (BT Avodah Zarah 11b), or in other words, that there was a large fair there. Trade and business, apparently at permanent stores which had a regular tax exemption, continued throughout the entire year, since it is difficult to assume that the fair itself functioned during this entire time. Thus, it was a permanent market which at some time or another officially became a fair. Sarifia is identified with H. esh Sheraf, a kilometer or so from the walls of Ascalon, indicating that this fair was also outside the established urban confines of the city. At the end of the third century CE a *polis* by the name of Diocletianupolis was established at this site or in its immediate environs.

Ptolemais. The fair at Acco (*mdbh'a* – see above) is mentioned in Talmudic sources a number of times together with Acco as one of the permanent pagan cultic sites in Palestine. It is also mentioned as one of the three major fairs in Palestine, together with Botnah and Gaza, which we have mentioned above.

Tyre. The fair at Tyre was established by Diocletian and PT Avodah Zarah I, 39d preserves a popular condensed form of the dedicatory inscription. This inscription has been discussed to a great extent in scholarly literature, and there is therefore no reason here to expand on the matter (Cohn 1929; Krauss 1909; Lieberman 1959).

Beth Gubrin. Chapter II of the Vita of Epiphanius (*Vita Epiphanii* 2. 6) discusses the fair that took place in this city.

Beth Shean. The fair in Beth Shean was in the city itself, and only some of the stores participated in it. This fair is cited in Talmudic literature as an example of a fair: "If a city has idolatry and some shops therein are decorated and others are not decorated – there was such a case in Beth Shean" (M Avodah Zarah 1:4). The tradition apparently dates to the Usha period (second century CE) since R. Meir discusses it.

Emmaus. We have already discussed the *atliz* at Emmaus. We have also already seen that Rabban Gamaliel came to this fair, together with R. Joshua (Javneh period and beginning of the second century CE) to buy a cow to slaughter for the wedding of his son. It is interesting that Rabban Gamaliel, who was quite rich, went from the *polis* of Javneh where he resided, to Emmaus to buy a cow. Undoubtedly it was possible to buy such an animal in Javneh, but the one in Emmaus was probably cheaper. Emmaus at this time was an important rural settlement with a high standard of living. It is possible that veterans of the Tenth Legion resided in this settlement (*BJ* 7.

217), although the identification of these veterans' settlements is somewhat difficult (Klein 1939, p. 150).

IV.3.5 The development of fairs in Eretz-Israel

A complete understanding of the development of fairs in Eretz-Israel requires that we begin the discussion in the Second Temple period. We have already discussed the phenomenon of the early Second Temple period of the small regional market which took place on Mondays and Thursdays. We have also seen that the traditions relating to the decline of these markets date to the Usha period.

In addition to the small regional markets just mentioned, a number of traditions referring to the period before the Bar-Kochba War mention larger regional markets such as Yeshuv, Patros and Antipatris. It is possible that such markets no longer existed after the Bar-Kochba War. As we saw above, it is quite clear that the three fairs which we just mentioned did not survive into the post-Bar-Kochba period.

It is possible that the *atliz* which we have discussed already in great detail represents this type of larger regional market. The *atliz* is mentioned in the sources before the Bar-Kochba War, and the one in Emmaus existed during the Javneh period (80–132 CE). The *atliz* is also mentioned in M Arachin 6:5. This chapter apparently reflects the Javneh period (and mentions such Javneh period sages).

It would appear, however, that the *atliz* continued to function after the Bar-Kochba War since a number of post-Bar-Kochba period sages were familiar with this institution. Thus, for example, R. Hiyya Ha-Gadol (beginning of the third century CE) cited an example of "one who sold a *talit* at an *atliz*" (Pesikta D'Rav Kahana 'Aser Te'aser 7, p. 168). It is impossible to know for certain whether the *atliz* was an internal Jewish market, but the sources seem to give the impression that it was not as pagan as the fair.

Perhaps the difference between the markedly pagan markets and those which were not so pagan can be seen in the *midrash* referring to Jewish fairs: " 'And it shall come to pass when thou shalt break loose' [Hebrew: *tyrd* – the same root (*yrd*) as *yerid* (fair)]. He said to him – you have your fairs and he has his fairs" (Genesis Rabbah 67:7, p. 762). "He" in the tradition represents Esau, the brother of Jacob, and "you" is Jacob himself. "Jacob" is the accepted symbol for the People of Israel, while "Esau" is the symbol of Rome. Isaac thus tells Jacob that the Jews will also have "fairs", although it is impossible to know whether they were fairs in the complete sense of the word or simply large regional markets.

The fairs appear in Palestine only after the Bar-Kochba War, and the first mention of *"yerid"* in Talmudic tradition appears from the Usha period (135–80) and afterwards. The fairs at Botnah and Gaza, for instance, were built by Hadrian and the one at Beth Shean is also mentioned at this time (although it is possible that it was established before). It is during the Usha period that we first find *halachot* dealing with particular aspects of the fair. It is true that some of these *halachot* are anonymous, making it possible to doubt the Usha attribution, but the historical situation at the time would still make the Usha period the most likely candidate for the first appearance of the markedly pagan fair in Eretz-Israel.

Until the Usha period the Romans followed a liberal policy of "civilizing" the province of Judaea, without forcing Roman cults upon other populations or without stressing too much the pagan nature of Roman civilization. After the Bar-Kochba War, Roman policy changed as is indicated by the pagan temples built on the Temple Mount in Jerusalem, at Schechem and at Botnah. It would seem, therefore, that the expansion of pagan fairs, and especially in the rural regions which were formerly Jewish, is connected to this change in Roman policy.

It is of no importance for our purposes, and the matter has been much debated in scholarly literature, whether it was this shift in policy which caused the Bar-Kochba War or whether the shift was the result of the war itself, a response to the severity of the revolt. It is interesting that it is R. Simeon b. Yohai, a contemporary of the Usha period, who complains about the markets that the Romans established (BT Shabbat 33b and cf. BT Avodah Zarah 2b), and it is not impossible that he is referring to the developments which we have just described.

IV.3.6 The geographic significance and the economic function of the fairs

Seasonal fairs existed throughout the world, and they can be found in different types of societies and under different geographic conditions (Skinner 1964; Nash 1966, pp. 58–80). Theoretically, the fair can serve a number of economic needs:

(1) An internal regional meeting-place. Such a fair would address itself to the lack of local balance between supply and demand of certain items. Needless to say, such a fair indicates a rather undeveloped region in terms of trade and commerce and the lack of a permanent market in the economic sense of the phrase.

(2) Connection between the residents of a region and inter-regional trade. Such a fair serves as a conduit for the marketing of the agricultural produce of every sub-regional unit on the one hand, and on the other hand as a fairly high-level source of supply for the residents of the region. This type of fair is most common in an area in which there is much economic activity, but rather limited external trade.

(3) A central and inter-regional meeting place for merchants. Such a fair

serves as a forum for large-scale merchants to come into contact with each other. In such a case, the particular region in which the fair takes place and the residents of that region play only a tangential role in the commercial activity of the fair, usually providing only services and a geographic base. Such a fair would generally take place at a commercial and transport center. Today, such fairs are essentially trade conventions generating publicity and business connections. In the past, goods in kind were sold at such a fair.

As we have seen above, slaves, land and animals were bought and sold at such fairs. Land transactions generally represent an aspect of high-level local trade. Slaves and animals were also basically intended for the local regional market. It is possible that the large-scale merchants engaged in the buying and selling of slaves among themselves, but it is still more likely that this sphere of economic activity was basically intended for the local market, with the large-scale merchants serving as either exporters or importers of the commodity.

The coins discovered at Botnah, discussed above, are a good indication of the level of external trade (transit). Literary traditions allude to the sale of pepper, an extremely rare and expensive item – another example of external trade.

One could also buy at a fair, however, sandals, *"keloskyn"* (see above), clothes, fruits, utensils and other such items characteristic of small-scale and local trade. The Babylonian Talmud also records instances in which local householders participated together with large-scale merchants (*tagar*) at fairs (BT Avodah Zarah 13a). This combination of local villagers and large-scale merchants coming together at a fair is also found in Epiphanius' description of the fair at Elathropolis (*Vita Epiphanii* 2. 4). Epiphanius himself, a simple villager and resident of one of the neighboring settlements, participated in this fair, as well as a Jewish merchant from Beth Gubrin called Jacob. Jacob is referred to as a *"pragmateutes"* and, as we remember, this is the term in Talmudic literature for a large-scale merchant. In spite of the fact that the account in *Vita Epiphanii* does not explicitly say that Epiphanius and Jacob participated in business transactions there, it would not seem too unreasonable to assume that this was the reason for their presence there.

The fair, however, does not seem to have been connected to the regular supplying of agricultural produce. Thus, for example, the "caravan," which was the usual instrument of marketing for agricultural produce, did not participate in the fair (T Avodah Zarah 1:7). It is possible, though, that the *"tagar,"* the large-scale merchant, did engage in some small-scale agricultural business since, as we have already seen, these merchants usually did engage in the sale of agricultural produce.

Thus, it is possible to see quite conclusively from the source material that local residents did participate in trade and commerce at the fairs, and that local items were bought and sold there. This, as we remember, characterizes the second type of fair mentioned above. The traditions pertaining to external trade show that the fairs also served as convenient forums for large-scale merchants, businessmen and local producers to meet. This characterizes the third type of fair discussed above. In such fairs the local population participated basically as customers and consumers. Such a fair offered the possibility of buying expensive and rare items usually brought from afar (spices, slaves and perhaps also animals) as well as local ones (real estate and animals). The local residents paid for these goods with their local surplus. One could, of course, also find the more common necessities at the fair and festival.

The traditions cited above give the clear impression that the fairs in Palestine were not identical, at least from an economic standpoint. This also seems to be clear from the traditions dealing with fairs in general found in Ammianus Marcellinus who tells of a large fair at which merchants from Persia and China met with Roman ones (14. 3. 3). At the same time we find in Libanius (11. 30 and Chapter 3.II above) reference to large villages whose commercial structure was based upon regional fairs in which trade and business dealings were transacted between the various villages themselves, a phenomenon characteristic of the first type of fair in our list above. It would appear, therefore, that there were different types of fairs in the same region itself. This would seem to have also been the case in Palestine. Likewise, a fair may have fulfilled more than one economic or trade function.

As we have already seen, trade in Palestine was quite developed. Those fairs which were intended for local commerce contributed only a small amount, however, to this trade. The importance of these types of fairs was perhaps that commerce there enjoyed large tax benefits. These tax benefits or reduction were meant to provide incentives to large-scale merchants to participate, and compensation for expenses involved in traveling to more removed areas. It is impossible, though, to compute the economic significance of these tax benefits, since although it is known that sales taxes were rather high, it is not known whether a complete or only partial exemption was granted.

Much of what we have just stated above would lead to the conclusion that some of the fairs during the Roman period in the more developed regions of the Empire as well as in Palestine were in actuality artificial economic creations, existing without real internal economic justification and surviving only on account of tax policy initiated from above. As we saw above, many of the pagan fairs centered around some local pagan festival or cult, and it is possible that some of the fairs did not begin as such, but came about as the result of local merchants or businessmen wishing to exploit the large gatherings at the festival or cultic site. It should be pointed out, however, that such explanations might fit regarding the type of fair found at such sites as Hamat

Gader, for instance, but not for such fairs as those at Botnah in which there was rather high-level and even international trade.

Be the economic justification of the fairs what it may, it seems clear that during the Roman period the fairs were an important economic, social and religious institution which greatly influenced commerce and trade in Palestine, to the extent that the *halachot* which had originally forbidden Jewish participation there were gradually abrogated.

V. THE NATURE OF REGIONAL TRADE

V.1 Seasonal trade in agricultural produce

Regional trade was to a great extent seasonal, and the price of a particular commodity was occasionally set only after the end of the season. Before the price was set, the only transactions undertaken were of a speculative nature and the sages forbade them, fearing that usury would result: "No arrangement may be made for [buying] produce [to be delivered at a future date] before its market price is set" (M Bava Mezia 5:7 and parallels). The discussion in the Talmuds on this Mishnah indicate that this was the law only in rural districts. In cities such as Tiberias and Sepphoris, there were usually permanent markets in which business continued throughout the entire year. However, even in the market of Tiberias, for instance, some of the trade was seasonal: "R. Johanan said – all of the towns near Tiberias, only when the price is set in Tiberias may they engage in buying and selling [of commodities]" (PT Bava Mezia V, 10c). This would seem to imply that the price was set in Tiberias itself only after the season. This tradition also shows the dominance of the city in establishing regional prices.

However, in spite of all the traditions pertaining to regional trade, its scope was probably quite limited. Thus, for example, in the *agora* of Curnub (Mampsis) there were only about 23 stores, and the market at H. Ta'mur had only 10 (see above, Figure 16 and below, Figure 67). This conclusion would be no different even if there were a few additional stores there and in spite of the impression one receives from the sources.

V.2 The chain of middlemen

V.2.1

The small-scale farmer sold his produce through the various market channels. It is important to determine the manner in which the produce was marketed and transported. The basic settlement pattern in the Roman world was based on the farmstead (*villa* – Chapter 1.V above). The farmstead was a large, organized agricultural unit which could take the necessary steps related to overland marketing. In other words, they required no professional middlemen to transport the produce to market. The farmsteads had their own wagons and drivers for this purpose. This was not the case regarding the transport of produce over bodies of water and various means of shipping and transport were set up for this purpose. The farmstead, as just stated, did not have its own ships and used instead the other means available. The situation described above probably pertained to those areas in Palestine with many villas and farmsteads (such as the Caesarea region, the upper *shephelah* east of the plain and the Lod area). The situation was undoubtedly different in the mountainous regions. In order to understand the marketing system it is necessary to understand two components: the number of times the commodity changed hands and ownership, and the manner of transport in each of these stages.

The more times that the produce changed hands, the higher the cost of transport. However, economic logic and principles dictate that the more developed the economic system, the greater number of specialties involved in marketing and transport. Thus, it is likely that anyone involved in marketing would participate in only one aspect of marketing and that the growers would not be involved in this at all. In a developed economic system, therefore, the produce will change hands a number of times. If this is not the case, then the economic system is apparently not very developed.

V.2.2

There are five ways to transport goods from economic station to station. (1) The owner of the goods markets them himself using his own means of transportation. (2) The owner of the goods markets them himself using professional means of transportation. He hires the means of transport, but undertakes the actual transport or supervision himself. (3) The original owner of the goods sells the merchandise to a professional to transport it to market and sell it there himself. (4) The owner of the goods sells the merchandise to a transport professional who brings the goods to market. This professional then sells them of his own volition to another merchant who will market them. (5) The owner of the goods sells them to a merchant located in the city. The latter then transports them himself to market, either through the use of professional services or by himself.

In primitive economic systems, the owner of the goods undertakes all labors himself, and therefore markets the goods himself without recourse to middlemen or transport professionals. As the level of the economy rises, more and more stages of marketing and transport are taken over by professionals undertaking their tasks with increasing levels of efficiency. This allows the grower to divert more of his energy to growing his crops. It is necessary to note, however, that there are differences between the various types of merchandise and it is necessary to examine the transport network of each individual type.

The criteria pertaining to the establishment of a transport system in the ancient world are quite complex. The basic principle is that in spite of the fact that the grower often has a surplus of free time at his disposal, during his "season" he is extremely pressed for time. The marketing of the produce takes place after the necessary stages of preservation, partly when the grower is still under pressure of harvest or related tasks and partly when the pressure has been relieved and the grower has time at his disposal and desperately seeks work. Marketing agricultural produce does not take much skill. It is logical, therefore, that the grower would prefer to market the produce himself. At the very most he would have to hire an ass from his neighbor and perhaps a driver, but it is hard to imagine the farmer who would not have these at his disposal without recourse to his neighbors. It should not have been too difficult then for the farmer to have brought his produce to the regional center.

The donkey and camel caravans discussed above undoubtedly had merchants attached to them. These were not representatives of the growers, but rather merchants who transported the produce directly to a harbor city (Tyre). A caravan like this also used to frequent Caesarea (PT Moed Qatan II, 81b). The *midrash* provides a rather realistic description of this phenomenon in relation to the sons of Samuel: "A caravan used to pass by and they [= sons of Samuel] used to abandon the cares of Israel and engage in business" (PT Sotah I, 17a). When the caravan came to the settlement, the residents would stop their regular activities in order to engage in business with the merchants in the caravan.

Additional *halachot* describe the donkey-drivers in the caravan as merchants, such is the permission that they had to buy wheat and other agricultural produce at a low price and to sell it for a much higher one someplace else (T Bava Mezia 4:8 and parallels). It should be pointed out that these driver-merchants did not necessarily sell their merchandise in a big city. Another example of a law pertaining to this group is found in T Bava Mezia 3:25 (and BT Bava Mezia 58a): "If the donkey drivers sought to buy wine and oil – one should not send them to someone who never sold wine and oil." From these traditions, as well as from others cited above, it is possible to see that there were independent merchants in the donkey caravans who transported merchandise directly to the central city or even to a coastal city. They spent only a short time in the large city and thus it is possible to conclude that they did not engage in retail trade or small-scale business but only in wholesale trade of a greater scope.

PT Bava Mezia V, 10b provides an interesting example of the relationship between the donkey caravans and the farmers. The tradition pertains to donkey-caravan drivers who receive payment from residents of a settlement to buy fruit intended for them and to sell it to them at the low price (of the place of original purchase) and not at "the expensive rate." The sages permitted this transaction in spite of the fact that it might have appeared to have the trappings of usury, as long as the fruit was bought nearby "from someplace to where one could go and return home on the same day," or in other words, a half day's distance away. The sages most likely permitted the transaction because there probably was not much of a variation of prices within such a limited area. Talmudic literature mentions distances of a half-day's travel and a full day's travel quite frequently, but this is not the appropriate forum to examine this phenomenon.

V.2.3

In addition to the transport network mentioned above, there were other means of commerce. Midrash Psalms 12 tells of R. Jonathan who came to buy wheat in a certain settlement. R. Jonathan, as is well known, lived in Sepphoris and the tradition, therefore, would seem to describe a merchant from a central city seeking merchandise in small settlements. The continuation of the tradition there describes a similar case. R. Hiyya of Sepphoris went down to Surta to buy wheat (this is the correct reading and does not refer to Sura in Babylonia. It is inconceivable that wheat should be imported to Palestine from Babylonia). The tradition cited above regarding the donkey-drivers who came to Hamuniya to buy wheat should also be understood in this manner. Such is the case also regarding the tradition about the merchant from Laodicea who came to buy oil in Gischala (BT Menahot 85b).

There were, however, undoubtedly donkey-caravan drivers who were not independent merchants, but rather hired workers who received a salary. It is difficult at times to determine whether a particular tradition relates to the hiring of a donkey to market merchandise or the hiring (or borrowing of it) to bring produce to the house of the renter. Both of these possibilities existed. We shall cite a number of traditions pertaining to the latter:

> A man says to his fellow – and my donkey shall go with you today and yours shall go with me tomorrow. However, he cannot say to him – mine shall go with you today to the east and yours with me tomorrow to the west . . . and if the payment is equal it is permitted.
>
> (T Bava Mezia 6:14)

The first part of the *halachah* apparently pertains to bringing the fruit from the field to one's house (and we have already commented above regarding this possibility). The second part, though, pertains to the transport of crops over greater distances, or in other words the marketing of agricultural produce by the farmer with the aid of a rented or borrowed ass. It is interesting to note that the Tosefta takes it for granted that both farmers are not marketing their produce in the same place, another proof of the "net" model discussed above and the apparent lack of a permanent center.

Many traditions deal with the rental of an ass and they probably pertain to

265

transport over long distances. Thus, for example, it is stated: "If one hired an ass to drive it over hilly country and he drove it in a valley. [If one hired an ass to drive it over a] valley and he drove it across hilly country" (M Bava Mezia 6:3; T Bava Mezia 7:7. See also T Bava Mezia 7:12).

It was common practice that one gave a meal to hired workers (M Bava Mezia 7.1 and many parallels). One of the most common instances of this *halachah* pertains to the feeding of the donkey-drivers (T Bava Mezia 3:27; 4:9; T Demai 5:14 and parallels). The numerous *halachot* on this matter indicate the frequency that these drivers were hired. The actual cultivation of the crops was based on the labor of the farmer. The transport of the crops was apparently dependent to a great extent on the hired labor of a driver (and sometimes his animal).

PT Bava Mezia VI, 11a cites an example whereby an ass is hired to go from Lod to Caesarea. Avot D'Rabbi Nathan (version B, chapter 27, p. 55) cites a conversation between Hillel the Elder and the donkey-drivers of Jerusalem. It is interesting to note that according to this tradition there were set rates for each section of a journey. If one hired a donkey for only part of an official section he still had to pay the full rate.

The *halachah* also cites as a regular phenomenon the fact that the rental fee for a driver is composed of three components: driver's fee, donkey's fee and "hotel" expenses (T Bava Mezia 3:23; BT Hagigah 9b). Such a *halachah* would clearly take for granted that long distances were involved. Thus, it appears that the hiring of means of transport, whether a donkey, a wagon or even a ship, was a fairly common phenomenon (T Bava Mezia 7:9, 14 *et al.*) and that a good many of the hundreds of traditions relating to the rental of means of transport refer to the marketing of produce over long distances.

Sometimes the owner of a donkey would hire out just the animal, while at other times he would go along with the animal. A clear indication of this phenomenon is found mainly in the traditions dealing with the hiring of an animal to transport people, such as the driver who provided the means of transportation for R. Jonathan on his way to Jerusalem (Genesis Rabbah 32:10, p. 297 and parallels). The tradition we cited above regarding the components of the fee for hiring a donkey ("He gives him the fee of the driver, the fee of the donkey and the fee of the inn") is also indicative of this phenomenon (see also T Bava Mezia 7:1). The owner or driver would most logically accompany his animal on long journeys. He would hardly be needed for short ones, proof once again of the frequency of long-distance transport.

The donkey-driver often appears in Talmudic tradition as a hired worker of a householder. The householder can pay his salary in goods and he is permitted to borrow money from the moneychanger in order to secure funds to pay his salary (T Bava Mezia 4:8 and parallels). The second instance cited in the Tosefta, the payment in cash, does not add too much to our understanding. The first instance, the payment in kind, is quite interesting.

There exists the fear that if the driver is paid in kind, he will sell the produce at a higher price and that this might be construed as interest. A similar case is found in T Sheviit 6:26: "The donkey drivers, camel drivers and merchant sailors who engaged in commerce in the Sabbatical Year, received their fees in produce of the seventh year." The mentioning of these three different types of transport workers clearly indicates that the *halachah* does not pertain to transport over short distances in the village sphere. It is likely that other cases dealing with the fees of donkey-drivers, such as the case in Avot D'Rabbi Nathan cited above (version A, ch. 12) also deal, therefore, with long distances, although, of course, it is impossible to prove this.

It is possible to sum up and state that Talmudic literature mentions all the different types of transport systems, including those that were quite organized. This fits in nicely with our conclusions above regarding the socio-economic organization of the donkey-drivers.

V.2.4

The issue of middlemen is much more complicated. It would appear to be quite clear that the donkey caravan did not use or need the services of middlemen of any kind and that the donkey caravan did not sell produce to small-scale retailers. Beyond this, it is difficult to arrive at any conclusions. The ancient road network might be of some aid in understanding the nature of this trade. It is possible to discern a number of basic models (Figure 54). These are not simply theoretical models, but rather the result of the analysis of remains existing today. The explanations and arguments pertaining to the establishment of the road network are based on functional and logical analysis. It is not possible to prove anything relating to this matter based on literary sources.

In model B, and perhaps also in model C, it seems that roads 1 and 2 were meant to serve transportation from the village to the cities at the ends of the road. Road 3, however, connected the village directly with the road. The only explanation for the additional connection would be that the means of transport was changed at the road: the farmer transported his produce by donkey up to the road, and from there he loaded it upon a wagon. If this explanation is correct, it might indicate the existence of an additional middleman who transported the goods in his wagon.

There is no proof in the first three models that there was any change whatsoever in the mode of transport. The lack of a direct road to the main highway might be the result of historical, economic, topographic or any other type of unknown reason, in spite of the fact that in model B the absence of a direct route is quite prominent. Proof of this may be found in diagrams of the transport network of a number of settlements in Samaria (Figure 55) near Roman roads. The road network in Samaria has been quite extensively examined. This is not the case, however, regarding the Galilee.

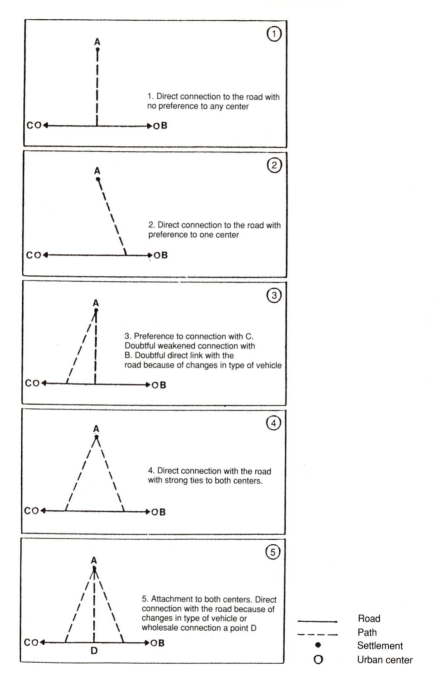

Figure 54 Transport connections between village settlements: possible models.

Most of our examples, therefore, will be from Samaria. It is likely that the economic structure in both regions was similar.

It is not always easy to discern examples of model B. There are a number of reasons for this. (1) The purpose of the road is not always clear. Sometimes it reaches the main highway and even connects to an additional settlement. In such a case it does not serve our present purposes. Sometimes the road continued to another settlement, but it is quite apparent that the function of the road was to connect with the main highway, and it was only by accident that another road was connected to this main highway from the other direction. Thus, for example, path no. 1 continues on to the village of a-Levad (Figure 55d), but it is not the shortest path from Ramin to this village since it winds around for no apparent reason. Moreover, at this point two paths meet, one from Ramin and the other from a-Laved. It is quite clear that this is not one path, but rather different sections. (2) It is not always possible to find remains of the road. (3) It is possible that the connection to the road was meant to serve as an access to agricultural terrain between the road and the settlement and not to the settlement itself.

The road network system in Samaria and the Galilee (pp. 276–87 below) points to the fact that model 5 was chosen quite often (Figure 54). It is impossible to state that this was the only system which actually existed, but in most cases in which it is possible to reconstruct the road network there seems to be proof that at the point on the main road which deviated or connected to a settlement there was some type of commercial activity. This is most likely additional proof of the reconstruction we have suggested above. See also below (VII).

VI. INTER-REGIONAL AND INTERNATIONAL TRADE

VI.1 Inter-regional trade

Basically, each of the major regions of Eretz-Israel – Judaea, Peraea, Galilee and Samaria – were separate units. The impression that one gets from Talmudic tradition is that there was hardly any travel between the various regions. However, the economic conditions and reality in Palestine necessitated inter-regional trade. Thus, for example, there are hardly any wine presses in the Golan, and therefore it is quite certain that the residents of the Golan imported wine from other regions of Palestine. The cities in the Peraea and Transjordan maintained trade ties with the coastal cities via Samaria and Judaea. The coastal cities were dependent on the agricultural produce of the hill region. Thus, for example, the *halachah* mentions an instance of one who "takes up fruit from the Galilee to Judaea" (M Maasrot 2:3).

It is most likely that the inter-regional trade was conducted by the

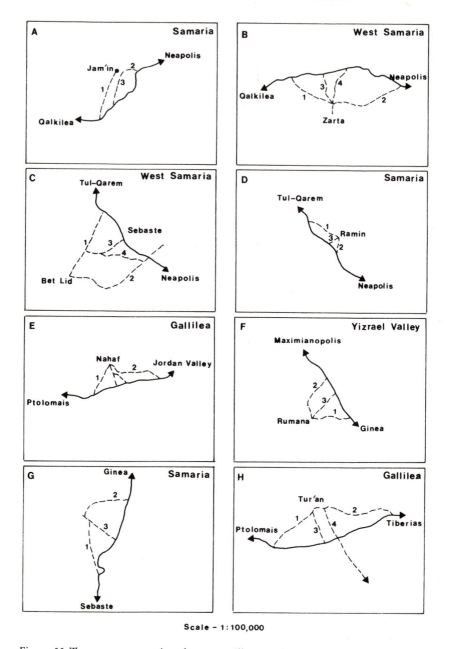

Scale – 1:100,000

Figure 55 Transport connections between village settlements and roads of Samaria.

large-scale merchants and *tagarim* (see above) in the *poleis*, and for all intents and purposes it was really inter-urban trade. We have already stated that the sources mention quite often the caravan which travelled rather long distances (and see below). The fairs, which we have also already discussed, served to foster inter-regional trade, and it would appear that it was therefore unnecessary for any special trade or commercial networks to be developed to fulfill the needs of this type of trade.

VI.2 International trade

As we have already seen, Palestine was dependent on a trade network in order to export produce as well as to import various necessities. In the next chapter (VII.2) we shall present a list of all imported and exported goods. Some of these goods, such as dates, oil and wine which were exported, and fish which were imported, were rather heavy and therefore their transport was no easy matter. Most of this type of trade was, most likely, conducted via the harbors in the coastal cities. The produce or goods was loaded onto ships and transported throughout the world.

The shippers transported the goods, but did not usually own them. The owner usually sailed with his goods, but this was not always the case. The *midrash* describes the situation quite nicely: "One has a ship, but the merchandise in it is not his. And if one has merchandise, then the ship is not his" (Midrash Psalms 24:2, p. 102; Krauss 1911, II, pp. 333–49). This reality was also the basis for some of the code of maritime law (see below).

The Roman Empire succeeded in developing trade in the Mediterranean basin and its fringes, and turned this area into an open trade region. One of the means of accomplishing this was to set up trade stations of a particular city in another country. Thus, for example, we know of such trade stations of Tiberias and Gaza in Rome. There were other such stations, of course, in Rome (Ostia). There were also trade stations of foreign cities in Palestine. Tiberias was not one of the major commercial cities of Palestine, and it is therefore likely that other cities such as Caesarea, Beth Shean, Ascalon and Gaza, for instance, were more active in this sphere. Representatives of the mother city were found at these stations and they also served as hostels for visiting merchants (Avi-Yonah 1964, p. 113; Brehier 1903).

Many merchants from Palestine were to be found engaged in commerce and trade throughout the cities of the world, and merchants from all corners of the Roman and Persian Empires were also to be found in Palestine. Greek merchants were in Acco as early as the mid-fourth century BCE and Athenian merchants visited Jerusalem. It is possible to learn about the many foreign merchants operating in Palestine from conditions in Joppa, which was a city of only secondary importance in terms of trade. Among the many funerary inscriptions found in the ancient necropolis there are those that mention a seller of cumin, apparently a native of Joppa, a dealer in a junk from Alexandria and two linen merchants from Tarsus (Klein 1939, pp. 80–8). What is interesting regarding the linen is that Tarsus was also an important producer of linen. Since linen was also produced in Palestine it is difficult to know whether these merchants bought Palestinian flax or linen or sold Tarsian linen in Joppa.

It is safe to assume that most of the international trade was not conducted by Jews. Thus, it is likely that the number of foreign merchants or agents found in the non-Jewish cities of Palestine such as Caesarea, Gaza or Ascalon was far greater than the number of such agents in Joppa. Thus, for example, merchants from Neapolis, or a trade station from that city, were found in Moesia in Asia Minor (*IGR* 1964, nos. 630–1).

The trade with Syria and the cities of the desert was obviously overland trade. The donkey caravans of the Galilee which engaged in regional trade used to frequent Tyre, Sidon and Acco, as we have already seen above, which were all regional trade centers (T Demai 1:10; see also III.2 above). The regular "caravan" and the "camel caravan" used to travel even further. The camel caravan used to travel up to a month's distance from its home base (M Ketubbot 5:6; BT Ketubbot 62b). The use of camels which were especially appropriate for desert travel, as well as the great distances it would travel, indicate that this type of caravan would trade with the desert regions, bringing them agricultural produce and taking back spices and rare metals indigenous to these regions. Such caravans are quite well known from the Palmyra region (Heichelheim 1938, pp. 198–203; Rostovtzeff 1967, pp. 153–72).

The regular caravan served as another means of marketing goods. This type of caravan would also travel great distances and is even mentioned in Talmudic literature together with traveling by ship as an example of traveling long distances. This is the background, therefore, to the traditions and discussions pertaining to this type of caravan and the Sabbath or crossing the desert with such a caravan under difficult conditions (see, for example, T Eruvin 3:2; T Bava Mezia 7:13; 8:25; M Gittin 6:5; M Tevul Yom 4:5 *et al.*).

Such caravans are mentioned pertaining to Syria and there are inscriptions on the organization and distances traveled by caravans frequenting Palmyra. The caravan did not engage in internal trade, and therefore the sages permitted a caravan to pass by a fair since it was generally clear that this was not its destination (unlike the case, for instance, of a regular merchant, a *tagar* or a householder – T Avodah Zarah 1:9). One exception was the fair at Botnah, discussed above, which catered to international trade which is clear from the many foreign coins (from Syria, Egypt, Rome, Asia Minor and even Gaul) found there, while very few local Palestinian coins have been uncovered at the site. Thus, the fair clearly was of the international (or at least transit) trade network (p. 256 below).

As we have pointed out, though, most of the international trade was maritime, passing through the various coastal cities.

The large-scale merchant was referred to in Greek as a *"pragmateutes"* or *"emporos."* The word found most frequently in Talmudic literature is *"tagar,"* which we have already discussed, and occasionally *"pragmateutes"* also appears in this literature. We have also seen that *"emporos"* is rather rare in Talmudic literature. The *tagar* was found in all types of settlements, bought merchandise or produce in the rural sector and sold it at mobile or temporary stalls in the city or village. At times, he also wandered from city to fair. The sources which deal with international trade at this time mention the *"pragmateutes"* as traveling by ship from one coastal city to another and selling his merchandise from a mobile stall at every city he frequented (Sperber 1978, p. 86, no. 34; Heichelheim 1938, pp. 204–8. On the wandering *"pragmateutes"* going from coastal city to city, see A. H. M. Jones 1964, p. 825. See also PT Moed Katan II, 81b; Dan 1971; Doctrina Jacobi; Pesikta D'Rav Kahana, U-Va-Yom Ha-Shemini, p. 420; Ha-Hodesh Ha-Zeh 2, p. 81; 'Aser Te'aser X, p. 172 *et al.*).

VI.3 Transit trade

VI.3.1

During the Biblical period and to some extent during the Second Temple period, transit trade was of great economic and political importance and the traffic between Syria and Egypt was often the background to many political events in Judaea. The western Roman Empire imported spices, metals and luxury items from the East. One of the major routes of this trade passed the harbor city of Gaza. Another important route was the "King's Highway" along the base of the mountains in the Transjordan. Some of the battles during the Hasmonean period were to gain control of this important highway.

Important information on the transit trade from Syria and Greece to Egypt via Palestine is found in the Zenon Papyri from the Ptolemaic period, but this is outside the scope of our discussion.

Things changed, however, during the Roman period. Direct trade between Egypt, Greece and Syria became much more limited and most of it passed through Rome, which was the regional trade center of the Empire. Any direct trade that did take place was maritime and Palestine perforce hardly benefited from it. With the establishment of the Nabatean kingdom, and its incorporation later on into the Roman Empire, the spice routes were removed from Palestinian control, and only the coastal city of Gaza was occasionally to benefit from this trade.

We do not know how the the spice trade was organized. It is impossible to know whether those who transported the spices also owned them or whether they were simply middlemen or hired laborers. It is also not known whether merchants from the cities of Palestine or from Gaza at least served as middlemen in this trade or not. In any event, the volume of this trade was not too great, in spite of the high prices. If the residents of Palestine did not serve as middlemen, but rather only as transporters or providers of auxiliary services, then their profit from this trade was probably quite modest.

As we have already seen, the fair at Botnah essentially served transit trade. Another branch of transit trade pertained to marketing produce of the rich cities of the Transjordan. Their market was oriented to the West – to the coastal cities, since most caravans would naturally have to pass through Neapolis or Beth Shean and would arrive most likely at Caesarea or Acco. Thus, the role of transit trade and road services provided to this trade for the economy of Palestine was limited. An example of profits to be made from road services provided for this type of trade is found in the itinerary of the Egyptian official who passed through Palestine on his way to Syria and once again on his way home (see Schwabe 1954).

VII. THE TRANSPORTATION SYSTEM

VII.1 The main road system

The active and developed economic system described above necessitated the establishment of a road system to serve as the vibrant basis for any economic activity on a large-scale basis. Until the Roman period there were almost no constructed roads in Palestine, although there were recognized highways. The first constructed road in Palestine was apparently that built by the Hasmonean kings which connected Jerusalem with Lod via Emmaus (M. Fischer 1989), by the Hasmoneans or by the house of Herod. Josephus uses phrases which seem to refer to main roads at this time, but for the present it is impossible to know to which roads he is referring and to point out constructed roads from this time.

The first Roman road in Palestine from which there are clear-cut remains is the Beth Shean-Caesarea road which was built in 69 CE by the Tenth Legion (Roll 1976), although it is likely that they built other roads before this one. Both Trajan and Hadrian continued to construct roads in Palestine. The construction of most of the roads of Roman Palestine was completed with the rise of the Severan dynasty at the end of the second century CE (Roll 1976, Figure 56). Some of the roads were constructed out of military considerations alone such as the road from Maaleh Deragot to Ein Gedi and the road that passed along the periphery of the desert from Bethlehem to Carmel. Most roads, however, also fulfilled an economic function, in addition to the military one.

The geographic outlook of those who planned and constructed the road network is unknown. It appears, however, that generally each *polis* was

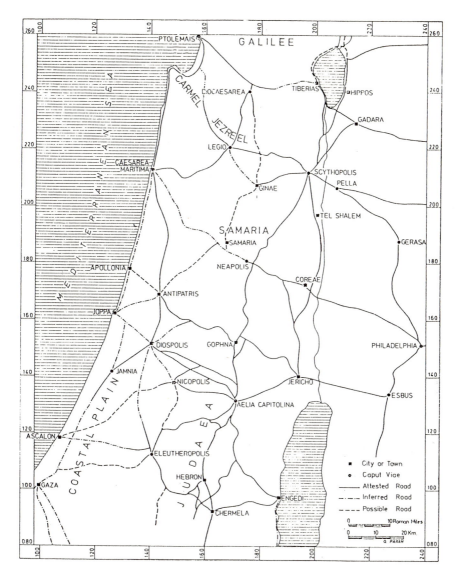

Figure 56 The roads of the Land of Israel. After Roll 1976.

connected to at least its nearest neighbors. In addition, roads were built which connected various cities with major highways such as the road from Lod and Antipatris to Gophna which eventually intersected with the Jerusalem–Neapolis road, or the road from Jericho which also reached this route, or the road from Sebaste which connected with the Beth Shean–Legio road near Jezreel. The major purpose of all these roads, then, was to connect the various *poleis*, and thus it was only the great number of cities, and consequently the roads that connected them, that allowed for the possibility of uninterrupted travel throughout the length and breadth of Palestine.

We do not know which were the most important routes in Palestine. It is likely, however, that the most important road was the route from Gaza to Acco via Caesarea which was essentially made up of roads connecting the individual cities along the coast. This road served the rich coastal cities as well as the traffic from Egypt to Syria. The *Itinerarium Antoninianum* (190–200; 149.5–150.4) lists five major routes in Palestine: from Syria to Neapolis via Beth Shean; from Sarina in northern Syria to Beth Shean; from Caesarea to Eleutheropolis; from Jerusalem to Ascalon; and in a different section of his work he describes the fifth route – the coastal road. These would seem to be the major routes during the time of the author of the itinerary, but this was apparently not the permanent situation. Changes were apparently dependent on developments in certain cities, but this is beyond the scope of our present study. However, it is important to point out that this work stresses the Syria–Palestine connection especially via Beth Shean. Beth Shean was also connected to the Transjordan through the road to Pella. All of this would seem to reflect the economic and commercial importance of Beth Shean at this time.

It is possible, therefore, to state that the road system in Palestine was as sophisticated as those in other developed provinces of the Roman Empire (Von Hagen 1967, etc.). The system was for the most part built by imperial authorities through the agency of the army, and the villages were usually required to pay towards the construction and maintenance of the roads through *liturgiae*. Proof of this last point, though, has been found only pertaining to other provinces, but it is likely that this was the case in Palestine (Frend 1956; Poulter 1980; Avi-Yonah 1946).

VII.2 The local road system

VII.2.1

In addition to the road network there was also a developed system of rural or village roads, although obviously not constructed on the same level as the main highways. These rural roads had a basic foundation and they were narrower than the inter-urban roads (usually 3–5 meters including the shoulders – Figure 57). These village roads, however, were much more

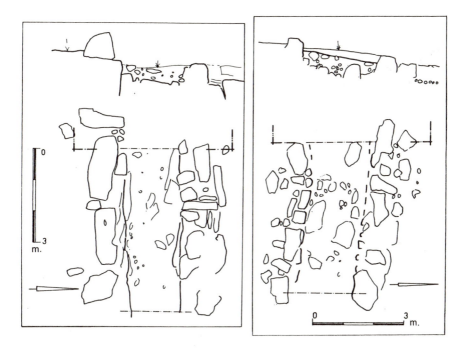

Figure 57 Sections of village road. After Dar *et al.* 1986, pp. 98–9.

numerous than the other kind and they numbered in the thousands throughout Palestine. This type of rural road system has been preserved almost in its
entirety in Samaria and it is likely that the situation was the same in the other
regions of Palestine. Every village, it seems, was connected to its neighbors
within a radius of 3–5 kms and such roads extended even farther in the case
of large villages. All this was in addition to the system of regional rural roads
and the main routes which occasionally connected villages to the Roman
road system. The village roads were built and maintained by the the local
authorities, Jewish or Samaritan (Chapter 1 above and Dar 1986, pp. 126–
46). This road system began to appear in the early Hellenistic period and
perhaps even earlier, but most of the roads that belonged to this network
were constructed in the Roman–Byzantine period when the system reached
its zenith.

VII.2.2

The theoretical models of this system have been extensively studied in
scholarly geographic literature, and the various models have been summarized by Bunge (1962, pp. 187–93, and see above, Figure 50).
These models, as in any theory, are always plain and homogeneous in

nature, and not subject to external influences. In reality, every region is influenced by its environment. In spite of the fact that we are dealing with a relatively small rural area, there are at times important roads which may pass through the region and this should certainly be taken into consideration. It is for this reason that we present an additional road model (G).

This model actually represents further development of model E of Bunge. It is also conceivable that this model could be combined with other models cited above. Thus, for example, there could be an equality model (model D of Bunge) or a hierarchical model (model C) with a major highway included. The settlements are usually near a main road and also connected to it in addition to the roads between them or parallel to them. Since Samaria and the Galilee are mountainous regions, it is also necessary to take this into account and a deviation from the norm of the theoretical models is not to be unexpected.

Understanding the form of the road system allows for further insight into a number of issues pertaining to economic structure:

(1) Settlement hierarchy. Is there a central settlement (model C) or a central axis (model G) or is trade undertaken between settlements of equal rank and standing (models A, B, D, E, F)?
(2) Is the trade or commerce internal or local with mutual commercial relations between the settlements, or is the trade with a central settlement or with the coastal region?
(3) What is the level of commercial development of the region? The more developed the road system, the greater number of roads in general and the more lively is the economy and trade.

One of the difficult problems facing the scholar was the manner of determining a means of quantifying the level of development. There are two criteria. The first is expressed thus:

$$\text{index} = \frac{\text{actual number of roads}}{\text{optimum number of roads}}$$

The optimum number of roads represents the number of routes that will allow for direct connection between every settlement (model D). This number changes in accord with conditions of the terrain. The second means of quantification (Taaffe and Gauthier 1973, pp. 100–15) is expressed as:

$$\text{level of accessibility} = \frac{\text{length of the roads}}{\text{size in sq. km}}$$

We shall not use this second equation since its results are not conclusive due to difficulty in measuring and evaluating different levels of roads. These difficulties exist only in relation to the analysis of ancient roads, since there is no efficient means of distinguishing between roads of different levels in the case of these early roads.

It is important to note, though, that both instruments of measurement are

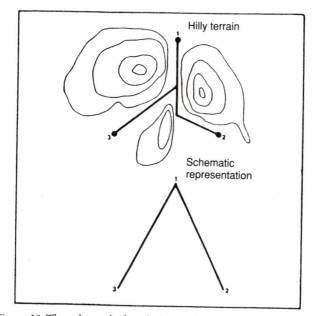

Figure 58 The schematic descriptive method of the road network.

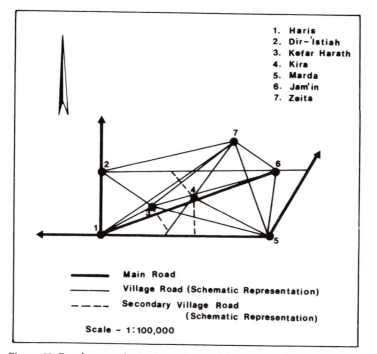

Figure 59 Road networks in the vicinity of the village of Haris, Samaria.

279

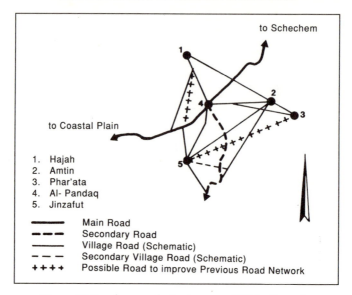

Figure 60 Road networks in the area of Haja, Samaria.

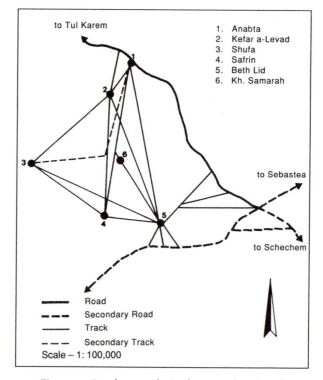

Figure 61 Road networks in the area of Beth Lid.

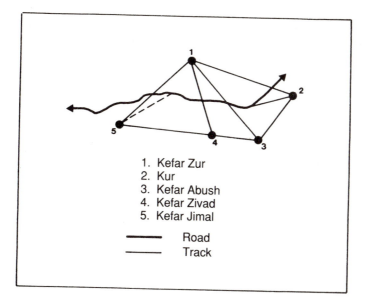

1. Kefar Zur
2. Kur
3. Kefar Abush
4. Kefar Zivad
5. Kefar Jimal

——————— Road
——————— Track

Figure 62 Road networks in the area of Kur, Samaria.

not completely appropriate for evaluating ancient roads, since they do not distinguish between the different natures of the road. Later on, we shall discuss village roads which were usually fit only for ass (or camel) travel. The two instruments, however, are not able to properly evaluate a road which allows for the passage of wheeled vehicles. Moreover, the state of scholarship today does not always allow for a correct evaluation of the very nature of an ancient road. In spite of all this, we shall make use of the second instrument in order to give us some indication of the level of development.

In order to evaluate the nature of the system both from a quantitative and from a functional point of view, we have chosen to examine randomly the roads in two regions: Samaria, in which there is a fairly high level of preservation of ancient roads, and the Galilee, in which fewer ancient roads are preserved, and therefore the reconstruction is more in the nature of hypothesis.

Figures 59–66 have been prepared according to the following principles: (1) major settlements and roads have been indicated at their exact location, and (2) the village roads are marked off schematically and in terms of their final destination and not their exact course. Thus, it is possible that two roads may be united, as it were, into one (Figure 58), in spite of the fact, for instance, that both section 1–2 and section 1–3 (on the right-hand side of Figure 58) represent the shortest distance between both settlements. In such a case, the schematic model is drawn as from the left in relation to the destinations of the roads and not their exact course. It is possible, therefore,

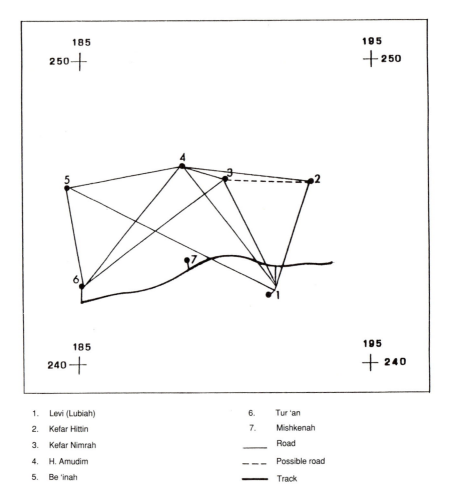

1.	Levi (Lubiah)	6.	Tur 'an
2.	Kefar Hittin	7.	Mishkenah
3.	Kefar Nimrah	____	Road
4.	H. Amudim	_ _ _	Possible road
5.	Be 'inah	━━━	Track

Figure 63 Road networks in the area of H. Amudim, Lower Galilee.

that a road may appear twice in the same diagram, intersections may not appear, or on the other hand fictitious intersections may be drawn.

The path, therefore, is basically drawn in terms of its major function (points of origin and destination) and not in terms of reality which is a product of topographical or physical considerations.

VII.2.3 *The road network in Samaria*

Roads 2–5, 1–7 and 1–4 in Figure 59 actually pass through settlement 3, since this is the shortest topographic line connecting these settlements. The terrain is difficult and the roads do not progress in a straight line. Thus,

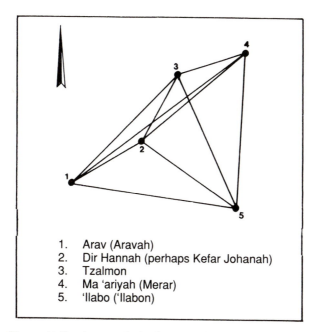

1. Arav (Aravah)
2. Dir Hannah (perhaps Kefar Johanah)
3. Tzalmon
4. Ma 'ariyah (Merar)
5. 'Ilabo ('Ilabon)

Figure 64 Road networks in the area of Arab, Lower Galilee.

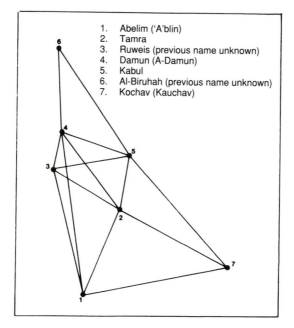

1. Abelim ('A'blin)
2. Tamra
3. Ruweis (previous name unknown)
4. Damun (A-Damun)
5. Kabul
6. Al-Biruhah (previous name unknown)
7. Kochav (Kauchav)

Figure 65 Road networks in the area of Cabul, Lower Galilee.

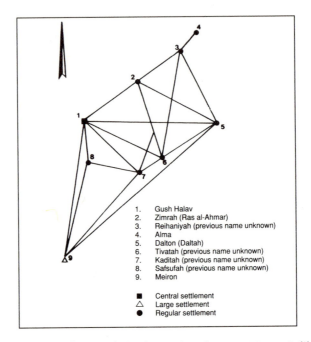

1. Gush Halav
2. Zimrah (Ras al-Ahmar)
3. Reihaniyah (previous name unknown)
4. Alma
5. Dalton (Daltah)
6. Tivatah (previous name unknown)
7. Kaditah (previous name unknown)
8. Safsufah (previous name unknown)
9. Meiron

■ Central settlement
△ Large settlement
● Regular settlement

Figure 66 Road networks in the Gush Halav area, Upper Galilee.

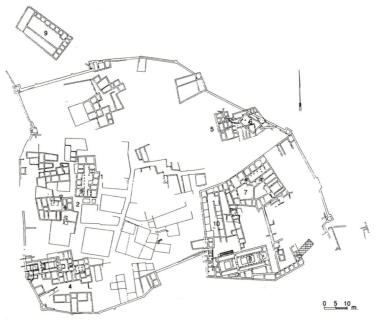

Figure 67 Mampsis (Mamshit): the city and inn (9, the inn; 10 the *agora*). After Negev 1988.

settlement 3 extends to the transitional zone from Heres (1) eastward. The more distant settlements are not always connected to one another. It is important to note that Heres was the major regional settlement and was connected, therefore, to settlements 6 and 7. This road network can be described as being almost ideal and there was no need for additional roads to facilitate direct connection between the settlements. An additional road might have existed between 5 and 2, but it would have little advantage over the existing routes (5–3–2–). The effect of the major roads is also felt in this region (model G in Figure 50).

The central basis for the network in the Hajah region (Figure 60) is the Neapolis (Schechem)-Kalk Iya road. There are only six roads in the network between the settlements when the theoretical optimum amount would be ten. However, due to the terrain and the location of the settlements, it is possible to build only an additional two roads. This network, therefore, would receive an index of $6/8 = 75$ per cent.

There are additional roads in this area. Three of them connect with main roads. Once again, thus, the influence of the main road is felt (model G, Figure 50). The road network in Figure 61 is also not optimum and two roads are missing (from H. Samara to Kefar a-Levad and to Anabta). Road 2 is the shortest route between 1 and 3. This area would receive an index of $13/15 = 84$ per cent. The index is rather low because of the condition of the terrain. H. Samara is at the center of the area and it is easily accessible from each of the settlements. The other roads more than compensate for the lack of one from H. Samara to Anabta. Thus, the lack of roads in the model is not an indication of an inferior road network. In this region the prominent roads are also those that connect to the main highways. The network in Figure 62 is complete and the connection between settlements 2 and 5 is almost direct. At most there might have been the possibility of building a short additional sector to further shorten the distance between the two settlements. The index of this region is 90–100 per cent.

The study of the road maps (Figures 59–62) leads to a number of conclusions: The transportation level was rather developed. The number of roads was generally close to the optimum number, 85–100 per cent. Also, every settlement was apparently connected to its neighbors within a radius of 3–4 kms, in addition to secondary roads and connections to main roads. When this is not the case, there are usually a number of reasons: (1) the difficult nature of the terrain; (2) boundaries between secondary regions; and (3) administrative boundaries. As an example of the last reason, only two roads pass through Nahal Zerredah which was the administrative boundary between Judaea and Samaria. The mountain road, in that section in which it served as the boundary between the toparchy of Acraba and Samaria, was intersected by only two or three roads. The situation was the same in Mt Gilboa and in Wad Ara.

VII.2.4 The road network in the Lower Galilee

The examination of the network system in the Lower Galilee is of great importance since it enables us to compare the data and verify it with literary traditions regarding the nature of various settlements in the area. Moreover, the description of the trade and commercial network described above is based almost entirely on literary sources pertaining to the Galilee. It is likely, therefore, that they basically reflect the situation in the Galilee. However, the available data on which we shall base our description below is lacking in that it does not allow for sufficient understanding of chronological differences and developments which took place in the Galilee. This was also the case regarding Samaria, although the general dearth of literary information made this particular problem less acute. In spite of all this, it appears that the problem may be ignored for the following reasons: (1) The stability of the structure of Galilean settlement in the period under discussion (135–300). (2) Economic conditions were generally stable; moreover, there were no far-reaching ethnic or administrative changes in the Lower Galilee during this time. Needless to say, we shall deal with the matter of chronology to the extent that it is possible. As can be seen in Figures 63–66, the road network was quite developed and testifies to vibrant internal trade which was not dependent on urban centers. This would seem to be clear-cut proof regarding the function of the donkey caravan which we discussed above. This road network reflects a reality of an open and specialized economic system as we suggested at the beginning of our discussion.

The road network in the vicinity of Amudim, between settlements 1–5, is almost at optimum level (Figure 63), despite severe topographic disturbances. In spite of the fact that Mt Tura'an protrudes between Turan and and Beina, a number of internal roads climbing up the mountain connect the two settlements. Ilabon belongs to another region (Figure 64) and its connection, therefore, to the present area under discussion is quite limited. H. Mishkana was only a satellite settlement and road station and its role, therefore, in the road network was rather limited.

Figure 65 shows that the road network suffered from medium-level topographic disturbances. The general regions of settlements 2, 5, 6, and 7 are all missing a road. The index of the region is relatively low – 83 per cent, undoubtedly the result of the topography. The most convenient route between 2 and 6 would pass very close to 5, and therefore it was not worthwhile to build an additional route.

There was only one road missing between settlements 1–5 in the Cabul region and this road was really unnecessary, since the most convenient route in terms of local topography (between 1 and 5) passed through 2. Thus, the region received an index of 90–100 per cent. There was one additional road missing in the region of settlements 2–6, since it was not worthwhile to build another long road (6 kms) when the actual road between 2 and 6 was 7.5 kms. This region would receive an index of 90 per cent.

The entire region has twelve roads and is actually only missing one from the optimum amount (2–6). The non-construction of the other roads was the result of the small profit that could be expected from their construction.

In the region depicted in Figure 66, a number of settlement clusters – 1, 5, 6, 7, 8, 9 – can really be considered one large settlement cluster, and villages 1, 2, 3, 5 and 6 can be considered another settlement cluster. Village 4 belongs to another settlement cluster and Nahal Baram separates it from village 3. This *nahal* also served as the administrative boundary between Provincia Judaea and Phoenicia, and therefore its connections with the settlements to the south were rather limited.

VII.2.5

It is possible, thus, to sum up and state that there was vibrant trade between the various settlements. The need for such a complex road system between the settlements can be understood in light of the donkey caravans, as we have discussed above.

VII.3 Road services

Inns were built in the cities and along the major roads which offered the traveler room and board in return for payment. Such inns were found in Palestine as early as the first century CE. These inns were private property, although they may have been built at times through government initiative. The Romans themselves built way stations (where drivers could also change their horses) which were built specifically for the use of the imperial mail system (*Itinerarium Antoninianum* 149.5–150.4; 190–200), but were also at the service of the regular wayfarer. Cisterns were also built along the village roads and sometimes trees were also planted alongside. The towns also provided services related to hospitality (see Chapter 1.III.3 above) (Figure 67).

In spite of all this, travel conditions were not good. Internal security conditions were poor and bands of armed robbers operating on the roads often made travel quite perilous. Talmudic tradition refers to one setting out on the road to travel as someone who has endangered himself. One who goes out in a caravan is, according to the law, just like one who sets out for a journey at sea and is similar to a prisoner or to one on the verge of death (M Gittin 6:5). The protected road stations (*burganim*) were locked at night out of fear of armed robbers (Midrash Psalms 10:2 pp. 92–3 and see B. Isaac 1984; Herr 1981; Krauss 1911, II, pp. 317–23; MacMullen 1966).

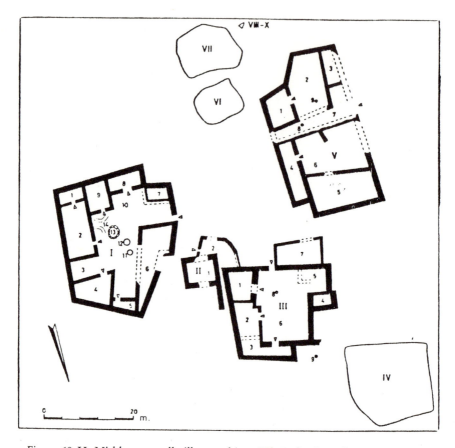

Figure 68 H. Mishkena: small village and inn. No. I after Z. Safrai 1985, p. 217.

During the Roman period there was not much danger of piracy (Ormerod 1924, pp. 258 ff.). In spite of this there were still pirates at sea and the residents of Eretz-Israel suffered from them at times, or as the *midrash* states: "A tale is told of a king who said to his son, 'Go out and engage in business.' He said to him: 'Father, I fear the roads on account of the brigands, and the seas on account of the pirates' " (Leviticus Rabbah 25:1, p. 567).

It is possible to learn about the network of inns and the services of the *cursus publicus* for the most part from information pertaining to the Empire in general (Tengström 1974, pp. 26–34; Holemberg 1933; Kleberg 1957). The minimal amount of specific information about the situation in Palestine makes it clear that this province fitted into the existing framework. The *Itinerarium Antoninianum* (see the reference above) also tells us about postal stations. An inn has been excavated at Tel Megadim (Broshi 1969), and one was surveyed at Mishkenah in the Lower Galilee (Z. Safrai 1985, pp. 167–72, Figure 68). Literary sources tell of many different kinds of additional inns such as a civil one, community, imperial and monastic ones, but all this is beyond the purview of our discussion.

VII.4 Means of transport

VII.4.1

The most common means of land transport was the donkey which is mentioned quite often in Talmudic sources. The horse was far more rare; the wagon was even rarer, and the few times it is mentioned in the sources are in relation to the transport of stones or the transport of children ("the wagon of a young child"). Another type of animal mentioned in the sources is the camel, which was employed essentially for transport in the desert. There are, however, references to camels being used for regular overland transport (Krauss 1924, I. 1, p. 170).

As in other countries in the Roman Empire, transport by donkey was cheaper in Judaea than by wagon (Duncan-Jones 1982, pp. 364–6 and many other studies). This was because the donkey could travel much faster than the wagon, in spite of the fact that more could of course be carried in the wagon. The Mishnah provides information regarding how much weight animals could carry (M Bava Mezia 6:5; T Bava Mezia 7:10 and BT Bava Mezia 80a–b). According to these sources, it is possible to provide the following figures (the computations from measures of volume to those of weight are based on the transport of wheat mentioned in this Mishnah):

1. Porter – 5 *seahs* (42.7 liters = 32 kgs)
2. Donkey – 15 *seahs* (128 liters = 96 kgs)
3. Camel – 30 *seahs* (256 liters = 192 kgs)
4. Wagon – 90 *seahs* (768 liters = 576 kgs)
5. Regular-sized ship – 180 *seahs* (2304 liters = 1728 kgs)
6. Large-sized ship – 540 *seahs* (6912 liters = 5184 kgs).

The figures regarding the ships, however, are found only in the Babylonian Talmud and they may, therefore, reflect the situation only there (pp. 296–7 below).

The figures on overland transport are similar to those available regarding Africa (Duncan-Jones 1982, pp. 364–6). The roads of Eretz-Israel were quite capable of supporting wagon transport, but as stated above, donkey transport was more common since it was cheaper. Transport via wagons was next to impossible on village or rural roads. We shall deal later on with costs pertaining to transport (Appendix to Chapter 5).

Transport by water was not very common in Eretz-Israel. Ammianus Marcellinus already states that there were no navigable rivers in Palestine (14. 7. 12) and indeed only a few streams are navigable, and this in any case seems to have had no economic impact. The situation was different, however, along the Mediterranean coast and the coasts of large lakes in Palestine.

Thus, harbors were built along the coast of Palestine such as Gaza, Anthedon, Ascalon, Azotus, Jaminiton Limen (= Javneh Yam), Joppa, Apollonia, Caesarea and Dor. There were also many small piers (Figure 53). These city harbors were built to service international trade, but also served to facilitate trade between themselves. This phenomenon is described in Talmudic tradition. Thus, for example, one who vows not to derive any benefit from seafarers is not forbidden to derive benefit from those "who go from Acco to Joppa, but from one that is wont to sail afar" (M Nedarim 3:6). These traditions also mention, for instance, fruit which arrives at the port of Caesarea and is considered fruit from the Land of Israel, meaning that it came from another port in Eretz-Israel (T Demai 1:11). Trade between the ports of Palestine is mentioned in additional sources such as the interesting story, from the end of the Byzantine period, regarding the Jewish merchant who traveled from Acco to Sycaminun (= Shiqmona) (Doctrina Iacobi; Dan 1971).

The Dead Sea and the Sea of Galilee were also water transport routes. The port of Ein Gedi, of Eglatin and of an additional site are mentioned in the Bar-Kochba letters (Yadin 1971, p. 176, p. 233, p. 236, etc.). The Madeba Map also depicts two boats transporting either wheat or salt on the Dead Sea. A number of piers along the coast of the Dead Sea were discovered by P. Bar-Adon. Boats on the Dead Sea are mentioned by Xenophilus (*Historiarum Mirabilium Collectio*, p. 151) and by Galen (*De Simplicium Medicamentorum Temperamentis ac Facultatibus* 4. 20), although it is possible that the latter refers not to transport vessels but to the boats which collected the asphalt of the Dead Sea.

In terms of transport, the Sea of Galilee was more important. Merchandise from the Golan to Tiberias and the Galilee was often transported via the Sea of Galilee (PT Sheviit VIII, 38a). Thus, for example, Noah's ark is described in the *midrash* in the following manner: "And thus the ark used to float on the water like two beams floating slowly from Tiberais to Susita (= Hippos)" (Genesis Rabbah 32:9, p. 296). The plain meaning of the text is that the ark was similar to the vessels which regularly plied the route between these two cities, and there might even have been a special type of ship on this route. Another midrashic tradition describes the furrows, as it were, made in the Sea of Galilee by the many boats on this route (Genesis Rabbah 31:13, p. 287). The many piers along the shore of the Sea of Galilee

(Nun 1977) were for the most part for fishermen, but some were also used for the transport of items from Tiberias to Hippos and from the northern regions of the Sea of Galilee to the southern ones. It is likely that the boats used for transport on the Sea of Galilee were relatively small. The boat discovered along the coast at Ginossar (Wachsmann 1990) is probably a good representative of this type of vessel which could carry less than two tons all told (see p. 289).

VIII. TRADE ARRANGEMENTS

VIII.1 Business guilds

The nature of commerce required some kind of mercantile organization. It is likely that in order to facilitate marketing of goods, transport and the financing of capital (Frank 1936–40, IV, p. 97), merchants, at least in some locations, banded together into guilds which could also represent them *vis-à-vis* the authorities. Such guilds were common in various fields (Chapter 2.II.2 above). The donkey-drivers were also organized within the framework of a guild and the rabbis permitted them, as well as sailors, to reach agreements of mutual responsibility for each other (T Bava Mezia 11:25–6; Midrash Psalms 12: 1 pp. 104–5).

VIII.2 Moneychangers

Problems of finance were solved through the moneychanger. The moneychanger (Hebrew: *shulhani*; Greek: *trapezites*) was more than just one who exchanged various currencies, but was also a banker of sorts who supplied credit and kept watch over the temporary surplus capital of various individuals. A number of traditions also describe the *shulhani* as a channel for payments from one partner to another, or to artisans or to participants in various business deals. Thus, for example, sources mention payment through a check to a *shulhani* to a donkey-driver, for the *ketubbah* of a woman and even for the sale of a cow and donkey (Gulak 1931. On sources relating to payment to donkey-drivers and the supplying of merchandise through a check to the *shulhani* see Gulak ibid., pp. 158–60. This was apparently an accepted practice. See also PT Bava Mezia IV, 9c; Albeck 1957, 273–7; Sperber 1978, p. 49). In Babylonia there are terms which clearly relate to selling on credit and the like. Such terms, however, are not found in Palestinian sources. Nevertheless, Palestinian tradition does describe similar transactions taking place in a village in Eretz-Israel in which payment in cash is through one of the residents of the village to whom debts are passed over (PT Kiddushin III, 64a. This passage is quite difficult. (See the explanation of Nahmanides cited in Assaf 1935, p. 94.) On "checks", the "transference of debts" and obligations see Albeck 1957, esp. pp. 273–4; id. 1966, pp. 586–775).

The *shulhani* in Palestine was not only a private institution, but was also found in the Temple in Jerusalem (Gulak ibid.). Josephus even mentions a government bank in Sepphoris (*Vita* 9. 39). Needless to say, though, the *shulhani* was found only in the *polis* (M Bava Mezia 4:6; T Bava Mezia 3:20), and it is likely that most were non-Jews, since the Jewish laws against the lending of money for interest would not have made it very profitable for a Jewish practitioner of this trade. Jewish law, however, did show some leniency for the few Jews involved in this occupation. In the rural sphere where there was no *shulhani*, as we have just seen above, his functions were at least partially fulfilled by the shopkeeper, especially regarding the examining and supplying of cash, as well as providing credit (M. Bava Mezia 9:12; T Bava Mezia 3:20; M Bava Mezia 3:11; M Shevuot 7:5 *et al.*). In summary, therefore, the *shulhani* in Palestine functioned in the same capacity as the *shulhani* in the rest of the Empire (Rostovtzeff 1957, pp. 179–81; M. Crawford 1970; Johnson and West 1949, pp. 127–73).

VIII.3 Commercial laws

VIII.3.1

The realities of commercial life necessitated the establishment of a detailed system of commercial law, some of which is known from the various collections of imperial edicts and others only from the late Byzantine collections of laws (Ashburner 1909, pp. 26–7). A papyrus from Egypt, for instance, tells of a maritime loan given to a merchant from Ascalon (Casson 1956). The Church Father Johannes Moschus tells of a similar law regarding the cargo of a merchant which was lost at sea during a storm, and therefore the merchant could not repay a maritime loan. The merchant was subsequently arrested, but later released through the intercession of his wife with the authorities (*Leimanarion* (or *Praatum Spirituale*), *Letters* 186–7; Dan 1971). It would appear, therefore, that the laws which existed in the East were included within the commercial laws of the Roman Empire.

The Jews, of course, enjoyed their own autonomous system of laws, and therefore it is interesting to examine the relationship of the *halachah* to the commercial law of the time. Although the details of Jewish commercial law are not within the purview of this study, we should nevertheless like to examine a number of elements relative to the attitude of Jewish law to Roman commercial law. Jewish law on these issues deals, of course, only with matters relating to Jews, since non-Jews would obviously not seek recourse in Jewish law. Internal Jewish commerce, however, was totally isolated from the reality of commerce in general. In any case, we shall

discuss only those Jewish laws which deal with helping the Jewish autonomous system to adapt to the framework of the Roman commercial system.

VIII.3.2

The open economy and widespread commerce and trade both in Palestine
and in the Roman Empire resulted in a number of halachic difficulties. The
difficulties did not relate to problems of "ideology" regarding commerce,
but to problems that resulted from it such as interest, trade with non-Jews,
trade in items connected to pagan cults and the like. It is possible to discern
changes in the attitude of the rabbis over the generations regarding some of
these issues, and others which developed as a result of the meeting of the
Jewish and Roman systems.

VIII.3.2.1 Laws of interest

The laws of interest in the Talmud are quite strict and clear-cut, and their
main purpose was to prevent interest or usury in any form or fashion.
However, Eliash (1978), for instance, has shown that the Palestinian Talmud
showed a quite lenient approach on numerous occasions, apparently reflecting some kind of attempt to come to terms with credit and interest. It would
appear that Katz (1965) was correct in attributing this to a rabbinic response
to commercial needs and problems. In the thirteenth century the rabbis
established the "*heter 'isqa*" – a legal fiction in which the loan theoretically
becomes a transaction between partners – in order to allow for the acceptance of interest. A papyrus from the fifth century dealing with a loan
between two Jews specifically refers to interest, and it is possible that the
document refers to a fifth-century CE version of the *heter 'isqa* mentioned
above. In any case, the details of the loan are far from clear (Friedenberg
1939).

VIII.3.2.2 The functions of the moneychanger (*shulhani*)

We have seen above that the *shulhani* or moneychanger, the banker of the
ancients, fulfilled an important role in the commercial system of the ancient
world. However, their entire existence was dependent on the interest that
they took, whether for loans or for credit. As we have also seen above, the
shulhani was found only in the *polis* and not in the settlements of the rural
sphere. Most of the residents of the *polis* were, of course, non-Jewish, and
therefore the great number of sources pertaining to the *shulhani* in Talmudic
literature is quite surprising. It would seem, thus, that the many traditions
reflect the fact that this profession was also considered a respectable occupation for a Jew.

There were even a number of rabbis who were money-changers. Thus, it appears that R. Hiyya was also a moneychanger in addition to his other avocations (BT Bava Kama 99b). Once when he made a mistake and approved a coin which was later discovered to be counterfeit, he told his assistant Rav: "Go and exchange it and write in your ledger that this was a bad transaction." Another sage who was a moneychanger was R. Hana Petora'ah (BT Hullin 54b). Thus, it would seem that in some manner or another it became possible for the Jewish moneychanger to operate within the framework of Jewish commercial law and to receive interest. There were also moneychangers in the Temple, and in the Gospel account Jesus rails against them. The criticism, however, does not seem to be against them in general, but rather against their conducting business in the Temple Mount (Luke. 19:45; Matt. 21:12; Mark 11:15).

Gulak (1931) points out two means by which the *shulhani* could more or less take interest. Thus it was taught:

> Donkey drivers and laborers were standing next to him and he said to the *shulhani* – 'Give me coins worth a dinar so that I may pay them and I shall return to you coins worth a dinar and tressis from the coins which I have in my purse.' If he has them in his purse it is permitted, but if he does not have them it is not permitted.
>
> (T Bava Mezia 4:9)

To all intents and purposes, this is a transaction revolving around credit and interest (at 12.5 per cent) and the only reason that it is permitted is because the borrower actually has the sum, but not where he needs it. The Babylonian Talmud (Bava Mezia 46a) had great difficulty in understanding this decision and cited the opinion of the Palestinian *amora* Ulla who did not understand it at all, and that of R. Abba who claimed that the transaction involved coins whose denominations had not been marked, and thus was really nothing more than an exchange of coins. The far-fetched explanation highlights the absurdity of this legal fiction.

In any case, the *shulhani* was allowed to charge interest only because the transaction was not considered a loan, but rather as making fluid capital available to one who had funds, but not necessarily fluid at that time. Thus it was a matter of organization, and the transfer of monies and not of a loan. In addition to Gulak's understanding of the situation, it might conceivably be argued that the case could be construed as a short-term loan ("until the lender came home" to the source of his capital). The high rate of interest, however, does not allow for this explanation and it would therefore appear that the entire purpose of this law was to enable the *shulhani* to participate in regular banking transactions. We shall return later on to deal with these types of transactions.

Another means allowing the *shulhani* to charge interest was "the renting out of money." According to Gulak (1931), T Bava Mezia 4:2 reads as follows:

One rents out his monies to the *shulhani* to beautify himself with them, to practice with them, to embellish himself with them. If they were stolen or lost he is responsible for them. If they were taken from him in an unavoidable situation, he is like one who receives a salary. If he divided them into three, it is forbidden on account of interest.

Thus, one "rents out" monies to the *shulhani* not as interest but in return for another usage of the money. The *shulhani*, however, is allowed to use the money as it is explicitly stated in other *halachot* (M Bava Mezia 3:11). The amount of the payment was not explicitly stated, and it was therefore possible to use this "lenient measure" of the rabbis to charge regular interest, although the interest was supposedly referred to as rent. According to Gulak, it is possible that the phrase "if they were taken from him in an unavoidable situation" refers to a case wherein the money was stolen from the *shulhani* before he had the chance to use it, and the phrase we translated above as "if he divided them into three" actually refers to a case in which the *shulhani* served as a "third party," one who was simply trusted to hold on to the funds without being allowed to use them.

Both of these legal fictions allowed for the smooth functioning of the Jewish *shulhani* and prove that the rabbis were interested in and sensitive to the successful operation of both the *shulhani* and the Jewish economic system in general.

VIII.3.2.3 Trade with non-Jews

We have already discussed to some extent the restrictions regarding trade with gentiles and scholarship has also shown why these restrictions were eventually limited. Basically there were two reasons for this phenomenon. There was, for instance, no longer much fear that those doing business with non-Jews would be swept up into the web of paganism (Urbach 1964) and economic pressure made such trade necessary at times. Limiting these restrictions regarding trade with non-Jews is proof of the willingness of the rabbis to espouse a lenient position in order to facilitate Jewish participation in the economic life of the time (Sperber 1978, pp. 160–76).

VIII.3.2.4

Jewish participation in fairs was forbidden on account of fear lest benefit be derived from tax or customs exemptions dedicated to the gods. As we have already seen, this restriction was also limited, beginning in the Tannaitic period, and was for all intents and purposes almost entirely abolished (IV.3 above). It is important to point out, however, that this case is different from the other examples of trade with non-Jews since the decree could not be abolished on account of a changing attitude to paganism. The decree against deriving benefit from exemptions dedicated to the gods was not abolished, or the principle on the matter did not change. Moreover, the fear of Jewish participation at pagan festivals was not any less serious. Proof of this is the fact that there was Jewish participation at the "interdenominational" festival at Botnah near Hebron, and it is difficult to claim that the rabbis agreed to Jewish participation at such a fair, in which both Christians and pagans participated.

The three previous examples relate to the inclusion of Jews in the world of Roman trade and business. The fourth one relates more to economic pressure in general. However, it is sometimes difficult to distinguish between these two factors.

VIII.3.2.5 The halachic authorization for artisan guilds

Artisan guilds were a common phenomenon in the Roman world. The organization of the workers into guilds was primarily for the convenience of the Roman authorities, which saw the guilds as a representative organization of a particular trade and allowed for a convenient means of taxation and the supplying of necessary goods. There was a degree of cooperation between the authorities and guilds beyond the limited scope of taxation, but the guilds did not really come into their own and flower until the Middle Ages.

There were guilds in Palestine just as there were in other provinces (Chapter 2.II.2 above). For the sake of our present discussion, it is important to point out that the rabbis considered these groups in a quite positive manner and, in fact, the *halachah* was quite explicit in allowing them to function. Thus, for example we find the following *halachah*:

> The wool workers and the dyers are allowed to say respectively that they shall all be partners in every deal that comes to the town. And the bakers can make a deal among themselves. And the donkey drivers are allowed to say that if someone's donkey should die then they shall provide him with another. . . . And the merchant shippers are allowed to stipulate that they will provide a ship to someone who has lost his own.

> (T Bava Mezia 11: 24–6)

An analysis of the text shows that it deals with mutual guarantees and the organized dispersion of supplies or goods arriving at a settlement. The example in the Tosefta relating to wool-workers and dyers is quite instructive, since these are undoubtedly local products coming from nearby. Thus, the decision to form the "partnership" is not connected solely to any considerations pertaining to supplies under government supervision, but rather could be a local and internal matter, albeit influenced by common procedures in the Roman world.

There may have been halachic problems when one of the sides involved sought to abrogate the agreement or when it was necessary to invoke the mutual guarantees. In such a case the *halachah* was quite innovative, since usually any partner could pull out of a deal whenever he wished. In this case, however, he had to continue his partnership within the context of the guild.

VIII.3.2.6 Lenient measures in order to facilitate the operation of donkey caravans

As we have already seen, there were donkey caravans which traveled from village to village buying surplus crops and selling to the villagers those necessary items not produced locally (III above). The *halachah* was aware of the fact that this was almost the only trade and business option available for the rural sphere, and therefore stated: "Donkey drivers came into a town: One said – mine [produce] is new and my companion's is old, mine is not completely tithed, but my companion's is completely tithed; they are not to be believed. R. Judah says that they are to be trusted" (M Demai 4:7). PT Demai IV, 24b states that R. Judah's opinion was "on account of the lives of the townspeople" while the more stringent view of the rabbis was based on the premise "that they were able to support themselves from another town." In any case, in spite of the fact that the donkey-drivers were united by profession and guild and their testimony regarding each other somewhat suspect, the rabbis were willing to be lenient and give them some type of artificial credibility in order to facilitate the existing economic order. R. Judah was willing to be lenient in making provisions for allowing this economic institution, one characteristic of the Roman business world, to function smoothly. The rabbis agreed in principle with this lenient position, but since in their view the economic problem could be solved in a different manner, they expressed a more stringent opinion in this particular case.

VIII.3.2.7 Prozbul

The Prozbul edict which prevents the forced dissolution of debts in the Sabbatical Year has been much discussed in literature. The purpose of the edict was to facilitate the continued lending of funds in the final years of the seven-year Sabbatical cycle, and was therefore intended for the benefit of the lender (M Sheviit 10:1–6 and numerous parallels). Prozbul can also be described as a business or commercial decree, although in this case the dependence on the Roman economic system is much less pronounced and it is possible to explain the edict as a reflection of rising standards of living, and not necessarily as directly related to economic structure.

VIII.3.2.8 Business provisions

We include under this heading trade and business provisions which are not considered to be explicit changes from existing *halachah*. Rather, they represented innovations or development of *halachah*. It appears that a number of laws developed in the period which we are studying which were intended to make commercial activity easier, and apparently reflected the transition from a closed agro-economic system in which business decisions were quite rare to an open system in which business decisions were an everyday fact of life. A complete discussion of these innovations would require a rather long and detailed study, beyond the scope of our present work. We shall, therefore, make do with a number of examples (for details see Z. Safrai 1989).

VIII.3.2.8.1 Acquisition through the scarf

VIII.3.2.8.1 Acquisition through the scarf The earliest primitive form of acquisition was of course barter, in which one good was exchanged for another. In this primitive exchange, the real relationship between both components of the deal was preserved. Sometime at the end of the Tannaitic period there developed a fictitious form of barter whereby the seller gave the buyer a valueless item which, when the buyer received it, symbolized another more expensive acquisition. It is difficult to determine the exact time when this innovation developed, but it is not mentioned in Tannaitic traditions. The first sages associated with this development in the Babylonian Talmud were Rav and Levi, two of the earliest Amoraim (BT Bava Mezia 47a; Gulak 1922, II, pp. 123–4). Rav and Levi had studied in the Land of Israel, and it is therefore possible to claim that this form of acquisition originated there.

However, this form of acquisition is not mentioned in the Palestinian Talmud and in PT Kiddushin I, 60c (with a partial parallel in Ruth Rabbah 7:11) the discussion on the matter is referred to in the form of "there (Babylonia) it is said," the phrase commonly used for a Babylonian tradition brought from Babylonia to Palestine. Moreover, the discussion in PT deals with the historic "*k'tsatsah*" ceremony (a means of taking possession of an estate or heirloom) or with the acquisition undertaken by Boaz as described in the Book of Ruth (4:7), and not with concrete legal forms of acquisition. It is possible, therefore, that this form of acquisition did originate in Babylonia, and the Amoraic tradition was used for the purpose of introducing it, even though the basis of the tradition was another similar but different aggadic matter (see also De Vries 1962). In any case, this form of acquisition is not mentioned or discussed in the Palestinian Talmud, while the opposite is true pertaining to the Babylonian Talmud. Even if it was introduced at some time into the Land of Israel, it was apparently popular only in Babylonia. For our purposes, then, this form of acquisition does not serve as proof of the *halachah*'s willingness to accommodate itself to the reality of business and trade in the Land of Israel.

VIII.3.2.8.2 Acquisition through land

VIII.3.2.8.2 Acquisition through land The Mishnah states that it is possible to buy movable items through the land on which they are found. This is also a primitive form of acquisition which reflects the position of land in general within the framework of ancient property and economy. Eventually, however, the *halachah* came to the conclusion that the items did not have to be piled up on the particular piece of land, and this type of acquisition became a means of facilitating a fictitious sale in which the item did not have to be physically transferred. The following tradition in PT can give us some indication regarding the date and nature of this halachic innovation:

> It happened regarding a native of Meiron who lived in Jerusalem . . .
> and he had many (movable) possessions which he wished to distribute.
> . . . What did he do? He went and bought a rocky piece of land at one
> side of Jerusalem and said, the northern side of this land I give together
> with a hundred barrels of wine. . . . And the case came before the
> Rabbis and they upheld his words.
>
> <div align="right">(M. Peah 3:6 <i>et al.</i>, PT Kiddushin I, 60c–d;
BT Kiddushin 27a)</div>

Thus, it appears that this innovation regarding the turning of the dependence on land into a fiction was the result of private initiative at the end of the Second Temple period, and that the rabbis agreed with it.

Later on during the Amoraic period the fictitious nature of this type of transaction was further expanded, and it was also applied to cases of borrowing and renting out land; it was further decided that there was no need to designate a specific plot of land (Gulak 1922, II, pp. 118–20).

VIII.3.2.8.3 *'Iska* A new form of partnership was established somewhere around the beginning of the Amoraic period called the *'iska* or "throwing in of goods." Both partners in this arrangement contribute merchandise to a joint venture. One of the partners engages in active business, buying and selling, while both partners share in both profits and losses. Later on it developed that only one partner contributed merchandise while the other partner contributed only his labor. The profits and losses were split in such a manner that the partner who provided capital received a greater share of earnings and suffered a smaller share of potential loss (Gulak 1922, II, pp. 196–8; Beer 1975, pp. 211–15). Rabbi Judah the Prince tried to institute a somewhat similar arrangement regarding maritime trade which was called "danger (Hebrew: *klyto*) of the sea." The rabbis, however, opposed this innovation because of problems regarding interest. The details of this arrangement were apparently that the partner providing funding gave merchandise to a salesman, and that the profit was split between them in some form or fashion (most likely with the partner providing the capital or merchandise receiving more than half of the profits). The potential for loss, however, was entirely the problem of the salesman (PT Bava Mezia V, 10c; Lieberman 1984, pp. 31–2). This arrangement was apparently quite common in Roman maritime trade and many times resulted in rather heavy losses for the salesman who traveled with merchandise funded by someone else (VIII.3.1 above).

VIII.3.2.8.4 Brokership Laws of brokership or agency were instituted at the very latest by the Usha period. There is no proof that the broker was a fixed institution or in other words that he had a general power of attorney, as it were, from either the buyer or seller. The broker or agent was apparently appointed only for specific transactions.

VIII.3.2.8.5 The transference of debts The ability to transfer debts from one debtor to another or from one lender to another is of great importance for the smooth operation of any free trade system. The transference of debts in Talmudic law is quite complex and it would appear that it is possible to sum it up in the following manner (Albeck 1957; id. 1969, pp. 577–95): in general the transference of debts is forbidden. However, it is possible to allow it, even without setting up a new loan, under the following conditions:

(1) "In the presence of three." The debt is transferred in the presence of the debtor, lender and a third individual. All of the traditions attesting to this arrangement are Babylonian, in spite of the fact that the innovation is mentioned in the name of Rav and Levi who both studied in the Land of Israel at the academy of Rabbi Judah the Prince. The arrangement, however, is not mentioned in the Palestinian Talmud, a situation reminiscent of the acquisition through the scarf which we discussed above.

(2) The handing over of writs or bills. It is possible to hand over the writ of debt to another person. The *Tannaim*, however, were not in agreement as to whether this required the writing of a new writ (BT Bava Bathra 75b–76a). A requirement to write a new writ would be a severe impingement on free trade since to all intents and purposes this would be the equivalent of a new loan.

(3) It was possible to transfer the debt from one lender to another. This practice was popular both in the Land of Israel and in Babylonia and served as a common means of making payments without recourse to actual capital. The *shulhani* played an important role in this procedure in the city while the shopkeeper played a similar role in the towns. PT Kiddushin III, 64a, for example, describes an interesting instance of the transference of debt through a *"tanna"* in a village. This arrangement, as we have stated, is mentioned within explicit mercantile contexts.

(4) Power of attorney. In this instance, a representative is appointed in order to collect the debt. Formally speaking, the debt belongs to the first debtor. It is doubtful, however, whether this concept was used in order to transfer debts to another debtor. Most of the traditions on this matter are also Babylonian. The principle itself, though, was formulated in the

Tannaitic period, indicating that the concept was Palestinian in origin, dating at the latest to the beginning of the third century CE.

VIII.3.2.8.6 A transaction without payment or the transfer of goods   In a regular transaction goods are usually handed over in return for payment. The basic difficulty attendant upon this idea is that it is necessary for both elements to be "fluid," or in other words, the merchandise must be such that it can be handed over to the buyer upon payment. In the ancient business world, there were a number of ways in which this principle could be circumvented.

(1) Futures (Hebrew: *pesikah*, lit. the setting up of a future agreement or deal). In this instance a deal is struck to sell merchandise at a future time in exchange for immediate payment at a future rate. The sages permitted this arrangement only if the rate or market price was known. This eliminated the danger that in the future, when the merchandise would be supplied, the buyer would have to pay interest if the price had meanwhile gone up (M Bava Mezia 5:7). Talmudic tradition also records an instance of extremely complicated transactions in futures of a somewhat speculative nature when neither of the sides really intends to transfer or receive merchandise. Rather, the intent of such complicated dealings was usually simply to continue to transfer around the same capital, in a manner similar to the workings of a modern-day stock exchange (Lieberman 1975).

(2) A bill of indebtedness signed on trust (Hebrew: *amanah*, lit. trust or faith). This transaction was a sale of future merchandise for immediate payment based on the present rate. This deal also had inherent difficulties with forbidden interest. In any event, though, this practice became quite common. The first traditions mentioning this practice are related to Rav and R. Jannai (BT Bava Mezia 62b). This would seem to imply that the system originated before their time, at the beginning of the third century CE, since these rabbis already had detailed discussions and controversies as to its workings. According to traditions in the Tosefta and in BT, it appears that the owner of the merchandise was responsible for providing it as well as for its transport, but the expenses incurred in this were the reponsibility of the buyer.

The similarities and relationship between the business laws and transactions described above and the realities of imperial Roman law is a quite difficult matter, and we shall not discuss it here (see, for example, B. Cohen 1966). Moreover, it would probably be more instructive for us to compare those rabbinic traditions not with imperial law, but rather with the legal situation in the provinces. Egypto-Roman law is known through the study of legal papyri (see, for example, Taubenschlag 1955) and Sachau and Bruns have published a book of Syrian-Roman laws (1880), giving us a glimpse into this legal system. However, a comparison of this eastern law with Jewish law is beyond the scope of our study and we shall refrain from dealing with this matter. However, even without going into a detailed comparison here, it is possible to sum up and state that Jewish law made every effort to facilitate the transaction, and thus showed an openness and understanding of the economic and business reality of a province within the Roman Empire.

IX. MEANS OF PAYMENT

From the general traditions describing the period we are studying, it seems to be clear that in spite of marked economic development, merchandise itself or payment in kind was still often considered a common means of payment. Much of the local trade, it would appear, was operated through a barter system and Talmudic tradition also tells of payment in kind to those transporting merchandise or doing some type of work associated with it (as, for example, T Sheviit 6:26). Barter was extremely popular in the rural and village regions and a special form of barter acquisition was even established there. It is thus likely that the barter system was extremely ancient (see also VIII.3.2.8 above).

Another means of payment was through the coins minted in the various cities of Palestine and in other imperial institutions (Figure 69). We shall not deal here with the monetary problems of the period, a subject beyond the purview of our discussion. In any case, it is possible to state that payment through this means was generally reliable and accepted.

Thus, for example, it was usually possible to use a coin from one Roman province in another one, and the *shulhani* could take care of any minor problems in exchanging coins or evaluating them, for a small charge of course, if such were indeed to arise. Talmudic literature makes many references to coins, and the problems attendant upon these traditions have been examined by A. Ben David (1974), and a second time in a most successful manner by Sperber (1974, pp. 27–97) who also devoted extensive discussion to problems related to monetary policy in the Land of Israel.

Tens of thousands of coins have been discovered in the course of excavations in Palestine. It is still difficult, however, to evaluate the extent to which they represent a more popular means of payment than barter. A great many coins have also been found in the rural and village regions of Palestine, but it is difficult to utilize this material since there does not exist, as of yet, any statistical study on this matter. The only real statistical study, relating to Jerusalem, does allow some preliminary conclusions to be drawn pertaining to this site (Ariel 1982). A limited amount of material has also been collected from settlements in the Galilee (Chapter 4.VIII below). More than ten cities in Palestine minted coins (Figure 69), but as yet no economic synthesis of the material has appeared, such as, for example, how many coins from each city have been discovered or from which periods. All of this leads to the conclusion that it is impossible to present an analysis of monetary policy in Palestine, even though the matter was undoubtedly of great importance.

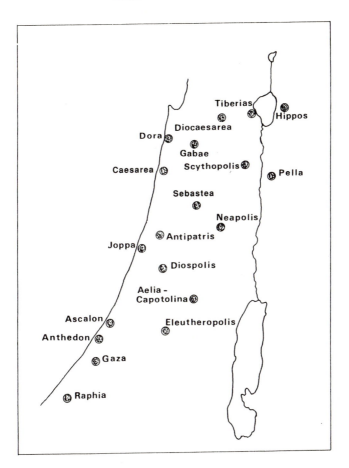

Figure 69 Cities which minted coins.

X CUSTOMS

X.1 Sales taxes

Taxes on business transactions were an important source of capital for the Empire. Only transactions at a recognized fair were exempt from such taxes. The Romans also levied taxes on the use of ports and bridges in addition to those taxes related to the preparation of the merchandise and its sale. Most of our information on these matters is derived from papyri relating to Egypt (Wallace 1969). Rabbinic literature has preserved only a few references to the names of particular taxes and the means by which they were collected. These traditions refer to harbor and bridge taxes and to a number of trade taxes and excises (for specific taxes in Palestine see, for example: BT Shabbat 33b; BT

303

Avodah Zarah 2b (bridge tax); PT Demai VI, 25b (ofna (?) tax); PT Peah I, 16a (tax on flax merchants); Leviticus Rabbah 34:12, p. 796–9, (tax on silk merchants). See also Midrash Psalms 118:18, p. 486 and additional sources). The matter still must be studied (cf. Gulak 1938 and Heichelheim 1938, pp. 231–95).

The *polis* also levied taxes on trade and commerce there, but not on transit trade. The religious obligation to set aside heave-offerings and tithes was the obligation of the grower or producer. However, if he had not done so it became the responsibility of the buyer or consumer. Talmudic tradition does mention a tithe set aside from merchandise, but this appears to have been only a moral obligation and not an actual requirement (S. Safrai 1983, pp. 126–7).

Trade and commerce in the Empire, however, did not proceed only in accordance with the economic rules of the market-place. Imperial and municipal authorities and institutions took an active interest not only in the supervision of the fairness of trade in the market, but also to some extent in control of prices. These institutions also guaranteed the regular supply of produce to the army and various cities of the Empire. This intervention applied both to agricultural production and to trade. Although there is no explicit information regarding such intervention in Palestine, it would seem certain that the general situation in the rest of the Empire prevailed in this province as well.

Moreover, a number of economic fields were controlled by government monopolies. Thus, for example, the production of perfumes and the salt trade were government monopolies. Cities were also occasionally able to establish local monopolies within the confines of their borders.

Since the tax and customs framework was similar to a great extent to that existing in the rest of the Empire, there is no reason to delve into this matter in great detail here (see pp. 349–50).

XI. THE ECONOMIC UTOPIA OF RABBINIC THOUGHT

XI.1 The Hellenistic period

After the conquest of the coastal cities of Palestine by the Hasmoneans, we hear of the encounter between the Jewish nation and the economy of the Hellenistic world. It would appear that until then there was really no connection between the Jewish nation, composed for the most part of farmers, and the realities of trade and commerce of the ancient world. To the extent that such a connection did previously exist, it probably pertained to Jerusalem or to one of the Hellenized *poleis*, and in any case we have no source material on this matter. With the conquest of the coast, it now became necessary for the Hasmoneans to decide whether to continue to foster and develop the cities which, of course, were also the centers of trade and commerce, or to initiate a policy of repression and decline. As Applebaum has shown (1980), although most of the cities which were conquered were not totally abandoned, they did suffer a serious decline and trade and commerce there suffered as well. The exception to the rule was apparently Joppa whose harbor continued to function, but the importance of this should not be exaggerated.

Applebaum determined that the Hasmoneans, at least at the beginning of their reign, opposed trade and commerce and sought to base their rule on agriculture. The author of the *Letter of Aristeas* also praises the agriculture of the Land of Israel, but adds that "the land is also good for commerce" (114). It is possible that this reference is not enough to teach much regarding the nature of the land, but it does indicate a positive attitude regarding commerce and trade, and shows that they were considered to be important economic components. However, this work was basically apologetic and written for the most part to impress its intended audience (cf. *BJ* 3. 53). According to most scholars, the work was intended for a Hellenistic audience (Egypt?) and was therefore meant to impress them. The classical Hellenistic economic utopia preferred manual labor and production. Commerce was only of secondary importance. This, though, was true more in theory than in practice, and the fostering of trade and commerce was considered an important economic development and beneficial in terms of the cultural and social climate (Mundolfo 1954; D'Arms 1981; Wheeler 1955). The *Letter of Aristeas*, therefore, might well be closer in spirit in this matter to the Hellenistic world and might not reflect the economic ideology of the residents of the Land of Israel.

XI.2 The attitude to commerce

Jewish writings from the end of the Second Temple period and from the Mishnah and Talmud periods clearly indicate the negative Jewish attitude to commerce. Josephus, for instance, states: "The coast is not our home, nor does commerce gladden our hearts. On account of this we do not come into the company of foreign nations. For our cities are built far away from the sea and our portion is good and fruitful. This is the land which we cultivate." Josephus continues: "The residents of the coastal region [= Phoenicians] expended much effort in selling and trading out of greed" (*Contra Apionem* 1. 12). Josephus makes these points to explain why the ancient Greek writers mentioned the Jews so infrequently. The lack of contact based on the Jewish inimical attitude to commerce and trade resulted, theoretically, in a great deal of non-Jewish ignorance regarding the customs of the Jews living in Israel. In any case, it seems that Josephus stresses the non-commercial interests of the Jews as part of his presentation of the Jewish-gentile polemic. However, in spite of the danger of exaggeration, the basic idea is probably correct. The elements of greed and the commerce which does not "gladden

(Jewish) hearts" may be overdone and probably represents Josephus' personal opinion. In any case, the attitude prevailing in the text is anti-trade and commerce, considered to be inspired by avarice and at the expense of labor and production.

The Testament of Issachar more or less voices the same opinion: "Place your interest in the cultivation of the land and toil in all labors of the field." In the fiery prophecy of Jacob relating to the end of days, he states: "And know my sons that at the end of days your sons will abandon their innocence and cling to the love of greed which shall know no satisfaction . . . and they shall forsake the cultivation of the land" (*Test. of Issachar* 6:1–2). Just as in Josephus, the only reason for abandoning cultivation of the land is greed. Moreover, the prophecies in the Testaments of the Patriarchs are of two different natures. The "first prophecy" usually relates to the period of the author such as the period of the Hasmonean revolt and the beginning of their reign, and this is usually a realistic portrayal. The second prophecy relates to the future. The prophecy above would seem to relate to the time of the author or at least to a condition beginning to exist at this time, and probably reflects the period of the Hasmonean reign.

A similar sentiment is found in Philo's description of the Essenes: "For they have not the vaguest idea of commerce, either wholesale or retail or marine, but pack the conducements of covetousness off in disgrace" (*Quod Omnis Probus Liber Sit* 12. 8). It is possible, of course, that this represents only the feelings of the Dead Sea Sect or the Essenes, but the Testament of Issachar, Josephus and Talmudic literature which we shall discuss later on express similar views. Thus, the sentiment of the Essenes would appear to be a popular one of the time which the Essenes observed in their own unique fanatic way.

This general sentiment probably continued to reflect the social reality of the Second Temple period when the majority of the population made their living from the land and had little need for trade or commerce. The anti-trade sentiment had probably become somewhat outdated by the end of the Second Temple period, and later on the opposition to trade and commerce was to become completely anachronistic.

The rabbis sought to return to a closed economic system with little need for trade and commerce. The following *derashah* gives clear expression to this sentiment: " 'And there was no strange god with Him' – that there should not be among you those who engage in worthless commerce" (Sifre Deuteronomy 315, p. 358; Midrash Ha-Gadol on Deuteronomy 32:12, p. 707). Thus business and commerce are compared to a "strange god" and characteristic of non-Jews. When the Children of Israel shall be blessed, there will be no merchants among them. This *derashah* was formulated at the same time as those praising the tribe of Zebulun who traded with the fruits of Issachar (Sifre Deuteronomy 354, p. 415), when many supported themselves through export, as we shall see later on (Chapter 4.VII).

This is also the sentiment of the Amora R. Hanin:

"And thy life shall hang in doubt before thee" – this is one who buys
a supply of wheat for a whole year. "And thou shalt fear night and
day" – this is one who buys from a small retailer. "And thou shalt have
no assurance of thy life" – this is one who buys wheat from a large
store. And I depend on the large-scale merchant for wheat.

This *derashah* is repeated a number of times in rabbinic literature
(PT Shabbat VIII, 11a and parallels). The verse is taken from Deuteronomy
28:66 which is the chapter of reproof and curses, and comes from the section
of the chapter describing the most difficult conditions that will prevail in the
Land of Israel. Thus, one who has to buy a whole year's supply of wheat at
one time (because he has no land) is in a rather difficult situation. One who
has to buy grain in the market from a small retailer fears day and night and
one who has to buy from the large-scale merchant does not have much of a
life. According to the rabbis, all of the curses mentioned in the verse began
to appear during their days. The rabbis, thus, considered the necessity to
buy grain in the market to be an awful situation and a punishment from
heaven. Thus, for instance, it is stated: "One who has to buy from the
market – this is a decline for him" (Tanhuma Buber, Miketz, p. 195).

The teaching of R. Hanin is a further development to some extent on the
derashah of the *tanna* R. Aha b. Josaiah who says:

What is he like who buys wheat from the market? He is like a babe whose
mother has died and he is passed from wet nurse to wet nurse but is never
really satiated. What is he like who buys bread from the market? He is
like one who is buried in his grave. One who eats his own food is like one
who suckles and thrives at the breasts of his mother.

(Avot D'Rabbi Nathan, version A, chapter 30)

R. Aha is quite explicit in calling for self-sufficiency in the cultivation of
grain. One who does not have land and has to buy grain in the market is
miserable, and one who has to buy his bread there is described as the most
wretched of the wretched.

It is necessary to remember that the importing of grain was quite a
common phenomenon in the Land of Israel. Moreover, even in Sepphoris,
R. Hanin's town, there was a grain market which was in operation during
the entire year (PT Bava Mezia V, 10c) and R. Hanin indeed sorrowfully
admits that in his time people had to frequent this market out of necessity. In
spite of the fact that there was a good deal of land in the vicinity of Sepphoris
which was appropriate for the cultivation of grain, most people preferred to
use these lands to cultivate different crops (flax?) and buy grain in the local
grain market (Chapter 2.I.2 above). The opinions of the sages cited above
then did not represent a realistic picture of the situation, but rather the
concept of the economic utopia which they espoused.

R. Zera, who was born in Babylonia and later came to live in the Land of Israel, stated that: "It is the way of the world that when someone sells something to his fellow – he sells in sorrow, but buys happily" (BT Berachot 5a). Such a claim is obviously inappropriate for a free-market system in which both partners in the transaction should more or less be satisfied. In a closed economic system, though, every sale represents somewhat the dissolution of permanent property and takes place only out of dire necessity.

R. Aibo the Babylonian advised his son that it was preferable to have: "a *kab* from land and not a *kur* from payment" (BT Pesahim 113a). According to this rabbi, then, it was better to earn less from one's own land than to receive more money from some type of payment; he was most likely referring to speculation in trade or business. This is also the spirit of the *midrash* supposedly quoted by the Patriarch Isaac: "He said – since blessing pertains only to the work of one's hands, he stood and planted" (T Berachot 7:8). The opposition of the rabbis to trade and an open economic system is based on a number of their views pertaining to both morality and *halachah*. We shall attempt to point out their positions on this, although the individual traditions may represent more than one reason for their objections.

XI.3 Attachment to the land

According to the rabbis, land should not be sold, or if it is necessary to do so then only as a last resort.

> From where do we learn that one is not permitted to sell his field and put the proceeds in his vest, or buy an animal or utensils or a house, unless he has been impoverished? Thus it is written, "If he should become impoverished and sold from his portion," – from his portion and not all of his portion.
> (Sifra Behar 7:1 and parallels; T Terumot 1:11; BT Gittin 52a)

There are really two teachings here: one is forbidden to sell agricultural land even to make a profit (or to buy a house!) and one cannot sell, even if impoverished, an entire holding. Since there is nothing inherent in the *derashah* to indicate that it refers to the Second Temple period, there is no reason to restrict it only to that time.

A number of traditions describe the custom of "*kezazah*" which was the joyful ceremony (for the buyer at least) in which one sold his patrimony in shame (T Ketubbot 3:3 and parallels). This custom clearly reflects a society which opposed the sale of land, even if this had to be done at times rather frequently. Alon (1980, p. 155) was probably right in claiming that this tradition does not reflect only the Second Temple period. All of these traditions are cited by rabbis in whose time obviously much land was sold. Their opinion, however, was their view of utopia and not reality.

XI.4 Self-sufficiency

The rabbis much preferred self-sufficiency in all spheres to specialization in one sphere and the marketing of a single product, as we have already seen in a number of traditions cited above. A tradition in Genesis Rabbah (91:6, p. 1122 and parallels) states along those lines: " 'And go down [Hebrew: *u-rdu*] there,' from this you learn that anyone who buys wheat in the market is downtrodden [Hebrew: *yarud*]." The famous teaching that one should divide his resources into three parts should also be understood in this manner: "one-third in grain, one-third in vineyards and one-third in olives" (BT Bava Mezia 107a). The rabbis, thus, would seem to prefer that one should raise all the major crops and not specialize in just one.

It is interesting to compare this sentiment with the following *midrash*: "In this world, one who has a field of wheat (lit. a white field), does not have an orchard and one who has orchards does not have a field of wheat" (BT Bava Bathra 122a). It is difficult to know whether this sentiment or the one cited above reflects the reality of the time in the Land of Israel. There were certainly people with only one field, just as there were those possessing a number of plots. In any case, the directive of the rabbis that one should cultivate all the important crops and not just one would appear to reflect the former economic sentiment described above.

The desire for self-sufficiency is also found regarding meat and milk: "It is enough for a person to support himself from the milk of goats and lambs in his own house" (BT Hullin 84a). It is also stated that one should not buy meat from the market, but should secure his supply of meat from his own flock. A drastic formulation of this idea is found in Midrash Proverbs 5: "Blessed is the man whose wife is from his own town, whose Torah is from his own town and whose livelihood is from his own town. To him applies the verse, 'Let your source be blessed'."

XI.5 Limitation on trade

The rabbis sometimes place such drastic limitations on trade that its very legitimization was almost invalidated and profit was to all intents and purposes made impossible. Thus, for example, T Bava Bathra 5:13 states: "One may not make a profit twice from eggs or fruit. This is the opinion of R. Judah. The rabbis permitted it." (See also BT Bava Bathra 91a and cf. BT Bava Mezia 40b and BT Menahot 77a.) The meaning of this law is that one who bought these items can sell them only to a consumer, but not to another merchant or retailer who will then proceed to sell to a consumer. A *baraita* in BT states that R. Eleazar did not heed this law. The law is also found with some variation in T Avodah Zarah: "One is not allowed to make a profit from grain but is allowed to do so from wine, oil and legumes. It was said regarding R. Eleazar b. Azariah that he dealt so in wine and oil all his life"

(T Avodah Zarah 4(5):1). In T Bava Bathra there is the added provision that the prohibition refers to a double profit from these commodities, and the opinion of R. Eleazar b. Azariah was formulated as a difference of opinion between him and the sages. The *baraita* in BT adds an additional explanation pertaining to the matter and formulates the explanation as an addendum: "as for example wines and oils and flours." T Avodah Zarah states that the prohibition refers only to wheat but not to wine and oil, and thus provides a means of explaining the economic behavior of R. Eleazar who traded only in wine and oil. The development and different formulations of the tradition refer undoubtedly to different stages of economic development in Palestine. Thus, for example, the export of oil and wine took place much before the export of grain (Chapter 2.I.2; I.3 above).

The *baraitot* most likely reflect the Usha period (R. Judah) and the Javneh period (R. Eleazar b. Azariah), and there is therefore no reason to claim that they reflect only the depression immediately after the Bar-Kochba revolt.

Needless to say, all of these laws limiting the rate of profit to a maximum of 100 per cent, or forbidding any profit at all regarding certain agricultural produce, are quite negative in the sense of economic development. Moreover, they do not reflect at all the reality of a vibrant trade in agricultural produce and do not take into account (expensive) costs of transportation, taxation and other expenses. If our understanding of the development of the texts quoted above is correct, this represents once again the rabbinic view of economic utopia which was not connected to any economic reality.

Another law relates to a prohibition against hoarding agricultural produce:

> One may not hoard in the Land of Israel those products which are basic commodities such as wines, oils, flours and fruits. But those which are not basic commodities such as cumin and condiments may be hoarded. When does this law apply? Only regarding those products bought from the market. If they are produced, however, by oneself they may be stored away for even ten years. During a year of drought one should not even hoard a *kab* of carobs since it introduces a curse into the prices.
>
> (T Avodah Zarah 4(5):1)

BT cites a large number of traditions dealing with and illustrating the principles mentioned in the source above (BT Bava Bathra 90b). The most important aspect of the Talmudic discussion, at least for our purposes, is the establishment of a chronological framework; in addition to citing a *baraita* which is not found in the Tosefta, the Talmudic tradition mentions a statement in the name of R. Johanan (third century CE) regarding a person called Shabtai who used to hoard fruits in spite of the opposition of the rabbis, as well as additional views of the Babylonian sages. In any case, the traditions cited in BT prove that the *baraita* was observed in the third century CE in Palestine (the period of the anarchy) as well as in Babylonia.

The third law in this series of *halachot* (T Avodah Zarah 4(5):2) deals with the prohibition against the export of fruits from the Land of Israel abroad and to Syria:

> One does not export to Syria foodstuffs which are basic commodities such as wines, oils and flours. And Rabbi (Judah the Prince) says: I say that it is permitted to export wines to Syria because that lessens foolishness. Just as one may not export to Syria, one may not export from district (lit.: *hyparchia*) to district. R. Judah permits from district to district.

This *baraita* also appears in BT (90b) with minor variations. The permission granted to export from district to district pertains it would seem from the border region of the Land of Israel to Syria, as a number of Talmudic commentators have already stated (Rashbam, R. Gershom and others).

Thus, the sages appeared to have forbidden the exporting of agricultural produce. The decree is from the Usha period and from the period of Rabbi Judah the Prince. There is no indication in these sources that the restrictions pertain only to times of drought and other difficult times. However, the export of agricultural produce (to Egypt and Syria), especially wine and oil, was the lifeblood of the Palestinian economy. Galilean oil was regularly found in the markets of Tyre and Sidon (Chapter 1.I.3 above). The restrictions on this type of trade set forth by the sages, therefore, do not necessarily reflect reality. They reflect once again, however, the rabbinic view of a closed economic system with no buying and selling of agricultural produce.

XI.6 The attitude to commerce as a profession

The large-scale merchant (Hebrew: *tagar*) was considered a cheat who could not be trusted. Thus, for example, he could not be trusted regarding water which he might claim fell into the wine which he was selling (M Bava Mezia 4:11). The rabbis deprecated this type of merchant quite often even though it was not always clear what offense they were guilty of (II.3 above). It is likely, though, that this attitude was justified, at least in some aspects. The sources clearly indicate that the residents of the rural sphere, as well as the great majority of urban dwellers, regarded these merchants with some degree of suspicion, and the sources cited above should be regarded as an expression, albeit exaggerated at times, of this suspicion.

The attitude of the rabbis was clearly hostile. The series of traditions contrasting commerce with the study of Torah clearly express this attitude: "Nor can one who occupies himself overmuch in business grow wise" (M Avot 2:5); "If he occupies himself much in the academy and little in business, at once the holy spirit rests within his internal organs" (Tanna

D'Ve Eliyahu 2); "One does not find Torah either among pedlars or among merchants" (BT Eruvin 55b); The Torah "does not rest among those who sail the seas" and even among those who go from Acco to Joppa (Deuteronomy Rabbati Nitzavim, p. 119). We have also cited above an additional source viewing trade in a negative manner (Sifre Deuteronomy 315).

These sayings are clearly opposed to the favorable traditions (see above) regarding the attitude of the rabbis to labor and agriculture. The negative traditions are related to the problem concerning the relationship between the study of Torah and Derech Eretz (behavior in everyday life). We shall therefore briefly discuss this important matter.

Without a doubt, there is an inherent contrast between the requirement that one devote himself entirely to the study of Torah and the observance of commandments, and the "way of the world," as it were. This is not just a matter of the correct utilization of time, but rather an issue of the highest spiritual importance. Early on in scholarship it was clear that the rabbis generally demanded some sort of combination and symbiosis of these two different spheres. The ideal postulated by most of the rabbis was not a sage devoting his entire life to Torah, but rather the lay person who could combine the study of Torah with his everyday affairs. Undoubtedly there were those who demanded a more religious life-style dedicated to heavenly pursuits only, but there were probably few who could meet such demands (Alon 1980, I, pp. 173–5; Beer 1964; Ayali 1982; Ben Shalom 1985).

As we stated above, there are hundreds of traditions in Talmudic literature praising labor and crafts. All these traditions stress the positive aspects of labor and the like, but do not praise commerce or business. This is very important. None of the numerous traditions which stress the importance of working and of supporting oneself mention business or commerce as an economic or professional option, which is not surprising in view of their opposition to these pastimes.

XI.7 The opposition to the *polis*

The sages opposed not only business and commerce, but also life in general in the *polis*. The *polis* in their view is synonymous with sin: "The People of Israel said: Lord of the Universe, don't judge me as a resident of a *polis* with thievery and immorality and oaths in vain and false ones" (BT Eruvin 21b). "A bachelor who lives in a *polis* and who does not sin" (BT Pesahim 113a–b) faced greater temptation since the *polis* was usually a hotbed of immorality and especially of fornication. The Palestinian Amora R. Jose b. R. Hanina makes the general statement: "From whence do we know that living in a *polis* is difficult, as it is written" (BT Ketubbot 110b. In M Ketubbot 13:10 the *polis* appears as a type of residence different from a town. The Mishnah, however, does not state which is the preferred form). Ruth Rabbah 2:6 mentions an additional complaint against the *polis*: "They came to the *poleis* and found them lacking in water." It is difficult to know whether this reflects reality or not, since most *poleis* had a regular system of aqueducts. They did not, however, always reach the residential areas of the masses and there might have been a shortage of water there at times.

In the Greek and Roman world, the *polis* was considered the ideal form of settlement as well as the cradle of civilization, even though Greco-Roman literature still preserved to some extent the old utopian view of village life. This is not the correct place, however, to discuss the contrast between these two different types of cultures, and in any case it is not clear that such a discussion will provide worthwhile results. In any event, though, it is possible to sum up and state that rabbinic literature contains no appreciations of commerce and city life.

Talmudic literature describes the *polis* as the source of wealth and comfort on the one hand (Chapter 1.II.3 above), yet as the bastion of sin on the other hand. Moreover, there is no particular appreciation of this wealth in those sources which mention the wealth. Rabbinic literature in general does not think too much of a life of luxury, and this is no exception to the rule.

It would appear that the sources mentioned above describe a rather naive and simplistic economic system. The rabbinic ideal is that everyone should be able to support himself from his own labors. There should be no commerce in food commodities and, in any case, commerce should be limited and profits restricted. Commerce is invalid by its very nature and, moreover, it corrupts. It derives only from greed and clearly does not lead to fear of God. Not only is the *polis* not an accepted form of settlement, it is also the source of sin and corruption. However, only a limited number of traditions extol poverty as a virtue (Urbach 1961).

XI.8 The realistic economic approach

Until now we have discussed traditions pertaining to the utopian rabbinic view of economy which negated commerce. However, it is also not difficult to find traditions praising trade, or perhaps to be more exact, traditions recognizing trade and commerce as a legitimate means of making a living. Job, according to the Testimony of Job (second century BCE) was willing to give monies to be used in trade and commerce in order to provide for charity: "And now do a service for us and lend us money in order that we shall go to the large cities and trade, and thus we may be able to serve the poor" (Testimony of Job 11:3). Job, who fulfills their request, has no problems with the trade and commerce involved. This apparently was also the view of the rabbis in the Second Temple period, who stated that tithes also had to be set aside on profits from commerce. They voiced no objection to this commerce (p. 304 above).

Similar sentiments are found in many other traditions. Thus, for example, many of the leading sages of Eretz-Israel such as R. Isaac, Rabbi Judah the

Prince and R. Ishmael b. R. Jose were active in the world of commerce. R. Hoshaiah b. Simi was a merchant who was accustomed to travel the seas and R. Isaac b. R. Eliezer advised him how to conduct himself (PT Moed Qatan II, 81b). We could cite numerous other examples. The sages discuss business profits in hundreds of traditions. It is true that they do discuss such problematical matters as interest, price-gouging and trade with gentiles, but they do not specifically state any objection to trade itself or to the profit which derives from it. There are also many laws dealing with the limitations pertaining to trade with non-Jews or selling them land, but once again there is no opposition to trade in general or the selling of land per se.

The tribe of Zevulun which engages in commerce is described in a favorable manner (Sifre Deuteronomy 354, 18, p. 415 and many parallels). R. Isaac even advises that one should divide funds into three parts: "one-third in land, one-third in commerce (!) and one-third as ready capital" (BT Bava Mezia 42a). Jerusalem is described in the sources as a wondrous city because, among other things, there is much business and trade there (Lamentations Rabbah 1:1, p. 44). The upshot of all this is that many sources clearly see trade and commerce as legitimate. In addition to the rabbinic sources, one must also take into consideration the numerous testimonies relating to Jewish merchants whether from Eretz-Israel or the diaspora. These have not been collected or analyzed in a systematic manner (pp. 315–16 below). However, the importance of all this is rather tangential for our purposes and in spite of the large amount of archeological and literary material on this matter, it is impossible to determine to what extent these merchants, even those who were the leaders of their times, represented national and communal aspirations.

The traditions describe, therefore, two different ideological approaches to the economy. However, it would be incorrect to describe them as conflicting approaches or as diametrically opposed to one another. They were not even really two different ideologies. On a theoretical level, commerce and business was looked down upon. On a practical level, however, the sages realized that trade was inevitable, and both the sages and the public in general accommodated themselves to this reality. It was necessary, but there are no rabbinic traditions praising it as a means of spiritual purification or as an educational tool as was the case regarding agriculture and physical labor. A similar approach is found in Hellenistic thought. The words of the philosophers in praise of labor, and in particular manual labor and production, do not necessarily contradict encouraging business and commerce. Augustus boasted, for instance, that he did not wear a tunic which his wife did not weave. He also, however, did much in terms of legislation favorable to commerce and also encouraged it within the Empire.

The question of the attitude towards commerce for the most part pertains to ideology and theory and not to actual reality. The same was true in the Roman Empire. Trade and commerce was considered degrading, but it was this trade and commerce which served as a vital part of the Roman economy and society and which also, to a great extent, gave political force to the Empire (see, for example, D'Arms 1981; Mundolfo 1954 *et al.*).

XII. THE ETHNIC BACKGROUND OF MERCHANTS

Those studies dealing with the economy in the Roman–Byzantine period often claim that the Jews played an important role in the international trade of the time and that the Jewish community in the diaspora served, as it were, as a trade station for itinerant Jewish merchants (Avi-Yonah 1964, p. 131; Krauss 1924, I, 1, pp. 201 ff.). According to this theory, the ties between the various diaspora communities were economic in nature and they gave the Jews a decisive advantage over their neighbors. Proof of this situation is found in the many references to Jewish merchant shippers and sailors in Talmudic literature, while they are hardly mentioned in the literature of the Roman Empire. It therefore appears likely that a Jewish merchant would have probably availed himself of the services offered by the various communities in the diaspora. Thus, for instance, the *midrash* places in the mouth of a Jewish merchant arriving by ship in a strange city the following sentiments: "I am not a stranger, who does not know where to go. And someone said to him – Are there Jewish strangers?" (Devarim Rabbah 2:10).

However, the view that the Jews in the Roman Empire were a nation of merchants and traders is apparently an anachronism and reflects a much later reality. There is no proof that such was the situation in the Roman Empire.

During the period of the Restoration of Zion the term "Canaanite" was synonymous with merchant (Proverbs 31:24; Nehemiah 13:16). Later on, during the Hellenistic period, the Jews are described as farmers who despise commerce. The Greek coastal cities which were captured by the Hasmoneans were not restored, except for Joppa, and certainly did not become new Jewish centers of commerce (Applebaum 1980). Later on, the war fleet of Herod was mentioned in the sources, but the fleet was apparently quite small and without much economic significance. The important merchants of the Roman and Byzantine periods lived along the coast and the residents of the cities or settlements there were for the most part non-Jewish. As we mentioned above, Jewish literature has many references to Jewish merchant shippers or moneychangers, but this same literature, which by its very nature concerns itself much more with Jews than with non-Jews, also quite often mentions non-Jewish merchants, caravans, ships and moneychangers.

There is no doubt that the Jews participated in international trade during the Roman period. There is no proof, however, that their participation in this sphere was greater than their relative place within the population. There is also no means of arriving at any figures regarding Jewish participation in this trade. The role of Eastern merchants in the trade of the Empire began to grow during the Byzantine period and there are, for instance, traditions pertaining to Syrian merchants found throughout the Empire (Brehier 1903; A. H. M. Jones 1964, p. 865). The rise in the number of Jewish merchants, for the most part from Judaea, in imperial trade (Synesius 4, Dan 1971, *et al.*) and in Indian Ocean trade (Dan 1980) should be understood in the light of this phenomenon.

APPENDIX 1:
THE WHEAT TRADE

As we saw above (Chapter 2.II.2), massive import of wheat to Eretz-Israel began in the third century CE It is necessary, however, to determine whether this was the result of free trade or of government intervention. The wheat supply in the Empire was a rather sensitive matter. Grains were of great importance for the economy in general, and the economy was to all intents and purposes dependent on this economic sphere. The fact that there were regions in the Roman Empire in which grains were not cultivated may have encouraged and perhaps even required a system of regulations. Moreover, in the Roman Empire, and especially during the Byzantine period, the economy was to a great extent centrally controlled. Means of production and marketing were dependent on central government regulations, and it is quite likely that the same was true regarding the cultivation of wheat. The organization of the supplying of wheat in the Empire has been much discussed in scholarly literature (Rostovtzeff 1959, pp. 142–5; Rickman 1980). It is possible to point out a number of major components of this system.

(1) The imperial government supplied grain *gratis* to the residents of Rome, and during the Byzantine period this was also the case regarding Constantinople. In order to facilitate this, the government ordered the cultivation of massive quantities of grain in Egypt and Cyranaica and then demanded payment of customs and excises there in grain. A system of transport and marketing was also developed in order to further facilitate the distribution of this grain in the capital (Tengström 1974).

(2) The imperial government levied grain taxes (payable in kind) to supply the soldiers of the Empire as well as the imperial bureaucracy. This was the *annona* or "*arnona*" of the Jewish sources. Sometimes, however, the government would make do with a cash payment and not require the actual cultivation of the grain. Grains composed a great amount of the food which was supplied to the soldiers of the Roman Empire through the *annona*.

(3) In the course of central imperial regulation of the economy, the government was also likely to regulate the level of grain cultivation in certain provinces. This was especially the case in the Byzantine period.

(4) Many of those cities which had to import grain were afraid that grain

merchants would not come there of their own volition. This fear forced the government to take steps to guarantee a regular supply of grain. This practice was already common in the early Hellenistic period and continued afterwards (A. H. M. Jones 1966, pp. 217–18). The official in charge of economic matters in the *polis*, generally the *agoranomos* or the *logistes*, but at times the *astonomos*, also dealt with this matter (Lieberman 1944–5, pp. 37–8; Sperber 1970).

(5) The municipal government occasionally regulated prices of produce and foodstuffs in general, as well as the prices of grain and bread (and also quality control). This practice was common already in early Greek cities and continued in different forms for quite a long time. The grain market was the "*sidke*" and was under the supervision of the *agoranomos* or *sidkearchos*. Somewhat infrequently, the city subsidized the prices of foodstuffs and agricultural produce and there were even times when such foodstuffs were distributed free of charge. The subsidies were, of course, an important means of regulating prices, but they had an additional and more far-reaching importance. The official in charge of these subsidies was the *siton*. Subsidizing the price of grain was especially common during periods of drought or famine.

For our purposes, however, it is necessary to determine what the situation was in the cities and villages of Eretz-Israel. The practices mentioned above were not obligatory and there were many differences between the individual cities of the Roman Empire.

There were two different local administrative systems in Eretz-Israel. In the Jewish villages there was a highly developed autonomous communal system. In the cities there was the mechanism of the *polis* (Chapter 1 above). It is necessary, therefore, to examine both systems independently, even if the sources do not always clearly distinguish between them.

The sources give no indication that the Jewish town subsidized the price of wheat and they also do not mention any special measures regarding the supplying of produce to the city. It is also not clear to what extent the *agoranomos* was responsible for the regulation of prices and it would appear that according to the Palestinian sources, at least, the *agoranomos* dealt for the most part with weights and measures, making sure that there was no chicanery (Sperber 1977; Chapter 1.III above). The few sources dealing with price regulation are not specifically connected to the *agoranomos* (T Bava Mezia 11:23; Genesis Rabbah 98(99):4, p. 1255). If, however, price regulation was fairly uncommon, it would appear that subsidization was almost non-existent (and indeed there are dozens of traditions referring to Jewish communal and economic activity; if such subsidization existed there is no reason why it should not have been mentioned). The matter of supplying grain to the *poleis* of Eretz-Israel and the question of subsidization of grain prices are difficult due to the lack of material pertaining to these issues. Even if subsidization was common in Roman cities, there is no proof that this was the case in every city in every province. Thus, it is necessary to find proof in the case of the *poleis* of Eretz-Israel.

Talmudic tradition does have a number of references to direct action of various *poleis* regarding the sale of grains at subsidized prices. Some of these traditions also refer to the establishment of prices in general and to the selling of wheat only to professional bakers (Yankelevich 1983). Thus the most important and direct tradition is that of Ulla regarding the bakers whom the members of the *boule* or town council "strike every twelve months and say – sell at a cheap price, sell at a cheap price" (BT Yoma 9a). Or in a similar vein the words of R. Samuel b. Isaac who said: "The matter may be solved in this manner – it was a non-Jewish *agoranomos* who forced him to sell cheaply" (PT Demai II, 22c).

The second tradition clearly deals with an *agoranomos* in a *polis*, and it is likely that those who strike the bakers were also in a *polis*. An important tradition regarding the role of the *agoranomos* is, according to Sperber, found in Yalkut Shimoni Deuteronomy § 808:

> It happened that a city was in dire need of bread. The residents came and pleaded before the *heshbon* (or *hasban* = *agoranomos*). Two bakers got up and ground wheat the entire night. The continuation of the tradition relates that these bakers mixed in a low-grade wheat into the bread and the *heshbon* reprimanded them, saying: "You are worthy of having the blade put against your necks."

Our conclusions, based on an exacting analysis of the tradition, however, are somewhat different than those of Sperber. The people complain to the *agoranomos*, but he apparently does nothing regarding the supplying of the bread. He only seems to be interested in quality control. Since the people apparently do seek the active intervention of the *heshbon* in this case, it is possible, therefore, that in some unusual instances he did concern himself with matters of supply.

According to Yankelevich (1983), the dependence of the city on external factors to provide grain explains the deliberations of the rabbis regarding the permissibility of bread baked or provided by non-Jews. According to Yankelevich, the grain was supplied to non-Jewish bakers and if such bread were forbidden, the Jews would not be able to enjoy the subsidies on bread. In spite of all this, Yankelevich does not claim that these traditions serve as proof regarding the matter of subsidies, but only to explain the developments pertaining to the *halachah*. It is possible, however, to offer a different explanation for the permission given by the rabbis to eat this non-Jewish bread. Thus this particular matter is related to a similar decision regarding the use of non-Jewish oil (see, for example, BT Avodah Zarah 37a and M Avodah Zarah 2:6). It is therefore likely that there is a similar reason behind both instances. The matter of non-Jewish oil was explained by the fact that it became difficult and indeed dangerous for the Jews to acquire oil prepared only by Jews ("For they used to go up to Har ha-Melekh and were killed on account of it" – PT Avodah Zarah II, 41d). The tradition appears to refer to the Lod area in which there were Jewish landowners who also had land in the hostile non-Jewish region of Har ha-Melekh (cf. PT Demai VI, 25b and BT Avodah Zarah 40b). This makes sense in Judaea in the Lod area, but certainly not in the Galilee where olive oil production was to a great extent a Jewish operation. However, since the rabbis decided to permit the non-Jewish oil in Judaea, they also permitted its use in the Galilee.

According to this, it is possible to explain that the Jews of the cities became more and more dependent on the non-Jewish bakers. And indeed, the reason stated by the Palestinian Talmud regarding the permissibility of non-Jewish bread relates to Rabbi Judah the Prince: "Once Rabbi Judah the Prince went to a certain place and saw that the sages only had a meagre amount of bread. Rabbi Judah said – is there not a baker here? The people thought that he was referring to a non-Jewish baker when he really meant a Jewish one" (BT Avodah Zarah 35b – and according to PT the decision pertained only to permission to buy from a baker). It would seem, therefore, that the root of the problem was the dependence on non-Jewish bakers. As is well known, in most *poleis*, wheat was ground in large mills and not in private homes (T Pesahim 1(2):13 and parallels). It is likely that these mills belonged to non-Jewish bakers and the Jews were forced, therefore, to buy bread from non-Jews.

There are conceivably a number of other sources which might be cited regarding the supplying of wheat and the subsidization of grain prices. Rabbinic literature mentions the *siton* a number of times, but this *siton* appears to have been Jewish (see, for example, M Demai 2:4 *et al.*). This particular term seems to have taken on the general meaning of a large-scale merchant. This is the meaning of the phrase "*cheese siton*" found in a relatively late source (Tractate Cuthim, chapter 2:3). Moreover, the *siton* and the baker are allowed to sell wheat that is *demai* (= it is not clear whether tithes have been set aside from it). This is not because of pressure from the non-Jewish *agoranomos*, but rather because they sold in "large measures" and generally gave the customer somewhat more than they really paid for (M Demai 2:4). Since the term *siton* took on the meaning of a large-scale merchant, the only thing that can really be learned from Talmudic sources is that the Jews were familiar with the term, but obfuscated its original meaning.

Ruth Rabbah 1:4 mentions a member of a boule upon whom a city depended to provide for its needs during a year of famine. Unfortunately, this seems to have been a matter of a private donation and official responsibility. It is possible, however, to bring indirect proof attesting to the fact that the city did not engage in the supplying of food to the city and did not subsidize grain prices in any permanent manner. The fact that there is no reference to any of this in the numerous sources of Talmudic literature cannot be pure coincidence. Moreover, we have also seen above (Chapter 2.I.1) that a number of traditions mention private grain merchants in such cities as Ascalon and Sepphoris. In Sepphoris, there was the permanent grain market (*sidke*) and the Palestinian Talmud is quite clear in indicating that prices changed in accordance with supply and demand, and that fluctuations in prices had an effect not only on the market but in the entire area. Thus, all aspects of the market, buyers and sellers, appear to have been of a private nature.

Talmudic tradition has some sources of a positive nature regarding the Empire and its institutions. There are also many such parables regarding the "king" which clearly represents the government in some form or fashion. These traditions usually refer to activities related to "civilization" such as the supplying of water, the building of aqueducts, the construction of roads and bridges. None of these traditions mention the supplying of food to the city, a phenomenon which certainly would have been mentioned if it had taken place (BT Shabbat 33b; BT Avodah Zarah 2:2; Mekhilta De-va-Hodesh 5, p. 219). It is possible then to sum up and state that the wheat trade was more or less in the domain of private enterprise. The role of the government in this matter more or less revolved around the collection of taxes in kind and the sale of this produce, or part of it, to private customers in the market. In spite of all this, however, the basic governmental control of the imperial economy undoubtedly influenced, to some extent, the critical and important trade in grains.

APPENDIX 2:
TRADE DURING THE SABBATICAL YEAR

It was forbidden to work the land during the seventh year of the sabbatical cycle, or the Sabbatical Year. Among the various prohibitions listed by the sources, it was also forbidden to sell fruits or produce which grew during the Sabbatical Year (which grew of its own accord without being cultivated). However, this prohibition was not always observed and some of this trade was apparently allowed, at least within the framework of certain restrictions. Thus, at the end of the Second Temple period the sages of the House of Shammai (Beth Shammai) state that this trade should be allowed to take place only in the form of barter: "Beth Shammai say that the fruits of the Sabbatical Year should be sold only for fruit . . . and Beth Hillel permit them (to be sold for money) (T Sheviit 6:19). The opinion of Beth Hillel was accepted, however, and in the generations following, trade in the fruits of the Sabbatical Year became an accepted practice, although the rabbis did try and prevent those who engaged in this trade from making exorbitant profits (M Sheviit 8:3 and many parallels). The rabbis also forbade deals of brokering in this produce as well as wholesaling and the like (M Sanhedrin 3:3 and parallels). They also forbade the collection of this type of fruit on a large scale for the specific purpose of selling it (T Sheviit 6:22 *et al.*). Only "primary" trade was allowed, or in other words the sale of the small amount of produce by one who had picked it up himself or by his neighbor who lived nearby the potential consumer (M Sheviit 7:3; T Sheviit 6:22). All of this requires further study, but this is not the correct forum for this matter.

The fact that the rabbis did not forbid this type of trade would seem to indicate that it was necessary for the farmers of both country and city in order to survive during the Sabbatical Year. During the Javneh period, a system was devised whereby all such fruits were collected by the local court which was responsible for its distribution to local residents (T Sheviit 8:1; 7:9; T Peah 4:16). This system is referred to in both classical and scholarly literature as "Otzar [lit. treasury] Beth Din." The system became more sophisticated in the modern *halachah* later on but still remained local in nature. In fact, "Otzar Beth Din" is not mentioned in post-Javneh period sources. There are, however, numerous sources from this period which refer to private citizens operating their own businesses without community guidelines. We do not know, though, whether Otzar Beth Din was abolished or whether it simply did not function from its very inception in certain regions. In any case, the villages were allowed some degree of trade and commerce with this produce and apparently it was quite necessary. All this would seem to indicate that the agricultural sector produced surplus crops and it was necessary to market them even during the Sabbatical Year. It is likely, though, that this surplus was not any form of grain. Grain was not cultivated at all during the Sabbatical Year and it is impossible that there would be such a large crop which had grown of its own accord, untended. The surplus was probably either olives or grapes or similar types of fruit. It was forbidden to store or hoard the fruits of the seventh year; therefore it was often a matter of survival to sell them.

In light of all this, it is possible that Otzar Beth Din was abolished because the local distribution of the produce was not sufficient to guarantee economic survival and it was necessary to market some of the surplus outside the immediate local region. The local community leaders apparently were not able to organize this within the strict guidelines of the complicated laws of the Sabbatical Year. Thus, it is likely that Otzar Beth Din was abolished some time during the Usha period, although for the moment this theory does remain hypothetical. In any case, the fact that commerce in this produce was essential for survival and was consequently permitted, in spite of the fact that it had previously been forbidden, goes to show that we are dealing with an open and developed economic system which depended to some extent also on commerce and not just on self-production.

4

The organizational framework of farming

I. AGRARIAN STRUCTURE

I.1 Introduction

Since the land was an important means of production, it is worthwhile to determine who owned it. In the Roman Empire in general and in Eretz-Israel in particular there were a number of different types of landowners. They can be divided according to either social or legal criteria:

(1) government estates (Duncan-Jones 1964a; D. J. Crawford 1976);
(2) private estates which belonged either to the rich or to those close to government circles, whether the estates were granted by the government or not;
(3) a small tract of land held by a small-scale independent farmer;
(4) city lands;
(5) church lands.

We shall try in this chapter to prove the existence of these different types of lands and to determine the different agricultural and economic organization of these individual types of land. We shall also try to determine the agrarian process of each, or in other words, the quantitative relationship of these different types of land to one another, and how much land of the province was held by public institutions, by rich individuals and by small-scale farmers.

I.2 Government estates

When the Romans officially took over the province in 6 CE they found a quite developed system of government-owned estates. Royal lands and estates were a common phenomenon already during Biblical times and the Persian period. The Persian crown lands passed directly to the Ptolemaic and Seleucid regimes when they conquered Palestine. Sources tell of a 50 per cent tax on fruits and a 33 per cent tax on cultivated fields during the Hasmonean

322

period (I Mac. 10:30). This tax rate is much higher than any rate levied on private estates. It does, however, conform to rates levied on crown estates in Egypt and Syria. Scholars therefore suggest that all the lands of Judaea had been turned by the government into royal estates and then officially confiscated by the government at the outbreak of the Hasmonean revolt (Mittwoch 1955).

The confiscation of the lands of Judaea, if indeed such had actually taken place at the outbreak of the Hasmonean revolt, lost all meaning as a result of the success of the rebels. However, it is likely that the Hasmoneans appropriated for themselves the former crown lands such as the estate at Jericho which we have already discussed above (Chapter 2.I.7). The large number of wars and conquests which took place between 110–76 BCE offered many opportunities to further expand Hasmonean royal possessions. The areas which were conquered and the Greek cities whose inhabitants were exiled would most likely have become Hasmonean crown lands, even though it is impossible to prove this. Herod, who followed the Hasmoneans, gave his veterans lands in Geba Hippeum and Sebaste (Schalit 1969, pp. 358–65) which were, most likely, crown lands. An additional crown estate was at Jamnia (Javneh), further proof of crown lands near these Greek cities.

The arrival of the Romans in 63 BCE did not change the situation in Judaea itself. The re-founding of the Greek cities and their renewed construction at that time undoubtedly did result in changes related to the land there, and probably allowed for the introduction of new elements in the settlement of these lands. Sources pertaining to the end of the Second Temple period mention great tracts of land which were considered to be crown lands. Herod, for instance, had much of this land (PW, supp. II, p. 92; Schalit 1969, pp. 257 ff.; Applebaum 1958–9, p. 44).

Agrippa I, Herod's grandson, had estates in the vicinity of the Jezreel Valley. The center of these estates was at Beth Sheraim (*Vita* 24). Previously, Hyrcanus II apparently also had estates in the Jezreel Valley (*Ant.* 14. 207; Mazar 1958, p. 15). There was an additional estate at Asochis, although it is not clear whether it belonged to Agrippa II or to the emperor himself (T Shabbat 13(14):9; PT Shabbat XVI, 15d; BT Shabbat 121a). Gischala served as a central depot for collection of grain taxes during the War of Destruction (66 CE), but this serves to prove only that it was the capital of a toparchy and not a royal estate (*Vita* 13). Herod gave the estate at Jamnia to his sister Salome and she, upon her death, gave it to Livia (*Ant.* 17. 189, 321; *BJ* 2. 98; *Ant.* 18. 31; *BJ* 2. 167). Sources somewhat later mention the procurator of the royal estate at Jamnia who managed affairs for the emperor there (*Ant.* 18. 150 and cf. Philo *Legatio ad Gaium* 199 and Smallwood 1981, p. 261). A funerary inscription of the daughter of an imperial procurator was found at this city (Avi-Yonah 1946, p. 84). An imperial procurator of Jamnia was also mentioned much later on in the fifth century CE (Petrus the Iberian, p. 123) and the hostel of the empress Eudocia was apparently related to this.

However, the entire city of Jamnia was apparently not a royal estate since the city is mentioned as a *polis* already in the first century CE (Avi-Yonah 1963, p. 49). Jewish sources also mention rabbis such as Rabban Gamaliel and others who were private landowners in this area (M Demai 3:1). The phrase Har ha-Melech, literally the "king's mountain," which is mentioned a number of times in Talmudic tradition, also apparently refers to crown lands (Applebaum 1967). We shall discuss the size of this territory later on.

According to Josephus, Vespasian confiscated all the lands of Judaea after the War of the Destruction. This would seemingly imply that all of Judaea became crown property (*BJ* 7.216). However, S. Safrai has already shown that this was not actually so and that there are many traditions regarding the private ownership of lands in Judaea after the War of Destruction (M. Gittin 5.6; S. Safrai 1966, pp. 306–10; Büchler 1912). The legal option of turning all the lands in a rebellious province into crown territory may have been possible in legal and political theory, but need not have taken place. B. Isaac (1988), continuing along the same line of reasoning and closely analyzing the pertinent text in Josephus, has shown that Josephus did not actually write about the confiscation of land in Judaea. In any case, there are numerous traditions which attest to the fact that there was much private ownership of land in the generation after the War of Destruction. These traditions describe, for instance, the buying, selling and leasing of land.

The Bar-Kochba War, much more intense than the War of Destruction, conceivably offered another chance to widen the extent of crown lands. Eusebius even explicitly states that Rufinus confiscated the entire territory which participated in the war (*Hist. Eccl.* 4. 61). A Talmudic tradition from this time even tells of a large vineyard in Eretz-Israel owned by Hadrian (PT Taanit IV, 69a; Lamentations Rabbah 2:2 p. 104). Rabbinic sources from the period after the Bar-Kochba War, or immediately before, also mention the "*mezikim*" which Applebaum identified with the "*conductores*," officials who were in charge of crown lands. At this time after the war, the sources also begin to mention the law of "*sikarikon*" which, according to S. Safrai, pertained to private lands expropriated by the crown (S. Safrai 1983, pp. 57–70). Undoubtedly, there were lands which were confiscated after the Bar-Kochba War, probably of rebels or rich landowners, just as the lands and property of Archelaus were confiscated in 6 CE (*BJ* 2. 111; *Ant.* 17. 344, 18. 26).

Sources from this period also tell of many tenant farmers and of farmers who lost their property and left for other regions (see Introduction p. 3). Apart from this general information, though, it is impossible to determine the exact extent of crown lands at this time. Royal estates were undoubtedly confiscated by Bar-Kochba during the revolt, and a number of leases, probably of these lands, were found among the Bar-Kochba documents discovered in the Judaean Desert (DJD II, no. 24; Applebaum 1967).

There was hardly any distribution of lands to veterans in Eretz-Israel. We do know of a settlement of veterans established near Jerusalem after the War of Destruction (*BJ* 7. 216). Remains of a lone veteran were found at Azzun in Samaria (Bull 1966). A single veteran, or perhaps an entire colony apparently lived at Aphek in the Golan. Apart from this we have no other information (Mann 1983).

Other lands were occasionally given to local rich residents favored by the government such as Rabbi Judah the Prince who received lands in the Golan from the emperor (PT Sheviit VI, 36d). The phrase "vineyard *doron*" (Dan 1972) might also indicate a vineyard which had been given to a local rich resident. However, we have no additional information regarding these grants.

During the second and third centuries CE there was an area encompassing all of northern Judaea which was called the "King's Mountain" (Har Ha-Melech) (Klein 1939, pp. 239–48 *et al.*). If the name actually implies a mountain which belonged to the king (Applebaum 1967), this would serve as excellent proof of the wide extent of crown territory. However, caution should be exercised since even if the term originally did imply crown territory, it eventually took on its own independent meaning. Originally the phrase referred to an area that was quite small. Later on, when it took on a more general meaning, it also began to incorporate a much larger territory. By this time, though, the phrase had no connection with its original legal standing. Thus, for instance, Talmudic literature tells of private landowners from the Lod area who had lands in this region (PT Avodah Zarah I, 40a; II, 41d). During the second and third centuries we hear of a rich landowner called R. Eleazar b. Harsom who owned lands in this area (Lamentations Rabbah 2:2, p. 105). During the fifth century, there was a village there called Ganthah which was the property of the empress Eudocia and was donated by her to the church (see p. 325).

There is not much information from the Roman-Byzantine period. Byzantine sources mention a number of villages such as Ganthah mentioned above which belonged to the emperor (Johannes Rufus, *Plerophoriae* 20, p. 39). Another such village was Prophyrion which was owned by a resident of Caesarea and was confiscated by Justinian without any legal explanation (Procopius, *Anecdota* 30. 18–19). Such capricious confiscations served as a means of expanding crown territory, in spite of the opposition that such actions aroused. Caphar Turban was also apparently a crown village whose day-to-day affairs were under the supervision of an imperial manager (Zacharias Rhetor, *Historia Ecclesiastica* 262 and parallels). All of the crown territories were governed by an appointed supervising manager. Procopius mentions a Samaritan, native to Palestine (*Anecdota* 27. 31).

The lists of the administrative units of Palestine mention two regions referred to as a "*saltus*". The term implies a large imperial holding which was an independent administrative unit (Clausing 1925; Kehoe 1988). This particular term refers to two areas in southern Eretz-Israel which served as bases for the line of border forts (*limes*). These regions were called Saltus Geraiticus and Saltus Menois. Zoar, which according to Anastasius of Sinai had large imperial tracts which continued to be cultivated after the Arab conquest (*PG* 89:745A), should be added to the other areas mentioned above which were connected to the *limes*.

The tax inscription from Beer Sheva mentions tax payers from Zoar (Alt 1921, and for a different opinion, Berchem 1952, p. 33) as well as *limitanae* from Zoar. This would seem to imply that the entire settlement was not considered crown land. Zoar is also mentioned as one of the settlements of the *conductores* (Sifre Deuteronomy 357, p. 426 and parallels). It should be remembered, however, that even during the second century when *conductores* abounded, there were still private landowners. One of those was the woman Babata whose legal documents, or at least part of them, were discovered in caves in the Judaean Desert (Lewis 1989). A "king" who gives land to tenant farmers is also mentioned in a number of Rabbinic sources (Genesis Rabbah 49:2, p. 499 and parallels p. 328).

The villages of the king which are mentioned in the sources were not, as we have mentioned, regular estates. Ein Gedi and Porphyrion were not only villages but were also administrative centers (we have already mentioned Ein Gedi above). Porphyrion had a boule and a bishop, proof of the fact that it also had free independent citizens and perhaps even private landowners in addition to those who worked on the imperial estates (Honigmann 1939–45). We shall return later to this complicated legal structure.

As already mentioned above, the village of Ein Gedi belonged to the king, or in other words was the property of the Roman *fiscus* (Lewis 1989, p. 42, etc.). However, it was an independent village and at least some of its inhabitants were independent. There was an *agora* (market) in the village, and some private landowners. We learn this from the legal documents found in caves in the Judaean Desert which belonged to the woman Babata (Lewis 1989, p. 42).

I.3 Non-imperial estates

I.3.1 Private estates

We have already discussed this matter (Chapter 1.V).

I.3.2 Urban estates

There is very little information available on this matter and we have studied it in a previous chapter (Chapter l.II).

I.3.3 Church estates

The Church had a great deal of land, but only from the fourth century onwards (Dan 1984, p. 90 ff.); therefore we shall not deal with this matter.

I.3.4 Private lands

The rest of the Land of Israel was in private hands and we shall now examine this matter.

I.4 Agrarian development

Private estates, imperial lands and small farmsteads were found in Eretz-Israel at various times during the ancient world. The major problem is not establishing the existence of these individual types of farmsteads, but rather in determining the numerical relationship between the amount of land that was held by the government and the amount that was in private hands, and specifically also how much land was in the form of small farmsteads.

I.4.1

There is no data available regarding the amount of land in the province which was owned by the rich or which belonged to the government. Büchler and Safrai (I.2 above) who examined the situation during the Javneh period (70–132 CE) came to the conclusion that the majority of land was held by small landowners, in spite of the fact that there were also, of course, imperial lands and large estates. In any case, there seems to be a clear trend of the expansion of imperial lands and large estates at the expense of the small, traditional plot of the independent farmer. The Bar-Kochba revolt, for instance, offered an excellent opportunity for the confiscation and expropriation of lands and their transfer to the government. The government also had the right to confiscate the land of criminals, which also helped to increase the scope of imperial lands. Moreover, there are many sources which mention the expropriation of private lands by the emperor without any particular justification, such as in the case of the village Prophyrion (Procopius, *Anecdota* 38. 18–19). Despite all this, and despite the fact that we cannot determine the actual extent of imperial lands in the province, it would appear that they were not all that extensive. Thus, for example, a Novella of Justinian (no. 144) which deals with the Samaritan revolts and certain decrees related to lands concerns, for the most part, private estates and does not even mention imperial holdings. Many Amoraic *midrashim* relate parables in which the "king" gives out parcels of land, but this Talmudic king seems to have simply been a rich person and not necessarily related to the government (Ziegler 1903).

It is even more difficult to determine how much land was in the possession of rich landowners. Most Tannaitic sources, and for fairly clear reasons, deal with Jewish owners of small farmsteads. Some sources, however, do deal with the cultivation of crops in fields owned by rich landowners. Tenant farmers are mentioned in traditions from the Second Temple period and from the Javneh period, but the majority of traditions relating to them, and the intensity with which legal problems pertaining to their status is discussed, date from the second to fourth centuries CE. There are, of course, no statistics on the matter, but it would seem that during the Amoraic period the number of estates increased, although there are still a goodly number of traditions which mention the small farmer.

Dozens of traditions from the end of the Tannaitic period and the Amoraic period mention the "king" in relation to land and, as we have seen above, this king is none other than the rich landowner (see, for instance, Genesis Rabbah 8:3 p. 59; 9:9 p. 72, 41(42):3 p. 404; 61:6 p. 664 *et al.*). Sperber, who dealt with this matter to some extent, has pointed out an increase in the phenomenon of patronage at this time and even if we do not accept all of his conclusions, it seems that there was a general trend towards an increase in the amount of land held by the rich (Sperber 1978, pp. 119–35; 177–86; Gulak 1929). The archeological remains of the time also corroborate the existence of this trend, since the majority of estates which have been discovered date to the end of the Roman period and especially to the Byzantine period.

The majority of Byzantine sources relate to rich landowners, even though there are a few which imply that there still were a number of small, private holdings.

Our book, however, deals with the Roman period and it seems that during this time, the majority of land was privately owned. In any case, Talmudic literature, which serves as an important source for our discussion, mentions estates only a limited amount of times and for the most part describes a reality of the small landowner. We shall return to discuss this matter below.

At the end of the fourth century CE, the Lex Colonatus was instituted in Palestine (Goffart 1974, pp. 84–6). The decree which promulgated this law in the Empire in general dates to 332 CE (*Cod. Just.* 5. 17.1). This law has been discussed to a great extent in scholarly literature and its basic intent was to tie tenant farmers to the land which they worked and to prohibit movement from one plot of land to another. The inclusion of Palestine within the framework of this law at the end of the fourth century CE would seem to indicate that by this time the phenomenon of tenant farmers was quite prominent. On the other hand, the fact that it took a number of decades from the origin of the law until it was instituted regarding the Land of Israel can be explained by the large amount of land that remained in private hands until the end of the fourth century. In any case, we have already stated that even during the Byzantine period there were still a number of private small landowners, even if their number had declined.

I.4.3

As we have just stated, there was a general trend from the small independent farm to large estates, whether private or imperial. The trend, however, was not in one direction. Imperial lands were occasionally given as gifts to the rich or to other supporters of the government. Roman veterans often enjoyed the benefits of such gifts. In the Land of Israel there were not many veterans, but even so Josephus tells of one such settlement established near Jerusalem in 70 CE after the War of the Destruction for those recently released from service in the Legio X Fretensis (*BJ* 7. 216). There was another settlement in Egypt for veterans of this legion, and therefore it appears that not all veterans of this legion received land in Judaea. The former settlement, the one near Jerusalem, was undoubtedly destroyed during the Bar-Kochba War, although it is impossible to know exactly what happened to the lands of the veterans. There were individual veterans who apparently settled in Azzun in Samaria (Bull 1966) and in Aphek in the Golan (see p. 325), and there were undoubtedly other individual estates which were given to veterans, even if there is no specific information available on them.

As mentioned above, the rich also received land grants from imperial lands. Thus, for instance, Josephus received lands in the plain (*Vita* 76 (422)) and Rabbi Judah the Prince received two grants in the Golan (PT Sheviit VI, 36d). It is even possible that the Talmud has preserved the terminology related to such grants and the "vineyard *doron* (= gift)" had been one such gift (PT Peah VII, 20a; Dan 1972). Many sources also mention the "king" who gave "gifts" to his servant or supporter.

Private estates were likely to be dissolved when they were transferred to the imperial treasury such as in the case of the estates of Salome, the sister of Herod, which were bequeathed to Livia (*Ant.* 18. 31) or through cases of expropriation or confiscation, a phenomenon which we have already discussed above. Talmudic sources also mention lands from estates being transferred to small farmers or vice versa. Thus, for instance, they talk of a "town of the many" which became a "town of one" or in other words a private *villa*, or the other way around (M Eruvin 5:6). These phenomena were quite prevalent in all the provinces of the Roman Empire, but as we shall see, there were a number of unique conditions in Judaea.

In Judaea the conflict between the small farmer and the rich landowner was not just social and economic, but also ethnic; it was part of the general struggle between Jews and non-Jews. Of course, not all Jews were small farmers or tenant farmers and there were certainly rich landowners who were Jewish. For the most part, though, the matter was as we stated it in general terms. The Jewish community and the rabbis began to develop a land ideology which was devoted to the concept of maintaining as much of the Land of Israel as possible in Jewish hands as well as redeeming lands held by pagans. Much has been written about this peaceful yet heroic economic struggle (Sperber 1978, pp. 160–76). It is not clear how successful the Jews were during the course of the struggle, and in the final result they did lose the battle. The struggle, however, did buy time for the Jews and did result in a degree of fluidity of lands which allowed Jewish farmers to redeem at least part of their lands and ancient patrimony.

I.5 The economic significance of estates

I.5.1

The private or government estate also had a great deal of social and political importance. The system contained an inherent social injustice since the profits of the "producers" were capriciously transferred in such a manner as to be for the benefit of a consumer who had nothing to do with the actual labor in the fields. In terms of the economy of the ancient world this would mean that the sector which produced was limited and poor, while another sector derived the profits and income from the former group's labor. This situation was a major cause of social tension. Many a revolt or disturbance in the history of nations in the ancient world was caused by these agrarian factors. In this sense, therefore, Palestine was not an exception to the rule, even though there are scholars who argue regarding the actual impact of this particular factor on the history of settlement, on disturbances and on other events and political developments.

Our present study does not deal with moral, social and political factors. We shall focus our discussion, therefore, on an attempt to evaluate the economic significance of agrarian structure. Needless to say, such an evaluation is dependent to a great extent on quantitative analysis, or in other words on determining how much land was held by this or that estate owner. Unfortunately, it has not been possible to answer this question; thus our discussion on the economics of the matter is somewhat deficient.

I.5.2

The influence of the estate system on agricultural or industrial production is not clear. On the one hand, it would seem that large tracts of land under the control of a single owner could produce large yields. In such great tracts of the land, the owner could often undertake large-scale measures and prepare big tracts of land in such a manner as would often not have been worthwhile for the small farmer. On the other hand, though, the remains of ancient farms have shown us that the farmers of yore were capable of undertaking fairly large-scale drainage projects and thus of preparing relatively wide tracts of land for their use. This is clear from the remains of terrace agriculture in the hills. Often the cultivation was over extensive areas and all of this would have required a great deal of planning and organization. In many areas, or to be more exact, in all the hilly areas of the Land of Israel, there was terrace farming and this would indicate that the private and independent farmer was also capable of such type of organization and labor. As we have already seen, the rural towns had a communal network which could have taken care of such organization; therefore the estate owner, in this matter at least, would not have had much of an advantage over the small farmer.

The rich landowner or imperial estates did have better and cheaper sources of financing than the small farmer. However, in the ancient world, the major means of production was the work force or labor and once again, therefore, the advantage enjoyed by estate owners in such matters was not all that great. Cultivation on a large-scale manner was most likely cheaper. This can be discerned in the Talmudic discussion regarding neighbors (of adjoining fields). The essence of this law is that if a field is put up for sale, then a neighbor owning an adjoining field is to be given the first opportunity to buy the field since its value is obviously much greater for him. This, in an indirect manner at least, seems to recognize the economic importance of large tracts. However, it is still necessary to point out that in the ancient world and in the final analysis, the size of the plot is really not of supreme importance. Unlike the situation in modern agriculture in which the cost of operating the machinery is directly related to the size of the plot, in the ancient world, one who plows with the aid of a cow, for instance, is limited to the size of the plot which the beast can plow. According to the Talmud, this area is approximately nine *kabs* or less than 1.5 dunams (BT Bava Bathra 12a). Beyond this area, size played a limited role and it is likely that in a plot 5–6 times greater in extent (about 10 dunams), size played a relatively minor part in the agricultural framework.

In the Late Roman and especially in the Byzantine period, the large estate became much more important. The owners of large estates gave the small farmer legal, economic and especially social protection from the oppressive measures of corrupt government officials. The measures of such government officials often brought the small farmer to seek the protection and patronage of the local rich estate owner. Such oppressive measures were also of economic importance since they represented an inefficient use of economic resources, at least from a national point of view.

It is, of course, likely that the owner of land was more efficient, in terms of agricultural labor, than those leasing the land or tenant farmers. The private landowner was more sensitive to the correct use of the terrain as well as to its preservation and ecology than a foreman or an absentee landlord. Proof of this is found in the system of laws meant to clearly formulate the rights of landowners and to grant them the legal means to protect the value of their holding (see, for example, M Bava Mezia, ch. 9 and T Bava Mezia, ch. 9, and the many parallel traditions). However, no legal system can serve to replace the goodwill and diligence of the owner of the small agricultural farm who fears for the source of his income. Part of this problem was solved by the development of the permanent tenant-farmer system since the tenant farmer had some type of long-term interest in protecting the value of the land, the land he hoped to cultivate for many more years. It did not completely resolve the problem, though, and was also not a perfect defense against the whims of the absentee landlord, often unfamiliar with the nature of the land and perhaps not always interested in fulfilling the maximum potential of the land.

I.5.3

The imperial estate served as an indirect means of raising funds from the residents of the province as well as of exporting capital. The profits were not returned to the inhabitants of the province, but rather were funneled to an imperial center, whether in Rome or later in Constantinople. It is possible to estimate the economic significance of this phenomenon. Hopkins has estimated that about 10 per cent of agricultural income arrived at court in the form of taxes. The farmer, however, was paying a rate of about 30 per cent of his income. The difference found its way into the pockets of tax collectors and government officials (Hopkins 1980). The average annual rent of the tenant farmer in the Land of Israel was about 50 per cent (Gulak 1929, pp. 110–14). Such being the case, there was a 20 per cent differential between agricultural income and the regular rate of taxes levied on the independent farmer and the rate paid by the tenant farmer which was taken out of the province and transferred to the imperial treasury. This differential can be described as damage to the economy of the province, providing that the costs involved in administering the imperial estate are similar to those costs involved in collecting the taxes. (The costs of administration are those sums which the manager or *epitropos* or the tax collector deducted for themselves and thus provided for their support while in the Land of Israel. Some of these sums, however, were transferred to other provinces in which the officials in question maintained their permanent residences.

The rent paid to the owners of the land, in spite of the fact that it was a heavy burden for the tenant farmers, did not directly harm the rate of production or, within a larger framework, the gross national product. This was the case since the payments were transferred to persons who also lived in the same province. Obviously, therefore, the matter was different when the owner of the land, or his agents, lived in a different province. It is impossible to determine how many of the rich landowners in Judaea actually lived in that province. It is likely that some of them did live on a regular basis in other provinces (and see Sifre Deuteronomy 37, p. 54 which seems to hint at such a possibility). It is also possible that some of the local rich land-owners had income from lands abroad. In any case, it would seem to be the general rule that the income from agricultural estates was spent in the province itself and not in any other one.

I.5.4

The estate system served as the economic foundation for the social and economic structure of the Roman Empire (and for that matter also for most of the Hellenistic kingdoms). The rich landowners who lived in the cities together with their slaves enjoyed rather respectable incomes from the rural sphere. They were also the prime consumers of all that Roman urban life had to offer such as services and merchandise, and therefore were actually the ones who funded these frameworks. It is impossible to describe the *polis* without including these rich landowners and it would have been impossible to establish an urban Roman trade network without these people as con-sumers and without all those whose task it was, at least at the beginning of the process, to serve this class of rich landowners residing in the cities. The success of the cities was dependent on the estates and this was true for all aspects of Hellenistic-Roman life.

Hopkins (1980) mentions an additional economic factor. The rent, as is well known, was either paid in kind or in cash. Payment in cash would seem to indicate that the grower is producing a surplus which he sells at the market and thus secures the cash to pay the landowner in the city. If indeed the rent is paid in cash, this indicates that there was a market in the village and that not only were there producers of agricultural products in the village, but also consumers not involved in agriculture (such as artisans and those providing various services). These consumers apparently also had incomes which provided them with ready cash. The farmer who received this cash transferred it to the various official institutions in Palestine.

Rabbinic sources, however, usually describe the sharecropper or tenant farmer and these usually paid the landowner in kind. The "hired" renter, mentioned only a few times in rabbinic literature, is the one who pays his rent in cash (see, for example, T Demai 6:2). This does not necessarily indicate that the "hired" renter was a rather rare phenomenon, since the Tosefta (ibid.) does state that the legal status of this renter is the same as that of the tenant farmer and the like and, therefore, there was no real need for independent traditions and discussions pertaining to the "renter." In any case, the Bar-Kochba letters speak for the most part of leases of tenant fees paid in kind (see, for example, DJD II, no. 24, A-F etc. and Yadin 1971, pp. 175 ff.).

In addition to the model suggested by Hopkins, the transfer of mer-chandise paid in kind to the landowner would require some sort of transport network and this might not have been cheaper than a system based on private trade. In any case, such a large number of estate owners would imply the existence of a wealthy class and all those serving it who were obviously not involved in agriculture, and this clearly requires agricultural surplus and everything implied by the existence of this surplus. Thus, the system itself may contain elements of social injustice and may result in political tension, but from an economic point of view, it was likely to result in the economic success of the city at the expense of the village or rural sphere.

I.6 The operation of the estate

The system used to operate agricultural estates had a great deal of social and economic significance; it is therefore necessary to briefly discuss what is known about the operation of these estates. It is likely that there was not much difference in these matters between imperial estates and those which were privately owned.

I.6.1 The estate which was dependent on slaves or laborers

In this system of operation the foreman or supervisor lived in the estate house itself and the slaves or workers lived in houses nearby. The work revolved around some form of central planning. The workers or slaves were supported from the income of the estate and the profits were sent, according to the instructions of the foreman, to the landowner. This was the accepted form of estate operation in the Roman Empire and archeological excavations of villas in the Roman Empire have uncovered many of the shoddy houses of the workers, as well as elements of the central estate house (Percival 1976). Such structures have been found, for instance, at H. Muraq (Damati 1982 and see above, Figure 23), Um Rihan (Dar *et al.* 1986, pp. 105–12), Tirat Yehuda (Yeivin and Edelstein 1970) and at many other sites. It is generally rather difficult to differentiate between slaves and free workers. A number of small kitchens were found in the rooms of the estate near Aderet and, in our view, these would seem to indicate that they were inhabited by families of free laborers who were allowed to make use of these kitchens. An olive press installation found in the building, however, would seem to indicate that tasks pertaining to agricultural products were undertaken in a centralized manner characteristic of a regular estate (*Hadashot Archiologiot* 78/79 (1981), pp. 81–2).

There are traditions pertaining to estates operated by slaves, such as that source which mentions the "town" (*'yr*) which was bought together with all its pagan slaves (PT Yebamot VIII, 8d). Moreover, the laws pertaining to the selling of an estate mention the "*santer*" and the "*eukonomos*" who were important functionaries in the operation of the villa *vis-à-vis* its relationship to the town and those elements of the town sold together with it (M Bava Bathra 4:7; T Bava Bathra 3:5). There is an interesting story in midrashic literature regarding a matron who sought to wed slaves from one estate with slaves from another one (Numbers Rabbah 22:11) and there are many other similar traditions.

There are also many traditions which mention the hiring of free workers on an estate. These are usually in the form of a king who hires workers (Midrash Psalms 26:3, p. 217; 37:3, p. 253 *et al.*)

I.6.2 An estate given to tenant farmers

Tenant farming was a rather common phenomenon in the Land of Israel during the Roman period and there are many laws, tales, *aggadot* and the like which deal with tenant farming. There has not yet been a serious discussion of this matter in Talmudic literature; therefore collecting the sources on the matter is quite important. Some of the legal material has been discussed by Gulak (1929, pp. 109–37), but this is not within the present scope of our study. The sharecropper or the tenant farmer were independent and a series of laws and customs ("the custom of the country") defined the relationship between them and the owner of the land. The various laws protected the tenant from the whims of the landowner and provided him with certain rights and protection, such as the inability to remove him from the land during certain seasons. They also offered protection to the landowner so that no harm would come to his holding.

A village of tenant farmers would seem to a visitor to be like any other independent village, except that the residents paid a good part of their income from the land to the landowner instead of paying taxes. The various labors after the harvest were governed by established rules and customs. This was the situation in other provinces and there was no real innovation in Palestine *vis-à-vis* the social and economic framework in these matters. In the manner described above, therefore, it is possible to understand the existence of an estate at Ein Gedi in which those who worked the land were free farmers, at least in terms of their own persons (Chapter 1.V above). The situation was similar in the village of Porphyrion which was actually the private property of a rich landowner which later became an imperial estate. In many respects, however, this village was like any other, with a boule and other local institutions (Honigmann 1939–45).

I.6.3 Permanent tenancy

A permanent tenant was like any other, except that he had the right to pass on his holding to his sons upon his death; to all intents and purposes, his behavior was that of the owner of the land. The connection of the actual landowner to the land was only financial in terms of receiving rent (Gulak 1939, pp. 124–9). The connections between this permanent tenancy and the Byzantine *emphyteusis* needs more discussion (Clausing 1925, pp. 307–9).

Tenant farming was apparently more popular in Jewish society than any direct system of operation such as the running of the estate based on hired labor or slave labor. This is clear from the great number of *halachot* which deal with tenant farmers and sharecroppers and the small amount of legal discussion pertaining to the operation of an estate based on hired or slave labor. It should be pointed out, though, that this may have been the case only in certain parts of the Land of Israel, namely the Jewish areas, and in the pagan or non-Jewish ones the estate system was more prevalent. There are, however, no sources pertaining to such a distinction. It is important to remember, however, that the majority of the traditions on such matters are internal Jewish traditions and there would have been no reason for the *halachah* to deal with cases in which the landowner or those who worked the land were not Jewish, and thus were not bound by the *halachah*. As we have already mentioned, most of the lands in Palestine were probably in non-Jewish hands; therefore the *halachah* does not provide a true reflection of this phenomenon which, as we just pointed out, it preferred to ignore.

In aggadic literature and in midrashic parables there is more of a tendency to make reference to those elements of society which were not bound by *halachah*. In this type of literature, therefore, there is more of a chance of finding traditions relating to Jewish tenant farmers and the like and non-Jewish landowners. This literature also has many traditions regarding tenant farmers. Thus, for example, a parable tells of a "king" (rich landowner) "who had a field and wanted to give it to tenant farmers" (Exodus Rabbah 27:8). Many of the "king" parables (Ziegler 1903) mention tenant farmers, but they also deal with parcels of land given out to laborers or slaves. There is no purpose in counting the traditions, but the general impression one gets is that there are more tenant farmer traditions in this type of literature. All of this would seem to imply that at least until the fourth century, this was the most popular system of operation.

It is necessary to determine the means of organization of agricultural labors in an estate of permanent tenant farmers or sharecroppers. There are sources which seem to hint at the fact that in this type of estate in particular, the labors attendant on the produce after harvest were undertaken in common. The Palestinian Talmud deals with the relationship between tenants and landowners and mentions what was apparently a common phenomenon of a joint effort of tenants and landowners regarding post-harvest labors. From the discussion there, it also seems to be quite clear that the tenants were "permanent" ones. (This is based on a combination of commentaries to M Halah 4:7. See also T Halah 2:5 and PT Halah IV, 60a.) As we have also seen above, the estate of R. Judah the Prince in Mahalal (modern Nahalal) was operated by permanent tenant farmers, and a large number of wine presses, indicating communal labors, were found there (Raban 1982, pp. 68–9 and Figure 27).

It is likely that there were no iron-clad rules in the operation of such estates and possibly many had some degree of joint labor and efforts. There were probably also estates in which the produce was divided before any additional labors were undertaken. A number of traditions deal with the relationship between the regular tenant and the landowner. Thus, for instance, it was accepted practice that the necessary labors to produce wine from the grape crop would be undertaken by the tenant. Olives, however, were divided among all those concerned such as tenants and landowners and each produced the oil himself (T Bava Mezia 9:19). There were also various rules as to the payment of taxes and how the burden should be divided between landowners and tenants. The Tosefta, however, stresses that "the custom of the region should not be changed" (T Bava Mezia 9:14). This, though, would seem to indicate that there were different types of customs (compare for example, Kehoe 1988, pp. 29ff, De Neeve 1984, etc.).

It is possible, then, to sum up and state that there were apparently many estates in the Galilee, and the lack of specific information is explained by the common system of organization in which the landowner had very little to do with the everyday life of the farmers.

The entire matter, though, still requires much more study and thought. Our discussion should be considered as a prolegomenon to that more detailed discussion.

I.6.4 Private village

This type of estate operated by tenants or permanent lessees required the special structure of a private village. Such a village had to include residences for the farmers and a central building for the overseer or for the landlord to stay on his visits. We have no direct textual evidence of such a building. However, a spacious structure of this type is probable in light of the social-organizational structure of the tenant-operated estates. As we have seen, both the Mishna Challa and the Jerusalem Talmud to this Mishna refer to the landlord gathering the harvest together with his tenants. Thus the landlord, or his representative, lived in the same village as the tenants.

There is an example of this type of village in Palestine from the Byzantine period. Prophyrion, on Mount Carmel, was a large rural settlement which had a council, and a Christian bishopric (episcopacy). Yet at the same time, it was a private village belonging to a wealthy resident of Caesarea which the emperor Justinian expropriated for himself as a royal estate (Procopius *Anecdota* 30. 13; Honigmann 1939–45). It seems that settlements of this type were more common in the Byzantine period, when estates in general were more accepted and widespread. Perhaps Ein Gedi in the early second century also bore similar legal status. Ein Gedi is described in the papyri from the early second century as a 'village of a lord' (Lewis 1989, no. 11. 16), but in this village there were independent people who were property owners and land owners (ibid.). Later a synagogue was built there from the donations of members of the community (Naveh 1978, pp. 105–11).

In a number of sites in Israel a large and ornate residential building has been found, with a number of modest dwellings around it. It is likely that this type of village was a private village. The central structure was a villa and the simple buildings housed the farmers. This distinction has already been suggested by Hingley (1989, pp. 100 ff.), on the basis of findings from Roman Britain. A settlement of this kind was excavated by Safrai and Dar at Hurbat Bira (Z. Safrai and Dar, in press).

In one of the residential buildings (17–29) two kitchens were found; this indicates that several independent families lived in the building. The authors believe that a total of about eight or nine households lived in the settlement and they have proposed a reconstruction of the division of land in the settlement.

Hurbat Najar may have been another settlement of this type. The settlement was surveyed and charted by Dar (1986, pp. 47–51, Figure 10 in this title). At the summit of the hill on which the settlement lay is a large, relatively ornate building (building A), and around it smaller, more modest buildings. The settlement is from the "Roman–Byzantine" period, but without excavating it is difficult to verify additional details on its character and date.

The private village type of settlement explains another kind of finding that is very widespread in the southern section of Mt Hebron. In this area a number of huge wine presses were found, each with a capacity to process the harvest of hundreds of dunam of vineyards. They are closely associated with townlets that seem to have been independent, such as Ashtamoa, Susiya and similar settlements. (These wine presses are well known to hikers, and were surveyed by the author, among others. However, they have not been widely publicized and no systematic research has been devoted to them.) Perhaps these wine presses provide significant evidence of common processing of produce by a landlord and his tenants. An alternative explanation is that all the local residents processed their harvest together at such facilities. However, we have no other textual evidence of common processing of produce. Evidently, the vineyards in the area belonged to the owner of a private estate, and his tenants lived in the rural townlets. Thus, for instance, there was a large townlet in Susiya, covering an area of about 60 dunams (Negev 1985), and there was an organized community there with educational institutions (Naveh 1978, no. 77–8) as well as a court (Naveh 1978, no. 75). A security-related structure, a sort of wall surrounding part of the settlement, has also been excavated here (Negev 1985).

On the basis of all this evidence, it seems that in the province there was a special type of private rural settlement which belonged to the land owner, where the residents were independent but their property was mortgaged. At this stage it is difficult to determine how common this type of settlement was in the Roman and Byzantine periods.

II. THE INFLUENCE OF THE ROMAN ARMY IN JUDAEA

II.1 The Roman army in Judaea

The situation of the Roman army in Judaea underwent many far-reaching changes which are beyond the scope of our discussion. For the purpose of our study we can briefly point out four stages.

(1) Until 66 CE the Roman army in Judaea was rather small: 3–6 auxiliary units, some of which were composed of local militia from Sebaste and Caesarea (Mor 1986).

(2) During the period from 70–120 CE (or perhaps a little later), the Tenth Legion was stationed in Judaea, together with a number of auxiliary units. Generally, 6–12 auxiliary units were attached to a legion, providing, in terms of manpower, about as many soldiers as in a legion. We do not have a complete list of all the forces in Judaea. On the other hand, it is also conceivable that there were fewer forces than usual in Judaea. It is possible to estimate the number of forces at this time at approximately 10,000 soldiers.

(3) From 120 CE to the beginning of the fourth century CE there were two legions in Palestine: Legio X Fretensis and Legio VI Ferrata. Auxiliary units composed of about 25,000 soldiers were attached to these two legions. The exact date of the arrival of VI Ferrata in Palestine and whether another legion preceded it are not relevant for our discussion (Lifshitz 1960; Kennedy 1980; Isaac and Roll 1979; B. Isaac 1982). Legio X Fretensis was based in Judaea proper and had military camps in Jerusalem and Caesarea. Legio VI Ferrata was based in the Galilee and its headquarters was in Legio (= Kefar 'Otnay). Numerous additional forces were sent to Palestine during the Bar-Kochba revolt, but they were in Palestine for only a short period.

(4) During the fourth century Legio VI Ferrata was transferred out of Palestine and Legio X Fretensis was transferred to the south of Palestine, essentially along the *limes*, and was headquartered in Aila (Gichon 1974; Avi-Yonah 1963); this is also beyond of the purview of our discussion (Figure 70). During this time there were a relatively small amount of forces in Palestine, probably numbering no more than 7,000–8,000 soldiers. The transfer of numerous forces to the *limes* region was of great economic significance. It was necessary, for instance, to extend supply lines to this desert region from the central regions of the province. The unique problems of this matter, however, fall within the purview of the Byzantine period and, therefore, not within the scope of our discussion of the Roman period.

To sum up then, we have seen evidence as to three camps appropriate for a cohort. The rest of the army was probably stationed in rural outposts. This situation would explain the intense confrontation between the Roman army and Galilean Jewry, since indeed there are hundreds of traditions which

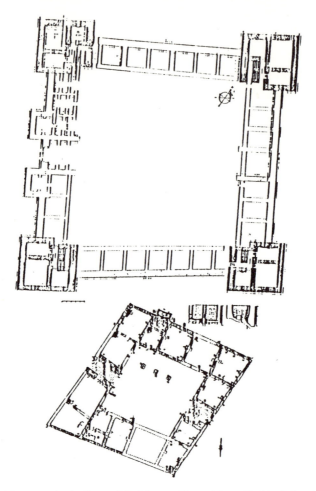

Figure 70 Fortresses in the *limes* of the Negev. Above, Kazer Baskir; below Beer Scheva.

attest to the fact that as far as the Jews of Galilee were concerned, the presence of the Roman army was a common and far from unusual phenomenon. Thus, for Galilean Jewry during this time, an encounter with the Roman "government" was probably really an encounter with a local military unit or with troops passing through.

II.2 The influence of the Roman army during peacetime

II.2.1

The general opinion of scholarly research regarding the Roman Empire was that every province was responsible for supporting and funding the forces located there both in peacetime and during periods of war. This implies that the larger the forces in a particular province, the greater the burden on the residents of that province. This view was originally challenged by Gren (Gren 1941) and later by a number of other scholars (A. H. M. Jones 1974, p. 274; Blagg and King 1985; Birley 1981, pp. 39–53; Burnham and Johnson 1979; MacMullen 1968; Davies 1974; Rivet 1969). Even if theoretically, in terms of political and economic policy, the residents of the province were responsible for supporting the army, in practice the forces were actually supported by the central government or treasury. Thus, there was a dual cash flow in the Roman Empire. On the one hand monies were sent from all provinces to the central government in Italy. On the other, the rich provinces (Gaul, Egypt, Syria, etc.) sent funds to the border provinces to support the large forces that were concentrated there.

The German provinces and Britain are generally portrayed in scholarly literature as those poor provinces, relatively speaking, in which large forces were concentrated. Thus, they enjoyed, on account of the large Roman forces encamped there, a great degree of funding. Much has been written to examine the influence of this flow of capital on the economies of these provinces, and attempts have also been made to analyze the component parts of this process and its economic results.

In light of all this it is necessary to examine the influence of the Roman army in Judaea on the economic framework of this small province. The above information proves that during the Roman period (approximately 120–300 CE), Judaea contained the greatest amount of Roman forces of any province relative to its size (approximately 18,000 square km, and half of this army was stationed in Galilee which is only 25 per cent of Judaea.

The examination of the influence of the Roman army on the residents of Judaea would therefore seem to be of great importance. Amazingly enough, there is hardly any data or direct information on this matter and it is necessary to make do with general speculation and with similar conditions in other provinces.

II.2.2

The commanders of the Roman army had recourse to what was available in the specific province in order to support the army as well as to external funds sent to the province, as we have already pointed out. The tax rate was not influenced by the presence of military forces in a province, since the tax base in the various provinces was more or less similar. It is known that the taxes were particularly high in Judaea (Appian, *Syr.* 50) and that a special tax was levied on the Jews after 70 CE. However, if this small province really had to support the military forces there, it would have been an unbearable and indeed unique burden and there is no testimony to this fact. Based on the above stated and somewhat inexact principle that the tax base levied on the provinces was identical, it is possible to estimate the inflow of capital for the support of the army in Judaea.

In an important study, Hopkins suggested a method of arriving at cost quantification of the Roman army (Hopkins 1980). In his opinion, the government levied a tax of 10 per cent of the gross national product (GNP) of the Empire. Moreover, about half of the expenses of the Roman army were spent on the support of the army (M. Crawford 1970). Hopkins does not reckon into his account unique or unusual income, such as from estates, since it is impossible to evaluate it. Hopkins does, however, take into consideration the fact that the residents of the Empire undoubtedly had to support the corrupt structure of tax collection. From an economic point of view there is really little difference whether the monies went straight to the Roman *fiscus* or to the corrupt freedmen collecting the levies.

Hopkins' calculations are essentially dependent on the evaluation of the cost of the army based on the rate of salary paid to its soldiers. In our view, Hopkins' cost estimations are too low. As is well known, the Roman soldier had to pay for his food, as well as for that of his horses, out of his salary. There is no certainty, however, that a realistic price was charged. On the contrary; there seems to be an indication of the fact that those prices were not realistic, but this matter is beyond the scope of our discussion.

If the cost estimates suggested by Hopkins must be raised, it is clear that the rate of taxes collected was different. Moreover, it is difficult to accept the figure of 10 per cent cited above regarding the GNP which would appear to be too low. The accepted rate of payments in estates was 33.3 per cent in grain fields and up to 50 per cent in orchards and the like (Johnson *et al.* 1961, pp. 173–5). Even in Judaea payments of up to 50 per cent of the produce were customary (Chapter 4.I.6.3) and would seem to indicate that the average family could support itself, albeit with difficulty, with half the produce it was able to cultivate. If the rate of taxation was only 10 per cent, the farmer would have been in a much better position since he would have had approximately 40 per cent surplus beyond his subsistence needs, which could have been marketed at a profit. It is possible that the tenant farmer had larger tracts of land at his disposal than the average independent farmer, but even so, the question mentioned above still pertains. During the days of John Hyrcanus II, the Roman Empire took a tax rate of 12.5 per cent from wheat fields in Judaea. Another 10 per cent was the customary rate handed over to the semi-autonomous rulers there and to the Temple (*Ant.* 14. 203). Was it possible that later on, when autonomous rule was abolished, the tax rate was actually lowered?

It is impossible to determine the tax rate exactly, whether in Judaea or in the Roman Empire in general, although as mentioned above, Hopkins' estimations would appear to be low. We shall, however, use his low estimates in the course of our discussions, bearing in mind that when the tax burden becomes greater, the support of the army becomes more expensive for the inhabitants, and this in turn leads to a greater influx of capital into the province for the support of the army. Judaea was less than 1 per cent of the entire Roman Empire. Thus it would seem likely that the tax revenues from that province did not exceed this 1 per cent. For the sake of caution, however, we shall assume that the tax revenues from Judaea reached 1.5 per cent of the sum collected in the Empire. Approximately 8 per cent of the Roman forces of the Empire were encamped in Judaea (25,000 soldiers), and thus the Empire would have to allot 4 per cent of its income for the support of these forces (based on the supposition that the support of the army constituted 50 per cent of Roman expenses). Thus, for every 1.5 dinars which reached the Roman treasury from Judaea, it was necessary to allocate an additional 2.5 dinars for the support of the army in Judaea, and more to support the army in Galilee. If taxes constituted 10 per cent of the GNP of every province in the Roman Empire, it would be necessary for the Roman government to allocate to Palestine 16.6 per cent of its GNP for military support in this province. In our view, the tax burden was greater, and the support of the army was also more expensive. The flow of capital to the provinces, therefore, would have had to be even higher. Not all this money reached the residents of the provinces in the final result, since some of it constituted wages that were saved until the soldier left the province. All these numbers are of course estimates and should be treated as such. However, if these are inflated, it is clear that the contribution of the Roman army to the province, especially to Galilee, was of great importance.

It is not difficult to see that this inflow of capital was rather significant for the economy of a province. After the period of the Bar-Kochba War the land was devastated and the income from taxes was obviously low. During this time, and at least until 139 CE (Applebaum 1976), there were additional legions in Palestine, in addition to those mentioned above, and thus the inflow of capital to support them would have had to be rather high. Thus the army unwittingly helped somewhat to restore the economy of the province. During this time there is evidence of the transfer of commodities from Egypt (P. Ryland II. 189, p. 237). During the period of the anarchy when government or imperial support was delayed, the legions obviously took care of themselves at the expense of the local residents. This economic disaster was part of the economic catastrophe of that time.

It is likely that the army based in Judaea had large sums of money at its disposal in order to buy food supplies, clothing and weapons on a regular basis. Cassius Dio, for instance, gives a specific instance of Roman forces buying weapons from local producers in Judaea (Cassius Dio, 69. 12. 2; MacMullen 1968, pp. 23–40, no. 2; Davies 1969; Speidel 1984, pp. 329–31). This was probably the case regarding other supplies necessary for the army. There has been much scholarly discussion as to the supplying of Roman forces (Middleton 1979; Wild 1979; Davies 1969; Lesquier 1918). There is no direct information on this matter, however, pertaining to Judaea. In any case, the situation in Judaea was probably no different from that in the other provinces, except that the army was relatively large in Judaea, and thus the buying power of the army in this province was relatively larger than in other provinces.

This would also seem to be the case regarding the supplying of linen. The army probably was supplied via the imperial weaveries in Scythopolis (Chapter 1.II.1). Some, however, was undoubtedly bought, on the open market, as was the case in other countries that produced flax, as for example in Egypt (Wipszycka 1966; Wild 1979). The food supplies of the Roman army were naturally dependent upon the customs storehouses and it is clear that taxes in kind or commodities found their way essentially to the Roman army. These were usually earmarked for the forces garrisoned on a regular basis in the province. Thus, it would seem likely that a good deal of the tax debt in Judaea would have been paid in kind. The relationship between the amount of taxes paid in kind and that paid in cash is difficult to determine and the situation in the provinces, perhaps apart from Egypt, is not really clear. In the talmudic literature there are many *halachot* about payment of taxes in cash but also in kind.

It appears that every province had its own policy in keeping with the particular situation there. In Judaea, it is likely, as we just suggested in light of special circumstances there, that the Romans would have been more interested in being paid in kind so that what was collected could be transferred directly to the units serving there as part of their necessary food supplies. This, however, does not seem to have been the case. A number of references in Talmudic literature seem to indicate that commodities which reached these storehouses were sold to the general public. Two independent traditions specifically mention merchants (from Galilee) buying commodities (wheat?) from the storehouse in Jamnia (Javneh) which is also specifically referred to as belonging to the government (T. Demai 1:12–13). One of these traditions dates to the Usha period (140–80 CE). The second tells of two sages, Rabbi Judah the Prince and R. Jose b. Judah (180–225 CE) who go to buy wheat at the storehouse of Jamnia (Javneh – Genesis Rabbah 76:8 p. 960). There are also a number of *halachot* which deal specifically with produce bought from such storehouses, and the buying of produce there would seem to have been a common phenomenon. It would appear, therefore, that even in a small province, the government preferred to sell commodities collected as taxes and transfer the money to the military units. Perhaps the structure of the local economic framework dictated this situation. Those units stationed in the plains in areas like Jamnia had a plethora of grain at their disposal. However, those units stationed in the Galilee suffered from a dearth of grain supplies, while the surplus of tax revenues in kind from olive oil or flax could not make up for the lack of grain. All of this was, of course, the result of the trend to cultivate less grain in the Galilee in order to free lands for the cultivation of other crops there (see Chapter 2.I.1; I.7 below).

Moreover, the soldiers of the Roman army stationed in the provinces usually enjoyed a diet different from that of the local residents, which was usually much richer in meat (Davies 1971; 1974; King 1984). There was not much production of meat in Palestine and the opportunities for securing pig meat, a staple of Roman forces, were also not very great in Palestine (see Chapter 2.1.8.3). This imbalance between the agricultural complex and the commodities paid as taxes on one hand, and the needs of the Roman army on the other hand, probably resulted in the sale of local tax commodity surplus in order to purchase other supplies. An additional testimony as to what was happening in Palestine, and particularly in the region of the *limes*, is found in a Roman law from the end of the fourth century CE (*C. Th.* 7. 4.30). However, as we have mentioned already, this period is beyond the scope of our discussion. We shall return below to discuss the systems used to collect taxes and the economic implications of this matter.

Based on our analysis above, it would seem that the Roman army had two extremely positive influences on the economy of Palestine. (1) The support of the standing army there required an inflow of 16.6 per cent of the GNP of Palestine; this money was used to buy various supplies from the residents of the province. (2) Supplying the army encouraged further business activity; we shall return to deal with this matter later.

II.3 The social-economic influence of the Roman army

The presence of such a large army in a small province would undoubtedly have had many effects on the socio-economic framework of the country. Our analysis of this situation makes use of MacMullen's short summary of the matter (MacMullen 1968; Jones 1974; Birley 1981; Burnham and Johnson 1979; Rivet 1969, pp. 173–216; Cunliffe 1979), as well as those studies mentioned at the beginning of this discussion. In particular, it is necessary to examine to what extent their conclusions are operational regarding Palestine.

(1) The Roman soldier received a rather good salary. From the period of Diocletian the salary was about 300 dinars. Auxiliary forces received 75 per cent of this (Speidel 1984, pp. 83–90; Watson 1959; Brunt 1950). A more or less set rate, however, had to be set aside by the soldier to pay the army for his food supply. Some of the money was saved by the soldier in the camp treasury and was withdrawn only upon his release. Another part of the salary, which it is impossible to estimate, was used for personal expenses or towards the purchase of communal sacrifices. The amount of money put aside for savings established the sum which could be spent in the province. There was undoubtedly no set rule and individual soldiers made their own decisions on these matters. We do not know how much money a soldier spent on average in his camp. We do know, however, that around the camps there sprang up both large (*canaba*) and small (*pagus*) civilian settlements.

These settlements usually housed those who provided services for the military camp and personal services for the soldiers. The soldiers' families also usually lived here, even if their families were not recognized by Roman law (Fink 1971, nos. 68–70; 77; 83; Thomas 1989, pp. 46–7; etc.). It is likely that the situation was similar in Judaea. This perhaps might explain how Legio, the civilian settlement next to the headquarters of Legio VI Ferrata, was a large village with a theater (Schumacher 1908). We do not know about any other theater in villages in Judaea or Galilea. This village later turned into the *polis* Maximianoupolis in the third century CE. It would appear that even the civilian settlement of Beer Sheva developed out of a *canaba* at the military headquarters of the *limes* there, as can be learned from the large number of Byzantine inscriptions found there and from the relatively large size of the town. There were undoubtedly other such settlements in Palestine.

(2) The army base as a consumer of services and supplies automatically turned into a natural merchandising center surrounded by markets. There is no information available on this phenomenon in Palestine, but it seems to have been fairly common in other provinces. In Judaea there was found a weight measure of the Fifteenth Legion (Qedar 1981, p. 45).

(3) The army was a consumer of technology and of a Roman life style. The soldiers and officers of the legion consumed great amounts of high quality wine (Middleton 1983, *contra* Tchernia 1983) and used Roman pottery (Greene 1979), and other such implements (King 1984). This encouraged local producers to raise the quality of their goods as well as local residents to buy them. Tiles stamped with the imprint of Legio VI Ferrata have been discovered in H. Hazon and in Kefar Hananiah and in Legio (Bahat 1974; Adan Bayewitz 1987). It is not known whether these finds are indicative of a local factory producing for the Roman army, or for the private use of the residents of the villages (see below). Another factory for the production of such tiles for the Tenth Legion was found near Jerusalem. Likewise, it is not clear whether this was a civilian or military establishment (Barag 1967). Bricks from this factory have been found in Joppa (60 km from Jerusalem), as well as at Ramat Rahel near Jerusalem. The latter site, however, was clearly civilian (*contra* Aharoni 1962, 1964), and in a *villa* near Jerusalem (unpublished).

(4) The army produced utensils and sold them in civilian markets (p. 343 above).

(5) The army produced utensils and services (such as bathhouses) and served, thus, as a role model for local residents as to the quality of Roman life.

(6) The army provided and built services for the province itself. The army, for instance, constructed many roads in Judaea; in Galilea the roads between Scythopolis and Caesarea, Diocaesarea and Legio were constructed by the army and for its use (Isaac and Roll 1982; Roll 1976).

However, many sources throughout the Empire show that the local rural residents often found themselves participating in the paving of these roads or in providing towards their upkeep through the various *liturgiae* imposed by the Romans (see, for example, the interesting inscription published by Frend from Asia Minor (Frend 1956). Avi-Yonah published an inscription testifying to the contribution of villages from Ptolemais valley (in Phoenicia) to the construction of the road from Ptolemais to Tyre (Avi-Yonah 1946, pp. 85–6). Local aqueducts providing cities with water were occasionally built by Roman forces. There are explicit inscriptions, for example relating to the construction of the aqueduct to Caesarea (Figures 71, 72).

IMP TRN	Imp(eratori) Tr(aia)n(o)
HADR	Hadr(iano)
VEX LEG	vex(illatio) leg(ionis)
X [F] RETE	X [F]rete(nsis)

Figure 71 Inscription of the 10th Legion on the aqueduct at Caesarea.

(7) The army served as a sort of roving ambassador of Roman culture, religion and economics. The presence of large Roman forces in Judaea was undoubtedly difficult for the local residents on account of the numerous *angariae* imposed, most likely, by Roman officers. During certain seasons of the year, a large military presence could result in shortages of various commodities and in rising prices, as was the case once in Antiochia (Downey 1951). However, the presence of the army was usually beneficial for the economy of the province. This might explain why rabbinic literature evinces a positive attitude to the Roman army in spite of the marked hostility and pent-up hatred which this same literature evinces towards the Roman Empire (S. Safrai 1971, pp. 224–30; Sperber 1969a, pp. 164–8).

Rabbinic traditions attest to a sort of cooperation and reciprocity between the army and residents of Palestine in terms of everyday life. These traditions do not stress the hatred and animosity usually associated with everything Roman. Thus, for example, Talmudic tradition relates how members of a military unit in Sepphoris sought to aid in extinguishing a fire at the house of a senior Jewish official (T Shabat 13(14):9 and parallels). Another tradition describes how a Roman soldier aided an ordinary Jew in the fulfillment of a commandment (M Bechorot 5:3). In spite of the hostility to Roman rule in general, it seems that there developed occasionally rather good relationships with local forces, at least on the personal level. Needless to say, this relationship was of great economic potential. On the other hand, the relationships between the Roman government and army and Galilean Jewry was also marred at times by a great deal of hatred. Our present discussion deals only with economic aspects of the matter.

A number of sources refer to the appearance of Roman army officers

Figure 72 Stamps of Legio X Fretensis on bricks. After Barag 1967, p. 175.

within the social and economic framework of both urban and rural settlements in the Land of Israel. Thus, for example, Talmudic tradition tells of a Roman officer who lent water to Naqdimon b. Gurion, one of the richest inhabitants of Jerusalem at the end of the Second Temple period (BT Taa'nit 19b).

A loan document discovered in the Judaean Desert mentions a Roman officer lending money to a rich inhabitant of Ein Gedi (Lewis 1989, no. 11). An inscription in Ascalon praises a centurion who most likely contributed a large sum to the city or to some municipal institution there

(Hogarth 1922). A number of other interesting testimonies on the matter are found in inscriptions and papyri found in the northern Negev. These, however, reflect the conditions of soldiers serving in the *limes* in the Byzantine period. The lifestyle and conditions of those soldiers serving in the Byzantine *limes* were different from those of the soldiers and officers of the Roman legions earlier, and therefore are beyond the purview of our discussion.

II.4 *Territorium legionis*

Another manner of providing supplies for the army was through the *territorium legionis* (Kandler 1975; Schulten 1894). The army was given a region through which it could provide its supplies. The region was divided similarly to the Roman century, and each sub-unit received a portion with which to provide for its needs. The details of this system, however, are not entirely clear, such as whether the legion received a government estate or whether the army simply collected the taxes from a regular *territorium*. Only in *territorium legionis* were the soldiers acting as tax collectors. Such a *territorium* existed, maybe, in the Jezreel Valley near the camp of Legio VI Ferrata at Legio (*contra* Isaac and Roll 1982, pp. 105–6). It is important to point out that rabbinic literature does contain references to officers functioning as tax collectors (Sperber 1969). The Jezreel Valley contained government estates, but there is no way of knowing exactly where they were located. This system, therefore, apparently did exist in Galilea, but it is impossible to determine its economic implications there.

III. TAXES

Taxes were an important component of the gross national product. In spite of a few preliminary studies, the tax framework in the Land of Israel has not yet been sufficiently examined (Gulak 1938; Alon 1977, I, pp. 64–70; Dinur 1990). We shall, therefore, refrain from a detailed discussion of this matter and make do with a number of general comments. As we have seen above (I.1), there are a number of different estimates regarding the rate of taxation. The lowest estimate is a rate of 10 per cent, but as we have seen, in actuality, the tax rate was much higher.

Hopkins has shown the economic significance of the manner in which taxes were collected (Hopkins 1980). Taxes paid in kind had no bearing on the business framework of the province since those taxes were transferred directly from the producer to the consumer, viz., the Roman army. The payment of taxes in cash, however, required, according to Hopkins, an operative business framework. The producer had to sell his surplus in the market in order to secure the cash to pay his taxes and, most likely, even after the payment of these taxes he was left with a degree of capital. The producer, for this system to have worked, obviously found customers in the market, implying that there were in the regions artisans and the like, probably working for the well-to-do or for the community which did not raise its own agricultural produce. They were undoubtedly paid in cash for their labor or services and served, therefore, as potential customers for the agricultural produce. This also implies that there were wealthy inhabitants or government officials in the region who had the cash to pay these artisans. Thus, the payment of taxes in cash, just as the payment of agricultural rents in cash, proves the existence of vibrant trade as well as of an economic system based on this trade.

Based on these important considerations, it is possible to reach a number of additional conclusions. The Roman imperial system had three means by which to collect taxes: (1) payment in cash; (2) payment in kind of agricultural produce grown by the farmer himself; (3) payment in kind of agricultural produce not produced by the farmer himself.

The first means of payment was entirely dependent on business conditions in the market. Payment in kind is not really dependent on the existence of such a framework, but does require that there be a transport framework, an absolute necessity for getting the payment to its final destination. The farmer would bring the produce to some kind of storehouse. Those in charge of collection had to have some means of preserving it, as well as of recording the amounts brought as payment, and of distributing it to its ultimate destination, whether in the Land of Israel itself or in some other part of the Empire. All of these procedures are business procedures. Those undertaking them, however, were not businessmen, but rather clerks and government officials.

Practice and reality often showed that this imperial and centralized system was often much more expensive than the "capitalist" system of open trade. This is certainly the case today and was undoubtedly the case in the ancient world, particularly regarding the Roman officials who were quite corrupt, thus adding more expense to the system.

Moreover, and as we have seen above, some of this tax produce was sold to residents of the province in which it was produced. This, of course, requires the existence of a market, since otherwise the produce collected as tax would have no economic benefit. Jewish sources also attest to the third type of payment. Thus, for instance, the *midrash* states:

> At a time when a person desires to eat a piece of bread made from barley but is unable to find one, then the nations demand of him a piece of bread made of fine flour and meat and oil . . . at a time when someone desires to drink just a drop of wine vinegar or beer but is unable to find these beverages, then the nations demand of him the best wine of all the countries in the world . . . at a time when someone has a desire to wear a garment of wool or linen but cannot afford it, the

nations demand of him garments made of the finest types of silk in all the world.

(Avot D'Rabbi Nathan, version A, chapter 20, p. 71;
Midrash Ha-Gadol on Deuteronomy 28:47–8)

The tradition is attributed in Midrash Ha-Gadol to R. Nehuniah b. Ha-Kaneh who lived at the beginning of the second century CE. In Avot D'Rabbi Nathan it is attributed to another sage from the same time. In Tanna D've Eliyahu Zuta (chapter 16, pp. 2–3), however, it is attributed to R. Simeon b. Yohai, who lived during the latter part of that century. This tradition reflects tragic business conditions in which a poor small-time farmer is theoretically forced to trade in luxury items about which he can only dream at best. Tacitus portrays similar conditions of harassment in Britain (*Agr.* 19).

The methods of collection were not the same in all the different kinds of taxes. Such taxes as business taxes, *aurum coronarium* and other types of special taxes were collected in cash on a much more frequent basis than taxes on land or agricultural produce. The traditions attest to the collection of taxes in kind from agricultural produce (see, for instance, T Demai 6:3; PT Maaser Sheni IV, 54d). There are traditions which even refer to the "liberal" option available to the owner of the field to exchange tax in kind from one type of crop for another such as paying barley instead of wheat (in such a case, though, it was necessary to pay more barley than wheat since the price of barley was only half of that of wheat – Chapter 2.I.1 above) or legumes such as *ful* instead of barley (T Bava Mezia 9:10). Other sources, however, attest to payment in cash (Mechilta D'Ba-Hodesh, Jethro 1, p. 203).

Another source describes a situation in which a farmer gives money to an intermediary to go buy some type of agricultural produce to bring to the treasury as payment of taxes (T Demai 6:4). There is no way of knowing whether this tradition represents a requirement to pay taxes with agricultural produce not grown by the farmer, or in his original possession, or whether this simply was an elaborate means of trying to avoid the payment of tithes. According to the *halachah*, one had to set aside tithes for the priests and Levites before the payment of taxes in order that they not lose their portion. The owner of the field was obviously interested in setting aside tithes only after the taxes had been paid. The *halachah* in the Tosefta may hint at a procedure by which the farmer did not pay taxes directly from his produce. Rather he sold it, before the setting aside of taxes, to a non-Jew, which was permitted according to the *halachah*, and the non-Jew then gave it over to the authorities as payment of taxes. The original Jewish owner was thus able to avoid double taxation. This option opens up the possibility that the Romans permitted the Jews to pay taxes in cash as a special favor to the Jews who could then avoid religious taxation; of course, the Romans had nothing against receiving cash. A law of Theodosius from the fourth century

CE (*C. Th.* 7. 4. 30) mentions tax collectors who apparently became too enthusiastic in the collection of taxes and levied payment in kind, and established that taxes from that point on were to be paid in cash. The law, however, refers to the region of the *limes* in the Byzantine period and undoubtedly reflects the situation there. It is not known whether this law pertained to the entire province.

To sum up, it is basically impossible to determine how much taxes were paid by the inhabitants of Palestine and the percentage of those taxes that were paid in cash. It is also impossible to point out the various processes which were instrumental in shaping tax policy. Chance references to the tax system such as the comment of Appian that a property tax of 1 per cent was levied on Syria and that the Jews had to pay a higher rate (Appian, *Syr.* 50) are of little value in trying to understand the general situation. We are, therefore, missing information on one of the most important components of the economic system of that time.

IV. THE RURAL ECONOMIC SYSTEM

IV.1 Farming versus labor and trade

In the previous chapters we have discussed the various components of the economic system: the different branches of agriculture, labor, services and trade (Chapters 2–3). Now it is necessary to discuss the balance between these different components. It is clear that there was no single economic framework or balance for all of these components in all the different regions of the Land of Israel and throughout the various periods of the ancient world which we are discussing. Even so, it is worthwhile to attempt to point out a few general trends regarding the economic system and the place of the various components which we have just mentioned within this system.

We have pointed out a number of times in the course of our study the many references to labor and trade in the rural villages of the Land of Israel. We have also discussed the importing of and trade in food staples, especially wheat, from the third century CE. In other words, a resident of the rural sphere could choose to make his living through some non-agricultural occupation and subsequently buy food for himself and his family at the market. In spite of this, though, it is clear that agriculture was the economic basis of the Land of Israel and that most residents of the province engaged in an agriculture-related occupation. There are a number of proofs for this assertion. (1) The majority of examples cited in the cases in halachic litera-ture refer to agriculture. (2) Land alone was considered to be a stable possession that one could depend upon either to pay taxes or to earn a living (Gulak 1929, pp. 94–131). (3) Many people, sages and commoners, rich and poor, made their living from the various branches of agriculture. R. Tarfon, for instance, had agricultural estates. R. Eliezer b. Hyrcanus came from a family which owned land. Rabban Gamaliel also possessed land. R. Akiva was a shepherd in his youth (although the historical value of this *aggadah* is negligible). Beytus b. Zonin owned animals and R. Zadok also had animals. R. Eleazar b. Azariah had animals and other farm-related possessions. These sages should probably be considered as representative of the entire population.

The accepted reality was usually that the farmer also functioned as an occasional artisan or laborer and at least part of his time was devoted to non-agricultural work. Only a few traditions reflect this situation. We shall discuss some of them now.

(1) The textile industry was based on the farmer raising flax or sheep who used his free time to weave thread and to sew (Chapter 2.I.7, I.8 above)

(2) Midrash Psalms 12:1, pp. 104–5 tells of a group of donkey-drivers whose leader was also a farmer. According to the tradition, his agricultural pursuits were of more importance than his transport tasks.

(3) The slaughterers in a town plied their official trade rather infrequently, as can be learned, for instance, from the need for a law to discuss the obligation to slaughter on the eve of a festival (M Hullin 5:3–4; T. Hullin 5(6):9). If he slaughtered so infrequently, it was impossible that he made his living and supported his family from such an occupation.

(4) The Tosefta mentions the case of a hired worker in a store, who is an "artisan" but is forbidden to ply his trade. Thus, the artisan also works as hired labor for a storekeeper (T Bava Mezia 5:12 and parallels). It is possible, though, that the store owner hired a worker to be in his store because he himself went out to work in his fields (as, for example, M Bava Mezia 5:4 and parallels). There could have been other reasons, though, for this phenomenon. In any case, the storekeeper could not have been busy the entire day selling wares in his store because otherwise the hired worker could not have had time to think about plying his original trade while at the store.

(5) Lamentations Rabbah (1:1, p. 48) mentions a wine merchant who also grew grapes. This certainly refers to a merchant in a *polis*.

(6) Many lime pits have been discovered within an agricultural context (in a field or in a terrace). Moreover, in many instances a wine press or lime pit have been discovered next to an agricultural tower (Dar 1986, pp. 111–13). These finds show that the farmer worked at labors associated with the wine press or lime pit in addition to his agricultural work in the field.

(7) There are sources attesting to a hired laborer who was also a farmer. Thus, for example, a tradition states: "a laborer is not permitted to do his own work at night and then to hire himself out during the day to

plow with his cow and to hire it out in the morning . . . on account of stealing the labor of the employer" (T Bava Mezia 8:2).

(8) A number of sages were both farmers and businessmen, although since a number of them were quite wealthy it is hard to know whether this is indicative of the rest of the population (as, for example, R. Hiyya b. Ada – BT Ketubbot 111b; Genesis Rabbah 20:6, p. 189; R. Hoshaiah, BT Pesahim 113b; PT Shabbat VI, 8a; *et al.*).

(9) The baker in a village usually baked only once a day and it is clear that this was not sufficient to support his family (T Pesahim 1(2):13 (2:3) and parallels).

(10) As we said above (Chapter 3.II.2), only the store is described in the sources as an example of a workhouse which is open the whole day, and only the storekeeper deals with cash. Thus, the worker or laborer worked at his trade only part of the day.

It would appear that based on these examples it is possible to conclude that most professionals in the township were also farmers, and they plied their professions only to supplement their income. Therefore, it is especially important that the Jewish town, as an organized institution, encouraged artisans. Thus, the slaughterer who was obligated to slaughter on the eve of a festival undoubtedly received some kind of bonus or benefit from the city. Otherwise, it is difficult to assume that the municipality could force him to lose money simply for the benefit of the city residents.

In T Bava Mezia 11:30 it was taught:

> Wool workers and dyers fill (their pails or buckets) in order to drink, but not for merchandise. Bakers and food wholesalers do not fill (their buckets) for merchandise. The digger of wells and the bathhouse attendant and the barber fill to drink, but not for use. One may, however, soak in vinegar and the like in a store those things which are to be pickled and one can wash off vegetables in a store.

This law deals with the use of public or communal water. The various artisans and laborers can use these waters for their businesses, but not in all cases. It is not exactly clear from this *halachah* which instances are permitted and which are not. In any case, the law states in a positive manner ("[they may] fill . . . they may not fill"). This would seem to imply that in any case they had the use of some of the public water supply. The *halachah* also mentions such terms as "merchandise", "use" and "drink" in terms of the use of this water supply. The terms, which are not really clear within their present context, relate to the services provided by a city to its inhabitants. The town clearly supplied water to artisans and service providers. It also developed the transportation system for the comfort of its inhabitants.

IV.2 The size of the agricultural holding

IV.2.1

The major question regarding the standard of living of the individual farmer revolves around the size of the plot of land which was at his disposal. If his land was his major means of production, then the size of his holding determined the level of his income. This matter can be examined from two standpoints: (1) the size of a holding which can support a family based on crop and price calculations known in literary sources; (2) the actual size of agricultural holdings.

IV.2.2

We have already determined the size of a plot necessary to support the average family (Chapter 2.I). Based on our information regarding the prices of food and calculations regarding harvests, we saw that to feed an average family of four persons the following size plots were necessary:

wheat	10 dunam (p. 110)
barley	18–20 dunam (p. 106)
olives	4.9–9.8 dunam (p. 123)
grapes	0.88 dunam (p. 131)
figs	8.8 dunam (p. 136)

These calculations are, of course, quite schematic and based on literary sources and are meaningful only in an economic framework which allows for the selling and buying of foodstuffs.

A family, however, which was interested in growing its entire food supply itself (a closed or self-sufficient economic system) required a minimum holding of 11 dunams based on the following:

wheat	6 dunam
olives	2.8 dunam
figs	1.2 dunam
wine	0.37 dunam
legumes	although the estimate is uncertain, probably no more than 1 dunam was necessary

The figures above add up to approximately 11 dunams which, as stated above, was the size of the theoretical holding which would enable a family to be self-sufficient in their food needs. As can also be seen, 50 per cent or so of this was cultivated with wheat. No family, however, could have been totally self-sufficient to the extent that it never needed to make outside purchases, and there were also taxes to pay.

Thus, it is likely that the real minimum figure was 20 dunams in order to

	Value of land in dunams needed to support a family based on M Ketubbot	Value based on Syrian-Roman Law Code
Wheat	1	1
Olives	2.04	2.4
Grapes	11	4

Figure 73 Value of lands in the Land of Israel. Base value = 1

support a family. The weak part of this system was the cultivation of the wheat, since of the crops mentioned above, this was the least profitable, yet the demand for grains was relatively great. If, indeed, there was an open agricultural-economic system and the farmer could buy wheat in the open market, and if wheat was also imported to the Land of Israel (Chapter I.1.2 above) then the size of the average holding may have been much smaller than the estimate made above.

An additional source aids us in evaluating the value of agricultural holdings. In the Syrian-Roman code of laws we find the following:

> The lands were surveyed in the days of the Emperor Diocletian. It was established that 5 *iugera* (= 12.5 dunams) which are ten *plethra* of vineyards should be considered as one *iougon* (= a tax unit). 20 *iugera* (50 dunam) of seed which are 40 *plethra* shall be considered as 1 *iougon*
> (Bruns and Sachau, 1880, no. 151; Jones 1953).

In other words, trees were planted in the Land of Israel at a density of 10 trees to a *beit seah* and 11–12 were planted in a dunam. Thus, approximately 225 trees represent an area of 20 dunams. If, for arguments sake, we set the price of a wheat field at 1, then an equivalent sized vineyard would be worth four times as much, while an olive grove would be worth 2.5 times as much as the wheat field. In Figure 73 above there is a comparison between the relative prices of fields according to the Syrian-Roman law code and expected profit based on the figures we have seen above in Mishnah Ketubbot.

Thus, the relationship between an olive grove and a wheat field is almost identical. On the other hand, the price of a vineyard in the Land of Israel was much higher than the price of one in Syria. Perhaps this reflects difficulties in the cultivation of grapes in Syria and indeed the Land of Israel was renowned for its grapes. Moreover, since M Ketubbot reflects the southern region of Palestine (Chapter 2 above), a region in which the cultivation of the grape was quite profitable, the figures pertaining to the vineyard in the Land of Israel.

The continuation of the same section in the Syrian-Roman law code mentions three different types of land. Second-rate land was priced at half the value of first-rate land (40 *iugera* of grain was valued at one *iougon*). In the case of third-rate land, 60 *iugera* are considered one *iougon*. Talmudic literature also refers to "superior" land, to "average" land and to "low quality" land. The differences then in the quality of the land were of great importance. The numbers in Talmudic literature referring to quantities and harvests most likely refer to average yields. In any case, the economic computations are modular and the quality of the land in any particular site was of maximum importance.

IV.2.3

There are additional sources which can tell us something about the size of the average agricultural holding. Alon (1980, I, p. 156) attempted to calculate the size of a plot by analyzing a literary source mentioning two average farmers having thirty-four dunams (Euseb. *Hist. Eccl.* 3. 20. 1–2).

Field research, though, is probably of greater value. S. Dar, for instance, has examined two villages in Samaria (Dar 1986, pp. 73–6, 237 ff. and Figures 74 and 75). The average plot in H. El-Buraq was approximately 25 dunams (including non-arable or difficult terrain). In Qarawat Bene Hasan the sizes run from 39.7 dunams to 45.6 dunams. The latter may have been a village of tenant farmers, a possibility a number of sources seem to hint at. In a number of sites examined by Safrai in the Galilee (Z. Safrai 1985, p. 129), the size of the average plot varied from 6–11 dunams (Figure 76). Safrai also examined the plots of the settlers in Neapolis in the Schechem region. The size of the plots there varies from 15–18 dunams (Z. Safrai 1986, pp. 99–100, Figures 77 and 78).

None of these figures, however, offers a complete understanding of the matter since they do not take into consideration the nature and type of the land which, as we saw above, was of great importance. Another problem which cannot be completely solved was whether every settler had only one plot. All the studies on land usually take this for granted, although there is absolutely no proof that this was indeed the case.

It should be stated, though, that there seems to have been a uniformity, more or less, in the size of the plots examined. This allows for a number of preliminary conclusions. (1) The checking procedure in the field was correct. (2) There was limited economic stratification in the villages which were examined or, in other words, there were no extremely wealthy residents. Needless to say, this matter also requires further study and in any case this fact is just one of the many which have to be taken into consideration. (3) Land use in the villages was more or less uniform.

As we have already stated, the matter requires much more study and we only intend here to show the basic agreement between the data collected in the field and the literary sources discussed above.

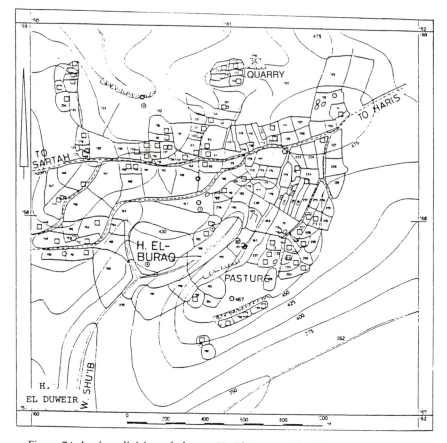

Figure 74 Ancient division of plots at H. El-Buraq. After Dar 1986, Figure 43.

V. THE STRUCTURE OF THE FARM SYSTEM

Agriculture on Jewish farms and most likely in the entire rural sector was small-scale and private, intensive, professional and dependent upon self-labor.

V.1 Private agriculture

As we said above, most of the farmers in the Land of Israel were small-scale and independent. The tenant farmers should also be included in this category since to all intents and purposes they ran their farms independently, apart from having to pay rents of about 50 per cent or so, which was usually higher than the 30 per cent or so tax rate.

Small-scale and independent agriculture. As we have seen, the plots which were at the disposal of the average farmer were rather small. Such small plots

358

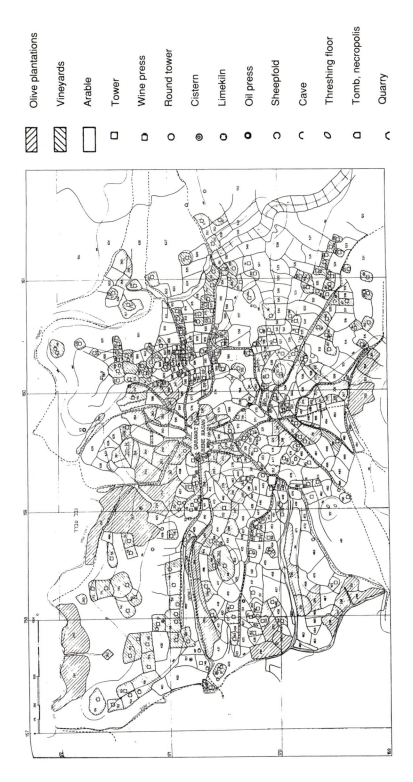

	Olive plantations
	Vineyards
	Arable
□	Tower
◗	Wine press
○	Round tower
◎	Cistern
◖	Limekiln
●	Oil press
◠	Sheepfold
◡	Cave
◔	Threshing floor
◗	Tomb, necropolis
◡	Quarry

Figure 75 Division of plots at Qarawat Bene Hasan. After Dar 1986, Figure 43.

Region	Reference point	Size of the area (dunams)	Number of plots	Average size (dunams)	Number of plots					
					0–3	3–5	5–11	11–14	14–20	20+
Bir Macksur	244/172	464.6	32–53	8.6–8.8	–	6	35	6	4	2
Yoda-phata										
1	176/245	118	22–24	4.9	–	10	12	–	–	–
2	176/245	72	7–10	7.2–10.3	–	–	6	–	–	–
Kh. Kana										
1	178/247	115	14+	8.2	–	–	6	1	–	–
2	180/298	163	22–25	6.5–7.4	3	5	15	–	–	–
Kh. Ruma	179/242	92	8–11	8–11	–	0–2	3/4	3/4	1	1
1		33	4	8.2	–	1	31	1	–	–
2		336	32–38	8.8–10.4	1	1	31	4	1	–
3		301	24	12	–	1	9	3	6	3
4		185	16–18	10–11.5	–	1	9/12	2	2/4	1?

Figure 76 The sizes of plots in the Galilee. After Z. Safrai 1985, p. 129.

Note: It is possible that every man had more than one plot

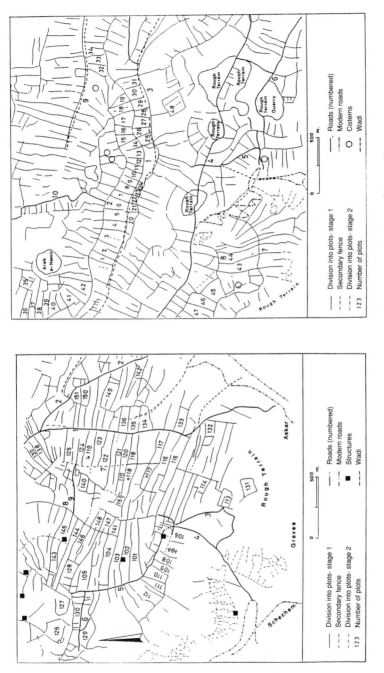

Figure 77 Land allotments to settlers in the Neapolis region. After Z. Safrai 1986b, pp. 93–4.

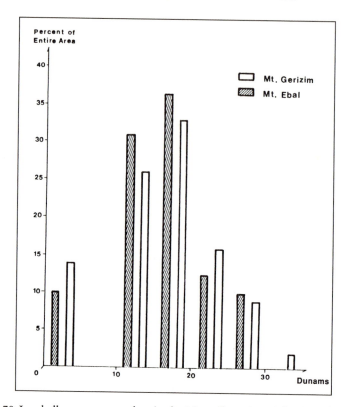

Figure 78 Land allotments to settlers in the Neapolis region. After Z. Safrai 1986b, p. 78.

could support a family only if they were worked rather intensively. Talmudic traditions relating to agricultural labors often bear testimony to the intensive manner in which the land was worked. As Feliks has stated: "The Land of Israel supported its many inhabitants through the steadfastness of its farmers, the intensity of agricultural labor, the strong connection between the farmer and his land and the vast store of agricultural knowledge at the disposal of the farmers," (Feliks 1963, p. 21). We shall not go into the details of all agricultural labors. We shall, however, bring a few examples of such labors which testify to the intensity of agricultural labor.

(1) Large-scale fertilization of up to five tons per dunam (Feliks 1963, p. 109).
(2) Multiple plowings of up to 5–6 times with rather deep furrows (27 cms) (Feliks, pp. 26–37).
(3) Picking figs every day so that a fig would always be picked on the exact day on which it became ripe (PT Berachot II, 5c).
(4) Every tree being treated separately (M Sheviit 2:5)

362

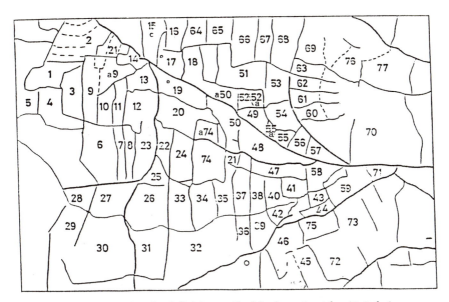

Figure 79 Ancient land division at Shufah, Samaria. After Z. Safrai unpublished survey.

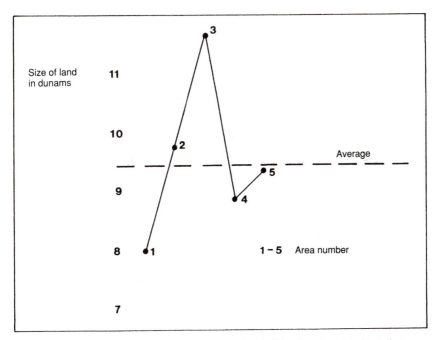

Figure 80 Ancient land division in the *shephelah* of Lod. After Z. Safrai unpublished survey.

(5) The cultivation of plots in difficult and rocky terrain and even in those areas which could not be plowed (M Peah 2:2 *et al.*). All this was so prevalent in the hill areas that remains of this type of agriculture are visible even today.

The high level of agricultural cultivation of the ancient farmers is also quite evident in the nature of the system of the various labors and in the choice of crops. All of this led to very high yields. There was a very high population density and it was possible to support this population only through these large yields.

V.2 Self-production

Working the land was dependent to all intents and purposes on one's own labor, taking into account the occasional drafting of family members to help. This assumption, however, is hard to prove since there are many sources which mention the hiring of farm workers. In any event, though, the assumption made above is certainly correct. As we shall see below, the tilling of the land and private agriculture were the economic backbone of the town. If there were many landless segments of the population, then private agriculture would not have played this role *vis-à-vis* the town, and the selling of the labor of the workforce would have replaced agriculture as the prime economic mover of the town (cf. Jameson 1992).

The plots were quite small and this would seem to indicate that they had to be divided among a good many people. Agriculture based on hired labor would imply the existence of large farmsteads and a good deal of social stratification. This was not the case, however, in the Jewish town. Needless to say that this type of settlement did have both rich and poor, but for the most part, the economic level was quite uniform.

Moreover, most of the sources mentioning hired workers refer to the harvest or to special tasks. It is no coincidence that the Mishnah, for instance, mentions 37 instances of hired laborers. Of these instances, 20 deal with communal labors such as the harvest (15 cases) or processing the crop (drying it, wine or oil), 5 refer to cases of weeding, 14 are not specific and 3 refer to different types of cases. As a typical example of the type of hired agricultural labor found in the Mishnah we find the following: "If he had to build his house, or put up his wall, or to reap his field . . . he goes among the laborers" (M Nedarim 4:7). On the other hand, the Mishnah mentions in the same chapter one who was accustomed to do his own plowing as opposed to one who used to hire laborers for this task (4:6).

Another proof of the prevalence of independent labor is the fact that many of the rich farmers mentioned in the sources worked their holdings themselves. Thus, for example, the sons of Hyrcanus, a rich farmer and landowner and the father of the sage R. Eliezer b. Hyrcanus, plow their own fields (Genesis Rabbah 41(42):1, pp. 397–8 and parallels). Likewise, R. Hiyya who was quite rich also worked by himself (PT Peah IV, 18a) and there are many other such similar cases. In spite of all this, it is clear that hiring additional laborers in busy seasons was a common phenomenon. It is also quite clear that the rich hired laborers on a much more frequent basis and often their estates were actually run by hired labor or by slaves.

Sometimes the problem of additional required work during busy seasons was solved by communal labor. An interesting *halachah* in PT Berachot II, 5a (and BT Berachot 16a) records an example of this. According to the law, hired workers are supposed to recite a short version of the grace after meals and to say only the first blessing. A private individual, however, is required to recite the entire four blessings of the grace after meals. The principle behind this is that the average person has to recite the entire grace. A worker, however, was exempt from saying the grace in its entirety since it was not accepted that the worker would spend all this extra time at the expense of his employer. The Talmud adds that "if they were taking their meal with him together then they are exempt." The usual explanation is that this refers to workers whose entire salary was their meals. This explanation, however, is far from satisfactory. It is hard to imagine that there were workers whose entire salary was limited to meals. And in any case, why should their status be different from other workers?

In our view this *halachah* hints at a custom which was common also in traditional Arab agriculture. The men of the village used to assemble at the field of one of their neighbors to harvest it. At night they would all gather for a festive meal provided as recompense by the owner of the field. Thus, all the fields were harvested in order. This custom is called "to take their meals together" and reflects communal and joint labor during the busy harvest seasons which required extra labor (Figure 81).

V.3 Regional specialities

Agriculture in the Land of Israel was based on specialization. Every region cultivated essentially those crops for which it was best suited in terms of the conditions of the land and its ecological limits. G. Alon (1980, I, pp. 161–8, Figure 82) was the first to prepare a map of regional agriculture. Actually, it is necessary to differentiate between two different types of testimonies on the matter: (1) traditions relating to the cultivation of a specific crop at one place or another and reflecting specialization; (2) coincidental agricultural traditions which happen by chance to mention the cultivation of a crop at a particular place.

Obviously, the second type of tradition is less important than the first type which clearly and specifically reflects specialization. These specific traditions indicate the following.

Vegetables. These were apparently cultivated throughout the entire Land

Month / Crop	1	2	3	4	5	6	7	8	9	10	11	12	
Grain					+++	+++			——	——	– –	– –	
Legumes				+++	+++				——	——	– –	– –	
Olives	··········								+++	+++	+++	+++	
Grapes	············					+++	+++	+++	+++				
Figs							——	——	,				Small Amount Cultivated
Flax					+++	+++ ··	··········		——		– –		
Squash Family	——	——	– –	– –	–		+++	– –	– –				Attendant Labors During Free Time
Onions						+++	+++			——		– –	
Vegetables				+++	+++	·····	······	··········	——	– –		– –	Dependent upon Types and Kinds Grown
Rice			– –	– –	······	··········	··········		+++				Intensive Irrigation
Dates				······	······	······	+++	+++					

——— Plowing ++++++ Harvest — — — Sowing–Planting ·········· Miscellaneous

In Hebrew Months

Figure 81 Theoretical ancient yearly work schedule in the Land of Israel. After Z. Safrai 1986, p. 41.

of Israel and not in any one particular place. Moreover, the cultivation of vegetables was tangential to other more important crops. A farmer growing some type of cash crop would also grow a few hundred square meters of vegetables through irrigation.

Olives. Olives were cultivated for the most part in the Galilee in general and in the Upper Galilee in particular. Among those places mentioned in the sources regarding the cultivation of olives are Meiron, Gush Halav and the Galilean Tekoa (M Menahot 8:3 and parallels). Many other traditions mention the Galilee in general as the center of olive cultivation in contrast to Judaea in which the cultivation of the vine and grain were more prevalent. Thus, for example, in the letter sent by the elders of Jerusalem to the Galilee regarding *biur* of tithes (= having to remove those tithes after a number of years already set aside and handing them over to the priest or Levite), the elders mention olives in relation to the Galilee, but grain in their missive to Judaea (Midrash Tannaim on Deuteronomy 26:13 and parallels). Also, a good many *midrashim* praise the portion of the tribe of Asher, identified for

366

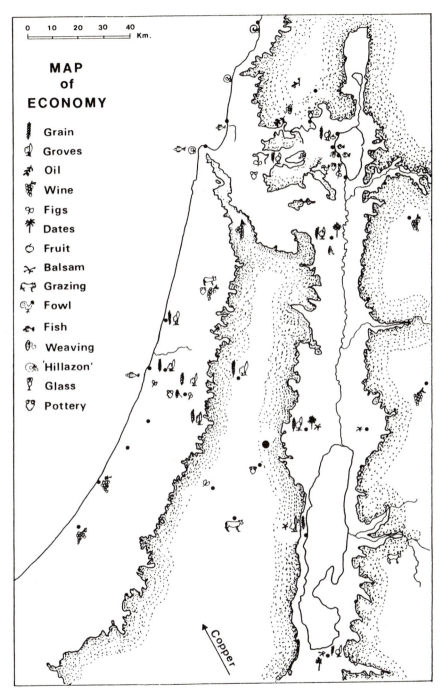

Figure 82 Map of crops.

the most part with the Galilee, regarding olive oil: "as it was taught that the land of Asher draws forth oil like from a fountain" (Midrash Tannaim on Deuteronomy 33:24 and parallels – and here the tradition is related regarding an elder from Gush Halav, a settlement, as we have seen, already associated with the cultivation of oil). Another source in a similar vein states: "that the portion (of Asher) supplies the oil for the Temple" (Genesis Rabbah 97:20, p. 1222 and parallels). One of the sons of Asher was "Bar Zait" (Hebrew: lit. son of olive). This name offered the rabbis many opportunities for *derashot* on connections between Asher and olives or olive oil (Agadat Bereshit 83; Z. Safrai 1985, pp. 108–10). Most of the Agad of Bereshit traditions referring to the specialized cultivation of olives refer to the Upper Galilee (Asher), but they were undoubtedly also cultivated in the Lower Galilee.

Grapes. As we have already seen, the grape was cultivated especially in Judaea. M Menahot 8:6 mentions a number of sites which were renowned for their grapes: "Keruhim and 'Atulin (or *crutin* in Judaea, see Yadin and Naveh 1989, p. 449) are of the best quality (lit. *alpha*, best quality wine to be brought to the Temple) for wine. Second to them are Beth Rimah and Beth Laban in the mountain region (= the northern Judaean mountains) and Kephar Signah in the valley" (Klein 1939, pp. 138–42). Kefhar Signah in the Mishnah is not Sikhnin in the Galilee, but rather a settlement in the Lod region, since questions from this village are directed to sages of Javneh and Lod. Other settlements or regions mentioned in relation to bringing wine to the Temple or regarding the production of a large amount of wine are Ein Gedi and Edom in general (Klein 1939, p. 141). Other sources, such as the many *derashot* on Genesis 49:8–12, mention the large amount of wine in the Darom (= Edom): " 'He washeth his garments in wine' – there is much wine within his borders" (Genesis Rabbah 98(99):12, p. 1281, and Targum Jonathan on Genesis 49:12). The tradition of the Jerusalemites (ha-Darom) reflects a rather developed culture of the vine (Genesis Rabbah 98(99):10 p. 1261) and indeed BT Nazir 31a stresses "in the Galilee they taught that wine is preferable to (= more expensive than) oil." Documents from Judaea even mention "trailers", those who trail or lift up branches of a vine on to a tree (DJD II, no. 29) and there are many other similar types of sources.

Based on the sources discussed now as well as those studied earlier on, it is possible to conclude that the specialty of the Judaean mountains was the cultivation of the grape. In spite of the fact that olives were undoubtedly also grown in Judaea and grapes also in the Galilee, the regions specialized in the crops which we have mentioned.

Dates. Dates grew in the valleys, and those grown in the hills were considered inferior. The areas which specialized in dates were: Beth Shean, Jericho, Ein Gedi and Zoar (see also Chapter 2.1.3).

Grain. We have already discussed those areas which specialized in the cultivation of grains (Chapter 2.I.2). Barley, for instance, which was rather rare in the Land of Israel, was cultivated in the southern Mt Hebron region.

Flax and grazing. The cultivation of flax was basically limited to the Galilee while sheep were for the most part raised in Judaea (Chapter 2.I.7 and I.8 above).

Fishing. This occupation was for the most part limited to the area around the Sea of Galilee or along the coastline (Chapter 2.I.8).

Some of the regional specialities were based on local geographic conditions. Thus, for example, the cultivation of dates or balsam as well as the fishing industry required specific natural conditions which were not found in other regions. These natural conditions may not have been all that prominent or obvious in every case, but they always had some bearing on the specialized agriculture of a particular region.

V.4 Agriculture of non-irrigated and irrigated fields

In order to understand ancient agriculture in the Land of Israel, it is important to remember that most agriculture depended on natural rainfall and not on irrigation. Although Talmudic literature contains many traditions regarding irrigation, it is clear that fields were irrigated in only a few areas because the Land of Israel does not have many springs. It is likely that irrigation was practiced in those places or areas in which there were springs. Even so, the amount of water available was limited. Also trenches or channels were usually not dug for the purposes of irrigation. Thus, for example, during field work in Samaria, it was noticed that only rather infrequently does one find such cisterns in open agricultural fields. Such cisterns are usually found in connection with settlements or with roads, but not too often just in connection with fields. An interesting phenomenon, however, is that in many settlements cisterns were found around the settlement at a distance of 10–100 meters from it. This was most likely the area in which the vegetable gardens were cultivated and the water necessary for the gardens was collected in the cisterns. The water collected in these cisterns also served to water sheep.

The large extent of agriculture not dependent on irrigation is clear from the many *midrashim* which praise the Land of Israel in terms of the large quantities of rainfall which it receives as against Babylonia and Egypt which were dependent on rivers (Sifre Deuteronomy Eqev 38 pp. 73–4; Numbers Rabbah 17:6). Regions in which irrigation was prevalent were, for example, the Sea of Galilee Basin, the Beth Shean Valley, the Hulah Valley and the regions of Acco and Sepphoris. In most settlements, though, agriculture was simply dependent on rainfall. Those small areas irrigated were usually for the purposes of a local vegetable garden. Rice, it seems, was also grown in irrigated fields.

The Land of Israel is quite temperate, but limited in arable land.

Therefore, the only way to increase agricultural production was to irrigate. Proof of this is found in the *midrash* which tells of a person who bought a neglected field and managed to turn it into a blooming orchard by digging ditches (for irrigation) or a well. This tradition would also seem to imply that the ancients knew how to drill deep enough in order to reach the aquifer (Mekhilta D'Rabbi Ishmael Beshalah, pp. 87–8 and parallels). In any case, it is likely that most of the area was not watered with irrigation channels and the ancients probably realized quite quickly that it was usually not that worthwhile to dig irrigation trenches. It is also important to remember that adding water to vineyards or olive groves reduces the level of sugar in the grapes or of oil in the olives for the sake of the volume of the fruit. Also, irrigated fruit was considered to be of secondary quality (M Menahot 8:2, 6 *et al.*). In summary, one can say that in certain instances, irrigation may have been worthwhile, but the profits were small and the trouble involved was great.

VI. THE ECONOMY OF THE *POLIS*

VI.1 Agriculture versus labor and trade

The majority of our study, based to a great extent on historical traditions and archeological material, deals with the reality of the rural sphere. This does not exempt us, however, from some type of discussion regarding the differences between the *polis* and the rural sphere in terms of economy. The very fact that a settlement was defined as a *polis* indicates that the standard of living there was on a higher level than in the rural sphere. The same can be said regarding the level of services (Chapter 1.II above). The upper-echelon officials dealing with this or that element of administration were clearly rich residents of the *polis*. The *polis* was undoubtedly the home and sphere of activity of most of the rich upper class, including those who also owned villas or farmsteads in the rural sphere. The *polis* was also the center of trade and business and the *shulhani* (see Chapter 3.VIII.2 above) also operated only in the *polis*. The question which we wish to discuss at present is the impact of the agricultural sphere on the *poleis* of the Land of Israel.

In his discussion of urban economy, A. H. M. Jones (1974, pp. 36 ff.) states that even in trade cities, the most important component of the economy was agriculture and not trade or business. His major proof, however, is not so convincing. He compares the taxes on commerce of a trade city like Edessa with the taxes received from agriculture from Heracleopolis which was a regular city. The income from the agricultural taxes was indeed higher. However, our information on commercial taxes in Edessa is based on a literary source (Joshua Stylites 31). The value of a such a source in terms of quantifying the rate of taxes is rather problematical. Moreover, it is possible that the tax rate on agriculture in Egypt was higher than the rate on commerce in Edessa, and thus the higher taxes received on agriculture simply reflect a higher tax rate and not higher production rates. Another point made by Jones relates to the high cost of transport. We shall, however, examine this matter in a following chapter (Chapter 5.VI) and we shall see that this economic component was lower than the figure that appears in the Edict of Diocletian which served as the basis for Jones's computations. Most of the cities of the Land of Israel were port cities and it was rather cheap in terms of transport to supply them with merchandise. Jones's arguments, therefore, are far from convincing and it would be wise to examine once again the figures which pertain to the Land of Israel (see also Pleket 1984).

VI.2 Agriculture in the city

VI.2.1

Little attention has been paid to the question of the economy of the cities of the Land of Israel. It is clear that on one hand the trade, labor and service networks in the city were quite developed. On the other hand, there was also agriculture in the cities. Thus, for example, Talmudic tradition knows of a certain kind of *ethrog* grown in Caesarea, or at least in the surrounding fields (PT Demai III, 23c; Levine 1975, pp. 51–2) as well as of a particular kind of wine produced there (PT Megillah I, 72d). Ascalon was famous for its onions (Pliny, *HN* 19. 101; Strabo 16. 2. 29) and the capparis plant used as a herb (*HN* 12. 109). 12. 109. There are also many traditions about Sepphoris which was well known for its irrigated fields which were at the disposal of its residents (the *"skyy"* – of Sepphoris; see discussion below). All of these facts are very important, but they do not offer a complete quantitative picture of urban agriculture. A number of other cities, however, provide better data.

VI.2.2 Gaba

Dozens of agricultural installations, such as olive presses, wine presses and especially installations to soak flax, have been excavated in the vicinity of Gaba Hippeum. All of these testify to the great deal of agriculture around the city (Z. Safrai and Linn 1988, Figure 83).

VI.2.3 Schechem (Neapolis)

Z. Safrai (1986b, pp. 92 ff; and see Figure 4 above) found an area surrounding Schechem which was apparently divided into agricultural plots for the residents of that city. This surrounding area includes a region of some 35 square kms surrounding the city and, therefore, it is likely that this was the agricultural periphery of that city. Based on his computations regarding the size of the average plot, Safrai came to the conclusion that there were

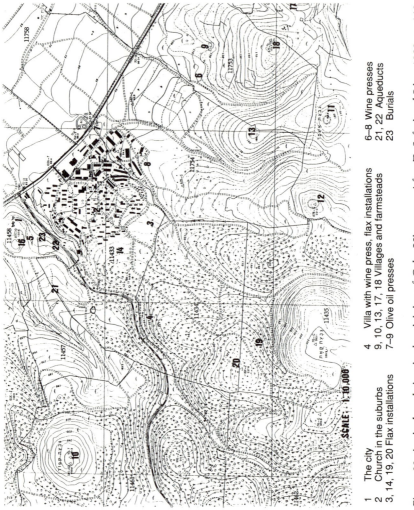

1   The city
2   Church in the suburbs
3, 14, 19, 20 Flax installations

4   Villa with wine press, flax installations
9, 10, 13, 17, 18 Villages and farmsteads
7–9 Olive oil presses

6–8 Wine presses
21, 22 Aqueducts
23   Burials

Figure 83 Agricultural sites in the vicinity of Gaba Hippeum. After Z. Safrai and Linn 1988, p. 168.

approximately 2,600–3,100 plots surrounding the city. The size of the city was approximately 300 dunams and based on the accepted population density of 30–40 people per dunam, there were no more than 3,000 families in the city, assuming that every family received a plot. It is, of course also possible that some families had more than one plot which they gave to tenant farmers and that some families engaged in commerce and trade and not directly in agriculture. It is also necessary to take into account that within the agricultural region surrounding Schechem there were five towns and 15 villages (Figure 4 above). It is true, though, that the size of all of these settlements was no more than 120 dunams.

It is impossible to determine whether the residents of these settlements within the agricultural periphery of Schechem were tenant farmers or independent farmers living in quasi village suburbs of the *polis* (Chapter 1.II.3 above). In any case, all of this would seem to lead to the conclusion that there were no more than 4,000 residents in the entire region and only 3,000 plots. This would also imply that no more than 25 per cent of the residents of the city did not engage in agriculture and that most of the residents of the city did possess agricultural plots in one form or another. It is, of course, possible, that some of those owning plots and even working them also engaged in some other form of labor or craft like the average village farmer (Chapter 4.IV.1 above). After all of this, however, it should be remembered that these numbers are not absolute and the same may be said, therefore, for the conclusions derived from them. In the final analysis, though, it seems that the majority of the inhabitants of Schechem (50–75 per cent) were either independent farmers or tenant farmers with small plots.

VI.2.4 Sepphoris (Diocaesarea)

Sepphoris appears in many literary traditions as an agricultural city. Thus, for example, the sources mention wine from Sepphoris (PT Megillah I, 72d). The sources also mention the "irrigated region of Sepphoris" and the rabbis often praised the agricultural nature of the region and the fruits cultivated there (PT Bikkurim I, 63d; 64b; PT Sheviit V, 35d; BT Megillah 6a). The "irrigated area of Sepphoris" had groves and the sources mention a pear which grew there (T Kilayim 1:4) and apparently also almonds (PT Maasrot I, 49a). The sources also praise various kinds of vegetables which grew in the city, and it is likely that they were also cultivated in the irrigated fields (Sifre Deuteronomy 317, p. 360; Midrash Tannaim on Deuteronomy 32:14; T Makhshirin 3:6).

It is possible to evaluate the extent of the irrigated region around Sepphoris. The irrigated region was apparently in the Nahal Sepphoris (Zippori) area. The agricultural area of the city in general can be determined based on the towns which surrounded Sepphoris such as H. Rumah (Sihin?), Tel Hanaton, Rumanah and perhaps also Bir el-Makhsor in the north. Also in the Sepphoris region are Qana, Reine and Meshed in the east. Nazareth 'Alut and Sur el-Musheirifia were located in the south (Raban 1982, no. 70, p. 63). This agricultural region extends over an area of 26–30 sq. km and only part of it can be irrigated. Sepphoris itself was a medium-sized city and according to rough estimates it was about 800 dunams. According to the accepted density coefficient mentioned above (30–40 people per dunam), there were no more than 32,000 people in the city or about 8,000 families. Thus, every family had approximately 3–4 dunams at its disposal. Even if part of this were irrigated, it certainly was not enough to support the average family. Thus, it is possible to sum up and state that agriculture was important in this city and possibly also one of the main forms of income there, but apparently not the major one. It is possible to estimate that only about 50 per cent of the income of the city derived from agriculture since the average "nuclear" family required a plot of about 10 dunams to support itself. As was the case regarding our computations above, all of our conclusions by their very nature are general and schematic.

VI.2.5 Caesarea

Caesarea was the epitome of a commercial center with a large port. The city is located on rather poor agricultural land which is for the most part covered with sand dunes. Serious efforts to use these lands for agriculture were undertaken only in the Muslim period (Porat 1975). In the third century, the sages decided to exempt the city from commandments dependent upon the land since most of the inhabitants of the city were non-Jews (Z. Safrai 1984). At first, only the city itself and the immediately surrounding region were exempted. It is likely, though, that within the territory exempted were the fields belonging to the residents of the city, since if most of the residents of the city were pagans, their fields would also almost automatically have been exempted.

It is possible also that the exemption extended over an area larger than the immediate fields surrounding the city. There is a list of agricultural produce which was brought to Caesarea from outside the region of the exemption, or in other words, the list pertains to imported produce. Most of the produce found in the city did not grow in fields belonging to the city. The list is found in PT Demai II, 22c as well as in the Rehob inscription (Y. Sussmann 1973–4, pp. 131–2). The exempted fruits and produce included wheat, wine, oil, dates, rice, cumin and the bolbos or wild onion. This would seem to indicate that almost all agricultural staples were imported to the city and that the residents of Caesarea produced none of them themselves. The sources mention only pressed dates and a number of vegetables (except the bolbos) in relation to produce grown in the exempted fields of Caesarea.

VI.2.6 Beth Shean (Scythopolis)

There was a similar exemption in relation to Beth Shean. The list of imported produce to that city included wine and oil. Wheat, however, grew in the local "exempted" fields or in fields belonging to the city (PT Demai cited above and Y. Sussmann 1973–4, pp. 111–19; Feliks 1987, pp. 447–56 and see also Chapter 1.I.2). Flax was also grown in the city's agricultural periphery and this product was also considered characteristic of the produce of Beth Shean (Chapter 2.I.7 above). Dates, apart from the Ephes dates (Chapter 2.I.3 above) were also gown in Beth Shean as well as a number of different types of vegetables mentioned in PT Demai and the Rehov inscription. It is thus possible to conclude that agriculture played an important role in the economy of Beth Shean.

It is possible to estimate the exempted area as including approximately 50–60 sq. km (Z. Safrai 1984, Figure 84). The size of the city was about 1,100 dunams (Conder and Kitchener, 1882, II, p. 105) and therefore, according to the density co-efficient cited above, there were about 11,000 families in Beth Shean. Thus, every family had at its disposal a plot averaging 5–6 dunams. This is not very much, and is similar in size to the family plots at Sepphoris. Most of the Beth Shean area, however, was irrigated and it was possible, therefore, to cultivate produce with an extremely high profit rate such as dates, flax and vegetables. Thus, the average family plot in Beth Shean, although somewhat small, could probably support a family there without any difficulty. On the other hand, though, the legal phrase "exempt" included not only the agricultural region of the city residents, but also the territory of a number of nearby villages. It is difficult, therefore, to determine the percentile relationship of agriculture to the other components of the economy of Beth Shean. It can be assumed with a fair degree of certainty that agriculture provided for upwards of 80 per cent of the gross income of the city.

VI.2.7

It is possible, therefore, to sum up and state that despite the fact that there is no exact data on the matter, it would seem that there were two or three different types of cities in the Land of Israel. In cities like Jerusalem (at least until the end of the Second Temple period, see pp. 377–9 below) or Caesarea, agriculture was relatively unimportant in the city economy. In Jerusalem, for instance, the agricultural sector of the city probably accounted for no more than 25 per cent of the inhabitants. In the second type of city, agriculture was extremely important, accounting for 50–60 per cent of the residents of these cities. It is also possible that there were cities which were markedly agricultural in nature, and in this case agriculture would provide for 80–85 per cent of the city's income.

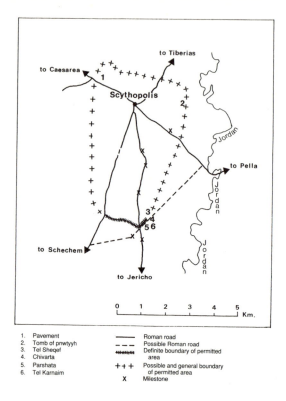

1.	Pavement	———	Roman road
2.	Tomb of pnwtyyh	- - -	Possible Roman road
3.	Tel Sheqef	┉┉┉	Definite boundary of permitted area
4.	Chivarta		
5.	Parshata	+ + +	Possible and general boundary of permitted area
6.	Tel Karnaim	X	Milestone

Figure 84 Map of permitted areas in the Beth Shean region.

All of the above goes to show that there was not all that much difference between the *polis* and the surrounding rural towns regarding occupations. In both types of settlements, the norm was a livelihood based on a combination of agriculture and labor or agriculture and trade. Except for a few unusual cases, agriculture represented the major source of production even in the cities, while there was also a degree of labor and industry in the villages. What is clear, though, is that in the village, the non-agricultural component was smaller than it was in the city. This was the case regarding most rural towns, although as we have seen in the course of our discussion, there were also towns which were exceptions to the rule, such as some located on the coastal plain, in which many, if not all, of the inhabitants there engaged in quarrying (Chapter 2.II.2, Figure 47).

VI.3 City–village relations

The relationship between the city and the village plays an important role in modern research and has been discussed by many major scholars (see, for instance, Rich and Wallace-Hadrill 1992). Our above investigation indicates that the socio-economic structure in the Judaean province was different from that in the western provinces.

Before discussing the activity in the province in the Roman era following the destruction of the Second Temple, we briefly address this aspect of life in the province in the period preceding the destruction of the Temple.

VI.3.1 Jerusalem at the end of the Second Temple period

At the end of the Second Temple period, over ten Hellenized cities and one central Jewish city – Jerusalem – were spread throughout Judaea. We do not know much about the relationship between the Hellenized cities and their surroundings, but we do have a wealth of information about Jerusalem and its role as a metropolis and a centre.

Second Temple period Jerusalem extended over an area of about 1,200 dunams (Broshi 1975). The suburbs around the city included another 3–4 sq. km (Chapter 1.II.3 above, Figure 5). It is possible to estimate the land which belonged to the residents of the city based on the density of graves surrounding the city. Hundreds of graves have been found in the area around the city. Kloner, who studied the matter, assumed, and rightly so, that the area in which the necropolis was so dense represented the region which belonged to the residents of the city (Kloner 1980, pp. 25 ff., and Figure 5). The area of the Jerusalem necropolis was approximately 36 sq. km (about 4 sq. km of this area was used for the building purposes of the city and its suburbs). An agricultural region of this size could hardly support the 13,000 or so families who lived in the city and the surrounding region. Only 3,000 or so families could be supported in an area whose size was 36 sq. km (or only about 25 per cent of the population of Jerusalem).

Jerusalem at the end of the Second Temple period was certainly unique in size and wealth. Many of its inhabitants undoubtedly engaged in Temple-related occupations, possibly as priests, or in administration as officials of the Herodian house. Many others engaged in trade or commerce including the supplying of food and sacrifices to those pilgrims coming to Jerusalem. Josephus states that there were 18,000 workers on the Temple Mount and Temple from the time of Herod until the time of Agrippa II, or in other words during the course of seventy years (*Ant.* 20. 219). The number is probably exaggerated, but does indicate that there were many residents in the city who had nothing to do with agriculture.

It is known that Jerusalem served as a social, national and religious centre, housing the central and only Jewish sanctuary, to which pilgrimages were made from throughout Palestine and the Jewish world (S. Safrai 1965). All the central political events were held in Jerusalem. The leaders of all the cults came to this city and considered it the central sphere of their activity (the pilgrimage of Jesus from the Galilee to Jerusalem was only one example of many). Jerusalem's elite led the Jewish masses in Palestine and the chief rabbis also worked in this city; this is all well-known and clear information (Schürer 1973, pp. 199 ff.). Jerusalem was a centre for its surrounding area in the economic sphere as well. Halachic sources reveal that all the agricultural produce in the Judaean district within one day's walk of Jerusalem was purified and sent to the markets of Jerusalem and the temple (M Hagiga 3:3–4).

Another halachic reference deals with the laws of second tithing. In the third and sixth years (in the seven-year cycle, in which the land is left fallow in the last year), the farmer was obligated to set aside a percentage of the harvest and to eat it in Jerusalem, in purity. If the produce was located further than one day's walk from Jerusalem, it was permitted to sell it, and bring the money to the city, while those who were close to the city had to bring the produce itself. This was in order "to adorn the markets of Jerusalem with fruits" (M Ma'aser Sheni V:2). We do not know what percentage of the Jews observed the tithing rules, but a great deal of agricultural produce was sent to Jerusalem in those days. Most donations and tithings were brought to Jerusalem even though by law they could be presented to any priest in Palestine. In the time of the Hasmoneans this was even formally legalized (Oppenheimer 1968). The leaders of Jerusalem were evidently responsible for the collection of money from the surrounding territory. Josephus, who tells us this, does not report from which territory taxes were collected. Was it from the district of Judaea? From the area surrounding the city? Or, perhaps, from the entire country? At any rate, the role of the city leadership and members of the boule in the tax collection network is clearly documented (*BJ* II 405).

Thus we derive an overall picture of the city as a magnet not only for pilgrims, but also for agricultural produce from the entire district of Judaea. It can be assumed that the agricultural products were followed by luxury items as well. Some of these, such as pepper (Echa Raba I.2), which was rare and expensive, are mentioned in the texts.

In the Roman Empire, the different national elites were located in cities. In the rural sector almost no elites developed. Members of rural families who became important found their way quickly to the large cities, and only there did they develop. In Judaea at the end of the period of the Second Temple the situation was slightly different. In Palestine members of respected families from different parts of the country had important positions. Thus, for instance, among the high priests were people from Sepphoris (Schürer 1979, p. 228) and Joshua of Gamla was from Gamla in the Golan Heights (T Shabat 2:5 and more). One of the leaders of the rabbis was Yohanan Ben Zakai, who worked in Gabara in the Galilee (PT Shabat VII, 15d) and other rabbis came from rural settlements, such as Rabbi Dustayi of the village of Yatma (M Orlah 2:5), Rabbi Tzadok of Tivon, Rabbi Yonatan of the Horan and Rabbi Eliezer from the area of Lod. All these rabbis moved to Jerusalem and evidently lived there permanently.

Some members of the council of Jerusalem were residents of the rural sector. The scribe of the council was from Emmaus (*BJ* V. 5.32), and Joseph who redeemed the body of Jesus was from Arimathea, a village in the area of Lod (Luke 23.50 and cf. Matt. 27.57; Mark 15.43). Another council member was from Sakhnin, and was called the man of "etza," which in Hebrew means "council"; according to the *midrash* he dealt with digging water-holes (Kohelet Raba IV, 12). Another Galilean council member may have been Nakadimon Ben Gurion, known from the stories of Jesus as "Bulutes" (member of the boule, Echa Raba I.31 but this term does not appear in the parallel in BT Gitin), and he or his family lived in the village of Ruma in the Galilee (T Eruvin 3:15; BT ibid. 51b).

Thus this partial list includes local leaders who became powerful in their birthplace but moved (partially?) to Jerusalem and worked in the central city. It seems that this period was one of transition, with migration of members of the elite from the rural sector to the central city. This is another aspect of the centrality of the city in the socioeconomic fabric.

The centrality of Jerusalem also aroused the animosity of the local leadership of the villages. Despite its great holiness, the admiration and honor given it, the leaders of villages such as Bethther did not refrain from rejoicing in the destruction of Jerusalem, and from bearing a grudge against the aloof leaders of Jerusalem (PT Taanit IV, 69a).

To sum up, Jerusalem fits the accepted model of relations between city and village in the Roman Empire. The wealthy members of the city owned land and estates in the area of the city and throughout Palestine and the residents of the region sent consumer products to the city and worked there as laborers and service providers.

VI.3.2 City–village relations after the destruction

With the destruction of Jerusalem, the city of course ceased to serve as a social and economic centre. Its religious sanctity and its appreciation grew, but this had no economic consequence. Despite the tremendous wealth of sources dealing with social and economic life, we have no evidence of a "normal" city–village relationship in Palestine. As we saw in the field of employment, there was great similarity between the city and the village. The city produced a large part of its own agricultural needs, and industrial products were produced in both the city and the village. For instance, manufacturers of ceramics in Kefar Hananiah and Sihin supplied vessels to their area, including the city of Sepphoris, and we have already discussed the widespread industry in the rural sector. In the city, of course, trade was much more developed, and the network of services was also much more developed (Chapter 1.II.3 above). There is no evidence, however, that the rural residents were dependent on a day-to-day basis on the city's network of services and trade, as there were also artisans and shops in the rural villages.

As shown, trade was not conducted directly between the city and village, but by means of the donkey caravan (Chapter 3.III.2; V.2 above). The caravan set out from the city and was loaded there and also brought surplus from the rural sector to the city, but this is not sufficient to constitute a regular city–village relationship.

Of all the sources available to us only a few pieces of evidence indicate direct trade between the city and surrounding villages. Above we summarized the little information available that deals with this (Chapter 3.III above). These are the only explicit pieces of evidence of "normal" city–village relations and of a direct tie between the rural masses and the market in the city. Needless to say, the cities were the commercial centres in Palestine, but because of the power of the rural sector, the common relationship of dependency did not emerge in city–village relations here. Perhaps the social tension between the Hellenized population and the autochthonic inhabitants of the rural sector also contributed to the detachment between the economy of the *polis* and that of the village. It seems, though, that the effect of the cultural and social gap was secondary, and it is difficult to believe that this determined the economic structure in the province. This summary statement requires detailed study, which is beyond the scope of the present work.

VII. THE BALANCE OF TRADE

VII.1 Methodological problems

The ancient sources contain many traditions regarding both the importing and exporting of goods. A number of important scholars have also compiled at least partial lists of the traditions (Heichelheim 1970; Avi-Yonah 1958; Sperber 1976). A list of such products, however, does not provide a reliable economic picture of the balance of trade in Judaea during the Roman period for a number of reasons which we shall now discuss.

(1) Knowing that a product was imported or exported does not tell us the extent of the phenomenon. It is impossible to know from a single literary reference whether this was a common occurrence, and the entire supply of the product was either exported or imported, depending upon the context, or whether the literary tradition simply reflects a single episode. It is also possible that the literary tradition reflects only one branch or type of the product and not the commonly accepted one. Moreover, it is impossible to know whether such a tradition represents general conditions in the Land of Israel or conditions in an unusual year such as during a famine.

(2) The mentioning of the importing or exporting of a product in ancient

literature in general and particularly in Talmudic literature is for the most part only a matter of coincidence. Talmudic literature was not composed for the purpose of imparting economic information, but rather to record *halachot*. Therefore, Talmudic literature does not have many references to the importing of ivory and metals such as silver and gold (and as we know, there were no quarries of such metals in the Land of Israel). Talmudic literature, though, does mention the importing of cheeses to the Land of Israel and particularly cheese from "Beth Uniyaki", apparently from Bithynia in northern Asia Minor (M Avodah Zarah 2:4; T Avodah Zarah 4(5):13 *et al.*). The importing of cheese to the Land of Israel had undoubtedly only minimal economic importance, but since there were many halachic problems involved regarding whether these cheeses could be eaten or not, the matter was mentioned quite often. The importing of precious metals was undoubtedly much more important, but since no halachic issues were involved, the matter was not discussed in Talmudic literature.

This methodological problem does not exist to the same extent in the Roman sources or in archeological remains. Archeological material is of great importance for this matter and it is necessary, therefore, to utilize this type of source material to the greatest extent possible.

(3) A number of *halachot* had a good deal of influence on importing and exporting. As a result of this, there is often a plethora of information on the particular product involved, as we mentioned above. This also resulted occasionally in the fact that certain products were exported from the Land of Israel or imported to that province even though there was no economic justification for it. It is possible to furnish a number of prominent examples of the importation of sanctified objects to the Land of Israel. According to the *halachah*, there is no obligation to set aside heave offerings and tithes outside the Land of Israel. However, individual Jews as well as entire communities of Jews abroad often were quite stringent in their observance of these non-obligatory matters. The heave offerings and tithes naturally were sent quite often to the Land of Israel since it was the center of Jewish life, whether formal halachic distinctions required this or not. Moreover, technically, according to halachic understanding, heave offerings could be eaten only in the Land of Israel, since one could eat them only in a state of ritual purity, and any land outside the Land of Israel was by its very nature defiled. Also, the second tithe could be eaten only in Jerusalem. There are even cases recorded in which heave offerings were brought to the Land of Israel in spite of the fact that the sages may have forbidden this (on the importing of heave offerings see M Sheviit 6:6; T Sheviit 5:2 *et al.*; Beer 1974, pp. 350 ff.). On the importing of the firstborn to the Land of Israel, see · T Sanhedrin 3:5). There is also specific reference to the setting aside of the poor man's tithe in Egypt during the Sabbatical Year for the express purpose of supporting the poor of the Land of Israel, as well as to the setting aside of the second tithe in Babylonia during the Sabbatical Year for the support of

the indigent in Israel. The same traditions also discuss which tithe was to be set aside in Ammon and Moab (M Yadayim 4:3 and parallels).

All of this leads to the conclusion that some of the import items mentioned in the sources were sanctified produce being imported to the Land of Israel, and these were not connected to regular trade and commerce.

(4) It is not always possible to differentiate between imported produce and a particular type or local variety which was simply named after a foreign country. Thus, for example, Egyptian *ful* is mentioned many times in the sources as growing in the Land of Israel (see, for example, PT Sheviit II, 34b). This is also the case regarding Egyptian lentils (M Maasrot 5:8 and many parallels). Both of these were mentioned among the produce from which tithes had to be set aside, and as is well known, tithe had to be given only from crops grown in the Land of Israel.

In spite of all this, there is still a great deal of importance in the very act of gathering this material and analyzing it in the light of the methodological problems mentioned above.

VII.2 Imports

VII.2.1

The most detailed list of imported products to the Land of Israel has been prepared by Sperber (1976). The list actually only relates to those products or goods imported from Egypt, but since most imported goods to the Land of Israel came from that country, his list more or less serves our purposes. Sperber points out that except for an isolated instance during the Second Temple period, there is no proof that wheat was imported from Egypt. During our discussion of this crop (Chapter 2.I.2 above), we saw that there was massive importing of wheat to the Land of Israel during the third century CE, although it is not clear from where the wheat was brought.

M Hallah 2:1 provides some testimony to the importing of wheat to the Land of Israel. The Mishnah states: "Produce from outside the Land of Israel which had been brought into the Land of Israel is liable to hallah [the priest's share of the dough]. If it had been taken out from here [Land of Israel] to there [outside the Land of Israel], R. Eliezer declares it liable and R. Akiva exempts it." The "produce" mentioned in the mishnah is obviously grain, since only grain is liable to hallah. This source then coincidentally records the importing and exporting of grain to the Land of Israel as early as the second century CE, when the sages quoted in the mishnah lived. Another source recorded three times in the Palestinian Talmud mentions "Median wheat" from Media (PT Shabbat VII, 9d; IX, 12b; XII, 13c). The last source cited indicates that it relates to a Babylonian Tannaitic tradition (cited in the form of "it was taught there" = Babylonia) and it is likely, therefore, that the entire matter pertains to Babylonia since it is inconceivable that grain would have been imported all the way from far-off Media to the Land of Israel.

Oil and wine were apparently imported to the Land of Israel on a rather infrequent basis. Testimonies to the importing of apples, fish (*garum*) and wine from Italy have been found in the palace of Herod in Masada (Cotton and Geiger 1989, pp. 148, 177). The *halachah* does forbid the drinking of non-Jewish wine, but finding such "luxury" imported wine in Herod's palace should not be too surprising.

Talmudic literature mentions a number of times "a quarter measure of Italian wine" and the Babylonian Talmud states that this wine was apparently exceedingly strong (BT Eruvin 64b). This explanation, however, is not correct. Lieberman has already shown that most of the references to a quarter measure of Italian wine should really read "a quarter litra of wine in the Italian measure" and the reference, therefore, is to a weight and not to a type of wine (Lieberman 1988, T Ki-Fshutah IV, p. 499). Indeed, Talmudic tradition also mentions an Italian *issar* (see, for example, M Kiddushin 1:1; PT Kiddushin I, 58d and many parallels), an Italian *pondion* (pound) (M Kelim 17:12 and parallels), an Italian *maneh* (M Sheviit 1:2–3 and parallels), and the Mishnah even mentions in general that regarding the Temple, liquid and dry measures are Italian measures (M Kelim 17:11). Also, one who was obligated to provide food for his wife had to do so according to the "Italian measure" (T Ketubbot 5:8). A number of weights found in the Land of Israel have inscriptions explicitly mentioning an "Italian litra" written on them (see, for example, Qedar 1983, p. 36).

Moreover, "Italian" wine is described as a regular type of wine and according to this measure, many normal and commonly accepted ones were established, such as how much wine it is necessary to drink on the evening of the Passover *seder*, or how much wine makes one officially drunk in relation to a number of laws. It is highly unlikely that these laws and measures would have been established in relation to an expensive imported wine and it would appear that the examples cited above reflect normal and everyday usage. Talmudic tradition does not refer at all to the importing of wine from Italy, but rather to Roman measures of weight and volume. Talmudic tradition does refer to the importing of wine from Cilicia (T Sheviit 5:2; PT Hallah IV, 60b). This, however, refers to one who brought a heave-offering from abroad, even though according to Jewish law a heave-offering did not have to be brought from outside the Land of Israel. Thus, this does not reflect the importing of wine on a regular basis.

Cyprian wine is also mentioned (PT Yoma IV, 41d; BT Keritoth 6a). The last instance, however, may refer to the fruit of the capparis which is also called "Cyprus" and which may have been used to flavor local wine (Feliks 1968, p. 132). Talmudic literature also mentions Ethiopian wine (*Hebrew*: *Kushi* = dark or black), but the phrase may just refer to dark wine and not necessarily to wine from Ethiopia. Talmudic literature also mentions the importing of apple wine by ship (T Avodah Zarah 4(5):12) and it appears that the law which discusses the buying of wine in Syria also refers to the importing of wine from Syria to the Land of Israel (T Avodah Zarah 4(5):13). A Byzantine source tells of many wine merchants from Egypt found in Maioumas Gaza (the port city of Gaza) during the fifth century CE who were active in the many religious struggles taking place in that city and in the general area (*Vita Porphyrii* 58), although it is not clear whether they were engaged in the importing or exporting of wine.

Talmudic tradition also tells of a shipment of raisins brought to Tiberias in the Galilee (PT Demai II, 22d; PT Nedarim VIII, 41a). The *Amoraim* disagree as to whether the shipment had been imported or not (thus in the version of MS. Vat. on PT Demai). It is important to remember, though, that the source does refer to the Galilee which did not produce much in the way of grapes (Chapter 4.V.3 above).

Byzantine traditions provide more information regarding the importing of wine to Palestine. Thus, for example, in the collection of Byzantine Christian questions and answers (Barsanuphias and Ioannes, Biblios, paragraph 835), one of the leaders of the Church complains that government officials wish to levy taxes on wine brought in through one of the harbors belonging to the church.

It is also possible to learn about the extent to which wine was imported to the Land of Israel from the vast number of imported amphorae found in various excavations in the Land of Israel and which were undoubtedly used for wine. There are no final or official figures on this matter, but it is quite clear that imported amphorae have been discovered at many sites. Important information on five Palestinian sites have been collected by Grace (Grace 1962). Thirty-eight amphorae have been discovered in Nessana in the Negev, a Byzantine military-agricultural settlement, and 33 have been found in the important *polis* of Scythopolis. In Gezer, which served as a center of government during the Hellenistic period, 653 amphorae have been discovered while 308 have been found in the Idumean *polis* of Maresha. In the important Hellenistic–Roman *polis* of Samaria 2,077 amphorae were found. For the sake of comparison, though, it is worthwhile to mention that 53,362 such amphorae were found in Alexandria. Approximately 10 per cent of the amphorae discovered at the sites mentioned above were imported. This, of course, indicates that there was wine imported to the Land of Israel, but does not provide a statistical framework as to the extent of the phenomenon or as to whether the phenomenon took place in the rural sphere.

It is difficult to determine whether the minimal amount of imported wine was the result of religious factors or perhaps may have been the result of economic conditions, since after all, the Land of Israel produced wine itself and was basically self-sufficient. At any event, most of the few references which do relate to the small amount of imported wine refer to non-Jewish settlements, and it would therefore appear that the religious factor was rather important in limiting the importing of wine to the Land of Israel.

There was also some exporting of wine from the Land of Israel (see pp. 394ff. below). Thus, it would appear that the wine imported to the Land of Israel was for those who would style themselves connoisseurs. It is also possible that government or military officials preferred wine more familiar to their palates than the local varieties, as was the case regarding the Roman military who continued to maintain Roman customs regarding the eating of meat even when stationed in Britain (King 1984).

VII.2.2

Preserved or pickled fish were also imported to the Land of Israel in one form or another. As we have already seen, the fishing industry was of extreme importance in the Land of Israel in general and in the Sea of Galilee region in particular (Strabo 16. 2, 45 and other sources – see also Chapter 1.I.8 above). Despite this, most local requirements in terms of the consumption of fish were supplied from abroad. The sages stated, therefore, that a "preserved" fish in general was probably imported (see also below). The Mishnah (Avodah Zarah 2:4 *et al.*), for instance, specifically mentions non-Jewish fish brine. Talmudic literature also tells of a shipment of fish brine which came from very far away (T Avodah Zarah 4(5):11; BT Avodah Zarah 39b). BT Avodah Zarah 34b relates a tale of fish brine brought to the Land of Israel from "Aspamea" to Acco. In Talmudic literature, "Aspamea" is often Spain, but occasionally should be understood as Apamea in Syria. According to the account there in BT Avodah Zarah, the fish arrived at Tyre from a region in which wine was more expensive than fish. Accordingly there was a degree of fear that at Tyre the fish underwent some type of additional procedure involving wine. All of this lends credence to the theory that Aspamea of the Talmud was in this case Apamea, since wine was quite cheap in Spain and Tyre was certainly not on the route from Spain to the Land of Israel.

Aspamea is mentioned by the rabbis as a place in which there is much fish brine to be found, and Acco is described in rabbinic literature as a city in which fish is even more plentiful (Exodus Rabbah 9:4). Another source mentions in particular the fish of Acco, Sidon and Aspamea (Genesis Rabbah 5:8, p. 38). It is likely that the rabbis would not have mentioned these cities if they were not major sites of the fishing industry.

Fish brine in general was considered to be of non-Jewish origin (T Avodah Zarah 4(5):13) – the parallel Mishnah (Avodah Zarah 2:4) deals only with fish brine specifically bought from a non-Jew. R. Abahu, a sage living in Caesarea in the fourth century CE, decreed that any fish (bought in that city?) was probably from Aspamea or Pelusa (BT Avoda Zara 34a). Pelusa is Pelusium, the port on Lake Bardewil in northern Sinai which was especially rich in fish. Talmudic tradition also relates that R. Judah the Prince (third century CE) imported more than three hundred barrels of fish (PT Avoda Zara II, 42a). Another type of imported fish was the Spanish tunny fish (M Shabbat 22:2; M Makhshirin 6:3). The Mishnah in Makhshirin (6:3) also mentions a fish from Egypt packed in baskets. Indeed, the fish of the Nile were famous throughout the entire East and remains of such fish have been found in other countries in this part of the Empire (Reese *et al.* 1986).

Thus, imported fish were apparently quite important in the fish industry and markets, and even in the coastal settlements a majority of the fish at the market was imported.

VII.2.3 Vegetables and gourds of the cucurbitaceae *family*

There are many laws which indicate that vegetables were imported. Thus, for example, there is a dispute between R. Eliezer and the sages (100–25 CE) regarding the status of dirt "which came on vegetables" (T Ahilot 17:6), which reflects the fact that the vegetables are imported. Other traditions refer to the importing of vegetables during the Sabbatical Year (T Sheviit 4:16, 18, 19; BT Nedarim 53b), but as we have already seen, such laws deal with a year and situation which were the exception to the rule and not the rule itself.

Talmudic sources mention such vegetables as Egyptian mustard (M Qilayim 1:2 and parallels); the Egyptian gourd (as, for example, BT Pesahim 39a; PT Qilayim I, 27a); the Egyptian lichen (BT Bechorot 49a); the Aramean gourd (BT Nedarim 21a; PT Qilayim 1, 27a *et al.*); the Greek gourd (PT Qilayim 1, 27a *et al.*) and the Greek and Roman hyssop (BT Sukkah 13a; M Negaim 14:6). There is, of course, no certainty that all of these were imported, and some of them indeed were grown in the Land of Israel. Many of the species mentioned above appear in Talmudic literature in regard to the laws of Qilayim or mixed kinds, and these laws theoretically pertain also to lands outside Israel. It is difficult to assume, however, that the rabbis would have gone into so much detail regarding mixed kinds *vis-à-vis* these vegetables if they were not commonly cultivated on the local scene.

There is more clear-cut information regarding onion and garlic. M Maasrot 5:8 mentions the "garlic of Baalbek" (Heliopolis in northern Syria) and the "onion of Richfa (or Dichfa)", perhaps Raphanah in Syria, together with "large beans of Cilicia" and "Egyptian lentils" as produce which grew semi-wild in the Land of Israel, and were therefore not too important. However, these crops are also mentioned in PT Demai II, 22b and in the course of the discussion regarding them two views are cited. One is that they are indeed imported from abroad to the Land of Israel, and only similar species are cultivated in Israel, while the other view is that they are actually cultivated in Israel and exported abroad, where they are not cultivated. In any case, these species are named after a geographical entity related to them in some form or fashion and are described in T Maasrot 3:15 and PT Maasrot V, 52a. Their name would seem to imply, though, that they did originate abroad and not in the Land of Israel, and it is therefore difficult to claim that they were not cultivated abroad. Thus, these species were imported. It would also seem, though, that they were cultivated in Israel, or grew semi-wild, and that the majority of produce of these species in the Land of Israel was grown locally. In any case, though, they probably were not of much importance.

The "Cilician bean" is mentioned in other sources (M Kelim 17:12; M Negaim 6:1 and parallels). The bean is used to illustrate or describe a "bright spot on the skin" related to Levitical impurity and the like. This would seem to imply that the species was fairly common in the Land of Israel and was cultivated there. The same is true regarding the Egyptian lentil (M Kelim 17:8). The end result of our discussion, though, is that the importing of these vegetables and the like was a rather negligible phenomenon.

VII.2.4 Legumes

We have already mentioned the importing of legumes from Egypt and Cilicia. Ancient sources also mention Egyptian and Libyan *ful* (PT Shabbat V, 7b; PT Qilayim VIII, 31c; M Kelim 17:8). The latter were the same species and the different names pertained to degrees of wetness (Feliks 1967, p. 44; id. 1980, pp. 153–5). We have also mentioned above that this type of *ful* was grown in the Land of Israel. Another type of *ful* was the Persian *ful* (Feliks 1967, pp. 72–3). An interesting story told by R. Jose relates that once a large shipment of *ful* was brought from abroad to Meiron in the Galilee and R. Akiva (beginning of the second century CE) exempted the entire shipment of *ful* in the marketplace from tithes (T Demai 4:13). From the story it is clear that most *ful* found in the markets in the area was locally grown, and imported *ful* was the exception to the rule. Thus, in spite of the many "foreign" species, there was only a minimal amount of imported *ful* in the Land of Israel.

VII.2.5 Fruits

The Land of Israel was almost entirely self-sufficient in fruit. There were, though, a few fruit products which were imported such as dried figs from Bostra, carobs from Bachiari (?) and dates from Alexandria (PT Demai II, 22a). Although these fruits were imported, there were also similar locally grown fruits. This is of extreme importance, since these types of fruit were apparently of rather high quality, and it is therefore quite significant that they were also grown in the Land of Israel. It should be remembered, though, that transporting dates by sea from Alexandria to Caesarea, for example, was cheaper than transporting them over land from Jericho. Transporting dried figs from Bostra, however, was undoubtedly very expensive. A Tannaitic tradition adds an additional instance of figs imported to the Land of Israel by boat at the beginning of the second century CE (M Avodah Zarah 5:2).

Talmudic literature also mentions a few other imports such as the *'itsarin*, apparently a type of pistachio, the regular pistachio (*'pistakin*) and the fruit of the pine (PT Demai II, 22d). Talmudic literature also mentions Damascene plums (PT Shabbat I, 4a; PT Bezah III, 62a *et al.*). T Demai 1:9 tells of Damascene nuts in Palestine as well as Phaselos *ful* and pistachios which were imported quite often but still cultivated quite frequently in Israel. Thus, the importing of fruits to the Land of Israel was apparently quite limited and for the most part only exotic fruits not cultivated locally were imported, or special products such as apple wine (T Avodah Zarah 4(5):12 and see VII.2.1 above).

VII.2.6 Livestock

There are also only very few traditions attesting to the importing of animals or livestock. The sources mention, for instance, the Libyan and Egyptian donkey (M Qilayim 8:4; PT Qilayim VIII, 31c *et al.*). Even so, the name is not proof that these species were actually imported, and the nomenclature may simply be genetic. A number of traditions attest to the importing of sheep (see, for example, T Bava Kama 8:11), but these traditions for the most part refer to sheep for the Temple such as "rams from Moab" (T Menahot 9:13) and "sheep from Kedar" (PT Hagigah II, 78a; BT Bezah 20b and perhaps also PT Berachot IX, 13c, but this is not certain).

The Lyddan doctor Todos relates an interesting tradition (100–30 CE): "No cow or sow leaves Alexandria before they cut out its womb so that it cannot bear offspring" (M Bechorot 4:4; BT Sanhedrin 93a; BT Bechorot 28b). This tradition describes the exporting of animals from Alexandria, sterilized in order to prevent breeding of superior livestock with local stock. In any case, the source proves that at least some of these animals were imported to the Land of Israel, since this is the only way in which the phenomenon would have been familiar to the Lyddan doctor. However, it should be remembered that the testimony of the doctor here is "professional" as an expert witness, in an attempt to show that R. Tarfon, who claimed earlier in the Mishnah that an animal could not live if its womb was cut out, was incorrect. R. Tarfon was the owner of a number of estates and if the phenomenon described above pertaining to Alexandria were so prevalent, then R. Tarfon would have been familiar with it. Moreover, it is difficult to believe that the womb was completely cut out in Alexandria and it is likely that the procedure was somewhat more simple. Todos's statement, therefore, is probably exaggerated and does not derive from first-hand knowledge. It can be of little help, then, in determining the situation in the Land of Israel, and provides no proof regarding the importing of livestock from Egypt.

All of the above would seem to prove that the importation of livestock to the Land of Israel took place to a rather limited extent.

VII.2.7 Clothing

As we have seen above, the Land of Israel was a center for the production of linen clothing during the second century CE (Chapter 2.1.6 above). In spite of this, the sources record many instances of the importing of clothing. The Mishnah in Qilayim, for instance, mentions a number of imported products (9:7): "Dalmatian undergarments," "shoes from Pinon (?)," "Bera and Brundisian cloaks" (which were obviously imported). PT Qilayim *ad loc.* (IX, 32d) adds a number of other types of clothing and explains that the law is reflecting the situation during the Usha period (140–89 CE – the time of R. Jose mentioned in the Mishnah). PT then explains that the situation "today" regarding these articles of clothing is different, proving that these types of clothing were still common in the Land of Israel and still, most likely, imported. BT Bava Mezia 29b also mentions "Roman cotton," which was very expensive and very fragile, maybe only in Babylonia.

Superior quality linen was imported to the Land of Israel. The Mishnah mentions, for instance, *"pilusin,"* which was linen imported from Pelusium and *"hinduyin,"* linen which came from India (M Yoma 3:7). This Mishnah refers to the garments of the High Priest and reflects, therefore, the reality of the end of the Second Temple period before flax began to be cultivated and produced in great quantities in the Land of Israel.

As we have already stated above (Chapter 2.1.6), the production of silk in the Land of Israel was a rather limited affair. The large number of traditions regarding the silk trade, therefore, and especially with Tyre (Genesis Rabbah 77:2, pp. 910–11), reflect the importing of silk to Israel and connection of the local merchants and traders with the international silk trade. One of the types of silk, the *"kalach"* is called *"cissaros* of Caesarea" (PT Qilayim IX, 32a), indicating, most likely, that it was imported to Palestine via Caesarea. When the sages had a problem with the term *"kalach,"* they sought the aid of sailors (PT Qilayim ibid.), assuming that they would be familiar with the meaning of the terms relating to the different types of silk.

Imported shoes, such as the Laodicean sandal, are also mentioned in Talmudic literature (M Kelim 26:1). Talmudic tradition also tells of the buying of sandals from Tyre (PT Avodah Zarah I, 39d), although this tradition does not reflect the importing of sandals from Tyre, but rather a single merchant who visited the fair there and was buying products for everyday use.

VII.2.8 Metals, glass, pottery, wood and salt

VII.2.8.1 Metals, stone and glass

The Land of Israel is quite poor in natural metals, and therefore metal implements had for the most part to be imported. There are indeed few literary traditions pertaining to this, but it is clear that there was no substitute source for such metals as gold, silver, tin and copper. A number of sources do seem to indicate that metal "junk" was occasionally imported as a source of raw material (T Kelim Bava Mezia 1:3). Tin was imported from the British Isles and was called "*kasteron*" in Talmudic literature after the Kasteron Islands (T Kelim Bava Mezia 1:8; Y. Brand 1953, p. 234). Silver goblets were imported from Seleucia in Babylonia (BT Bava Mezia 84a and parallels. It is difficult to determine whether the tradition reflects the reality of the Land of Israel or of Babylonia). It is also necessary to mention imported marble (*marmeron* in Aramaic because most of the marble was brought from the Marmara Sea), remains of which have been discovered in the excavations of houses of the wealthy or of public buildings (Fischer 1988; Russo 1987). Marble was also imported to Palestine to build a church in Gaza during the time of Bishop Porphyrius (*Vita Porphyrii* 84–5).

Imported glassware has been discovered in many excavations, although there has yet to be a work collecting and analyzing the relevant material. We can only state, therefore, that the phenomenon existed.

VII.2.8.2 Pottery and glass

There is some data regarding the importing of pottery to the Land of Israel, but this subject has also not been sufficiently examined. The relevant material has already been discussed above (Chapter 2.II.2) and we saw that a good deal of imported pottery has been found in the various excavations throughout the Land of Israel. Imported wares have been found in remains from the first century CE, at least until 70 CE and the end of the Second Temple period. It is not clear, however, whether the utensil itself was imported or only the raw material, and the pottery itself was made locally.

Imported wares have also been found in remains from the third century CE (Hayes 1972, maps 7–12; 27; 1980; Riley unknown date, pp. 106 ff). There are, however, not many remains of imported wares from the Tannaitic period (70–250 CE). However, in a few excavations, imported wares have been discovered from the first and second centuries CE, such as in Caesarea (Levine and Netzer 1986, pp. 161 ff.). The remains of imported pottery up to the year 70 have been discovered for the most part in excavations of cities or administrative centers. The material from later times (see above) has also been found in excavations undertaken in villages or in the rural sphere and at such sites as Capernaum, Nazareth, Sumaka and others both on the coast and in inland settlements. There is, however, no statistical data which would enable us to evaluate how much pottery was imported, and this of course limits our ability to provide a complete economic picture. According to S. Dar, the excavator of Sumaka (a village settlement in the Upper Carmel about 20 km from the coast), about 80 per cent of the pottery wares discovered there were imported (not yet published). We shall be able to evaluate the matter further only when we have such data from other sites. The imported wares are for the most part delicate serving utensils and food dishes. More simple utensils and the like were clearly provided by local artisans. Imported wares were also often utensils needed for specific purposes such as imported dishes for pounding and crushing, which have been found in a number of Late Roman sites (Ysraeli 1970; Ben Arieh 1974). Other vessels were "imported" only because they were used for storing something of importance such as the amphorae used to store imported wine which we have discussed above. In such cases, the pottery was clearly only of secondary importance. Talmudic literature mentions the importing of pottery wares only coincidentally in regard to the laws of ritual purity: "If one brings chests and ovens and cups and pottery from abroad . . . they are ritually impure." This seems to imply that this was a fairly common phenomenon.

The source just cited, however, is one of the few references to the importing of pottery or glassware. Tannaitic and Amoraic literature has, for the most part, little to say on the matter. Most of the wares mentioned are Semitic in origin, and this would seem to imply that the local Jewish market satisfied most needs in this area. There are a few specific types of pottery or glass whose names seem to reflect the fact that they were imported, such as "Alexandrian cups" (BT Menahot 28b) and the Sidonian "*kyzin*" or "*kysom,*" which were perhaps identical with the famous Sidonian glass cups mentioned in a few sources (Y. Brand 1953, pp. 210–15).

It is difficult to know why there was only limited importation of pottery wares to the Land of Israel during the Tannaitic period. Perhaps this phenomenon reflects an economic decline (drop in buying power) or the exact opposite, that the local producers were on such a high professional level that they could provide all local needs, and there was therefore no need to import such wares. It is also important to remember the halachic aspect of this matter: imported pottery wares, as well as imported glass wares, were considered to be ritually impure and could not be purified. In spite of the fact that the majority of the population in the Land of Israel were "*Amei Ha-Aretz*" who were not very particular about the laws of ritual purity, there still were a good many "*Haverim*" who were, and it is likely that even some of the "*Amei Ha-Aretz*" were particular about such matters. It is very possible, therefore, that this halachic dimension prevented any large-scale importing of pottery and glassware.

VII.2.8.3 Wood

The Land of Israel was not particularly known for its tall trees, and it was therefore necessary to import wood required for building purposes, and especially cedars of Lebanon which were long enough to serve as beams for roofing. An inscription mentions two wood merchants in Byzantine Gaza (Ovadiah 1968), and although it is impossible to prove, it is likely that these two merchants engaged in the importing of wood. A discussion of the architecture of the Land of Israel is beyond the purview of our study, but it is clear that using wooden beams or planks for roofing was not very common, most likely due to the scarcity of appropriate wood. The transport of wood suitable for construction purposes was also very expensive, since the beams were approximately 5–6 meters in length and weighed hundreds of kilograms apiece, more than the average wagon could handle. It is likely, therefore, that there was not much large-scale importing of wood to the Land of Israel.

VII.2.8.4 Salt

Salt was another raw commodity imported to the Land of Israel. As we saw above (Chapter 2.1.10), part of the salt requirement of the Land of Israel had to be imported, and one of the main sources of this salt was Ostarkine or Sabkhat el Bardawil in northern Sinai. According to Dar (1980), the settlements along the coast of the northern Sinai were meant to serve as road stations for the salt trade. These settlements are known from literary sources as well as from archeological surveys (Oren 1980, pp. 123–51). Most of the salt was probably transported in boats and the settlements were most likely supposed to provide port services. On the other hand, the salt may not have been transported by boats due to the fear of damage to the salt from the sea water. It is also important to point out that there is really no proof that these coastal settlements serviced the salt trade and they may have been part of trade routes in general, or were perhaps connected with the fishermen plying the coast of northern Sinai whom we have mentioned above (VII.2.2).

VII.2.9 Miscellaneous

A number of other imported products are mentioned in the sources, such as oak (*Quercus suber*) bark from which it was possible to make shoes that was brought via Susita to Tiberias (PT Sheviit VIII, 38a; Feliks 1987, pp. 176–7). "Egyptian" rope (M Sotah 1:6) is also mentioned, but it is impossible to determine whether this was actually imported or whether it was simply the name of a local rope. As we remember, this has been a problem in other similar instances. Cumin from Cyprus is also mentioned (PT Demai II, 22b), as well as peppers (PT Avodah Zarah I, 39d), pearls (Krauss 1910, I, pp.

659–60), Babylonian sour-milk bread porridge, Egyptian and Median beer (M Pesahim 3:1; PT Pesahim III, 29d), scribe's glue (Greek: *kolla*) from Alexandria (PT Pesahim III, 29d and on *kolla* see Sperber 1976), Alexandrian soap (Hebrew: *neter*, BT Shabbat 90a and parallels), an Egyptian straw strainer (M Kelim 26:1; M Shabbat 20:2; Y. Brand 1953, pp. 319–20), and Bithynian cheese (M Avodah Zarah 2:4 and parallels).

All in all then, the list of imported products is not that long and they are certainly of secondary importance. Thus, the example that the Mishnah brings when it discusses imported fruit which are, by nature, different from those indigenous to the Land of Israel, is the bark of the oak mentioned above (*Quercus suber*) which was used for making shoes (PT Sheviit VIII, 38a; Feliks 1987, p. 177). If this is the example brought of fruit imported to Israel during the Sabbatical Year, then the importing of fruit must not have been a very large-scale phenomenon. Additional traditions regarding imports are phrased in somewhat more general language as, for example, the following in T Terumot 2:13: "A boat which came from abroad and had fruits etc." As we just stated, the law is quite general and there is also the possibility that it does not describe a real situation and, at best, cannot be considered to reflect a common or widespread reality. A more realistic tradition is found in PT Demai II, 22c regarding a question of R. Jonah: "A boat which came from Rome, how many types of produce does it contain etc?" The question *per se* is halachic and does not really concern us.

An interesting tradition on the matter is found in T Demai 1:11. According to this Tannaitic tradition, the majority of produce which reached the ports of Caesarea and Joppa came from the Land of Israel. This would seem to reflect the limited extent of imported produce at this time.

Thus, once again we can state that those goods imported to the Land of Israel were not of great economic significance. The most commonly imported product from the third century onwards was grain. Metals and luxury items (and the like) were also commonly imported.

VII.3 Exports

We have already discussed most of those products or produce which was exported in the course of our discussion on production (Chapter 2 above). Textiles were among the most important products exported (from the second century CE – see Chapter 2.I.6 above). Oil was also an important product to be exported from the Land of Israel (Chapter 2.I.3 above). We have already seen that the majority of olive groves were intended to produce fruit for the production of exportable oil. There are many sources reflecting the exporting of olive oil and especially to Egypt (Sperber 1976, pp. 142–3). Sifre Deuteronomy 355, p. 421 tells of an oil merchant from Laodicea buying tremendous quantities of oil from Gush Halav in the Galilee. Even if the tradition does exaggerate somewhat, it does reflect basic economic reality. Jerome, in his commentary on Hosea 12:1, tells of large-scale exporting of oil from Samaria to Egypt. The *midrash*, in describing what were supposed to be the relations between Israel and Egypt during the Biblical period, writes: "What did the tribes used to do . . . they used to send oil there and take back grain" (Lamentations Rabbah 5:6, p. 156). The buying of grain reflects the Biblical story of Genesis 42 and following. The selling of oil, however, reflected contemporary Roman-period reality.

Another important export was wine. We have discussed this matter above (Chapter 2.I.3) and there we saw that the majority of vineyards in the Land of Israel were cultivated with export in mind. There are many sources indicating that wine exported from Israel was found in many markets abroad. The *Expositio Orbis Descriptio* (31), describing the cities of the Empire, praises the wine of the Land of Israel. Many wine merchants from Egypt were found in the fourth century CE in Maiumas Gaza, the port city of Gaza (*Vita Porphyrii* 58). The fifth-century Sidonius Apollinaris praises the wine of Gaza (*Carmina* 17. 15–16). Cassiodorus in the sixth century (Marco Aurelii Cassiodorii Variae 12.12) and Corippus (*In Laudem Iustini* 3. 87–8) do the same, and Gregory of Tours also praises the wine of Gaza imported to France (the most important producer of wine in Europe; *Historia Francorum* 7. 29). Moreover, he was not the only one to continue praising this wine (*Vita S. Martini* 20. 80–3; Isidore of Seville, *Etymologiae* 20. 7).

Gaza produced a special kind of amphora. We can assume that in these containers the famous wine from Gaza was exported. These wares were found in the whole east and in the west; 2.5 per cent of the whole ceramic containers in Crimea, 1–2 per cent in Bangazi (Bernice) in north Africa, and 3 per cent in Carthage (Riley 1975, 1981, unknown date). Pottery from Gaza was also found in Caesarea and this would probably indicate that Gazan wine was also sold here, brought to Caesarea in these jugs (Riley 1975, pp. 27–31; Mayerson 1992). We do not have information about fine wares from other Palestinian cities in other provinces of the Roman Empire.

A number of Egyptian sources mention Gazan wine in Egyptian markets (*P.Oxy.* 1929; Johnson and West 1949, p. 148; Sperber 1976; Mayerson 1985; 1992). The wine of Judaea was especially known for its good taste and was quite expensive, as can be learned from the "Life" of John the Alms-Giver (ch. 10 – Dawes and Baynes 1948), a cleric of the seventh century CE. This archbishop refused to use Judaean wine for the agape or holy meal because it was too expensive. The exported wine did not, however, come from the Gaza region but apparently from the Hebron Mountains, an area known for its excellent wine. From there it was exported via Gaza.

The Land of Israel also exported dates, and we have already discussed the matter to some extent (Chapter 2.I.3). It is possible to add some more proofs (Heichelheim 1938, pp. 204 ff.). Balsam and bitumen from the Jericho region were exported especially to Egypt. They were apparently no longer exported after the end of the first century CE (Chapter 2.I.6 above).

It is likely that Jewish law aided the export of fruits and especially of wine and oil. Thus, for instance, the *halachah* states it is forbidden to use wine and oil of gentiles. In the third century the sages became more lenient regarding the use of non-Jewish oil. This encouraged Jews to buy wine and oil from the Land of Israel. A clear expression of this is found in the events of the War of Destruction (66 CE). The *Vita* of Josephus (13; and see also *BJ* 2. 592) tells of the selling of kosher Galilean oil to Caesarea Philippi. The *halachah* mentioned above probably also spurred the export of Jewish wine and oil and probably also accounted for the high price of these commodities in world markets. Oil was also exported from the Land of Israel during the Byzantine period, as can be learned from the small, unique Jewish and Christian oil flasks discovered at various sites throughout the Land of Israel and abroad (Barag 1970, pp. 6 ff.)

Ancient sources mention a number of other export items, but they were, apparently, only of secondary importance. Thus, for example, we hear of cotton from Jericho (Gregory of Tours, *Liber de Gloria Martyrum, PL* 71:721) and onions from Ascalon (Strabo 16, 2, 28; Pliny, *HN* 19. 32. 101–5,107; Stephanus of Byzantium, s.v. Ascalon). An Egyptian papyrus also mentions fish from Gaza (Sperber 1976). It is unlikely, however, that there was much in the way of exported fish from the Land of Israel to Egypt, since most of the fish imported to the Land of Israel came from that country. Thus, it is more likely that this refers to a specific type of fish or a particular vessel which was named after Gaza and which was marketed in Egypt.

Many sources also attest to the fact that slaves were exported from the Land of Israel. T Avodah Zarah 3(4):18 states the law regarding one "who sells his slave abroad" (and see additional laws on this and similar matters in T Kelim Bava Kama 1:5; BT Gittin 8a). A document found in Egypt explicitly mentions a female slave and her daughter from Ono in Judaea sold into slavery in Egypt (*P.Oxy.* 1205). Those who came to redeem her were municipal functionaries from Ono, and it is likely that they came for the specific purpose of freeing their townswoman. The export of slaves from the Land of Israel was probably related to the general export of slaves from most eastern lands to the markets of Rome (Wilken 1884; cf. *P. Oxy* 3054). The revolts in Judaea also facilitated the capture of many high-class and capable potential slaves. It is difficult to determine the economic implications of this trade during peacetime and in any case, as far as the residents of the Land of Israel were concerned, this economic sphere was only a source of aggravation and concern and certainly not a means of economic prosperity.

We have already discussed the export of glassware above (Chapter 2.II). The Land of Israel was an important exporter of glass. Glass blowing was apparently developed in southern Phoenicia and northern Israel, and glass wares produced in this manner were sold throughout the entire world (Barag

1970, pp. 230–77). Most of this export took place in the first century CE. After that production centers developed in Egypt, and therefore the export of glassware to that country was probably severely curtailed (Harden 1936). The export of glass to other countries and regions, such as to Cyprus and Dura Europos, though, continued (Barag ibid.).

Most export from the Land of Israel was, therefore, agricultural (wine, oil, flax, etc.). The Land of Israel also provided tourist services for pilgrims and an opportunity for an eternal resting place for those interested in burial in the Holy Land. It also provided lodging for soldiers serving there, as we have already seen (Chapter 4.II). The list of exported commodities may have been limited, but since these commodities were widely exported, they were of great economic and financial importance for the Empire.

VII.4 The role of external trade in the economy of the Land of Israel

VII.4.1 The size of ships

The capacity of harbors or ports could be of great importance in helping to determine the extent of trade. There were a number of important ports in the Land of Israel such as those in Gaza, Ascalon, Joppa, Dor (?) and Caesarea. There were also a number of smaller ones such as those in Anthedon, Raphia, Azotus Paralius, Javneh-Yam (Jaminiton Limen), Sycaminum (Shikmonah), Haifa and at a number of other sites (see above, Figure 53). Of all of these mentioned above, none has been completely excavated and only the port of Caesarea has been partly excavated (Raban 1989. On the port of Acco which is in Phoenicia, see Raban 1986). The port of Caesarea was rather large, but it is still not clear what its capacity was. The information regarding the other ports or harbors is quite minimal.

Many vessels from many different countries visited the ports and harbors of the Land of Israel. We have already mentioned above a ship from Rome of indeterminate size. Two other types of ships are mentioned in Midrash Psalms 19:11 (pp. 168–9): "R. Berechia said: Like a ship coming from Karkonia [Archemonia] which has three hundred and sixty-five ropes, as many as there are days in the [solar] year, and like a ship which comes from Alexandria which has three hundred and fifty-four ropes, as many as the days in the lunar [year]" (and see also Yalkut Shimoni on Psalms 19:11). The first name – Karkonia – appears in a number of different forms in different manuscripts (Sperber 1986, pp. 44–5). An unusual version which appears in Yalkut Shimoni is "Brittania". The preferred reading is most likely "Karmonia" which is Acarmonia, a western province in Greece or "Karkidonia" which probably represents Chalcedonia. The second ship was from Alexandria. Both ships were apparently quite large as can be learned from the number of ropes. The sources also mention a ship from Sarmantia

(Sarmatia) which had three hundred and sixty-five ropes (Midrash Ha Gadol on Genesis 23:1, pp. 364–5). This apparently was also quite a large ship (Casson 1971, pp. 229–69).

It would be interesting to determine the size of the ships which sailed along the coast of Israel. Jewish traditions record many traditions and much information on this matter (Krauss 1924, I, pp. 187–213; Sperber 1986). Most of the traditions reflect Babylonian reality, but some do reflect or apply to the Land of Israel. The sources, for instance, mention a "large boat" and a "small boat": "And what is a large boat? R. Judah (140–80) says – any such as cannot heel with [the movement of a] person [in it]" (M Zavim 3:3). This means that the boat is large enough so that one would not wobble in it while standing up. Another source gives more exact information. M Oholoth 8:1 (and many parallels) mentions "the water tank of an Alexandrian ship – [tanks] that have [flat] bottoms and which hold at least forty *seah* [= 340 liters]." This amount of water would be sufficient for 28 people on a four-day trip (according to the calculation of three liters per traveller). Once again, the source seems to describe quite a large vessel.

A *baraita* in BT Bava Mezia 80b gives additional information regarding the measurements or size of a boat. According to these measurements, the volume of a regular ship was 30 *kur* or 7.686 cubic meters, while that of a "*burni*" or Liburna was 23 cubic meters. These then were rather small vessels. The *baraita*, however, appears only in the Babylonian Talmud. In the Palestinian parallels the version is "a ship in whatever form" (T Bava Mezia 7:10; PT Bava Mezia VI, 11a). This leads to the conclusion that the 7.7 or so cubic meters mentioned above represents only Babylonia. The Babylonians lived along the banks of the Tigris and the Euphrates, and since these rivers served, for the most part, for internal or local travel, the ships that plied those waters were appropriate for that type of travel and not very large. In spite of the fact that the tradition regarding the cubic metrage of the vessels described above is from a *baraita* and introduced with the formula "our rabbis taught" (*tannu rabbanan*), it is possible that the *baraita* is of Babylonian origin, since, as we have seen, the situation in the Land of Israel was different.

To all intents and purposes, therefore, it is impossible to determine exact measurements or size regarding the ships which frequented the ports and harbors of the Land of Israel. This, then, cannot serve as an additional means of estimating the extent of foreign trade.

VII.4.2 Trade with neighboring provinces

The sum total of imported and exported items mentioned in literary traditions is not very great. As we have seen above, most of the imported items mentioned in the sources were not of much economic importance. As we have stated, though, in any case at the beginning of this chapter, a list of such items, whether imported or exported, cannot provide an estimate of the foreign or external trade of the Land of Israel. The lists we have studied do, however, show a rather close commercial relationship with Egypt. Most of the imported items are Egyptian and the more important exported goods, such as textiles, wine and oil, were sent from Judaea to Egypt. Theoretically, this might reflect the vitality of the Egyptian–Jewish community. Until the Jewish rebellions in the time of Trajan (115–17 CE), the largest Jewish diaspora was in Egypt. However, after the suppression of these revolts, the Jewish community in Egypt began to decline. Since our sources indicate that there was a good deal of trade going on between Egypt and Judaea after this period, it would seem that all of this had nothing to do with the Jewish community in Egypt.

In any case, however, it would seem that the very claim that most of the external or foreign trade of Judaea was with Egypt is quite doubtful. Syria was also a neighboring province and its ties with Judaea were of a more simple nature and more natural than those between Judaea and Egypt. Indeed, there is much information on trade between Judaea and southern Syria (Chapter 3.III above). Produce from the Land of Israel was found quite often in the markets of Tyre and Sidon, and the *halachah* even stated that so much produce in Tyre came from the Land of Israel that it was taken for granted that produce found in the markets there came from the Land of Israel; it was therefore necessary to set aside tithes from this produce (T Demai 1:10). The Tosefta also discussed the halachic status of the produce in the markets of Sidon. Moreover, and as we have already discussed above, even some of those sages who did not allow trade or commerce with those countries outside the Land of Israel allowed it with southern Syria (T Avodah Zarah 4 (5):2 and Chapter 3.XI above). A Jew from the Land of Israel might buy land in Syria (T Kelim Bava Kama 1:5) or might become a tenant farmer there (see, for example, PT Hallah IV, 60a) and there were even cases in which a Jewish landowner in the Land of Israel might have holdings which were worked by tenant farmers from Syria (see, for example, PT Demai VI, 25d).

Trade with Syria, therefore, was simple and natural and the political boundary between the two provinces might not have been a clear-cut economic one. Trade with Egypt, however, was dependent on boats and ships. The nature of the trade between Judaea and Syria and Judaea and Egypt was different in a number of other aspects. The agricultural nature of Syria was similar to that of the Land of Israel. Egypt, however, grew a number of different types of crops, and therefore trade between Egypt and Judaea was far more "colorful" than that between Syria and Judaea. The goods involved in the Judaean–Egyptian trade were unique, and consequently are reflected more in the sources.

Based on the logic and arguments outlined above, it is likely that there was also a good deal of trade between Judaea and the cities of the Transjordan, in spite of the very few sources attesting to it.

VII.4.3 Numismatic evidence

Conceivably, numismatic evidence might supply a good deal of material helpful in the evaluation of external trade. Up until the third century, cities minted local copper coins of low denominations. Finding foreign coins in the Land of Israel and coins from the Land of Israel abroad might serve as a good indication of foreign trade, as well as of those countries engaging in commerce with the Land of Israel. However, the question as to which mint supplied imperial coins has no economic implications and was related only to matters of Roman administration.

Unfortunately, there are no complete sets of statistics regarding the finding of city coins from the period which we are studying. The general impression that one gets from studying the available material is that foreign city coins have been found at a great number of sites in the Land of Israel, including in the rural or village sphere. The coins discovered in the Galilee could serve as an indication of this phenomenon. Foreign city coins have been found at Capernaum (Spijkerman 1975), Migdal (Meshorer 1976), Gush Halav (Hamburger 1954), Meiron, a synagogue near Gischala and H. Shema' (Barag 1982–3). A large quantity of coins found at Migdal, a large township along the shores of the Sea of Galilee, contained 168 city coins: 89 were from Syrian cities (47 per cent), 44 were from cities of the Land of Israel (23 per cent), 19 were from cities of the Transjordan (10 per cent), and most of the coins were from the cities of the general neighborhood such as Tyre and Gadara. Trade, therefore, was more or less of a local nature. Merchants or traders from the surrounding cities were the ones found in most towns, and provincial boundaries had little impact on all this economic activity. It is not surprising, therefore, that there were so many Tyrian coins found in the cities of the Galilee. We shall return later to discuss this phenomenon.

The numismatic evidence from Gischala shows how this rural township fitted into the international trade complex. Hamburger has compared the coins of Gischala with hoard 19 of Dura Europos and with the additional hoard of unknown origins published by Newell (Hamburger 1954, p. 203). The hoard from Dura had 187 coins. Eight of these were from Tyre (4.2 per cent), 1 was from Sidon (0.5 per cent) and 24 were from cities of Judaea (12.8 per cent). Of the Judaean coins, 9 were from Jerusalem and 10 were from Caesarea. The Newell hoard had 93 coins; 10 were from Tyre (42 per cent) and 4 were from Judaea. The hoard of Gischala had 161 coins; 157 of these were from Syria and Phoenicia (98 per cent), 1 was from Gadara in the Transjordan, 1 was from Cyprus and only 2 were from cities in the Land of Israel. The conclusion from all this is quite clear. Most of the trade and commerce in the rural sector of northern Israel was with cities outside the Land of Israel. Also, the relatively large amount of Palestinian coins found in the commercial city of Dura shows how extensive its trade ties were with the Land of Israel. The hoard in Gush Halav had an especially large amount of coins from Syria: 37 from Tyre (23 per cent), 38 from Antioch (24 per cent) and 29 from Laodicea (18 per cent). As we have already seen above, there are literary traditions which attest to the trade connection between Gischala and Laodicea (Sifre Deuteronomy 355, p. 421 and parallels).

There are few city coins in Capernaum. Approximately 55 per cent are from the cities of the Land of Israel, 38 per cent from Phoenicia and 7 per cent from the cities of Arabia. As in the other cases seen above, Tyre is especially represented with 22–27 per cent of the coins coming from this city (Barag 1982–3; Hanson 1980).

Jerusalem of the Roman period (135–324 CE) was a small, insignificant city, lacking any special economic or religious importance. The coins discovered from Roman Jerusalem have been collected and classified, and in fact the only exact and trustworthy study on the matters we have been discussing deals with this city (Ariel 1982, especially pp. 317–18). Two hundred and fifty city coins were discovered in Jerusalem: 20 coins were from Syria and Phoenicia (8 per cent), 20 were from the cities of the Transjordan (8 per cent) and 115 were from cities of the Land of Israel (45 per cent). In addition to these, 75 coins were from Jerusalem itself (30 per cent). In sum total, 75 per cent of the coins were from the Land of Israel. There were also 22 coins from other cities in the Empire (9 per cent) and only 2 coins from Alexandria. These coins seem to provide a realistic picture of the commercial ties of a small city in central Palestine. Most of the trade was within the province. Twenty-five per cent of the commerce was of a local nature and 25 per cent was external.

Hundreds of coins were discovered in the excavations of Caesarea (Levine and Netzer 1986, pp. 137–48). Out of 77 city coins, only 8 come from cities in the Land of Israel. Sixteen are from cities in Syria, 15 came from Egypt and 37 from other countries, for the most part in Asia Minor. All of this represents, however, only one excavation at that site and not all the finds. There are thousands of coins, for instance, in the private collection of Hamburger, made up of coins found in the Caesarea environs. Most of the coins, however, have not been published.

The Eretz Israel Museum of Tel-Aviv has approximately 3,000 city coins. A detailed catalogue has yet to be published and we wish to thank the curator of the collection, Dr Aryeh Kindler for allowing us to examine the coins. Based on the catalogue that does exist, as well as on our perusal of the coins, the following results were obtained: 42 per cent of the coins are from the Land of Israel, 28 per cent are from Phoenicia and only 8 per cent are from Transjordan, 10 per cent are from cities in Syria and 16 per cent are from Alexandria. Among the most prominent cities represented in the collection are Tyre (15 per cent), Sidon (4 per cent), Antioch (7 per cent), Acco (3 per cent) and Alexandria (16 per cent). Among the most prominent cities in the Land of Israel in the collection are Neapolis (9 per cent), Caesarea (8 per cent), Aelia Capitolina (6 per cent) and Tiberias (3.3 per cent). There are also dozens of individual coins from various cities of the Hellenistic–Roman world.

The value of all this, however, is problematical since the collection is to all intents and purposes eclectic. Coins from a new excavation or a chance hoard which the museum might receive or acquire could significantly change the statistics above. Much of the collection of the museum is based on contributions from private collections, for the most part from western countries. Collections from such countries could possibly change the statistics in favor of cities from the West. We have therefore not included these cities in our list. In spite of all these problems, though, the list does have some value.

Kindler (1986) found that in the Golan the majority of coins were from Sidon, while there were hardly any from Tyre. This, as we remember, is different from the situation in the Galilee in which the coins of Tyre were dominant.

From all of the above, it seems that the numismatic evidence is far from uniform and all of the conclusions above should be considered only as rather preliminary ones. It appears that we should distinguish between two types of data. The evidence from the towns of the Galilee, Golan and Jerusalem represent the norm in the Land of Israel. Caesarea and Botnah (Mambre) represent international trade centers of the Land of Israel. Thus, very few local coins were found at these two sites, but many foreign ones were discovered there from as far away as Spain and Gaul as we have mentioned above.

Thus, trade and commerce in the Land of Israel seem to have functioned within two complexes. The first one was local. Every settlement usually traded with its neighbors. Provincial boundaries were of no importance for this type of trade and did not form an economic barrier. The second complex was international and trade within this framework was to a great extent with foreign cities such as Alexandria, Antioch, etc. Foreign trade accounted for about 35 per cent of the general trade of the time, although the data is somewhat colored by the fact that the cities of Syria and of the Transjordan were close by to many settlements, and thus trade with these cities might sometimes have fallen within the local complex. Thus, for example, the cities of the Transjordan are near, relatively speaking, to Jerusalem and the cities of Phoenicia and the Transjordan are near to many sites in the Galilee. Moreover, the picture that we get from city coinage is also not complete because these coins were minted from copper in low denominations and are therefore not totally representative of trade which undoubtedly was conducted to a great extent with gold and silver coins.

Among the city coins in general, coins from Tyre are most prominent. Barag has dealt with this matter and suggested that perhaps the great number of Tyrian coins found in the Galilee does not represent the extent of trade with this city, but rather the fact that neighboring cities, including Sidon, were not allowed to mint a sufficient number of coins, and there was therefore a need to make do with Tyrian coins. It is difficult, however, to accept this suggestion, since in the Golan nearby, many Sidonian coins have been found, even more than the number of Tyrian ones discovered there. Moreover, the numismatic evidence from the Museum of Beirut (Baramki 1974) proves that coins of Sidon were just as common as Tyrian ones. Also, the material from the Eretz-Israel Museum shows that the coins of Tiberias and Acco were also widely used and it is difficult, therefore, to believe that the government limited the minting of coins from these cities. It is more logical to suggest that the large number of Tyrian coins simply reflects the great amount of trade with that city.

As we just mentioned, Kindler has shown that the Golan apparently had extensive trade relationships with Sidon while the Galilee, like the rest of the country, traded more with Tyre. The difference between the Golan and the rest of the country apparently is the result of local custom which, it seems, was influenced by local road networks. Trade with the Golan revolved around the road which goes through the Biqa Valley, the valley between the Lebanon and anti-Lebanon ranges. In spite of the relative distance to Sidon, the road from the Golan was good. The road from the Golan to Tyre, however, was not because it passed through difficult terrain. In spite of this, however, the towns of the Galilee preferred to trade with Tyre. Caravans from the Galilee traveled westward along the mountain ridges and from there to the Via Maris to Tyre. We have already discussed above (Chapter 3.III) the role of Tyre within the marketing complex of Galilean towns. The difference between Tyre and Sidon in this matter might be hinted at in T Demai 1:11 which we discussed above. This Tosefta, as we remember, mentions differences between these two cities, although, as we also remember, the text of this Tosefta was quite problematical.

If there was extensive trade between the Land of Israel and its neighbors, then the numismatic remains of those neighboring provinces should also provide some indication of this. This matter has not been studied at all and requires at least some preliminary examination. A number of collections which have been randomly chosen and studied do give some indication of the external or foreign trade of Judaea.

The collection in Gerasa (Bellinger 1938) was found in the course of the excavations of that city, in which 126 city coins were found. Of these, about 31 per cent are from cities of Syria, 22 per cent are from cities of the Land of Israel, 27 per cent are from cities of the Transjordan, 4 per cent are from Alexandria and 2 per cent are from cities of Asia Minor. Almost all of the Palestinian coins date to the Herodian period and afterwards. Thus, it can be seen that a good deal of the trade of Gerasa from the first century was with Palestine.

The collection in the Museum of Beirut is more problematic (Baramki 1968, 1974) since it is eclectic, and it is possible that it incorporated coins from the Land of Israel by chance, and not such coins that were local, due to their use in trade. In spite of all this, it is likely that the collection is for the most part local. A comparison of the catalogue of 1974 with earlier ones shows that most of the Palestinian material was acquired between 1966 and 1974, years in which political conditions limited traffic between Beirut in Lebanon and the State of Israel. Thus, the collection may be eclectic, but at least is regional in nature.

The Museum of Beirut has 1411 coins from Phoenicia and the Land of Israel. Fifty-seven per cent of these are from Phoenicia, 10 per cent are from Beirut itself, 28 per cent are from cities of the Land of Israel, 5 per cent are Hasmonean, 1 per cent are Herodian and 11 per cent are from first century Judaea. Thus, 43 per cent of the coins are from the Land of Israel. This would seem to indicate that the number of city coins that were minted was influenced for the most part by economic criteria and that the level of trade between the Land of Israel and southern Phoenicia was very great. Among the coins from the Land of Israel, 13 per cent were from Caesarea, 10 per cent were from Neapolis and 10 per cent were from Aelia Capitolina. However, there were not many coins from Sepphoris and Tiberias in spite of their proximity to Phoenicia, and between both cities there were only 26 coins in the collection or 4 per cent of the coins in the museum.

Almost all of the coins date to the first century CE and afterwards. Only 1 per cent of the coins date to the period before the Common Era. This would seem to indicate that the trade relations between the Land of Israel and Southern Syria or Phoenicia became extensive only at the end of the Second Temple period.

Hundreds of city coins were found in Antioch, the capital of Syria and one of the largest commercial cities of the East (Waage 1952, pp. 175–8). Most of the coins are from Antioch itself and the surrounding cities. Thirty-seven coins came from the surrounding region. Of these, 14 are from Judaea and 21 are Nabatean. Among the city coins, Judaea is represented by only one coin. However, a number of cities from other provinces are also not represented to the extent expected.

Of the 24 coins found at Tarsus, none are from cities in the Land of Israel (Goldman 1950). Thousands of coins were found at Dura. Of these, only 70 were from different provinces, with 46 of these from Judaea (Hasmonean, Herodian and Procurators). From 9,000 city coins, only 20 were from cities in Judaea. There were 104 from Phoenician cities, 3 from Egypt and Arabia, 9 from Cyprus and 14 from Cilicia.

Palestinian coins are found in just about every numismatic collection in European museums. Unfortunately, the coins' origins are rarely listed and thus cannot help us, since there is always the doubt that they were brought to Europe by dealers or tourists during modern times. Palestinian coins have also been found at the site of archeological excavations, even in quite remote areas such as Spain (Ripoll *et al.* 1976).

The evidence has not been collected in any systematic manner, and we can therefore only offer a tentative summary of the matter as it stands now. It seems that coins from the Land of Israel are found in foreign cities, and bearing in mind that Palestine was a rather small province, the amount of coins is quite impressive. It is interesting to note that in the more remote areas (Dura, Egypt) most of the Palestinian coins date to the period up to the year 70, while in the nearby cities (Beirut, Gerasa), the coins are for the most part from the end of the first century through the third century. However, due to the small amount of cities whose coins have been examined, it would be dangerous to arrive at any far-reaching economic conclusions.

VIII. THE CURRENCY

There are relatively few coins from the province of Palestine compared to the western provinces of the Empire. Among the thousands of coins found in all the excavations, these are fairly rare and were found at isolated sites. There are also dozens of extremely rich collections of coins exhibited in museums or hidden in private collections. However, access to these collections is problematic; they do not usually have an organized catalogue, and the source of the coins is not recorded. The private collections are also usually closed to researchers, and information about them is by word of mouth alone.

Furthermore, in the last century and the first third of this century, many coins were discovered, but most were sold to antique merchants and collectors. Today they are dispersed in numerous museums and among collectors throughout the world. Despite such difficult conditions of research, we can speculate that the currency in this province was no less developed than in the wealthier provinces of the Empire, considering its relative size. However, at this stage the number of coins available for research purposes is limited.

Here, the large number of coins found in the rural sector should be noted. As discussed earlier (VII.4.3 above), in many villages, hundreds of coins were found in small excavation areas.

The currency in Palestine is clear. From the first to the third century (70 CE to 284 CE) there were relatively few coins in the province. The number of coins increased dramatically, sharply and clearly in the fourth century, and clearly slowed down in the fifth century, that is, after the year 408. The reign of Diocletianus (305–84) represents a period of transition. There are sites in which the number of coins from this time is relatively large, and there are others with only a few of this emperor's coins. This discussion of the currency is based on all findings in Judaea, as summarized by Z. Safrai (in press).

The increase of the number of coins in the fourth century is consistent throughout the country and is indicated in almost all the sites, with the exception of a few isolated cities that declined in the third century, such as Dora (Stern 1992). This summary does not include settlements that were destroyed in the First Revolt (66–70 CE) and were not rebuilt (such as Gamla and Masada), nor those that were only partially renewed (such as Jerusalem, Herodion, and others). The summary information is displayed in Figure 85. Within the fourth century itself local changes occurred. In several regions, such as the Galilee, the peak period was the first half of the century, while in others (such as the Golan Heights) it was the second half of the century. These local differences are beyond the scope of our discussion.

In the fifth century there was a drastic drop in the number of coins. The decline encompasses almost the entire country, although its extent varies among areas. A few examples are illustrated (Figures 86–92) (Z. Safrai in press).

This currency is not unique to Judaea. Johnson and West's findings indicate a decrease in the number of coins in early fifth-century Egypt (Johnson and West 1949, p. 180) (Figures 93–4). A decline is also reported in the fifth century in many cities in Transjordan (Garasa, Amman Museum and other excavations) (Figures 93–6), as well as in many cities in Syria and Asia Minor (such as Antiochea, Tarsus, Tyre, Aphamea, Sardis, Ephesos and others) (Figures 94–101).

Discussion of these processes of growth and degeneration in the entire East is beyond the scope of this work. However, it should be noted that this is clearly not a local incidence but rather a general process in the eastern part of the Empire. (The conditions in the western Empire were different. Lewit (1991) recently showed that the fourth century was not a period of decline and slow-down in the western Empire, as it was in the eastern provinces. By all accounts, the fifth century was, of course, a period of degeneration, as a result of the invasion of Vandals and the collapse of the western Empire.)

These are the numismatic facts. The central methodological question is, What can we learn from these quantitative numismatic figures? This question is not specific to the province we are dealing with, and many scholars grapple with it. One group of scholars sees variation in the number of coins as evidence of fluctuations in the volume of trade and, to some extent, also changes in the economic strength of the area under study (Reece 1978; Hopkins 1980; Duncan-Jones 1990). In contrast, some cast doubt on the economic significance of this evidence. MacMullen (1988), for example, raises a number of reservations, such as the possibility that a large number of coins actually indicates inflation and not economic development. He prefers the evidence of regional surveys to quantitative numismatic findings (see also Grierson 1966; 1967; Howgego 1992).

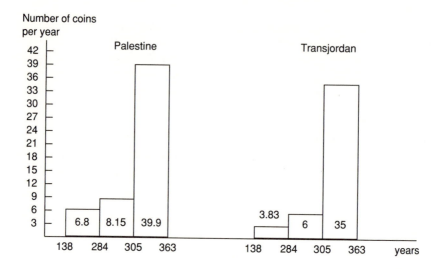

Figure 85 The currency in Palestine and Transjordan in the third and fourth centuries.

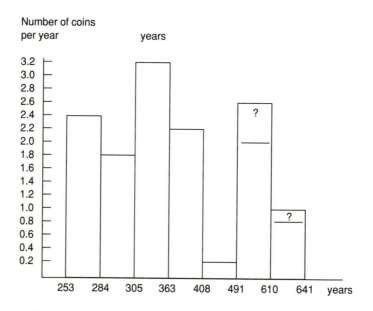

Figure 86 The currency in Jerusalem in the Roman–Byzantine period. After Ariel 1982.

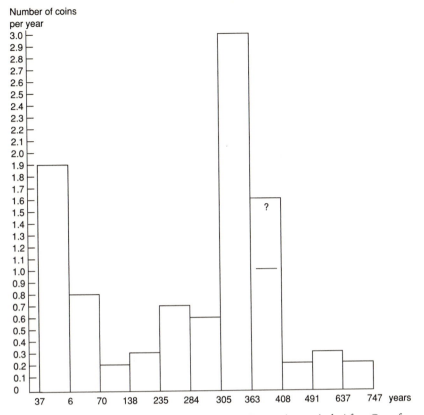

Figure 87 The currency in Sebastea in the Roman–Byzantine period. After Crowfoot *et al.* 1957, pp. 43–69; Fulco and Zayadin 1981; Reisner *et al.* 1924, pp. 252ff.

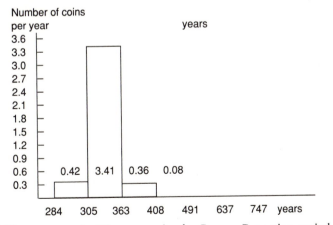

Figure 88 The currency in Diocaesarea in the Roman–Byzantine period. After Meyers *et al.* 1986, p. 9; Waterman 1931.

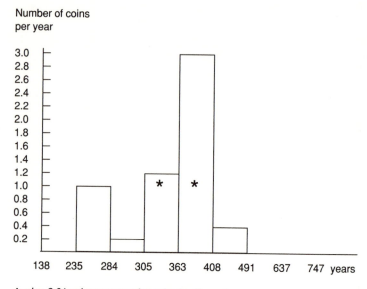

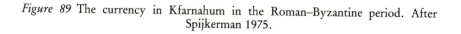

★ *plus 2.01 coins per year from the fourth century*

Figure 89 The currency in Kfarnahum in the Roman–Byzantine period. After Spijkerman 1975.

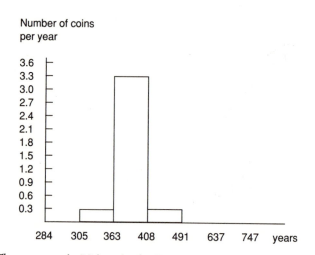

Figure 90 The currency in Meiron in the Roman–Byzantine period. After Raynor and Meschorer 1988.

408

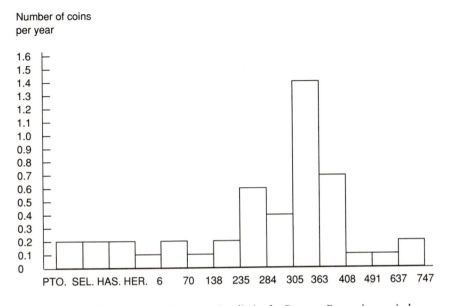

Figure 91 The currency in Jamanea Paralia in the Roman–Byzantine period.

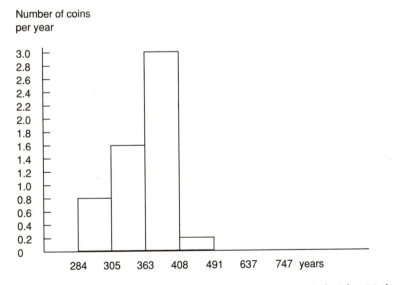

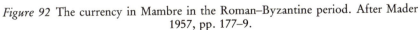

Figure 92 The currency in Mambre in the Roman–Byzantine period. After Mader 1957, pp. 177–9.

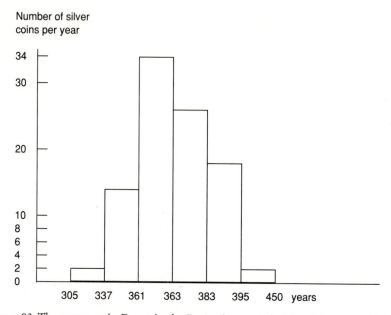

Figure 93 The currency in Egypt in the Byzantine period. After Johnson and West 1949, p. 180.

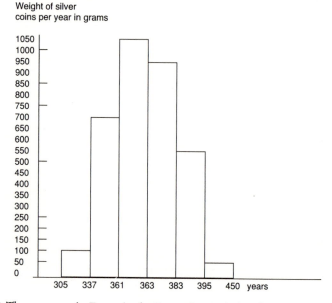

Figure 94 The currency in Egypt in the Byzantine period. After Johnson and West 1949, p. 181.

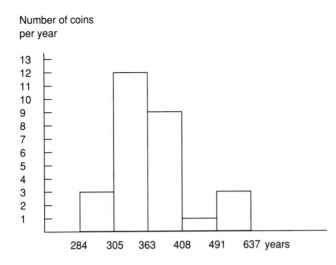

Number of coins
per year

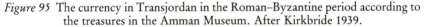

Figure 95 The currency in Transjordan in the Roman–Byzantine period according to the treasures in the Amman Museum. After Kirkbride 1939.

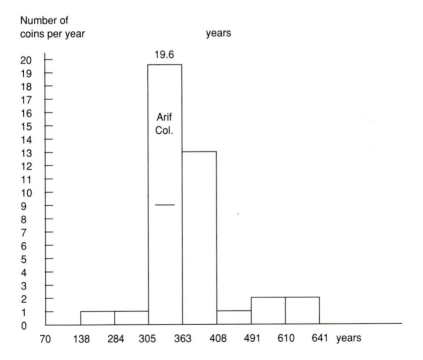

Figure 96 The currency in Garasa in the Roman–Byzantine period. After Bellinger 1938; Zayadin 1986, pp. 82–9, 257–62; Goicoechera 1986; Arif 1986.

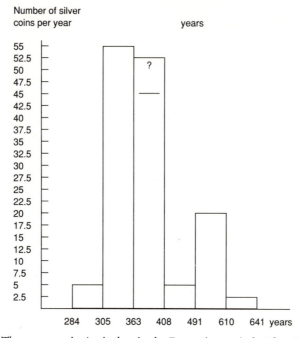

Figure 97 The currency in Antiochea in the Byzantine period. After Waage 1992,
p. 171.

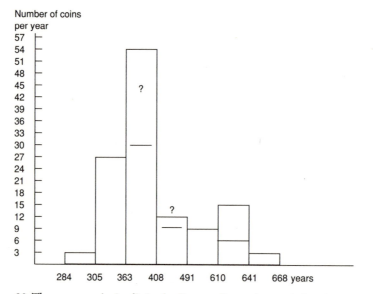

Figure 98 The currency in Sardis in the Roman–Byzantine period. After Buttrey
et al. 1981.

412

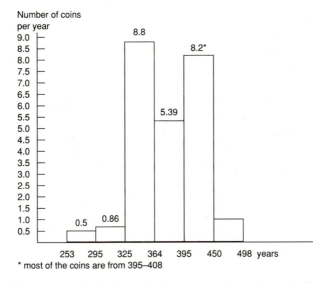

Figure 99 The currency in Aphamea in the Roman–Byzantine period. After Callu 1979.

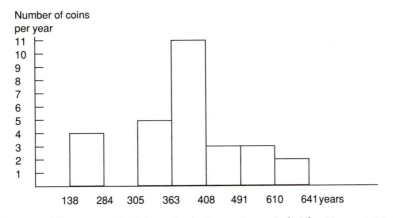

Figure 100 The currency in Ephesos in the Byzantine period. After Vetters 1979–89.

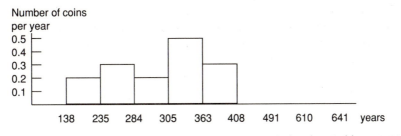

Figure 101 The currency in Tarsus in the Byzantine period. After Goldman 1950.

413

This theoretical debate is beyond the bounds of our discussion. I have expressed my views on this matter elsewhere (Z. Safrai in press). In the specific case at hand, a number of details testify to the reliability of the quantitative numismatic evidence. (1) The third century was a period of anarchy and inflation (235–84). This had no effect on the growth in the number of coins in that period in the province. Hence it seems that inflation has no critical impact on the growth in the number of coins. (2) We show below (Chapter 6.I.1) that the archeological surveys conducted in Palestine indicate a peak in the number of settlements in the Byzantine period, and our discussion in Chapter 6 also deals with the relationship between demographic growth and the development of industry and trade. The quantitative numismatic evidence indicates a peak period in the fourth century as well. According to the archeological surveys, then, the peak period was the fourth century. The evidence in the surveys and the numismatic findings corroborate one another, thus confirming the credibility of both these methods of investigation. (3) In many of the excavations, the archeological findings confirm the quantitative numismatic findings (Z. Safrai in press).

These last three points are not meant to substitute for a systematic discussion on the methodological problems and limitations of quantitative numismatic evidence, which should be placed in a wider context. However, they do provide additional information, as they are based on an empirical experiment in which the research method under discussion was applied in the study of parts of a province. This successful experiment may contribute to the discussion of the general reliability of quantitative numismatic evidence.

VIII.2 The use of coins for trade

Coins were, of course, used for the purpose of trade. It can be assumed that a considerable proportion of the coins were circulated in the market by military personnel (Chapter 4.II), and some were brought to Palestine by merchants. At the same time, other methods of trade, particularly barter, were also common. We do not know the percentage, but it is clear that a considerable proportion of trade was conducted in coins. We deal with this subject below in Chapter 5 (section IV.5)

The numismatic evidence of all the types which we have examined shows a rather extensive level of international trade. We cannot, at this time, provide exact statistics, but it would seem that most of this trade was with Syria and Phoenicia. Next came trade with Egypt and then commerce with the Transjordan and Arabia. Finally, there was only a rather small amount of direct trade with the cities of the western provinces.

5

Open or closed economy in the Land of Israel during the Roman period?

I. THE PROBLEM

In this chapter we shall examine perhaps the key question in our study of economy: was the economic system of Judaea an open one or a closed one? In other words, was the agricultural system made up of farmers who produced, more or less, their own food needs and what little surplus remained was sold for the occasional "luxury" item? In such a system, agriculture was almost the only means of production. This is what we have called a "closed economy." The other possibility, or what we have called an "open economy," is a system in which the individual farmer was extremely dependent on trade and commerce. The farmer in this system cultivated a number of different crops. Some he used himself, but a good deal he sold and with the profits bought all the other goods that he needed. It is generally accepted that the first suggestion, the closed system, was the system that existed in the ancient Land of Israel, including during the Roman period. It is our intention to re-examine the economic data pertaining to the Land of Israel in order to present a complete and balanced picture. Afterwards, we shall have to compare our findings regarding the Land of Israel with the situation in the rest of the Empire.

Our discussion will revolve around a number of economic spheres:

(1) To what extent was the individual farmer self-sufficient or dependent upon trade? If the farmer proves to be dependent upon trade then it will be necessary to examine the next point.
(2) To what extent were the village and town self-sufficient? In other words, did the farmer have reciprocal economic relations with only his neighbors? Or were goods perhaps brought to the local village from great distances? Did the village market its surplus production over great distances?
(3) Were the more extended regions such as Judaea, Samaria or the Galilee self-sufficient or did the residents depend on international trade?

The question to what extent was the entire Land of Israel able to provide

415

for its needs or be self-sufficient is secondary. This is the same regarding its national balance of trade. During the Roman period, the Land of Israel was a province which was part of a much larger administrative and economic unity. The economic system of the provinces was not autonomous and the established ties between the provinces make the Empire in general one large and unified economic whole.

The data which we shall use does not allow for a complete and orderly discussion according to the division which appears here. Thus, for example, a discussion on the economic activities of harbors might also be important for the other questions asked above. Therefore, we shall begin at present with a general discussion based on a summary of the data which we have collected in earlier chapters.

Since we do not have have any direct quantitative information, we shall have to make do with indirect references as well as with an examination of the characteristic economic indicators of a closed or open economic system. We shall now present the more important data.

II. SURPLUS PRODUCTION

The primary conditions for any open economic system are surplus production on the one hand and pockets of consumption on the other. The list of agricultural produce in the Land of Israel at this time is quite impressive. The backbone of agriculture in the Land of Israel were the major grains (especially wheat and barley in the south), olives and grapes. The sources mention these three crops numerous times, together and individually. Many a village or farm depended on the cultivation of these crops, in addition to supplementary crops and livestock. Most of the ancient agricultural installations which have been discovered were intended for one or another of these three main branches: olive presses, grape presses and threshing-floors (Chapter 2.I above).

II.1 Regional specialization

The great amount of material at our disposal shows that there were regional agricultural specialties. The agriculture of the Jordan Valley, for instance, was based on the cultivation of those plants which produced spices such as myrrh and balsam, or dates. The Galilee specialized in olives. The Judaean mountains were known for their grapes and wine. Southern Judaea was known for its barley and wine, and the *shephelah* of Judaea was recognized for its grains and wine. Judaea was the land of sheep while the Galilee was known for the cultivation of flax (Chapter 4.V.3 above). It is important to point out, though, that specialization does not necessarily imply an open economic system, since the level of specialization could have been rather local. However, careful study of the available information does indicate that there was a significant shortage of staples in many regions, implying the existence of an open economic system.

II.1.1 The production of olive oil and wine in the Golan

The Golan has been surveyed in a rather systematic manner and there has even been a survey of olive presses there. Interestingly enough, hardly any wine presses have been discovered there, with only two or three having been found within the administrative boundaries of Susita (Hippos) (Urman 1985; C. Ben David 1989). No others have been discovered. It has also been noted that the olive presses of the Golan have been found for the most part in the Lower Golan, where over 80 such presses have been discovered. In the Upper Golan, and in the northern Golan which belonged to Syria, only one olive press was discovered. It is of course possible that not all the presses were discovered or that some were destroyed in the course of time. However, the finding of over 80 olive presses in the Lower Golan and in the administrative boundaries of Susita, while only one such press was found in the rest of the entire Golan, can hardly be coincidental. The Golan, therefore, certainly imported wine and part of the Golan also had to import oil, undoubtedly from the Lower Golan where it was more plentiful.

II.1.2 The Jericho Valley

It is likely that it was not worthwhile to cultivate grapes in the Jericho Valley since the heat would have resulted in rather poor yields. There was probably also not much in the way of grain cultivated in this area since it was much more profitable to grow dates and produce spices (Chapter 2.I.3; 1.6 above). The many traditions attesting to the eating of dates there as a matter of fact would seem to indicate that there was also a degree of commerce and trade in this crop.

II.2 Exporting wine and oil; importing wheat

II.2.1

Historical traditions, especially from the Byzantine period, indicate that wine and oil was exported to Egypt and other countries (Chapter 4.VII.3 above). It is impossible, however, to evaluate the extent of this export. There are not all that many traditions on the matter and a chance reference hardly allows one to conclude whether the reference is to something of great economic importance or only of limited importance.

Two traditions pertaining to southern Syria may hint at rather widespread exportation to Syria. Acts 12:20 states that the residents of Tyre and Sidon "took their country's nourishment by the king's country." The phrase is problematic, but seems to mean that southern Syria was a large-scale and important consumer of food commodities from the areas ruled by Herod Antipas, who ruled over the Galilee and Golan. Another source, not dependent at all on the previous one, also seems to imply that during the Javneh period, most of the agricultural produce in Tyre came from the Jewish Galilee and food (oil) caravans from the Galilee arrived at Tyre via Achzib (T Demai 1:10; PT Demai I, 22a). Thus, in this region and at this time, at least, this export was not inconsequential, but rather an important part of the Galilean economy.

It would appear, therefore, that the region was able to afford the consumption of goods based on the value of the surplus agricultural produce which was sold (Chapter 4.VII.2 above). The list is quite impressive, but once again it is difficult to evaluate the importance of each economic sphere. The importance of most of the imported items is negligible. Thus, typical examples of imported agricultural goods are garlic from Baal Bek (Heliopolis), groats from Cilicia, and lentils and dates from Egypt. None of these can be considered staples (see also M Demai 2:1, T Demai 2:1). The most important one was apparently the import of grain which is mentioned in the sources as pertaining only to the Amoraic period (third century). At this time there was a good deal of importing of grain which was most likely financed by the goods exported, which we have mentioned above (Chapter 2.I.2). As we have seen above, much of the local needs of grain consumption was met by local cultivation and, as we have mentioned, the cultivation of grain was one of the major agricultural pursuits of the farmers of the Land of Israel. Thus, it is not possible to evaluate the economic importance of the importing of grain to the Land of Israel. It is clear that during periods of drought or famine every 2–3 years, imported grain was of more importance. However, it is impossible to determine how much grain was imported to the Land of Israel during regular years. The impression received is that the importing was quite massive, but it is, of course, impossible to provide numbers. We also quote some sources to show that there were regions in which the farmers sell most of their production to the market.

II.2.2 Scythopolis, Caesarea and Caesarea Philippi

A solitary piece of evidence in Talmudic sources enables us to reconstruct economic conditions in these city regions. All three of these cities were considered to be outside the halachic boundaries of the Land of Israel regarding "commandments dependent upon the land." The sources then go on to list the produce which was "forbidden," i.e. "commandments dependent upon the land" were applicable to it because it was grown within the halachic boundaries of the Land of Israel. This, of course, tells us that this produce was not locally grown, but rather imported over distances from the "Land of Israel." Regarding third-century CE Scythopolis, this meant that most of its wine, oil and *afas* dates were imported, while grain, regular dates and flax, mentioned in other sources (Chapter 4.VI.2 above), were grown locally within the administrative boundaries of Scythopolis. The extent of the "permitted" area of the city is unclear. According to the minimalists (Y. Sussmann 1975–6, pp. 114–19; Feliks 1985), this area was the region surrounding the city. According to the maximalists, the permitted area included a region of 30–40 square kilometers around the city (Z. Safrai 1984; see above, Figure 84). In any case, it is clear that the permitted area belonged to non-Jewish residents of the city. The late S. Lieberman brought an important proof for this (Lieberman 1976, pp. 54–63) by citing the halachic rule that vegetables grown by residents of the city were considered to have come from "permitted" areas, while those brought by merchants to the city were considered to have come from the "Land of Israel."

The "permitted" regions of Caesarea included a good part of the coastal region and it appears that this region provided residents of the city of Caesarea with most of their needs regarding wheat, wine and oil. The sweet potato, however, was brought from the Judaean mountains and this was also true regarding figs (Y. Sussmann 1973–4, pp. 131–2). Other sources mention the importing of wheat to Caesarea, apparently internal import from other regions of Palestine (Chapter 4.VI.2 above).

According to the ceramic finding at Caesarea, all the fine wares in this city were imported, and 30 per cent of the containers of wine were imported from Gaza (Riley 1975).

As far as Caesarea Philippi (Chapter 4.VI.2 above) was concerned, rice, nuts, sesame, *ful* and *Ahuniot* nuts were apparently imported. Other agricultural produce was grown within the halachic territory or "permitted" area of the city. Oil was imported from the Galilee at the end of the Second Temple period (according to Josephus – but this was the result of special conditions which existed during the period of the revolt, and therefore when regular conditions prevailed, there was no reason to import oil to this city). It is important to point out, though, that the southern part of the administrative territory of Caesarea Philippi was apparently included within the halachic boundaries of the Land of Israel, and therefore the source cited above does not provide a complete picture of the economic situation of that city.

As stated above, the decrees regarding "permitted" areas of Beth Shean and Caesarea allow us to reconstruct urban economies during the period which we are discussing. As we have also stated above, there are traditions regarding the importing of grain to these cities only during the third and fourth centuries. The developments and changes regarding the importing of grain are of great importance, but there is not enough information to clearly follow all of these developments.

The sources described above can be added to the general sources we have examined so far regarding import and export of agricultural produce. The picture received is that there was a good deal of self-sufficiency which occasionally had to be augmented by the importing of agricultural goods.

II.3 Oil

Production of olive oil has left clear-cut material remains in the form of olive presses; in terms of ancient agricultural installations these are usually the best preserved. At a number of sites more than an olive press has been found and, as can be seen from the chart that we presented above (Chapter 2.I.3, Figure 33), the presses were able to produce much more than the potential need of any community. The sites in which ancient olive presses have been discovered are scattered throughout the Land of Israel in the Galilee, Judaea, Samaria, Carmel and Lower Golan. It is only chance that has determined that some have been better preserved in this settlement or that. The sites in which these presses have been found can be considered representative of the rural sphere in general. It is interesting to note that only one such village has been found in the Mt Hebron region. This might be only coincidence due to the lack of remains or due to the state of research on the subject. However, since as we have seen, this area is described in the sources as a wine-producing region (Chapter 4.V.3 above), it is possible that the lack of olive presses is actually indicative of the fact that olive oil was not produced in this region.

II.4 Wine

We have seen that a great part of the wine was sold to the market, as a surplus production (Chapter 2.I.3.2.3 above).

II.5 Fish (see also Chapter 2.I.8 above)

Fish were a common festive dish and played an important role in the weekly diet. The fish were caught by fishermen living in the settlements along the Mediterranean coast as well as along the coast of the Sea of Galilee. Some of the fish consumed in the Land of Israel, though, were imported from Egypt. The transport of these imported fish to internal regions in the Land of Israel undoubtedly required marketing and commercial actions.

II.6 Raising doves (see also Chapter 2.I.9 above)

The raising of doves was an important economic pastime in the *shephelah* of Judaea in the Hellenistic and early Roman period. Even though there is not any data available on the matter, it is unlikely that the majority of the doves were consumed locally. The surplus was perhaps sent to Jerusalem to the Temple and marketed there. The breeding of doves is unusual in that it took place in a relatively early period and was connected to the Temple and not to regular or normal economic conditions.

Not all of the surplus production which we have discussed or which is mentioned in the sources was exported. Some of this production was probably transferred from region to region. This, however, should also be considered commercial activity, reflecting an economic system which is not based only on self-production.

III. BRANCHES OF INDUSTRY

In the Jewish village there were a number of branches of industry with a wide scope of production. Among the most prominent were:

III.1 Linen

This was undoubtedly the most important industrial export from the Land of Israel from the second century onwards, and linen from the Land of Israel was recognized throughout the Empire as the most important of its kind (Chapter 2.I.7; II.2 above). The growing of flax requires intensive agricultural cultivation, which means that in order to develop this economic sphere, it is necessary to use fields which, if they were used at all before, were used for the cultivation of food. Moreover, according to the well known rotation schedule, for every three years of grain cultivation, it was possible to cultivate flax once. Limiting the fields used for the cultivation of grain by approximately one-third resulted, most likely, in a greater dependence on trade, the profits of which were used to supply what had been lost by limiting cultivation, facilitating the regular export of linen.

III.2 Wool

The Galilee may have been known for the cultivation of flax and the production of linen, but Judaea was famous for its woolen cloth (Chapter 2.I.8; II.2 above). Although there is no proof that this wool was exported, it is clear that the clothing was produced on a rather extensive scale and thus export would not have been impossible.

III.3 Glass

This economic field was especially important in the Galilee and Carmel. Most of the glass produced was marketed abroad (Chapter 2.II.2 above).

III.4 Pottery production (see also Chapter 2.II.2 above)

Pottery constituted a rather common group of everyday utensils with a high breakage rate. These utensils often had to be replaced. There were pottery production centers in certain villages, such as those in Kefar Hananiah or

Asochis, which produced most of the pottery needs for an entire region, or the workshop in Beit Natif which produced lamps, and there were many other such sites. There is no proof that these vessels were exported, but there is proof of regional trade and the extended nature of this trade would seem to reflect an open economy.

III.5 Quarrying

In most parts of the Land of Israel, quarrying was only of minor economic importance and most people secured by themselves whatever rocks and the like were needed. This was not the case, however, in the coastal region of Mt Carmel. There were quite a number of quarries from Caesarea to Atlith and particularly from Dor to Atlith. A glance at the chart in Figure 47 (Chapter 2.II.3) shows that in this region, a good part of the workforce was involved in this work. This was obviously the case especially regarding those who lived in settlements near the quarries, but it is clear that those local residents could not have removed the amount of stone taken from the quarries, especially if we remember that this was also an agricultural region and some of those residents must have been farmers. Thus, the workers in the quarries probably included those living further away and for this region, at least, quarrying represented a major branch of industry.

The stones removed from the quarries were most likely brought to the coast and from there transported by boat to the major coastal cities such as Caesarea and perhaps also to Apollonia, Joppa, Javneh, Ashdod (Azzotus) and Acco. From the figures which we have seen above, it would seem that approximately 40 per cent of the residents of that region engaged in quarrying. With the profits from the sale of the stones they undoubtedly bought whatever necessities they could. Even if we made a mistake in the course of our evaluations, the deviation could not be more than 50 per cent. Thus, it is possible to estimate that at least 20 per cent, on the average, of breadwinners in this region engaged in this industry. The effects of this industry on the region and indeed the history of the region are beyond the scope of our study. In any case, and in spite of this industry, there does not seem to be any indication that the Carmel coastal region was especially well off, and economic conditions here were similar to the rest of the rural sphere at this time.

IV. SERVICE NETWORK

IV.1 Division of services (see also Chapter 2.II.3 above)

The average village in the Land of Israel had laborers and providers of services. Thus, in the rural town one could find, for instance, tailors, bakers, butchers, bathhouse workers, spice makers, notaries, stone cutters, carpenters and the like; it goes without saying that there were agricultural laborers for seasonal work and workers engaged in the food industry (olive press workers, fig pressers, etc.). This is the reality described not only in Jewish sources, but also in Byzantine sources; needless to say, if what we have described above was the reality in towns, this was certainly the case in cities.

The artisans and laborers mentioned above worked most likely for their neighbors and received payment for their toil. Large numbers of artisans reflect an open economic and agronomic system since these artisans were providing services for those who could pay for them based on profits from agricultural surplus, and this is indeed the definition of an open economic system. The traditions regarding self-service *vis-à-vis* the labors mentioned above, and similar ones, will be discussed later on.

IV.2 Volume of trade

We have already discussed the nature of trade and commerce (Chapter 4). For our present purposes, we shall simply sum up matters and point out once again the important issues.

As we have already seen, the trade system was rather limited during the Second Temple period, with the most important commercial institution of the time in the rural sphere apparently being the traveling salesman. The local market served, in addition to its commercial functions, as a convenient meeting place on Mondays and Thursdays. Such seasonal or temporary markets are usually good indicators of a small amount of commercial activity and the unimportant role of such activity in everyday life.

The situation changed, however, somewhere at the end of the Second Temple period or immediately afterwards. The sources from that time provide a picture of a developed trade system functioning at various levels. Sometimes the farmer would sell his produce directly at market without the benefit of any middlemen, and sometimes he would sell his produce to a merchant. There were also settlements in which most of the agricultural produce was intended for the market and not for local home consumption. Every town also had a number of stores which doubled as restaurants. In the rural town one could also rent a store for a short period of time. We also quote some sources to show that there were regions in which the farmers sold most of their production to the market (Chapter 3.II.1 above).

Surplus produce was sold to elements external to the immediate region. The most natural situation, accepted throughout the entire world, is that the farmer brings his produce to the big city. There are, however, only few traditions attesting to this phenomenon. Most sources seem to describe the "caravan" as the most common commercial institution. The caravan left the *polis* and traveled from town to town during the week, providing the necessities of the residents and buying surplus produce. At the end of the week the caravan returned to the *polis*. A commercial system employing middlemen is indicative of a developed system, while direct marketing reflects a commercial system of secondary importance. As we have already mentioned, the system in the Land of Israel was mixed, with the use of middlemen as well as direct marketing.

Large-scale merchants or middlemen were the most important players in inter-regional or international trade. These were the traders who traveled from coastal city to coastal city or from fair to fair. Sometimes these large-scale merchants would buy directly from the farmers living in the various towns, but for the most part their commercial activities were on a much higher level.

This commercial system described above is mentioned in the sources as existing only from the Usha period onwards. By this time the Monday and Thursday market-days had lost their importance, and fairs began to appear as part of the process of paganization taking place in the Land of Israel. A little later, in the third and fourth centuries CE, we begin to hear about large-scale wheat trade, while the cultivation of flax became extensive in the Land of Israel from about the second century.

Trade accommodations (Chapter 4.VIII above). A number of legal trade accommodations were set up for high-level trade. Some of these were set up based on trade accommodations of the Roman Empire. Such accommodations were probably most frequent in the cities. We also remember that the *shulhani*-banker which we discussed above was also found only in the cities. Some cities in the Land of Israel had *stationes municipiorum* in the cities of Asia Minor and in Rome, similar to the trade stations that other cities in the Roman Empire had. Most cities in the Near East had such *stationes*, and thus the cities of the Land of Israel fit into the accepted economic pattern. All of this, as far as the Land of Israel was concerned, took place from approximately the second century onwards.

IV.3 Road network

The early road system serves as a good proof of a high level of trade (Chapter 3.VII above). Every village had a road system connecting it with its neighbors within a radius of 3–4 kilometers (= 4–6 roads). Larger villages had a more developed and extended road system. This road system provided for good accessibility between the settlements of the Land of Israel. As we have just stated, the very existence of this developed system and the great number of roads (and above we even discussed a number of means to estimate the number of such roads) serve as important proof concerning the extent of trade and the great amount of merchandise and produce transported on these roads.

As we have also stated above, most of the traditions on a significant degree of trade refer to the second century onwards. The beginning of this road system, however, dates to the Second Temple period. The excavations at Um Rihan, for instance, have uncovered a section of road dating to the Hellenistic period and other surveys have uncovered similar phenomena.

IV.4 Jerusalem as a market center

Jerusalem at the end of the Second Temple period was a capital and full-fledged metropolis and a leader in terms of politics, society, religion and economics. The difference between Jerusalem and the secondary centers in all of these aspects was great.

It is quite clear from the sources that Jerusalem became an international urban center. Pliny's comment – "Jerusalem, the most famous of the cities of the East" (*HN* 5. 70) – refers not only to the religious status of the city, but also to the impression that various people had of Jerusalem in general and for whom religious status was not very important. Information from Josephus (*BJ* 5. 331, etc.) and Talmudic sources on various markets in Jerusalem, and the fact that the city was the destination of many international merchants, fits in with the general impression of Jerusalem as a vibrant city in terms of economy and life in general. Although we have shown above that agriculture was an important economic component of the city (Chapter 4.VI.3), it never exceeded 25 per cent in terms of meeting the city's needs or of supplying the residents of the city.

Many scholars have already discussed the size and importance of Jerusalem. However, there has been no real serious discussion on the importance of the Temple in terms of economic function. The Temple was not only a religious and national center, but also an economic "empire" and center of surplus production. In spite of the fact that most of the Jewish people did not maintain strict observance of the laws of ritual purity, the yearly production of wine, oil and pottery in Judaea was produced in purity, thus enabling its use in the Temple (Chapter 4.VI.3 above). There is no reason to doubt the economic implications of this *halachah* and it would seem to imply that within a radius of one day's travel from Jerusalem, much of the local agricultural produce would arrive at that city. This, of course, is in addition to the heave-offerings and various other religious levies that were brought to Jerusalem; in any case, it was good sense for local farmers to maintain a state of ritual purity regarding their produce so it could be used in Jerusalem or the Temple.

Many pilgrims came to Jerusalem. Many of them, and especially those who did not come from the Judaea region, bought all of their food supplies in the city as well as sacrificial offerings. The sources have descriptions of rather detailed arrangements regarding the purchase of sacrificial animals such as lambs, doves and the like and oil and flour to be used with the offerings (see, for example, M Sheqalim 5:3–4 and S. Safrai 1965, pp. 156–9).

The "bankers" or moneychangers of the Temple Mount (*shulhani*), handled vast sums of money of different types and nationalities on a daily basis, and especially around the festivals. Every type of coin from all countries of the world was recognized as legal tender in Jerusalem (T Sheqalim 2:13; PT Maaser Sheni I, 52d). The large number of coins found in the stores of Jerusalem is at least partial proof of the great commercial activity that took place in that city (Ariel 1982).

Jerusalem had many residents who did not meet their own needs such as the regular Temple workers, as well as the temporary ones serving in the "priestly courses." Government and municipal employees as well as resident soldiers likewise did not produce their own food requirements. The large-scale building activity in Jerusalem at the end of the Second Temple period required the hiring of many construction workers. Josephus states that 18,000 construction workers labored on the Temple and its environs during the time of Agrippa II (*Ant.* 20. 214). This number would imply that there were about 60,000–70,000 residents in the city connected with them, in addition to all the public officials who did not work in the Temple and the service network necessary for all these people. According to all this, it would appear that the majority of the residents of Jerusalem made their living in one form or another from the Temple or its environs. However, even if we assume that some of these Temple workers lived in neighboring villages, the numbers above would seem to be somewhat exaggerated. In any case, it is clear that a good many residents of Jerusalem did not produce their own food. The residents of this city, therefore, would have to buy food or have it supplied from the agricultural hinterlands. Such a center of consumption which we have just described would certainly be possible only if there existed an open economic system.

In addition to what we have just stated, the wealth of the Herodian empire was quite famous, with this wealth being reflected in a great amount of public building and contributions to various "luxury" projects in the Roman East. It is difficult to know how much this public opulence had an effect on private citizens, but it certainly had to have some effect on general economic structure and organization.

Thus, already in the Second Temple period Jerusalem and its Temple were an island of an "open" economic system within a general closed or self-sufficient economic system. The general picture would change during the Roman period, as we have already mentioned.

IV.5 To what extent was the market open?

Until now, we have discussed the traditions pertaining to the open economic system in the Land of Israel during the Roman period and especially during the second century CE and afterwards. There are also traditions pertaining to a closed, almost completely self-sufficient economic system. These latter traditions might indicate a low level of trade and a good deal of self-production.

Talmudic literature and the rabbis seem to have a marked preference for an ideology of self-production and look down upon trade, considering the profits deriving from it to be immoral. The utopian ideal of the sages is: " 'The Lord alone did lead him,' that there should not be among you people engaged in the business of nothing" (Sifre Deuteronomy 315, p. 358 and Chapter 3.XI above).

However, as we have seen earlier, it is quite unlikely that these rabbinic traditions reflect reality, and should be seen instead as utopian ideals stressing the importance of self-production similar to the idealization of agriculture in Greco-Roman literature. There might have been another reason for the negative view of the rabbis regarding trade. Trade and commerce, by their very nature, required contact with non-Jews and the rabbis might have feared this. As we just mentioned, the ideal was "The Lord alone did lead him," and therefore they preached self-production. Thus, these traditions do not reflect reality and on the contrary, they express sorrow over the gap between reality, an open system to some extent, and the ideal, a closed one.

We have assembled a number of traditions attesting to the fact that artisans traveled from settlement to settlement as salesmen (Chapter 3.II.4.1, pp. 229ff. above). It would appear that the many sources regarding the service network in towns and villages indicate that the village artisan was not an uncommon occurrence and the wandering artisan was the exception to the rule, either an anachronism from earlier times or common only in faraway districts.

Barter. Barter or trade in kind is characteristic of closed economic systems. This type of commerce apparently did exist in the Land of Israel during the period which we are studying. Payment of taxes in kind was, of course, quite popular both in the Land of Israel and in the Empire in general. All this is in addition to information regarding commercial transactions with cash or with bank checks at the *shulhani,* or through trade arrangements based on fixed or changing rates. As was the case above, there is no purpose in determining which system is more common in Talmudic literature, since at best the information is rather fragmentary and eclectic. It would seem that both systems operated simultaneously. It is important to stress, though, that the value of merchandise was determined by fiscal value and had no intrinsic worth. This was of great importance regarding laws of interest (Eliash 1978).

Barter as a legal means of acquisition lost its technical meaning (= the exchange of goods) in the course of time, and by some time at the end of the Tannaitic period or during the Amoraic period became a means of fictitious barter referred to as "acquisition through a shawl." This symbolic means of acquisition was not accepted in the Land of Israel and this might be the reason why it is not mentioned in the Palestinian Talmud (Chapter 3.VIII.3.2.8.1, pp. 298ff. above). The Babylonian Talmud has many constructions of legal fictions and this might be the reason why such a means of acquisition developed in Babylonia. It is also possible that there was more commercial activity in Babylonia, and therefore a more abstract means of acquisition developed there. This, however, is outside the purview of our study (Beer 1975, pp. 156 ff.). In any event, this attests to some degree to a good deal of barter in kind.

It is clear from the sources that the providers of services in rural villages were also farmers. The baker baked one oven-load a day and the butcher slaughtered a cow at rather infrequent intervals (Chapter 4.IV.1 above). Those fulfilling such functions could hardly have made a living from these endeavors. Even the head of the caravan mentioned in Midrash Psalms 12 engaged in agriculture, and this was probably no less important than his work as the head of a caravan and as a merchant. It would appear that only the storekeeper spent most of his time and effort in his store. Thus, only the store was open every day and most hours of the day as opposed to the services mentioned above (Chapter 4.IV.1; VI.1).

The synagogue inscriptions mention donations of money as well as donations of building parts (a column, an entrance or a door frame), and of grain. About sixty per cent of the donations mentioned in the Hebrew and Aramaic inscriptions were made in cash. The terms in the Greek inscriptions are more vague and therefore were not included in this examination (Z. Safrai 1987; Naveh 1978; Roth-Gerson 1987).

Cost of transport. The high cost of transport in general and of grains in particular prevented, most likely, the development of trade in the ancient world. The cost of transport is cited in many studies as the major reason for an economy remaining closed in spite of improvements and developments. Despite the fact that transport costs were certainly high, it would appear that this was not all that critical.

Based on the numbers found in the sources, it is generally claimed that transport of grain over a distance of 100 kilometers would double the price (Yeo 1946). Duncan-Jones, however, has shown that transporting grain over 100 Roman miles increased the price of the grain only by 55 per cent (Duncan-Jones 1982, pp. 366–9) or in other words only by 36.6 per cent over 100 kilometers. Transport by ship over the same distance in terms of Roman miles increased the price by 44 per cent or 29 per cent in terms of 100 kilometers. It would appear that even this more reasonable evaluation is exaggerated. Based on the expenses of a donkey-driver and the number of days which he used his animals, it would seem that the transport of wheat over a distance of 100 kilometers did not increase prices any more than 16–25 per cent (see Appendix at the end of this chapter). It is necessary to remember, though, that most imports to the Land of Israel were transported by ship over the seas to a port or harbor, and the rate of maritime transport was even cheaper. Only when the merchandise arrived at a port was it transported by land, which was relatively more expensive, to its final destination. Since most settlements were located no more than 50 kilometers from some point of maritime disembarkation, it would seem likely that overland transport added no more than 10 per cent to the cost of the product, not taking into account, of course, various fees of middlemen; in the ancient world these were probably rather low. The price of transport of grains, including various secondary fees, was much lower than corresponding prices today.

In spite of what we have said above, it is still clear that the cost of transport was high and was a serious impediment to an economy dependent on transport.

IV.6 The economy of Judaea within the context of the Empire

The province of Palestine (Judaea) was, of course, not an independent unit, but rather part of the complex whole of the Roman Empire. This fact has had a good deal of influence on our discussion of questions of economy. Our basic conclusion is that during the Roman period the economy of Judaea was for the most part an open one and dependent both on internal and external trade. It is important to examine this conclusion within the framework of the Empire in general; in other words, it is hard to imagine that a small independent "open" unit such as Judaea, and relatively poor at that, could operate within the greater whole of a closed, self-sufficient, yet undoubtedly more developed system.

This, of course, is not the proper forum for a detailed discussion on the economic structure of the entire Roman Empire, and our comments will deal only with the question at hand. Generally speaking, there are two basic approaches in scholarly literature. The first approach is that of A. H. M. Jones who sees the Roman economy as basically a closed, self-sufficient system with occasional open units (Jones 1974, pp. 35–60). During most historical periods the open unit was the capital of the kingdom or government in which there was, relatively speaking, a good deal of trade or commercial activity. During the Roman period, these open areas were very often found in the cities. However, even at this time, there were still many cities in which agriculture was the major means of production and most trade, therefore, revolved around agricultural products.

A group of scholars has proposed a different approach altogether. Thus, for example, Hopkins (1980, 1983) describes the Roman economy as a sort of circle of a closed economic system with a very thin covering layer of an open economic system. This image, or a similar description, has been accepted in a number of new studies (Whittaker 1983a; Fulford 1977; Pleket 1984).

Both systems recognize the importance of agriculture as the main source of production and see it basically as a self-sufficient economic sphere. This means that every farmer, or at least every settlement, grew its own basic needs; trade in agricultural produce over long distances was rather limited. Such trade when it did exist was the result of special circumstances. Thus, for

429

example, the wine trade in Gaul has been explained as necessary to supply the soldiers serving on the Roman border, and not as a regular or common trade in wine (Tchernia 1983; cf. Middleton 1983 who disagrees. See also Burford 1960).

The conclusions drawn from our study seem to be closer to the second approach described above, but are much more far-reaching. During the course of our study we have brought sufficient weight of evidence regarding the importing of wheat and the exporting of wine and oil, agricultural produce. Our study for the most part deals with the rural sector; the Land of Israel traditions are unique in that they allow examination and analysis of the economy of a rural sector. It would also seem that we have mustered sufficient evidence to show that the economic system within this sphere was also basically open (cf. Pleket 1984; de Ligt 1990–1).

From all of the above it is possible to receive a general picture of the village in the province of Judaea-Palaestinae in the Roman period. The major characteristics of the village are:

(1) The village is heavily populated (100–1,000 families; 10–100 dunams).
(2) Most of the inhabitants are small landowners with a minority being tenant farmers. There were also large villages which were included within private holdings (such as Porphyrion) or which belonged to the Roman *fiscus* (such as Ein Gedi).
(3) Most of the residents of the village engaged in agriculture, but there were also other means of making a living there and occasionally even industry was found in the village sphere.
(4) The village had a rather highly developed level of communal services, but of course much lower, relatively speaking, than that of the *polis*.
(5) The village had an autonomous system of administration which provided a developed level of social services.
(6) The village had a highly developed level of trade. Some, and in many cases even the majority of, agricultural produce may have been intended for outside markets.
(7) In spite of all this, the village did not enjoy economic prosperity and the standard of living there was much lower than in the *polis*.

This view of the village is different from the picture that one gets from the literature on the subject dealing with this sphere in the Empire in general. However, a number of studies have recently been published which present large and highly developed villages in the western part of the Empire too, as well as evidence of the various crafts and occupations which existed in them (Rodwell and Rowley 1975). In a new study, Whittaker proves that industry was not only found in the *polis* and in any case, the village economy was supported in no small manner on the trade of those items which it produced (Whittaker 1990). There were also extremely large villages in the eastern part of the Empire – in Syria, for instance – which were similar in many ways to a *polis*. Thus the village in the province of Palestine was not so unusual. It was different, though, in many aspects from villages in other provinces of the Empire. The amount of information available on the villages of Palestine also differs from the amount of data referring to the rural sphere in other provinces, whether in the eastern or western parts of the Empire (de Ligt 1990–1).

At this point we cannot learn about the Empire in general from the situation in Judaea or Palestine. However, since Judaea was not one of the richer or more developed provinces of the Empire, it could be argued that it is possible to reach conclusions *vis-à-vis* the Empire in general based on Judaea. This, of course, requires further study and it was not the intention of our study to examine economic conditions in the entire Empire.

Another question to which we have no answer relates to the peak period of trade in Palestine, and as part of this same question it is necessary to determine the peak of demographic growth which serves as prime mover of economic growth (Chapter 6 below). In the course of our work we have presented, or shall indeed do so in the final chapter, chronological data regarding demographic growth (Chapter 6.I.1), the importing of pottery (Chapter 4.VII.2), the importing of wheat (Chapter 2.I.2) and the like. We have seen, though, that in every single instance, the chronological data was problematic and insufficient in content and there were unique or special explanations for the supposed chronological development. Thus, for example, the increase in the importing of pottery could have been connected not only to the renewal of external trade, but possibly also to developments in the laws of ritual purity. Thus, we have no clear-cut answer for this crucial issue.

APPENDIX:
PRICE INDEX OF JUDAEA IN THE ROMAN PERIOD (METHODOLOGY)

Scholars of ancient economies have long had difficulties with attempts at quantification in terms of measuring and evaluating prices in the ancient world. The usual method is to collect all the prices mentioned in literature and in epigraphic material and to attempt through these to build some type of price index model which would also reflect changes during the course of time and *vis-à-vis* different provinces. It is, of course, necessary to take into account the reliability of the data, or lack of such, with the general assumption being that prices which fit into the general framework are more or less reliable. This has been the methodology of many important scholars such as Duncan-Jones (1974, pp. 63–256).

A good deal of information regarding prices mentioned in Talmudic literature has been collected by Sperber (1974, pp. 101–68), and to some extent he also compared this material with other prices. The major problem with this type of material is whether prices mentioned in a matter-of-fact manner in the course of a halachic discussion or as part of a demonstration of a halachic principle can be considered realistic. This question has absolutely nothing to do with the larger question concerning the nature of descriptions in Talmudic literature and whether they are realistic or not. Even if we assume that they usually are so, it is still possible that prices in this type of literature would be schematic.

The usual price for wheat in rabbinic literature is 4 *seahs* for a *sela* or 25.2 kilograms for 4 dinars (= 1 *seah* (6.3 kilograms) for a dinar). Talmudic literature does sometimes record different prices, usually higher (Sperber 1974, p. 102). However, the price mentioned above appears as a standard and schematic price in various Syrian works such as the Chronicle of Joshua Stylites (chs. 87, 29). Thus, a field which produces 75 kilograms per dunam in a year (or 150 in two years) makes a profit of about 3 *selas*. This should be compared with other findings. Thus, a number of papyri from the second century CE also provide information on this matter. These papyri are legal documents and thus the prices mentioned in them should be completely reliable. The prices found there are the following:

(1) 40 *zuz* (= 40 dinars) for a field as well as 4 *haruvin* for one (DJD II, p. 22. The *haruv* is *siliqua*, see Sperber 1974 p. 238). The size of the field is not mentioned.

(2) A *beth zera* of wheat of 5 *seahs* for 88 *zuz* (DJD II, no. 30). The measurement refers to the area in which 5 *seahs* are sown, and perhaps this is 5 *batei seah* or approximately 4 dunams. Within this area are a house and a grove or orchard (of figs, olives and a tree that "grows much" (?)). Thus, the price of a dunam was about 22 dinars (5.5 *selas*). However, there is also the possibility that the document refers to an area in which 5 *seahs* of wheat was cultivated. The ancients planted less than a *seah* of seeds in a *beth zera*, and therefore the document refers to a larger area and the price of a dunam would be even lower (Feliks 1963, pp. 156–7).

(3) The support of the son of Babata in terms of food and clothing for 3 months cost 6 dinars (Polotsky 1967, p. 50). Babta was rather well-to-do and the sum mentioned probably represented supporting her son on a high level.

(4) A house with a number of rooms for 36 *zuz* (Yadin *et al.* 1986).

(5) An archive found in the Judaean Desert has a number of prices. For the most part the necessary data needed to make use of this material is missing. Thus, for instance, it mentions rental fees, but not the size of the area being rented. It also mentions, for example, that a young son of Babta received 6 dinars for his support for a period of three months (Lewis 1989, no. 27). This archive also mentions that a rich woman received 500 dinars in her *ketubbah* (no. 18), or 200 dinars (DJD II, no. 116). The archive

provides other such examples, but as we stated above, it is hard to make use of the data there.

As we mentioned above, it is quite likely that the prices in the papyri are realistic and when these are compared with the prices mentioned in Talmudic literature, the latter seem to appear to be schematic. It is hard to imagine that the profit derived from a field cultivated with wheat would be 3 *selas* on the dunam, while the price of a dunam with a house and a grove was only 5.5 *selas*. Even if for the sake of argument we allow for a year of lower yields, the gap in prices would still be unexplainable. All this also applies to other prices such as the price of a *seah* of wheat being 2–3 dinars, as found in Avot D'Rabbi Nathan (version A, chapter 27, p. 55). There are also other examples of schematic prices in Talmudic literature such as, for instance, T Bava Mezia 5:13: "If one received a field for 10 *kur* of wheat (300 *seahs*) and then said give me 200 *zuz* and I will support it [the field] and give you then 200 *kur*". The agreement then was for a payment of 200 dinars in exchange for an additional yield of 2 *kur* or 60 *seahs*. According to the numbers mentioned above, the monetary value of the harvest was 60 dinars. It is difficult to believe that someone would pay 200 dinars in order to make a profit of 60 dinars. According to the context it seems to be clear that the 200 dinars is more or less a loan and the profit from it should be even higher.

The rabbis also mention a daily wage of 1–2 *selas* (T Bava Mezia 7:1; Mekhilta of R. Simeon b. Yohai, 21:19, p. 175). This is a rather high salary and is enough to provide wheat for a single person for a period of 48–96 days (according to a daily ration of 1 half a *kab*, as we established in Chapter l.I.2 and the price of wheat being 4 *seahs* for a *sela*). According to the prices mentioned in the papyri of the Judaean Desert (see above (2)), it would have been possible to buy a field with the wages of only 3–6 days of work. All of this leads to the conclusion that the wage rate mentioned above is quite exaggerated. Sperber (1974, pp. 101 ff.) also brings lower rates of a ½ dinar, 1 or 2 dinars for a day's work, but even these would seem to be too high, since it is difficult to believe that a grove or orchard of an area of 4 dunams, including a house, could be acquired with the profits of 44–88 days of work or even 176 days of labor. This is the same with other prices. The price of a *talit* (or outer garment) is quoted at either 8, 12, 25 or 50 dinars (Sperber 1974, p. 103). Is it even remotely possible that one could buy a field for the price of 2–4 such garments? The price of a lamb is 4 dinars (M Keritot 5:2; M Menahot 13:8; M Sheqalim 2:4 *et al.*) and even this would seem to be high in comparison with the price of wheat. According to the price of a lamb quoted above, this would just about be the profit from a dunam cultivated with wheat (3 *selas*, while the lamb cost 2).

During the period we are examining, prices remained rather rigid, for the most part, except for periods of rampant inflation such as during the anarchy (third century), and this was also the case regarding prices of seasonal agricultural produce which varied based on quality. The laws of "overreaching" ('*ona'ah*) which forbid one to take a price one-sixth more than the value of goods or merchandise (Sperber 1978, pp. 136–59) are based on an assumption of stable prices, and this assumption is also accepted in many other *halachot*. Changes in price, therefore, were not based on market fluctuations.

We could cite many other examples regarding contradictions resulting from the different prices cited in the sources. The final result of all this is that the prices mentioned in Talmudic literature are schematic and not to be trusted in any quantification analysis unless they can be verified from other sources. On the other hand, those prices which are part of a *halachah*, and not just cited as examples regarding some halachic principle, are most likely realistic. Thus, the *halachah* that someone who has 200 *zuz* is not allowed to solicit alms (M Peah 8:8 and parallels) is probably realistic, since after all, this was the figure which would theoretically determine whether the community had to support someone or not. The 200 *zuz* mentioned in the Mishnah would imply that that person had a house and a field, at least based on the data from (2) cited above.

We should like to suggest a different method of quantitative analysis based on prices. Talmudic literature mentions a number of price systems with the price of one set of goods or merchandise relative to another, such as the price of wheat in relation to barley or the price of wine in relation to oil. A good example of such would be the Mishnaic traditions which mention the amount of produce equal to food for two meals. The relationship between the various components of the tradition has been examined by Sperber (1974, pp. 112 ff.) who also pointed out the similarity between these traditions and Roman material. Since this Mishnaic material, which we also examined at great length (Chapter 1.I.2 above), relates to matters of legal import, it would seem likely that it reflects reality and can be used for establishing prices.

We should like to estimate transport costs in the same manner. A donkey-driver can lead a caravan of 3 or more donkeys, each carrying 90 *kav* of wheat (M Bava Mezia 6:5 according to the explanation of BT Bava Mezia 80a–b). Agricultural produce could be effectively transported over a distance of 35–40 km per day (see, for example, M Maaser Sheni 5:2 and many parallels). Therefore, the transport of 270 *kav* of wheat (90 × 3) over a distance of 100 km would require, at most, a week's work, assuming that additional merchandise was not transported on the way back. 13.5 *kav* of wheat were necessary to support a family of four (M Peah 8:5 and parallels. See Chapter 2.I.1). If we assume that payment for food and sustenance constituted approximately 50 per cent of family expenses, then the minimal payment which would suffice to support the donkey-driver and his family for the transport of wheat over a distance of 100 km was 27 *kav* of wheat or only 10 per cent of the value of the wheat.

However, it is unlikely that the donkey-driver returned home empty-handed. Even if the driver did not work during the entire week and even if it is necessary to add to the cost of transport expenses relating to the donkeys and their upkeep, it is clear that the cost of transport could not have been more than 20 per cent of the value of the merchandise.

The cost of transport of wine was even lower since only 4 *kav* of wine were necessary to support a family (4.IV.2). The cost of transport of oil was even cheaper. As the value of the merchandise goes up the cost of transport goes down.

Based on our assumptions above, the donkey-driver received rather good payment for his services and should have become quite rich. Unfortunately, the sources do not seem to describe this profession as all that lucrative, leading to the conclusion that perhaps he was not paid that much after all. This, of course, is problematical because it calls into question the authoritative scientific methodology of economic calculations based on literary sources and especially on the Edict of Diocletian. It is necessary, therefore, to examine the entire structure of quantitative calculations; clearly this is neither the time nor the place for such an endeavor. In any case, it is clear that general economic proof should be preferred to depending upon quantitative calculations rife with internal contradictions.

6

Demographic multiplication and economic growth

I. THE STAGES OF DEMOGRAPHIC MULTIPLICATION

I.1 The number of inhabitants in the Land of Israel

I.1.1

There was clearly a process of demographic multiplication and increase in the Land of Israel; this population increase eventually resulted in serious economic pressure. Unfortunately this assumption, in spite of its importance, cannot be proven. It is impossible to determine how many people lived in the Land of Israel during the Mishnah and Talmud periods. We do not know how many people lived there before then and we also do not know the "population threshold" of the Land of Israel or even how it can be determined. There have been a number of estimates regarding population numbers in the Land of Israel, but none is based on data which has been sufficiently examined (Broshi 1979; Avi-Yonah 1964, pp. 121 ff. See Byatt 1973 and Broshi 1979 for relevant literature).

Avi-Yonah based his evaluation on a theoretical division of settlements into different levels. This system may be correct in itself, but his conclusions regarding the number of settlements at each different level and his suggestions regarding the number of inhabitants in the various levels were unreliable. M. Broshi suggested that the level of wheat cultivation, after all one of the major crops in the Land of Israel, could provide the key. Based on this system, Broshi arrived at rather low figures, claiming that no more than a million people lived in the Land of Israel. In our view, Broshi's methodology is problematic and we shall briefly point out the reasons why this is so. (1) Broshi's figures on wheat production are based on wheat production in the Arab farmstead. The average Arab farm did not make use of all available land at its disposal. Thus, for example, the Arab farms in the Jerusalem corridor made use of only 60 per cent of available farm land in the period before 1948, and this constituted only 33.8 per cent of all available land. The remains of the terraces which were cultivated were appropriate for

436

the cultivation of wheat, yet the Arabs only cultivated 60 per cent of the land available to them (Ron 1977a, pp. 210–30). It is likely that there were additional ancient terraces which were cultivated that Ron did not discover since they may have been destroyed over the centuries. Moreover, the average Arab farmstead never arrived at a level of intensive production and its yields in general were quite low when compared with those of the Mishnah and Talmud periods (Chapter 2.I.2 above). (2) From the second century and afterwards, wheat was imported to the Land of Israel, making any supposed connection between the level of wheat cultivation and population rather irrelevant (Chapter 2.I.2 above). (3) As we shall see below, the population threshold of the Land of Israel was adjusted in accordance with population. This, therefore, would invalidate deterministic methodologies.

Another means of arriving at population numbers hinted at by Broshi is based on the amount of land used for construction and assuming that population density per square meter was more or less a constant. The methodology would appear to be acceptable, except for the fact that there is as yet no reliable information regarding the extent of this type of land in the Land of Israel during the periods which we are examining, apart from the Negev where it is possible to make use of estimations regarding the volume of water cisterns in order to arrive at population figures. In our view, there is not enough data at present to reach any sort of final number regarding population in the Mishnah and Talmud periods. The only means of arriving at some kind of solution is through systematic field work in various representative regions, and even this method depends upon being able to differentiate between the various levels of settlement in the regions under study, the number of settlements there and the average number of residents in each level of settlement. For all intents and purposes, this is the methodology of Avi-Yonah, which should be used with a good degree of care and caution.

I.1.2

Even though it is impossible to determine the number of residents in the Land of Israel during the Mishnah and Talmud periods, it is certainly clear that these were times of population growth. Proof of this is the large number of new settlements in various parts of the Land of Israel established in the Byzantine period (see Figures 102–3 for graphic representation of this phenomenon). It is still necessary to determine why the Jewish residents of the Land of Israel were not part of this demographic development and why their settlements decreased in number. It is also necessary to determine from where the new settlers came. All this, however, requires separate study and this is beyond the present purview of our work.

A perusal of Figures 102–3 clearly shows a great increase in the amount of sites with Byzantine remains. The demographic-economic growth is also

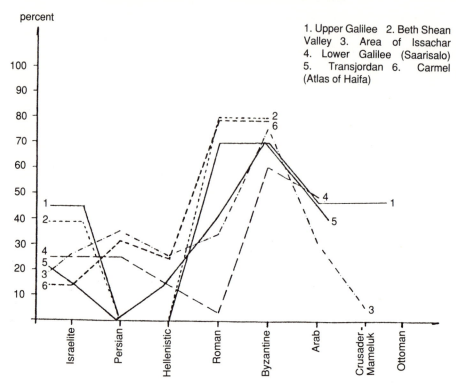

Figure 102 Demographic growth in the Land of Israel: archeological surveys.
After Z. Safrai 1986, p. 26.

reflected in the increase in the number of coins found in Palestine, as shown above in Chapter 4.VIII, and the figures fit in nicely. The manner in which the increase is represented in the illustrations, however, is somewhat misleading for a number of reasons.

(1) Identical means were not used for dating the pottery in the various surveys. Until recently, the knowledge regarding the ceramics of the Persian–Byzantine periods was rather limited, and therefore not all of this material was correctly understood or dated. This may explain the paucity of Hellenistic and Roman material in some of the surveys. Moreover, the scientific value of all the surveys is not the same, but we certainly cannot begin here to address the problem of the scientific basis of each and every survey.

(2) In order to be able to combine surveys from various regions, we have pointed out the number of sites in which remains were found from a particular period in relation to the entire number of sites examined in a survey (Figures 102–3). This, however, is not completely logical since the policy determining which sites should be examined is not the same in all

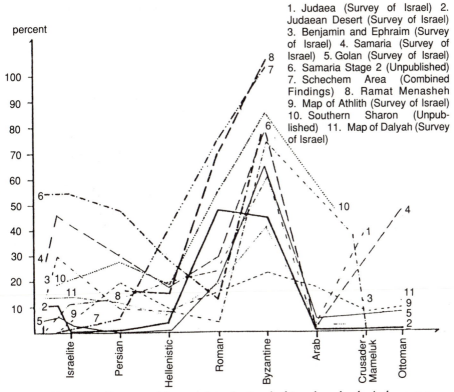

1. Judaea (Survey of Israel) 2. Judaean Desert (Survey of Israel) 3. Benjamin and Ephraim (Survey of Israel) 4. Samaria (Survey of Israel) 5. Golan (Survey of Israel) 6. Samaria Stage 2 (Unpublished) 7. Schechem Area (Combined Findings) 8. Ramat Menasheh 9. Map of Athlith (Survey of Israel) 10. Southern Sharon (Unpublished) 11. Map of Dalyah (Survey of Israel)

Figure 103 Demographic growth in the Land of Israel: archeological surveys. After Z. Safrai 1986, p. 27.

cases. Thus, for example, there are surveys in which the number of "all sites" refers only to settlements. Other surveys included in this number every cistern or quarry, which by their nature are difficult to date. This type of method, for instance, might lower the percentage of Byzantine sites, even though this particular method is far from scientific and it is the plethora of "undated" material which lowers the Byzantine final figures. Moreover, there are also regions which were particularly settled during the prehistoric periods such as the Upper Carmel. In such areas the percentage of Byzantine settlements is relatively low. This, however, is not the result of the situation in the Byzantine period, but rather of the fact that during that time there was no reason to live or settle in many of the caves which were inhabited during prehistoric times.

(3) There are a number of areas which have been surveyed almost completely from motor vehicles with a minimal amount of field work, while there are other areas which have been examined in a most systematic manner. It is likely that in those regions in which the survey was superficial, the sites near existing villages were the ones to be chosen for examination,

and such a survey could hardly be considered representative of the entire region.

(4) Most surveys do not discuss or deal with the size of the site during various periods. Clearly, the number of residents in a particular region is dependent on the number of settlements there as well as their size and density. Even if the number of settlements can be determined, the other two factors rarely can. Although it might be argued that population density would not change throughout different periods, it is still next to impossible to determine size during different periods. Size can usually be determined only in single stratum sites.

A survey which did take the size of settlements into consideration was the survey of the Jezreel Valley. The ceramic distinctions between various periods are also on a high level and quite exact, and it is therefore not surprising that this survey indicates a spurt of population growth in the Late Roman and Byzantine periods (Portugali 1986).

I.1.3

In spite of all the problems mentioned above, there is one clear-cut conclusion from all the surveys: there was a drastic increase in settlements in the Roman–Byzantine period. This would most likely seem to indicate that the population of the Land of Israel was greater at this time than in earlier periods. It is possible that this trend began in certain regions already in the Roman period. As we have seen above, though, this is often hard to discern because of the problems and limitations of the material and particularly regarding the identification of Roman period remains.

The first exact data regarding the number of inhabitants in the Land of Israel is the sixteenth century CE Turkish census. According to the census, there were 340,200 residents in Palestine, 200,000 of whom lived in what had been Roman–Byzantine (Hütteroth and Abdulfattah 1977, p. 43). If it were possible to consider the findings of the various surveys as a dependable means of determining population size at this time, then this figure would be of great importance even regarding other periods. This, of course, is based on the relationship between the number of sites in the sixteenth century and the number of active sites in the Roman period. Unfortunately, little is known about Ottoman period pottery and many surveys do not even include it in their findings. The Turkish census figure, therefore, must be used with great care.

As we shall see later on, all the stages and developments associated with population growth took place in the Land of Israel, proof indeed of that very population growth. In spite of this, there are still a number of questions regarding the process of demographic multiplication in the Land of Israel.

(1) It is still necessary to determine when this phenomenon took place and exactly when it began. It is also necessary to find out if and when there were

any economic problems and also when it reached its peak. Surveys under-taken in a systematic and exact method could probably provide some of the answers to these problems. Unfortunately, most of the surveys undertaken so far are not good enough in these aspects.

Palynological research may, however, provide some chronological answers. In a study undertaken by Baruch (1985), it was found that during the Roman period there was a marked increase in olive cultivation in the Galilee at the expense of "wild" trees such as the terebinth and the oak. This would seem to be clear-cut proof of an increase in cultivated terrain which would also be at least an indirect proof of an increase in population. This is so since we have already seen above that demographic growth and economic growth are connected one to another. Even so, it is difficult to discover the exact peak of this phenomenon which would appear to have been spread over a period of some 200–300 years. It began some time at the end of the second century BCE and finished in the second century CE, perhaps as a result of the Bar-Kochba War. The means of measurement, however, is far from exact and there is a possible margin of error of some 125 years. Thus, it is possible that the peak was much later and that the development in general lasted until the third century.

The dates mentioned above are based on an examination of sediment from the Sea of Galilee. Additional conclusions, though, require further study and examination from the Galilee to serve as a control for the Sea of Galilee sediment. The study in the Galilee is very important since this was the center of Jewish population during the period which we are studying and this is also the region to which most of our literary sources refer. However, it is necessary to expand this paleontological study to other regions of the Land of Israel, and only when this is done will it be possible to make complete use of this type of material.

(2) What was the force of this demographic growth and how severe was the economic pressure on the residents of the Land of Israel? Archeology does not provide answers for either of these questions.

As we have mentioned above, demographic growth was dependent on various economic and social developments. We shall examine some of these developments later on, and thus be able to provide at least partial answers for some of the questions raised above. For the moment we shall grant the assumption that demographic growth did pose a serious challenge for the residents of the Land of Israel. When we are able to determine how the residents of the province responded, then we shall finally have proof of the force of the development, the seriousness of the problems which existed and the period in which these developments took place.

The sources do not usually have any proof that a particular development was connected to an increase in population, and it is also generally possible to offer different causes for that particular development. In spite of this, an overview of these developments, the material from various surveys and the general situation all fit a society in the process of demographic growth. Thus, all of the individual developments should be considered as part of the larger whole and it would appear necessary to develop some type of paradigm of the stages of demographic multiplication and the economic implications of this.

Our study deals with the entire spectrum of the residents of the Land of Israel. In spite of the general population growth in the period under discussion, Jewish population was declining at this time. Talmudic literature implies that the condition went from bad to worse. This information, however, applies really only to the Jewish community and hardly provides a complete picture. It is, of course, necessary to determine why the Jewish population declined when the general population was thriving. However, this issue is really not part of our study and we shall deal with this matter only tangentially.

1.2 Economic implications of the stages of demographic multiplication based on conditions in the Land of Israel during the Roman period: a discussion

1.2.1

The discussion at present is based on the theoretical distinctions established by Boserup (1965; and see Grigg 1980) in her work which deals mainly with questions concerning the relationship of the population threshold of a particular region to the needs of that growing population. According to Boserup, the population threshold was rather flexible. During periods of demographic stability, the population threshold was adjusted to the size of the population. However, with a rise in population, new needs and demands also increase. There is increased development and investment which raises the population threshold of the particular region. Geographic conditions of course influence the nature of these investments, but they cannot really limit the demographic development entirely. Boserup points out a number of key stages in the increasing population threshold of a country. The major stages are:

(1) Limiting the amount of time a field remained fallow. Instead of sowing a field only once every few years, it was now sown every year and utilized as much as possible during all seasons of the year. This development took place in a number of stages.
(2) A "hydrological revolution" took place and new means of intensive irrigation and watering were developed.
(3) An increase of knowledge and a greater investment in the land at the disposal of the grower.

Not all of the stages mentioned above are appropriate for conditions in the

Land of Israel or for the period under study, and we shall discuss this matter later on. The economic and ecological problem is rather simple. If, for example, we assume that an area like the Land of Israel could support a million people or so, if this number remains more or less constant, then there is no reason for any economic framework to change. However, if the population increases, then the same amount of land must now feed additional people. It is important to distinguish between the need to "feed" additional people and the need to "support" them. Feeding requires supplying food to more people, while support is an economic matter and implies securing the means to be able to purchase food for a growing population.

Theoretically, the possibility exists that a particular society might seek to raise its standard of living, increase production and bring about an economic revolution of sorts with none of this connected at all to matters of demography. However, this did not seem to happen in the reality of conditions existing in the ancient world, and those poor societies with an extensive agronomic system did not exchange it for an intensive profitable one without some sort of external pressure or catalyst. Although this phenomenon might be an empiric fact, it should not be considered a law or social model.

I.2.2

In a closed, subsistence and self-sufficient economy, "feeding" and "supporting" are one and the same, and the residents of such an area undergoing an increase in population must find some sort of way to grow more food. However, in an open economic system, solutions to an increase in population might be found not only by increasing food production but also through such alternate means as increasing industrial production or trade and commerce. Wars and piracy also provided additional opportunities to solve the economic problem. All of this would provide the added capital to import the needed food. The transition from a closed economic system to a more open one was also likely to provide a means of dealing with the problems caused by an increase in population, and we shall deal with this matter in the course of time.

The Roman Empire as a unit maintained an almost completely closed economic system. There was little trade with countries outside the Empire, and that was usually limited to a few luxury items or perishables such as spices, expensive cloth, exotic animals and the like. The component geographic units of the Empire, the different provinces, did trade with one another and with Rome. Trade was also important in Judaea and we have already discussed the matter in Chapter 3. The need to pay taxes in ready cash also affected each economy (Hopkins 1980). Thus, the residents of the Land of Israel would solve the problem of "feeding" additional population not only through increasing agricultural production. It is those alternative

non-agricultural means of solving the problem which we shall now determine and examine.

In spite of what we have just said, it is still probable that most energy went
into solving the problem through agricultural means. There are two reasons
for this assumption.

(1) Agriculture, in its widest sense and including all those labors and the
like associated with it, was the most widespread and important source of
income in the entire Empire as well as in the Land of Israel (Chapter 2
above). It is no surprise, therefore, that this economic sphere should provide
most of the impetus for increased economic growth. Moreover, in accordance with modern standards, at least, most of the residents of the Land of
Israel had a rather low standard of living. It is well known that the lower the
standard of living, the more it is necessary to use a greater proportion of
income for basic survival. The average resident of the Empire needed first
and foremost to secure a source of food and used most of his income for this
purpose. Since agriculture was, and is, the major and often only source of
food, apart from such secondary items as salt, it would be of significant
importance in the Empire.

(2) Transport was very expensive. The Empire did develop a quite extensive transport system with roads and road services. In spite of all this,
transport was still expensive (Chapter 5 above). Food, in its various forms, is
usually large and bulky and commands a relatively low initial price. In such a
case, the cost of transport would be a significant factor in raising expenses.
However, as we have seen, this was less critical in cases of transport in the
Land of Israel (Chapter 5).

In any case, based on conditions in the Land of Israel, it was up to local
agriculture to make the first efforts to support any increase in population.
Only in later and more advanced stages of this development would there be
economic justification for alternative methods.

I.2.3

Increasing agricultural production is dependent upon a number of stages.

(1) *Using plots which had not been used before.* In the small Land of Israel
this factor was of secondary importance. Even in those periods of economic
decline there was little available agricultural land which was not used.
Regarding the Land of Israel, therefore, this could only serve as a temporary
solution.

(2) *Intensification of agricultural labor.* This implies more extensive working of the land, preparing plots for cultivation which had only been used
sporadically before, and turning low-profit crops into "intensive" ones
yielding a much higher level of profit. The process of intensification usually
takes place simultaneously at different levels. Those areas previously used
for pasture are now cultivated with grain. Those plots cultivated with grain

are now turned into orchards. Olive orchards now become grape arbors, producing a more profitable product. Choosing the type of produce to grow in accordance with optimal agricultural conditions is obviously dependent on the nature of the land and the conditions of market and we shall not go into detail here on the possible differences in the various regions of the Land of Israel.

The process of intensification requires additional investment in terms of various factors.

(1) *Labor*. Intensive agriculture demands more labor in terms of preparing a plot (which might not have been cultivated at all before) and more energy in terms of detail and care in farm work. There must also be greater efforts made to protect the crop from the vagaries of nature and more must be invested in agricultural installations for those labors associated with the produce and the preservation of the produce. Today capital investment is considered a necessary stage of any economic development. However, in the reality of the ancient world, self or hired labor was the most expensive economic component. Capital investment was necessary only for buying work implements (made of iron) or for hiring specialist labor. These were clearly secondary factors. The individual farmer could certainly have hired farm laborers instead of working by himself. In terms of the entire society, this was an investment in labor.

(2) *Knowledge and specialization*. It is possible to achieve higher yields through greater expertise and knowledge, or, in other words, by developing new systems of labor, sophisticated and beneficial machinery, new species which are adapted to local conditions and similar innovations. During modern times, most increases in crop production are the result of greater agricultural and genetic knowledge, and making this knowledge available to farmers who previously worked in more traditional manners. The dispersal of knowledge and the development of further agricultural expertise is dependent not only on economic pressure, but especially on the natural intelligence and cultural level of the farmers. It is also dependent on their willingness to implement new agro-technical innovations. In the ancient world there was no institution which engaged in systematic agricultural research. In spite of this, luck, natural intuition and a high agro-cultural level could result in new innovations. Usually, increasing knowledge is dependent on an additional investment in terms of days of labor, since the discovery is often made during work and the discovery may require more labor, or a new species may also require additional work or labor.

The farmer in the Land of Israel was in somewhat of a quandary regarding the necessity of additional investment of labor. Farm work here was seasonal. During the peak seasons the farmer was busy in the field and could have hardly made an additional investment in terms of labor. However, there were other times when the farmer was less busy (see Figure 81) and therefore the problem of the farmer was how best to use the off-season in order to make this time profitable. Theoretically, the farmer could raise some type of winter crop. The trick, however, was to find some sort of crop which would require an increase in labor investment only during these off-seasons. The peak season then sort of formed a bottleneck which dictated the conditions regarding labor during the rest of the year. We shall discuss below the realistic options available to the ancient farmer.

The possibilities of intensification and increasing yields are limited by the law of diminishing returns. According to this law, increased investment in the same plot of land, whether in terms of money, labor or knowledge, will result in less profit than the original investment produced. The farmer who continues to invest in developing his land does indeed make a profit from every unit of investment, but this profit consistently diminishes until additional investment is no longer profitable. The exact details of this process are beyond the purview of our study. It is clear, though, that the limits of profitability are determined by the options available to the investor. In other words, the farmer will probably be better off if, instead of continuing to develop his land and increase his investment in it, he could find additional channels for available labor. As we have just stated, there is a certain point beyond which additional investment is no longer profitable. Much before this, though, the wise investor will find another additional means of support and profit.

Boserup states in her book that a society in which the means of agriculture are not intensive is one in which there are few hours of labor. This is a society which does not have to face the challenge of increased population. It is interesting that in the ancient world, the desire for an increased standard of living did not serve as a catalyst for intensification. This matter should be explained, but it is also beyond the scope of our present work.

Now it is necessary to examine what actually happened in Judaea during the Roman period.

II. ECONOMIC GROWTH

II.1 Intensification of agricultural labour

II.1.1 Settlement in abandoned regions

There were actually no areas in the Land of Israel which were completely abandoned. Even in those regions in which it was difficult to eke out a living there were always a few residents, and those areas in which it was impossible to raise wheat were used for grazing. Therefore, we are not really dealing with absolutely newly settled regions but rather with a marked increase in settlements of those regions on the periphery which traditionally had a small population. All of these sparsely populated regions underwent a great demographic boom and many even became thickly populated. This was the case, for instance, in the *shephelah* of Lod (Z. Safrai, unpublished survey), the southern Sharon (Roll and Ayalon 1989), the Carmel (Olami 1981; Ronen 1983; Ronen and Olami 1978) and in other regions (see Kochavi 1972, pp. 196–293). The northern Negev should also be added to this list since this region also evinced similar demographic phenomena. However, at least part of this region was not included within the boundaries of the province of Palestine and demographic development in the Negev was dependent, in addition to other factors, on the actions of the Roman government in the east, in the Land of Israel in general and in the southern *Limes*, the line of border fortifications, in particular. In any case, this makes the Negev not completely indicative of what was going on in the rest of the Land of Israel. Further settlement was possible in these peripheral regions only by increasing the amount of cultivated land. In the Sharon this was dependent on the development of a regional drainage system. In the Beer Sheva Valley and in the Negev which, as we mentioned, is beyond the purview of our study, this required the installation of a water storage system. In the *shephelah* of Lod it was necessary to prepare more land for cultivation, particularly by removing the many stones. In this region signs of some systematic and centrally controlled organized distribution of lands into plots have even been discovered (see Figure 80).

In some of these regions, the inhabitants were able to achieve some degree of intensive agriculture, such as cultivation of the vine. In some regions they had to make do with achieving less in terms of intensification and cultivating olives and barley. The matter was certainly dependent to a great extent on the nature of the ecological problems of the region. Thus, for instance, in the *shephelah* of Lod many grape-pressing installations were discovered, but the olive still remained the major crop. Grape-pressing installations have not been discovered in the Beer Sheva Valley, while in the Sharon many have been discovered. These, of course, are only examples, and we shall refrain from a full agronomic discussion of the peripheral regions of the Land of Israel.

II.1.2 The establishment of satellite settlements

One of the more or less necessary components of the intensification process is the establishment of satellite settlements. Usually, the residents of a village will begin the intensification process in more outlying plots. However, in order to continue to further develop this plot, the farmer will generally prefer building a house near this particular area. The further away the farmer lives from the plot which he cultivates, the greater are his expenses, and this increased expense can often be quite critical. Thus, for example, if a certain plot requires 60 days of work per year, a farmer having to travel 2 kilometers from his village to the plot will increase the required labor by another 6 days of labor (the time it takes to walk 240 kilometers), or by 16 per cent.

Moreover, the farmer will think twice before he goes out to his field for short-term labor or for a seasonal check. All this is in addition to increased transport cost in terms of produce, fertilizer and other similar expenses. This entire matter is fairly well known throughout the world and has been much documented (Hudson 1969; Chisholm 1968).

As has been shown, it is certain that satellite settlements were also established in the Land of Israel (see also Chapter 1). This phenomenon started rather early, but it reached its zenith in the Byzantine period. Many of the sites which were established at this time were only 2–5 dunams and should be considered as satellite settlements. There are, of course, other reasons for the establishment of satellite settlements. Relevant data pertaining to the Land of Israel, though, seems to indicate that it was agricultural intensification that brought about the greatest increase in the establishment of satellite settlements.

In addition to economic pressure, there are two additional factors which play a role in the establishment of satellite settlements: (1) satisfactory security conditions; (2) a society which is not dependent on community services. It is very difficult for a satellite settlement to establish such necessary community services as supplying water, education, sanitation, trade, culture and the like.

During the Mishnah and Talmud periods there was generally peace and for the most part there were no wars. Even if there was fighting, this was usually between empires and did not affect residents of rural farm settlements. Security conditions, however, were not perfect, to say the least, and there was, for instance, a good deal of brigandage (MacMullen 1961, pp. 225–69; B. Isaac 1984). In southern Palestine, and perhaps also in the Golan, the situation was more serious because of Saracen incursions. The residents of rural villages were fully aware of this situation as can be clearly seen very often from the choice of location for the village as well as by the type of building there.

During the Mishnah and Talmud periods village-towns had a quite developed system of community services. This pertains particularly to Jewish settlements, but non-Jewish villages also provided their residents with a degree of communal services (Chapter 1.III above).

All of this leads to the conclusion that conditions during the Mishnah and Talmud periods were not all that conducive for the establishment of satellite settlements. However, the economic pressure was often so intense that many people were willing to give up the benefits of a good communal service system and to risk having to deal with brigands in order to survive and make a living; this resulted in the establishment of satellite settlements.

II.1.3 The development of systems of intensifying agricultural cultivation

II.1.3.1 Intensive cultivation

Agriculture in the Land of Israel was usually quite intensive with a great deal of labor, knowledge and expertise invested in certain types of crops (Chapter 2 above). The law which forbids the grazing of animals in agricultural lands serves as an indirect proof of this reality (Chapter 2.I.8). This *halachah* dates from the end of the Second Temple period and reflects the continuing struggle between those seeking pasture land and those seeking arable land. After the destruction of the Temple it became forbidden to graze sheep and goats on arable land. This provides a chronological testimony of sorts to the phenomenon of the expansion of arable land at the expense of pasture land. Josephus, for instance, still mentions the great amount of pasture land in Judaea, Samaria and the Galilee as a positive phenomenon (*BJ* 3. 42). After the destruction of the Temple there was opposition to this view.

As we mentioned above, the intensification process of agricultural cultivation was the result not only of increased labor but also of new botanical and agro-technical innovations. The stress in this sphere was most likely on the development of more fertile and profitable crops and species, even if they necessitated increased labor.

The sources mention a number of important watersheds on these matters: as we have already seen in our discussion of legumes (Chapter 2.I), the farmer often cultivated this type of crop when he left his fields fallow from other crops. It is impossible to date this innovation, but it does serve as a good example of the transference from a biennial system of cultivation to an annual one. As we have also mentioned above, Boserup mentions this process as the first stage of agro-economic growth.

II.1.3.2 The introduction of new crops and agricultural spheres

In our discussion above in Chapter 2 we have already mentioned the introduction of new agricultural species during the first and second centuries CE such as rice, flax and industrial-type crops which were all of great importance. Among the new agricultural fields developed at this time were the *ethrog*, silk, as well as others which we discussed above. Balsam and myrrh were also re-introduced at the end of the Hellenistic period and later on new crops or products were developed or introduced such as pepper, bee-keeping or the expansion of the fishing industry.

II.1.3.3 The introduction of new labor techniques

Due to the paucity of material before the Talmudic period regarding labor techniques, it is difficult to determine which techniques represented new developments. In spite of this, it is possible to suggest a number of such techniques which were developed in the Mishnah and Talmud periods such as the stringing and lifting of grapevines onto a trellis and grafting in orchards or groves.

During the Second Temple period the grapevines were not cultivated on a trellis, but stretched along the ground. Only when they began to ripen were the stems picked up off the ground and placed on stones. The sages of the Second Temple period expressed negative opinions regarding vines which were grown on a trellis, and did not allow them to be brought to the Temple (M Menahot 8:6; T Menahot 9:10). This technique became very popular, though, after the destruction of the Temple (Chapter 2.I.3 above). The use of the trellis was re-innovated apparently after the Second Temple period and then became popular. Thus, for example, the Bar-Kochba letters mention two workers who specialized in the cultivation of grapes on a trellis (DJD II, no. 29, p. 42) and R. Ishmael asks R. Joshua two questions connected with the construction of a grape trellis on other trees (M Kilayim 6:4 and parallels). From the tone of the question it would seem that the phenomenon was rather new and it was necessary for R. Joshua to actually see it in order to make up his mind.

As to grafting, it was undoubtedly known that new and better species could be developed through grafting even during early periods. A Tannaitic tradition describes a Galilean farmer who tried to develop two new and previously unknown types of grafts (T Kilayim 1:3–4). It was necessary for the sages of that time to express their views regarding the permissibility of this experiment, proving that this type of grafting was not common before this time.

II.1.3.4 Hydro-technical innovations

Irrigation is an important factor in the agriculture of the Land of Israel. In fact, water is such an important factor that if the amount made available to agriculture is increased, it may be possible to double and even occasionally triple crop yields. Researchers today wonder why the ancients did not develop more efficient means of irrigation. There are a number of answers to this question. What is certainly clear, though, is that the ancients did not really know how to harness great amounts of water to the service of agriculture, and when they did make such attempts, they were not very successful or efficient. The agriculture of the Land of Israel was for the most part not dependent upon irrigation. Irrigation basically required sources of water such as springs or rivers. The hydrological potential of the Land of Israel certainly was not maximalized, even in light of the limited hydro-technical innovations of the Roman period.

A number of impressive irrigation installations were constructed around and near fountains in Judaea and Galilee (Ron 1977a; 1977b), although it is not quite clear exactly when this construction took place. The development of irrigation installations in the Roman period was apparently connected with or dependent upon the central government. In the fourth century CE two water systems were built in the basin of the Sea of Galilee to supply the water and agricultural needs of the neighboring settlements of the area. These water systems apparently served as catalysts for the economic growth of the region and most of the settlements of the area underwent a spurt of growth and development at this time. The development of flax and rice cultivation during the Roman period was probably also dependent upon the expansion of irrigation systems (Chapter 5 above). The Jewish farmer was very educated, which enabled him to more easily accept these new techniques.

Thus, it is possible to sum up and state that during the Roman and Byzantine periods there were a number of important developments in the realm of hydrological projects. In spite of this, though, the high hydro-technical skills of the Roman Empire were not used for the most part for the further development of agriculture, but rather for the cities of the Roman Empire. Thus, there were no watersheds in the history of irrigation during the Mishnah and Talmud periods.

II.2 Development of new areas of craftsmanship

As we have already seen, agricultural development is limited by its very nature and the greater the relative increase in the amount and level of investment of capital, labor or knowledge, the lower the return on those investments. Thus, the most logical solution to the problems discussed above would be to find new sources of income. Moreover, the winter in the Land of Israel is a rather light agricultural season and it is only natural that farmers should seek additional means of sustenance during that time.

A good description of the agriculture of the Land of Israel at the end of the Second Temple period is found in the writings of Josephus (*BJ* 3. 41–50). Josephus, in his description of the Land of Israel, does not mention crafts or industry, but only agriculture. The same phenomenon is found in other works of that period (Chapter 3.I above).

During the Mishnah and Talmud periods the situation was different. There were many rural settlements with craftsmen and the sources even mention large groups of workers organized into professional guilds (Chapter 2.II above). In our discussion of crafts we have differentiated between those producing goods or services for the local market and those producing for export. The major industrial export from the Land of Israel was textiles. In the Galilee glass was also exported. The textile industry was extremely important. The major exporters were the cities of Beth Shean, Neapolis, Caesarea, Lod and Tiberias. There were factories, workshops and the like not only in the mother city, but also in the rural territory surrounding it

(Chapter 2.II). The raw material of this industry was mostly flax, with wool also being used mainly in Judaea. The raw material was turned into fibers and this in turn became fabric. The final product was a white or colored cloth. Sometimes the garment was even sewn in the local factory and the finished garment was then sold in local markets or abroad in cities.

As we have just stated, the basic material of this industry was flax, and thus it is possible to talk about the "flax revolution" which changed the agriculture and economy of the Land of Israel (Chapter 2.I.7).

The weak point of the agriculture of the Land of Israel was the cultivation of grains. Conditions in the Land of Israel were more appropriate for the cultivation of those crops which could be raised in orchards or groves; therefore there was always a chronic shortage of grains, especially serious in the light of the importance of flour in the diet of the inhabitants of the ancient Land of Israel. Flax was the most serious rival for those arable areas which were appropriate for the cultivation of wheat. Flax needs areas for soaking, rich in water. Such areas were also the major grain producers of the Land of Israel. Because of factors connected with crop rotation, flax was cultivated only once every four or six years while wheat was sown only once every two years. Thus, it appears that the cultivation of flax came at the expense of a third or a half of the long-term yield of wheat.

Thus, expansion of flax cultivation came at the expense of a cut in grain cultivation of those regions which provided the basic food commodity of the Land of Israel. It was necessary to import grain from abroad. Linen, produced from flax, was sold abroad and the profits were used to buy grain from the Transjordan regions or from Egypt. Thus, during the Talmud period grain was imported to the Land of Israel which was not the case during the Second Temple period (Chapter 2.I.2).

The "flax revolution", therefore, provided for a great increase of labor in a new intensively cultivated crop. Moreover, the farmer could now put in increased "industrial" labor time during the winter on those tasks related to turning the flax into linen. All of this required, however, changes in the agricultural-economic makeup of the Land of Israel and the introduction of an open economic system, which we have already discussed above. The cultivation of flax fits in quite well within the schedule of agricultural labors during the Mishnah and Talmud periods, as we shall shortly discuss.

Another field of export was glass utensils (Chapter 2.II.2). The raw material for their preparation was brought for the most part from the Acco Valley. The necessary fuel and combustible material came from the Upper and Lower Galilee. Many industrial installations have been found in the towns of the Carmel Range and the Galilee and there are also literary traditions pertaining to this phenomenon. From a geographic-economic standpoint, these industrial installations are not located at optimum sites. If the raw material was brought from the Acco Valley to Ptolemais (Acco), it would have been much more logical to build the installations in this general area. The construction of the installations in the Galilee and Carmel Range probably derives from the desire of the residents of these areas to find additional sources of income and support for their settlements.

II.3 The open economic system (see also Chapter 5)

II.3.1

The economy of the Second Temple period was a closed one. The Land of Israel was for the most part self-sufficient and most farmers produced for their own needs. This was not the case in the Mishnah and Talmud periods. This became the period of specialization and each region began to cultivate those crops for which it was particularly suited (Chapter 4.V.3 above). Thus, for example, the Galilee was an olive-raising region, Judaea was the center of grape cultivation and the Jordan Valley specialized in dates.

The province exported wine and oil (as well as textiles and glass) and imported industrial items, metals and especially grains. There was active trade between a mother city and its surrounding villages. There was also active trade between rural villages and the coastal harbor cities dealing in exports and imports. There were fairs and markets in the Land of Israel and donkey or camel caravans plied the roads between various settlements (Chapter 3.III.2). There were specialists of various professions in the villages as well as providers of necessary services such as bakers, cooks, slaughterers and cookers of meat, bathhouse workers and millers. There were also specialists and professionals related to agricultural tasks such as grafters, olive oil workers, flax soakers and the like (Chapter 2.II.3).

These professionals, service-providers, transporters of merchandise and the like were very often actually farmers for whom these tasks were the source of additional labor and income. Thus, for example, we saw above the tradition from Midrash Psalms 12 regarding the leader of the donkey-drivers' guild who was also a farmer. He and his friends considered agriculture preferable to transporting merchandise, even at a profit. There are other such traditions regarding farmers who held additional jobs or engaged in similar activities.

The development of all these new branches of labor as well as the market economy relieved the national economy from the burden of having to feed a large population. As we stated above, the major problem had been regarding the grain supply. Now grain was imported and the economy had only to produce labor and services of equal value in order to pay for it. The individual farmer no longer had to provide for all his food needs. Moreover, and as we have seen above, the return on agricultural investments becomes less and less in accordance with the "law of decreasing marginal output." Now the farmer could invest hours of labor, knowledge and capital in new fields and these investments would most naturally yield higher returns.

Moreover, the farmer could also engage in these profitable pastimes during the winter and rainy season when he had time on his hands in any case and when agricultural labor was quite unprofitable.

In spite of all this, self-production of food was of economic importance even in the open system. All of the basic food staples, except for wheat, were cultivated in the Land of Israel; thus the local and regional needs of these staples could be provided. Since, as we have seen, the Land of Israel exported dates, olives and oil, it would appear that the local and regional needs had been provided for.

II.3.2 The development of commerce in the Land of Israel

The open economic system as well as the production of items produced in industry required the establishment of a commercial framework. The details are beyond the scope of this chapter, but for our purposes it is important to point out that commerce certainly provided new sources of income in addition to agriculture and small-crafts labor. We have already discussed this matter in Chapter 3.

II.3.3 Urbanization in the Land of Israel

The development of a more open economic system, the dependence on land and sea trade and provision of services and the increase in population in general and of non-agricultural sphere population in particular, necessitated increased urbanization, as we have seen above (Chapter 1.II.2, Figure 104). The number of cities in the Land of Israel gradually began to increase. Urban development actually began during the Second Temple period. During those times when the number of cities did not increase, and even decreased, the urban fabric was not becoming weaker, but rather a major urban center was probably becoming stronger. This, of course, affected other cities. This process can be described as positive selection and reflects the strengthening of the urban sector, even if the number of cities did decrease. During the remainder of the Roman period, and during the Byzantine period, the number of cities in the Land of Israel continued to increase while the urban sector became stronger.

It should be pointed out, though, that the cities which made their appearance in the fifth or sixth centuries such as Geba and Sucomazon were for the most part small and "artificial" without a strong economic or settlement base. These are for the most part not "historical" cities and they did not serve as important urban centers, either during the Byzantine period or afterwards.

The construction of cities during the fifth and sixth centuries CE represents a degree of "over-urbanization." Many of these cities had been famous before such as Apollonia and Dora, but had declined after the

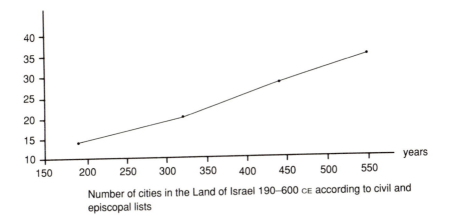

Number of cities in the Land of Israel 190–600 CE according to civil and episcopal lists

Figure 104 Urbanization in Palestine.

construction of Caesarea. Their "re-establishment" does not reflect a trend towards the strengthening of the settlements and economy of the region, but rather another example of "over-urbanization." However, even if this is so, the reconstruction and re-establishment of these cities do reflect an increase in population and a decision by those in charge to recognize additional settlements as cities, in spite of the fact that in terms of modern geo-economic thought, this decision seems rather strange. The question as to possible connections between urbanization and various agrarian processes is beyond the purview of our study.

II.4 Importing capital to the Land of Israel

The importing of capital was of extreme importance for the economic growth of the Land of Israel. This capital consisted of donations of individuals or funds transferred from the imperial treasury. The source of this capital revolved around three factors.

II.4.1

Contributions and taxes of diaspora Jews to sages and leadership institutions in the Land of Israel. Already by the end of the Second Temple period it was customary to send donations from abroad to the Land of Israel and the Temple (S. Safrai 1983, pp. 37–54). In the Javneh period, the payment of taxes, dues and the like from diaspora Jews was institutionalized. There are many traditions regarding the revitalization of this system during the period of Rabbi Judah the Prince (S. Safrai, ibid.; Alon 1984, II, pp. 692–5).

455

Another form of contributions of this type was related to the burial of diaspora Jews in the Land of Israel. This also became quite common during the period of Rabbi Judah the Prince in the third century CE (Gafni 1977). The monies collected as a result of this phenomenon were, of course, in addition to the regular and voluntary contributions of Jews given to sages and their students.

II.4.2

Contributions and official grants of Christians were sent to the Land of Israel for the purpose of building and supporting churches, "holy sites," monasteries and the like. All of this was in addition to profits of the pilgrim trade. Many of the monks and pilgrims were from the upper classes and came with large entourages. Needless to say, all of this was relevant only from the fourth century onwards and influx of Christian capital replaced Jewish capital to a great extent. It is difficult to estimate the relative effect of this imported capital on the economy of the Land of Israel. There certainly was a good deal of Christian capital brought to the Land of Israel, but there is no quantitative tool which would enable us to measure its effect on the economy. It is likely that the economic growth of Jerusalem in the fourth century CE and afterwards was the result of this process, but Jerusalem was always the exception to the rule and should not be considered indicative of the situation in general.

II.4.3

The Roman army was an important source of capital. After the Bar-Kochba War and until the end of the third century CE there were two legions in the Land of Israel, numbering together a little less than 10,000 legionnaires and most likely the same amount of auxiliary forces. Thus, there were about some 20,000–25,000 Roman soldiers in the Land of Israel, a relatively large number in terms of the population in general and the province of Judaea indeed had the highest ratio of soldiers in relation to per capita population in the entire Empire. This was of tremendous importance. The influence of the Roman army on the economy of a province as well as on culture in general has been studied in a number of provinces like Britain and Germany. Based on the large amount of Roman forces in the Land of Israel, the influence of the Roman soldiers on the economy should have been very great, greater than in the provinces mentioned above and certainly greater than the influence of the Roman soldiers in the border provinces just mentioned. We have already discussed a number of factors related to this phenomenon (see Chapter 4 II above). (1) In order to support the Roman expeditionary forces in the Land of Israel there was a need for an influx of capital and supplies of at least 10–20 per cent of the gross national product of the province. This influx was of great importance in changing the economic fabric of a province from a closed agricultural system to an open one based on trade and commerce. (2) The influx of capital was used to buy goods and services from local residents, providing, therefore, a source of income in addition to agriculture, labor and services. (3) The army was a consumer of luxury items and its presence in the province served as a stimulus for the production of high-quality items and merchandise. (4) Most likely settlements of merchants and providers of services were established near military camps (*vicus*, *pagus*) and near these camps there eventually developed markets, labor and commercial centers. All of this was, of course, in addition to all the other influences of the Roman army on a province which we have already discussed above.

Thus, it is possible to sum up and state that during normal, peaceful conditions the presence of the Roman army had a great positive influence on the national economy. It is quite likely, though, that the Jewish settlement in the Land of Israel did not consider this to be a positive phenomenon and instead felt debased and persecuted by the massive presence of the Roman army.

III. CONCLUSIONS

III.1 Demographic multiplication and economic growth: cause and effect

Demographic multiplication and economic growth are two parallel processes and it is important to determine cause and effect. Did the economic pressure that was caused by population increase bring about economic growth or was it economic growth that allowed for population increase? Regardless of the answer, both processes were parallel, as we just pointed out, and they both lasted for a rather long period of time (from 200 to 400 years). The question, therefore, is to some degree academic since in reality both processes were intertwined. The only real difference between the two relates to the perception of the population. If the catalyst of economic growth is population increase, then the general feeling of the population is one of pressure and strain. But if it is the other way round and the population increase is the result of economic growth, then the prevailing feeling will be one of well-being and optimism and the source material of the period will reflect these feelings and not those of scarcity and pressure.

The contemporary traditions would seem to indicate that the period under discussion was one of dire economic straits and the Jewish emigration from the Land of Israel would seem to be proof of this phenomenon. There are many Tannaitic and Amoraic sources which mention economic difficulties, even if this is not the main point of the source. The economic problems mentioned in the sources were for the most part solved, but their very mention in the source material does reflect existing conditions. Moreover, conditions in the rural sector or in the villages were certainly constrained. All the signs seem to indicate that it was population increase which resulted in economic stress and it was this stress which in the final analysis brought about economic growth.

III.2 The crisis: the end of the tale

Population increase resulted in the utilization of all potential resources in the land. Branches of labor and industry were also developed which were dependent on international commerce. This system was by its nature more sensitive to dangers which could make life difficult for the inhabitants of the Land of Israel and, indeed, even cause the collapse of the settlement. The international trade framework might become fossilized because of security and economic problems, and indeed by the end of the Byzantine period and with the Muslim conquest of the Land of Israel the commercial framework of the country began to fall apart, even if the collapse was not total. It would appear that conditions in the Land of Israel had begun to deteriorate before. Population increase and economic growth all but ceased and even started to decline. With the Muslim conquest, however, there was an especially sharp decline in population.

Population increase is a social process and like every other similar process it does not stop all at once in a drastic manner. Moreover, it takes 20–30 years from birth until maturity. The preparations for the crisis of economic stagnation had to begin a generation before the actual crisis and it is unlikely that anyone could foresee the problems so far in advance. Thus, at the end of the first generation of the period of the anarchy (225–84), conditions in the Land of Israel were quite bad. Population increase was still taking place and with it the need for additional sources of food and support, while economic growth and development had halted and there had maybe even been a decline in national production. This crisis was relatively short. At the end of the Byzantine period or at the beginning of the Muslim period, there was a much more serious crisis in which the entire commercial and market system collapsed. The process of demographic growth and multiplication, however, did not cease. The lack of economic balance catapulted the Land of Israel into a long depression from which it only really recovered in the twentieth century. The process of economic decline is, by its very nature, a long and continuous one. Traditional archeology is almost powerless to date this process. It seems the decline began before the end of the Byzantine period and ended during the mid-eighth century. The question of precise dating is still open.

Appendix I
Rabbinic literature:
an illustrated lexicon

INTRODUCTION

The rabbinic literature of the Mishnaic and Talmudic periods is a summary of the discussions that were held in the different *batei midrash* (schools), particularly in the period between the first and the fourth centuries CE. Some of the essays mentioned were written or edited later, between the fifth and ninth centuries, but these contain only a bit of "updated" material, such as proverbs or opinions from the sixth or seventh century. The essays that include material from this period are noted below.

The languages used for teaching in the *batei midrash* (schools) were Aramaic and Hebrew. The writing and editing were done mainly in Hebrew; in some of the essays some material in Aramaic was also incorporated.

BASIC CONCEPTS

(1) **Mishna**. The root *sh.n.n.* means 'to learn', so that *mishna* means learning *halachah* (see below) – the decision or the settlement of a controversy between two rabbis, without justification or explanation.

(2) **Talmud** (in Hebrew) or **Gemarra** (in Aramaic). The root *l.m.d.* in Hebrew means 'study'. The corresponding root in Aramaic is *g.m.r.*; hence the term 'Gemarra'. The Talmud is a study of the Mishna, an investigation of the rationale and precedents of each decision, a search for parallels and examination of its possible implications.

(3) **Midrash** is the study of the Bible, and particularly the Torah, in the light of the interpretations of the rabbis. In this context the focus is on identifying the relationship between the rules that appear in the Mishna and the verses of the Torah. Some of the teachings of the rabbis are interpretations; the majority are books far from literal readings. Similar to the Greek scholastics and the fathers of the Church, the rabbis adopted "creative interpretation" and took the liberty of removing things from their straightforward context so that they would fit with the *halakha* and the accepted views of their times.

Later, these three terms also became the names of written texts according to this method of study (see below).

Numerous *batei midrash* (schools) operated in Palestine and in Babylon; we have texts from dozens of such institutions. Representing hundreds of years of learning and study, the material of course comprises many literary strata. In general, these are not personal works but the summary of teachings of a social and intellectual stratum that invested tremendous cultural effort in their preparation.

THE CHRONOLOGY

We do not know exactly when the literature on the Oral Law was first written. The earliest specific mention is found in the second century BCE, and the first real information dates back to the days of the Second Temple. The rabbinic literature became a reliable and significant source from approximately the late first century to the mid-fourth century.

In terms of chronology and literary aspects, the known essays can be divided into two main groups: (a) *Tannaic* texts, which were written in the first half of the third century, and (b) *Amoraic* texts, most of which were written between the fourth and seventh centuries, the period known as the "Amoraic period" (230–400 CE). The essays combine Tannaic and Amoraic material. Sometimes they present sayings as Tannaic, but these have been somewhat edited and in some cases reworded by the *Amoraim*. In most of the essays there is almost no reflection of life in the Amoraic period, that is, after the fourth century.

MAIN TERMS

Torah or Scriptures

These are the books of the Bible, particularly the Pentateuch. Obligatory reading, they also served as a source of inspiration. The rabbis considered themselves bound to obey the Torah unquestioningly. This duty was also interpreted as the right to preach (see below) on the teachings of the Torah.

Oral Law

This term encompasses all the writings of the ages that involve interpretation and expansion of the **Scriptures**, as well as independent and new works.

Rabbi

'Rabbi' or 'sage' is the accepted term used to refer to the authors of the different generations. The rabbis assumed the right to interpret, to convey as tradition, and to renew and create (within limits, which we will not discuss here). In the Tannaic period (70–230 CE) the rabbis were known as *Tannaim*; in the Amoraic period, as *Amoraim*.

Midrash

The *midrash* was the method by which the rabbis learned and interpreted the Torah. The *midrash* sometimes ignores the simple content of the Torah and removes verses and even words from their contexts, shifting them to another subject. The *midrash* is, then, almost unrestrained "creative" interpretation. The *midrashim* are divided into *midrashey halakha*, in which "rules" are learned from the verses, and *midrashey agada*, which deal with legends, moral teachings, stories and the like.

Halachah

Halachah is the Jewish law as edited and developed in the discussions of the rabbis.

Mahloket (controversy)

The Oral Law evolved over many generations in different *batei midrash* (schools) and under the direction of different rabbis. In the course of time, differing opinions emerged. All these were considered legitimate and many were preserved in the oral tradition and in the rabbinic literature.

Baraitha

All the Tannaic traditions that were not collected in the Mishna are known as *Baraithot*. These are found in a number of volumes, such as the "Tosefta" and the "*Midrashey halakha*," and many of them are integrated into the literature of the *Amoraim*.

MAIN TYPES OF BOOKS

The *Mishna* is a collection or edited version of the rules and controversies on issues related to the *halachah*. Edited by Rabbi Yehuda Hanassi (early third century), it is written in the "*Mishna*" style. However, in some places excerpts of "*midrash*" and "*Talmud*" are incorporated. The Mishna is divided into six *orders*; in each order there are several *tractates*, which are divided into chapters and subchapters. Every tractate is devoted to a specific subject.

The Mishna served as a text book in the *batei midrash* (schools) in the Talmudic period, and it played a central role in the determination of laws that were established for the generations to come. It is unclear whether Rabbi Yehuda Hanassi saw his work as a text book alone, or also as a collection of rules (*Halachot*). It seems that the former possibility is more likely.

Tosefta

The Tosefta is a collection of *Baraithot*, organized according to the Mishna, which includes expansion on the teachings of the Mishna and various additions to the Mishna, examples of the rules in the Mishna, and the like.

The Jerusalem Talmud

This Talmud contains a collection of discussions of the Mishna, and was written according to the Talmudic teaching method. The authors of the Jerusalem Talmud considered the Mishna a textbook as well as a book of rules. The Jerusalem Talmud was written in the fourth century. It is not fully edited and is difficult to comprehend.

The Babylonian Talmud

The Babylonian Talmud is similar to the Jerusalem Talmud in character, but was written in Babylon in the fifth century. It includes Tannaic and Amoraic traditions from Palestine and Babylon. The Babylonian Talmud is known for its thorough editing and precise literary structure, which was improved by the different groups of editors. The internal editing in this Talmud is more developed than that of the Jerusalem Talmud; this facilitates study but makes it more difficult to use the text as a historical source.

Midrashey Halachah

This is a group of Tannaic *midrashim*, which interpret and teach the five books of the Bible in which there are rules (excepting the Book of Genesis). Although most of these *midrashim* are concerned with rules (*midrashey halachah*), some also deal with legends. The teachings of rules are Mekhiltah (by Rabbi Yishmael and Rabbi Shimon Bar Yohai) on the Book of Exodus; Siphra or the Law of the Priests on Leviticus; Siphre and Siphre Zuta on Numbers, and Siphre and Midrash Tannaim for Deutoronomy.

Midrashey Agada

This is a general term for numerous books that contain *midrashim*. All *midrashim* that are not included in the list of *midrashey halakha* are *midrashey agada*. Most of these are homilies on and interpret books of the Bible, such as the *midrash* Bereishit Raba on the Book of Genesis, and *midrash* Tehilim for the Book of Psalms. This group also includes some unusual essays, which are constructed in a different literary form.

Literature

In the last generation, a number of useful books and essays were written about the writings of the rabbis (such as S. Safrai *et al.*, 1976 and later; Starck and Stemberger 1991). For a selected list of translations to modern languages, see Starck and Stemberger 1991, pp. 390–401 (and below).

Appendix II
Rabbinic texts: abbreviations

(A) MISHNAH, TOSEFTA, TALMUDS

BT	Babylonian Talmud
M	Mishnah
PT	Palestinian Talmud
T	Tosefta

Abbreviations of the tractates of these works are the same throughout. The quotations are distinguished as follows: M is quoted according to chapter and *halakah* (e.g. AZ 1:1), BT according to folio, side a or b (e.g. AZ 2b); quotations from PT are preceded by 'p'. (e.g. pt. AZ 1, 39a: the first two digits represent the chapter, the third gives the folio and column).

Abot		Maas	Maa'serot
Arak	Arakhin	Mak	Makkot
AZ	Abodah Zarah	Makh	Makhshirin
BB	Baba Batra	MSh	Maa'ser Sheni
Bek	Bekhorot	Meg	Megillah
Besah		Me'ilah	
Bik	Bikkurim	Men	Menahot
BM	Bava Mesia	Mid	Middot
BQ	Bava Qamma	Miqw	Miqwaot
Demai		MQ	Moed Qatan
Eduy	Eduyot	Naz	Nazir
Erub	Erubin	Ned	Nedarim
Git	Gittin	Neg	Negaim
Hag	Hagiga	Ohal	Ohalot
Hor	Horayot	Orlah	
Hul	Hullin	Parah	
Kel	Kelim	Peah	
Ker	Keritot	Pes	Pesahim
Ket	Ketubbot	Qid	Qiddushin
Kil	Kilayim	Qin	Qinnim

RH	Rosh ha-Shanah	Tebul	Yom
Sanh	Sanhedrin	Tem	Temurot
Shab	Shabbat	Ter	Terumot
Shebi	Shebiit	Uqsin	
Shebu	Shebuot	Yad	Yadayim
Sheq	Sheqalim	Yeb	Yebamot
Sot	Sotah	Yoma	
Suk	Sukkah	Zab	Zabim
Taan	Taa'nit	Zeb	Zebahim
Tam	Tamid		

(B) OTHER TEXTS

ARN *Abot de Rabbi Nathan.* Text A or B; Sch. – Edition S. Schechter, Vienna 1887.

Bereshit Rabba   Genesis Rabbah; Th-A – J. Theodor and Ch. Albeck, *Midrash Bereshit Rabba: Critical editions with Notes and Commentary*, 2nd edn, Jerusalem 1965.

LevR   Leviticus Rabbah; = M. Margulies, *Midrash Wayyikra Rabbah* 5 vols, Jerusalem 1953–60.

Mek   Mekhilta de R. Ishmael; = J.Z. Lauterbach, *Mekilta de Rabbi Ishmael*, 3 vols, Philadelphia 1933–5.

Midrash Ha-Gadol (Haggadol)   Midrash on Genesis, ed. Margolies, M., Jerusalem 1947; Midrash on Exodus, ed. Margolies, M., Jerusalem undated; Midrash on Leviticus, ed. Rabinowitz, E.N., New York 1932; Midrash on Numbers, ed. Fisch, S., London 1957; Midrash on Deuteronomy, ed. Fisch, S., Jerusalem 1972.

Midrash Psalem   Midrash on Psalms; = S. Buber, *Midrasch Tehillim*, Wilna 1892; repr. Jerusalem 1966.

Midrash Proverbs   Midrash on Proverbs; = S. Buber, *Midrasch Tehillim*, Wilna 1892; repr. Jerusalem 1965.

Midrash Tannaim   Midrash Tannaim; = D. Hoffmann, *Midrasch Tannaim zum Deuteronomium*, Berlin 1908–9.

MRS   Mekhilta de R. Simeon b. Yohai; = Edition J. N. Epstein and E. Z. Melamed, Jerusalem 1965.

Tana D've Eliahu   Tana De'bei' Eliahu Seder Eliahu Rabbah; = Edition M. Friedmann, Vienna 1902; repr. Jerusalem 1960.

SZ   Sifre Zuttah; = Edition H. S. Horovitz, 2nd edn, Jerusalem 1966.

Tan   Tanhuma

TanB   Tanhuma Buber

Bibliography of ancient sources

Aeneas of Gaza, 1950, *Epistulae*, ed. Positano, L. M., Rome.

Ammianus Marcellinus, *Rerum Gesarum*, tr. Rolfe, J. C., (Loeb).

Antoninus of Placentia, 1891, *Itinerarium*, ed. Geyer, P., in: *Itinera Hierosolymitana, CSEL*.

Aruch completum I–IX, 1955, ed. Kohut, A., New York.

Baladuri, 1866, *Book of the Conquest*, ed. de Goeje, M. J.

Barsanuphius and Ioannes, 1960, Βίβλος ψυχωφελεστάτη, περιέχουσα ἀποκρίσεις, δια-φόροις ὑποθέσεσιν ἀνήκουσας, συγγραφεῖσα μὲν παρὰ τῶν ὁσίων καὶ θεοφόρων πατέρων ἡμῶν Βαρσανουφίου καὶ Ἰωάννου, ἐπιμελῶς δὲ διορθωθεῖσα καὶ τῇ τῶν ὁσίων βιογραφίᾳ, ed. Schoinas, S. N., Volos; Barsanuphe and Jean de Gaza, 1972, *Correspondance*, tr. Regnault, Lemaire and Outier.

Bruns, K. G. and Sachau, E., 1880, eds, *Syrisch-römische Rechtsbuch*, Leipzig.

Cassiodorus, 1865, *Marco Aurelii Cassiodorii, Variorum, PL* 69.

Cato, Marcus Porcius, 1967, *De agri cultura*, tr. Hooper, W. D. (Loeb).

Celsus, *De medicina*, tr. Spencer, W. G. (Loeb).

Choricius of Gaza, 1929, ed. Förster, R. and Richtsteig, E., Leipzig.

Chronicon paschale, 1832, ed. Dindorf, L., *CSHB*.

Cicero, *The Verrine Orations*, tr. Greenwood, H. G. (Loeb).

Codex Iustinianus, 1929, ed. Krüger, P., Berlin (second part of *Corpus iuris civilis*).

Columella, *De re rustica*, tr. Ash, H. B. (Loeb).

Corippus, 1886, *Flavii Cesconii Corippi Africanii Grammatici, in laudem Justini Augusti*, ed. Petschenig, M., *MGH (AA)* III Berolini.

Corpus Inscriptionum Graecarum, 1828–77, ed. Boeckhuis, A. (= *CIG*) Borussici.

Corpus Inscriptionum Latinarum, 1862– (= *CIL*), Berlin.

Cyprian, 1868, *De mortalitate*, tr. Wallis, E. R., *Ante-Nicene Christian Library*, ed. Roberts, A., and Donaldson, J., 8, pp. 452–68, Edinburgh.

Cyrillus of Scythopolis, 1939, *Vitae SS. Euthynii, Sabae etc.*, ed. Schwartz, E., *TU* 49, tr. Price, H. M., Kalamazoo, 1991.

Digesta seu pandectae (of Justinian), 1863–70 (includes Ulpian), ed. Mommsen, T., Berlin.

Dio Chrysostom, 1979, *Discourses*, tr. Cohoon, J. W. and Coosby, H. L. (Loeb).

Diocletian, 1940, *Edict of Maximum Prices*, ed. and tr. Graser, E. R., in Frank, T., *An Economic Survey of Ancient Rome* V, Baltimore 1940, and ed. Lauffer, S., Berlin, 1971. See also Crawford, M. H., Giacchero, M.

Doctrina Iacobi nuper baptizati, 1901, ed. Donwetsch, N. (*PO* VIII 1963) Göttingen.

Epiphanius, *Adversus haereses* (*Anecdota and Panarion*), ed. Holl, K., *Gr. Schr.*, 25, 31–7.

— 1935, *De mensuris et ponderibus*, ed. and tr. Dean, J. E., Chicago, *PG* 43: 238–94.

Eusebius, *Ecclesiastical History*, tr. Lake, K. L. and Oulton, J. E. L. (Loeb); *PG* 27.
—— 1966, *Das Onomastikon der biblischen Ortsnamen*, ed. Klostermann, E., Hildesheim.
Expositio totius mundi 1882 (= *Totius Orbis Descriptio*), ed. Muller, C. W. L., *Geographi Graecis minores*, II, Paris; ed. Rouge, J., 1966 (Sources chrétiennes 126); ed. Simisamtoni, 1972, Munich.
Fontes iuris Romani ante-iustiniani, 1940–3, (= *FIRA*) 1, ed. Riccobono, S.; 2, Baviera, J., Ferrini, C., Furlani, J.; 3, Arangio-Ruiz, V., Florence.
Gaius, *Institutiones iuris civilis*, 1870, ed. and comment. Poste, E., Oxford.
Galen, 1821–30, Claudii Galenii, *Opera Omnia*, ed. Kuhn, D. C. C., vols 1–19 (20 1965) Leipzig.
Georgius Cyprius 1890, *Descriptio orbis Romani*, ed. Gelzer, Leipzig.
Gregory of Tours, 1927, *History of the Franks*, intr. and tr. Dalton, O. M., Oxford.
—— *Liber in gloria confessorum*, 1885, *MGH* (Scriptores rerum Merovingicarum, 1), ed. Krusch, B., Hanover.
Hierocles, Synecdemus, 1893, ed. Burckhardt, A., Leipzig.
Imperatoris Iustiniani Institutiones, 1949, ed. Moyle, J. B., Oxford.
Itineraria Romana, 1929, ed. Cuntz, O., Leipzig.
Jerome, St., *Commentary to Isaiah*, *PL* 24; *CCSL* 73.
—— *Commentary to Jeremiah*, *PL* 24.
—— *Commentary to Osee*, *PL* 25.
—— *Die Chronik des Hieronimus*, ed. Helm, R., *Gr. Schr.* 47.
—— vitae S. Pauli, S. Hilarionis et malchi monachorum, *PL* 23.
John of Ephesus, 1860, *The Third Part of the Ecclesiastical History*, ed. and tr. Payne Smith, P., Oxford.
—— *Vitae sanctorum orientalium*, 1923, 1924, 1926, ed. and tr. Brooks, E. W., *PO* 17, 18, 19.
Josephus, *Antiq.* and *Wars* tr. Thackeray, J. *et al.* (Loeb).
Libanius, *Selected Works*, tr. Norman, A. F., ed. Förster, R. (Loeb).
Marcus Diaconus, 1930, *Vita S. Porphyrii Gazensis*: Marc le diacre, *Vie de Porphyre évêque de Gaza*, ed. Grégoire, H. and Kugener, M. A., Paris.
Malalas, John, 1831, *Chronographia*, ed. Dindorf, L., *CSHB*.
Malalas fragments, 1905: Constantinus Porphyrogenitus, *Excerpta*.
—— *Historica*, III–IV, ed. Boor, C., Berlin.
Moschus, John, *Pratum spirituale*, *PG* 87, cols 2851 ff.
—— 1938, ed. Nissen, T., *BZ* 38.
Nessana, P., 1958, Excavations at Nessana, Colt, H. D., vol. III. *Non-literary Papyri*, ed. Kraemer, C. J., Princeton.
Oxyrhynchus Papyri, 1898– , ed. Grenfell, B. P. and Hunt, A. S., London.
Petrus the Iberian, 1895: The Life of Petrus by John Rufus, ed. Raabe, R., *Petrus der Iberer*, Leipzig.
Plerophoriae, John Rufus, 1912, ed. and tr. Nau, F., *PO* 8.
Pliny (the Elder), *Natural History*, tr. Rackham, H., Jones, W. H. S. and Eichholz, D. E. (Loeb).
Pliny (the Younger), *Letters and Panegyrics*, tr. Radice, B. (Loeb).
Porphyrius of Gaza: see Marcus Diaconus.
Procopii Caesariensis (Procopius of Caesarea), 1953, *Opera Omnia* tr. Dewing, H. B. (Loeb).
Procopii Gazaei (Procopius of Gaza), 1963, *Epistulae et declamationes*, ed. Garzya, A. and Loenertz, R. J., Rome.
Sachau: *see* Bruns.
Scriptores historiae Augustae, 1953 (including Trebellius Pollio), tr. Magie, D. (Loeb).

Sozomenus, *Ecclesiastical History*, 1891, tr. Hartranft, C. D., in *A Select Library of Nicene and Post-Nicene Fathers*, ed. Wace, H. and Shaff, P., n.s. 2, Oxford.

—— 1960, *Historia Ecclesiastica*, ed. Bidez, J. and Hanson, G. C., *Gr. Schr.* 50.

Stephanus of Byzantium, 1849 (repr. 1958), *Ethnica*, ed. Meineke, A.

Strabo, *Geography*, tr. Jones, H. L. (Loeb).

Suidas (Suda), 1928, *Lexicon*, ed. Adler, A., Leipzig.

Synesius Cyrenensis, 1979, *Epistulae*, ed. Garzya, A., Rome.

Theodoret of Cyrrhus, *A History of the Monks of Syria*, (Cistercian Studies 88).

Theodosius, Codex, 1952 = *The Theodosian Code*, tr. Pharr, C., Princeton.

Theophanes, 1883, repr. 1967, *Chronographia*, ed. de Boor, C., Leipzig.

Timotheus of Gaza, 1914, *De animalibus*, ed. Bodenhimer, F. S. and Rabinowitz, A., Paris and Leiden,

Varro, 1967, *Rerum Rusticum*, tr. Hooper, W. D. and Ash, H. B. (Loeb).

Zacharias Rhetor (or of Mytilene), 1899, *Historia Ecclesiastica*, ed. and tr. Brooks, E. W., *CSCO* (Scr. Syr.), III, 25.

General bibliography

Abbot, F. F. and Johnson, A. C., 1922, *Administration in the Roman Empire*, Princeton.

Abel, F. M., 1927, Sappho et Arous, *Journal of the Palestine Oriental Society* 7.

— and Barrois, A., 1929, Sculpture du sud de la Judée, *RB* 38.

Adan Bayewitz, D., 1985, Manufacture and Local Trade in the Galilee of Roman–Byzantine Palestine: A Case Study, diss., Jerusalem.

— 1987, Kefar Hanania, 1986, *IEJ* 37.

— and Perlman, I., 1990, The Local Trade of Sepphoris in the Roman Period, *IEJ* 40.

— and Aviam, M., *Jodaphata*, in preparation.

Aharoni, Y., 1962, *Excavations at Ramat Rahel*, Rome.

— 1964, *Excavations at Ramat Rahel*, Rome.

— , Evenari, M., Shannan, L. and Tadmor, N. H., 1958–68, 'The Ancient Desert Agriculture of the Negev', *IEJ* 8 and 10.

Ahlström, G. W., 1978, 'Wine Presses and Cup-marks of the Jenin Megiddo Survey', *BASOR* 231.

Albeck, S., 1957, Hishtalsheluta shel Ha'avarat Hovot ba-Talmud, *Tarbitz* 26 (Heb.).

— 1969, *Introduction to the Talmud, Babli and Jerushalmi*, Tel-Aviv (Heb.).

— 1970, Ha-Ba'alut bi-Nechasim ve-ha-Derachim le-Siyyumah, Bar-Ilan, 7–8 (Heb.).

— 1972, Toldot Darke ha-Kinyan ba-Talmud, *Bar-Ilan* 9. 1 (Heb.).

Alon, G., 1977, *Jews, Judaism and the Classical World*, Jerusalem (orig. pub. [Heb.] 1953, 1958).

— 1980; 1984, *The Jews in their Land in the Talmudic Age* I, Jerusalem (orig. pub. [Heb.] 1952); II, Jerusalem (orig. pub. [Heb.] 1955).

Alt, A., 1921, *Die griechischen Inschriften der Palaestina Tertia westlich der 'Araba*, Berlin and Leipzig.

Applebaum, S., 1958–9, The Province of Syria-Palaestina as a Province of the Severan Empire, *Zion* 23–4 (Heb.).

— 1967, The Agrarian Question, and the Revolt of Bar Kokhba, *EI* 8 (Heb.).

— 1973, Ha-Kfar be-'Erez-Yisrael ba-Tekufah ha-Roma'it, in: *Ha-Tekufah ha-Roma'it be-'Eretz-Yisra'el* (Hosa'at ha-Mador Li-Yedi'at ha-'Arez ba-Tenu'ah ha-Kibbuzit) (Heb.).

— 1975, The Struggle for the Soil, and the Revolt of 66–73 CE, *EI* 12 (Heb.).

— 1976, Economic Life in Palestine, in: Safrai, S. *et al.*, eds.

— 1976a, *Prolegomena to the Study of the Second Jewish Revolt*, BAR S 7, Oxford.

— 1980, The Hellenistic Cities and the Judaization of Eretz Israel, in: Bar-Kochva,

B., ed., *The Seleucid Period in Eretz Israel*, Tel-Aviv (Heb.).

—— and Gichon, M., eds, 1971, *Roman Frontier Studies 1967*, Tel-Aviv.

Ariel, D. T., 1980, Coins from the Synagogue at Horvat Kanef, *INJ* 4.

—— 1982, A Survey of Coin Finds in Jerusalem (until the End of the Byzantine Period), *LA* 32.

—— 1991, Coins from the Synagogue at Dabiyye, *Atiqot* 20.

Arif, A., 1986, *A Treasury of Classical and Islamic Coins: The Collection of Amman Museum*, London.

Arim, K., Reynolds, J. and Crawford, M., *et al.*, 1971, Diocletian's Currency Reform: A new Inscription, *JRS* 61.

Arnon, I. 1963, *Giduleh Sadeh*, I–II, Tel-Aviv (Heb.).

Ashburner, W., 1909, *The Rhodian Sea Law*, Oxford.

Assaf, S., 1935, *Sifran shel Rishonim*, Jerusalem (Heb.).

Avi-Yonah, M., 1946, Newly Discovered Latin and Greek Inscriptions, *QDAP* 12.

—— 1953, The Madeba Mosaic Map, *EI* 2 (Heb.).

—— 1958, The Economics of Byzantine Palestine, *IEJ* 8.

—— 1963, *Geoggrafia Historit shel Erez-Yisra'el*, Jerusalem (expansion of his: Map of Roman Palestine, *QDAP* 5 (1935), 139–93). (See Avi-Yonah 1966.)

—— 1964, *Masot u-Mehkarim bi-Yedi'at ha-'Arez*, Tel-Aviv (Heb.).

—— 1966, *The Holy Land*, Jerusalem.

—— 1981, *Art in Ancient Palestine*, Jerusalem.

—— 1984, *The Jews Under Roman and Byzantine Rule*, Jerusalem.

Avnimelech, A., ed., 1976–1989, *Encyclopaedia of Agriculture*, Tel-Aviv (Heb.).

Ayali, M., 1982, Labor as a Value in the Talmudic and Midrashic Literature, *Jerusalem Studies in Jewish Thought*, I (Heb.).

Bacher, N., 1909, Der Jahrmarkt an der Terebinthe bei Hebron, *ZAW* 29.

Bagatti, B., 1969, *Excavations in Nazareth*, I, Jerusalem.

Bagnall, R. S., 1985, Agricultural Productivity and Taxation in Later Roman Egypt, *TAPA* 115.

Bahat, D., 1974, A Roof Tile of the Legio VI Ferrata and Pottery Vessels from Horvat Hazon, *IEJ* 24.

Balsdon, J. P. V. D., 1969, *Life and Leisure in Ancient Rome*, London.

Barag, D., 1967, Brick Stamp-impressions of the Legio X Fretensis, *EI* 8 (Heb.).

—— 1970, Glass Vessels of the Roman and Byzantine Periods in Palestine, I–II, diss., Jerusalem, (Heb.).

—— 1982–3, Tyrian Currency in Galilee, *INJ* 6–7.

Baramki, D. C., 1935, Two Roman Cisterns at Beit Nattif, *QDAP* 5.

—— 1968, *The Coins Exhibited in The Archaeological Museum of the American University of Beirut*, Beirut.

—— 1974, *The Coin Collection of the American University of Beirut Museum*, Beirut.

Baras, Z., Safrai, S., Tsafrir, Y. and Stern, M., eds, 1982, *Eretz-Israel from the Destruction of the Second Temple to the Muslim Conquest*, I, Jerusalem (Heb.; see also Tsafrir).

Baron, S. W., 1952–8, *A Social and Religious History of the Jews* (= *SRHJ*), I–III, New York.

Baruch, H., 1985, Shinuyei Tzomeach Be-ezor Kineret, *Rotem* 16 (Heb.).

Baud, M., 1959, The Dove Houses of Tinos, *Architektoniki* 17 (in Greek).

Baynes, see Dawes.

Beebe, H. K., 1975, Domestic Architecture and the New Testament, *Biblical Archaeologist* 38.

Beer, M., 1964, Talmud Torah and Derekh Eretz, *Bar-Ilan* 2 (Heb.).

—— 1975, *The Babylonian Amoraim*, Ramat-Gan (Heb.).

Bell, H. I., 1917, The Byzantine Servile State in Egypt, *JEA* 4.

Bellinger, A. D., 1938, Coins, in: Kraeling, C. H., *Gerasa: City of the Decapolis*, New Haven.

— 1949, *The Excavations at Dura Europus*, VI: *The Coins*, New Haven.

Ben Arieh, S., 1974, Survey between Raphia and the Brook of Egypt, II: The Finds, *Atiqot* 7 (Heb.).

Ben David, A., 1974, *Talmudische Ökonomie*, I, Hildesheim and New York.

Ben David, C., 1989, Olive Cultivation and Production in Roman and Byzantine Golan (unpubl. MA thesis), Ramat-Gan.

Bennett, R. and Elton, J., 1898, *History of Corn Milling*, Liverpool.

Benoit, P., Milik, J. T. and De Vaux, R., 1961, *Les Grottes de Muraba'at* (also cited as DJD), II, Oxford.

Ben Shalom, I., 1985, A Favourite Saying of the Rabbis in Jabneh, *Milet* 2 (Heb.).

Berchem, D., 1952, L'Armée de Dioclétien et la réforme constantinienne, Paris.

Bildstein, G. J., 1970–1, The Sale of Animals to Gentiles in Talmudic Law, *JQR* 61.

Birch, B. P., 1967, The Measurement of Dispersed Patterns of Settlement, *Tijdschrift voor economische en sociale geografie* 58.

Birley, A. R., 1981, The Economic Effects of Roman Frontier Policy, in King and Henig 1981.

Blagg, T. F. C. and King, A. C., eds, 1985, *Military and Civilian in Roman Britain*, BAR 136, Oxford.

Bloch, M. R., 1971, The Roman Limes: A Fortified Line for the Taxation and Protection of the Salt Trade, in: *Roman Frontier Studies 1967*, Tel-Aviv.

— 1976, Salt in Human History, *Interdisciplinary Science Reviews* 1. 4.

Boak, A. E. R., 1951, Tesserarii and Quadrarii in Egypt, in: Coleman-Norton, P. R., ed., *Studies in Roman Economy. . . . in Honor of A. C. Johnson*, Princeton.

Bodenheimer, S., 1950–6, *Ha-Chai Ve-Hzomeach Be-Artzot Ha-Mikra*, Jerusalem (Heb.).

Boneh, I., 1953, *The Olive*, Tel-Aviv, (Heb.).

Boren, H. C., 1983, Studies Relating to the Stipendium Militium, *Historia* 32.

Boserup, E., 1965, *The Condition of Agricultural Growth*, London.

Bradford, J., 1959, *Ancient Landscapes*, London.

Brand, C. M., 1969, Two Byzantine Treatises on Taxation, *Traditio* 25.

Brand, Y., 1943, Bait Habad, *Sinai* 12 (Heb.).

— 1953, *Klei ha-Heres be-Sifrut ha-Talmud* (Ceramics in Talmudic Literature), Jerusalem (Heb.).

— 1978, *Klei Hazechuchit Besifrut Hatalmud*, Jerusalem (Heb.).

Brehier, L., 1903, Les Colonies d'orientaux en Occident au commencement du moyen-âge (Ve–VIIIe siècles), *Byzantinische Zeitschrift* 12.

Brisay, K. W. de and Evans, K. A., eds, 1975, *Salt: The Study of Ancient Industry*, Colchester.

Brock, S., 1973, An Early Syriac of the Life of Maximus the Confessor, *Analecta Bodeliana* 91.

Broshi, M., 1969, Tel Megadim: A Phoenician City and Roman–Byzantine Road Station, *Qadmoniot* 8 (Heb.).

— 1975, La Population de l'ancienne Jérusalem, *RB* 82.

— 1979, The Population of Western Palestine in the Roman–Byzantine Period, *BASOR* 236.

— 1985, The Cardinal Elements of the Economy of Palestine during the Herodian Period, in: Gross 1985 (Heb.).

— and Qimron, E., 1986, A House Sale Deed from Kefar Baru from the Time of Bar Kokhba, *IEJ* 36. (See Yadin *et al.* 1986.)

Brothwell, D. and Brothwell, P., 1969, *Food in Antiquity*, New York.

Broughton, T. R. S., Roman Asia, in: Frank, T., *An Economic Survey of Ancient Rome*, IV, Baltimore.

Bruns, K. G. and Sachau, E., 1880, *Syrisch-römische Rechtsbuch*, Leipzig.

Brunt, P. A., 1950, Pay and Superannuation in the Roman Army, *PBSR* 18.
— 1966, The Fiscus and its Development, *JRS* 56.
— 1971, *Italian Manpower*, Oxford.
— 1972, review of White, K. D., *Roman Farming*, *JRS* 62.
Büchler, A., 1900, Du sens des mots 'poleach' et 'pagan' et 'Kartani Eirani' dans Le Midrasch, *REJ* 40.
— 1906, *Der galiläische Am Ha-'ares des zweiten Jahrhunderts*, Vienna.
— 1909, *The Political and Social Leaders of the Jewish Community of Sepphoris in the Second and Third Centuries*, London.
— 1912, *The Economic Conditions of Judea after the Destruction of the Second Temple*, London.
Buko, A., 1984, Problems and Research Prospects in the Determination of Pottery, *WA* 15.
Bull, R. J., 1966, A Roman Veteran's Epitaph from Azzun, *PEQ* 98.
— and Campbell, E. F., jun., 1968, The Sixth Campaign at Balatah (Schechem), *BASOR* 190.
Bunge, W. W., 1962, *Theoretical Geography*, Lund.
Bunnell, C. S., 1937, Catalogue of the Coins, in: Waterman, C. L., ed., *Preliminary Report of the University of Michigan Excavations at Sepphoris, Palestine in 1931*, Ann Arbor.
Burford, A., 1960–1, Heavy Transport in Classical Antiquity, *EcHr* 13.
Burnham, D. C. and Johnson, H. B., eds, 1979, *Invasion and Response: The Case of Roman Britain*, BAR 73.
Buttrey, T. V., Johnston, A., Mackenzie, K. M. and Bates, M. L., 1981, *Greek, Roman and Islamic Coins from Sardis*, Cambridge, Mass.
Byatt, A., 1973, Josephus and Population Numbers in First Century Palestine, *PEQ* 105.
Callu, J. P., 1979, *Les Monnaies romaines*, Brussels.
Carandini, A., 1983, Pottery and the African Economy, in: Garnsey, Hopkins and Whittaker, eds.
Casson, L., 1956, New Light on Maritime Loans, *EOS: Commentarii Societatis Philologae Polonorum* 48. 2.
— 1971, *Ships and Seamanship in the Ancient World*, Princeton.
Charanis, P., 1971, The Monk in the Byzantine Society, *Dumbarton Oaks Papers* 25.
Charles, C., 1942, Bees in Antiquity, *Antiquity* 16.
Charlesworth, M. P., 1926, *Trade-routes and Commerce of the Roman Empire*, Cambridge.
Chastagnol, A., 1977, L'impôt payé par les soldats au ive siècle, in: Chastagnol, A., ed. *Armées et fiscalité dans le monde antique*, Paris.
Chehab, M. H., 1986, *Fouilles de Tyr*, IV, Paris.
Chevallier, R., 1976, *Roman Roads*, London.
Chisholm, A., 1968, *Rural Settlement and Land Use*, London.
Chitty, D. J., 1966, *The Desert A City*, Oxford.
Clark, C. and Haswell, M., 1967, *The Economics of Subsistence Agriculture*, 3rd edn, New York.
Claude, D., 1969, *Die byzantinische Stadt im 6. Jahrhundert*, Munich.
Clausing, R., 1925, *The Roman Colonate*, Rome.
Cohen, B., 1966, *Jewish and Roman Law*, New York.
Cohen, G., 1967, *Abraham ben David ha-Levi*, Philadelphia.
Cohen, Y., 1974, The Attitude to the Gentile in the Halacha and in Reality in the Tannaitic Period, diss., Hebrew University, Jerusalem (Heb.).
Cohn, I., 1929, Die Marktbezeichnungen 'Atlas' und 'yarid' und ihr Verhältnis zueinander, *Breslau Seminar Festschrift*, Breslau.

Collingwood, R. G. and Richmond, I., 1969, *The Archaeology of Roman Britain*, London.

Conder, C. R. and Kitchener, H. H., 1881–3, *The Survey of Western Palestine*, I–III, London.

Cooper, A. B., 1977–8, The Family Farm in Greece, *CJ* 73.

Corbier, M., 1991, City, Territory and Taxation, in: Rich and Wallace-Hadrill, eds.

Corbo, V., 1975, *Cafarnao*, I, Jerusalem.

Cornell, L. A., 1981, Late Hellenistic and Early Roman Red-Slipped Pottery from Tel Anafa 1968–1973, diss., University of Missouri, Columbia.

Cotton, H. M. and Geiger, J., 1989, *Masada*, II, Jerusalem.

Crane, E., 1983, *The Archaeology of Beekeeping*, London.

Crawford, D. J., 1975, Price Control, *Classical Review* 25. 2.

— 1976, Imperial Estates, in: Finley, ed.

Crawford, M., see Arim.

Crawford, M. H., 1970, Money and Exchange in the Roman World, *JRS* 60.

— and Reynolds, J. M., 1975, The Publication of the Prices Edict: A New Inscription from Aezani, *JRS* 65.

— 1979, The Aezani Copy of the Price Edict, *ZPE* 34.

Crook, J., 1976, Classical Roman Law and the Sale of Land, in: Finley, ed.

Cross, F. M., 1969, Judean Stamps, *EI* 9.

Crowfoot, J. W., Crowfoot, G. M., and Kenyon, K. M., 1957, *The Objects from Samaria*, London.

Cunliffe, B., 1979, Some Concluding Thoughts, in: Burnham and Johnson, eds.

Cuntz, O., 1929, *Itineraria Romana*, I.

Curtis, R. I., 1983, In Defence of Garum, *CJ* 78.

Dalman, G., 1923–42, *Arbeit und Sitte in Palaestina*, I–IV, Gütersloh.

— 1935, *Sacred Sites and Ways*, London (orig. pub. in German 1919).

Damati, E., 1982, The Palace of Hilkiya, *Qadmoniot* 60 (Heb.).

Dan, Y., 1971, Two Jewish Merchants in the Seventh Century, *Zion* 36 (Heb.).

— 1972, Kerem Doron, *Tarbiz* 41 (Heb.).

— 1980, Jews in the Indian Ocean Commerce in the Pre-Islamic Period, *Studies in the History of the Jewish People and the Land of Israel*, V, Haifa (Heb.).

— 1982, The Foreign Trade of Palestine in the Byzantine Period, *Cathedra* 23 (Heb.).

— 1984, *The City in Eretz-Israel During the Late Roman and Byzantine Periods*, Jerusalem (Heb.).

Dar, S., 1980, Michrot Ha-Melach shel Zfon Sinaai, in Meshel, Z. and Finkelstein, I., eds, *Sinai in Antiquity*, Tel-Aviv (Heb.).

— 1986, Landscape and Pattern, BAR 308, I–II, Oxford.

— , Tepper, Y. and Safrai, Z., 1986, *Um Rihan: A Village of the Mishna*, Tel-Aviv (Heb.).

— and Safrai, Z., in press, Hurbat Bira, in: Schwartz, Y., Friedman, I. and Safrai, Z., eds, *Felix Yubelean Book*, Ramat Gan (Heb.).

D'Arms, J. H., 1981, *Commerce and Social Standing in Ancient Rome*, Cambridge, Mass.

Davies, J. H., 1969, The Supply of Animals to the Roman Army, *Latomus* 28.

— 1971, The Roman Military Diet, *Britannia* 2.

— 1974, Daily Life of the Roman Soldier under the Principate, *ANRW*, II. 1.

Dawes, E. and Baynes, N. H., 1948, *Three Byzantine Saints*, Oxford.

Day, J., 1985, Agriculture in the Life of Pompeii, *Yale Classical Studies* 3.

De Neeve, P. W., 1984, *Colonus, Private Farm Tenancy in Roman Italy during the Republic and the Early Principate*, Amsterdam.

De Vries, B., 1962, Kinyan Sudar, *Sinai* 50 (Heb.).

Dickstein, P., 1926, Mehir Zedek ve-Ona'ah, *Ha-Mishpat ha-Ivri*, 1, Tel-Aviv.

Dilke, O. A. W., 1971, *The Roman Land Surveyors*, Newton Abbot.

Dill, S., 1958, *Roman Society in the Last Century of the Western Empire*, New York.

Dinur, Y., 1990, The Taxes, in: Kedar, B. Z., Doton, T. and Safrai, S., eds, *Commerce in Palestine Throughout the Ages*, Jerusalem (Heb.).

Diringer, D., 1949, The Royal Jar-handle Stamps of Ancient Judah, *Biblical Archaeologist* 12.

Dore, J. and Greene, K., eds, *Roman Pottery Studies in Britain and Beyond*, BAR 30.

Downey, G., 1951, The Economic Crisis at Antioch, in: Coleman-Norton, P. R., Bourne, F. C. and Fine, J. V. A., eds, *Studies in Roman Economy in Honor of A. C. Johnson*, Princeton,

— 1958, The Size of Population of Antioch, *Proceedings of the American Philological Society*.

— 1961, *A History of Antioch in Syria from Seleucus to the Arab Conquest*, Princeton.

Drachman, A. G., 1932, *Ancient Oil Mills and Presses*, Copenhagen.

Duncan-Jones, R., 1962, Costs, Outlays and Summae Honorariae from Roman Africa, *PBSR* 30.

— 1963, Wealth and Magnificence in Roman Africa, *PBSR* 31.

— 1963a, City Population in Roman Africa, *JRS* 53.

— 1964, Human Numbers in Towns and Town-organisations of the Roman Empire: The Evidence of Gifts, *Historia* 13.

— 1964a, The Purpose and Organisation of the Alimenta, *PBSR* 32.

— 1965, An Epigraphic Survey of Costs in Roman Italy, *PBSR* 33.

— 1974, The Economy of the Roman Empire: Quantitative Studies, Cambridge; 2nd edn, Cambridge, 1982.

— 1974a, The Procurator as Civic Benefactor, *JRS* 64.

— 1976, The Size of the Modius Castrensis, *ZPE* 21.

— 1976a, The Price of Wheat in Roman Egypt under the Principate, *Chiron* 6.

— 1990, *Structure and Scale in the Roman Economy*, Cambridge.

Dupont, C., 1972, La Vente et les conditions socio-économiques dans l'empire romain de 312 à 535 après Jésus-Christ, *RIDA* 3. 19.

Elgavish, J., 1977, *Archaeological Excavations at Shikmona: The Pottery of the Roman Period*, Haifa (Heb.).

Eliash, B. Z., 1978, Ideological Roots of the Halakhah: A Chapter in the Laws of Interest, *Ha-Mishpat Ha-Ivri* 5 (Heb.).

Elon, M., 1988, *Jewish Law*, I–III, Jerusalem (Heb.).

Encyclopaedia of Agriculture, see Avnimelech, A. *et al.*

Encyclopedia la-Hafirot Archeologiot be-Erez-Yisra'el, ed. Mazar, B., Jerusalem, 1970 (Heb.).

Epstein, N., 1930, On Kefar Aris, *Tarbiz* 1b (Heb.).

— 1948, *Mavo Le-Nusah Ha-Mishna*, Jerusalem (Heb.).

Eshel, H., 1992, The Agriculture in Jericho in the Days of Bar Kochva, in: Dar, S., ed., *The 12th Conference for Ancient Agriculture and Economy in Eretz Israel*, Ramat-Gan.

— and Eshel, A., 1992a, Fragments of Two Aramaic Documents which were brought to Avior Cave during the Bar Kokhba Revolt, *EI* 23.

Evans, J. K., 1981, Wheat Production, and its Social Consequence in the Roman World, *Classical Quarterly* 31.

Evans, see Brisay.

Feliks, see Felix.

Felix, Y., 1963, *Agriculture in Palestine in the Period of the Mishna and Talmud*, Jerusalem and Tel-Aviv (Heb.).

—— 1963a, Rice in Rabbinic Literature, *Bar-Ilan* 1 (Heb.).

—— 1965, Ha-Ez ve-ha-Ya'ar be-Nofah he-Kadum shel Ha-'Arez, *Teva Vaa'Arez*, 8 (Heb.).

—— 1967, *Mixed Sowing Breeding*, Tel-Aviv (Heb.).

—— 1968, *Plant World of the Bible*, Ramat-Gan (Heb.).

—— 1971, Concerning the Expression Hei Ganeiv Zevutei De-Havrei, *Tarbiz* 40 (Heb.).

—— 1972, Gidulei Sadeh Bemekoroteinu, in: Halperin 1966–76, II (Heb.).

—— 1976, Azei Peri Ve-Ilanei Serak bemekoroteinu, in: Halperin 1966–76, III (Heb.).

—— 1980–6, *The Jerusalem Talmud-Talmud Yerushalmi-Tractate Sheviit*, I–II, Jerusalem.

—— 1980b, Raising Pheasant in Israel (the Kashrut Problem), *Techumin* I (Heb.).

—— 1982, The Jewish Agriculture in Eretz Israel, in: Baras *et al.* (Heb.).

Field, H., 1950, Pigeon Towers of the Faiyum, *Antiquity* 24.

Fink, R. O., 1971, *Roman Military Records on Papyrus*, London.

Finkelstein, I., 1981, Israelite and Hellenistic Farms in the Foothills, and in the Yarkon Basin, *EI* 15 (Heb.).

—— 1988–9, The Land of Ephraim Survey, *Tel-Aviv* 15–16.

Finley, M. I., 1965, Technical Innovation and Economic Progress in the Ancient World, *EcHr* 18.

—— 1973, *The Ancient Economy*, London.

—— ed. 1976, *Studies in Roman Property*, Cambridge.

—— 1976a, Private Farm Tenancy in Italy before Diocletian, in: Finley ed. 1976.

Fischer, M., 1988, Marble Import and Local Stone in the Decoration of Roman Palestine, in: Herz and Waelkens 1988.

—— 1989, The Road Jerusalem–Emmaus, in: Kasher *et al.*, (Heb.).

Fischer, T., 1979, Zur Seleukideninschrift von Hefzibah, *ZPE* 33.

Flach, D., 1990, *Römische Agrargeschichte*, Munich.

Flinder, A., 1985, The Piscinas at Caesarea and Lapithos, in: Raban 1985.

Foerster, G., 1985, A Cuirassed Bronze Statue of Hadrian, *Atiqot* 17.

Forbes, H., 1992, Ethnoarchaeological Approach to Ancient Greek Agriculture: Olive Cultivation as a Case Study, in: Wells ed. 1992.

Forbes, R. J., 1957–71, *Studies in Ancient Technology*, I–VI, Leiden,

Ford, A. B., 1960–1, Heavy Transportation in Classical Antiquity, *EcHr* 13.

Foxhall, L., 1992, The Control of the Landscape, in: Wells 1992.

Foxhall, L. and Forbes, H. A., 1982, Sitometreia: The Role of Grain as a Staple food in Classical Antiquity, *Chiron* 12.

Frank, K., 1936, Food in Early Greece, *University of Illinois Bulletin* 34.

Frank, T., 1924, Roman Census-statistics from 225 to 28 BC *CP* 19.

—— ed. 1933–40, *An Economic Survey of Ancient Rome*, I–V, Baltimore.

Frankel, R., 1987, H'Dani'la, *Hadashot Archiologiot*, 89 (Heb.).

Fraser, H. M., 1931, *Beekeeping in Antiquity*, London.

—— 1992, Some Oil-presses from Western Galilee, *BASOR* 286.

Frayn, J. M., 1979, *Subsistence Farming in Roman Italy*, London.

—— 1984, *Sheep Rearing and Wool Trade*, Liverpool.

Freidenberg, D., 1939, On Money Lending in the Fifth Century, *Yediot: Bulletin of the Jewish Palestine Exploration Society*, 7. 3 (Heb.).

Frend, W. H. C., 1956, A Third-Century Inscription Relating to Angareia in Phrygia, *JRS* 46.

Frier, B. W., 1980, *Landlord and Tenants in Imperial Rome*, Princeton.

Fulco, W. J. and Zayadin, Z., 1981, Coins from Samaria Sebaste, *Annual of the Department of Antiquities, Jordan* 25.

Fulford, M. G., 1977, Pottery and Britain's Foreign Trade in the Later Roman Period, in: Peacock, D. P. S., 1977.

—— 1984, Demonstrating Britannia's Economic Dependence, in: Blagg and King.

Gafni, Y. M., 1977, Bringing Deceased from Abroad for Burial in Eretz Israel, *Cathedra* 4 (Heb.).

—— 1991, *The Jews of Babylonia in the Talmudic Era*, Jerusalem (Heb.).

Garlan, Y., 1983, Le Commerce des amphores grecs, in: Garnsey and Whittaker, eds, 1983.

Garnsey, P., 1976, Urban Property Investment, in: Finley, ed.

—— 1992, Yield of the Land, in: Wells 1992.

——, Hopkins, K. and Whittaker, C. R., eds, 1983, *Trade in the Ancient Economy*, London.

—— and Whittaker, C. R., eds, 1983, *Trade and Famine in Classical Antiquity*, Cambridge.

Giacchero, M., 1974, *Edictum Diocletiani et Collegarum*, Genoa.

Gibbon, E., 1905–10, *The Decline and Fall of the Roman Empire*, ed. Bury, J. B., London.

Gibson, S., 1983, The Stone Vessel Industry at Hizma, *IEJ* 33.

Gichon, M., 1974, Towers of the Limes Palestine: Forms, Purpose, Terminology and Comparisons, *Actes du IX Congrès International d'Études sur les Frontières Romaines*, ed. Pippidi, D. M., Bucharest, Cologne and Vienna.

—— 1975, The Bar Kochva War: A Colonial Uprising Against Imperial Rome, *Revue international d'histoire militaire* 42.

Gil, M., 1968, Ha-ma'avak al ha-Karka, unpubl. MA thesis, Hebrew University, Jerusalem (Heb.).

—— 1970, Land Ownership in Palestine under Roman Rule, *RIDA* (3rd series) 17.

Goicoechera, E. O., 1986, *Excavationes en el Agora De Gerasaa En 1983*, Madrid.

Goffart, W., 1974, *Caput and Colonate: Towards a History of Late Roman Taxation*, Toronto.

Goldman, H., ed. 1950, *Excavation at Gözlü Küle (Tarsus, I)*, Princeton.

Golomb, B. and Kedar, Y., 1971, Ancient Agriculture in the Galilee Mountains, *IEJ* 21.

Goodenough, E., 1967, *Jewish Symbols in the Greco-Roman Period*, I, New York.

Goodman, M., 1983, *State and Society in Roman Galilee, AD 132–212*, Totowa, NJ.

Goulandris, D., 1979, *Dovehouses in the Cycladic Islands of Tinos and Andros*, Athens.

Grace, V., Stamped Amphora Handles, 1962, in: Colt, D. *et al.*, Excavations at Nessana, I, London.

Grace, see also Kraemer.

Graham, A. J., 1975, Beehives from Ancient Greece, *Bee World* 56. 2.

—— 1978, The Vari House, *BSA* 73.

Graser, E. R., 1940, The Significance of Two New Fragments of the Edict of Diocletian, *TAPA* 71.

Greene, P., 1979, Invasion and Response: Pottery and the Roman Army, in: Burnham and Johnson 1979.

Gren, E., 1941, *Kleinasien und der Ostbalkan in der wirtschaftlichen Entwicklung der römischen Kaiserzeit*, Uppsala.

Grierson, P., 1965, The President's Address, *NC* 5.

—— 1966, The President's Address, *NC* 6.

—— 1967, Byzantine Coinage as Source Material, *Proceedings of the XIIIth International Congress of Byzantine Studies*, London.

Grigg, D., 1980, *Population Growth and Agrarian Change*, Cambridge.

Groh, D. E., 1981, The Fine-wares from the Patrician and Lintel Houses, in: Meyers *et al.* 1981.

Gross, N., ed. 1985, *Jews in Economic life*, Jerusalem (Heb.).

Grossman, D. and Safrai, Z., 1980, Satellite Settlement in Western Samaria, *Geographical Review* 70.

Gulak, A., 1922, *Yesodei Ha-Mishpat Ha-Ivri*, I–IV, Jerusalem (Heb.).

—— 1929, *Le-Heker Toldot ha-Mishpat ha-Ivri bi-Tekufat ha-Talmud* I, *Dine Karka'ot*, Jerusalem (Heb.).

—— 1931, Banking in Talmudic Law, *Tarbiz* 2 (Heb.)

—— 1938, Le-Sidre ha-Missim ha-Roma'im be-Erez-Yisra'el, *Magnes Book* (= *Sefer Magnes*), ed. Epstein, J. N., Bodenheimer, F. S., Baer, F. I., Fekete, M., Fodor, A., Kliger, I. J. and Mayer, L. A. (Heb.).

—— 1939, *Toldot ha-Mishpat ha-Ivri be-Yisra'el*, I, *Ha-Hiyyuv ve-Shi'budav*, Jerusalem (Heb.).

—— 1940, Boule ve-Istratege, *Tarbiz* 11 (Heb.).

—— 1941, Al ha-Ro'im u-Megadle Behema Daka bi-Tekufat Hurban ha-Bayit, *Tarbiz* 12 (Heb.).

—— 1946, *Ozar ha-Shetarot*, Jerusalem (Heb.).

Gunneweg, J., Perlman, I. and Yellin, J., 1983, The Provenance, Typology and Chronology of Eastern Terra Sigillata, *Qedem* 17.

Gur, A., Spiegel, P. and Gratch, H. 1960, *The Olive*, Tel-Aviv (Heb.).

Gutman, S., 1981, *Gamla*, Tel-Aviv.

Haatvedt, R. H., 1964, *Coins from Karanis*, Michigan.

Hachlili, R. and Killebrew, W. A., 1981, The House of Goliath, *Qadmoniot*, 14 (55–6) (Heb.).

Hadashot Archiologiot, 1961, 1963, 1964, 1966, 1970, 1974, 1981, 1982, 1988: *The Bulletin of Archaeological Authorities of Israel* (without authors' names).

Hagen, W. von, 1967, The Roads that Led to Rome, London.

Halperin, H., ed. 1966–76, *The Encyclopaedia of Agriculture*, I-III, Tel-Aviv (Heb.).

Halstead, P., 1987, Traditional and Ancient Rural Economy in Mediterranean Europe: Plus ça Change? *Journal of Hellenic Studies* 107.

Hamburger, H., 1954, A Hoard of Syrian Tetradrachms and Tyrian Bronze Coins from Gush Halav, *IEJ* 4.

Hanson, R. S., 1978, Meiron Coins: 1974–5, *AASOR* 43.

—— 1980, *Tyrian Influence in the Upper Galilee*, Cambridge, Mass.

—— and Bates, M. L., 1978, Numismatic Report, in: Meyers *et al.* 1978.

Harden, D. B., 1936, *Roman Glass from Karanis*, Ann Arbor.

Hardy, E. R., 1931, *The Large Estates of Byzantine Egypt*, New York.

Harmand, L., 1955, *Libanius, Discours sur le patronage*, Paris.

—— 1957, *La Patronat sur les collectivités publiques*, Paris.

Harper, G. M., 1928, Village Administration in Syria, *Yale Classical Studies*, 1.

—— 1928a, A Study in the Commercial Relations between Egypt and Syria in Third Century before Christ, *AJP* 49.

Harris, W. V., 1980, Roman Terracotta Lamps: The Organization of an Industry, *JRS* 70.

Hayes, J. W., 1960, North Syrian Mortaria, *Hesperia* 36.

—— 1972, *Late Roman Pottery*, London.

—— 1980, *A Supplement to Late Roman Pottery*, London.

Heichelheim, F. M., 1938, Roman Syria, in: T. Frank, vol. IV.

—— 1970, *An Ancient Economic History*, I-III, Leiden.

Heitland, W. E., 1923, Agriculture, in *The Legacy of Rome*, ed. Bailey, C., Oxford.

Helen, T., 1975, *Organization of Roman Brick Production in the First and Second Centuries AD*, Helsinki.

Hengel, M., 1974, *Property and Riches in the Early Church*, Philadelphia.

Herr, M. D., 1961, The Problem of War on the Sabbath in the Second Temple, and the Talmudic Periods, *Tarbiz* 30 (Heb.).

Herszberg, A. S., 1924, *Hayye ha-Tarbut be-Yisra'el bi Tekufat ha-Mishna ve-ha-Talmud*, Warsaw (Heb.).

Herz, N. and Waelkens, M., eds, 1988, *Classical Marble*, London.

Herzfeld, L., 1894, *Handelsgeschichte der Juden des Alterthums*, Braunschweig.

Hill, G. F., 1913, *The Life of Porphyry by Marc the Deacon*, Oxford.

Hill, G. K., 1965, *Catalogue of the Greek Coins of Palestine*, Bologna.

Hill, P. V., *et al.* 1961, *Late Roman Bronze Coinage* AD 324–491, London.

Hingley, R., 1989, *Rural Settlement in Roman Britain*, London.

Hirschberg, see Herszberg.

Hirschfeld, Y., 1981, Ancient Vine Presses in the Area of the Ayalon Park, *EI* 15 (Heb.).

—— 1987, *Dwelling Houses in Roman and Byzantine Palestine*, Jerusalem (Heb.).

—— and Birger, R., 1988, Villa and Vine Presses in Ramat Hanadiv, *Qadmoniot* 20 (Heb.)

Hodder, I., 1974, Some Marketing Models for Romano-British Coarse Pottery, *Britannia* 5.

—— 1977, Some New Directions in the Spatial Analysis of Archaeological Data at the Regional Scale (macro), in: Clarke, D. L., ed. *Spatial Archaeology*, London.

—— and Orton, C., 1976, *Spatial Analysis in Archaeology*, Cambridge.

Hodkinson, S., 1988, Animal Husbandry in the Greek Polis, in: Whittaker 1988.

Hoenig, S., 1953, *The Great Sanhedrin*, Philadelphia.

Hogarth, P. G., 1922, Greek Inscriptions from Askalon, *PEF* 54.

Holemberg, E. G., 1933, *Zur Geschichte des Cursus Publicus*, Uppsala.

Honigmann, E., 1939–45, L'Évêche phénicien de Porphyrion (Haifa), *Annuaire de l'Institut de Philologie et Histoire Orientales et Slaves* 7.

Hoover, E. M., 1948, *The Location of Economic Activity*, New York.

Hopkins, K., 1978, Economic Growth and Towns in Classical Antiquity, in: Wrigley, E. A. and Abrams, P., eds, *Towns in Societies*, Cambridge.

—— 1980, Taxes and Trade in the Roman Empire, *JRS* 70.

—— 1983, Models, Ships, and Staples, in: Garnsey and Whittaker, eds.

Howard, H. E., 1902, *Garden Cities of Tomorrow*, London.

Howgego, C., 1985, *Greek Imperial Countmarks: Studies in the Provincial Coinage of the Roman Empire*, London.

—— 1992, The Supply and Use of Money in the Roman World 200 BC to AD 300, *JRS* 82.

Hudson, J. C. A., 1969, A Location Theory for Rural Settlements, *Annals of the Association of American Geographers* 59.

Huntingford, G. W. B., 1934, Defences against Cattle Raiding, *Antiquity* 7.

Hütteroth, W. P. and Abdulfattah, K., 1977, *Historical Geography of Palestine Transjordan and Southern Syria in the Late 16th Century*, Erlangen.

Isaac, B., 1979, Legio II Traiana in Judea, *ZPE* 33.

—— 1980, Trade-routes to Arabia and the Roman Army, in Hanson, W. S. and Keppie, L. J. F. eds, *Roman Frontier Studies 1979*, BAR 71.

—— 1982, *Roman Roads in Judea*, BAR S141, Oxford.

—— 1984, Bandits in Judea and Arabia, *Harvard Studies in Classical Philology* 88.

—— 1990, *The Limits of Empire*, Oxford.

Isaac, B. H. and Roll, I., 1976, A Milestone of AD 69 from Judea, *JRS* 66.

Isager, S. and Skydsgaard, J. E., 1992, *Ancient Greek Agriculture*, London and New York.

Jameson, M. H., 1992, Agricultural Labor in Ancient Greece, in: Wells 1992.

Jener, G. F., 1976, Hallazgo de los monedas de los procuradores de Judea en Iluro

(Mataró, Barcelona), *Numisma* 26.

Johnson, A. C., 1936, Roman Egypt, in: Frank, T., ed., *An Economic Survey of Ancient Rome* II, Baltimore.

— and West, L. C., 1949, *Byzantine Egypt: Economic Studies*, Princeton.

— *et al.*, 1961, *Ancient Roman Statutes*, Austin.

Jones, A. H. M., 1952–3, Inflation under the Roman Empire, *EcHr* (2nd series), 5.

— 1953, Census Record of the Later Roman Empire, *JRS* 43.

— 1960, The Cloth Industry under the Roman Empire, *EHR* Ser. II 13.

— 1964, *The Later Roman Empire 284–602*, Oxford.

— 1966, *The Greek City*, Oxford.

— 1969, *The Ancient Empires and the Economy: Rome, Third International Conference of Economic History, Munich 1965*.

— 1971, *The Cities of the Eastern Roman Provinces*, Oxford.

— 1974, *The Roman Economy*, Oxford.

Jones, C. P., 1978, A Syrian in Lyon, *AJP* 99.

Jones, J. E., Graham, A. J. and Sackett, L. H., 1973, An Attic Country House below the Cave of Pan at Vari, *BSA* 68.

Kandler, M., 1975, Territorium Legionis von Carnuntum, in: *Limes: Akten des XI Internationalen Limes-Kongresses*, Budapest.

Karmon, Y., 1978, *Eretz Israel*, Tel-Aviv (Heb.).

Kasher, A., ed. 1989, *Greece and Rome in Israel*, Jerusalem, (Heb.).

— , Oppenheimer, A. and Rappaport, U., eds, 1987, *Man and Land in Eretz-Israel in Antiquity*, Jerusalem (Heb.).

Katz, J., 1965, Laws Regarding Interest during the Mishnaic and Talmudic Period, *Third World Congress of Jewish Studies*, Jerusalem (Heb.).

Kehoe, D. P., 1988, *The Economy of Agriculture on Roman Imperial Estates in North Africa*, Göttingen.

Keller, O., 1909–13, *Die Antike Tierwelt*, I–II, Leipzig.

Kennedy, P. L., 1980, Legio VI Ferrata, *Harvard Studies in Classical Philology* 84.

Killebrew, W. A., see Hachlili.

Kindler, A., 1986, The Currency of Bronze Coins in Ramat Ha-Golan in the First Century, in: Yedaya , M., ed., *The Western Galilee Antiquities*, Tel-Aviv (Heb.).

King, A., 1984, Animal Bones and the Diety Identity of the Military, in: Blagg and King 1984.

— and Henig, M., 1981, eds, *The Roman West in the Third Century*, BAR 109, Oxford.

King, C. E., 1981, The Circulation of Coins, in: King and Henig.

Kirkbride, A. S., 1939, Ancient Coins Found in Various Parts of Trans-Jordan, *PEF* 71.

Klausner, J., 1975, The Economy of Judea in the Period of the Second Temple, in: Avi-Yonah, M., ed., *The World History of the Jewish People*, VII: *The Herodian Period* (Heb.).

Kleberg, T., 1957, *Hôtels, restaurants et cabarets dans l'antiquité romaine*, Uppsala.

Klein, S., 1928, Das tannaitische Grenzeverzeichnis Palästina, *Hebrew Union College Annual* 5.

— 1930, Kefar Aris, *Tarbiz* I. 2 (Heb.).

— 1934, Le-Korot 'ha-'Arisut ha-Gedola' be-'Erez-Yisra'el, *Yedi'ot*, 1 (Heb.).

— 1936, Be-'Ikvot ha-'Arisut ha-Gedola bi-Sevivot Lud, *Sefer ha-Yovel Li-Khevod Shemuel Krauss*, Jerusalem (Heb.).

— ed. 1937, *Trade, Industry, and Crafts in Ancient Palestine*, Jerusalem (Heb.).

— 1939, *Erez Yehuda*, Tel-Aviv (Heb.).

— 1939a, *Sefer Ha-Yshuv*, Tel-Aviv (Heb.).

— 1967, *Galilee*, Jerusalem (Heb.).

Kloetzli, G., 1970, Coins from Chorazin, *LA* 20.

Kloner, A., 1980, *The Necropolis of Jerusalem in the Second Temple Period*, diss., Jerusalem (Heb.).

—— and Hess, O., 1985, A Columbarium in Complex 21 at Maresha, *Atiqot* 17.

—— and Sagiv, N., 1989, Hellenistic Oil Presses in Maresha, *Niqrot Zurim* 15 (Heb.).

—— and Tepper, Y., 1987, *Hiding Complexes in the Judean Shephlah*, Tel-Aviv (Heb.).

Kloner, see also Wachsmann.

Kochavi, M., ed. 1972, *Judea Samaria and the Golan: Archaeological Survey 1967–1968*, Jerusalem (Heb.).

—— 1989, *Aphek–Antipatris*, Tel-Aviv.

Koder, J., 1986, The Urban Character of Early Byzantine Empire: Some Reflections on a Settlement Geographical Approach to the Topic, in: *The 17th International Byzantine Congress*, New York.

Kolendo, J., 1981, *L'agricultura nell'Italia Romana*, Roma.

Kraemer, C. J., 1958, *Excavations at Nessana*, Princeton.

Krauss, S., 1898–9, *Griechische und lateinische Lehnwörter im Talmud, Midrash und Targum*, Berlin.

—— 1909, Der Jahrmarkt von Batnan, *ZAW* 29.

—— 1909a, Honig in Palestine, *ZDPV* 32.

—— 1910–12, Talmudische Archäologie, I–III, Leipzig (repr. 1966).

—— 1924–9, *Kadmoniot Ha-Talmud*, Berlin and Vienna (Heb.).

—— 1929, Ha-Krach, ha-'Ir ve-ha-Kfar ba-Talmud, *He-'Atid* 3 (Heb.).

Landau, Y., 1966, A Greek Inscription Found near Hefziba, *IEJ* 16.

Landels, J. G., 1978, *Engineering in the Ancient World*, Berkeley and Los Angeles.

Lapp, P. W., 1960, Late Royal Seals from Judah, *BASOR* 158.

Lauffer, S., 1971, *Diokletians Preisedikt: Texte und Commentar*, Berlin.

Lesquier, J., 1918, *L'Armée romaine d'Égypte*, Cairo.

Levick, B., 1967, *Roman Colonies in Southern Asia Minor*, Oxford.

Levine, I. L., 1975, *Caesarea under Roman Rule*, Leiden.

—— 1975a, *Roman Caesarea: An Archeological–Topographical Study* (Kedem, 2), Jerusalem.

—— 1985, *The Rabbinic Class in Palestine During the Talmudic Period*, Jerusalem (Heb.).

—— and Netzer, E., 1986, *Excavations at Caesarea Maritima 1975, 1976, 1979*, Jerusalem.

Lévy, I., 1901, Cultes et rites syriens dans le Talmud, *REJ* 43.

Lewis, N., 1943, A Sidelight on Diocletian's Revival of Agriculture, *JEA* 29.

—— 1989, *The Documents from Bar Kokhba Period in the Caves of the Letters*, Jerusalem.

Lewit, T., 1991, *Agricultural Production in the Roman Economy 200–400*, BAR 568, Oxford.

Lieberman, S., 1934, *Hayerushalmi Kiphshuto*, Jerusalem (Heb.).

—— 1938, *Tosefeth Rishonim*, II, Jerusalem (Heb.).

—— 1939–44, The Martyrs of Caesarea, *Annuaire de L'Institut de Philologie et d'Histoire Orientales et Slaves* 7.

—— 1942, *Greek in Jewish Palestine*, New York.

—— 1944–5, Roman Legal Institutions, *JQR* 35.

—— 1945–6; 1946–7, Palestine in the Third and Fourth Centuries, *JQR* 36; 37.

—— 1955, *Tosefta Kipshutah* I: *Order Zera'im*, New York (Heb.).

—— 1959, Ten Words, *Eshkolot* 3 (Heb.).

—— 1962, *Tosefta Kipshutah*, II: *Order Mo'ed*, New York (Heb.).

—— 1962a, *Greek and Hellenism in Jewish Palestine*, Jerusalem (Heb.) (orig. pub. in English 1950).

—— 1963, How Much Greek in Jewish Palestine? in: Altmann, A., ed., *Biblical and Other Studies*, Cambridge, Mass.

—— 1970–1, A Preliminary Remark to the Inscription of En-Gedi, *Tarbiz* 40 (Heb.).

—— 1975, The Mishna of Baba Mezia 5. 1, and its Explanation, in: *Yad Reem, A. M. Lifshitz* (memorial volume without editor's name), Jerusalem (Heb.).

—— 1975–6, A Note to Tarbiz 45 (1976) p. 61, *Tarbiz* 45 (Heb.).

—— 1980, *Hellenism in Jewish Palestine*, New York.

—— 1983, Introduction and Commentary, in: Rosenthal, E. S., *Yerushalmi Neziqin*, Jerusalem (Heb.).

—— 1986, The Halakhic Inscription from the Beth-Shean Valley, *Tarbiz* 46 (Heb.).

—— 1988, *Tosefta Kipshuta*, IV: *Order Neziqin*, New York (Heb.).

Lifshitz, B., 1960, Sur la date du transfert de la legio VI Ferrata en Palestine, *Latomus* 19.

—— 1961, Inscriptions grecques de Césarée, *RB* 68.

—— 1967, *Donateurs et fondateurs dans les synagogues juives*, (Cahiers de la Revue Biblique 7), Paris.

—— 1969, Légions romaines en Palestine, in: Bibouw, J. ed., *Hommages à Marcel Renard* (Collection Latomus 102), II, Brussels.

—— 1970, Scythopolis: l'histoire des institutions et des cultes de la ville à l'époque hellénistique et impériale', *ANRW* II.18.

—— 1976, Bleigewichte aus Palästina und Syrien, *ZDPV* 92.

Ligt, L. de, 1990–1, Demand, Supply, Distribution: The Roman Peasantry between Town and Countryside: Rural Monetization and Peasant Demand, *Münstersche Beiträge zu antiken Handelsgeschichte*, IX, 1; IX, 2.

Linder, A., 1974–5, The Roman Imperial Government and the Jews under Constantine, *Tarbiz* 44 (Heb.).

Liversidge, J., 1976, *Everyday Life in the Roman Empire*, London and New York.

Loffreda, S., 1974, *Cafarnao*, II: *La ceramica*, Jerusalem.

—— 1975, La ceramica della sinagoga di Cafarnao, in: Corbo, V., Loffreda, S., Spijkerman, A., 1975, *La Sinagoga di Cafarnao dopo gli Scavi del 1969*, Jerusalem.

—— 1975, Un lotto di ceramica de Karm Er Ras presso Kafr Kanna, *LA* 25.

Lohman, H., 1992, Agriculture and Country Life in Classical Attica, in: Wells 1992.

Lopez, R. S., 1954, Silk Industry in the Byzantine Empire, *Speculum* 20.

Löw, I., 1923–34, *Die Flora der Juden*, I–IV, Vienna and Leipzig (repr. Hildesheim, 1967).

—— 1969, *Fauna und Mineralien der Juden*, Hildesheim.

MacAdam, H. I., 1985, *Studies in the History of the Roman Province of Arabia*, BAR 295, Oxford.

MacMullen, R., 1960, Inscriptions on Roman Armour and the Supply of Arms in the Roman Empire, *AJA* 64.

—— 1963, *Soldier and Civilian in the Later Roman Empire*, Cambridge.

—— 1964, Social Mobility and the Theodosian Code, *JRS* 54.

—— 1966, *Enemies of the Roman Order*, Cambridge, Mass.

—— 1968, Rural Romanization, *Phoenix* 22.

—— 1970, Market-days in the Roman Empire, *Phoenix* 24.

—— 1974, Peasants during the Principate, *ANRW* II. 1.

—— 1984, *Roman Social Relations*, New Haven.

—— 1988, *Corruption and the Decline of Rome*, Yale, New Haven and London.

—— 1990, *Change in the Roman Empire*, Princeton.

Mader, E., 1957–8, *Mambre*, I–II, Munich.

Magen, Y., 1984, Kalandia: A Vineyard Farm and Winery of Second Temple Times, *Qadmoniot* 66–7 (Heb.).

—— 1991, Elonei Mamre, *Qadmoniot* 93–4 (Heb.).

—— 1992, Samaritan Synagogues, *Qadmoniot* 99–100 (Heb.).

—— 1984, Jerusalem as the Center of Stone-ware Production in the Herodian Times, *Qadmoniot* 68 (Heb.).

—— 1992, Samaritan Synagogues, in: Eshel, Y. and Erlich, Z., eds, *Judea and Samaria Research Studies: The 2nd Annual Meeting*, Ariel (Heb.).

Magie, D., 1950, *Roman Rule in Asia Minor to the end of the Third Century after Christ*, Princeton.

Mann, J. C., 1983, *Legionary Recruitment and Veteran Settlement during the Principate*, London.

Manns, F., 1984, *Some Weights of the Hellenistic, Roman and Byzantine Periods*, Jerusalem.

Mantel, H., 1961, *Studies in the History of the Sanhedrin*, Cambridge, Mass.

Maoz, Z. A., 1986, *Ramat Ha-Golan Ba-Et Ha-Atika*, Jerusalem (Heb.).

Marany, A., 1955, *Hashpaa't Shitot ha-Gidul al Yevulei Pishtat ha-Sivim ve-Echuta bi-Tnaei ha-Aretz*, Jerusalem (Heb.).

Margoliot, M., 1974, *Hilchot Eretz Israel min ha-Gniza*, Jerusalem (Heb.).

Marmorstein, A., 1934, Dioclétien à la lumière de la littérature rabbinique, *REJ* 98.

—— 1937, Ha-Mazav ha-Kalkali be-Doro shel R. Yohanan, *Festschrift Dr Jakob Freimann*, Berlin (Heb.).

Marquardt, J., 1957, Römische Staatsverwaltung, I–III, Darmstadt.

Mayer, M. A., 1907, *A History of Gaza*, New York.

Mayerson, P., 1960, *The Ancient Agricultural Regime of Nessana and the Central Negev*, London.

—— 1985, The Wine and Vineyards of Gaza in the Byzantine Period, *BASOR* 257.

—— 1992, The Gaza 'Wine' Jar (Gazition) and 'Lost' Askelon Jar (Askalônion), *IEJ* 42.

Mazar, B., Dothan, T. and Dunayevski, I., 1966, En Gedi, *Atiqot* 5.

—— 1970, see *Encyclopedia la-Hafirot Archeologiot*.

—— 1971, The Inscription on the Floor of the Synagogue in En Gedi, *Tarbiz* 40 (Heb.).

—— 1973, *Beth Shearim*, I, Jerusalem.

Meiggs, R., 1982, *Trees and Timber in the Ancient Mediterranean World*, Oxford.

Melitz, J. and Winch, D., 1978, eds, *Religious Thought and Economic Society*, Durham.

Mellor, J. E. M., 1929, Beekeeping in Egypt, *Bulletin de la Société Entomologique d'Égypte* 12.

Meshorer, Y., 1967, *Jewish Coins*, Tel-Aviv.

—— 1974, Coins from the Excavations at Khorazin, *EI* 11 (Heb.).

—— 1976, A Hoard of Coins from Migdal, *Atiqot* 11.

—— see also Raynor.

Meyers, E. M., Kraabel, A. T., and Strange, J. F., 1976, *Ancient Synagogue Excavations at Khirbet Shema, Upper Galilee, Israel 1970–1972*, Durham, NC.

——, Meyers, C. L. and Strange, J. F., 1978, Excavations in Meiron in Upper Galilee, 1974, 1975: Second Preliminary Report, *AASOR* 43.

——, Netzer, E., and Meyers, C. L. 1986, Sepphoris, Ornament of all Galilee, *B.A.* 49.

——, Strange, J. F. and Meyers, C. L., 1981, *Excavations at Ancient Meiron, Upper Galilee, Israel 1971–72, 1974–75, 1977*, Cambridge, Mass.

Michel, H., 1940, *The Economics of Ancient Greece*, Cambridge.

Mickwitz, G., 1937, Economic Rationalism in Graeco-Roman Agriculture, *English Historical Review* 52.

Middleton, P. S., 1979, Army Supply in Roman Gaul: An Hypothesis for Roman Britain, in: Burnham, D. C. and Johnson, H. B.

— 1983, The Roman Army and Long-distance Trade, in: Garnsey and Whittaker, eds, 1983.

Millar, C. F., 1981, The World of the Golden Ass, *JRS* 71.

Millar, F., 1963, The Fiscus in the First Two Centuries, *JRS* 53.

Miller, J. I., 1969, *The Spice Trade of the Roman Empire 29 BC to AD 641*, Oxford.

Milne, J. G., 1926, The Currency of Egypt in the Fifth Century, *NC* 6.

— 1931, Woodeaton Coins, *JRS* 21.

Mittwoch, A., 1955, Tribute and Land Tax in Seleucid Judea, *Biblica* 36.

Mócsy, A., 1953, Das Territorium Legionis und die Canabae in Pannonien, *AAASH* 3.

Mommsen, T. and Blümner, H., 1893 (repr. 1958), *Der Maximaltarif des Diocletian*, Berlin.

Mor, M., 1986, The Roman Army in Eretz-Israel in the Years AD 70–132, in: Freeman, P. and Kennedy, P., eds, *The Defence of the Roman East*, BAR 297, Oxford.

Morel, J. P., 1983, La Céramique comme indice du commerce antique, in Garnsey and Whittaker, eds.

Moritz, L. A., 1958, *Grain-mills and Flour in Classical Antiquity*, Oxford.

Morris, I., 1992, The Early Polis as City and State, in: Rich and Wallace-Hadrill, eds.

Mumford, L., 1966, *The City in History*, Harmondsworth.

Mundolfo, R., 1954, The Greek Attitude to Manual Labour, *Past and Present* 6.

Muntner, S., 1957, *Assaph the Physician*, Jerusalem.

Nash, M., 1966, *Primitve and Peasant System*, Scranton.

Naveh, J., 1978, *On Stone and Mosaic*, Tel-Aviv (Heb.).

— 1978b, The Titles SHD/d MNHM in Jewish Epigraphic Texts, in: Avishur, A. and Blau, Y., eds, *Studies in the Bible and the Ancient Near East, presented to Schmuel E. Loewenstamm*, Jerusalem.

Negev, A., 1972, Nabatean Sigillata, *RB* 79.

— 1974, *The Nabatean Potter's Workshop at Oboda*, Bonn.

— 1985, Excavations at Carmel (Khirbet Susya) in 1984: Preliminary Report, *IEJ* 35.

— 1988, *The Architecture of Mampsis*, II (Qedem 29).

Netzer, E., 1984, Channels and a Royal Estate from the Hellenistic Period in the Western Plains of Jericho, *Leichtweiss-Institut für Wasserbau der Technischen Universität Braunschweig, Mitteilungen* 82.

— 1974, The Hasmonean and Herodian Winter Palace at Jericho, *Qadmoniot* 25–6 (Heb.).

— 1985, The Swimming Pools of the Hasmonean Period at Jericho, *EI* 18 (Heb.).

— 1987, Did the Nympheon in Magdala Serve as a Synagogue? in: Kasher, A., Oppenheimer, A. and Rappaport, U., eds, *Synagogues in Antiquity*, Jerusalem.

— 1989, The Hasmonean's Building Projects, in: Kasher, ed., 1989.

— 1989, The Hashmonean Buildings, in: Kasher, ed., 1989.

— see also Levine.

Neusner, J., 1979, *The Talmud as History*, Quebec.

— 1990, *The Economics of the Mishna*, Chicago.

Nezer, E., see Netzer.

Ninnen, P. van, 1987, Urban Craftsmen in Roman Egypt, *Münstersche Beiträge zu antiken Handelsgeschichte*, VI, 1.

Nun, M., 1964, *Ancient Jewish Fishery*, Merchavia (Heb.).

— 1977, *Sea of Kinneret*, Tel-Aviv (Heb.).

Olami, Y., 1981, *Archaeological Survey of Daliya, Map 31*, Jerusalem.

— unpublished, *Archaeological Survey of Israel, Carmel Map*.

— see also Ronen.

Opelt, I., 1971, Ein Edict des Kaisares Valens, *Historia* 20.

Oppenheimer, A., 1968, The Separation of First Tithes during the Second Temple Period, in: Melamed, E. Z., ed., Benjamin De Vries Memorial Volume, Jerusalem (Heb.).

—— 1977, *The 'Am ha-Aretz: Study in the Social History of the Jewish People in the Hellenistic–Roman Period*, Leiden.

—— 1978, Those of the School of Rabbi Yannai, *Studies in the History of the Jewish People and the Land of Israel* 5 (Heb.).

——, see Kasher *et al.*

Oren, A. D., 1968, The Herodian Doves in the Light of Recent Archaeological Discoveries, *PEQ* 100.

—— 1980, Seker Tzfon Sinai 1972–1978, in: Meshel, Z. and Finkelstein, I., eds, *Sinai in Antiquity*, Tel-Aviv (Heb.).

Ormerod, H. A., 1924, *Piracy in the Ancient World*, Liverpool.

Ostrogorsky, G., 1968, *History of the Byzantine State*, Oxford.

Ovadiah, A., 1968, The Synagogue at Gaza, *Qadmoniot* 4 (Heb.).

—— 1970, *Corpus of the Byzantine Churches in the Holy Land*, Bonn.

Packer, J. E., 1967, Housing and Population in Imperial Ostia and Rome, *JRS* 57.

—— 1971, The Insulae of Imperial Ostia, *Memoirs of the American Academy in Rome* 31, Rome.

Paret, R., 1960, Les Villes de Syrie du sud et les routes commerciales d'Arabia à la fin du VIᵉ s., in Dölger, F. and Georg Beck, H., eds, *Akten des XI. Internationalen byzantinischen Kongresses*, Munich.

Paul, S. M., 1975, Classifications of Wine in Mesopotamian and Rabbinic Sources, *IEJ* 25.

Peacock, D. P. S., ed. 1977, *Pottery and Early Commerce*, London.

—— 1977a, *Pottery and Early Commerce: Characterization and Trade in Roman and Later Ceramics*, London.

—— 1980, The Roman Millstone Trade: a Petrological Sketch, *WA* 12.

—— 1982, *Pottery in the Roman World: An Ethnoarchaeological Approach*, London.

Pekaery, Y., 1968, *Untersuchungen zu den römischen Reichsstrassen*, Bonn.

Peleg, Y., 1984, The Water System of Caesarea, in: *Leichtweiss-Institut für Wasserbau der Technischen Universität Braunschweig: Mitteilungen* 82.

Percival, J., 1981, *The Roman Villa*, London.

Perring, D., 1992, Spatial Organisation and Social Change in Roman Towns, in: Rich and Wallace-Hadrill, eds.

Pleket, H. W., 1984, Urban Elites and the Economy in the Greek Cities of the Roman Empire, *Münstersche Beiträge zu antiken Handelsgeschichte*, III, 1.

Pollard, J., 1977, *Birds in Greek Life and Myth*, London.

Polotsky, H. J., 1967, Three Greek Documents from the Family Archive of Babatha, *EI* 8 (Heb.).

Porat, Y., 1975, The Gardens of Caesarea, *Qadmoniot* 30–1 (Heb.).

—— 1986, Aspects of the Development of Ancient Irrigation Agriculture in Jericho and Ein Gedi, in: Kasher, Oppenheimer and Rappaport, eds (Heb.). See Porath.

Porath, Y., Applebaum, S. and Dar, S., eds, 1985, *The History and Archaeology of Emek-Hefer*, Tel-Aviv (Heb.). See Porat.

Portugali, Y., 1986, The Settlement Pattern in the Western Jezreel Valley from the 6th Century BCE to the Arab Conquest, in Kasher, Oppenheimer and Rappaport, eds (Heb.).

Poulter, A. G., 1980, Rural Communities (Vici and Komai) and their Role in the Organization of the Limes of Moesia Inferior, in: Hanson, W. S. and Keppie, L. J. F., eds, *Limes: Roman Frontier Studies 1979*, BAR 71, Oxford.

—— 1987, Townships and Villages, in: Wacher, J., ed., *The Roman World*, London.

Pritchard, J. B., 1971, The Roman Port of Sarafand, *Bulletin du Musée de Beyrouth* 24.

Qedar, S., 1978, *Gewichte aus drei Jahrtausenden*, I, Münz Zentrum-Aktion 32, Cologne.

—— 1979, *Gewichte aus drei Jahrtausenden*, II, ibid. 37, Cologne.

—— 1981, *Gewichte aus drei Jahrtausenden*, III, ibid. 45, Cologne.

—— 1983, *Gewichte aus drei Jahrtausenden*, IV, ibid. 49, Cologne.

Raban, A., 1982, *Archaeological Survey of Israel: Nahalal Map (28) 16–23*, Jerusalem.

—— ed. 1985, *Harbour Archaeology*, BAR 257, Oxford.

—— 1986, The Harbour of Acco, in: Yedaya, M., ed., *The Western Galilee Antiquities*, Tel-Aviv (Heb.).

—— 1989, *The Harbours of Caesarea Maritima*, BAR 491, Oxford.

—— *Mishmar Haemek Map* (unpublished).

Radcliffe, W., *Fishing from the Earliest Times*, London.

Rahmani, L. Y., 1973, The Erez Mosaic, *EI* 11 (Heb.).

Rainey, A. F., 1965, Royal Weights and Measures, *BASOR* 179.

—— 1982, Wine from the Royal Vineyards, *BASOR* 245.

Ramsay, H. G., 1936, Government Relief during the Roman Empire, *Classical Journal* 31.

Raynor, I. and Meshorer, Y., 1988, *The Coins of Ancient Mairon*, Vinnona Lake.

Reece, R., 1975, Roman Currency: New Thoughts and Problems, *WA* 6.

—— 1978, Bronze Coinage in Roman Britain and the Western Provinces AD 302–330, in: Carson, R. A. G. and Kraay, C. M., eds, *Scripta Nummaria Romana*, London.

—— 1979, Roman Monetary Impact, in: Burnham and Johnson 1979.

—— 1984, Mints, Markets and the Military, in: Blagg and King 1984.

Rees, R. K., 1952, The Defensor Civitatis in Egypt, *Journal of Juristic Papyrology* 6.

Reese, D. C. *et al.* 1986, On the Trade of Shells and Fish from the Nile River, *BASOR* 264.

Reisner, G. A., Fisher, C. S. and Lyon, D. G., 1924, *Harvard Excavations at Samaria*, Cambridge.

Rich, J. and Wallace-Hadrill, A., eds, 1991, *City and Country in the Ancient World*, London and New York.

Rickman, G., 1980, *The Corn Supply of Ancient Rome*, Oxford.

Rihll, T. E. and Wilson, A. G., 1985, *Settlement Structures in Ancient Greece: Model Based Approaches to Analysis*, Leeds.

—— 1991, Modelling Settlement Structure in Ancient Greece: New Approaches to the Polis, in: Rich and Wallace-Hadrill 1991.

Riley, J. A., 1975, The Pottery from the First Season of Excavations in the Caesarea Hippodrome, *BASOR* 218.

—— 1981, The Pottery, in: Humphrey, J. H., *Excavations at Carthage 1977*, Michigan.

—— (unknown date), The Pottery, in: Lloyd, J. A., *Excavations at Khrabish Bengazi (Berenice)*, II, Tripoli.

Ripoll, E., Nuix, J. and Villaronya, L., 1976, Monedas de los Judíos halladas en las excavadiones de Emporiae, *Numisma* 26.

Rivet, A. L. F., ed. 1969, *The Roman Villa in Britain*, London.

—— 1969, Social and Economic Aspects, in: Rivet ed. 1969.

Rodwell, W. and Rowley, T., eds, 1975, *Small Towns of Roman Britain*, BAR 15, Oxford.

Roll, Y., 1976, The Roman Road Network in Eretz-Israel, *Qadmoniot* 34–5 (Heb.).

—— and Ayalon, E., 1989, *Apollonia and Southern Sharon*, Tel-Aviv.

Roll, see also Isaac.

Ron, Y. D. Z., 1977a, The Distribution of Agricultural Terraces in the Judean Hills, in: Shmueli, A., Grossman, D. and Rechavam, Z., eds, *Judea and Samaria*, Jerusalem (Heb.).

—— 1977b, Utilization of Springs for Irrigated Agriculture in the Judean Hills, in: Schmueli, A., Grossman, D. and Rechavam, Z., eds, *Judea and Samaria*, Jerusalem (Heb.).

Ronen, A., 1983, *Archaeological Survey of Israel – Map of Haifa: East (23) 15–24*, Jerusalem.

—— and Olami, Y., 1978, *Archaeological Survey of Israel: Atlit Map*, Jerusalem.

Rosenthal, R., 1978, The Roman and Byzantine Pottery, in: Stern, E., *Excavations at Tel Mevorakh* (Qedem 9.)

—— 1978a, The Pottery, in: Stern, E., *Excavations at Tel Mevorakh* (Qedem 9).

—— and Sivan, R., 1978, *Ancient Lamps in the Schloessinger Collection* (Qedem 8), Jerusalem.

Rossene, S., 1975, A Note on Talmudic Maritime Law, *Dine Israel* 6 (Heb.).

Rostowzev (Rostovtzeff), M., 1910, *Studien zur Geschichte des römischen Kolonats*, Berlin.

—— 1932, *Caravan Cities*, Oxford.

—— 1957, *The Social and Economic History of the Roman Empire*, I-II, Oxford.

—— 1959, *The Social and Economic History of the Hellenistic World*, I-III, Oxford.

—— 1967, *A Large Estate in Egypt in the Third Century* BC (repr.), Rome.

Rot-Gerson, L., 1987, *The Greek Inscriptions from the Synagogues in Eretz-Israel*, Jerusalem (Heb.).

Rouge, J., 1966, *Recherches sur l'organisation du commerce maritime en Méditerranée sous l'empire romain*, Paris.

Rubin, N., 1972, For Whom Does One Mourn? A Sociological Analysis of Talmudic Sources, in: Hirschberg, H. Z., ed., *Memorial to H. M. Shapiro*, Ramat-Gan.

Runciman, S., 1956, *Byzantine Civilisation*, New York.

Russel, J. C., 1958, *Late Ancient and Mediaeval Population*, Lancaster.

Russo, E., 1987, La Sculptura del VI secolo in Palestina, *Acta ad Archaeologiam et Artium Historiam Pertinentia* 6.

Safrai, S., 1965, *Pilgrimage at the Temple of the Second Temple*, Tel-Aviv.

—— 1966–7, The Practical Implementation of the Sabbatical Year after the Destruction of the Second Temple, *Tarbiz* 35–6 (Heb.).

—— 1967, Monetary Development in Third and Fourth Centuries as Reflected in Talmudic Literature, in: Kindler, A., ed., *Proceedings of the International Numismatic Convention*.

—— 1968, Notes on Palestine Studies, in: Melamed, E. Z., ed., *Benjamin De Vries Memorial Volume*, Jerusalem (Heb.).

—— 1971, The Relationship between the Roman Army and the Jews of Eretz Yisrael after the Destruction of the Second Temple, in: *Roman Frontier Studies 1967*, Tel-Aviv.

—— 1974, Jewish Self-government, in: Safrai *et al.*, eds, 1974.

—— 1976a, The Jewish Town in Eretz Israel in the Mishna and Talmud Period, in: *Town and Community*, Jerusalem: Jewish Historical Society.

—— 1976b, Home and Family, in: Safrai *et al.*, eds, 1974.

—— 1976c, The Synagogue, in: Safrai *et al.*, eds, 1974.

—— 1976d, Education and the Study of the Torah, in: Safrai *et al.*, eds, 1974.

—— 1983, *Be-Shalhei ha-Bayit ha-Sheni u-be-Tekufat ha-Mishna*, Jerusalem (Heb.).

—— 1983a, *Eretz Yisrael Ve-Hakhameha bi-Tekufat ha-Mishna ve-ha-talmud*, Jerusalem (Heb.).

—— and Stern, M., with Flusser, D. and van Unik, W. C., eds, 1974, 1976, *The Jewish People in the First Century*, I-II, Assen.

— and Safrai, Z., 1975, Beth Anat, *Synai*, 78 (Heb.).

Safrai, Z., 1980, *Gevulot ve-Shilton be-Eretz Yisra'el bi-Tekufat ha-Mishna ve-ha-Talmud*, Tel-Aviv (Heb.).

— 1980, Urbanization in Israel in the Greco-Roman Period, *Studies in the History of the Jewish People and the Land of Israel* 5 (Heb.).

— 1982, The Security Organization in the Jewish Town in the Mishna and Talmud Period, *Cathedra* 22 (Heb.).

— 1983, Le-She'elat ha-Mivneh ha-Merhavi Shel ha-Yishuv ba-Galil bi-Tekufat ha-Mishna ve-ha-Talmud, in: Shmueli, A., Grossman, D. and Rechavam, Z., eds, *The Lands of Galilee*, I, Haifa (Heb.).

— 1983a, Family Structure during the Period of the Mishna and Talmud, *Milet* 1.

— 1983b, The Village in the Mishna and Talmud, in: Stern, M., ed. 1983, *Nation and History*, Jerusalem (Heb.).

— 1984, Leshelat Tchumei Eretz Israel Ha-Chayavim Be-Mitzvot, in: Refael, I., ed. 1984, *Soloveytzik Yubelean Book*, Jerusalem (Heb.).

— 1984b, Fairs in the Land of Israel, in the Mishna and Talmud Period, *Zion* 49 (Heb.).

— 1985, *The Galilee in the Time of the Mishna and Talmud*, Jerusalem (Heb.).

— 1986, Anab-Kabir: Village Pasture in the Roman Byzantine Period, *Israel: People and Land* 2 (Heb.).

— 1986b, Neapolis in the Roman Period, in: Dar, S. and Safrai, Z., eds, *Shomron Studies*, Tel-Aviv (Heb.).

— 1987, Financing Synagogue Construction in the Mishna and Talmud, in: Kasher, A., Oppenheimer, A. and Rappaport, U., eds, 1987, *Synagogue in Antiquity*, Jerusalem (Heb.).

— 1988, Beekeeping and Honey Production in Eretz Israel During the Roman Period, *Israel: People and Land* 4 (Heb.).

— 1989, The Jewish Nation and Roman Economy, in: Kasher, A.

— in press, *The Jewish Community in the Mishna and Talmud Period*, Jerusalem (Heb.).

— in preparation, *Byzantine Palestine*.

— and Linn, M., 1988, The Economic Basis of Geva, in: Mazar, B., ed., *Geva*, Jerusalem (Heb.).

Sauer, R., 1991, *The Ecology of the Greek World*, London.

Salway, P., 1965, *The Frontier People of Roman Britain*, Cambridge.

Schalit, A., 1969, *König Herodes*, Berlin.

Schürer, E., 1898–1909, *Geschichte des jüdischen Volkes im Zeitalter Jesus Christi*, I-III, Leipzig (rev. and trans. G. Vermes and F. G. B. Millar, 1973).

Schulten, A., 1894, Das Territorium Legionis, *Hermes* 29.

Schumacher, G., 1908, *Tell el Mutesellin*, Leipzig.

Schwabe, M., 1954, Document of a Journey through Palestine in the Years 317–323 CE, *EI* 3 (Heb.).

— 1967, Tiberias Revealed through Inscriptions, in: Hirschberg H. Z., ed., *All the Land of Naftali*, Jerusalem (Heb.).

— and Lifshitz, B., 1974, *Bet Shearim*, II: *The Greek Inscriptions*, Jerusalem.

Schwartz, J., 1984, Judea in the Wake of the Bar-Kochva Revolt, in: Oppenheimer, A. and Rappaport, U., eds, *The Bar Kochva Revolt: A New Approach*, Jerusalem (Heb.).

— 1986, *Jewish Settlement in Judea*, Jerusalem (Heb.).

Segal, A., 1983, *The Byzantine City of Shivta, Negev Desert, Israel*, Oxford.

Seligman, N., Raz, T. and Kazenelson, N., 1959, *Natural Pasture of Israel*, Merhavia (Heb.).

Sergé, A., 1942, Essays in Byzantine Economic History, I: Annona Civica and the

Annona Militaris, *Byzantion* 16.
— 1950, Note sulla storia dei cereali nell' antichità, *Aegyptus* 30.
Sheffer, A., 1987, Textiles from En Bokek, *EI* 19 (Heb.).
Siddle, P. V., 1970, Location Theory and the Subsistence Economy, *Journal of Tropical Geography* 31.
Siegelman, A., 1970, Herodian Columbarium near Ma'agan Michael, *Atiqot* 6 (Heb.).
Singer, C., ed. 1957, *A History of Technology*, Oxford.
Skinner, G. W., 1964, Marketing and Social Structure in Rural China, *Journal of Asian Studies* 24.
Skydsgaard, see Isager.
Smallwood, E. M., 1981, *The Jews under Roman Rule*, Leiden.
Snyder, W. F., 1936, Quinto Nundinas Pompeis, *JRS* 26.
Speidel, M., 1984, *Roman Army Studies*, I, Amsterdam.
Sperber, D., 1969, The Centurion as a Tax Collector, *Latomus* 28.
— 1969a, The Angaria in Rabbinic Literature, *L'Antiquité classique* 38.
— 1970, On Social and Economic Conditions in Third Century Palestine, *Archiv Orientalni* 38.
— 1971, On Pubs and Policemen in Roman Palestine, *Zeitschrift für deutschen morgenlandische Gesellschaft* 120.
— 1974, *Roman Palestine 200–400: Money and Prices*, Ramat-Gan.
— 1976, Objects of Trade between Palestine and Egypt in Roman Times, *Journal of the Economic and Social History of the Orient* 19.
— 1977, On the Office of the Agoranomos in Roman Palestine, *ZDMG* 127. 2.
— 1978, *Roman Palestine 200–400: The Land*, Ramat-Gan.
— 1986, *Nautica Talmudica*, Ramat-Gan.
Spijkerman, A., 1975, *Cafarnao*, III, Jerusalem.
Spurr, M. S., 1986, *Arable Cultivation in Roman Italy*, London.
Stark, H. L. and Stemberger, G., 1991, *Introduction to the Talmud and Midrash*, Cambridge.
Stern, E., 1973, *The Material Culture of the Land of the Bible in the Persian Period*, Jerusalem (Heb.). (Engl. trans. Warminster, 1982).
— 1992, *Dor, Ruler of the Seas*, Jerusalem (Heb.).
Stern, M., 1974–84, *Greek and Latin Authors on Jews and Judaism*, I-III, Jerusalem.
— 1980, Jerusalem, the Most Famous of the Cities of the East (Pliny, Natural History V, 70), in: Oppenheimer, A., Rappoport, U. and Sren, M., *Jerusalem in the Second Temple Period*, Jerusalem (Heb.).
Sukenik, E. L., 1942, The Meaning of Le Melekh Inscriptions, *Qedem* 1 (Heb.).
Sussman, V., 1969, Ancient Burial Cave at Rehovot, *Atiqot* 5 (Heb.).
— 1978, Samaritan Lamps of the Third and Fourth Centuries, *IEJ* 28.
Sussmann, Y., 1973–4, A Halachic Inscription from the Beth Shean Valley, *Tarbiz* 43 (Heb.).
— 1975–6, The Boundaries of Eretz Israel, *Tarbiz* 45 (Heb.).
Szilagyi, J., 1963, Prices and Wages in the Western Provinces of the Roman Empire, *AAASH* 11.
Taaffe, E. J. and Gauthier, H. L., 1973, *Geography of Transportation*, Englewood Cliffs, NJ.
Tabory, J., 1977, The History of the Order of the Passover Eve, unpublished Ph.d thesis, Bar Ilan University, Ramat Gan.
Taubenschlag, R., 1955, *The Law of Greco-Roman Egypt in the Light of the Papyri*, Warsaw.
Tchalenko, G., 1953–8, *Villages antiques de la Syrie du nord*, I–III, Paris.
Tcherikower (Tscherikower), A., 1933–4, Palestine in the Light of the Papyri of Zenon, *Tarbiz* 4–5 (Heb.).

—— 1951, Was Jerusalem a Greek Polis under the Procurators? *EI* 1 (Heb.).

—— 1959, *Hellenistic Civilization and the Jews*, Jerusalem.

Tchernia, A., 1983, Italian Wine Trade in Gaul at the End of the Republic, in: Garnsey *et al.*

Tengström, E., 1974, *Bread for the People*, Stockholm.

Tepper (Teffer) Y., 1986, The Rise and Fall of Dove Raising, in: Kasher, Oppenheimer and Rappaport, eds (Heb.).

—— 1986b, The Sun Dial from Dir Sima'an, in: Dar, S. and Safrai, Z., eds, *Shomron Studies*, Tel-Aviv (Heb.).

Thomas, J. D., 1989, *Masada*, II, Jerusalem.

Tsafrir, Y., 1984, *Eretz Israel from the Destruction of the Second Temple to the Muslim Conquest*, II, Jerusalem (see also Baras *et al.*) (Heb.).

Tzaferis, V., 1985, A Roman Bath at Rama, *Atiqot* 14.

Tzori, N., 1962, An Archaeological Survey of the Beth Shean Valley, in: *The Beth Shean Valley*, Jerusalem (Heb.).

—— 1973, The House of Kyrios Leontis at Beth Shean, *EI* 11 (Heb.).

—— 1977, *Nahalat Issachar*, Jerusalem (Heb.).

Urbach, E. E., 1951, Political and Social Tendencies in Talmudic Concepts of Charity, *Zion* 16 (Heb.).

—— 1959, The Rabbinical Laws of Idolatry in the Second and Third Centuries in the Light of Archaeological and Historical Facts, *IEJ* 9.

—— 1961, Ascesis and Suffering in Talmudic and Midrashic Sources, in: Baron, S. W., Dinur, B., Ettinger, S. and Halperin, I., eds, *Yitzhak F. Baer Jubilee Volume*, Jerusalem (Heb.).

—— 1964, The Laws Regarding Slavery as a Source for Social History of the Period of the Second Temple, the Mishna and Talmud, in: Weiss, J. G., ed., *Papers of the Institute of Jewish Studies in London*, Jerusalem.

Urman, D., 1985, *The Golan*, BAR 269, Oxford.

Ussishkin, D., 1992, Archaeological Sounding at Bethar Bar-Kokhba's Last Stronghold, *EI* 23 (Heb.).

Varady, L., 1950, *Justin the First*, Harvard.

—— 1962, Contribution to the Roman Military Economy and Agrarian Taxation, *AAASH* 14.

Vetters, H., 1979–89, *Ephesos*, Vienna.

Vincent, L. H., 1922, Une villa gréco-romaine à Beit Djebrin, *RB* 31.

Vitto, F., 1980, Potter's Kilns at Kfar Nahf, *IEJ* 30.

—— 1986, Potters and Pottery Manufacture in Roman Palestine, *Institute of Archaeology Bulletin*, 23.

Waage, D. B., 1952, *Antioch on the Orontes*, IV, Princeton,

Wacher, J. C., 1975, *The Towns of Roman Britain*, London.

Wachsmann, S., 1990, ed., The Excavations of an Ancient Boat in the Sea of Galilee (Lake Kinneret), *Atigot* 19.

—— and Kloner, A., 1981, A Graffito of a Warship at H. Rafia, *Qadmoniot* 14 (Heb.).

Wallace, S. L., 1969, *Taxation in Egypt from Augustus to Diocletian*, New York.

Wallace-Hadrill, see Rich.

Warner, A. H., 1961, *A History of Wine*, London.

Watson, G. R., 1959, The Pay of the Roman Army, *Historia* 5.

Watterman, E., 1937, *Preliminary Report of the University of Michigan Excavations at Sepphoris, Palestine in 1931*, Ann Arbor.

Webster, G., 1969, *The Roman Imperial Army of the First and Second Centuries AD*, London.

Weinberg, G. D., 1970, Hellenistic Glass from Tel Anafa in Upper Galilee, *Journal of Glass Studies* 12.

—— 1988, *Excavations at Jalame*, Columbia.

Weinberg, M., 1897, Die Organisation der jüdischen Ortsgemeinden in der talmudischen Zeit, *Monatsschrift für Geschichte und Wissenschaft der Judentums* 41.

Welles, C. B., 1938, The Inscriptions, in: Kraeling, C. N., ed., *Gerasa: City in the Decapolis*, New Haven.

Wells, B., ed. 1992, *Agriculture in Ancient Greece*, Stockholm.

Welten, P., 1969, *Die Königs Stempel*, Wiesbaden,

West, L. C., 1916, The Cost of Living in Roman Egypt, *CP* II.

—— 1924, Commercial Syria under the Roman Empire, *TAPA* 55.

West, see also Johnson.

Wheeler, M., 1955, Self Sufficiency and the Greek City, *Journal of the History of Ideas*, 16.

White, K. D., 1963, Wheat-farming in Roman Times, *Antiquity* 37.

—— 1967, Latifundia, *Bulletin of the Institute of Classical Studies*, 14.

—— 1970, *Roman Farming*, London.

—— 1975, *The Equipment of the Roman World*, Cambridge.

Whittaker, C. R., 1976, Agri Deserti, in: Finley, ed.

—— 1983, Trade and the Frontiers of the Roman Empire, in: Garnsey and Whittaker, eds.

—— 1983a, Late Roman Trade and Traders, in: Garnsey *et al.*, 1983.

—— ed. 1988, *Pastoral Economies in Classical Antiquity*, Cambridge.

—— 1990, The Consumer City Revisited: The Vicus and the City, *JRA* 3.

—— see also Garnsey.

Wild, J. P., 1979, Roman and Natives in Textile Technology, in: Burnham and Johnson eds, 1979.

—— 1980, Textile Manufacture in the Northern Roman Provinces, Cambridge.

Wilken, V., 1884, Papyruskunden über einen Sklavenkauf aus dem Jahre 359 n. Chr., *Hermes* 19.

Wilkinson, J., 1977, *Jerusalem Pilgrims before the Crusaders*, Jerusalem.

Wilson, see Rihll.

Wipszycka, E., 1965, *L'Industrie textile dans l'Égypte romaine*, Warsaw.

—— 1966, Das Textilhandwerk und der Staat im Römischen Ägypten, *Archiv für Papyrus forschung und verwandte Gebiete* 18.

Yadin, Y., 1966, *Excavation of Masada: Herod's Fortress and the Zeal*, London.

—— 1971, *Bar Kochva: The Rediscovery of the Legendary Hero of the Second Jewish Revolt Against Rome*, London.

—— , Broshi, Y. and Qimron, C., 1986, A Deed of Land Sale in Kefar Baru from the Period of Bar Kochva, *Cathedra* 40 (Heb.). (See Broshi and Qimron 1986).

—— and Naveh, J., 1989, *Masada I*, Jerusalem.

Yankelevich, Y., 1983, Granaries and Store Buildings in Eretz Israel, *Milet* 1 (Heb.).

Yeivin, Z., 1966, Turo Ancient Oil Presses, *Atigot* 3 (Heb.).

—— 1971, Survey of Settlements in Galilee and the Golan from the Period of the Mishna in Light of the Sources, unpublished diss., Hebrew University, Jerusalem (Heb.).

—— 1973, Excavations at Khorazin, *EI* 11 (Heb.).

—— and Edelstein, G., 1970, Excavation at Tirat Yehuda, *Atiqot* 6 (Heb.).

Yeo, C. A., 1946, Land and Sea Transportation in Imperial Italy, *TAPA* 77.

—— 1948, The Overgrazing of Ranch-lands in Ancient Italy, *TAPA* 79.

Youtie, H. C., 1936, Ostraka from Sbeitah, *AJA* 40.

—— 1978, Supplies for Soldiers and Stonecutters, *ZPE* 28.

Ysraeli, V., 1970, A Roman Pottery Mortarium, *Atiqot* 6.

Zayadin, F., 1986, ed., *Jerash Archaeological Project 1981–3*, Amman.

—— see also Fulco.

Ziegler, U., 1903, *Die Königsgleichnisse der Midrasch beleuchtet durch die römische Kaiserzeit*, Breslau.

Zori, see Tzori.

Index of places and subjects